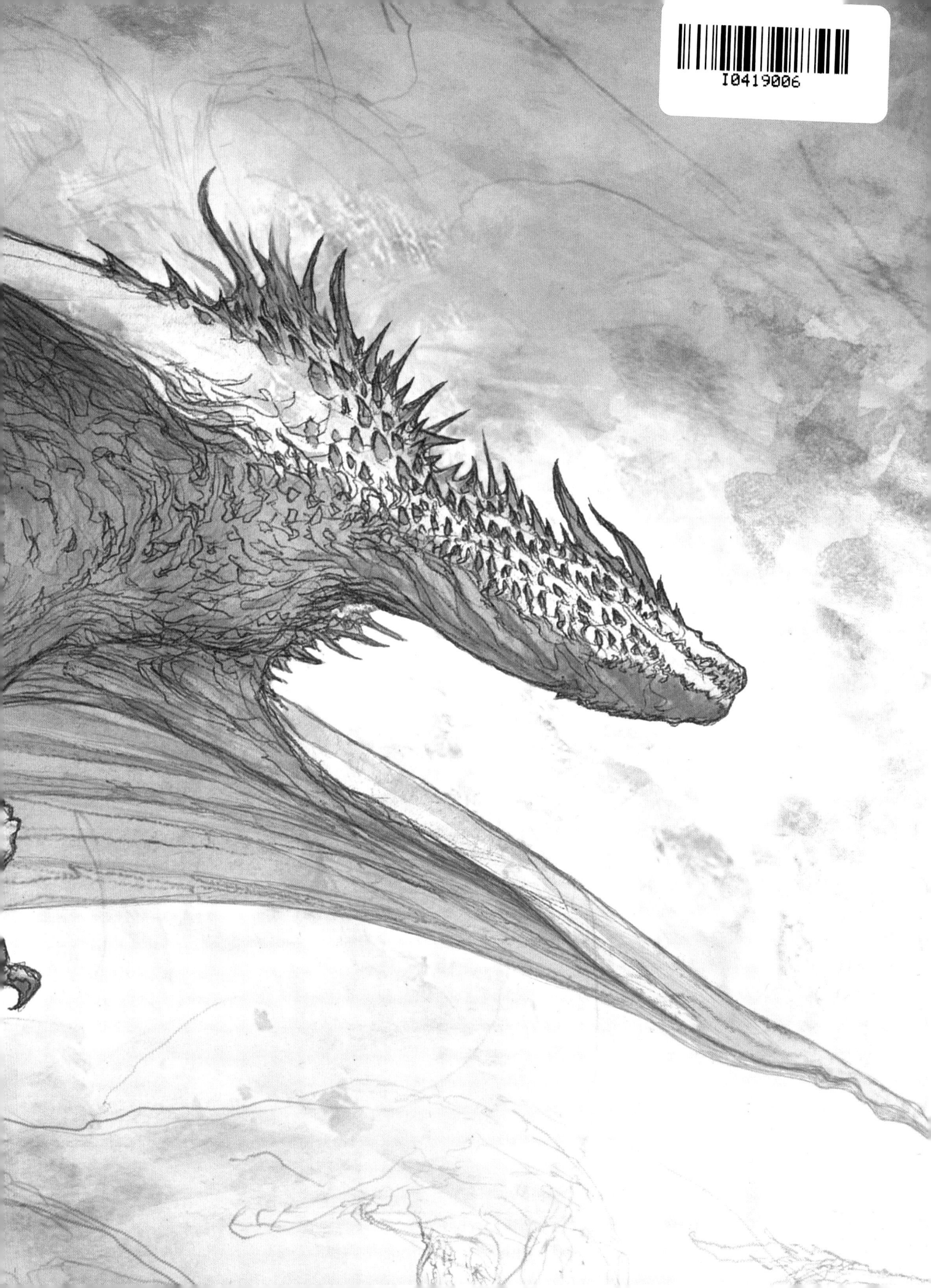

DESIGNING DRAGONS

AN ARTIST'S GUIDE TO THE LEGENDARY MYTHICAL CREATURES

3dtotal Publishing

DESIGNING DRAGONS

AN ARTIST'S GUIDE TO THE LEGENDARY MYTHICAL CREATURES

3dtotalPublishing

3dtotal Publishing

Correspondence: **publishing@3dtotal.com**
Website: **store.3dtotal.com**

Designing Dragons: An artist's guide to the legendary mythical creatures
© 2025, **3dtotal Publishing**. All rights reserved. No part of this
book can be reproduced in any form or by any means, without the
prior written consent of the publisher. All artwork, unless stated
otherwise, is copyright of the featured artists. All artwork that
is not copyright of the featured artists is marked accordingly.

Every effort has been made to ensure the credits and contact
information listed are present and correct. In the case of
any errors that have occurred, the publisher respectfully
directs readers to **store.3dtotal.com/pages/information**
for any updated information and corrections.

First published in the United Kingdom,
2025, by 3dtotal Publishing.

Address: 3dtotal.com Ltd,
29 Foregate Street, Worcester,
WR1 1DS, United Kingdom.

Hard cover ISBN: 978-1-915992-12-3

Printed and bound in China
by C&C Offset Printing Co., Ltd

Visit **store.3dtotal.com** for a complete
list of available book titles.

Editor: Marisa Lewis
Designer: Matthew Lewis
Lead Editor: Samantha Rigby
Lead Designer: Joseph Cartwright
Studio Manager: Simon Morse
Managing Director: Tom Greenway

Cover artwork © individual artists as credited throughout the book.
End papers artwork © Dibujante Nocturno (Fran Garcés)

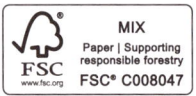

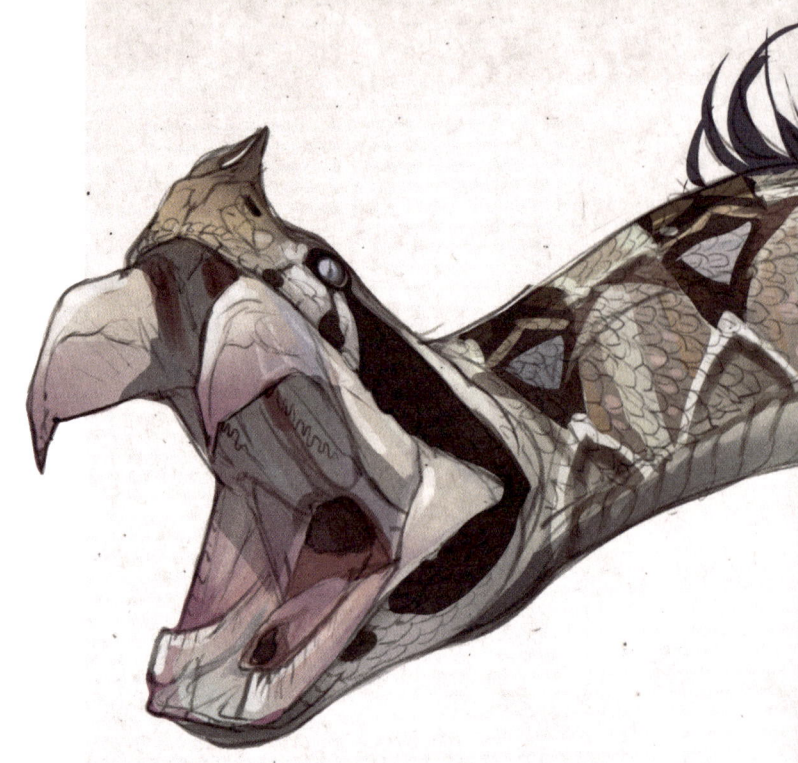

50%
of net profits donated
TO CHARITY

In 2022, 3dtotal Publishing became successful enough
to make a pledge to donate **50% of its net profits
to charity**. This continues to be possible due to the
incredible support from all our customers, employees,
and partners. At the time of printing, we have donated
over $1.62 million (USD) to charity.

We focus our giving on three charitable areas:
environmental, **humanitarian**, and **animal welfare**.
We use organizations such as Effective Altruism and
Founders Pledge to guide who we help within these
causes. Some ways of doing good are over 100 times
more effective than others, so donating this way hugely
increases the impact of our contributions.

See **3dtotal.com/charity**
for full details.

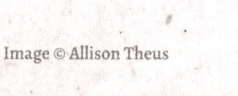

Image © Allison Theus

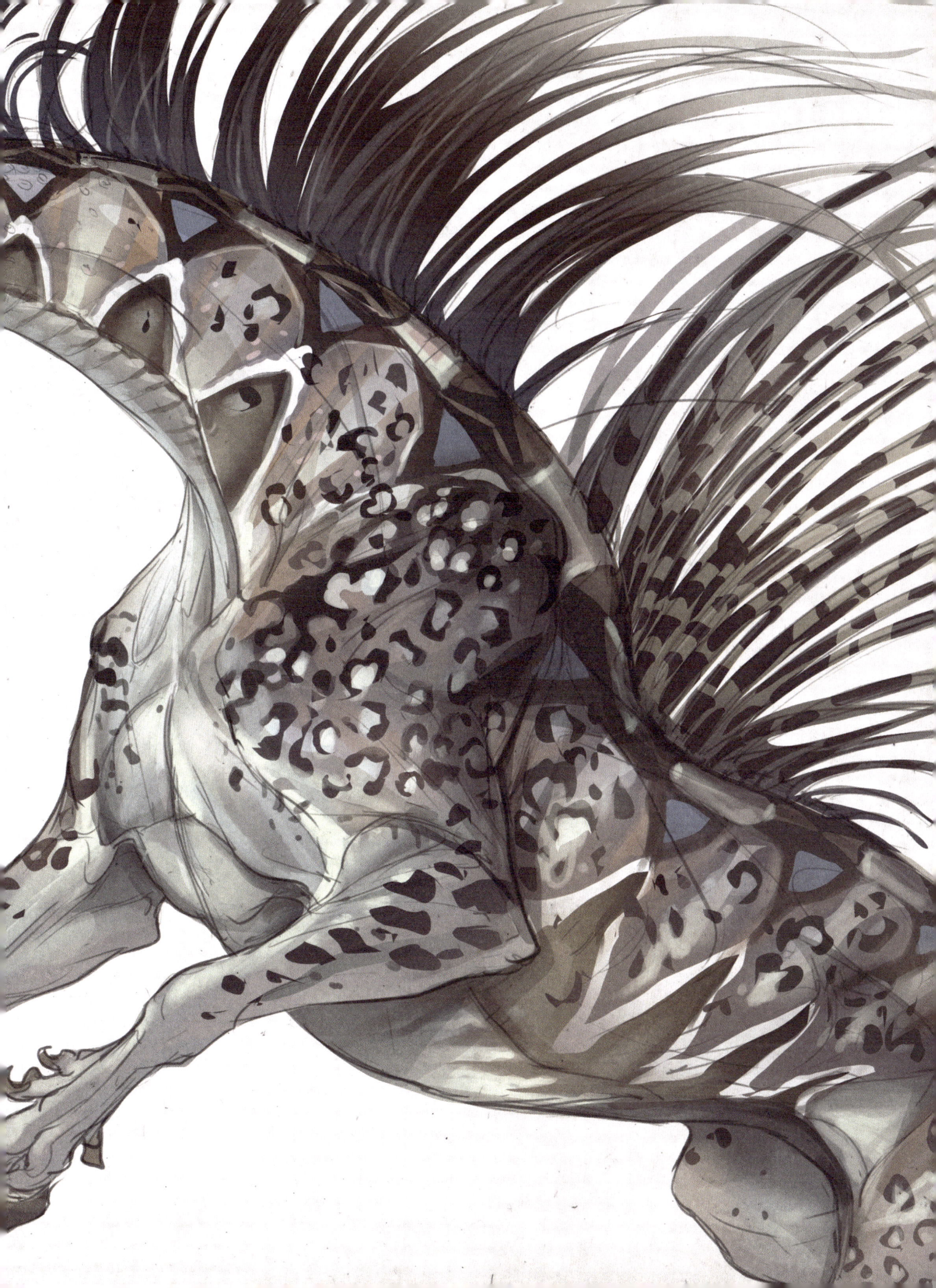

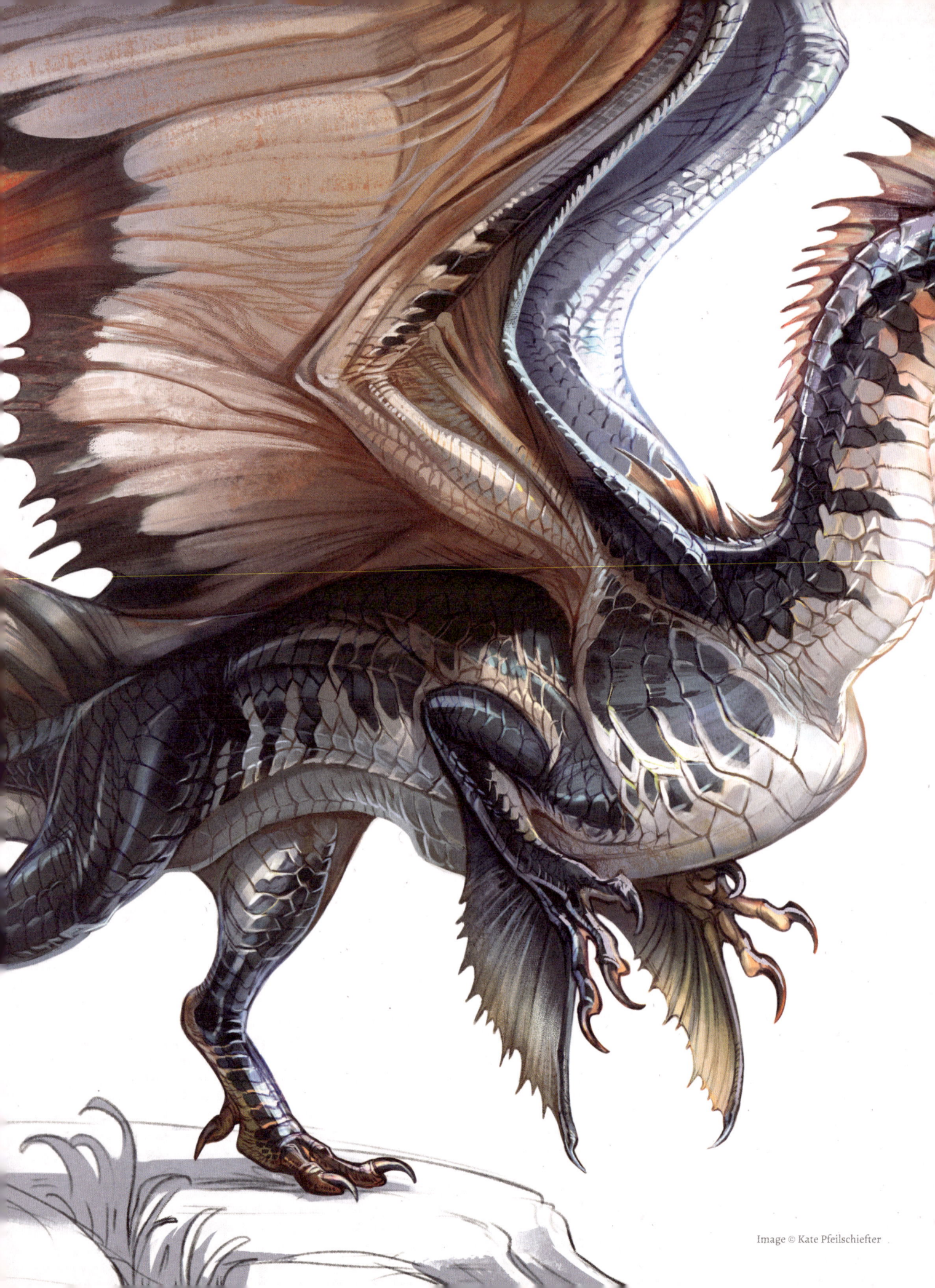

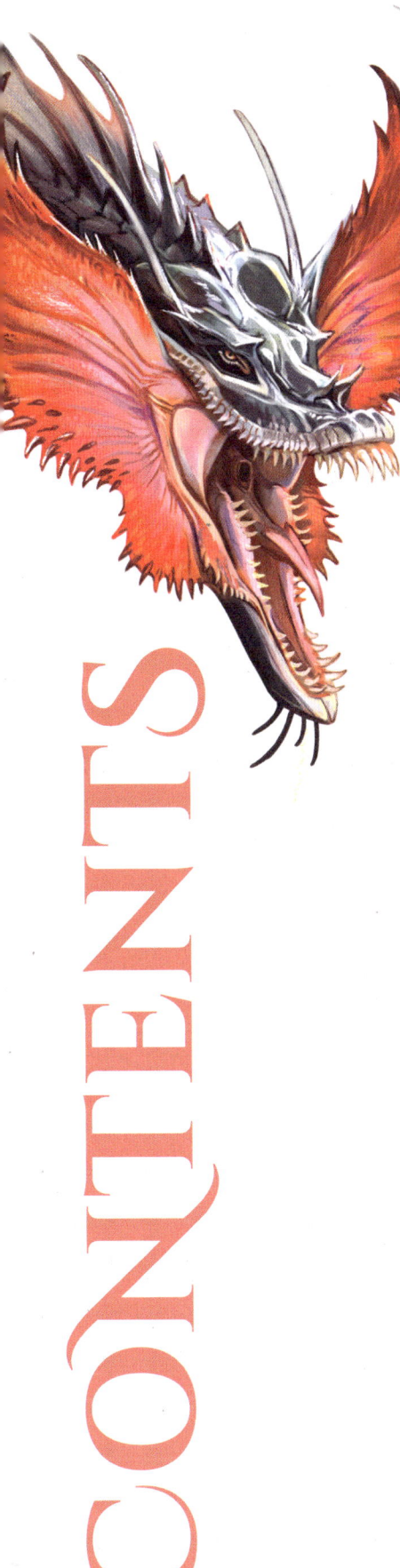

CONTENTS

Few mythical creatures have captured the human imagination like the dragon. Whether as a symbol of greed and devilry or wisdom and good fortune, whether flying through the skies or lurking beneath the waves, the dragon has loomed large in our consciousness across the centuries. Myths and folklore from all around the globe are filled with serpents and fire-breathers, adorning sculptures, murals, manuscripts, and coats of arms. In more recent memory, they appear on page and screen in forms such as Smaug, Falcor, Haku, Mushu, Paarthurnax, and Vermithor. Our appetite for these marvellous creatures never tires, whatever their size and temperament.

This book presents dragons from tales around the globe, reimagined by concept artists and illustrators with a passion for creature design. In a series of step-by-step tutorials, you'll see how each artist researches, interprets, and designs a dragon in their own unique way. They'll be putting a fresh, biology-inspired spin on famous beasts, and providing new interpretations for strange creatures rarely seen. We hope that you will discover not only some new dragons, but some new techniques and approaches for bringing your own fantastical creatures to life.

MARISA LEWIS | EDITOR

HOW TO USE THIS BOOK

We recommend starting by reading through the **Introduction** chapter (page 10), where Stephen Oakley and Alexander Ostrowski, two creature-designing professionals and friends, share an engaging, informative discussion about everything that dragon art entails. Their pearls of wisdom and insights into the design process will set you up for the tutorials to come.

In the **Dragons** section (page 48), you will follow thirteen artists as they illustrate thirteen different dragons. Ranging from winged predators to legless serpents, with scales or feathers, with fiery breath or deadly venom, this bestiary of diverse draconic creations will motivate you on your own fantasy-art journey.

The **Gallery** (page 252) features inspirational dragon designs from the portfolios and sketchbooks of further talented guests, and the **Glossary** (page 280) contains terminology you may find useful on your way through this book.

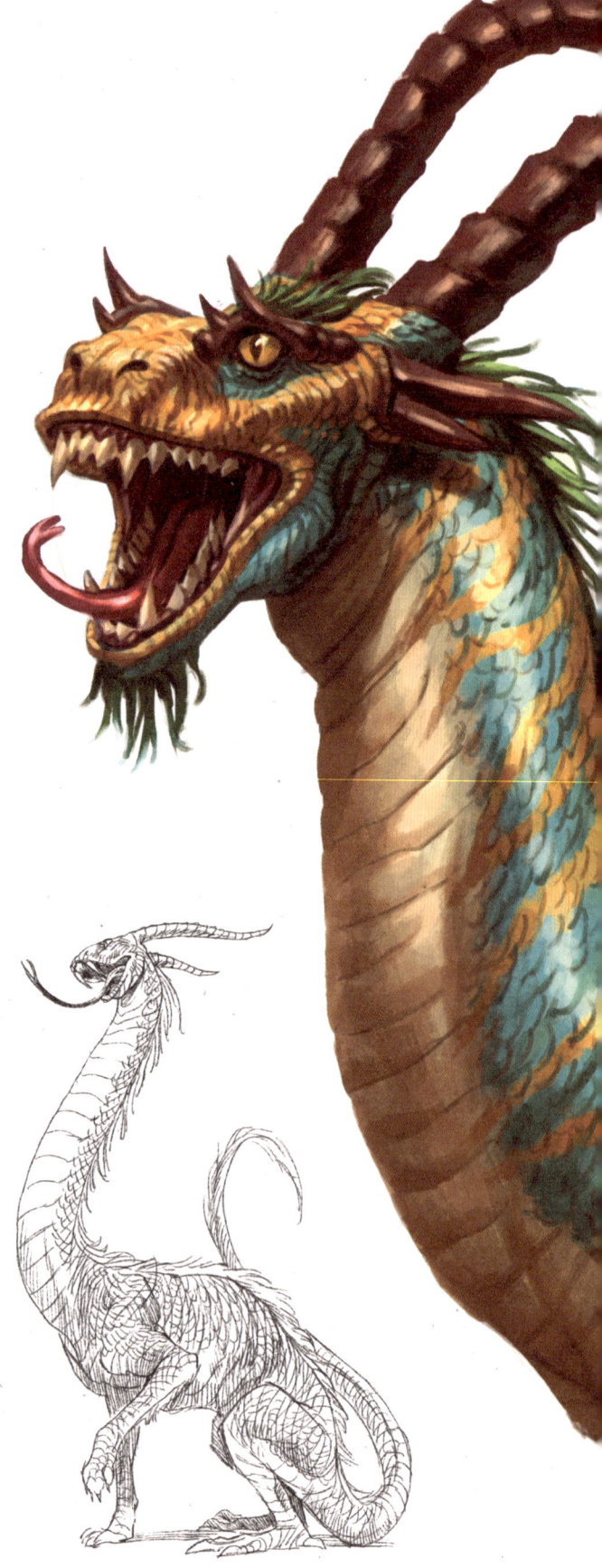

Image © Hazem Ameen

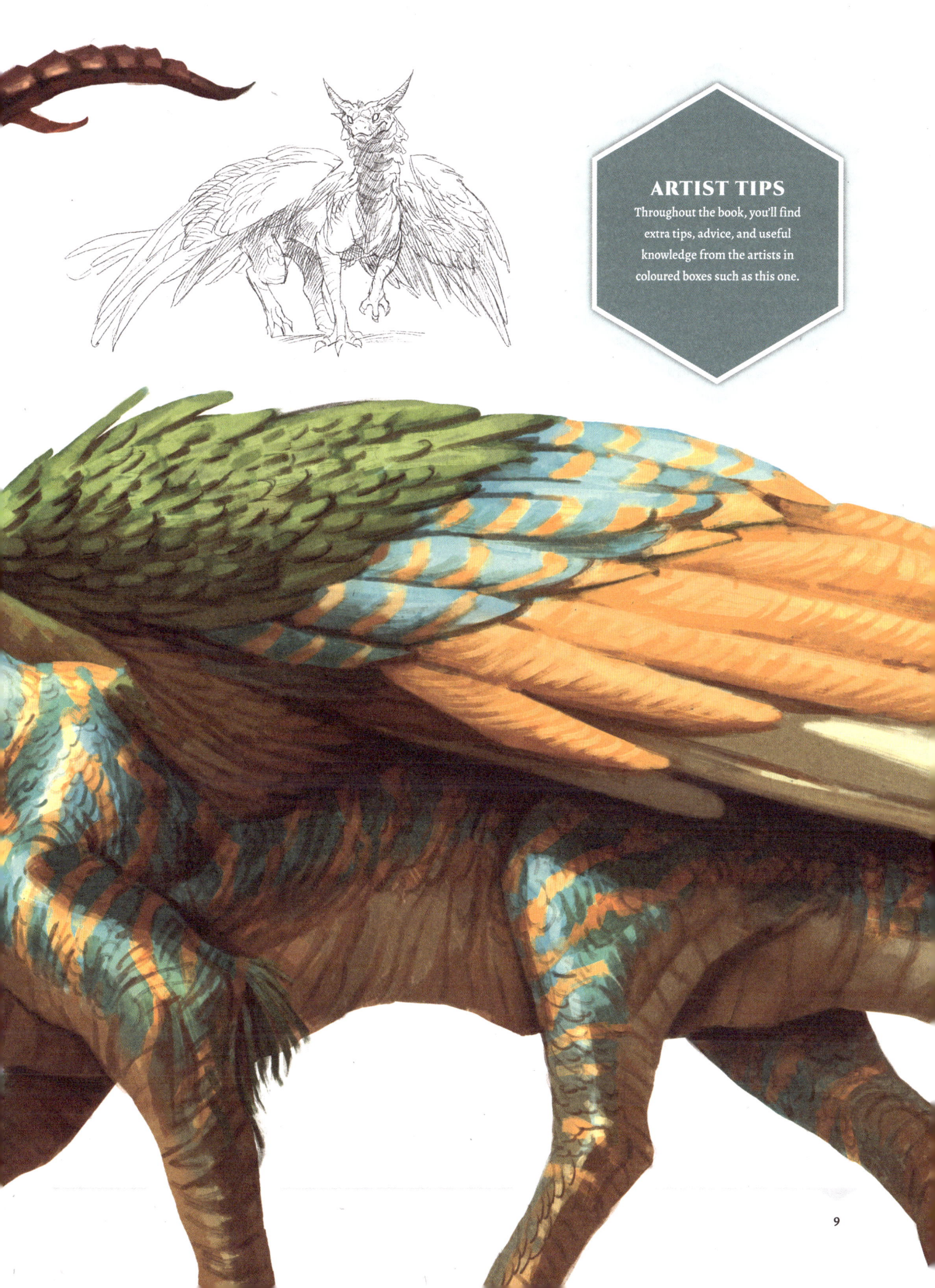

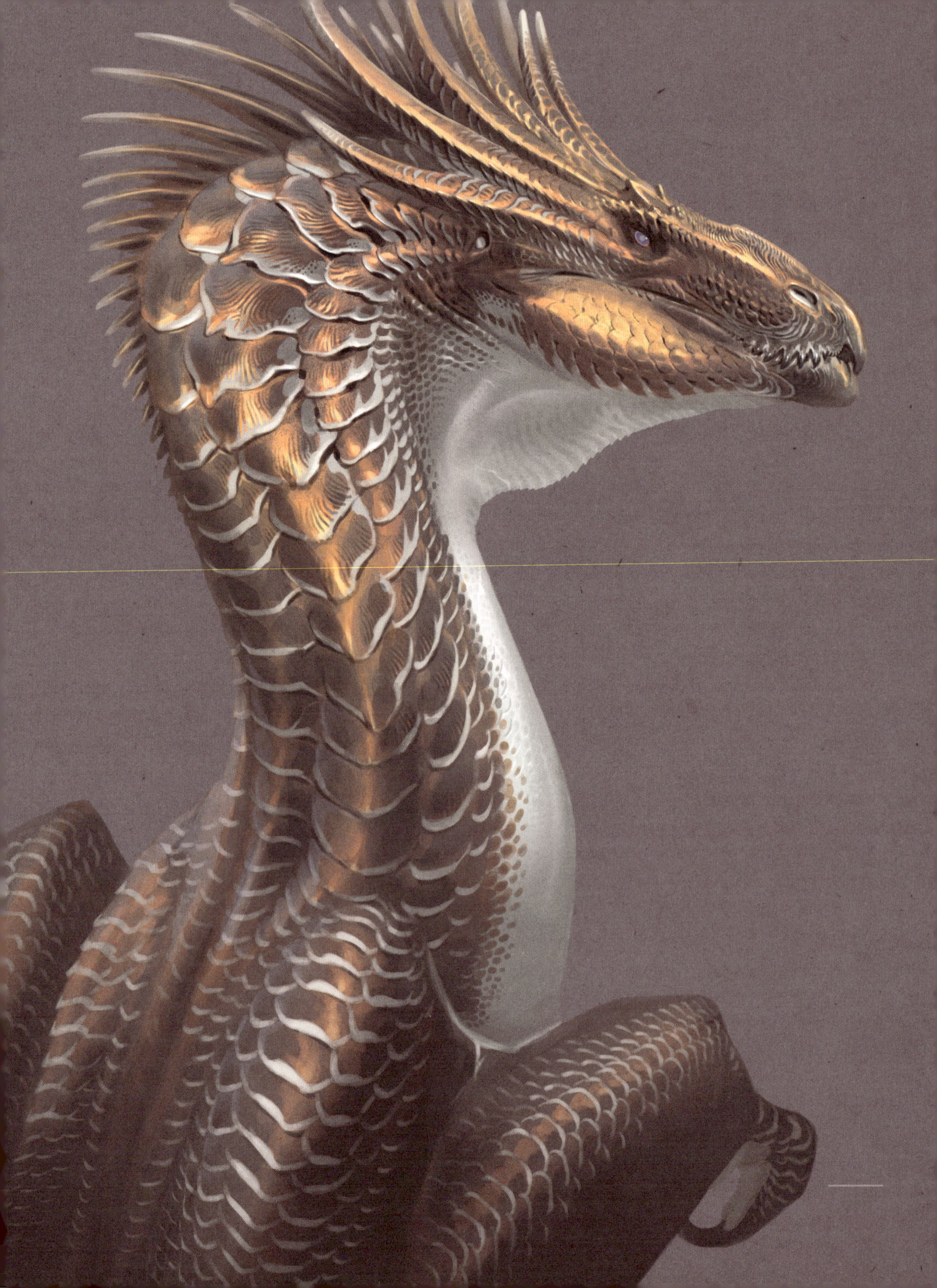

INTRODUCTION

In this chapter, Stephen Oakley and Alexander Ostrowski will introduce you to the key aspects of designing a dragon. They will share how they find ideas, their formative dragon inspirations, important factors to consider, common pitfalls to avoid, types of dragon anatomy, and how to strike a balance between the realistic and the fantastic.

STEPHEN OAKLEY & ALEXANDER OSTROWSKI

Images © Stephen Oakley & Alexander Ostrowski

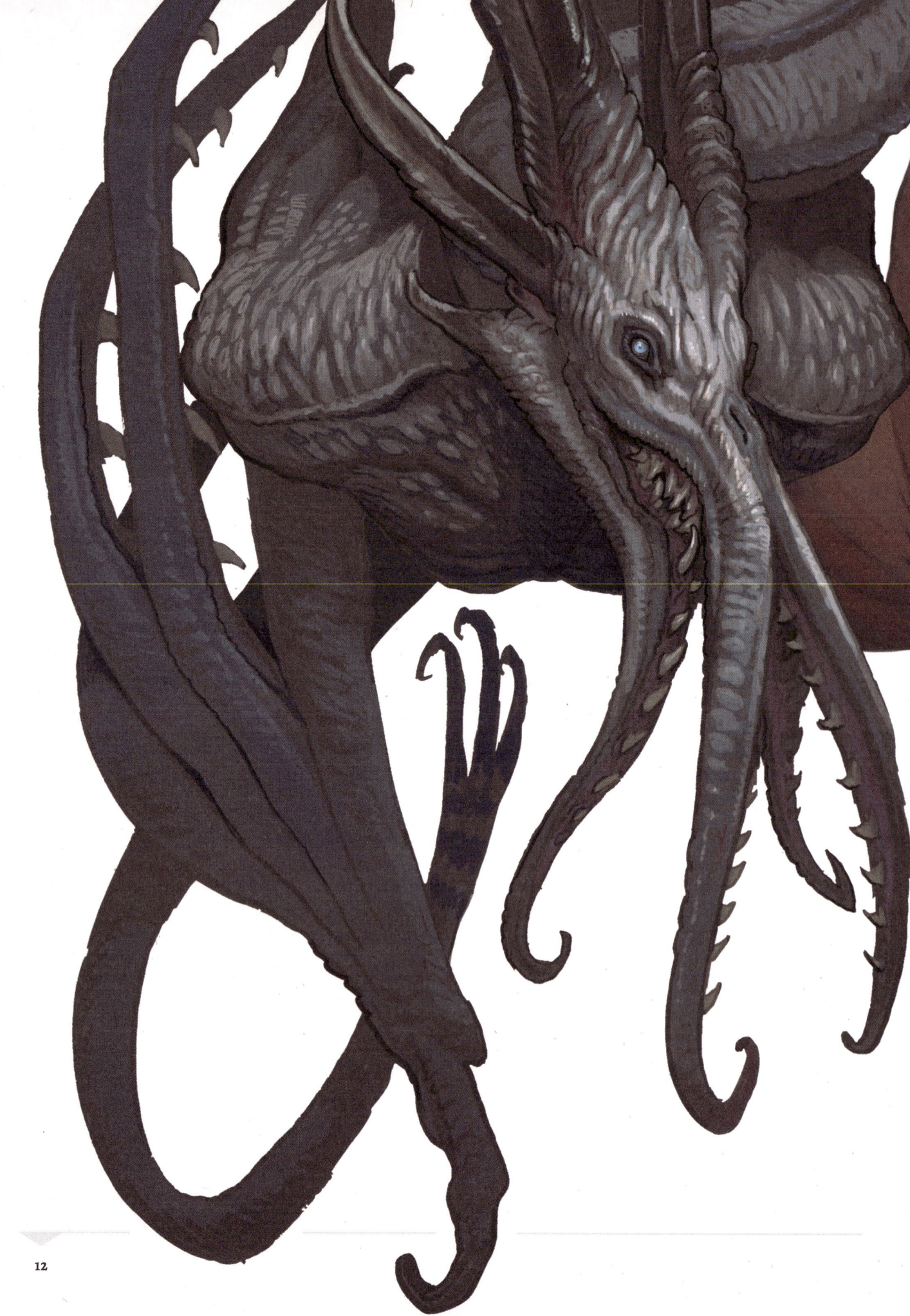

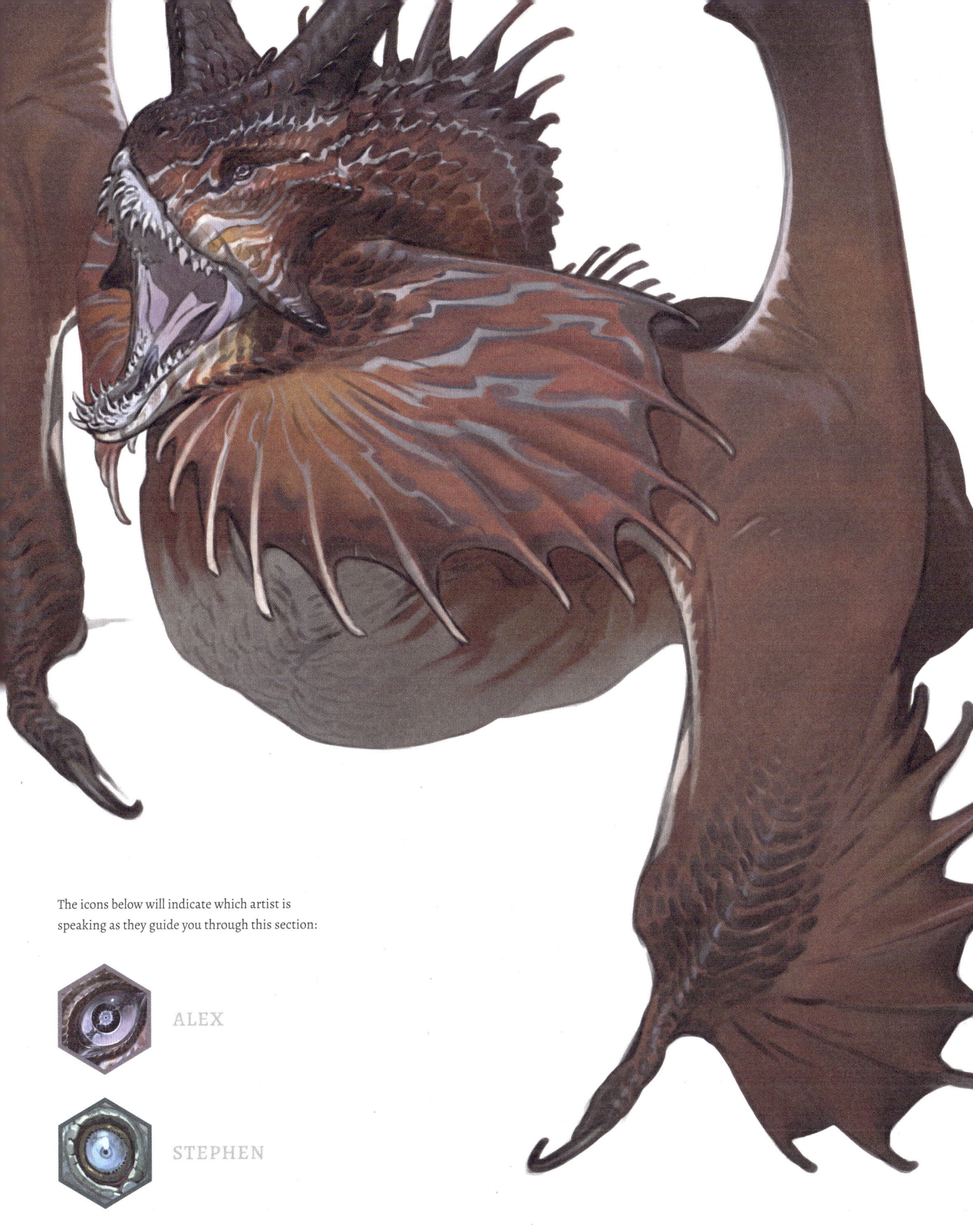

The icons below will indicate which artist is speaking as they guide you through this section:

ALEX

STEPHEN

FROM MYTHS TO POP CULTURE

 ALEX

Among mythological creatures, dragons hold a special place. Some form of the archetype of the dragon is found in mythology from all around the world, and although they differ greatly from culture to culture, they always stand out. They often symbolize the ultimate monster, a predator more dangerous than every living creature, the edge of the map. Here be dragons.

Ultimately, dragons are the unknown, there to be explored creatively as an idea and therefore open to interpretation, open to be approached from so many different angles. They could be symbols, characters, an arcane catastrophe, gods, or, as I like to approach them, animals – another fascinating part of the natural world, channelling my appreciation for what's already here living alongside us.

 STEPHEN

Myths are so often birthed by the natural world, and so designing from nature as a base will always yield a level of believability that makes for some of the strongest designs. Alex and I both have a deep-rooted love for nature and use it to inspire and shape our own dragons, each with textures and shapes that speak to us, in much the same way that each culture has created their own variations on these universal beasts. Our shapes and tastes differ but all start from a familiar, long-established blueprint.

I always try to channel the dragon's shapes and traits from unexpected places to try to mix up the blueprint, but keep it familiar to the dragon's purpose in the habitat or story they occupy. As Alex said, anything is on the table, but dragons have become almost established in their base forms from centuries of description and creation.

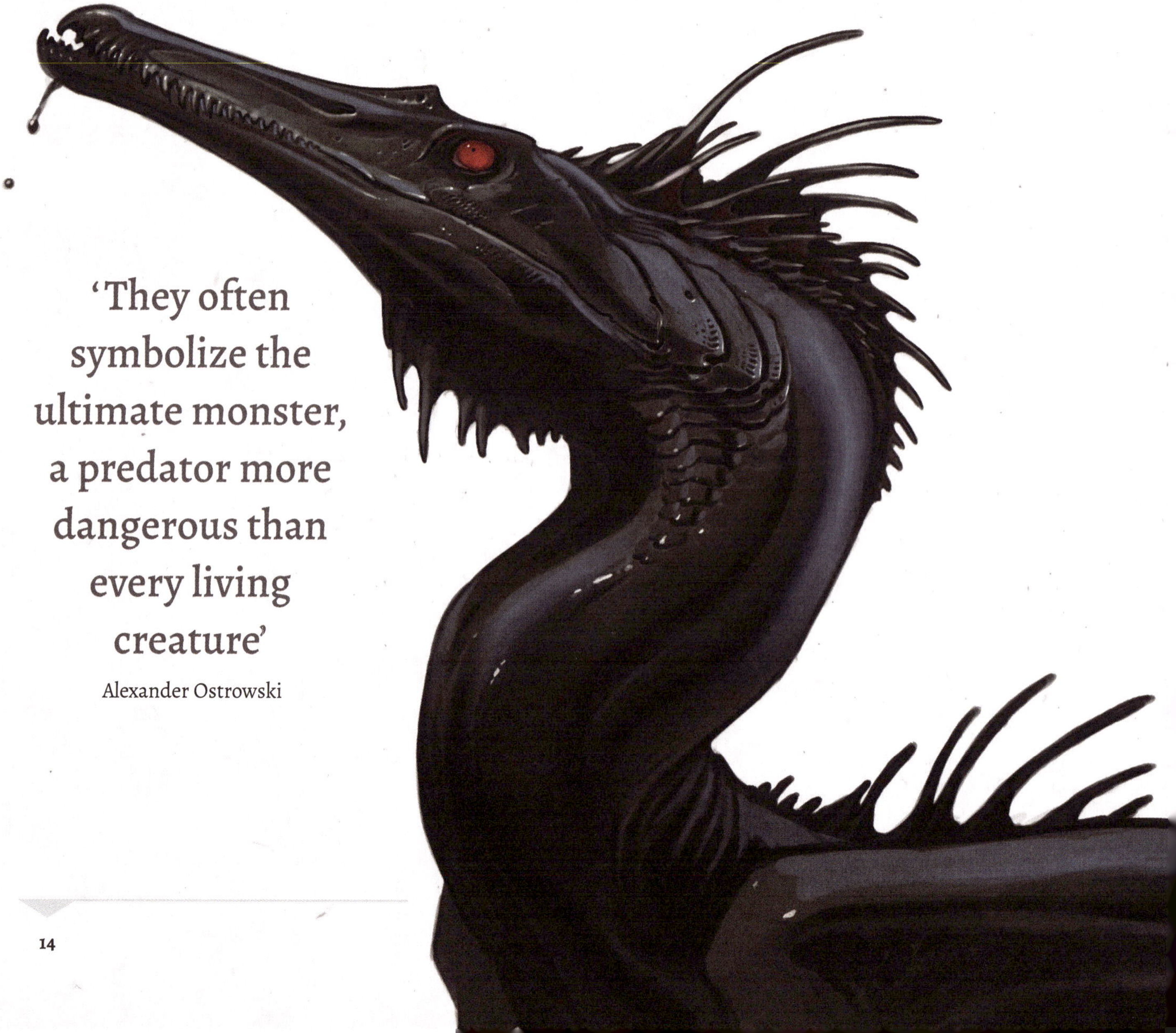

'They often symbolize the ultimate monster, a predator more dangerous than every living creature'

Alexander Ostrowski

14

ALEX

Generation after generation of human beings has been fascinated by the idea of dragons, so it is not surprising that, after all those centuries, dragons are still all over media today. They are in our favourite books, in movies, in video games and tabletop games, and both Stephen and I have been lucky enough to design some dragons and contribute to the pool of depictions out there. (Check out Stephen's dragons for *God of War* – they are amazing!) Some of my personal favourites include Smaug from *The Hobbit* (his role in the book and the movie design), all of the dragons in *How to Train Your Dragon*, and the beasts in *Reign of Fire*, *Game of Thrones*, *House of the Dragon*, and the *Harry Potter* movies – all realized by incredible artists.

STEPHEN

Reign of Fire has a special place in my heart as well for one of the coolest dragons, harkening back to the European depictions of the dragon being a manifestation of the Devil, but natural and world-ending. I am always drawn to classics like *Dragonheart*, *Dragonslayer*, and Smaug from the 1977 animated movie version of *The Hobbit*. Those dragons are old, wicked, or wise beings that are legends made manifest, and though some of the designs are older now, they are timelessly inspiring to me. For more recent depictions, the artists Jaemin Kim, Paul Bonner, Vincent Coviello (see page 238), and Alex, with whom I have the pleasure of sharing this chapter, sit high on my list of favourite dragon creators. In these following sections we will do our best to describe how we think of dragons and our methodology behind their creation.

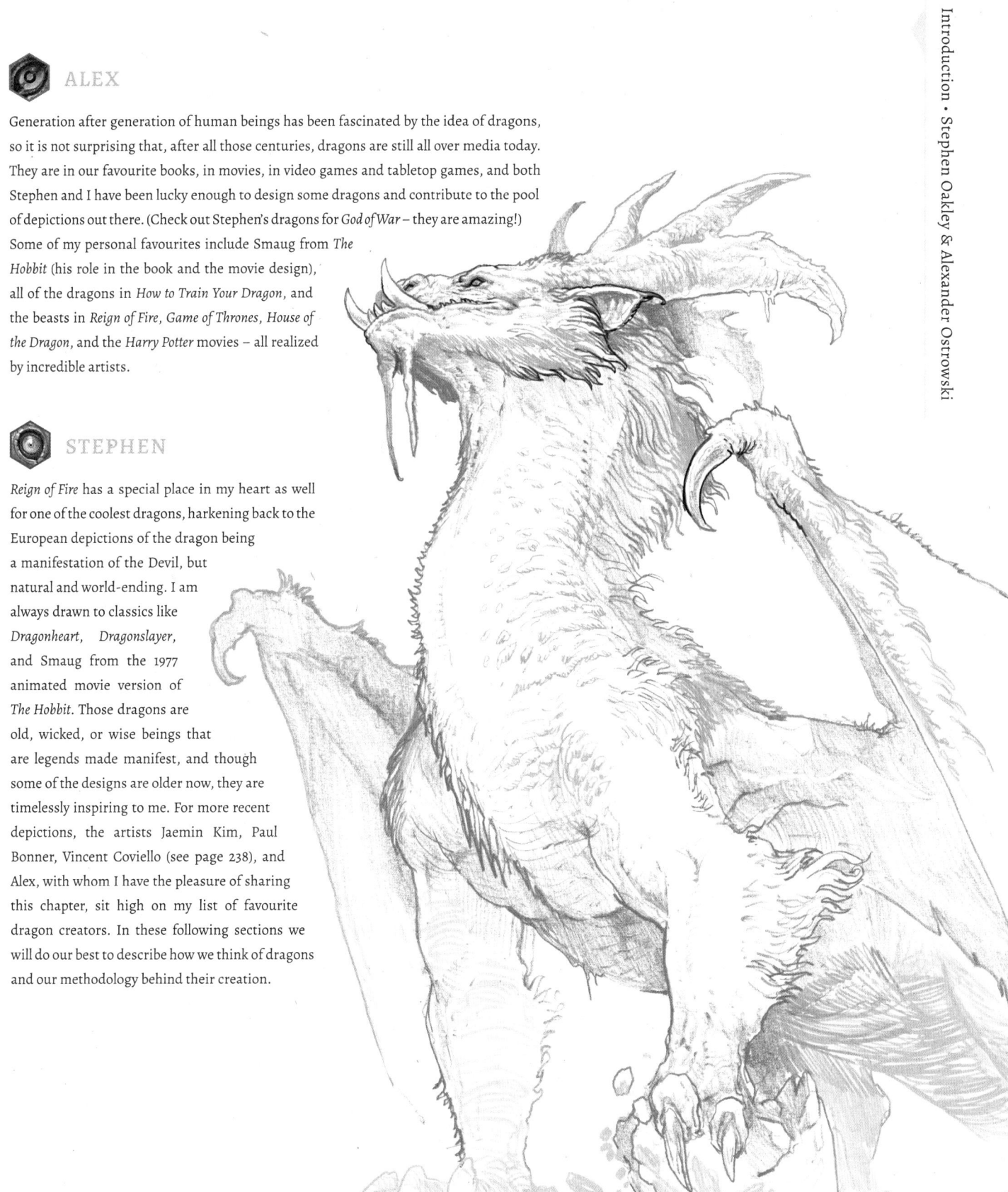

REAL-WORLD INSPIRATION

Learning about how the organisms of Earth have solved the problem of survival is the best inspiration you can get. It offers so many wonderful ideas that it's easy to lose track. Anything can be a dragon if you push and pull enough. Luckily, the descriptions and depictions of mythical dragons, just like the cultural perception of what a dragon is, offer a framework for us to design within.

Generally, some classic features are wings, horns, crests, beaks, sharp teeth and claws, long tails, and scaly integument. We might want to look at reptiles in general, including extinct dinosaurs and extant birds. Dragon wings are often similar to the wings of bats and their horns often call to mind rams and sheep.

While all these are a good starting point, it is worth looking beyond what's traditional. The options for wings alone are numerous. In our dragons on these pages you can see a lot of reptilian scales, monitor-lizard jaws, crocodilian teeth, flying-fox wings, raptor beaks and talons, and many more anatomical features, some of which are very unexpected or oddly specific.

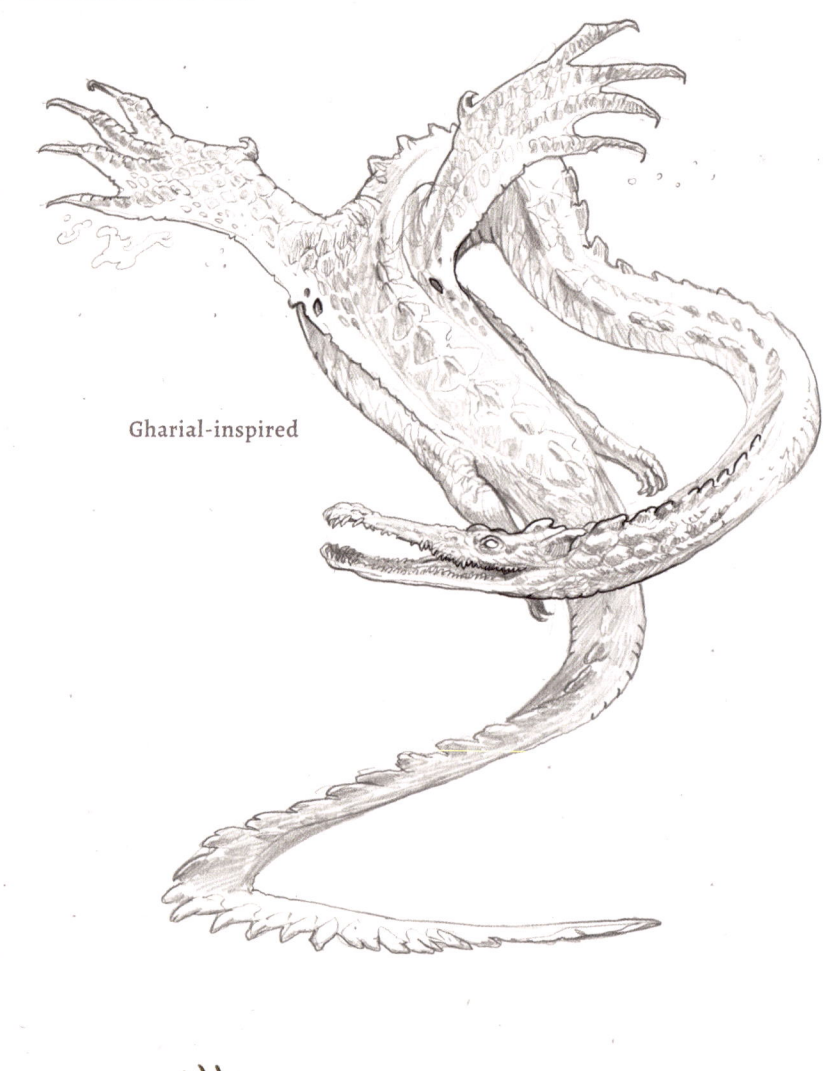

Gharial-inspired

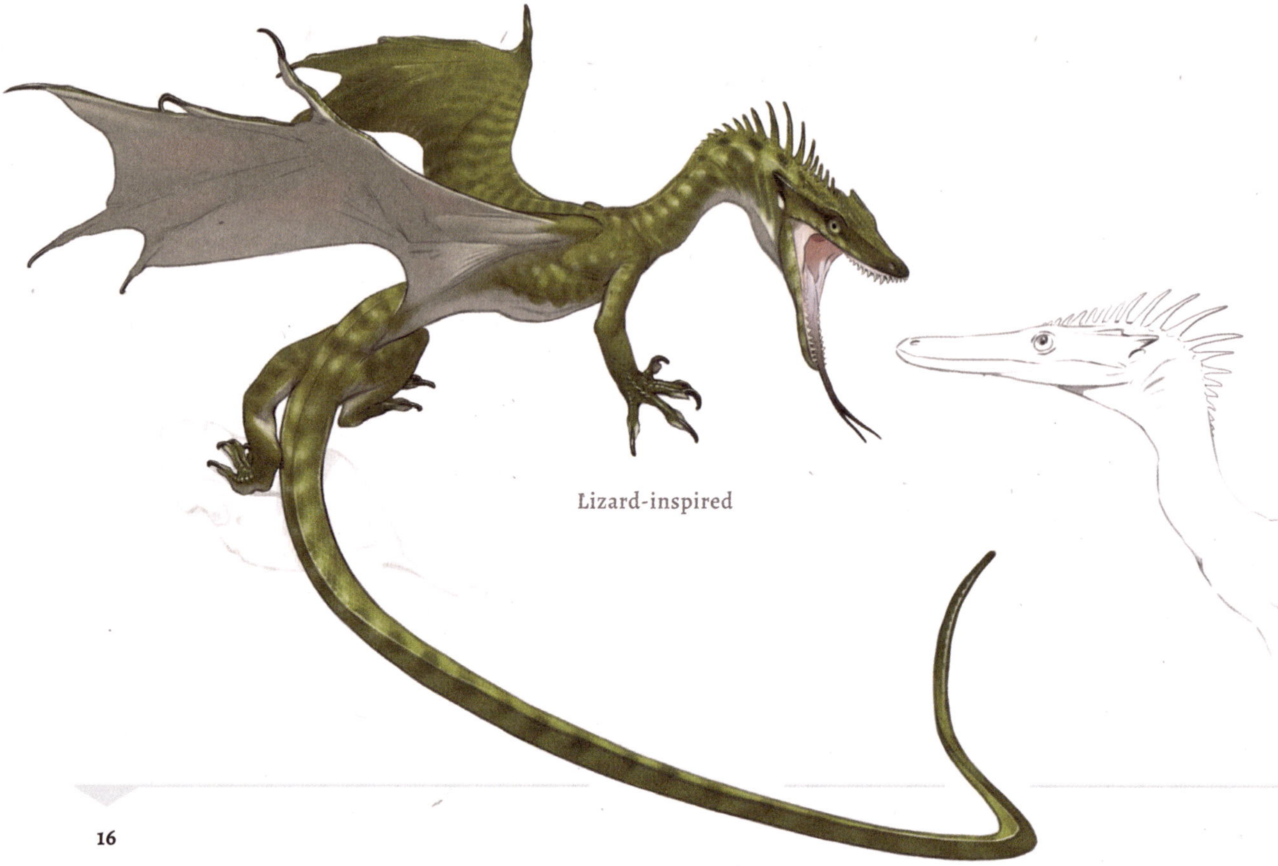

Lizard-inspired

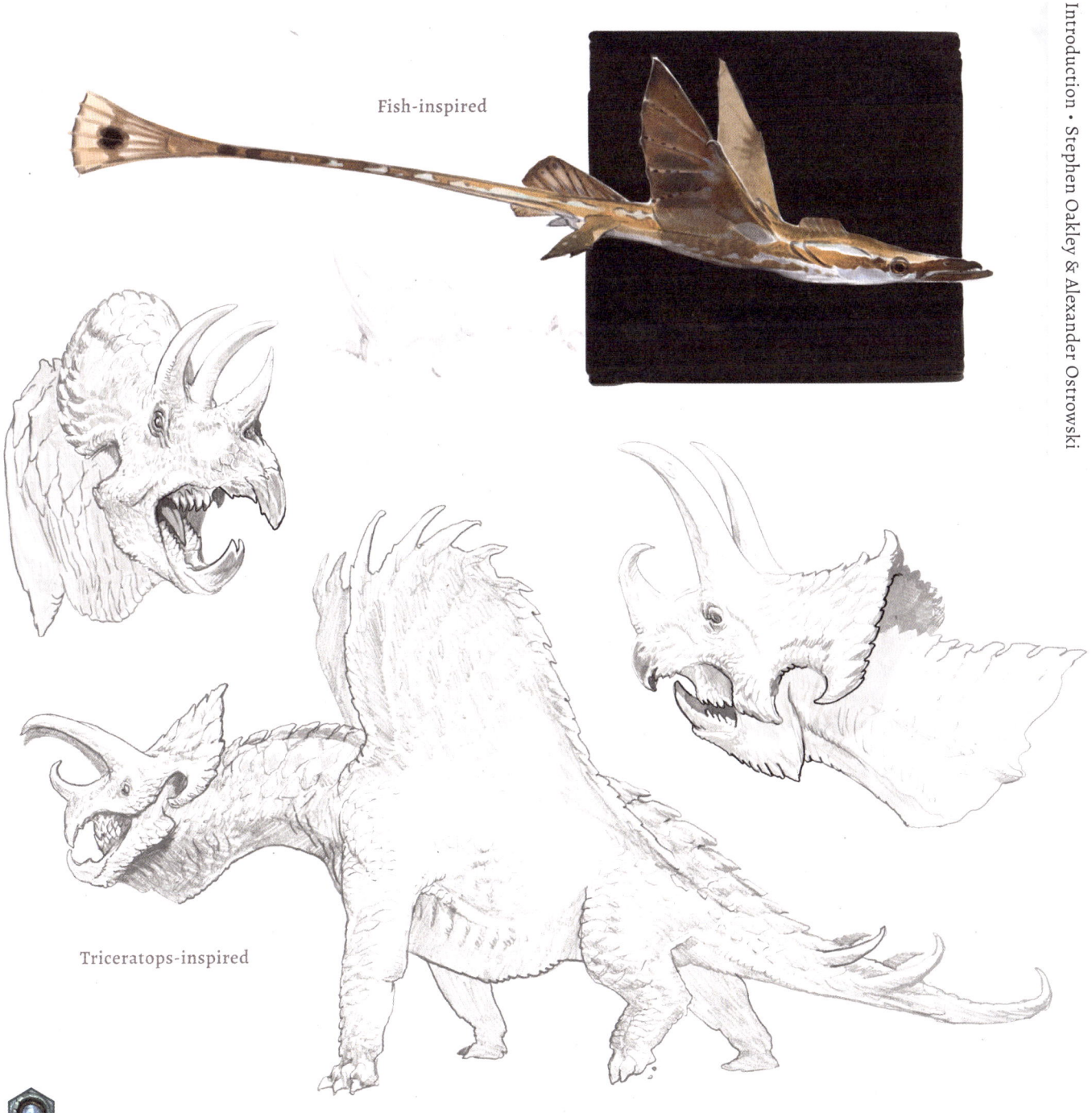

Fish-inspired

Triceratops-inspired

To Alex's point about the unexpected, I will frequently dig down deep into the ocean for many of my favourite inspirations, and will usually also pull from amphibians for many of the features and textures that add a little spice to the dragon of choice. A dragon that lives underneath large, damp boulders deep in a temperate forest, for instance, seems a prime choice for salamander-like traits.

However, if you are picking traits from certain animals, it's important to think of how the dragon would fare with those features in the wild. With softer skin, would that just make it large prey for something else? Nature solves these issues for you, more often than not, if you know where to look. Some salamanders have bright colours or orange spots to warn would-be predators that they are poisonous! That's a good solution for a squishier dragon that lacks hard scales. Not only that, but it could inspire what colours this poisonous salamander-drake would have.

Pulling ideas from deep-sea fish and invertebrates suddenly takes your dragon from the mountains of yore and makes it a space invader or otherworldly hoarder of treasures. Whether you are using their strange colours and patterns to build a luring or ambushing dragon, or using the massive mouths of gulper eels as a way for your dragon to snatch up large prey, the possibilities really are endless.

All animals are built with similar functions: to eat, breathe, and move through the world. By that account, once you understand the rules of established dragons, there is no animal or even plant that is off the table and can't in some way contribute to your dragon's design.

DRAGON DESIGN QUESTIONS

- How realistic or magical is this dragon?
- What is its habitat (terrain, climate)?
- What is its diet or prey?
- Does it have predators?
- How does it attack or defend itself?
- How does it walk, swim, or fly?
- How does it reproduce, socialize, and communicate?

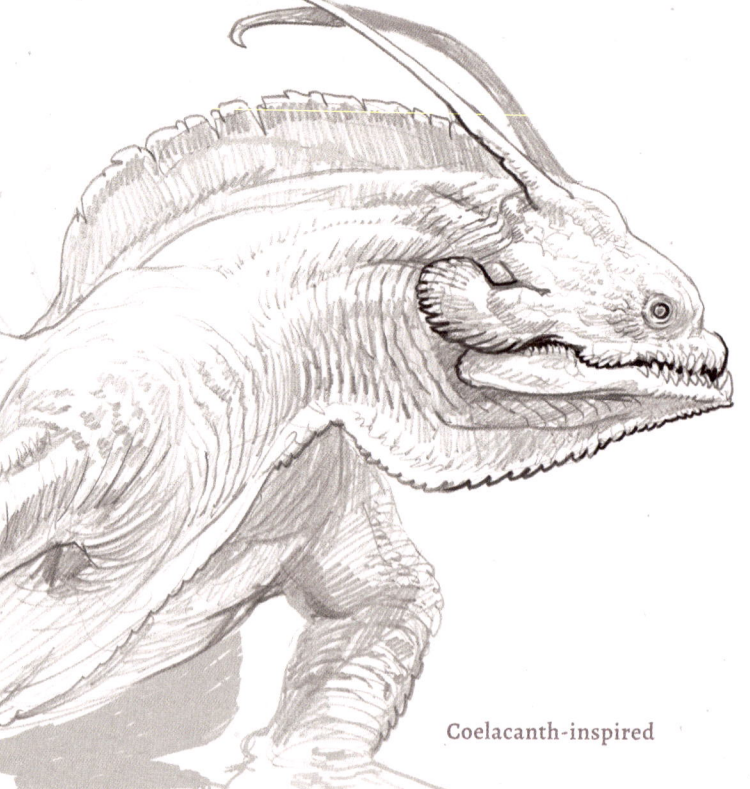

Coelacanth-inspired

There is also the possibility of a dragon not being a biological creature, but something else entirely – maybe a synthetic creation or a manifestation of magic, free from the constraints of evolution and phylogeny. This opens up the possible sources of inspiration even more, especially to include forces of nature, like the molten rock flowing from a volcano, creeping frost, or tidal waves.

As you can see, the options of where to look for references are endless, so it is really helpful to narrow down your idea and write a little briefing for yourself before jumping in.

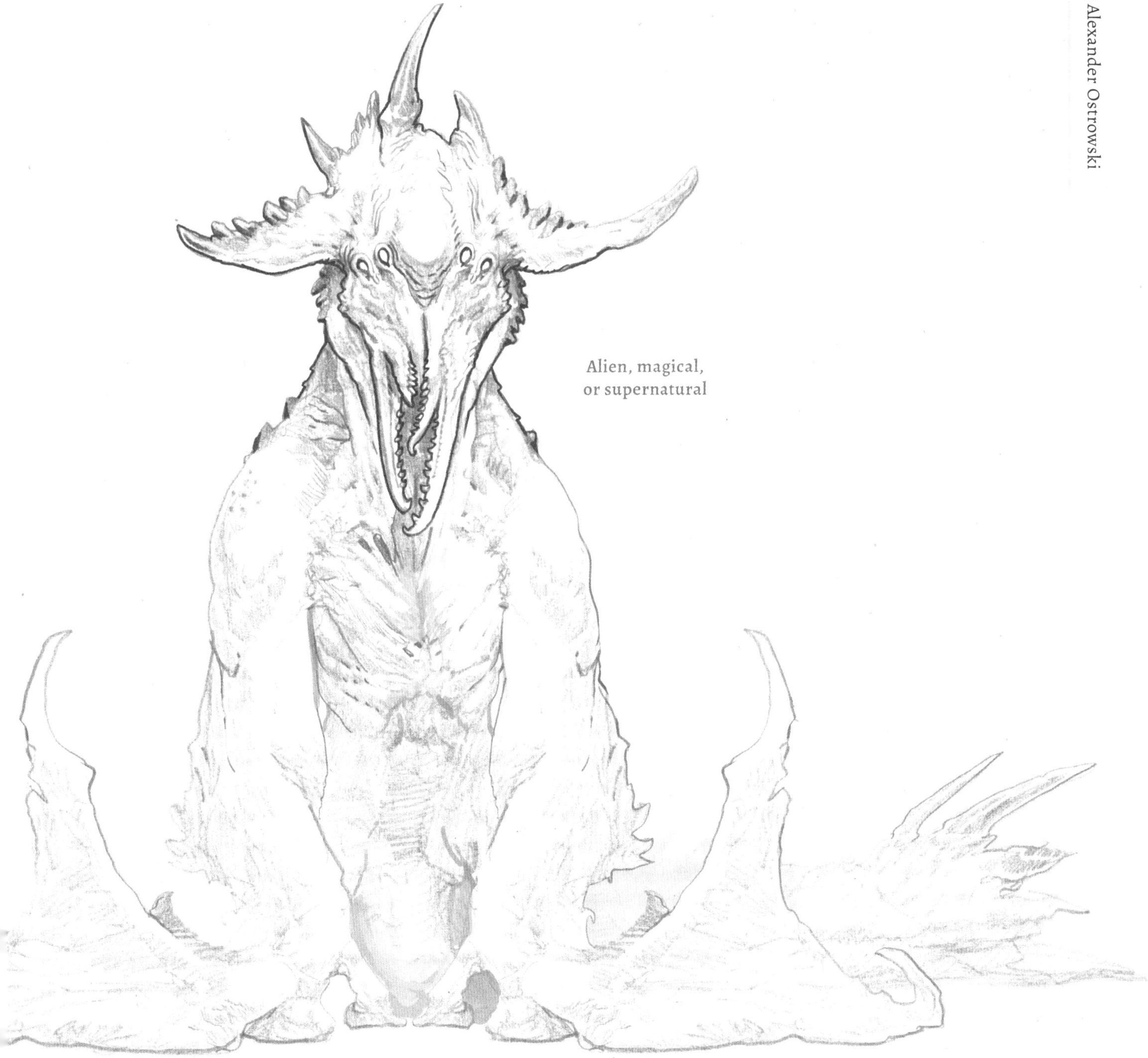

Alien, magical, or supernatural

DRAGON ANATOMY

The anatomy of dragons is always a balancing act between embracing the fantastical, through what different cultures have depicted dragons as looking like, and what nature has decided is possible. That being said, as long as a dragon bears the iconic traits of what dragons are expected to exhibit (physical or otherwise) there aren't too many rules for anatomy. I'd even go so far as to say that you will end up missing a chance of making something iconic by adhering to too many of the conventional anatomy tropes of dragon design.

As Alex explains later here, embracing the archetypes within dragons is often a great way to choose what anatomy to combine to create the perfect beast. If you are choosing a water-dwelling drake for instance, opt for wildlife with either immense tails or stout but powerful wings, or even immense bulk akin to whales or hippos. From there, choose their weapons to complement your chosen body type. Anything goes here, as long as the flow of the shapes is not abrupt. When shaping dragons from nature, you are able to create from a near-endless well of inspiration that has evolved to fulfil its role to the best it can.

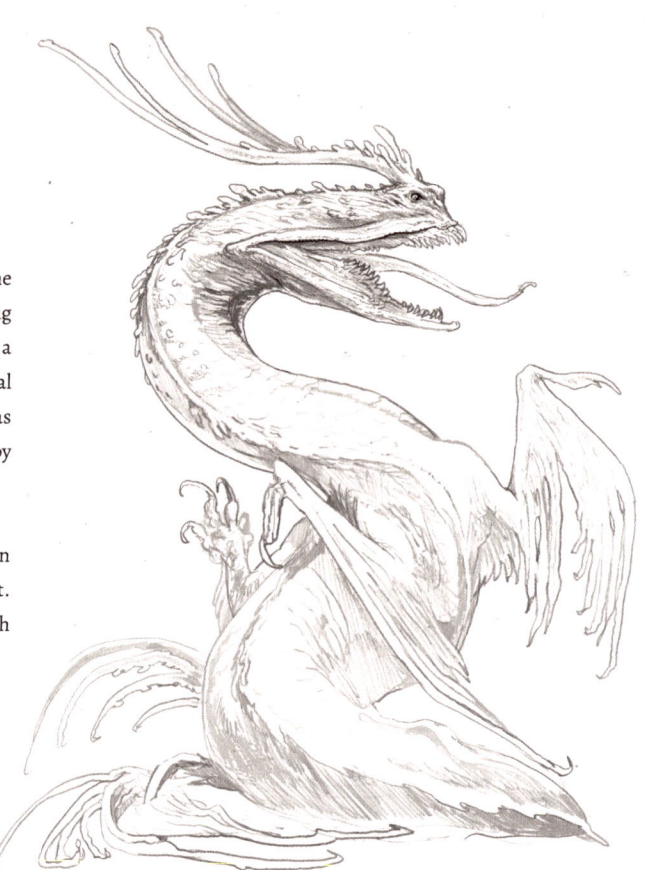

Deep-sea, eel-like, camouflaged

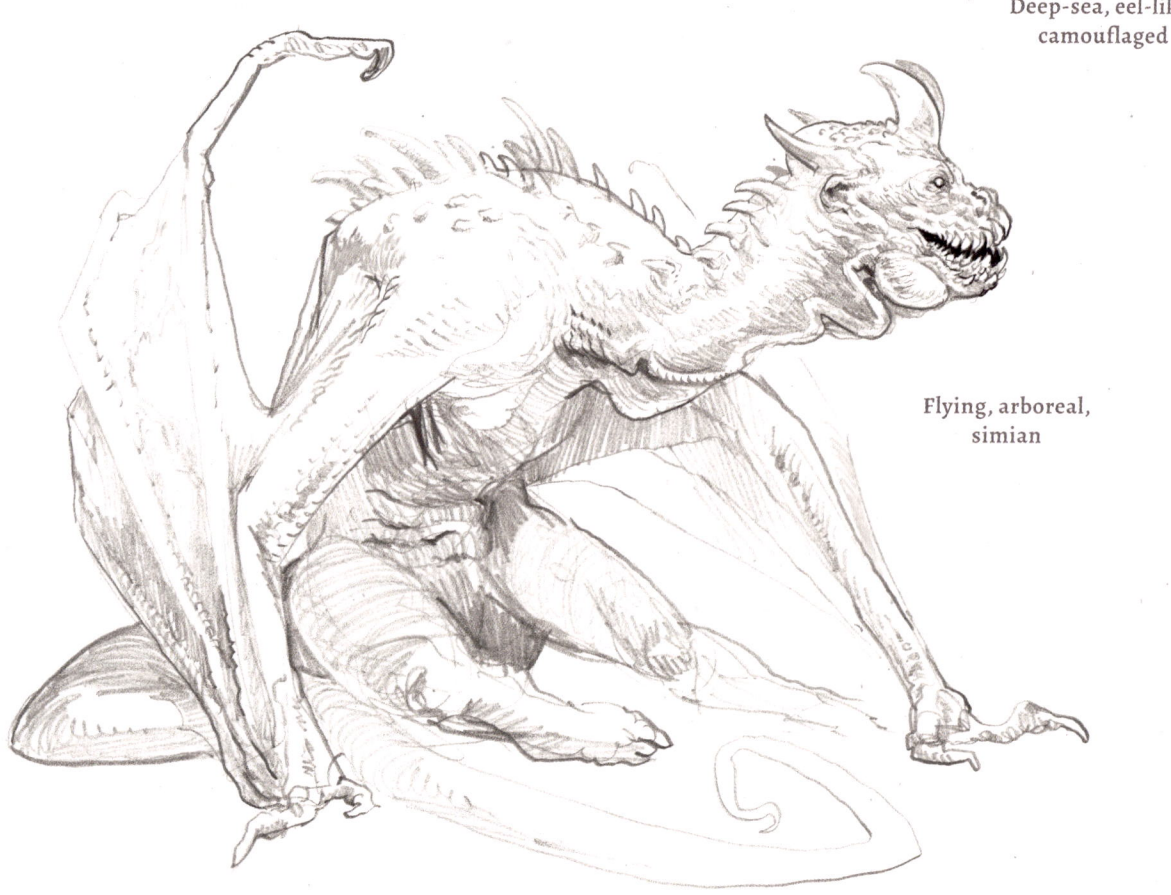

Flying, arboreal, simian

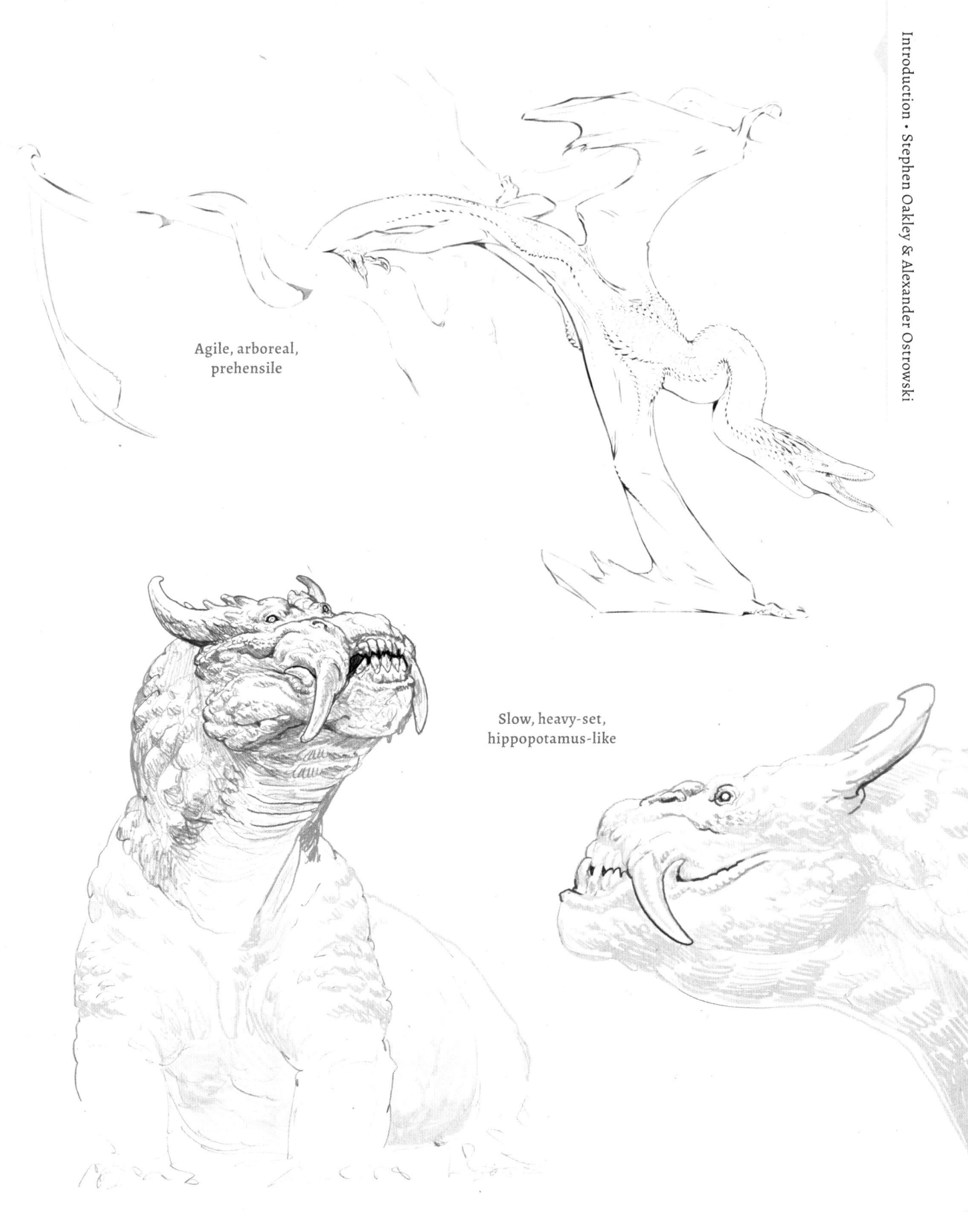

Agile, arboreal,
prehensile

Slow, heavy-set,
hippopotamus-like

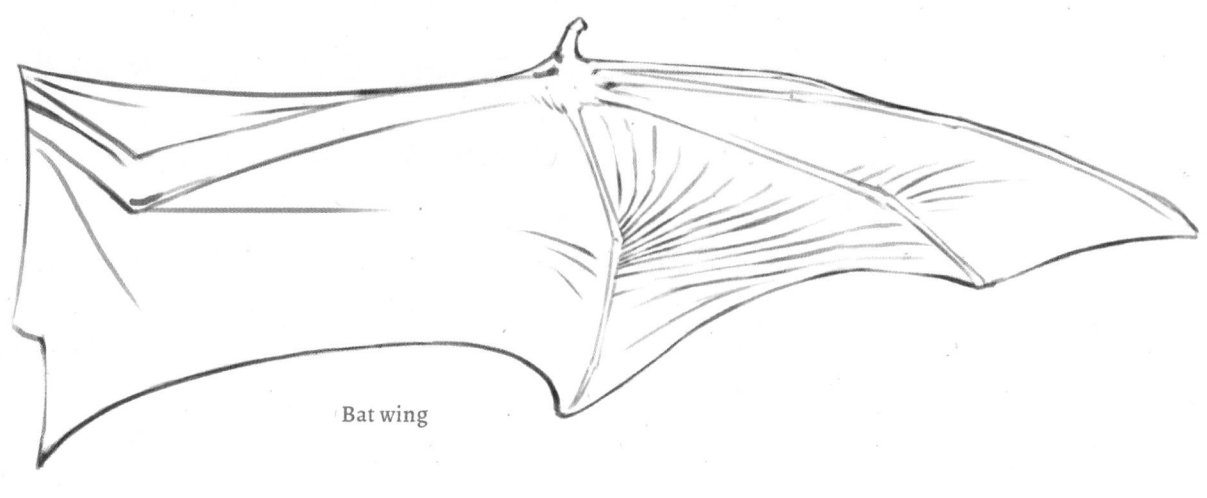

Bat wing

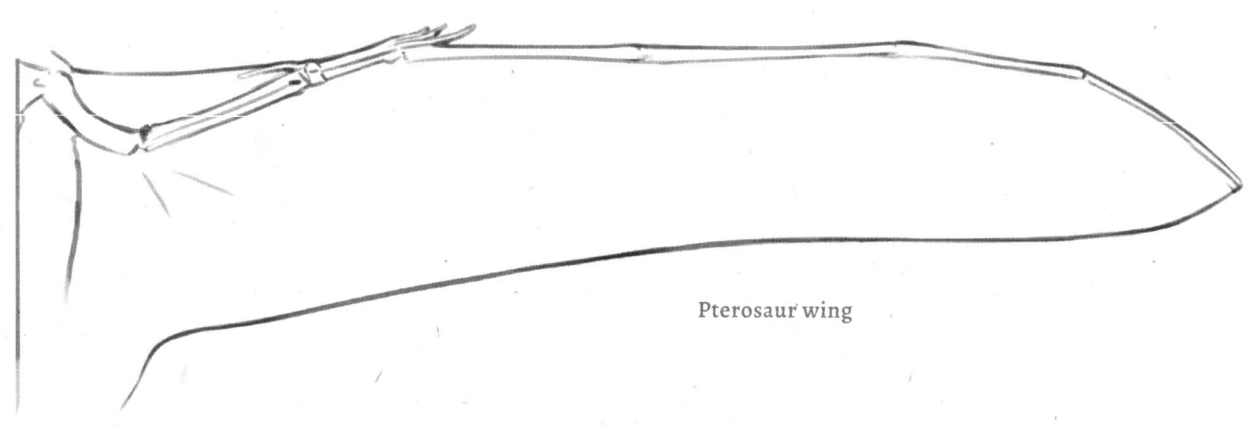

Pterosaur wing

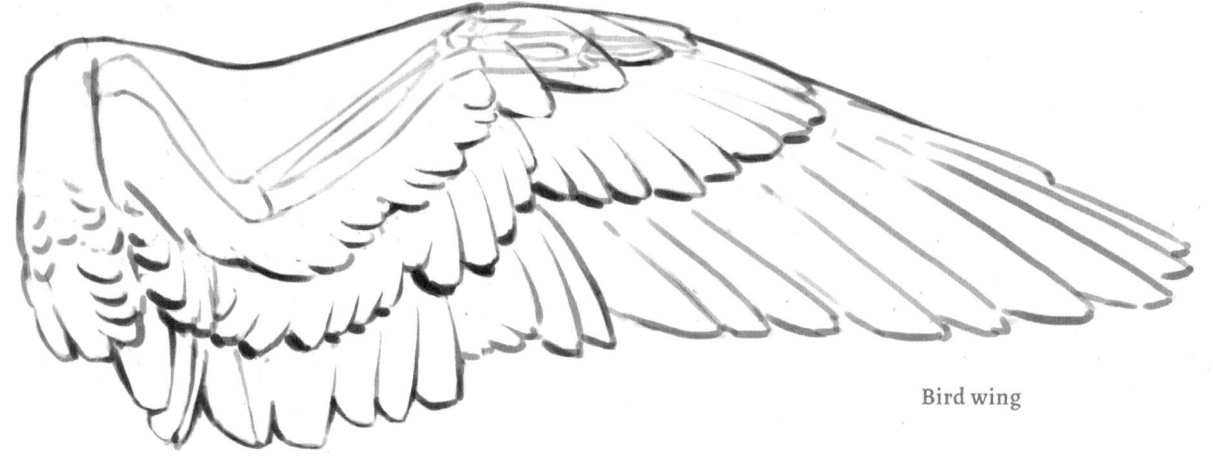

Bird wing

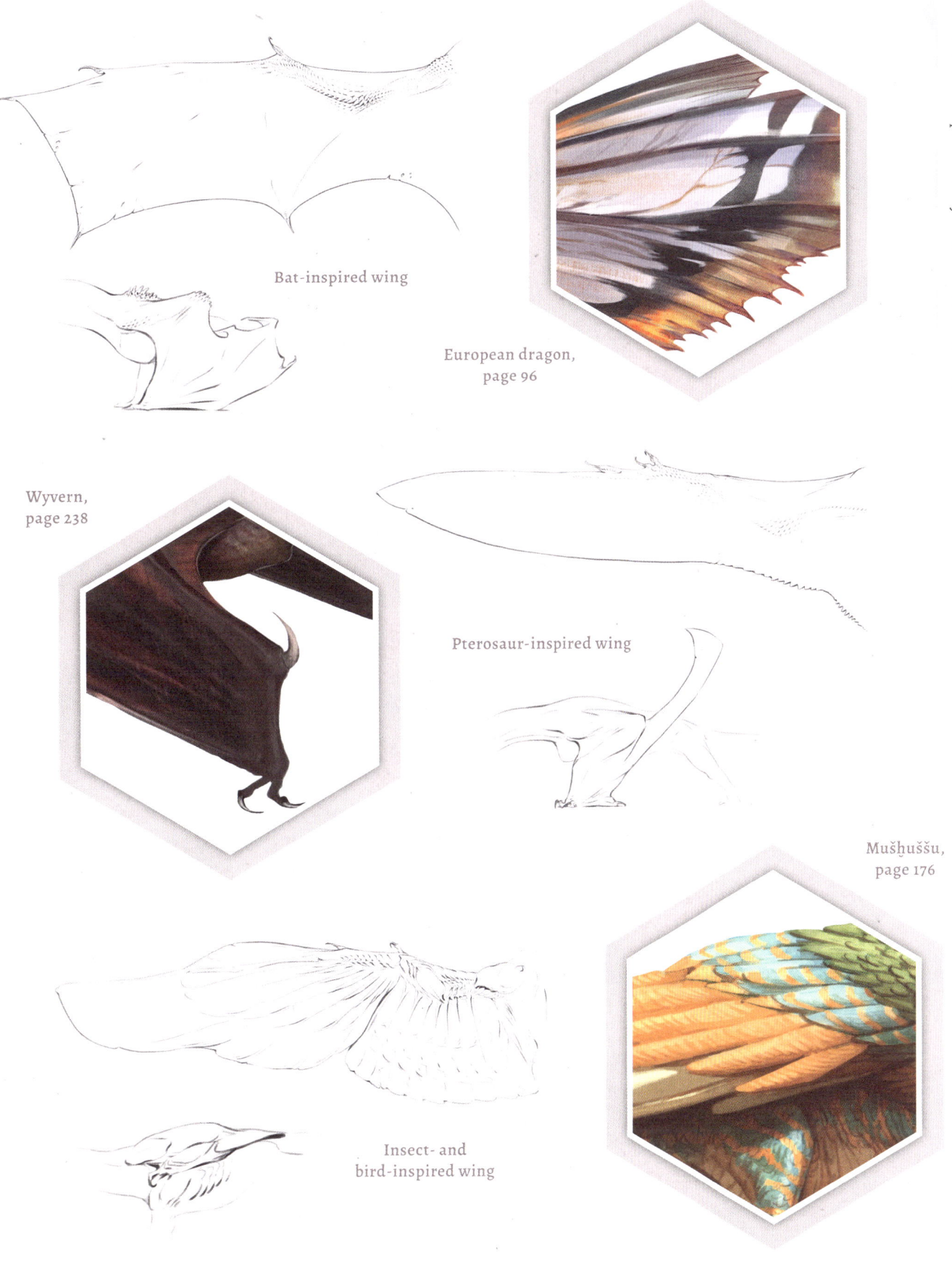

Bat-inspired wing

European dragon,
page 96

Wyvern,
page 238

Pterosaur-inspired wing

Mušḫuššu,
page 176

Insect- and
bird-inspired wing

DRAGON DESIGN QUESTIONS

- Does my dragon have/need legs?
- Does my dragon have/need wings?
- What type of wings, and how many?
- What type of legs, and how many?
- How does it move with those legs/wings?
- What real creatures can I reference for this idea?

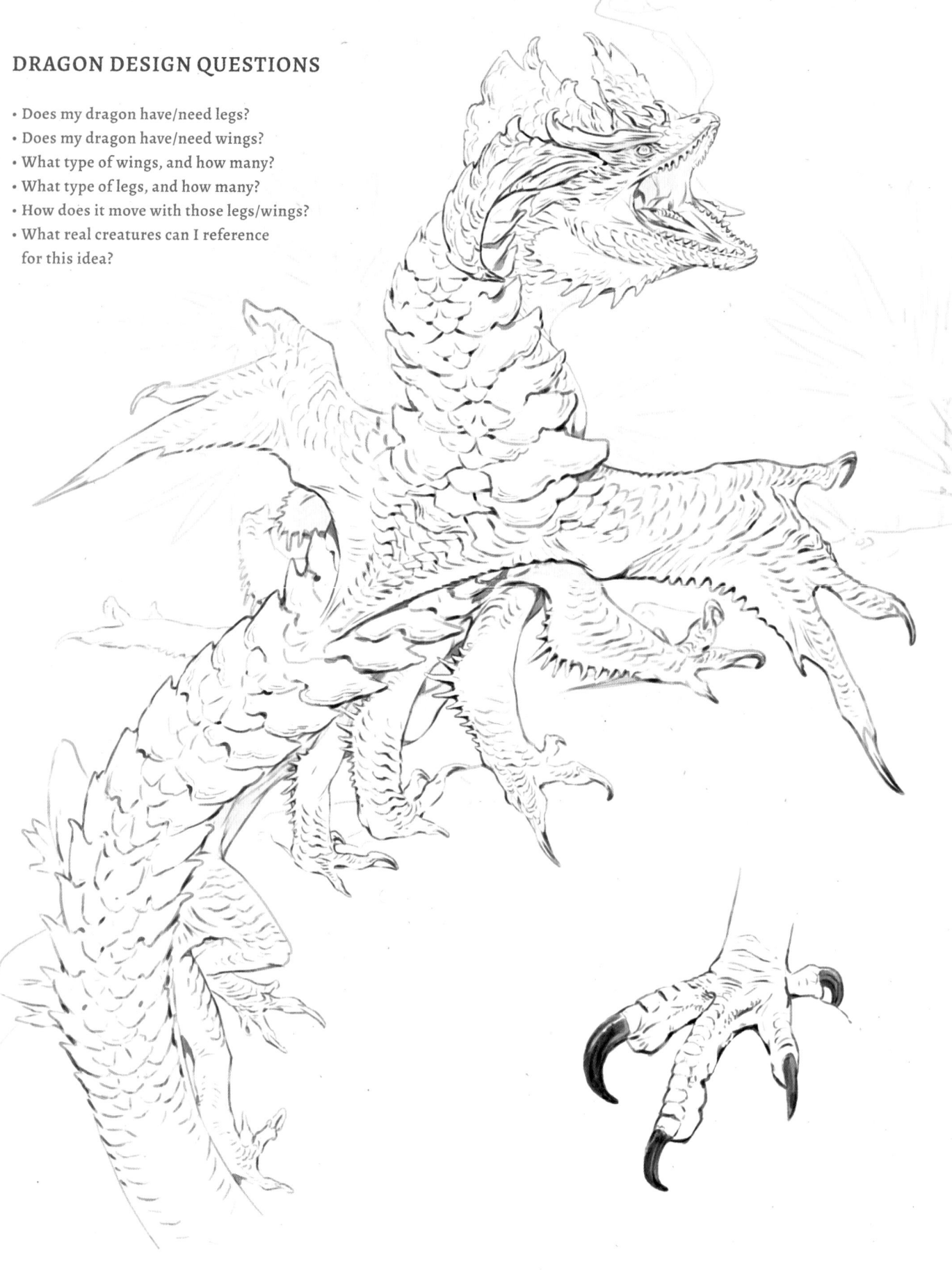

European dragon, page 96
(Classic type)

Salamander, page 206
(Drake type)

Lindworm, page 160
(Wyrm type)

Wyvern, page 238
(Wyvern type)

Ultimately the different types of dragons are options to explore, not rules to stick to, just as Stephen said. They can give you a good starting point and narrow down the places where you look for inspiration, and they might even be what's in your briefing. If you design for yourself, though, keep in mind that *you* decide what a dragon is. They are fictional creatures, after all.

The definitions of different types are also not entirely clear sometimes, although they mainly describe how many limbs there are and if they have wings or not. Among others, they range from wyvern-type dragons with two wings and two hind limbs, to drake-types with no wings and four legs, or even wyrm-types with no limbs at all. Maybe you want your dragon to have two sets of wings, though, or dozens of legs like a centipede, like the one pictured left. Don't let dragon archetypes hold you back from exploring!

When deciding how a dragon could stride, swim, fly, or burrow through the world, nature again can provide a strong base for limbs, mouths, or abilities that will shape the form of the dragon. The key to success is augmenting and enhancing these shapes and surfaces by pushing their forms, colours, and textures to communicate the dragon's personality or where it lives.

If this dragon is meant to live in the water, it should be shaped to accommodate movement through water. Does it camouflage from its prey above or below, or does it stand out, like the long fins of a venomous fish or the immense feathers of a gaudy bird, since it has nothing to hide from? What sorts of teeth support its diet in these waters? What horns rest on its mighty head to assert its dominion over others? Looking at regional animals from reality, depending on the climate, is a strong way to make your dragons feel like they have a real place in our world, or in a fantastical world. A northern European sort of environment might encourage a look of deer or elk antlers, versus a desert region inspired by Africa, which might inspire horns or antlers like those of a kudu or antelope.

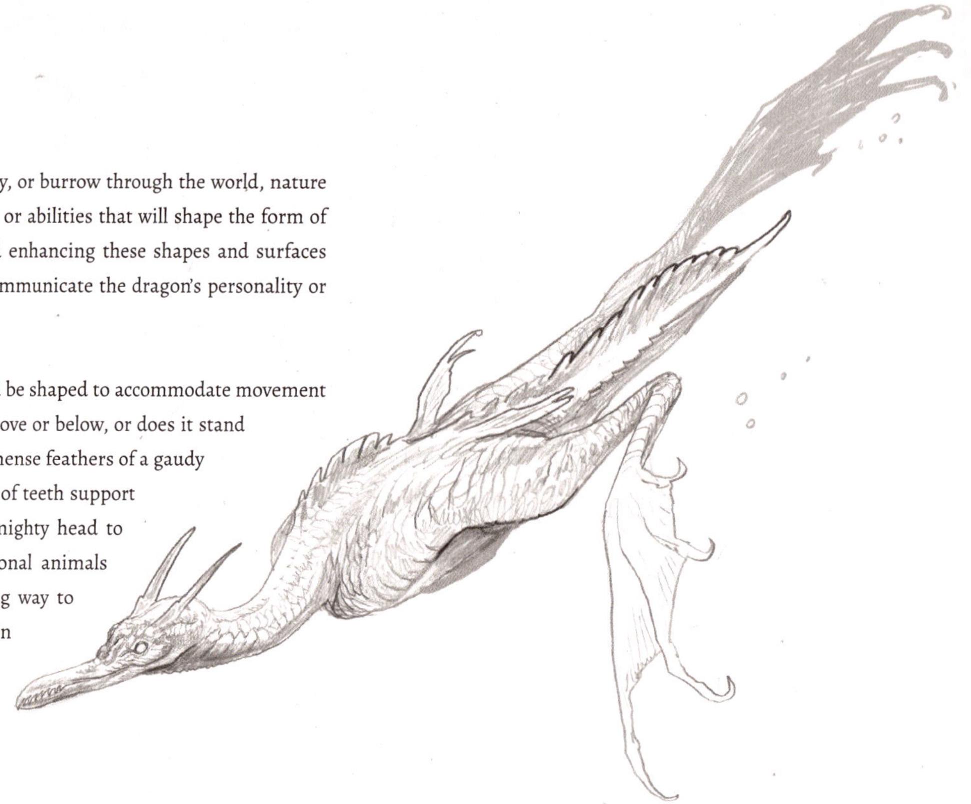

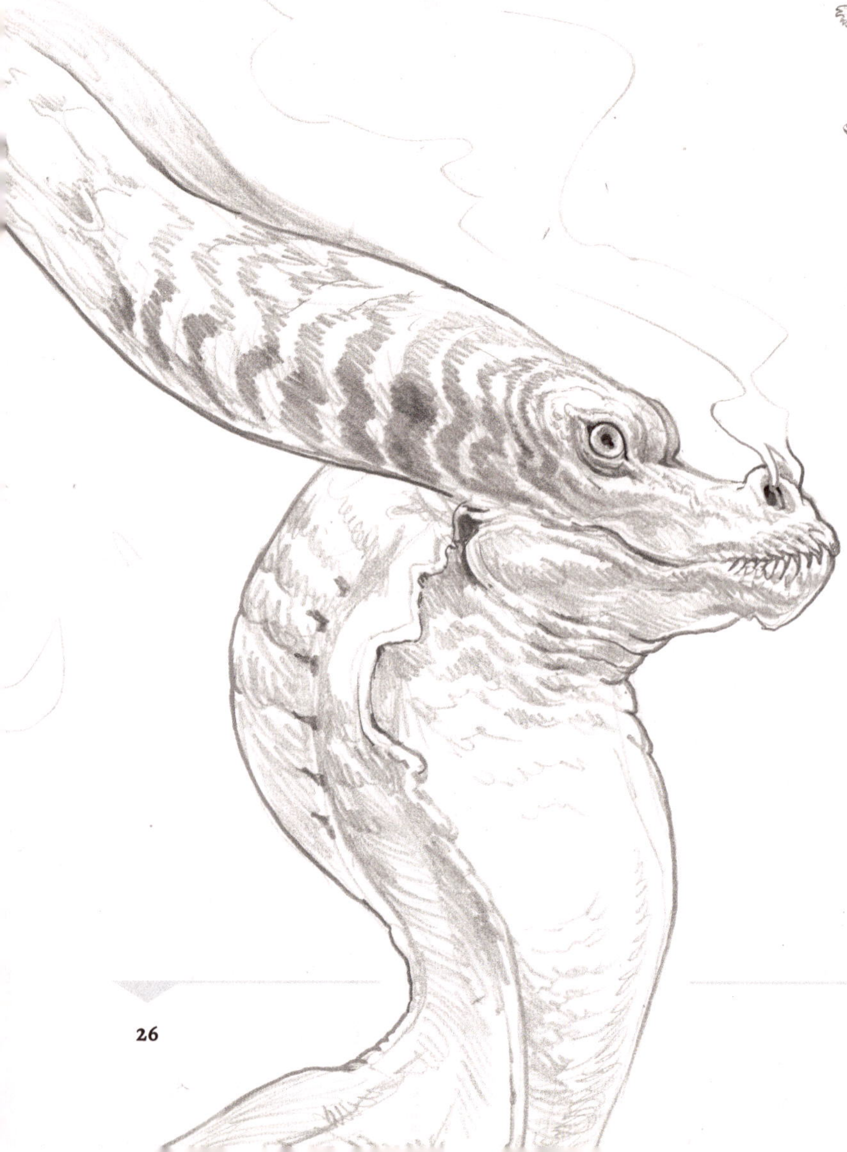

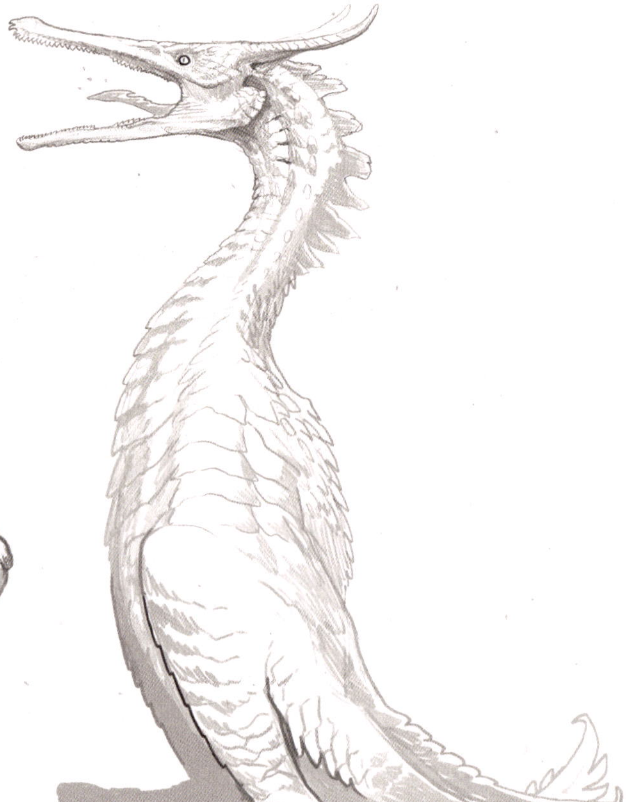

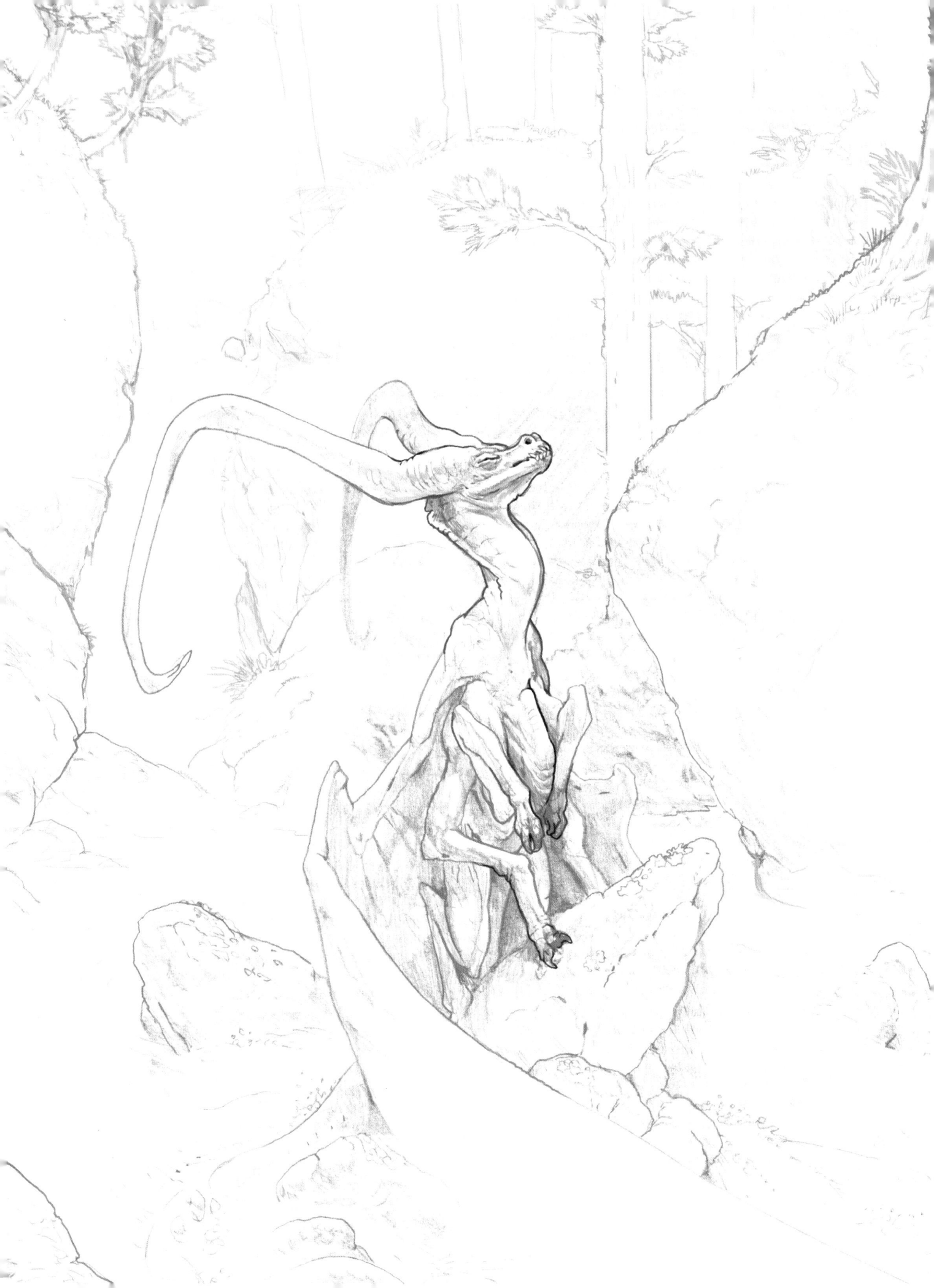

'Looking at regional animals from reality, depending on the climate, is a strong way to make your dragons feel like they have a real place in our world'

Stephen Oaklcy

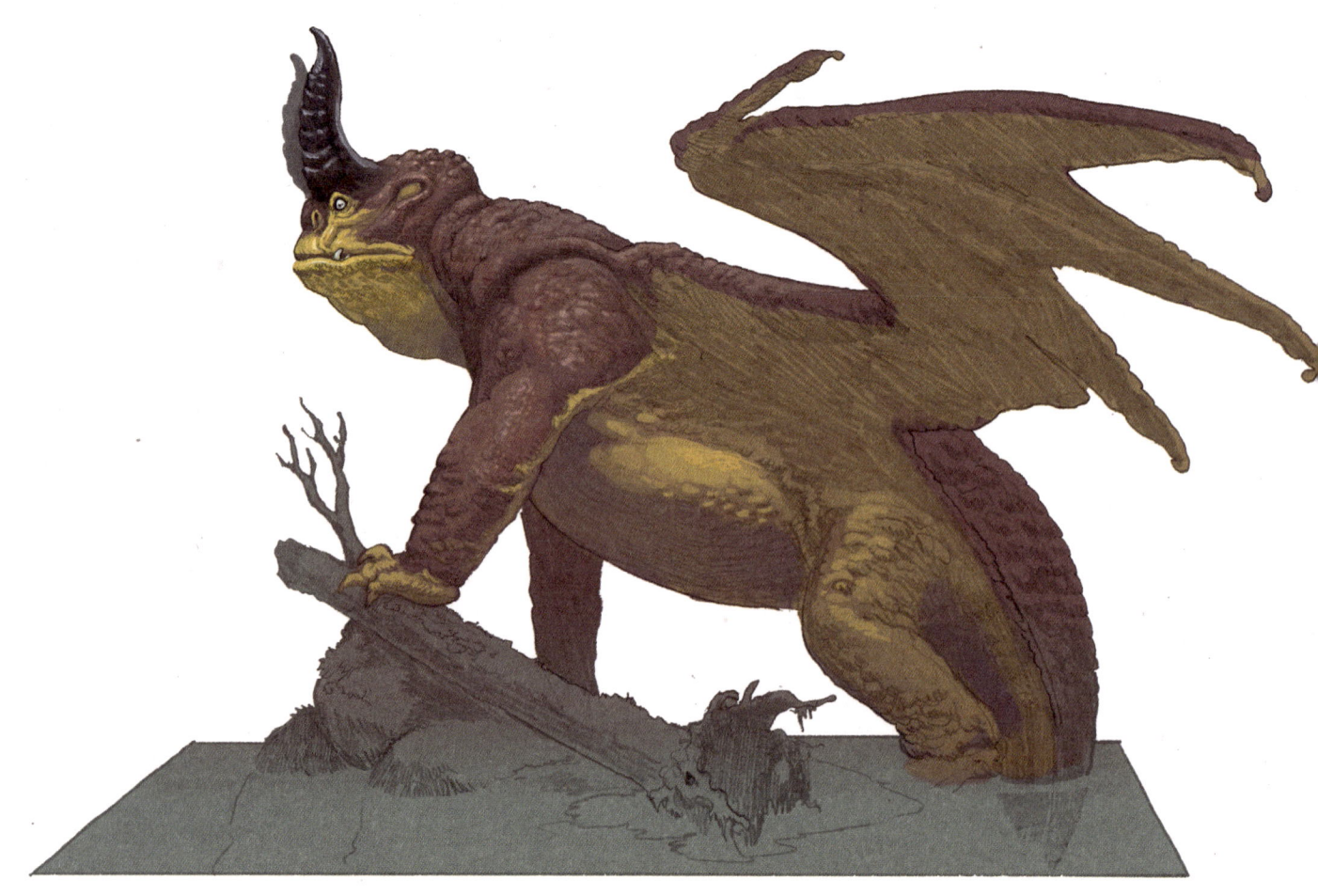

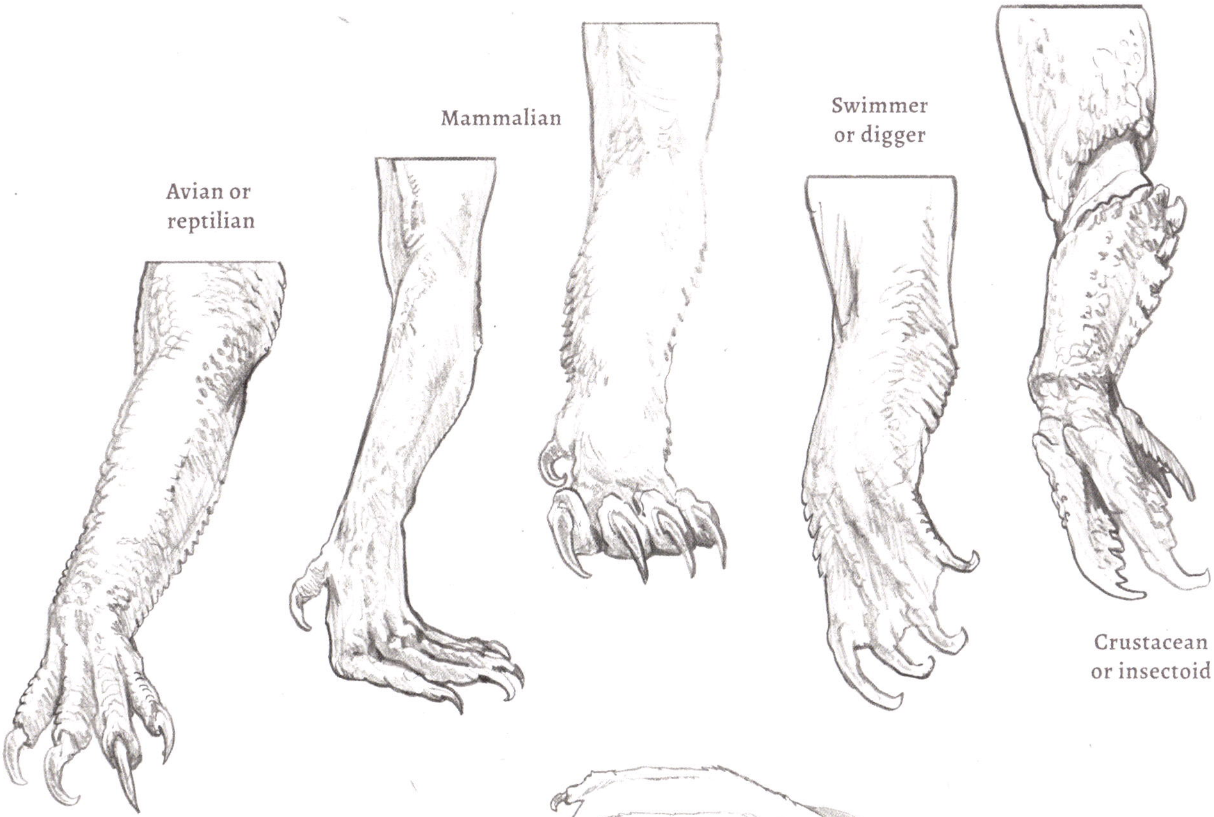

Avian or
reptilian

Mammalian

Swimmer
or digger

Crustacean
or insectoid

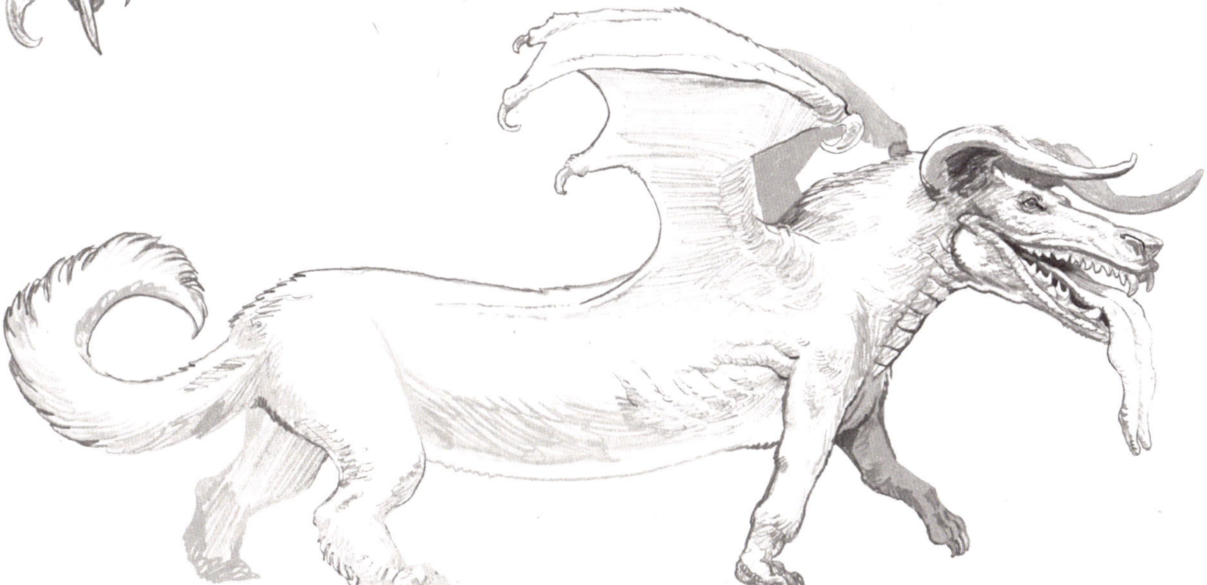

Dragons are often great and dangerous creatures, with features and defence mechanisms ranging from the natural to the fantastical. They can have thick scales, sharp claws, teeth, venom, tail barbs, maybe even frills and horns. Besides that, they are typically depicted as using some sort of breath weapon, the most common being fire breath. There are many other options, though, such as ice, poison, or lightning breath. How would these traits show in the design of the creature? Maybe the dragon uses a flammable gas or liquid – where would that come from? Maybe it has a special gland in its throat or even incendiary saliva. Perhaps your dragon is highly magical. Do they glow when they 'charge up' to attack? Are their scales lined with crystals that emanate magical force?

29

For me, the only time a dragon design really falls outside the realm of believability is if it is unable to eat or bite properly – usually if their horns get in the way of getting a bite to eat. Unless you can work around this by giving them a long, giraffe-like tongue to pull food to their mouth, or if their horns have siphons in them to drain their victims' blood for nutrients, you may need to rethink your approach! There are ample ways to get around this problem and still have ridiculous-looking horns. Dragons are ultimately just fun biological puzzles to make the coolest possible design, so never truly feel restricted if you can justify the shapes you have chosen through nature or plausible fantasy.

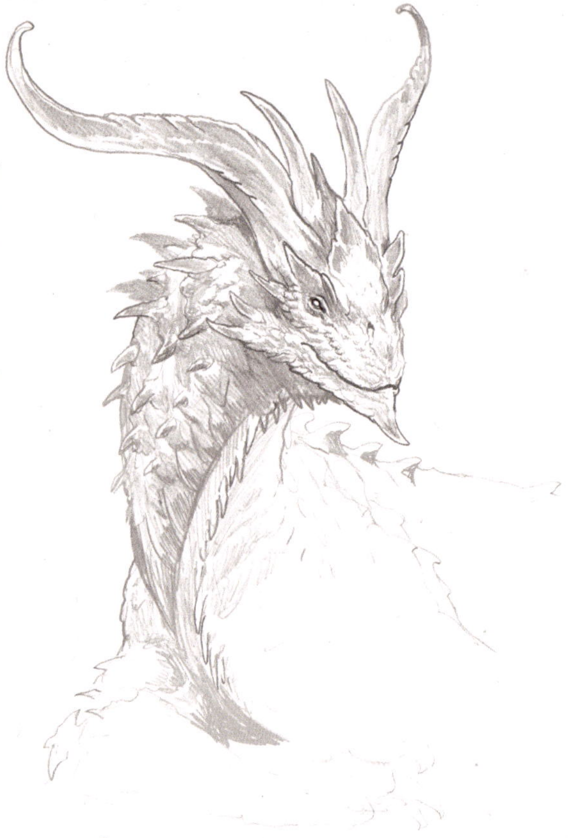

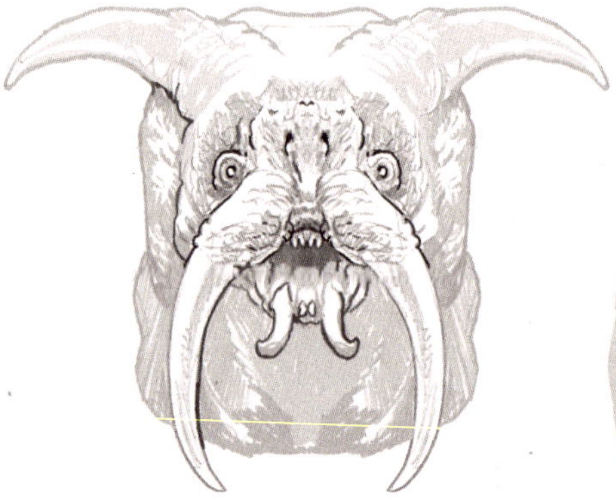

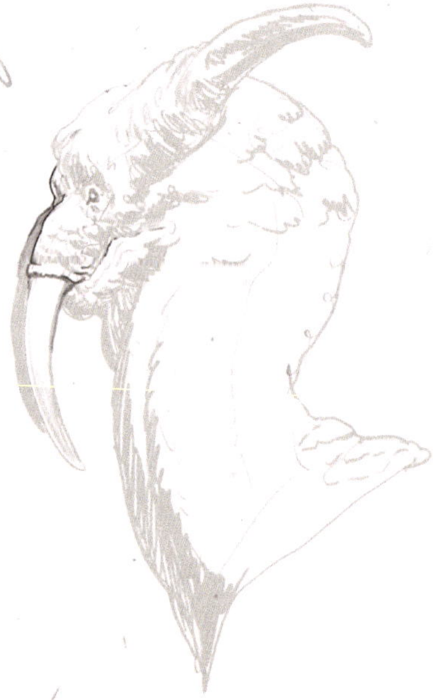

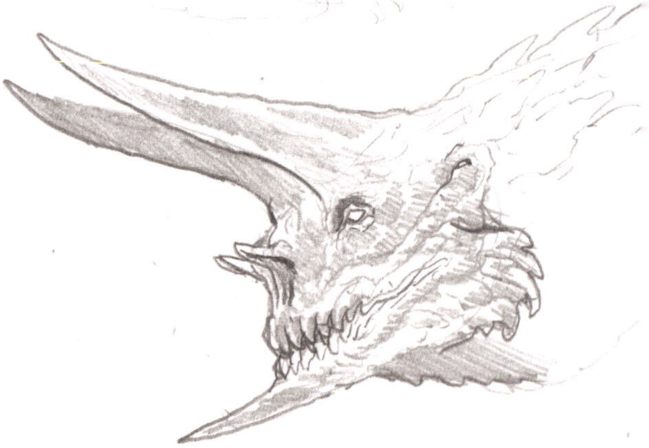

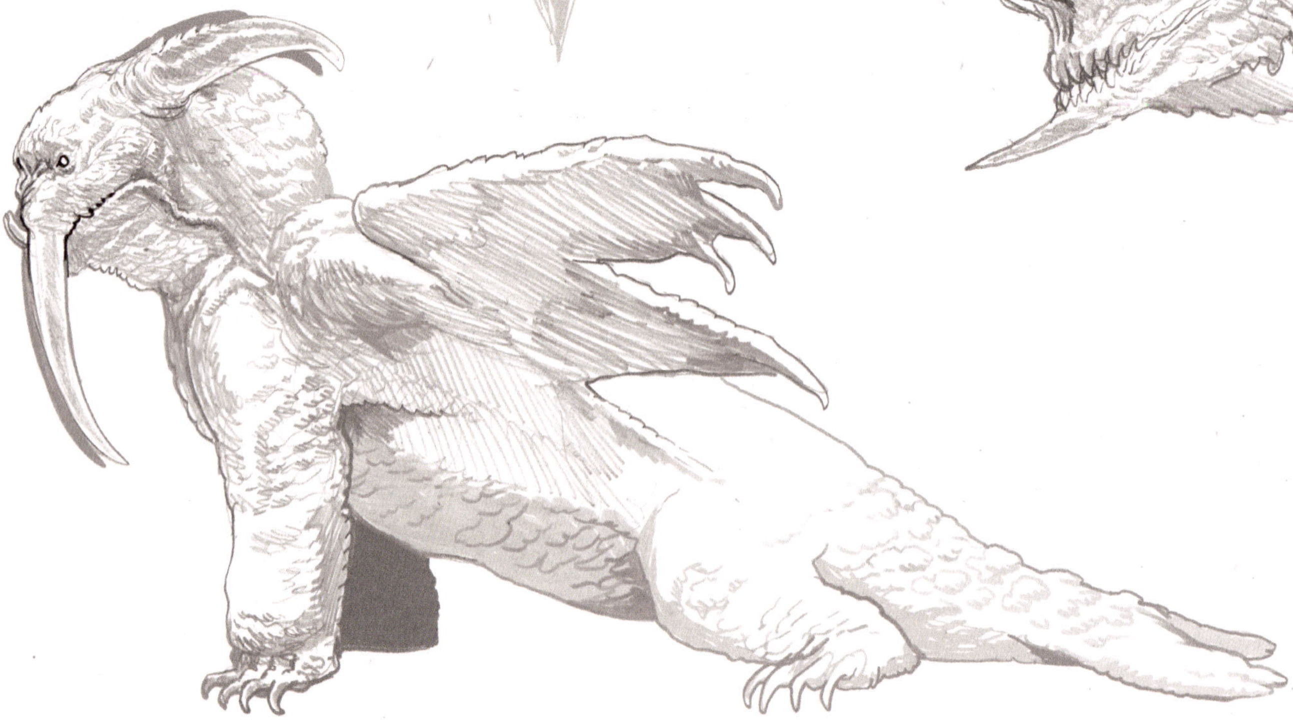

The best way to avoid such mistakes, like jaws that lock or wings that can't fold up, is to gain a solid understanding of animal anatomy. This is one of the most important skills for creature design as a whole. With an understanding of how different animals are built, it is much easier to use animals as a reference and to make your dragon design believable. If you know how a skeleton is structured and where the big muscle groups are located, you can also more easily make changes. You can add heft and bulk where it makes sense. You can shrink or elongate the wing fingers in a plausible way to create a more interesting or appealing wing shape. You can combine anatomical features and learn how to connect the muscle groups. You can solve the biological puzzle in a plausible way and have more fun while doing so.

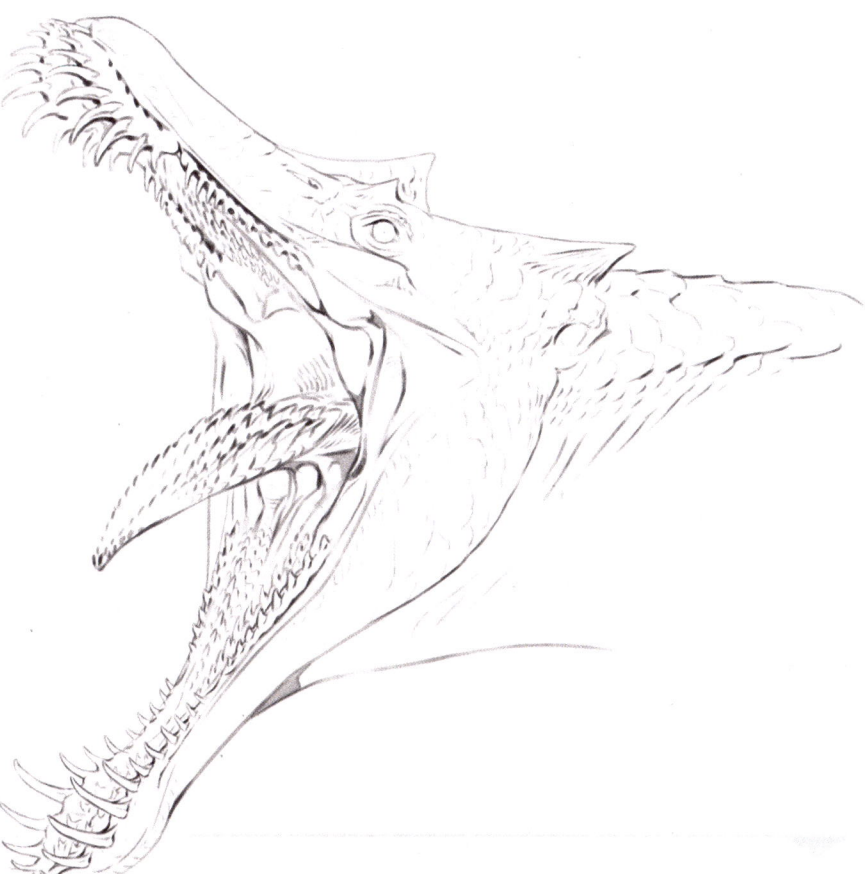

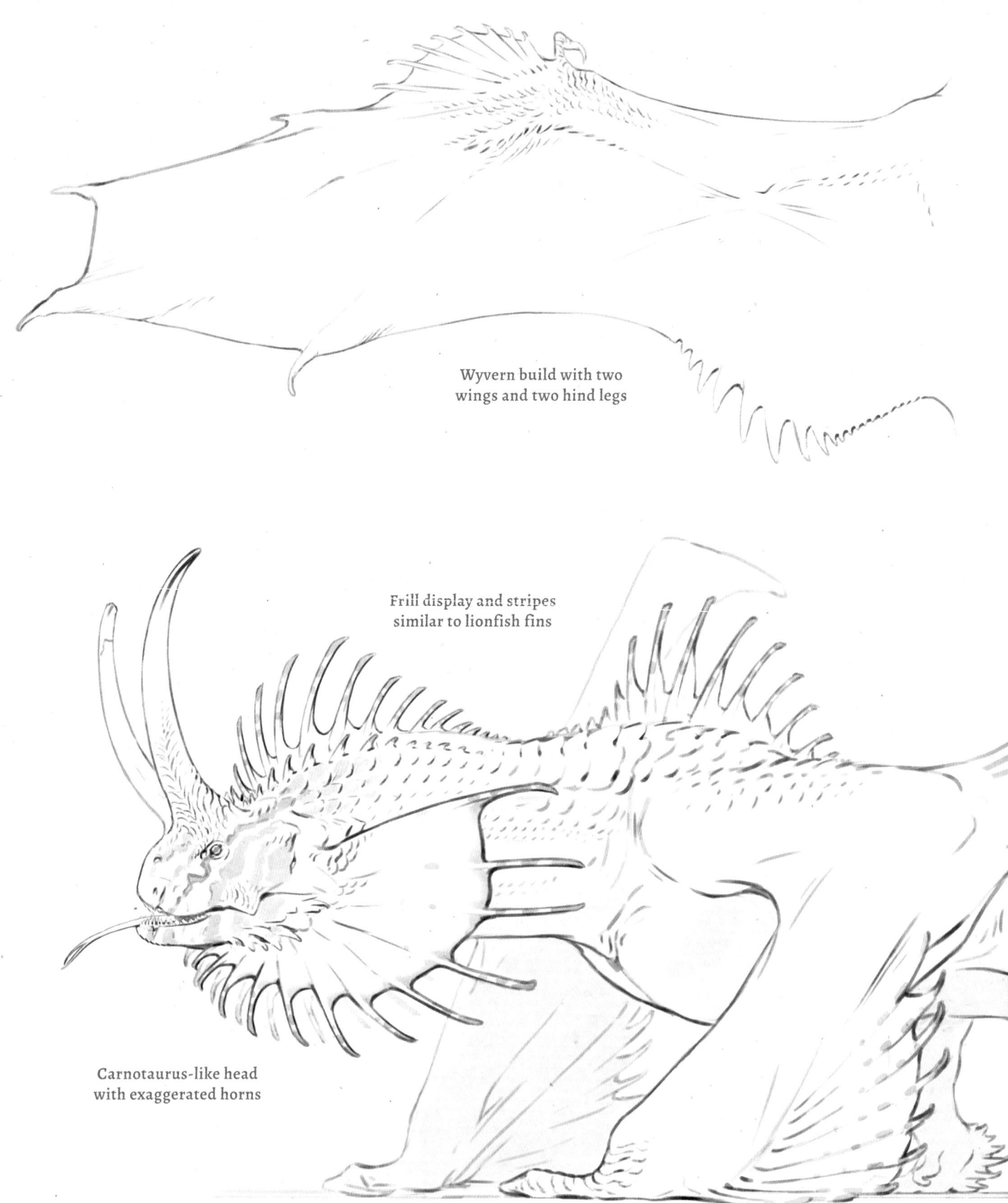

Wyvern build with two
wings and two hind legs

Frill display and stripes
similar to lionfish fins

Carnotaurus-like head
with exaggerated horns

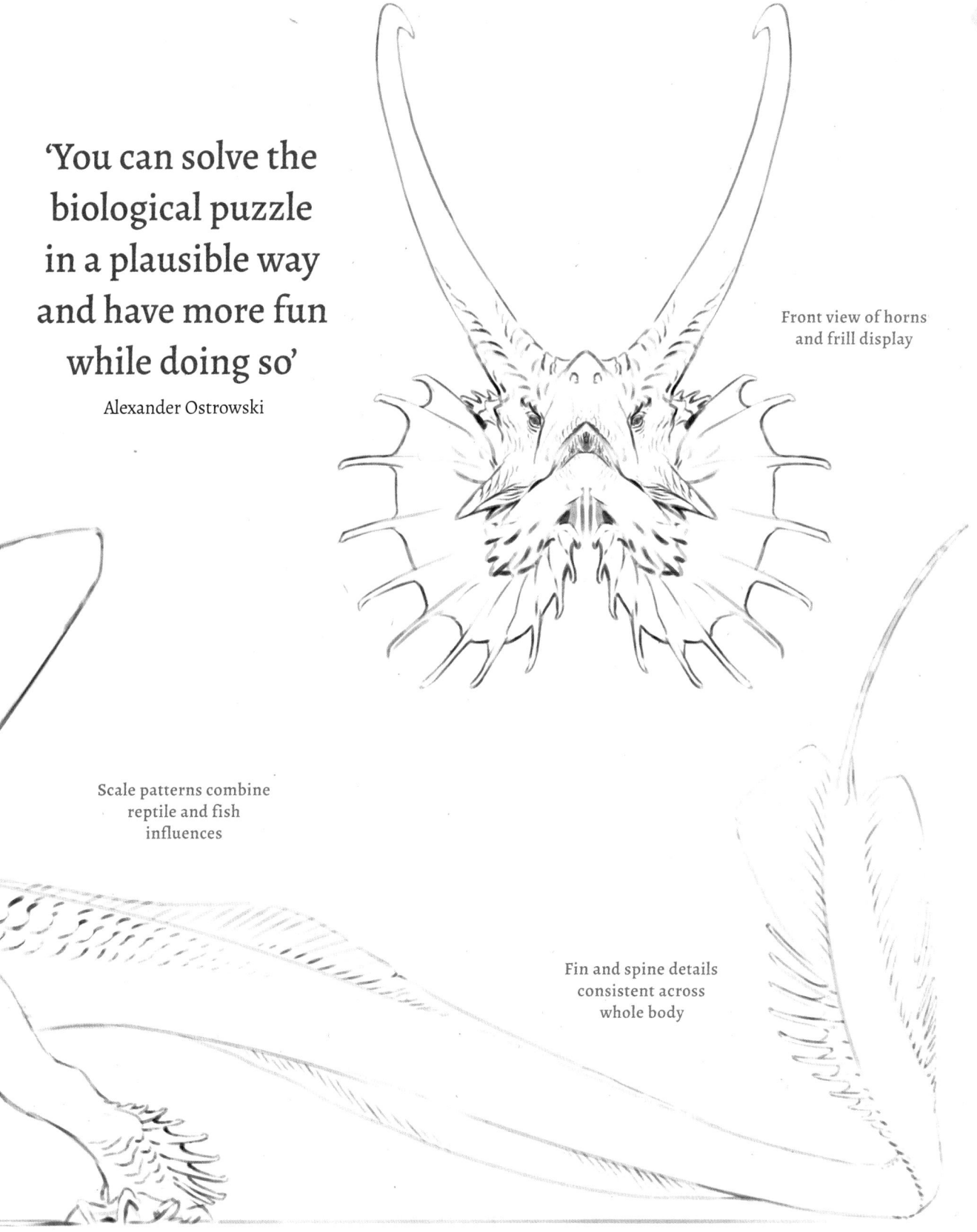

'You can solve the
biological puzzle
in a plausible way
and have more fun
while doing so'

Alexander Ostrowski

Front view of horns
and frill display

Scale patterns combine
reptile and fish
influences

Fin and spine details
consistent across
whole body

COLOUR AND TEXTURE

As form follows function, so do colour and texture. The lifestyle and habitat of an animal will influence their colour and texture a lot. Look at the markings and textures of different real-world animals that have a similar lifestyle or behaviour to your dragon. For an aquatic dragon, their scales might be smooth, their skin bluish-grey with white counter-shading on the belly for camouflage, just like Stephen suggested. A forest dragon might have non-reflective scales with a dappled pattern of greens and browns to hide in the foliage.

Besides the adaptations to their lifestyle, the story and character should also influence the dragon's appearance. A crown of horns can make a dragon more regal in appearance, rounded out by giving them gold and white scales, while a red-and-black snout riddled with scars can accentuate the violent character of a dragon. If your dragon is very magical, you might want to include magical elements into the design. What would a dragon made of fire look like? What colours and textures would an undead or magically corrupted dragon have?

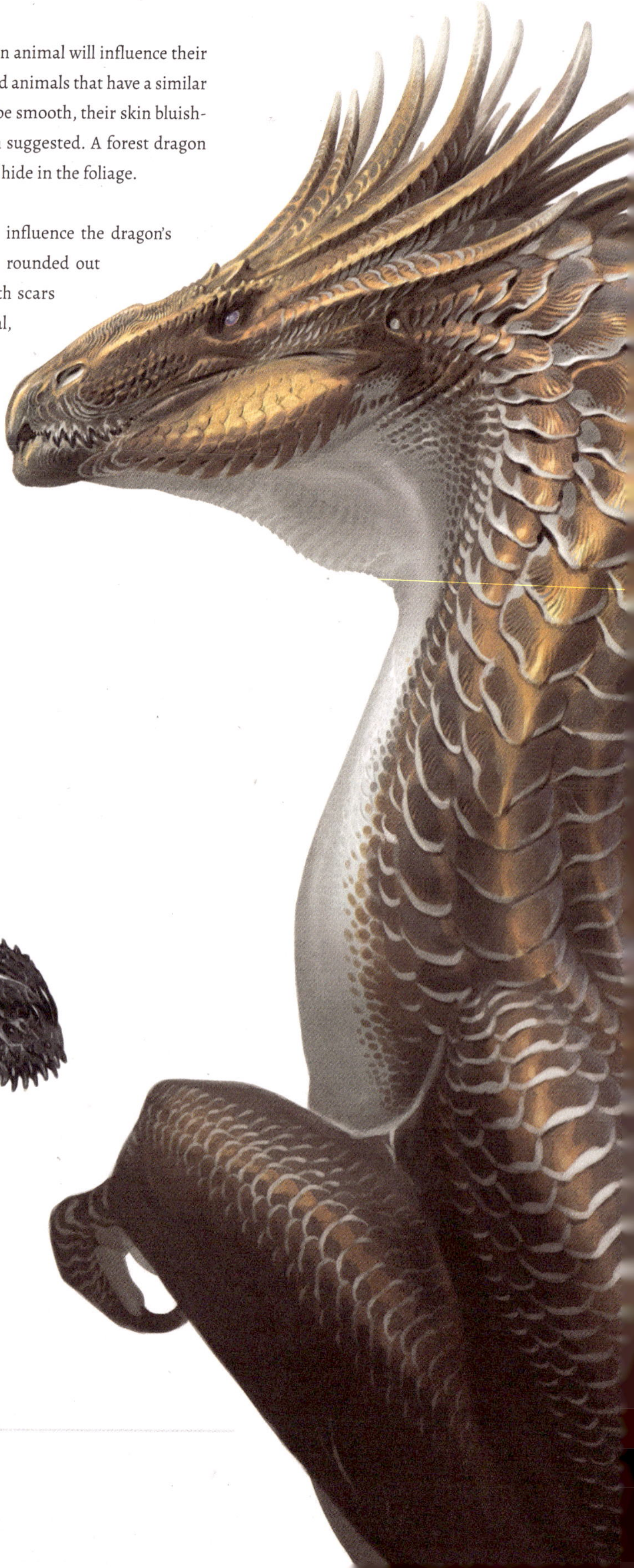

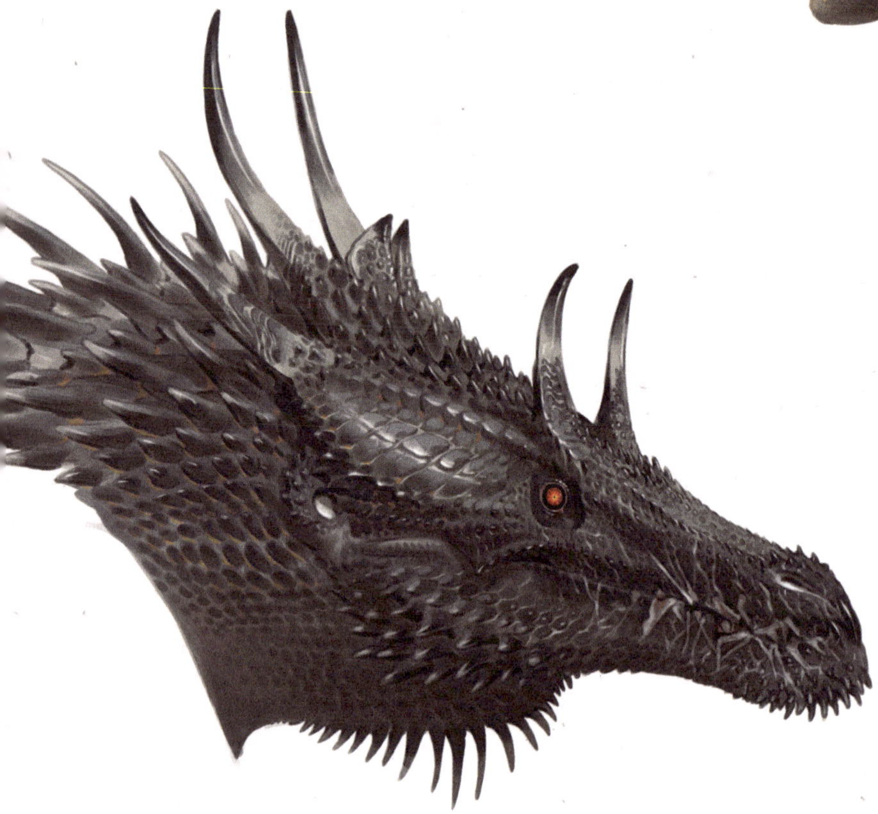

34

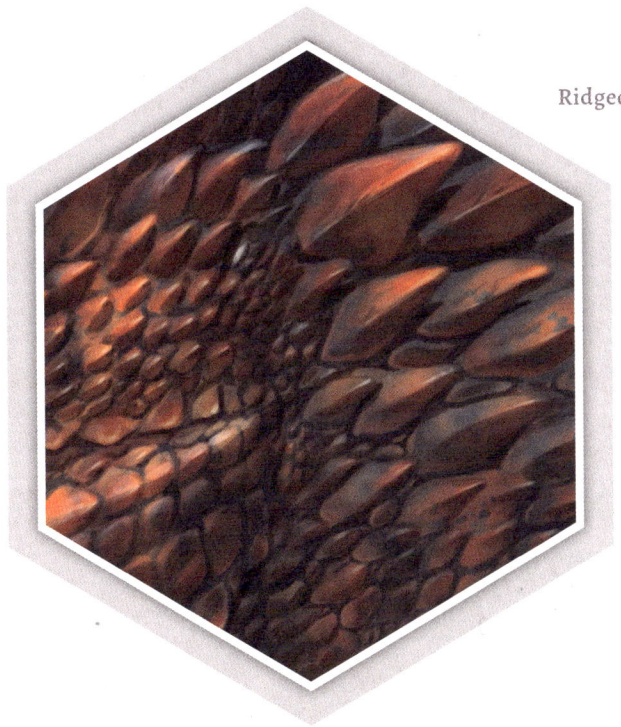

Ridged, keeled scales

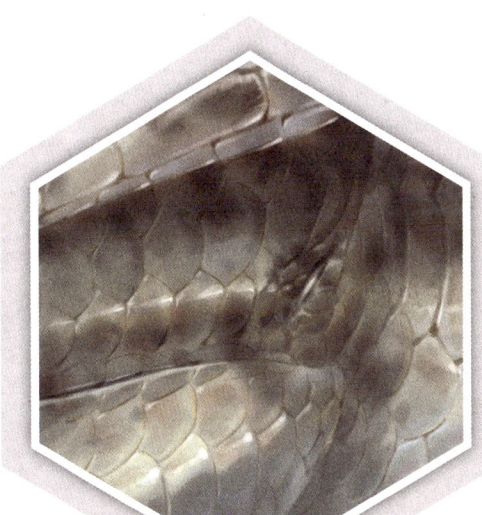

Shiny, smooth scales

Pebbled, crocodilian scales

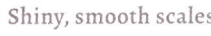

When it comes to palettes and patterns for dragons in games, colour and texture are the quickest ways to communicate what you can expect from the dragon's attacks and weaknesses. The strongest contrasting elements should be around the focal points or areas you need to watch out for as a player. I tend to reserve the bulk of the whitest whites, darkest darks, or most vibrant colours for around the heads, claws, tails, and weak spots.

Use patterns found in nature that mimic the abilities your creature may have. The sharp, zigzagging pattern of the Gila monster, tinted a bit more yellow, would be perfect for an electric-based dragon. Alternatively, sticking to and pushing the Gila monster's red colouration, or maybe swapping the black and red around its face, would help push the feeling that it's a fire-breathing monster. Pulling patterns and colours from what exists and adding a twist to them is the best way to preserve believability if you don't want to adhere to simple colours.

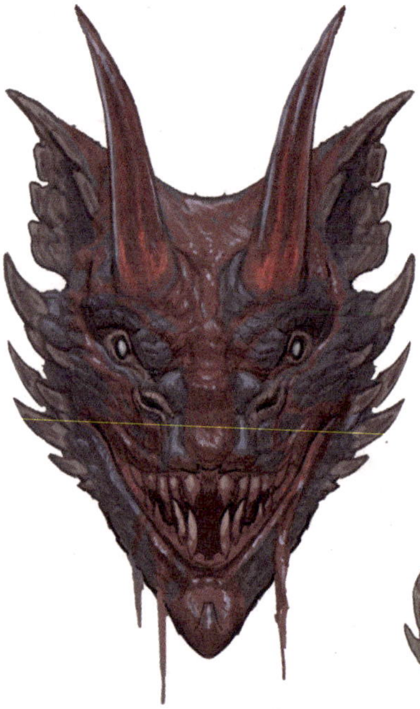

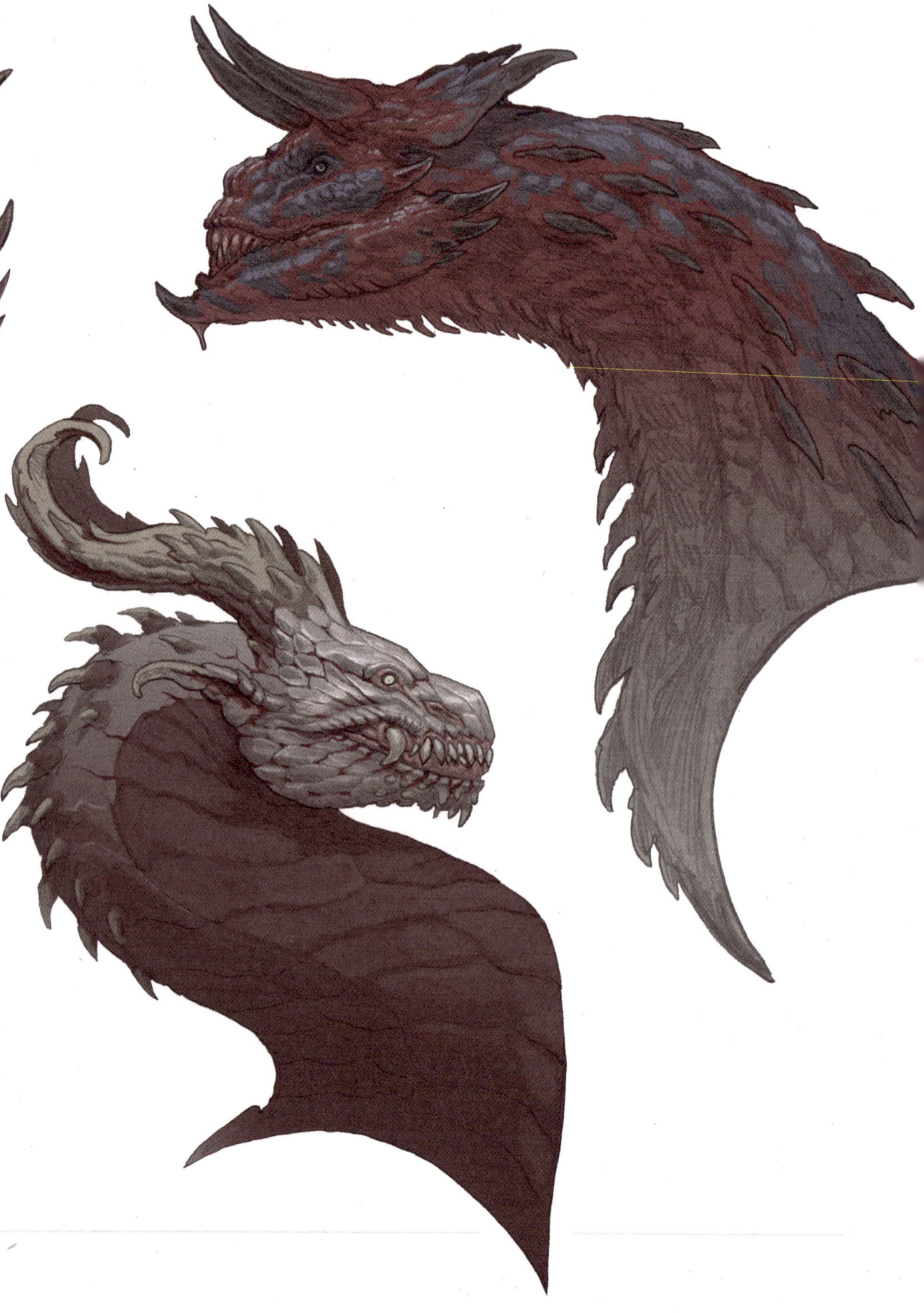

On top of all these ideas, the basics of design always apply. It is important to consider what you communicate with the shape language, colour palette, value range, and presentation. For an unpleasant or dangerous character, you might use more angular and sharp shapes. If it's a stealthy and sneaky wyrm, you might use sleek lines and shapes. Having a strong, physically imposing dragon be more robust and bulky helps to show their strength.

This also plays into the type of references you want to use, because audiences already have certain ideas about real-world animals, which need to be considered. If you evoke elements of a lion, like the stance and impressive mane, the connotations of royalty, pride, and power will be picked up by your audience. Be intentional with that. Every element of your design needs to be considered and every element has to work with every other.

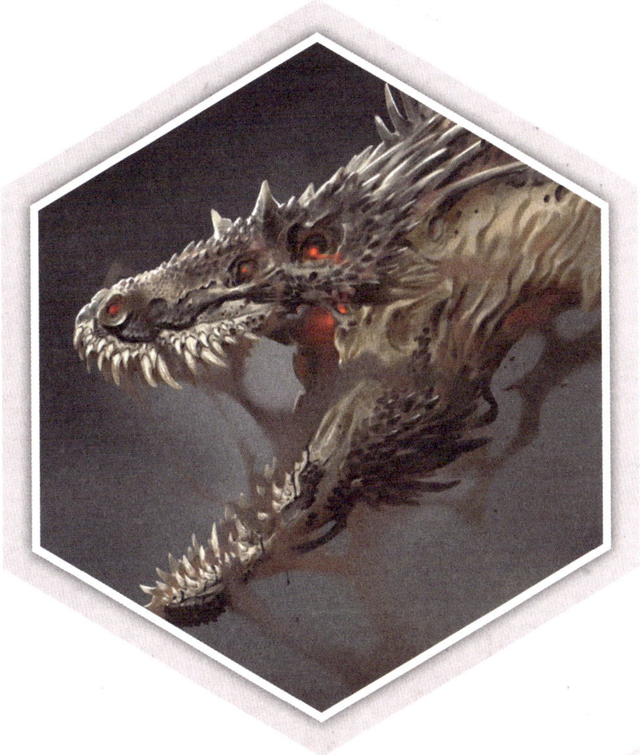

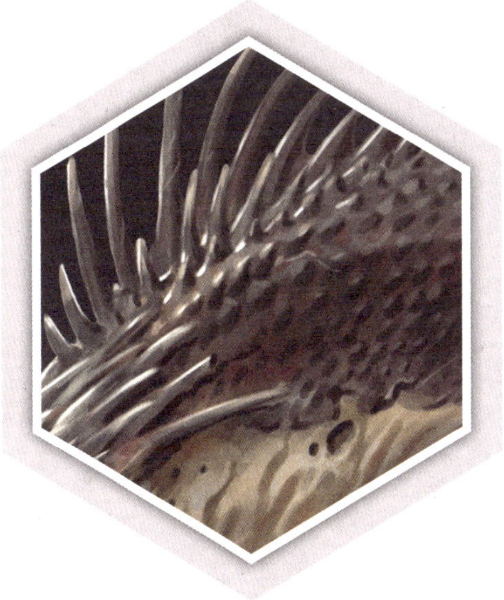

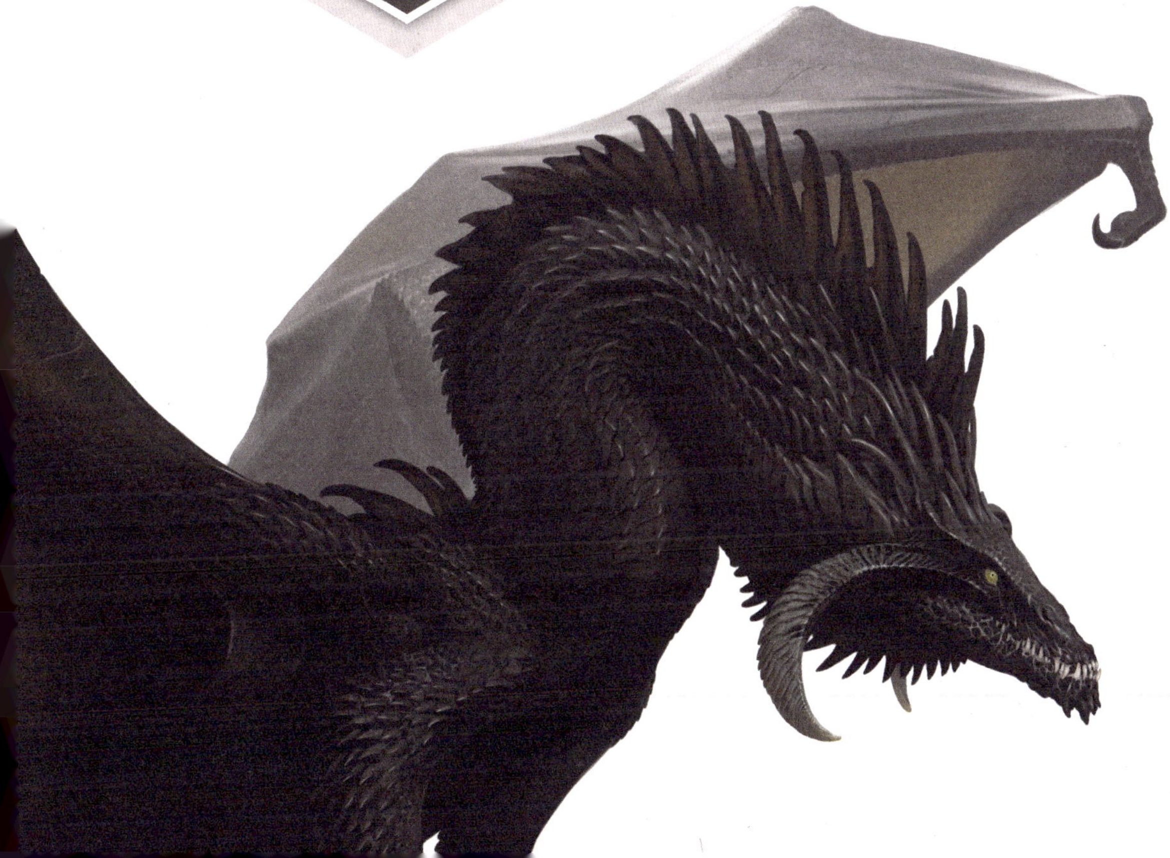

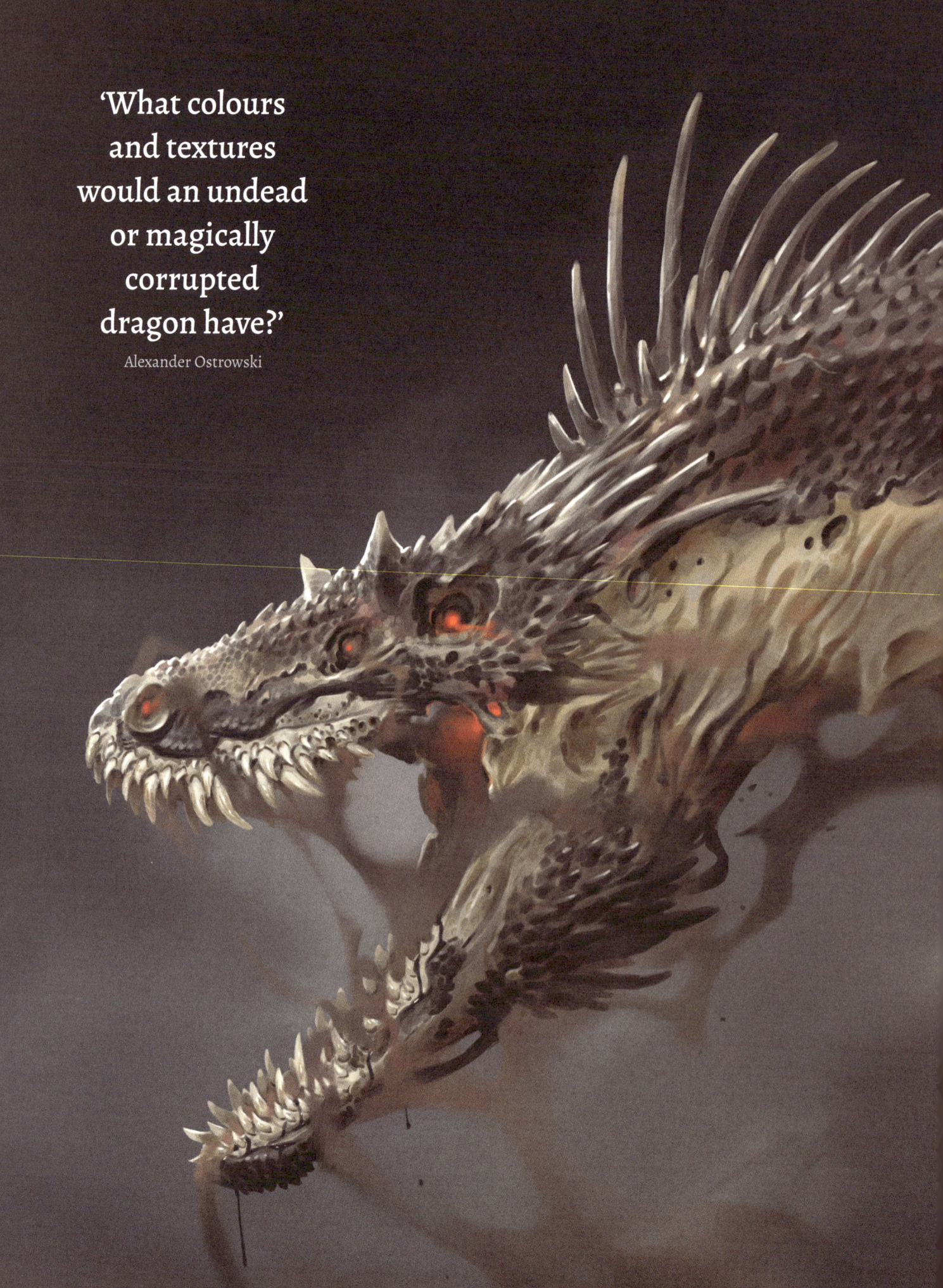

'What colours
and textures
would an undead
or magically
corrupted
dragon have?'

Alexander Ostrowski

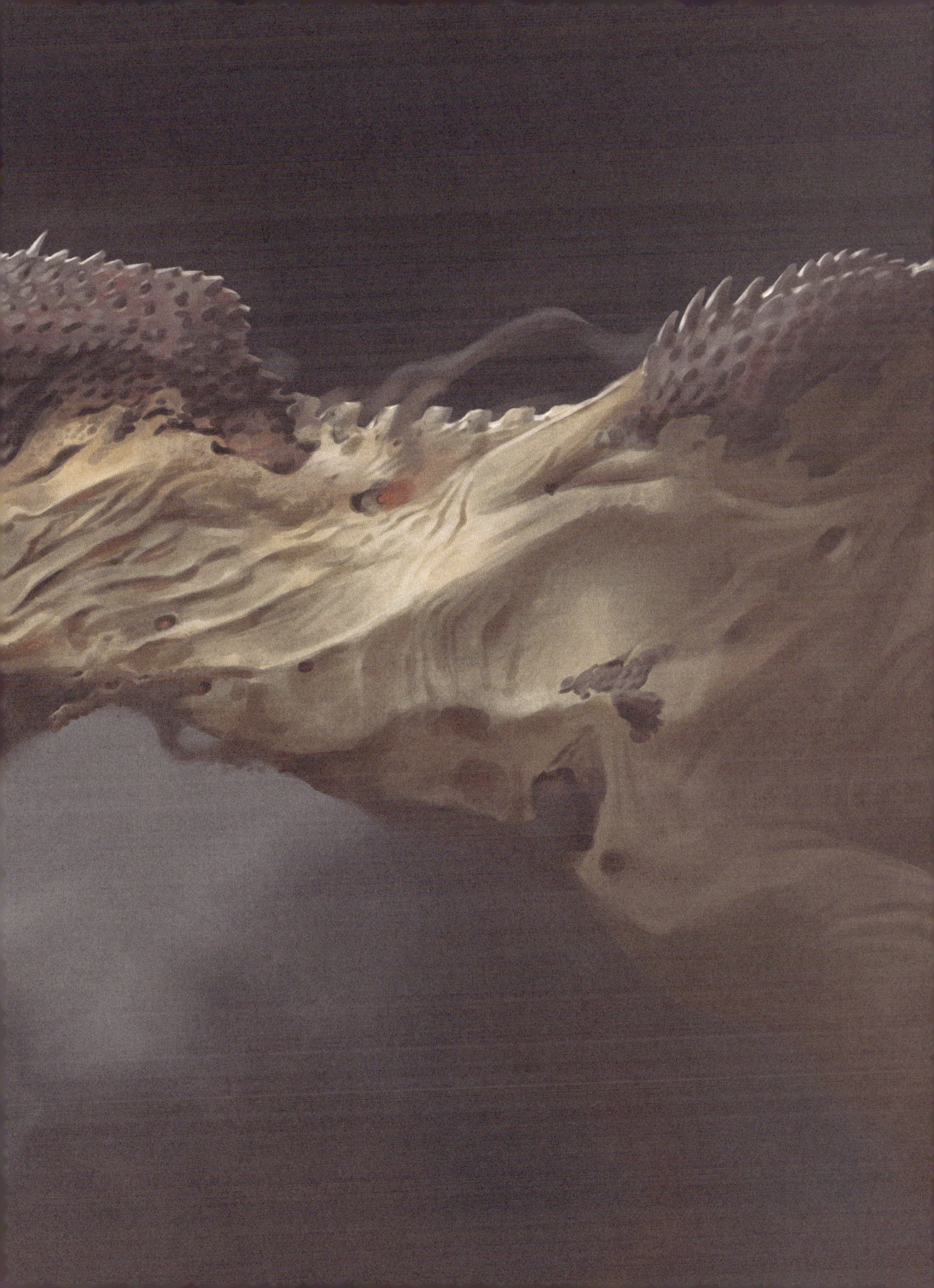

REALISTIC VERSUS FANTASTIC

Compatible shape language is important to make things more fantastical, and is something that I certainly lean into, convincing the various animals to achieve a purpose together. Finding unique animals to mix into the archetype of dragon is a refreshing way to make your design stand out. However, you could go another way and try composing a dragon with non-animal elements, just as ancient people used to see dragons in water spouts, mountain faces, trees, and hills! This can add an extra flair of the unbelievable, creating some truly next-level entities.

DRAGON DESIGN QUESTIONS

• How real-world or supernatural do I want this dragon to look?
• What genre or tone am I aiming for?
• What personality or character am I trying to convey?
• What is the story of this dragon?
• Do my dragon's features support those goals?

A fantastical hybrid clearly based on something real (polar bear)

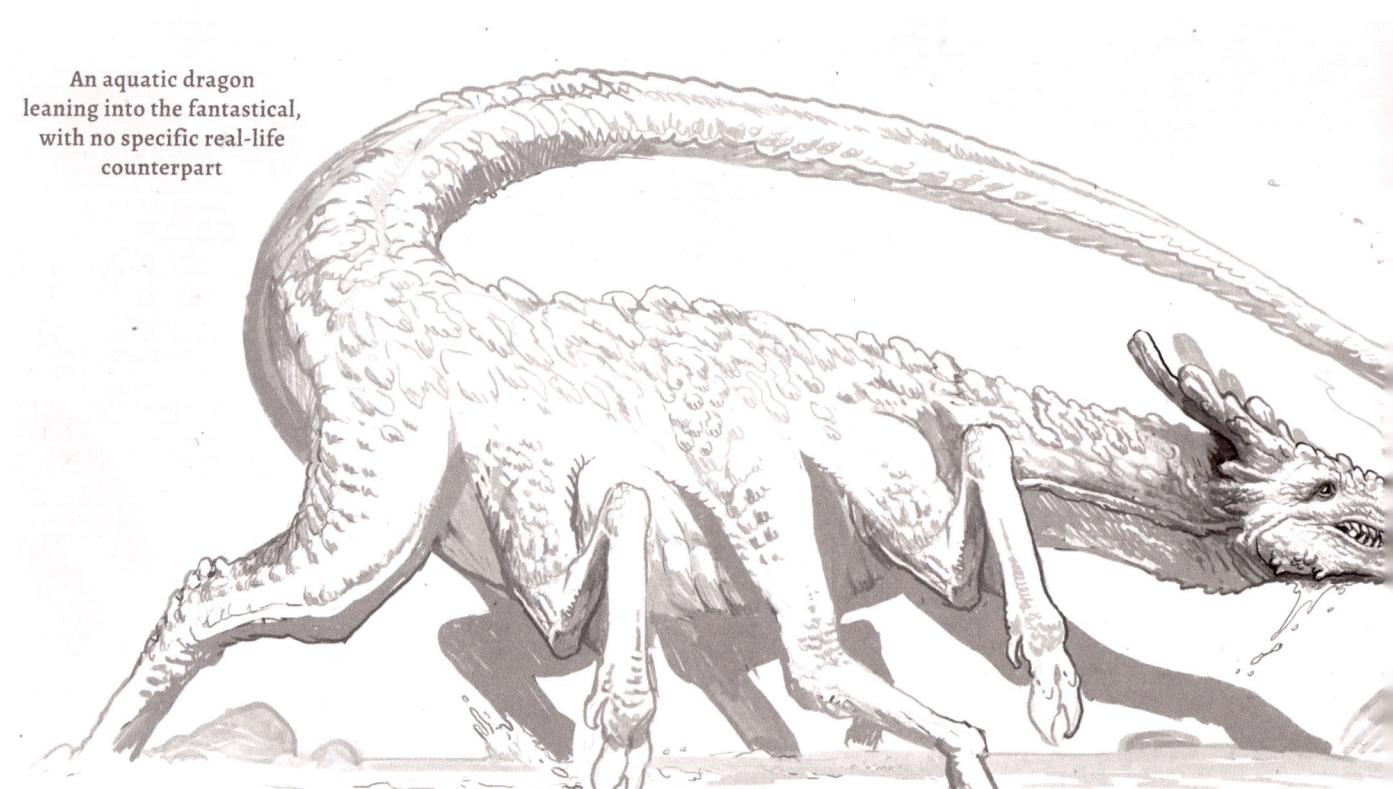

An aquatic dragon leaning into the fantastical, with no specific real-life counterpart

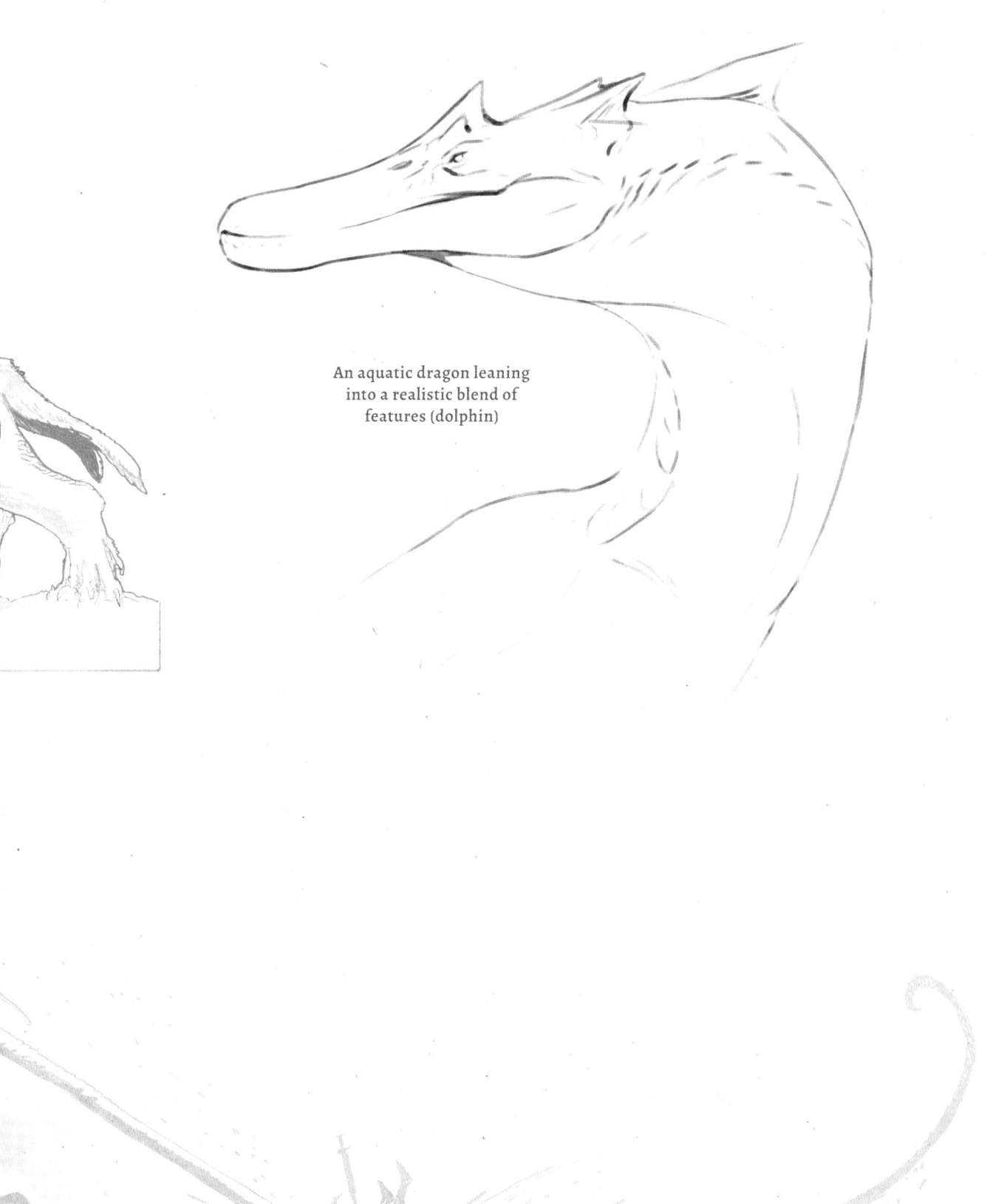

An aquatic dragon leaning
into a realistic blend of
features (dolphin)

When designing a true high-fantasy dragon, it's not about how believable the anatomy could be considered, but the supernatural elements you use to make it believable as a whole. If a dragon is a water dragon, it could be *made* of water, and its bones made of stones from the sea. Use the same building blocks of what makes up a real animal, but twist the elements involved in their make-up. Perhaps it is the bones of an ancient dragon, refusing to die and living on as a skeletal demigod of the sea and storm. In choosing what elements to play with, the stories surrounding them write themselves, not unlike the stories our ancestors told.

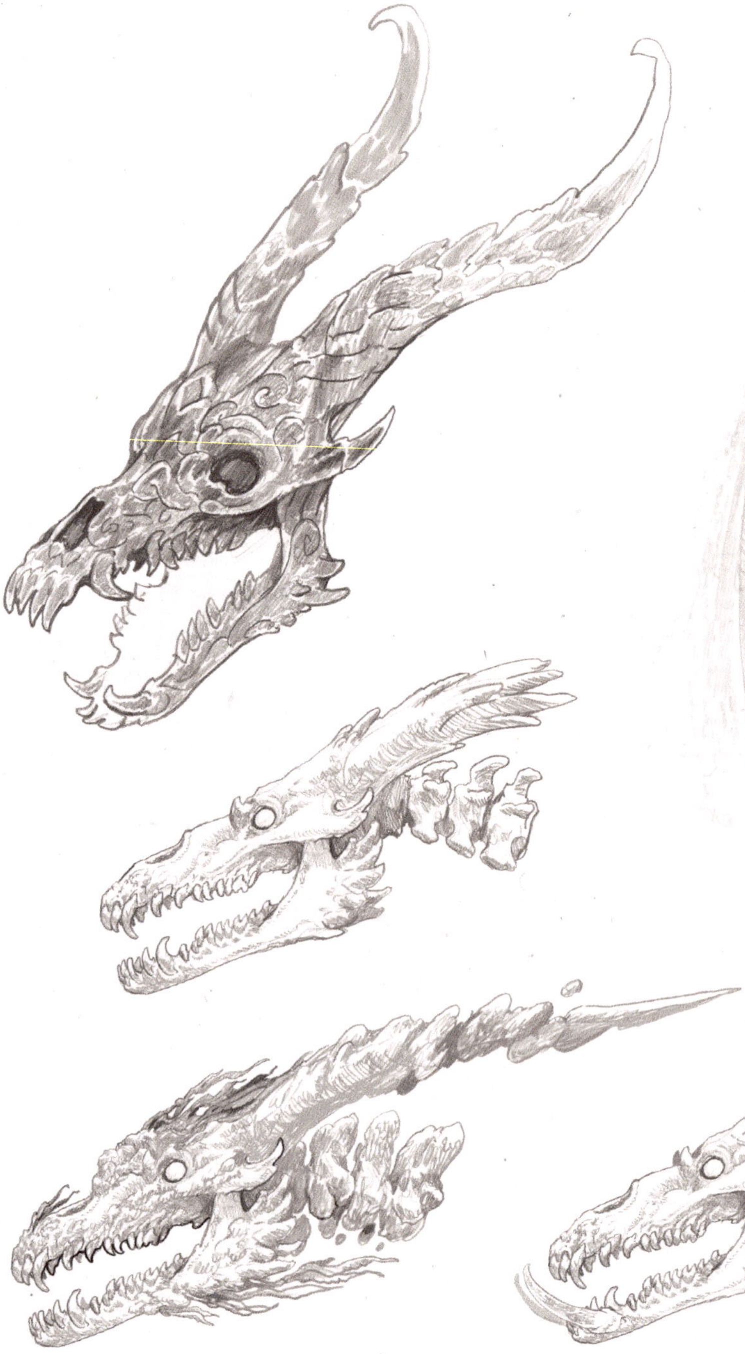

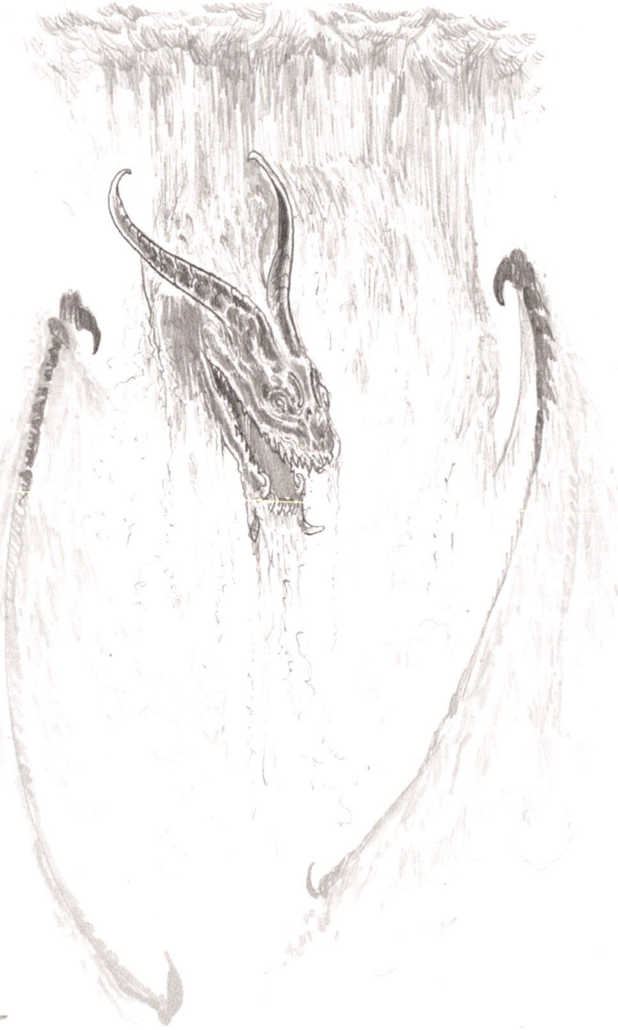

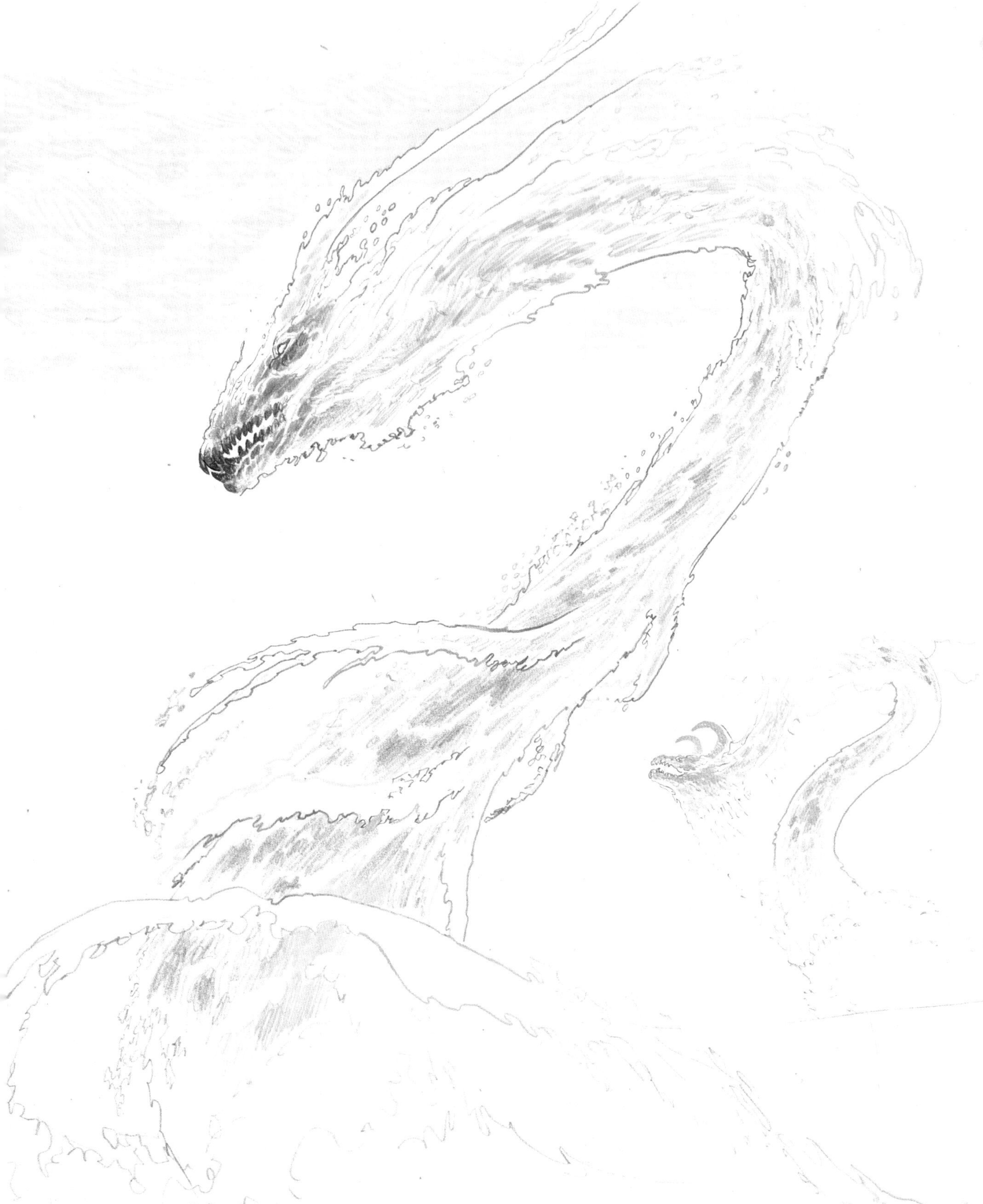

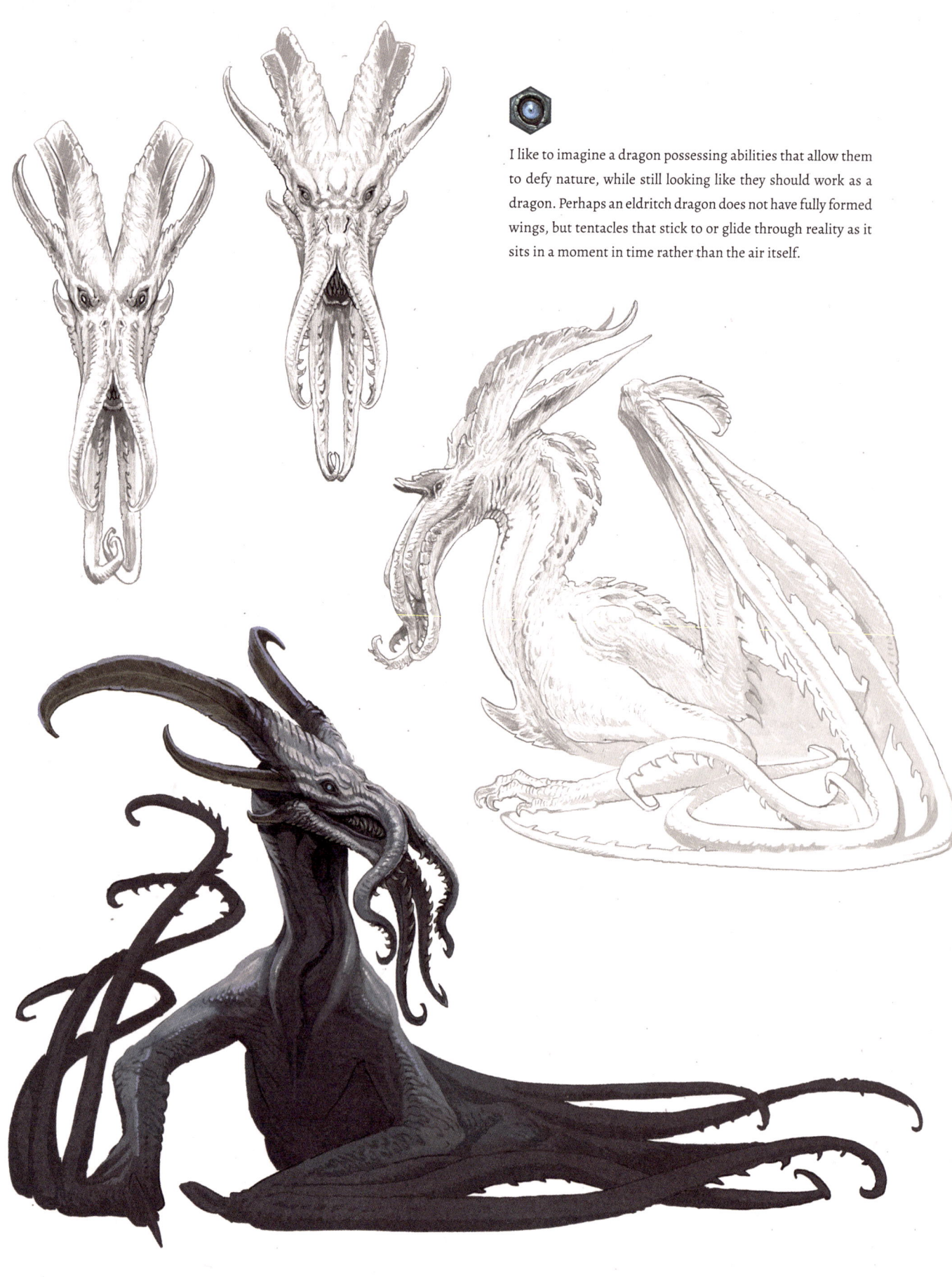

I like to imagine a dragon possessing abilities that allow them to defy nature, while still looking like they should work as a dragon. Perhaps an eldritch dragon does not have fully formed wings, but tentacles that stick to or glide through reality as it sits in a moment in time rather than the air itself.

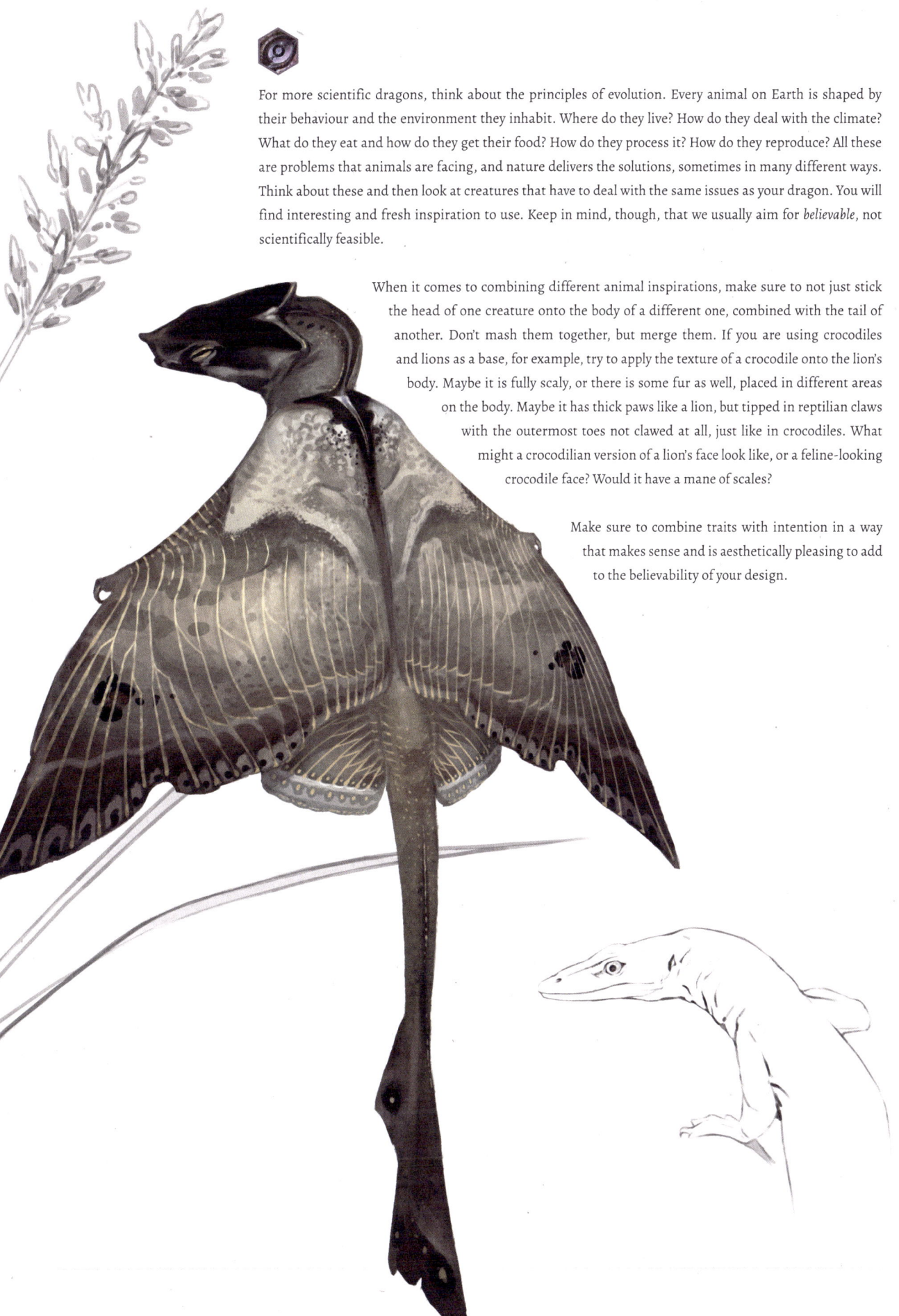

For more scientific dragons, think about the principles of evolution. Every animal on Earth is shaped by their behaviour and the environment they inhabit. Where do they live? How do they deal with the climate? What do they eat and how do they get their food? How do they process it? How do they reproduce? All these are problems that animals are facing, and nature delivers the solutions, sometimes in many different ways. Think about these and then look at creatures that have to deal with the same issues as your dragon. You will find interesting and fresh inspiration to use. Keep in mind, though, that we usually aim for *believable*, not scientifically feasible.

When it comes to combining different animal inspirations, make sure to not just stick the head of one creature onto the body of a different one, combined with the tail of another. Don't mash them together, but merge them. If you are using crocodiles and lions as a base, for example, try to apply the texture of a crocodile onto the lion's body. Maybe it is fully scaly, or there is some fur as well, placed in different areas on the body. Maybe it has thick paws like a lion, but tipped in reptilian claws with the outermost toes not clawed at all, just like in crocodiles. What might a crocodilian version of a lion's face look like, or a feline-looking crocodile face? Would it have a mane of scales?

Make sure to combine traits with intention in a way that makes sense and is aesthetically pleasing to add to the believability of your design.

DRAGON LIFE

It is really fun to speculate on the life of your dragons, as animals or magical creatures, or both. Their life cycles can be as wildly different as the dragons themselves. Reptiles usually lay eggs, but some extinct marine reptiles are thought to have given birth to live young in the water. So even if your dragons are reptiles, which they might not be, they don't necessarily have to lay eggs. As magical creatures, they might also reproduce in a completely different way. Maybe they emerge fully formed as adults, born from active volcanoes, or maybe they are transformed human sorcerers!

If they do have young, does the adult dragon care for them or leave them to fend for themselves? Maybe they have one chick every ten years or so and raise it over a long time. Maybe they lay a clutch of fifty eggs somewhere in a secluded nest and leave, with most of the hatchlings not surviving the first year of their life.

If they reproduce, is there a difference between the young and adult dragons? Are there male and female dragons at all? Are there more sexes, like in some fish? Do they differ from each other? If so, why and how? Males could be smaller, but have large, colourful crests to impress the females.

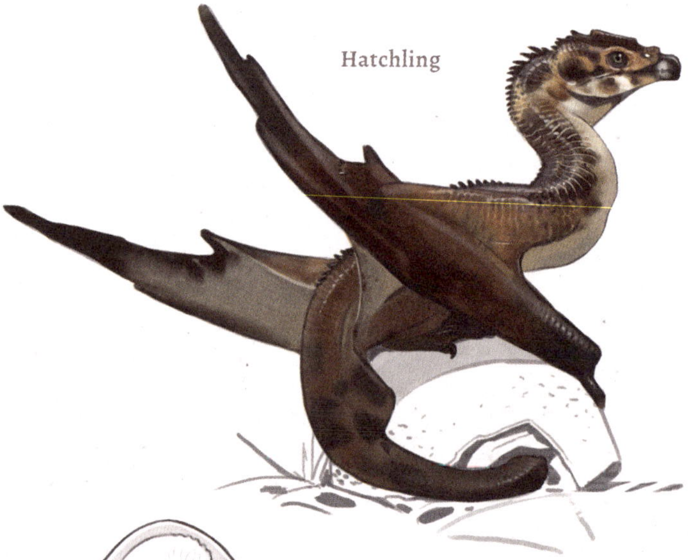

Hatchling

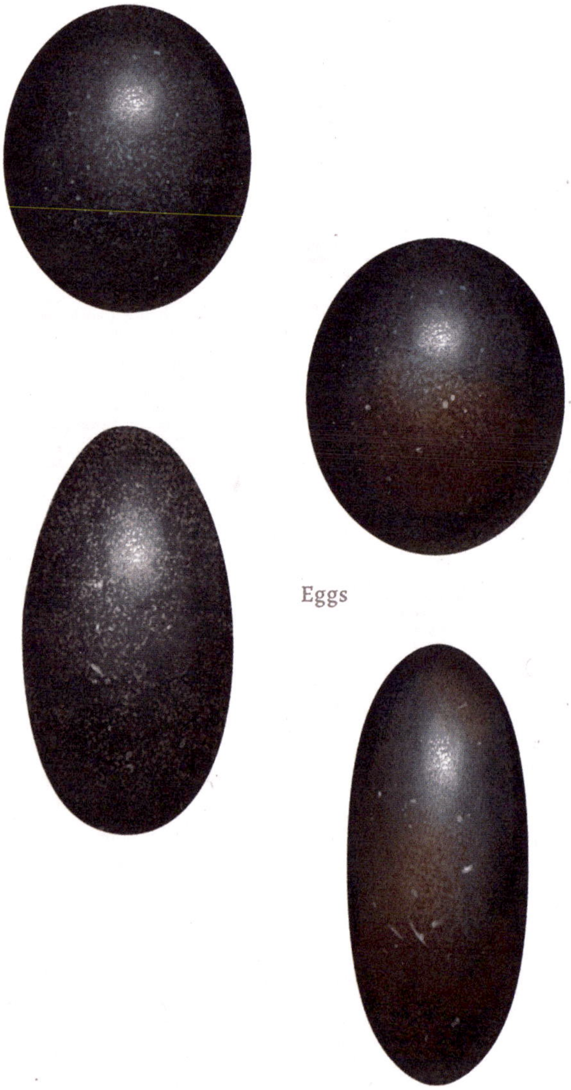

Eggs

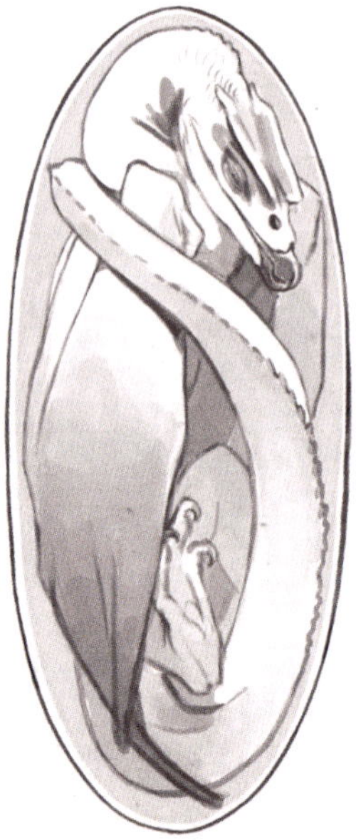

Embryo

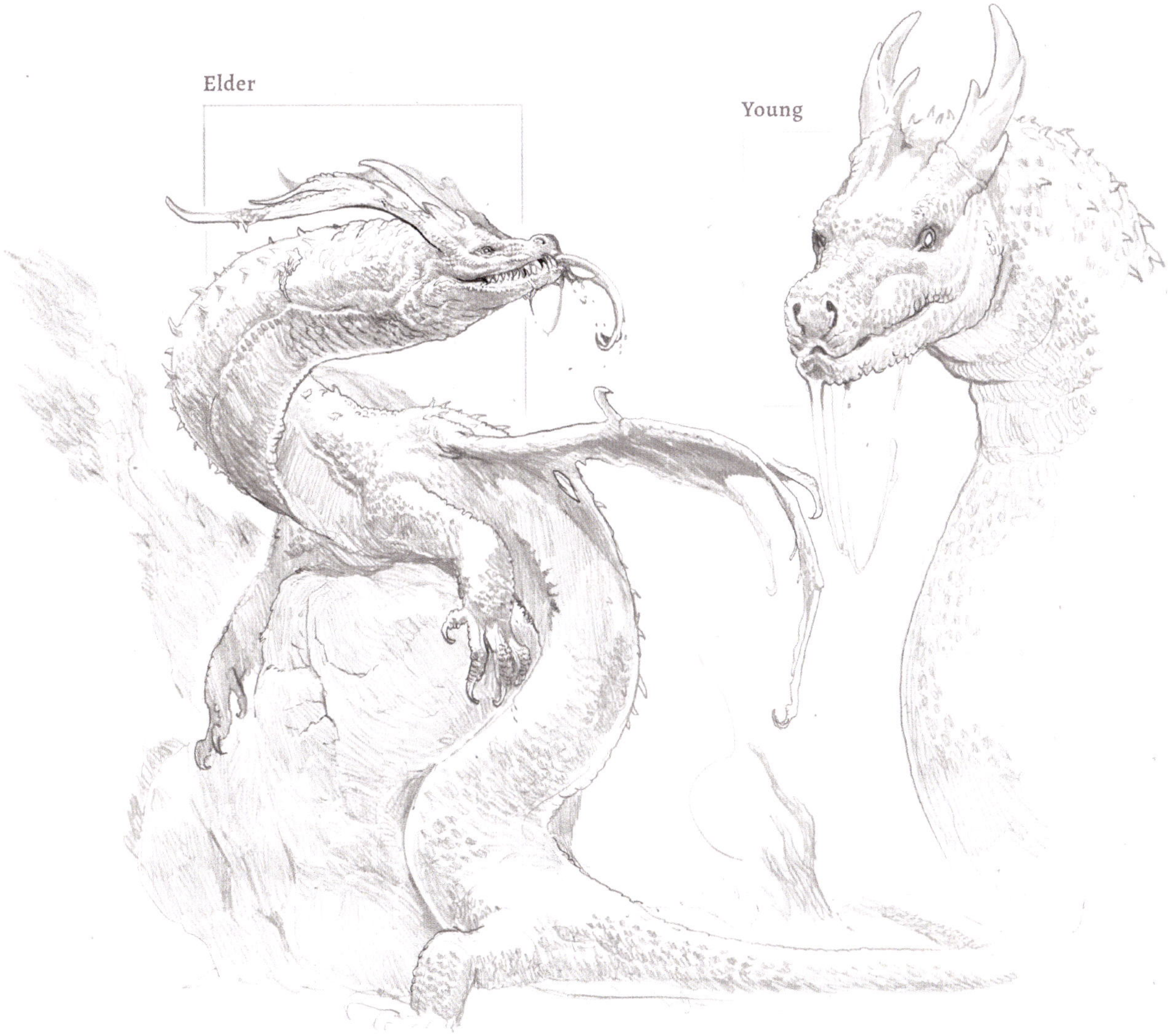

Elder

Young

Just as you can look to nature to make a believable life cycle, creating dragons that do not follow these rules but the rules of even stranger origin based in myth can make for unique designs. Ancient myths can be used as a jumping-off point, such as the Norse pantheon resulting from the mixing of fire and ice from the giant Ymir, or Athena being born from the skull of Zeus, or other, stranger ideas. Perhaps shooting stars are eggs from the moon that fall only once every thousand years, for dragons to hatch and grow here on Earth, only to return to the moon to live or die as adults. This idea plays with two familiar mystical elements (dragons and falling stars), while being rooted in a behaviour from our own nature (migrating salmon). When dealing in the dragons of high fantasy, respecting what it means to be a dragon is a fun thing to play with; but once you know the rules of creating dragons, you too can bend and break them.

With all that being said: go forth, beyond the edge of the map, and explore what a dragon is to you!

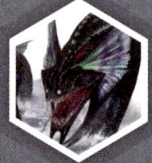

Jörmungandr • 144
Giovanni Lazzari

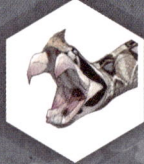

The Questing Beast • 192
Allison Theus

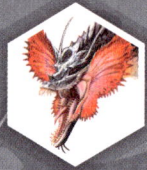

European dragon • 96
Kate Pfeilschiefter

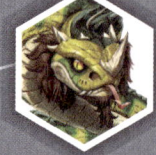

Lindworm • 160
Damien Mammoliti

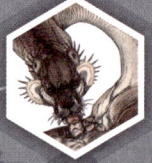

Tatzelwurm • 222
April Prime

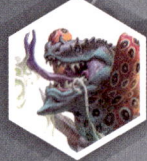

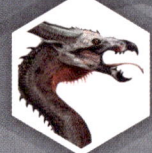

Salamander • 206
Jordan K. Walker

Wyvern • 238
Vincent Coviello

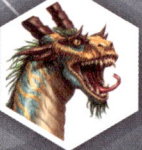

Mušḫuššu • 176
Hazem Ameen

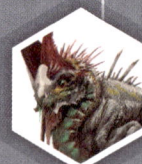

Cockatrice • 66
Gabriel McAlpine

Amphisbaena • 50
Dominique Vassie

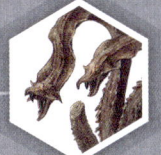

Hydra · 112
Anna Podedworna

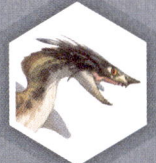

Jaculus · 128
Allie Irwin

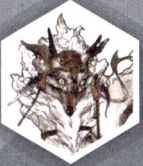

East Asian dragon · 80
Entei Ryu

THE DRAGONS

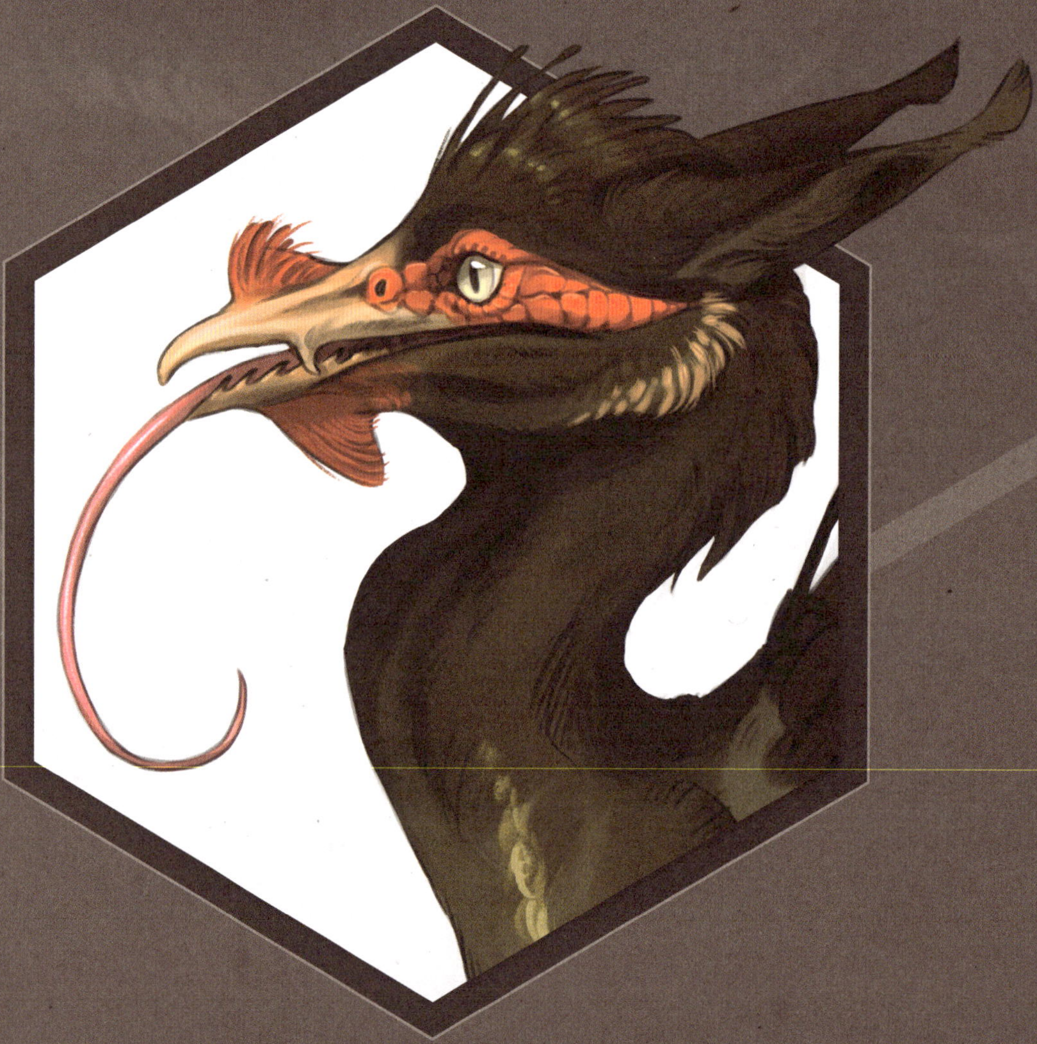

AMPHISBAENA

In this tutorial, I'll be designing a new version of the amphisbaena: a dragon-like creature famed for having a head at either end of its body. The word 'amphisbaena' comes from Ancient Greek, meaning 'to go both ways'. After learning about the depictions of this beast in European myth, I will explore real animals whose anatomy, behaviour, or ecology links to the descriptions of the amphisbaena. The new dragon will be a combination of the historical descriptions and the amazing real creatures with which we are lucky to share this world.

DOMINIQUE VASSIE

Final image © Dominique Vassie

⬡ 01 HISTORICAL RESEARCH

First, I'll research the story of the amphisbaena. It is originally a creature from Greek mythology that spawned from the blood dripping from Medusa's severed head as Perseus flew with it in hand over the Libyan desert. It is described as a venomous, ant-eating serpent with a head at either end of its body, and the ability to travel in two directions. In later medieval depictions, the amphisbaena is portrayed as more bird-like and is colourful with legs and wings. I have chosen to go with this later portrayal depicted within my home region of the United Kingdom, but there is scope for many directions.

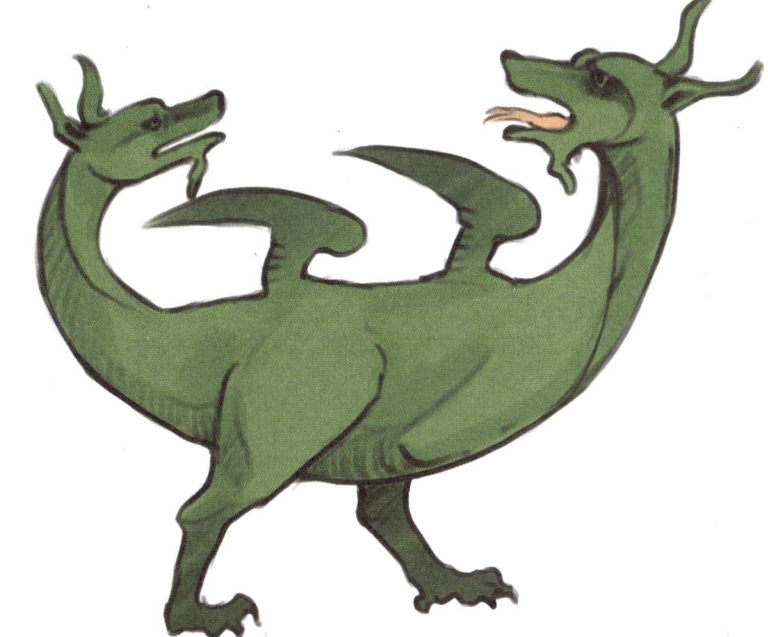

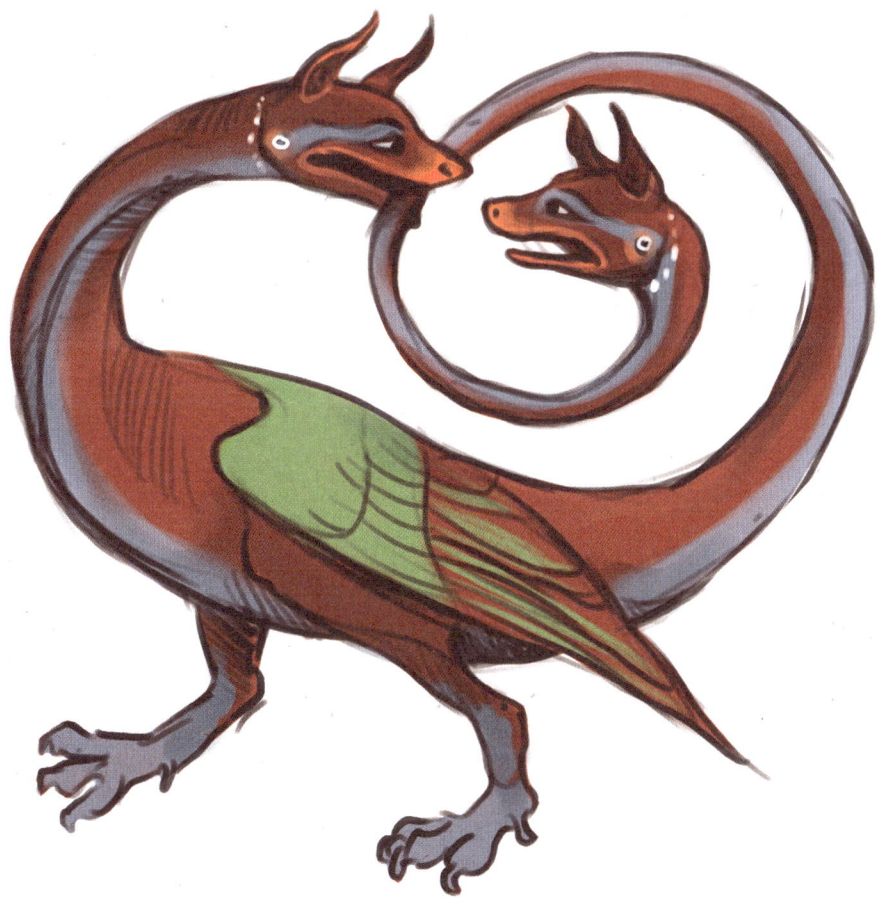

Broad-tailed gecko

The amphisbaena's most consistent trait is the head at the end of its tail. Biologically, two heads would be costly and probably of limited value, but it is not unusual for real animals to have fake body parts as lures or decoys. For example, animals with tails that look like their heads include worm lizards (scientifically named Amphisbaenia!), house centipedes, shingleback skinks, and broad-tailed geckos. Spider-tailed horned vipers have tail-tips that resemble spiders to attract their bird prey. Insects come in all forms of complex mimicry of both plants and other animals.

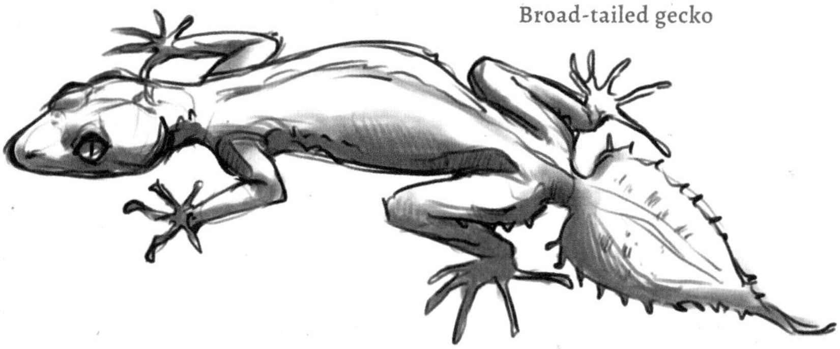

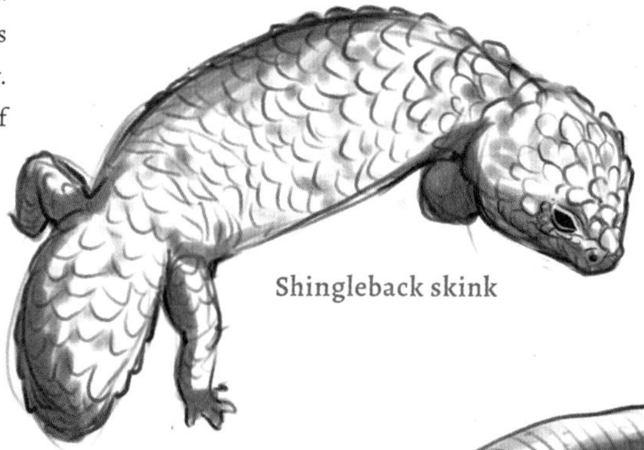

Shingleback skink

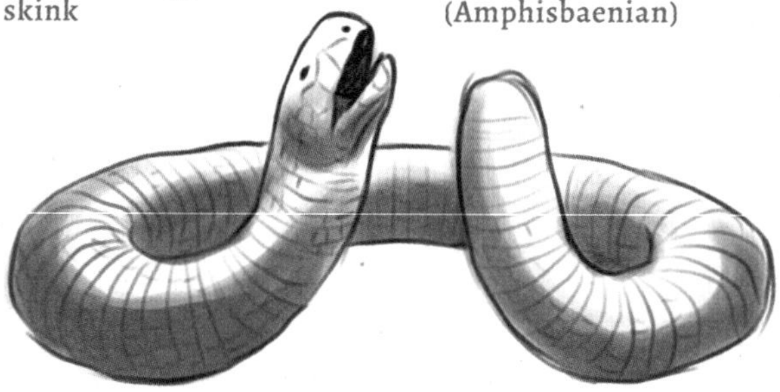

Worm-lizard
(Amphisbaenian)

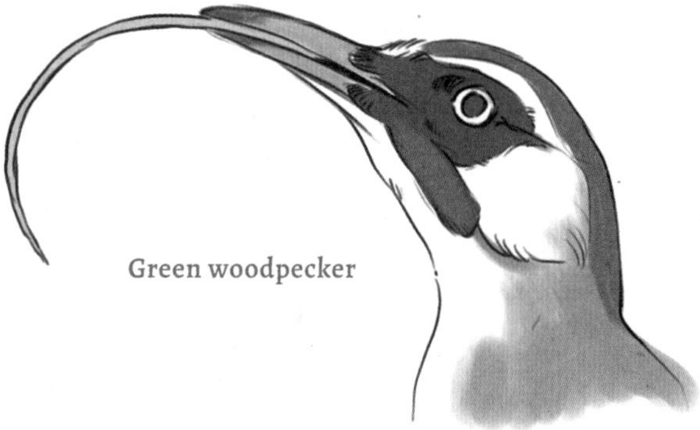

Green woodpecker

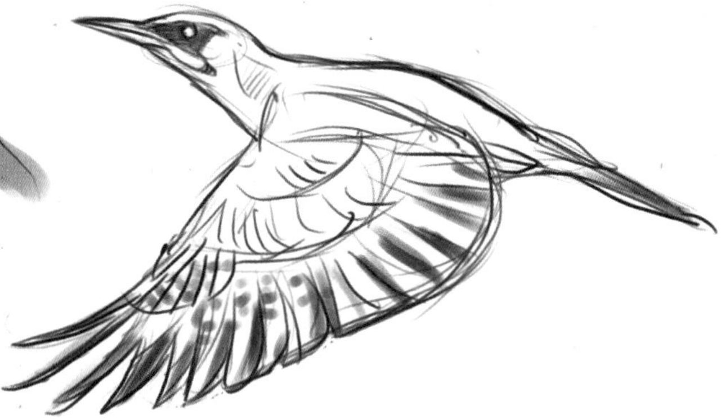

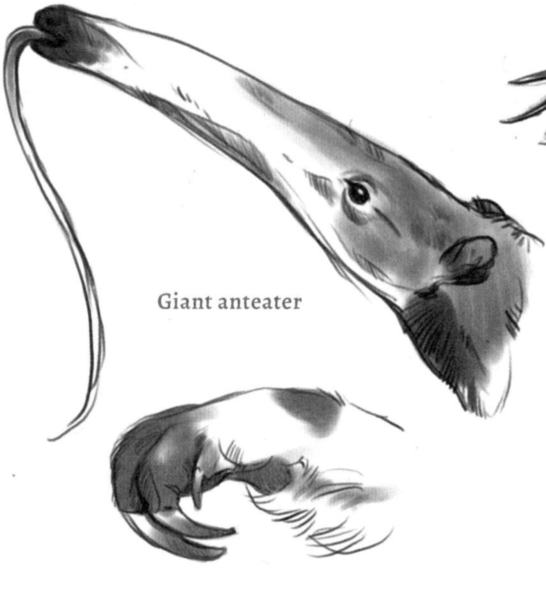

03 ANT-BASED DIET

Giant anteater

Ecologically, the amphisbaena is described as primarily feeding on ants, and so I will look to real ant-eating animals for inspiration. As this dragon will be more based on medieval bird-like depictions, I will focus primarily on green woodpeckers. These birds, like anteaters and echidnas, possess narrow faces and long, sticky tongues for accessing ants in their tunnels. Ant-eating mammals also usually have large claws for breaking up nests. I want to try introducing some of these characteristics into the new amphisbaena to make it suited to its ant diet.

04 DESERTS & SERPENTS

The amphisbaena is described in myth as a desert animal, and so I am choosing the roadrunner (a desert-dwelling cuckoo of the Americas) as an elegant base for this little bird-like dragon. I do also want to include some references to the original snake-shaped descriptions of this creature, and so I will be studying the United Kingdom's only venomous snake, the adder, for inspiration. At this stage, I'm considering working in just the eyes and scales of a snake somehow, as well as hints of their beautiful curves.

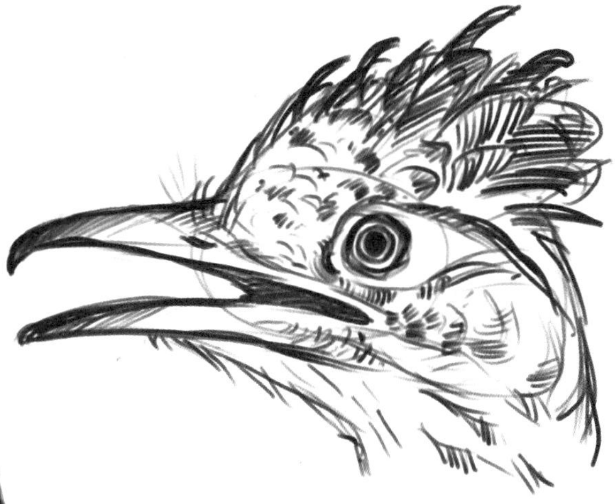

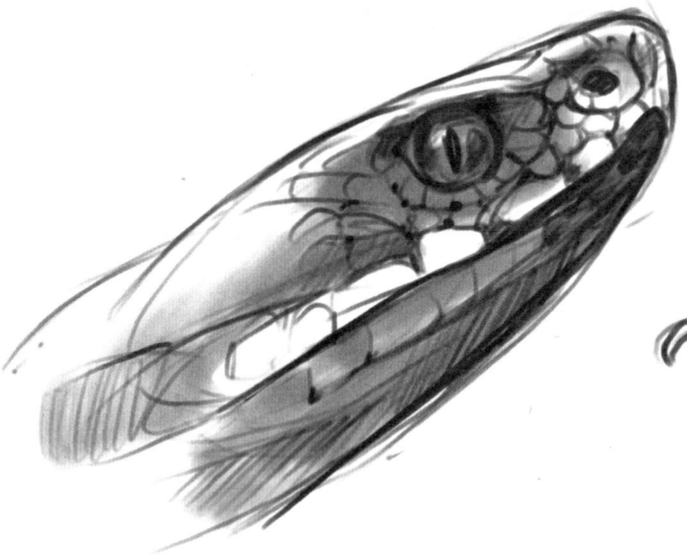

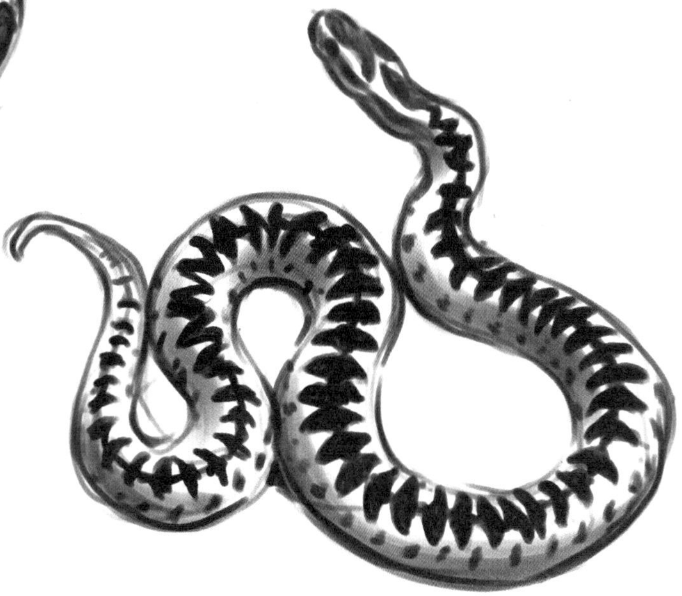

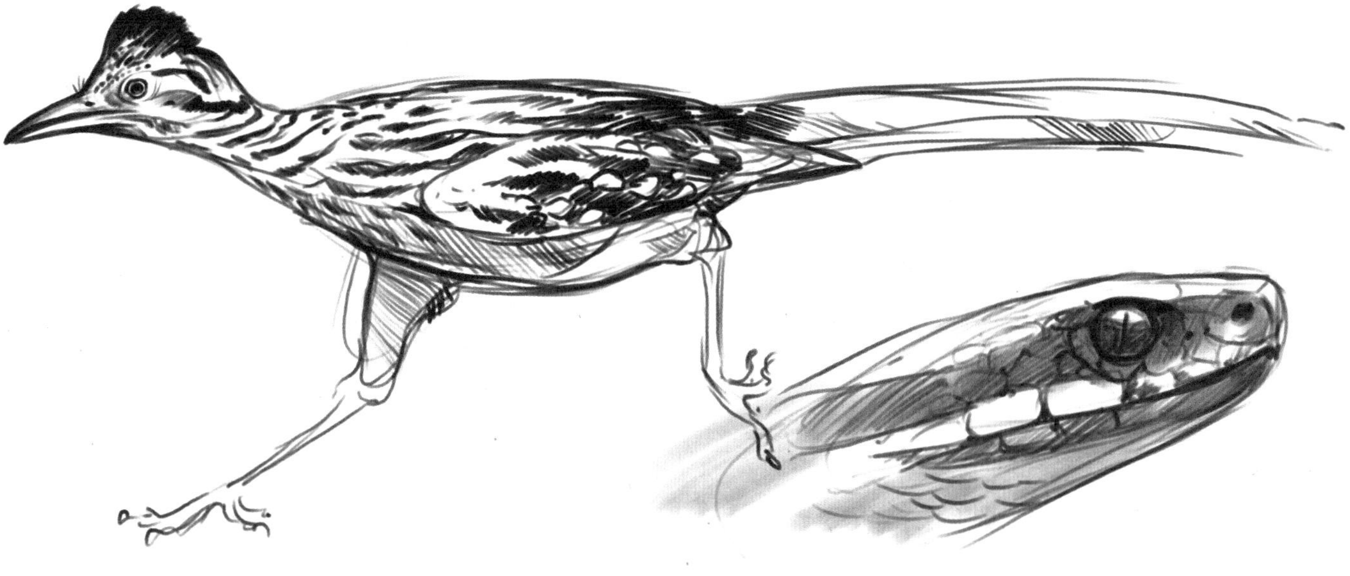

05 THUMBNAIL IDEAS

Now that I've had time to sketch some real animals, I can begin playing around with some quick, tiny thumbnails for the potential major shapes of the amphisbaena. Don't be precious about this stage, just put down any ideas that come to mind! Here, I am really sticking to the basic roadrunner body-plan while trying to work on depicting the symmetry of the two heads. Also, my amphisbaena will only be a small dragon, sustained by its diet of ants, so I want the proportions to suggest that if possible.

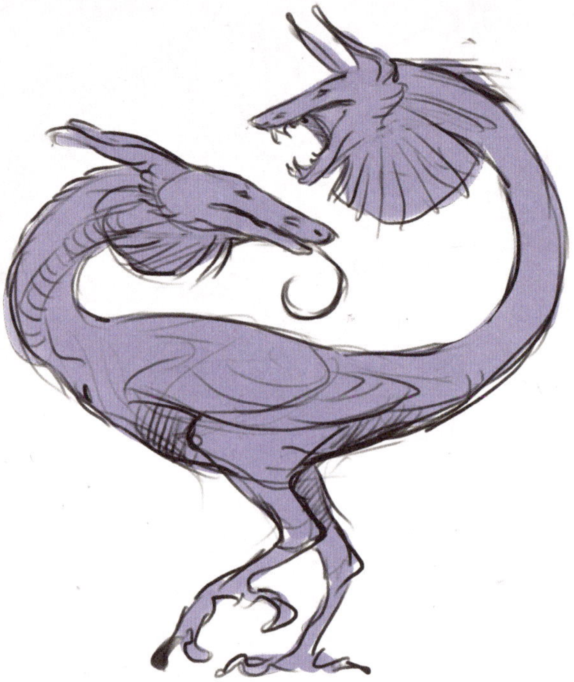

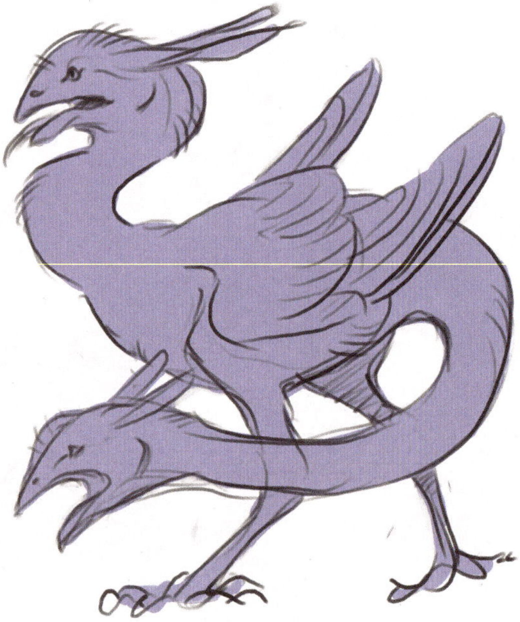

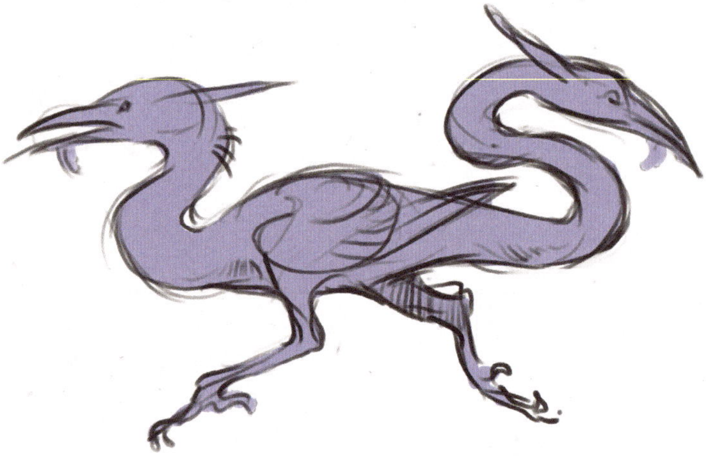

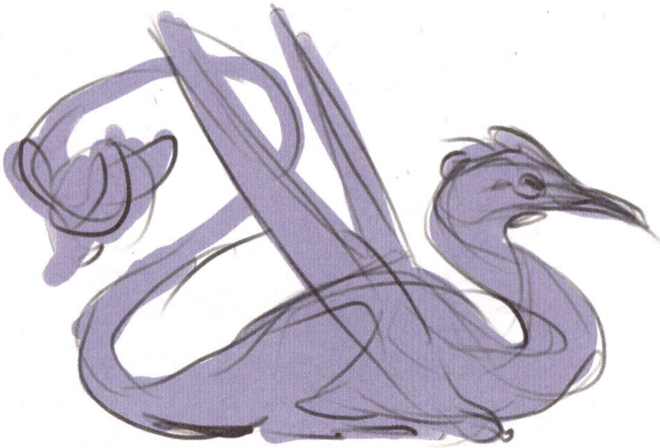

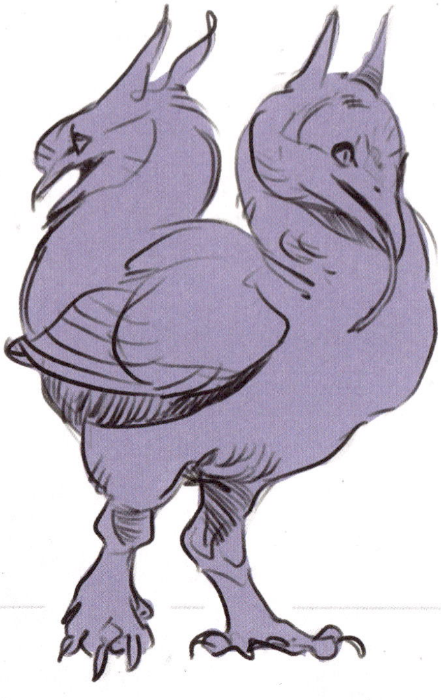

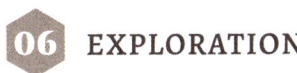

06 EXPLORATIONS

Now that I have a general idea of its shape, I sketch the dragon at different angles and in different poses to explore its anatomy, behaviour, and ecology. What does it eat? How does it sleep or communicate? Does it have predators? I feel this little dragon is certainly at risk of being eaten! This leads me to imagine that when under threat, it displays a fake head on its tail, adopts a symmetrical pose and jumps back and forth to confuse its predators before making a quick getaway. Real amphisbaenians (worm lizards) adopt a similar defence strategy.

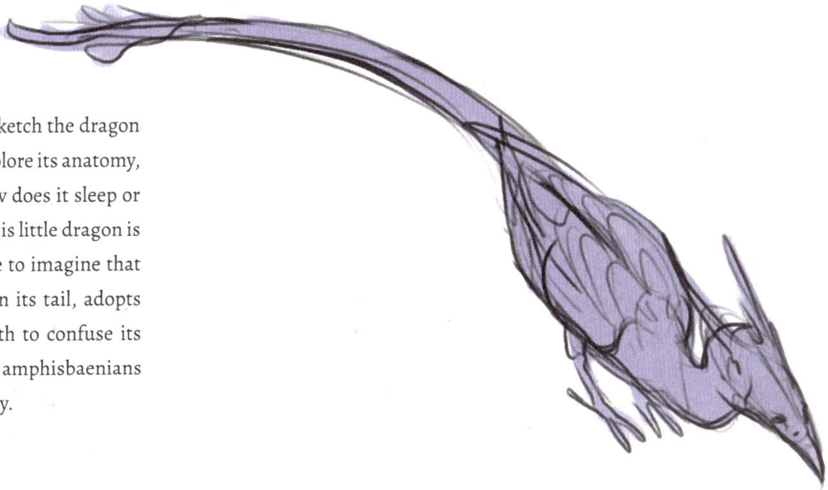

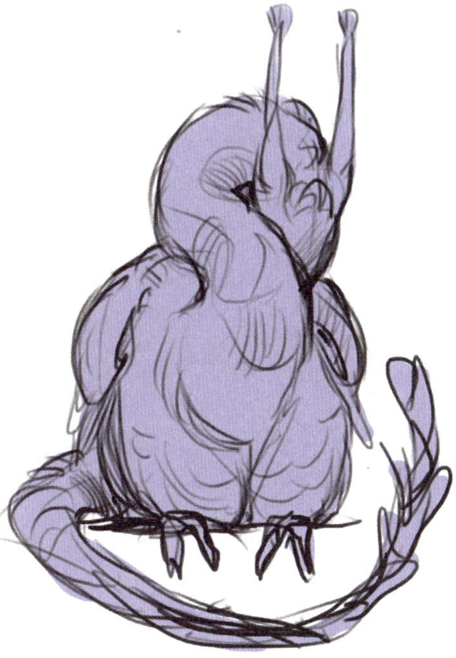

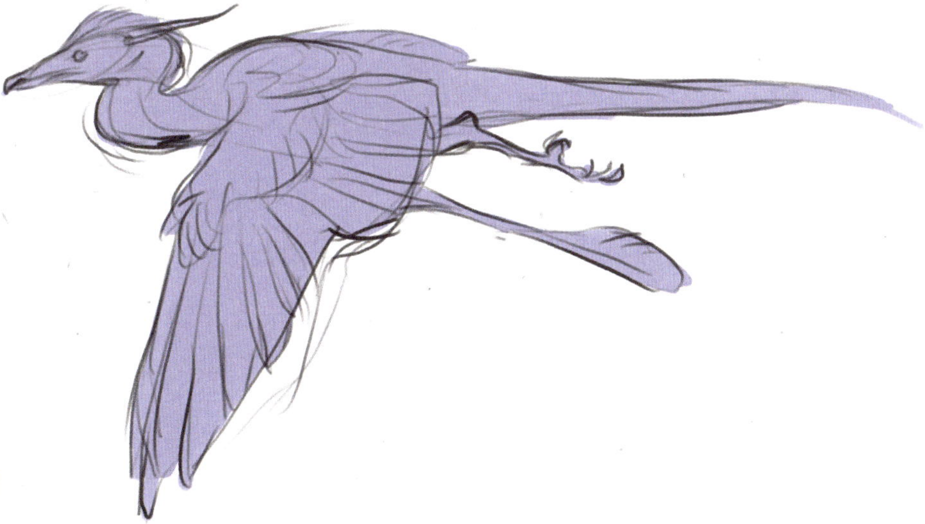

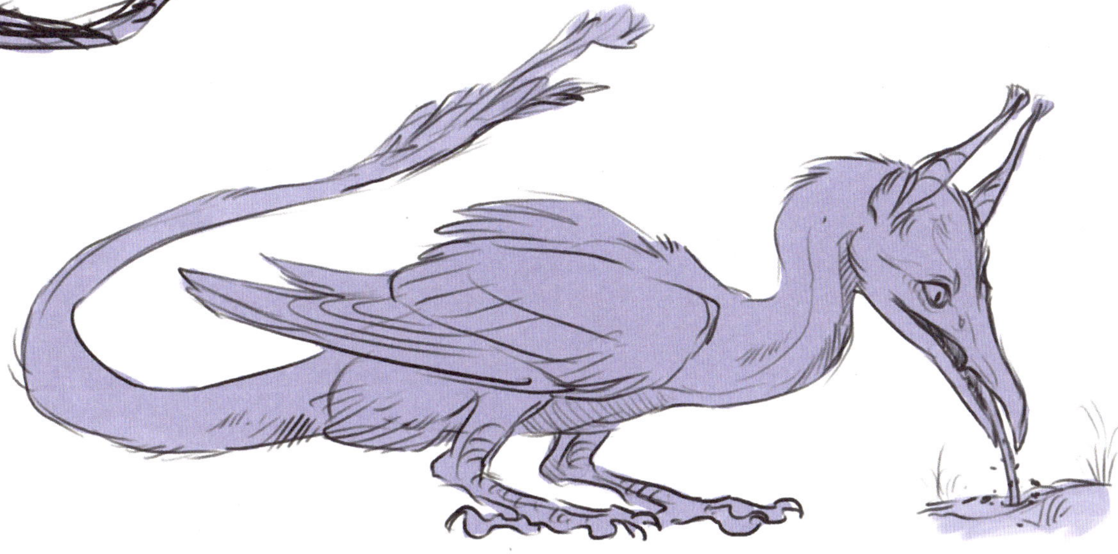

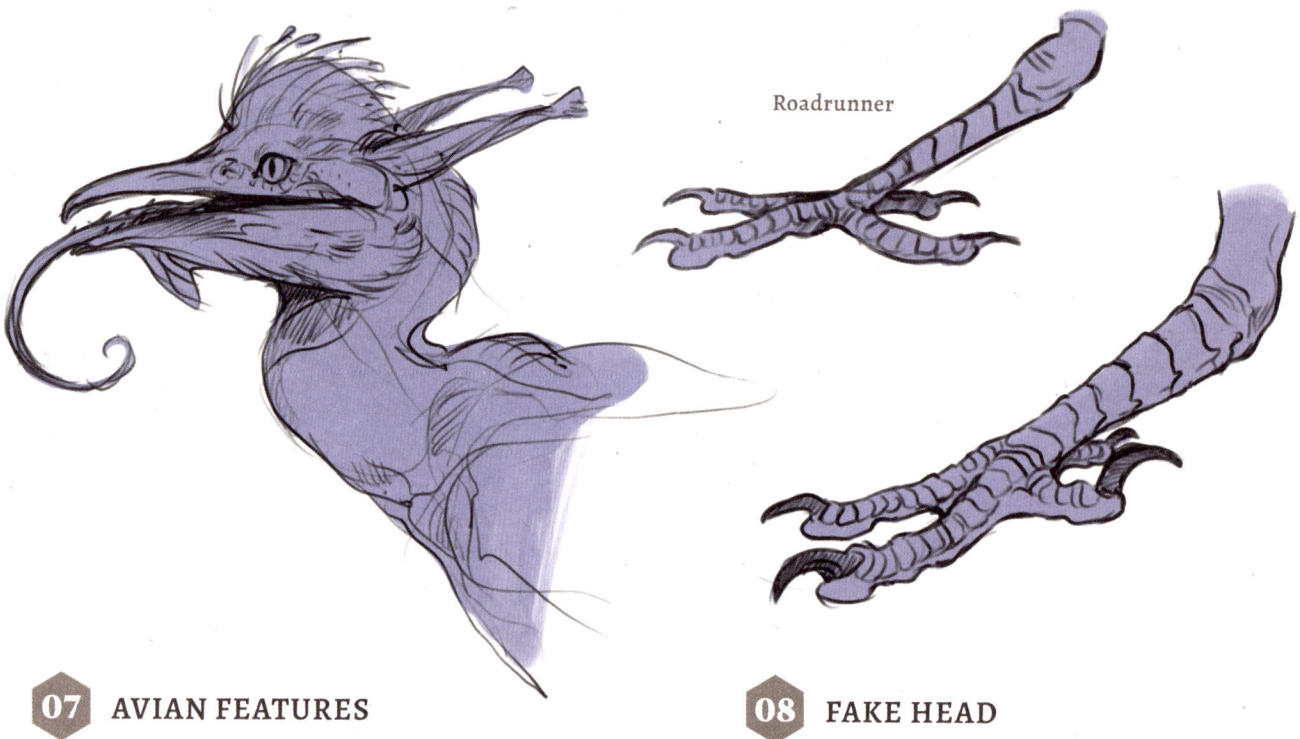

Roadrunner

07 AVIAN FEATURES

Now I have a general body shape, it's time to sketch some of the details of the dragon. For the head, I will take inspiration from both the roadrunner and woodpecker for the beak and long tongue. However, I don't want the amphisbaena to just look like a bird, so some snake-like eyes and scales will help make it a bit more 'dragon'. I love the long ears in the medieval paintings and have to include them. Furthermore, as I feel the amphisbaena is all about symmetry, I will try to include the roadrunner's almost symmetrical feet with two toes facing forwards and two facing backwards.

08 FAKE HEAD

A key detail to work out is the amphisbaena's fake head. I want this head to be made from feathers that can be folded flat when the second head isn't needed and raised upright when a display is required. Real bird feathers come in a huge variety of individual shapes and can be manipulated en masse to make very weird forms. For this, I look to those with arguably the most ridiculous feathers of all: the birds-of-paradise. I recommend researching the black sicklebill and superb bird-of-paradise as great examples of feathers' potential for shape-shifting.

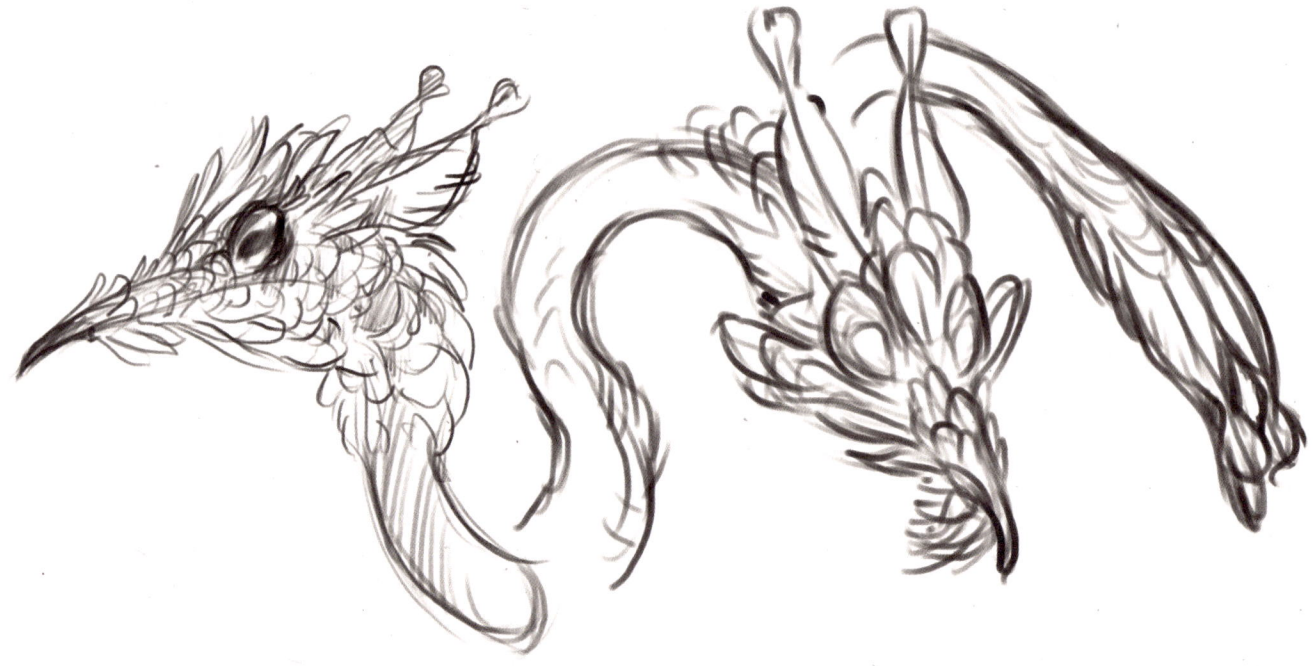

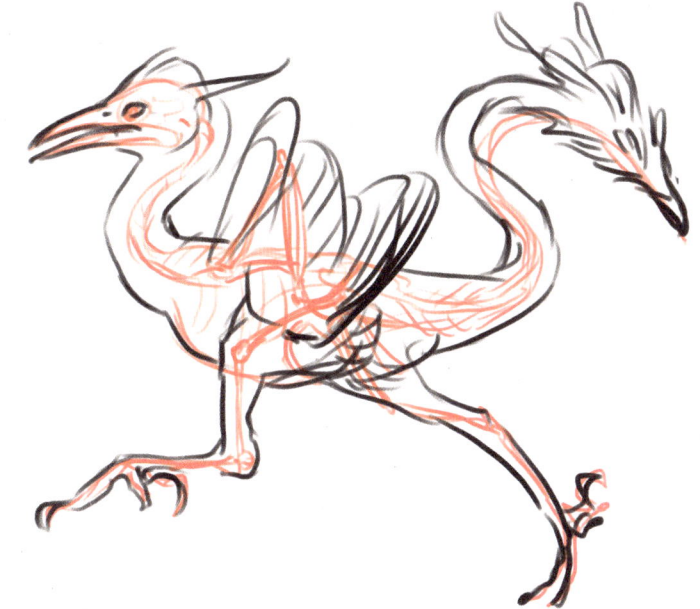

09 ROUGH SKETCH

Next, I need to decide on a pose for the final illustration. What pose would best exhibit this dragon's unique biology and features? The amphisbaena is all about those double heads, so I want to depict it in its defensive pose. I want the tail feathers arranged as the second head and held in a way that mimics the real neck and head. This, combined with raised wings, would make the dragon seem bigger and more threatening to its attacker. Curves and symmetry will also be good references to those original medieval paintings.

SKETCH THE SKELETON

It can be really helpful to try drawing a very rough skeleton under your dragon sketch, to help you make sense of the anatomy and draw it from different angles. Use real bird, mammal, and reptile skeletons for reference and try to figure out how your animal works.

10 REFINING

Once I have settled on a pose, I use a simple digital brush to create a neater, refined sketch to act as the base of the illustration. I am using Procreate for this image, but any digital painting software will have similar brushes and tools. In this stage, it's helpful to iron out as many details as possible as it will save time later on, so don't worry if your sketch gets messy. Here, I am debating whether to give the amphisbaena the longer, functional wings I sketched earlier or shorter wings (below-left) for display and more limited flying.

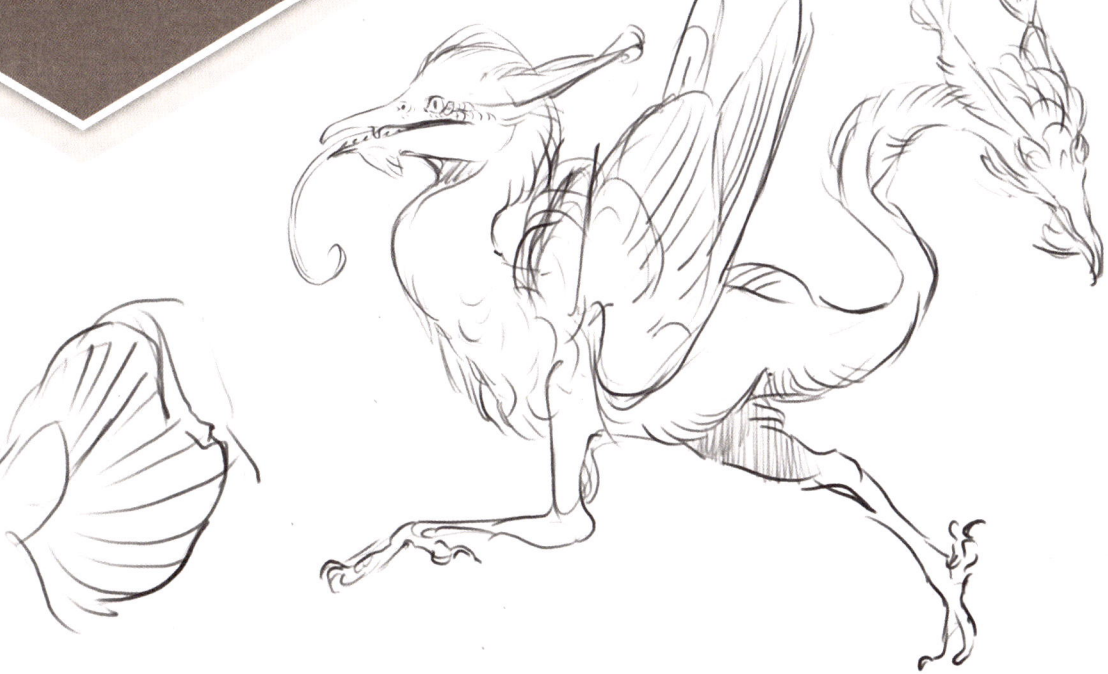

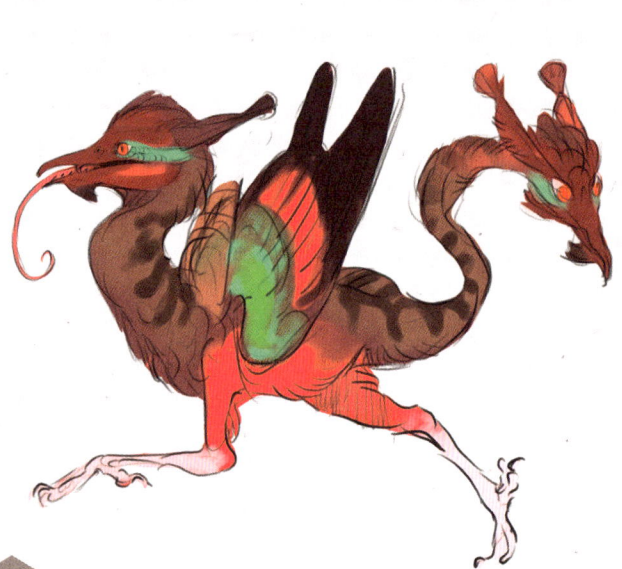

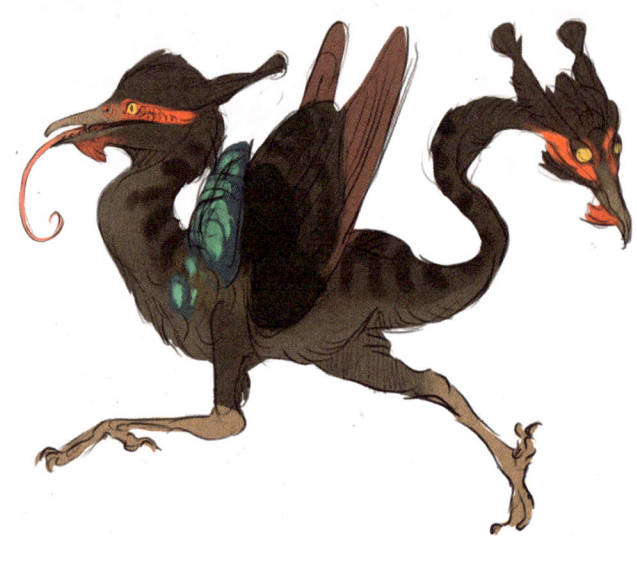

11 COLOUR IDEAS

Next, I want to start playing with colour. I block in a simple base on a new layer beneath the sketch and play with some colour combinations. I choose reds and greens as an homage to the colourful medieval depictions of the amphisbaena. I like the roadrunner's bright eye-skin, which also resembles some of the markings drawn in the old paintings. I also enjoy the bold stripes of adders and the patches of iridescence of the birds-of-paradise, so I try to find places for them in the design.

12 LINE ART

I reduce the opacity of my sketch layer and create a new one above it to work on the cleaner drawing. I use a simple round airbrush to sketch in the details of the face and feathers, still turning back to my photos of real animals for reference when needed. It can be a good idea to vary the weight and thickness of the lines to suggest shadow even at this stage, but in this particular illustration I'll mostly be adding shading later on, so I try not to add too many hatching details.

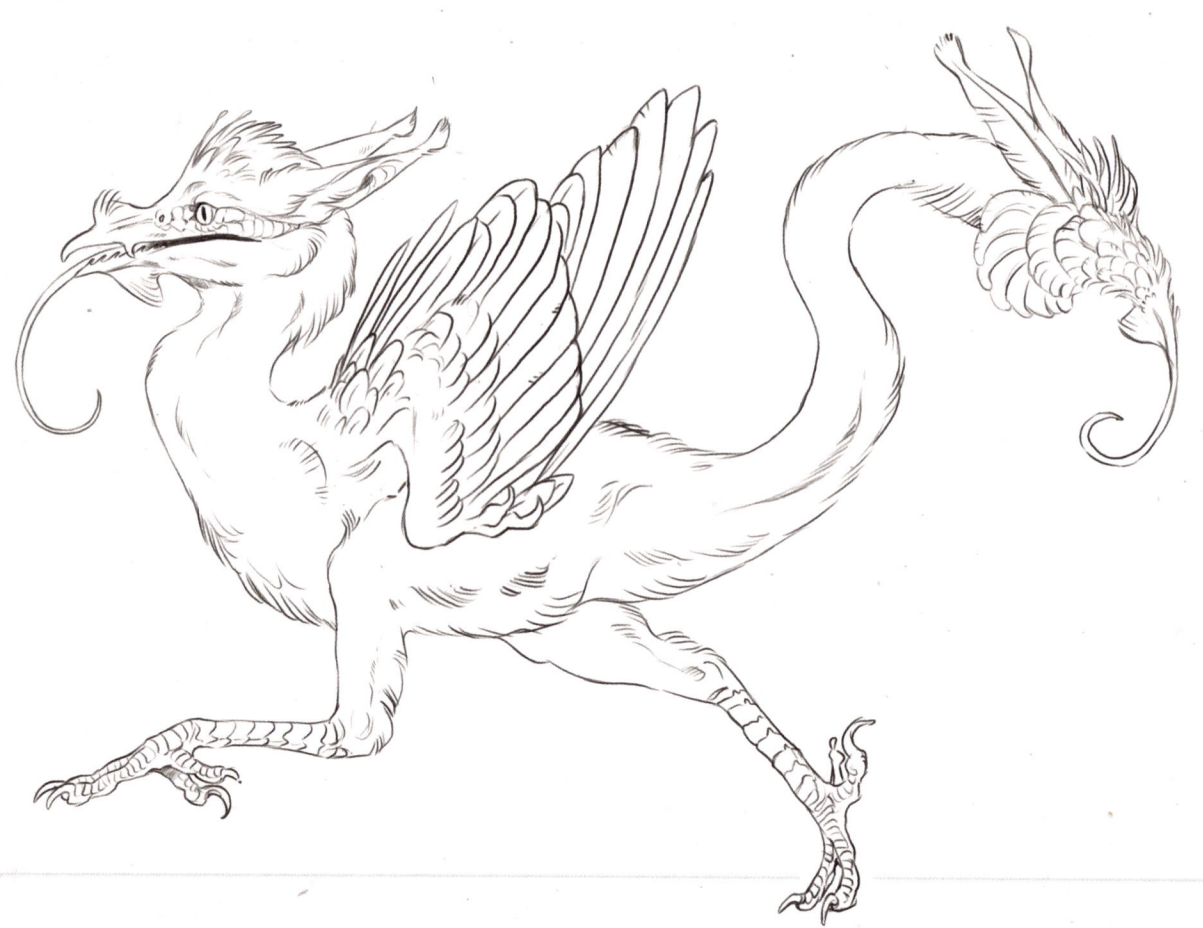

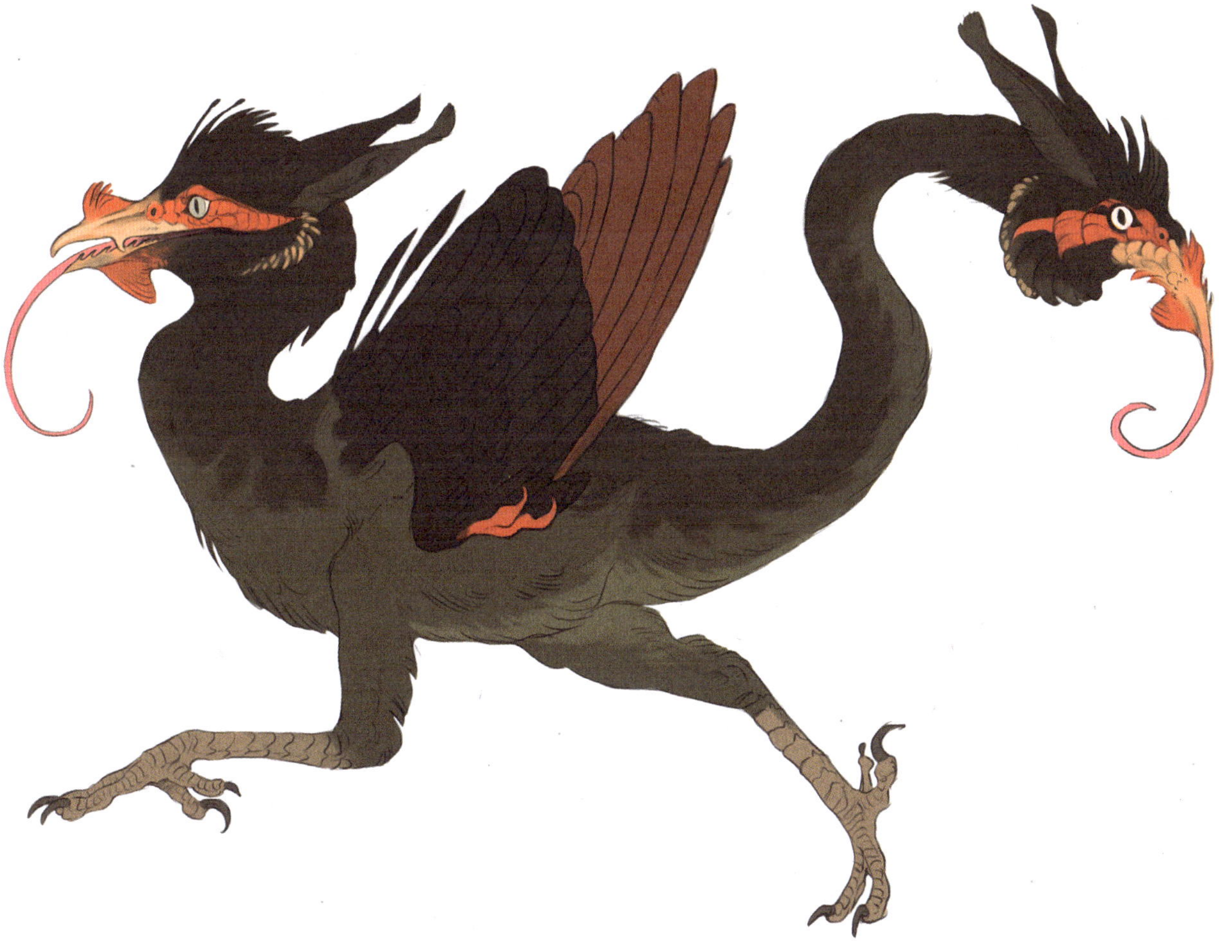

13 BASE COLOURS

I create a new layer beneath the final drawing and use the selection lasso to lay down a solid base upon which I'll colour the dragon. Colouring within a selection is helpful to ensure the base of your drawing is fully opaque. It's also useful at this stage to use your software's layer-locking and clipping-mask functions to fill separate body sections to make recolouring areas more efficient. I am leaning towards quite earthy colours for this dragon, with some pops of colour inspired by real birds. I realize the snake stripes would be too distracting, so decide to leave them off.

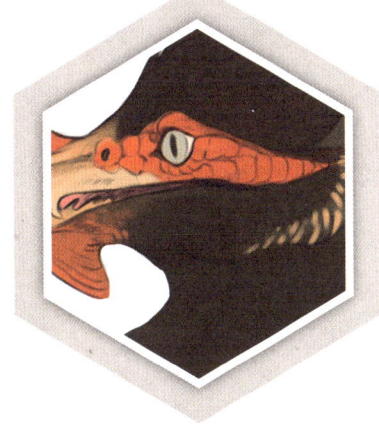

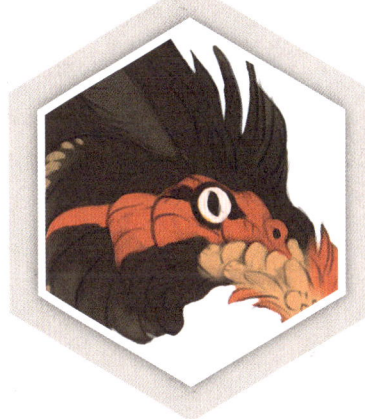

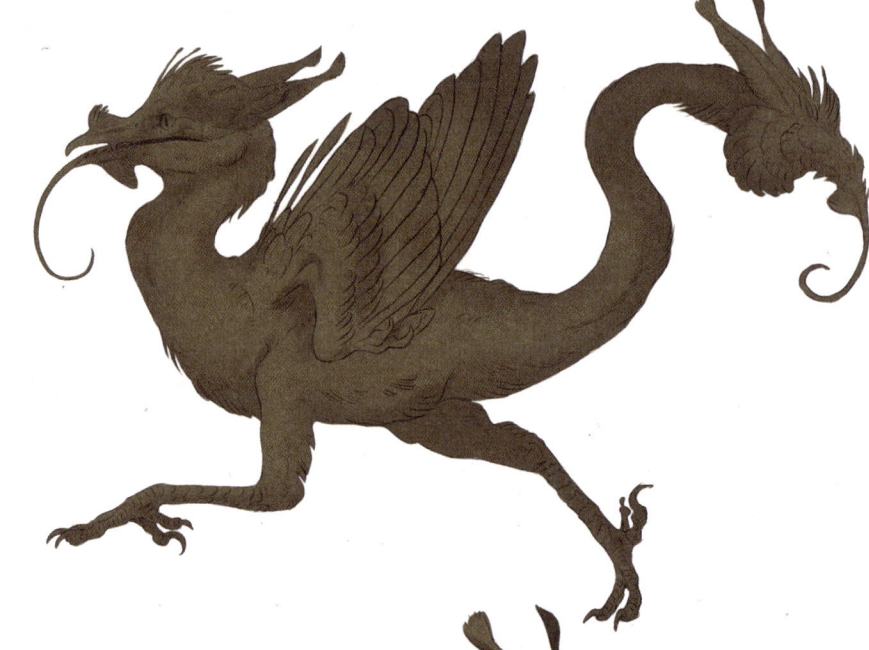

14 SOFT SHADOWS

Next, I choose a direction for the lighting and begin shading. I hide all but the base colour layer, create a new layer on top of everything, and set this to Multiply mode for my initial shadows. Mostly using a big airbrush and a light neutral-brown colour, I begin blocking in the larger, softer shadows over the dragon's body, taking care to suggest the curves of the neck and tail especially.

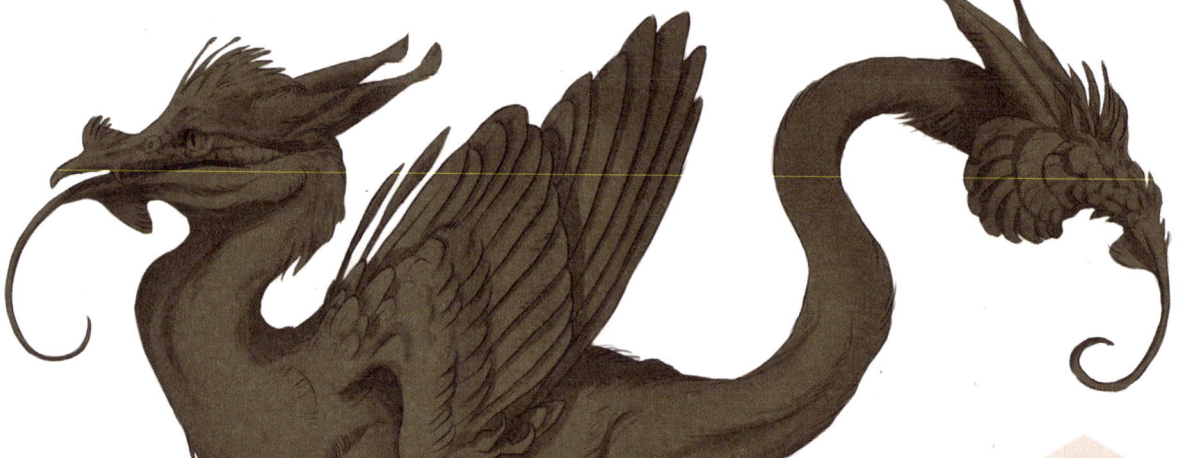

15 DEFINED SHADOWS

On another new layer in Multiply mode, I paint the more detailed shadows. Consulting photos of real birds, I use shadows to help define the feathers of the wings into their major layers and groups. It is also the time to look closely at the head structure and scales of the feet, and use shadow to help define the subtle textures and forms of those parts. I pay attention to where the planes of the body join and shade in those nooks, such as under the jaw and brow, and between the toes.

TRY USING CLIPPING MASKS

When shading in this style, sometimes the colours of the subject can be a little distracting and cause you to miss areas. It's helpful to make a new 'clipping mask' layer of solid colour over the other colours, which can be toggled on and off to allow you to see better how the form is looking.

16 COLOUR DETAILS

Once the major shadows are blocked in and all the colour layers are turned back on, I like to create a new layer over the top of everything (lines included) and paint details. I use the eyedropper tool to help pick colours, and a finer brush for detailing feathers, fur, and scales where needed. I like using a rougher and more painterly brush for this process; depending on the style you are going for, you could remove the lines entirely here by making them very transparent and defining areas with colour instead. For this image, I reduce the opacity of the lines but keep them in.

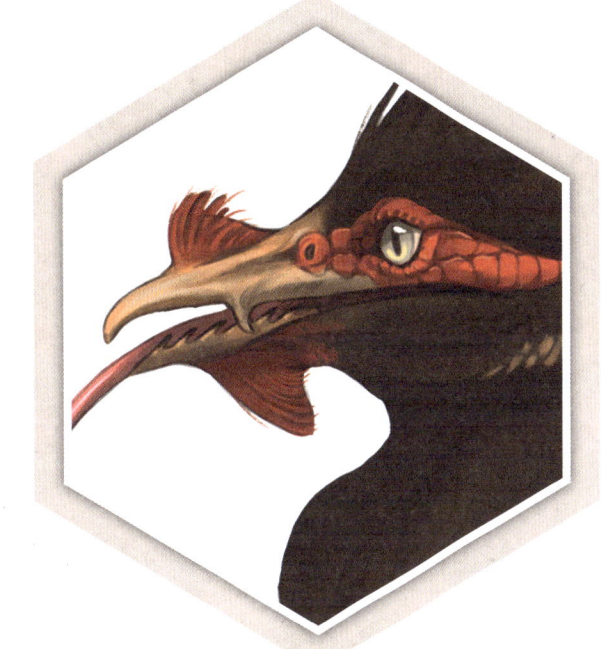

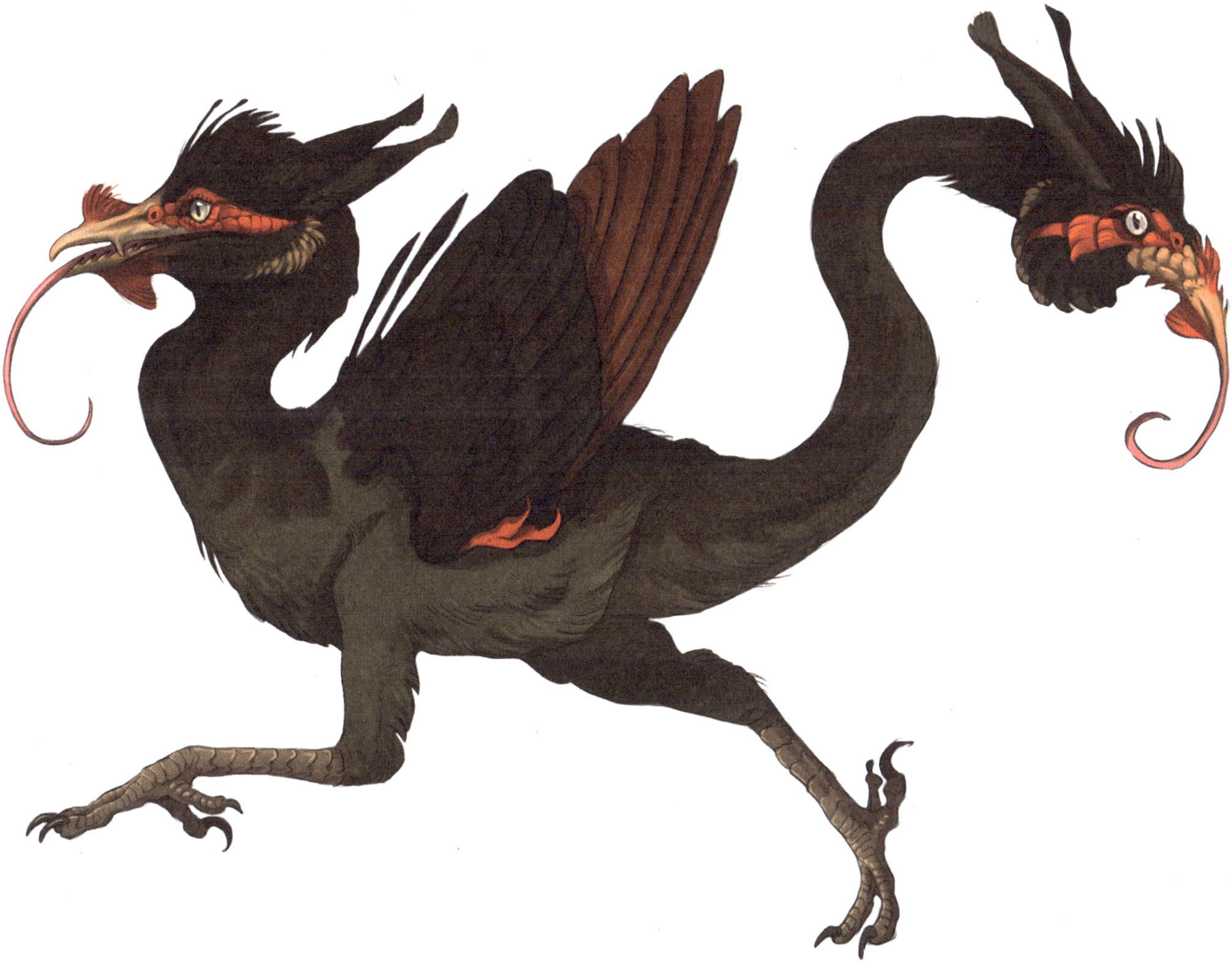

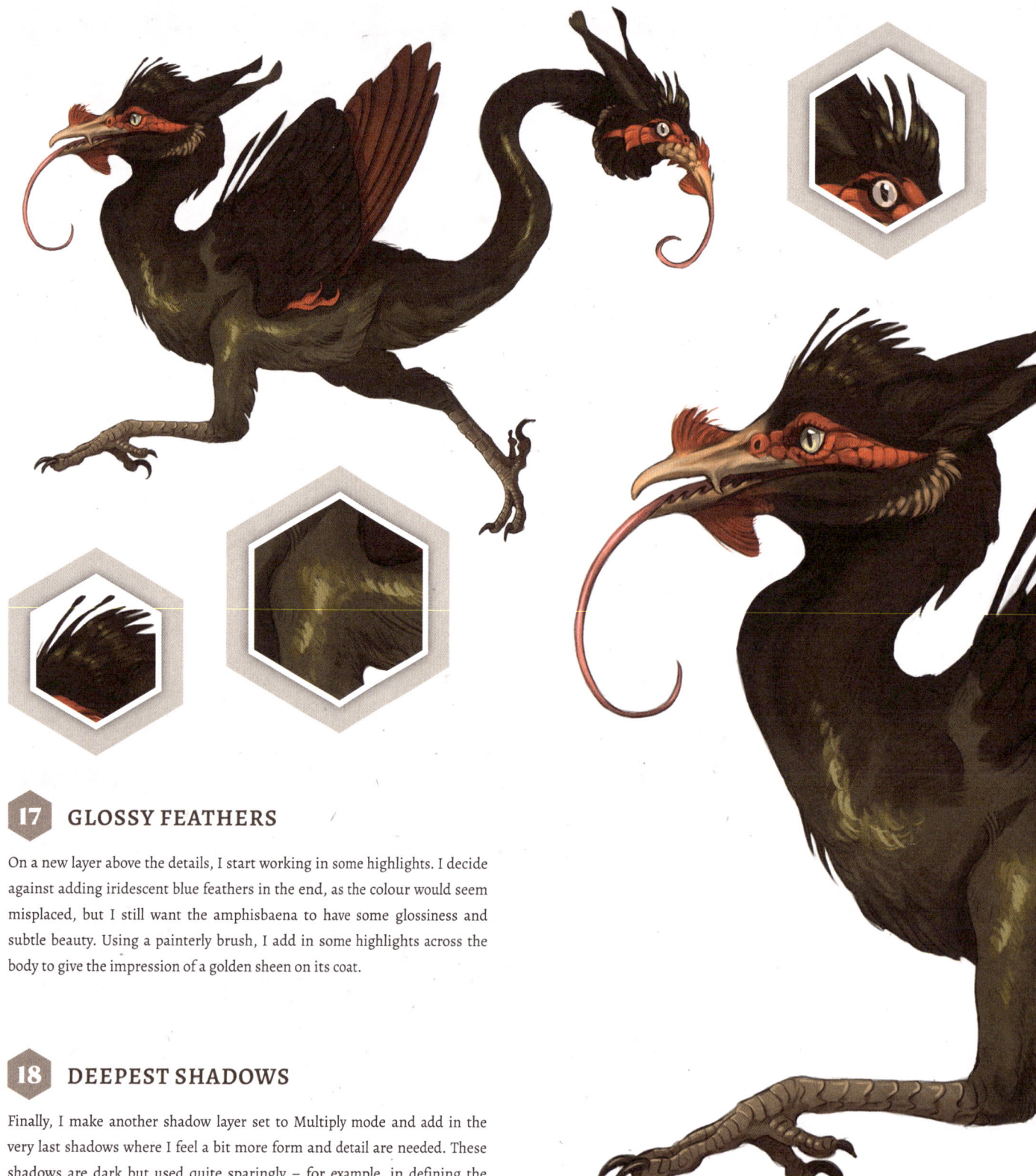

17 GLOSSY FEATHERS

On a new layer above the details, I start working in some highlights. I decide against adding iridescent blue feathers in the end, as the colour would seem misplaced, but I still want the amphisbaena to have some glossiness and subtle beauty. Using a painterly brush, I add in some highlights across the body to give the impression of a golden sheen on its coat.

18 DEEPEST SHADOWS

Finally, I make another shadow layer set to Multiply mode and add in the very last shadows where I feel a bit more form and detail are needed. These shadows are dark but used quite sparingly – for example, in defining the scales of the face and legs and the feathers of the tail. This is also the point where I add any last details on top of the whole drawing, especially if I have let go of the lines completely, and make any overall colour corrections needed for the final presentation.

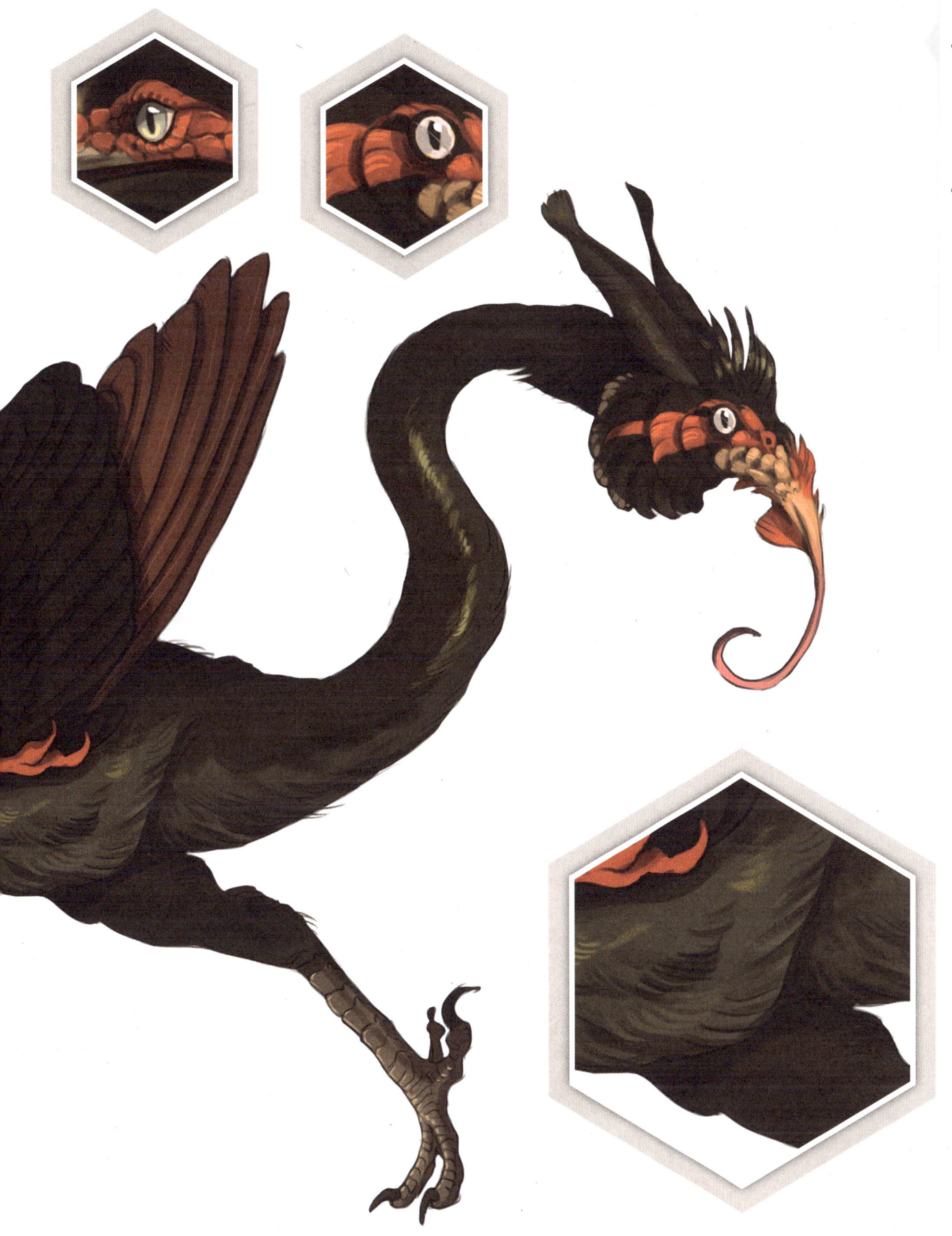

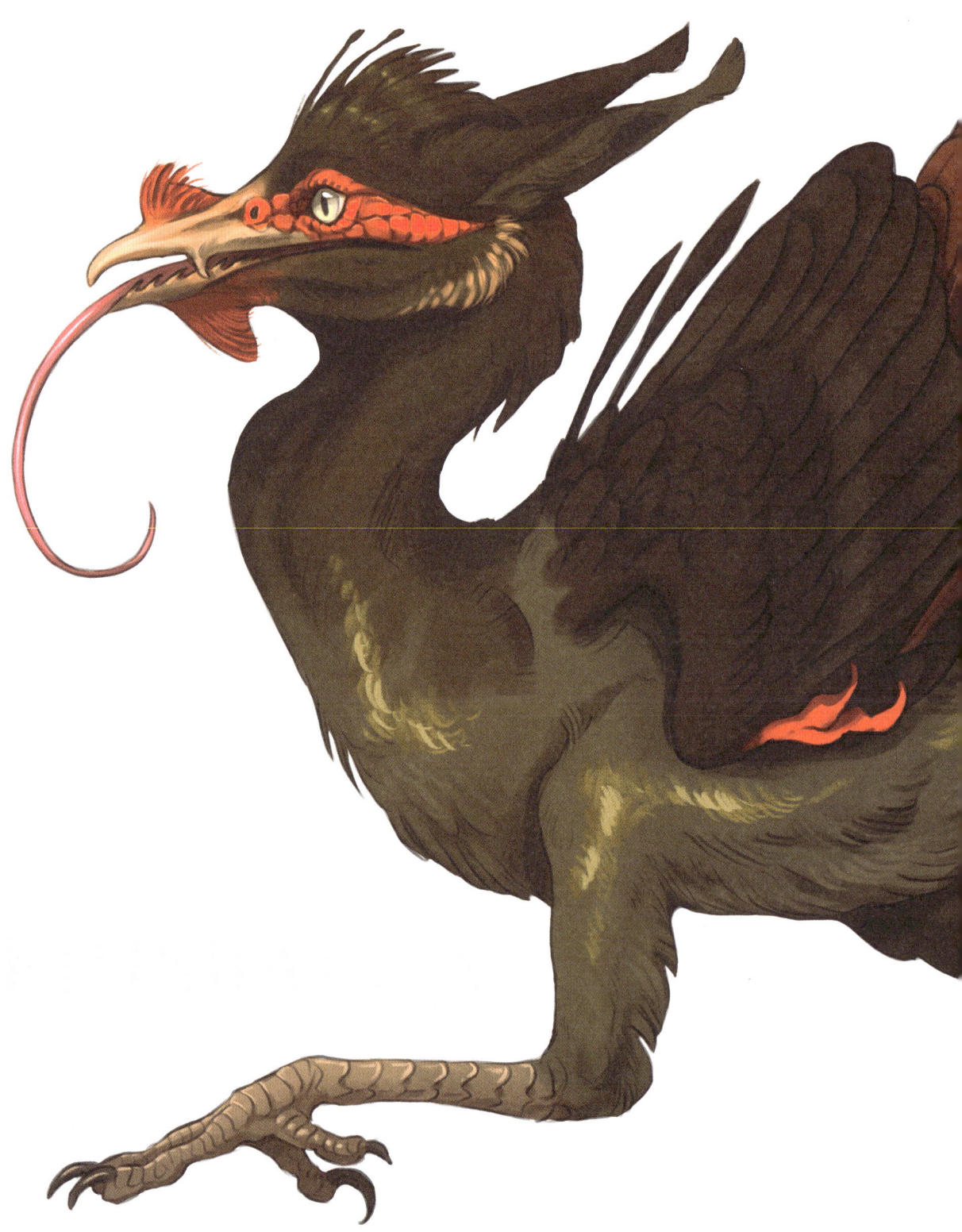

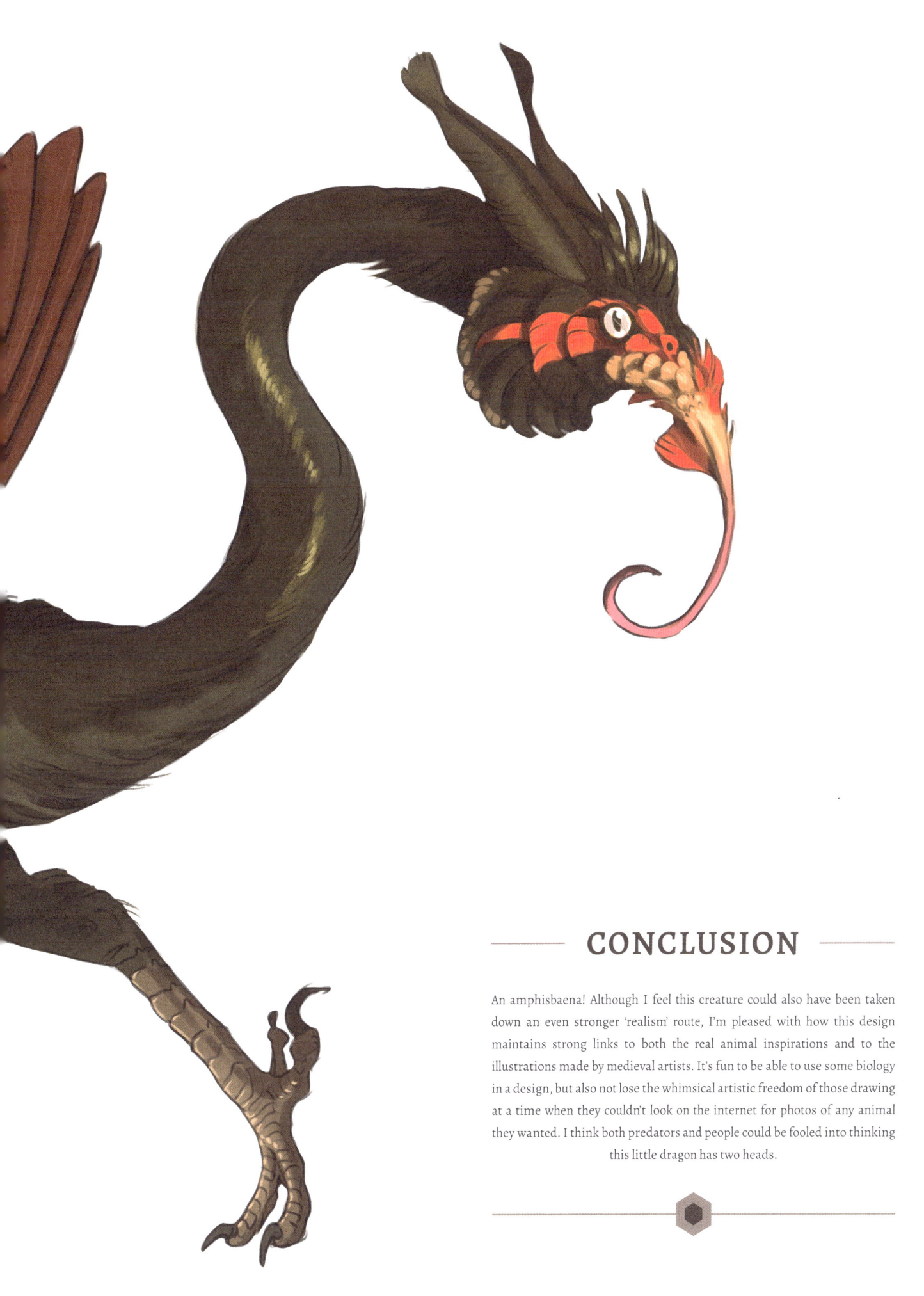

CONCLUSION

An amphisbaena! Although I feel this creature could also have been taken down an even stronger 'realism' route, I'm pleased with how this design maintains strong links to both the real animal inspirations and to the illustrations made by medieval artists. It's fun to be able to use some biology in a design, but also not lose the whimsical artistic freedom of those drawing at a time when they couldn't look on the internet for photos of any animal they wanted. I think both predators and people could be fooled into thinking this little dragon has two heads.

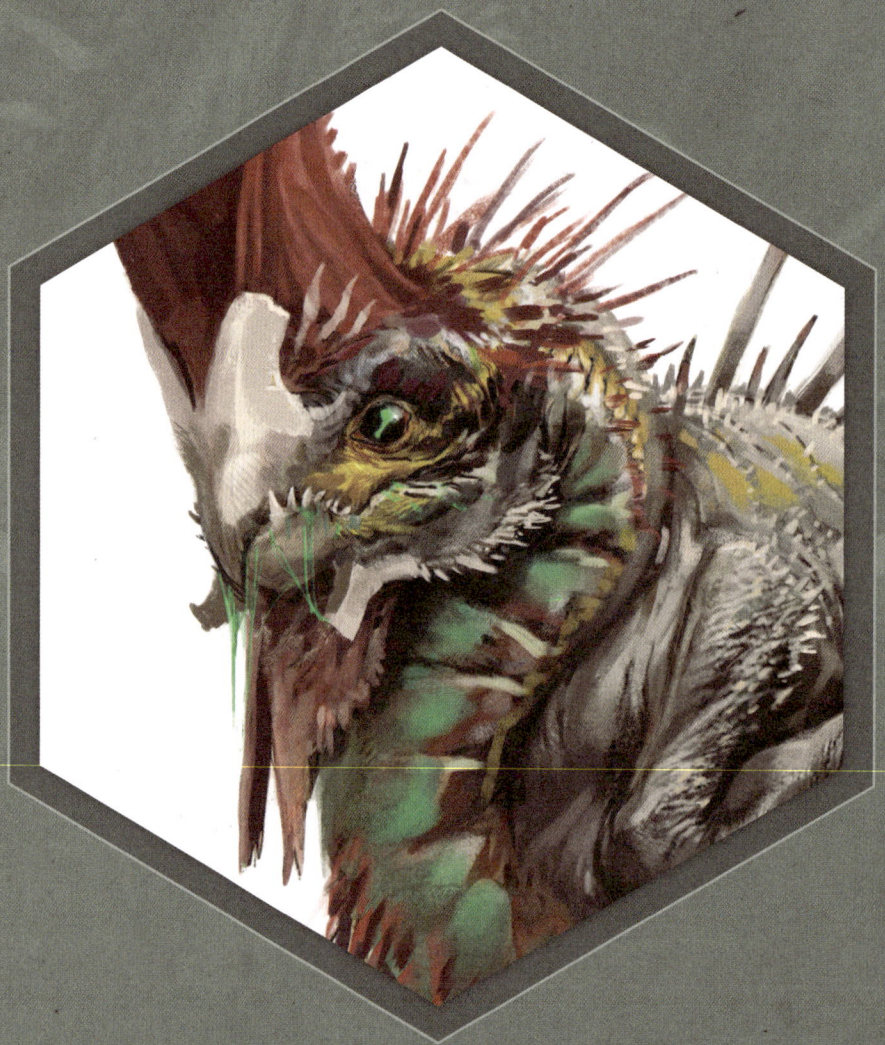

COCKATRICE

The cockatrice is a winged creature, usually represented as a bird-like beast with scaly wings and a serpent's tail. It apparently hatches from an egg laid by a cock and incubated by a serpent or toad. Old Latin tales describe the cockatrice as having a crested head and deadly poison that contaminates everything it touches. It also has a deadly gaze, but it can be killed by the crowing of a cock, or by a weasel, the only animal immune to its power.

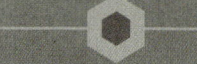

GABRIEL McALPINE
Final image © Gabriel McAlpine

01 SILHOUETTE IDEAS

I start out by creating a rough set of silhouettes to explore head designs, working with a rough-textured brush and neutral grey tone in Procreate. I try to create a diverse range of shapes so that each sketch is different from the next – some of these are more avian, while others lean into the cockatrice's more reptilian side.

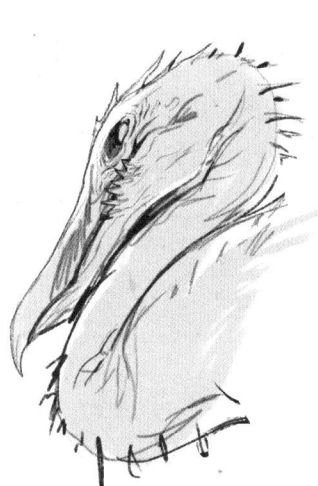

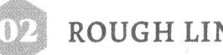

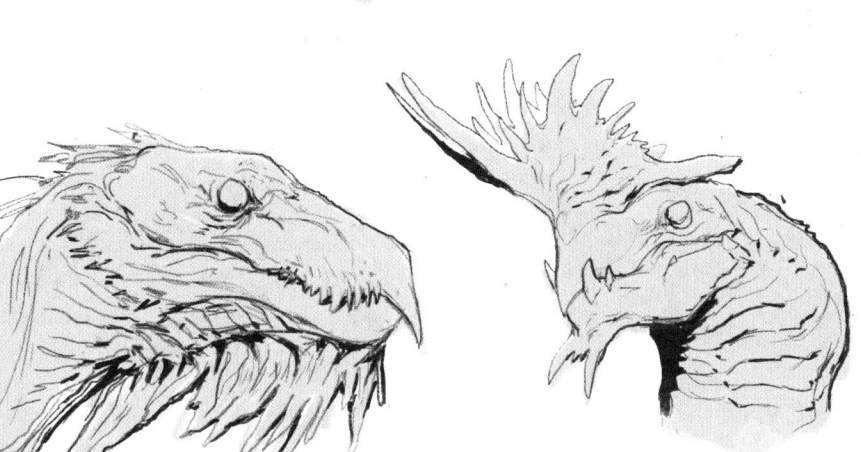

02 ROUGH LINE ART

I sketch over the top of my silhouettes, using rough lines to flesh out the concepts. I want to honour the cockatrice's part-chicken nature, drawing on some of those bird features for inspiration, but I want to remix the features rather than take them too literally. For example, instead of simply having a chicken's feathers and fleshy wattle, the cockatrice might have spines and hard crests on its head.

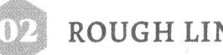

ROUGH SHADOWS

Before moving on to visualizing the full body, I add some quick greyscale shading to the heads, just to explore different materials and the three-dimensionality of the concepts. The cockatrice has lots of potential for bristles, spikes, ridges, and wrinkles that could add plenty of interest to the whole body.

 MORE EXPLORATION

I sketch another exploration, this time for the full body, with a hunched, vulture-like back and sharp spines that create a monstrous, menacing look. It's a striking concept, equal parts avian and reptilian, that I want to take forward as a basis for further explorations.

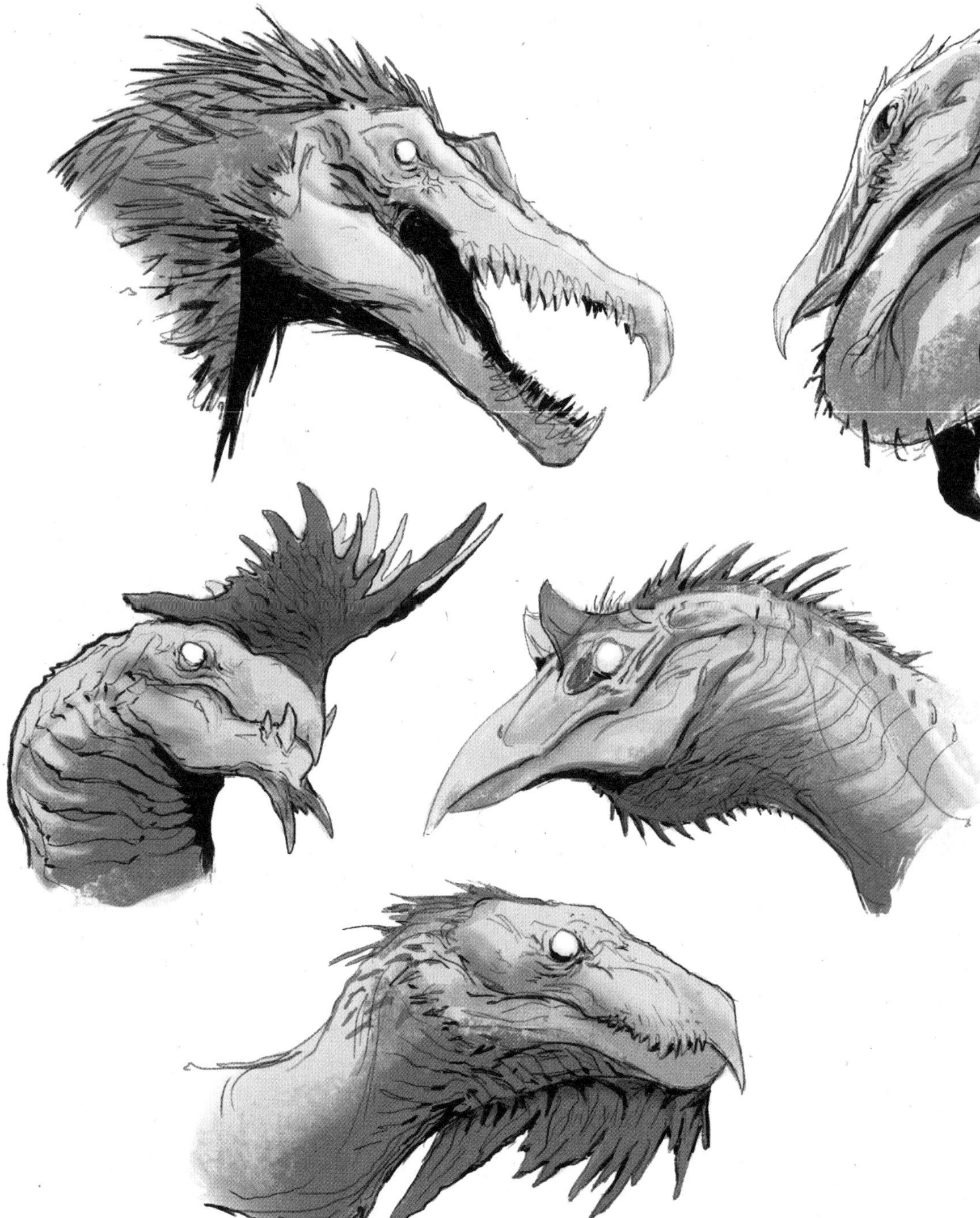

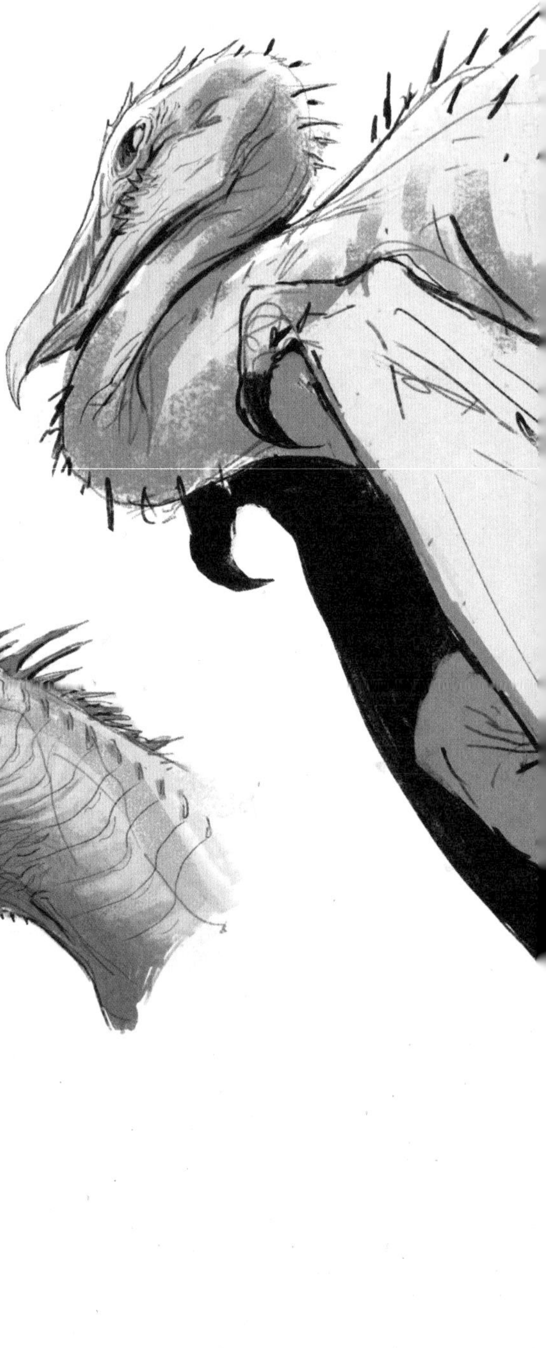

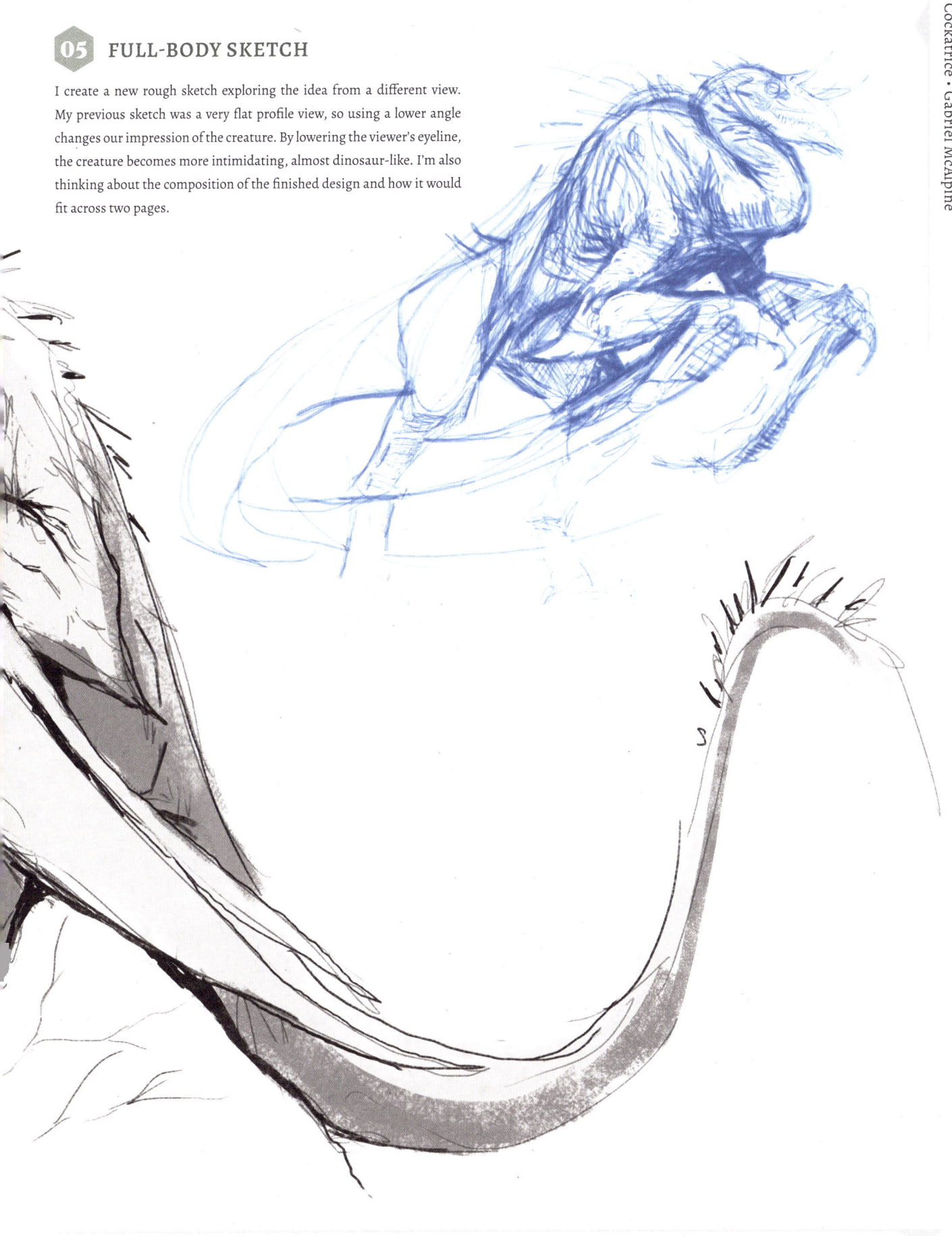

05 FULL-BODY SKETCH

I create a new rough sketch exploring the idea from a different view. My previous sketch was a very flat profile view, so using a lower angle changes our impression of the creature. By lowering the viewer's eyeline, the creature becomes more intimidating, almost dinosaur-like. I'm also thinking about the composition of the finished design and how it would fit across two pages.

06 ADDING DETAILS

I reduce the opacity of the new sketch and start drawing more details. In this version, I'm taking inspiration from the unfeathered areas of vultures' skin. Vultures have bare heads, revealing very wrinkled skin – the baldness facilitates their diet of messy carrion, enabling them to eat without spoiling their plumage. While this is a strong idea for the biological side of the creature, I'm not quite satisfied with the design and drawing yet.

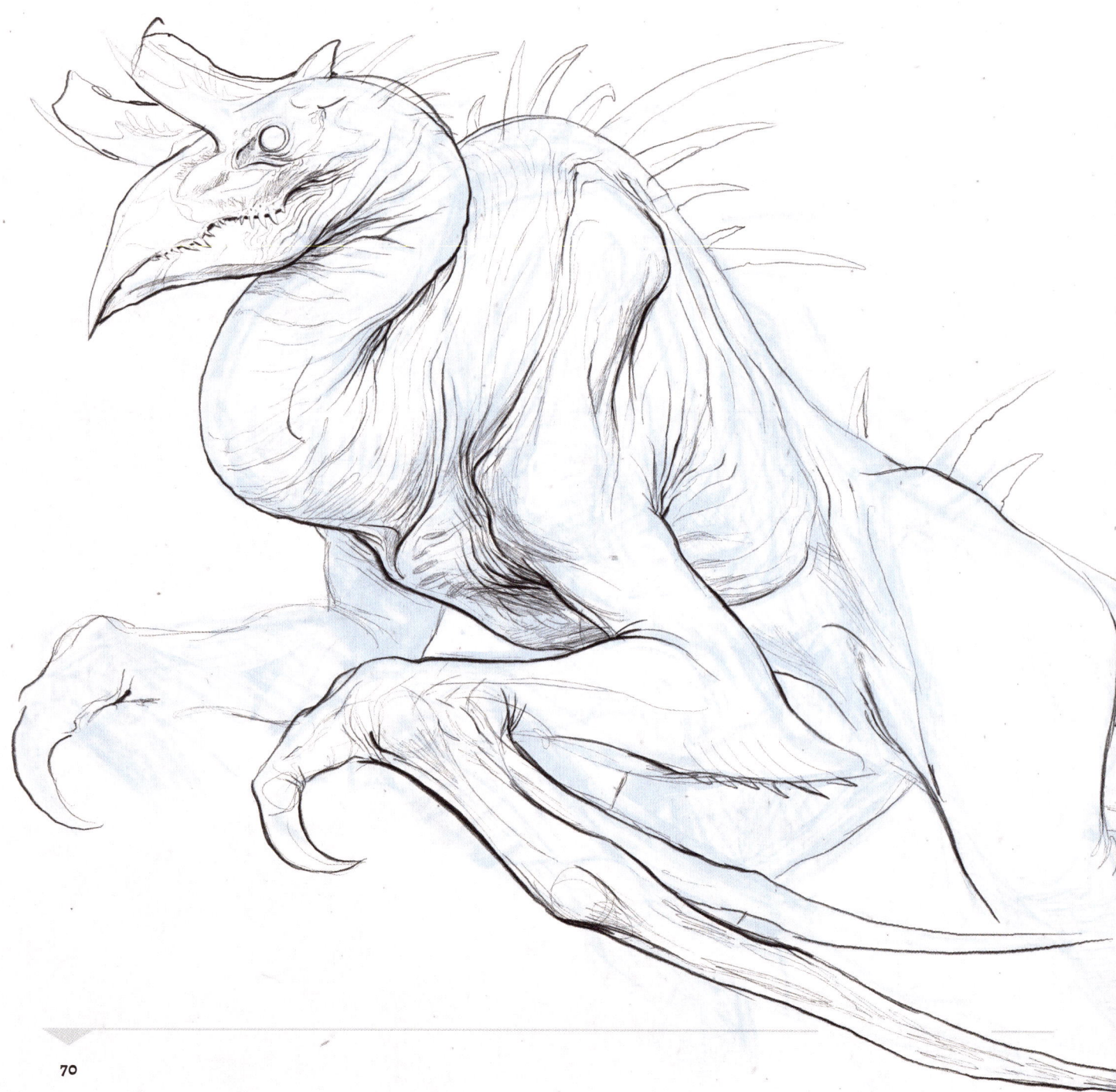

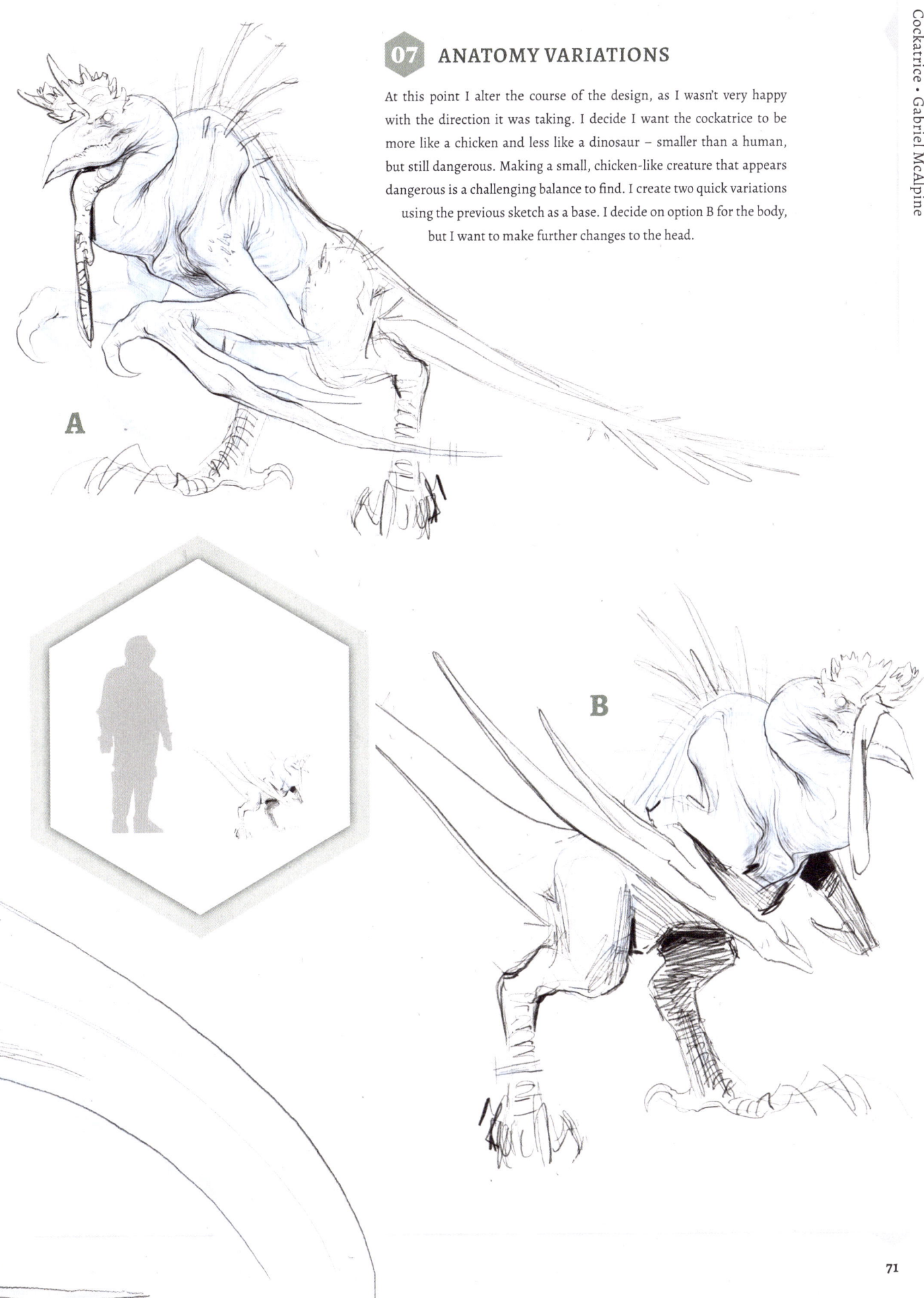

07 ANATOMY VARIATIONS

At this point I alter the course of the design, as I wasn't very happy with the direction it was taking. I decide I want the cockatrice to be more like a chicken and less like a dinosaur – smaller than a human, but still dangerous. Making a small, chicken-like creature that appears dangerous is a challenging balance to find. I create two quick variations using the previous sketch as a base. I decide on option B for the body, but I want to make further changes to the head.

A

B

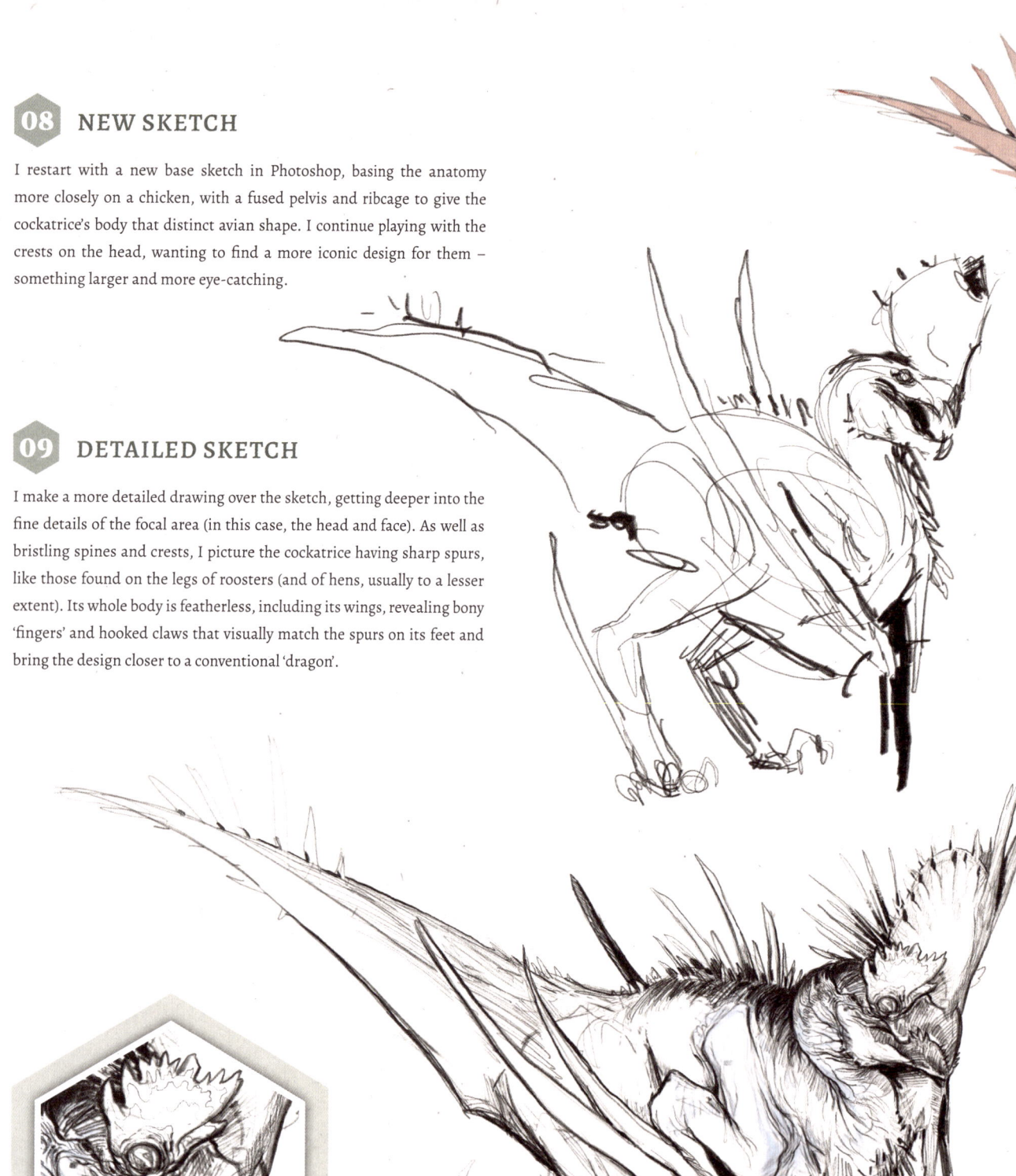

08 NEW SKETCH

I restart with a new base sketch in Photoshop, basing the anatomy more closely on a chicken, with a fused pelvis and ribcage to give the cockatrice's body that distinct avian shape. I continue playing with the crests on the head, wanting to find a more iconic design for them – something larger and more eye-catching.

09 DETAILED SKETCH

I make a more detailed drawing over the sketch, getting deeper into the fine details of the focal area (in this case, the head and face). As well as bristling spines and crests, I picture the cockatrice having sharp spurs, like those found on the legs of roosters (and of hens, usually to a lesser extent). Its whole body is featherless, including its wings, revealing bony 'fingers' and hooked claws that visually match the spurs on its feet and bring the design closer to a conventional 'dragon'.

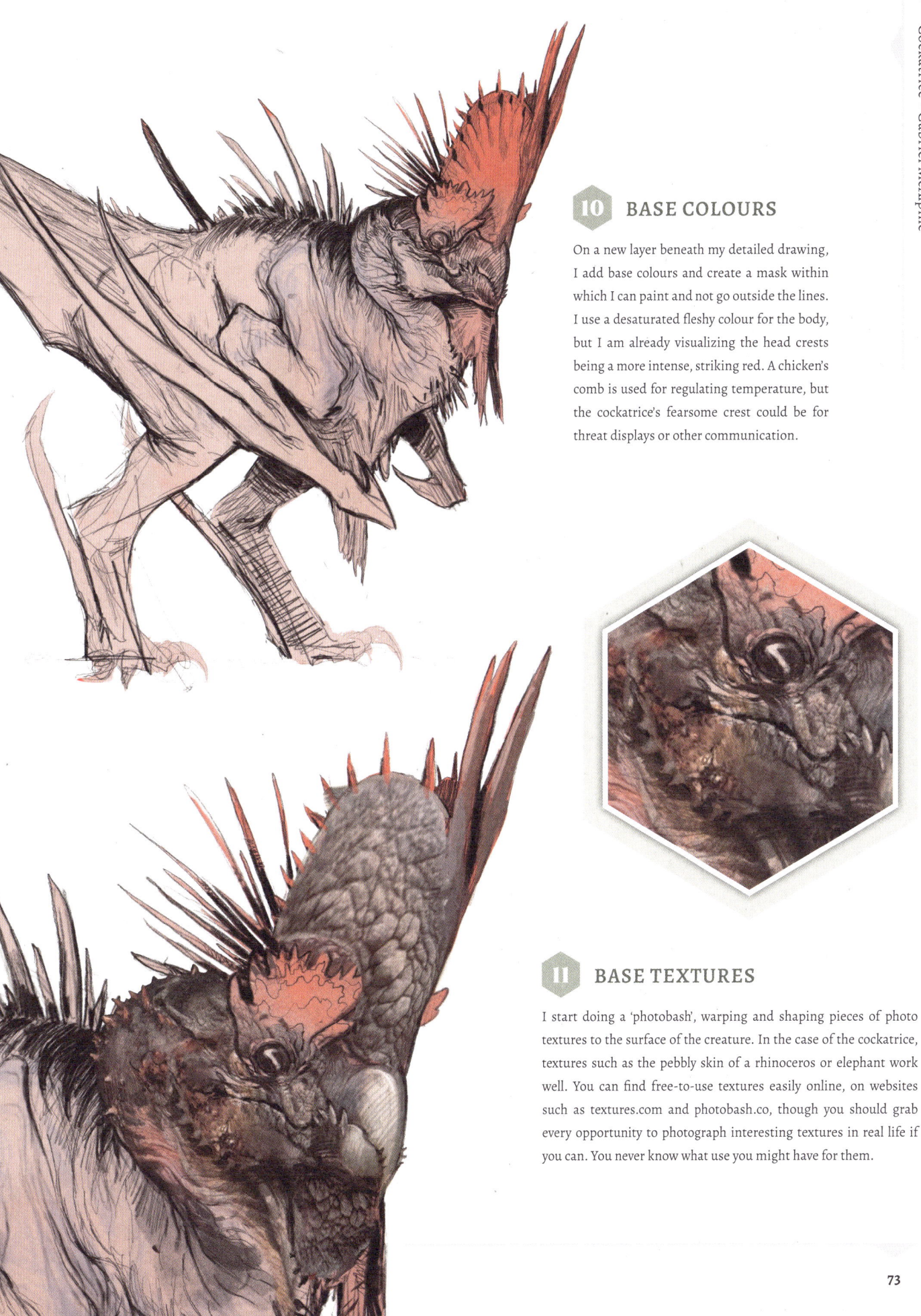

Cockatrice • Gabriel McAlpine

10   BASE COLOURS

On a new layer beneath my detailed drawing, I add base colours and create a mask within which I can paint and not go outside the lines. I use a desaturated fleshy colour for the body, but I am already visualizing the head crests being a more intense, striking red. A chicken's comb is used for regulating temperature, but the cockatrice's fearsome crest could be for threat displays or other communication.

11   BASE TEXTURES

I start doing a 'photobash', warping and shaping pieces of photo textures to the surface of the creature. In the case of the cockatrice, textures such as the pebbly skin of a rhinoceros or elephant work well. You can find free-to-use textures easily online, on websites such as textures.com and photobash.co, though you should grab every opportunity to photograph interesting textures in real life if you can. You never know what use you might have for them.

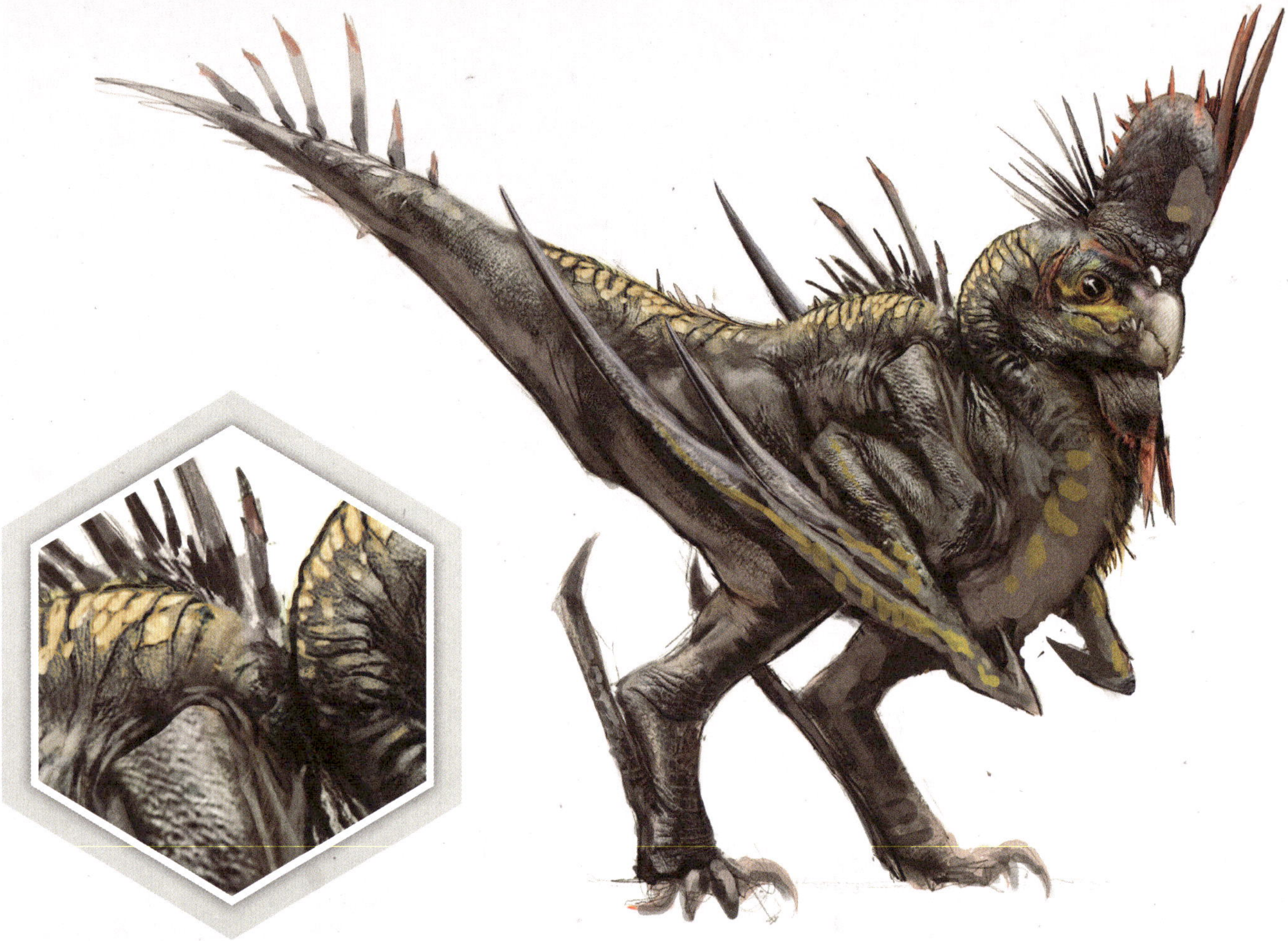

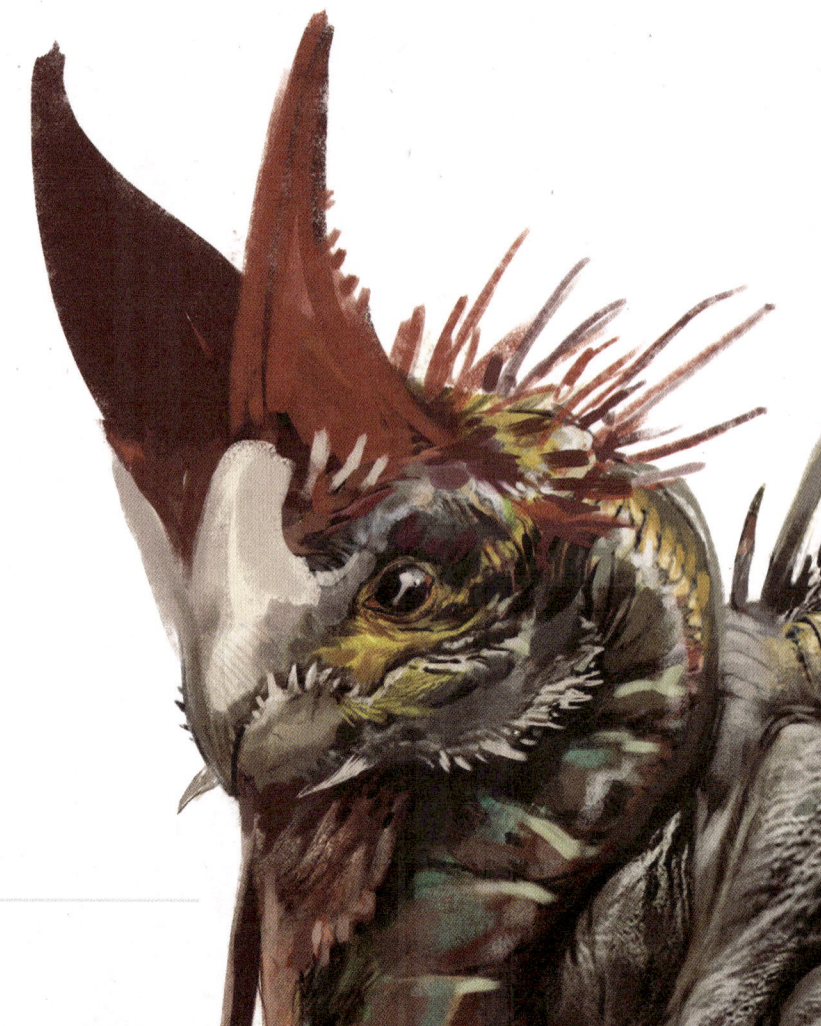

 WARNING COLOURS

After applying textures to the entire creature, I begin painting details manually. I want to use yellow warning patterns to suggest the cockatrice's poisonous nature. The head crests are spiked with red, and the face is a mix of dark and warning colours for high contrast. This palette emphasizes the creature's dangerous, reptilian side to offset its more 'chicken-y' size and shape.

 HEAD REDESIGN

Thorough overpainting starts to hide all the photograph textures. I'm still redesigning the head to make it unique and iconic, finally settling on two red sails that have a lighter, brighter, sharper look than the previous leathery crest. Bony bristles and a fanged beak give the impression of a hostile creature that is not easily fought or preyed upon.

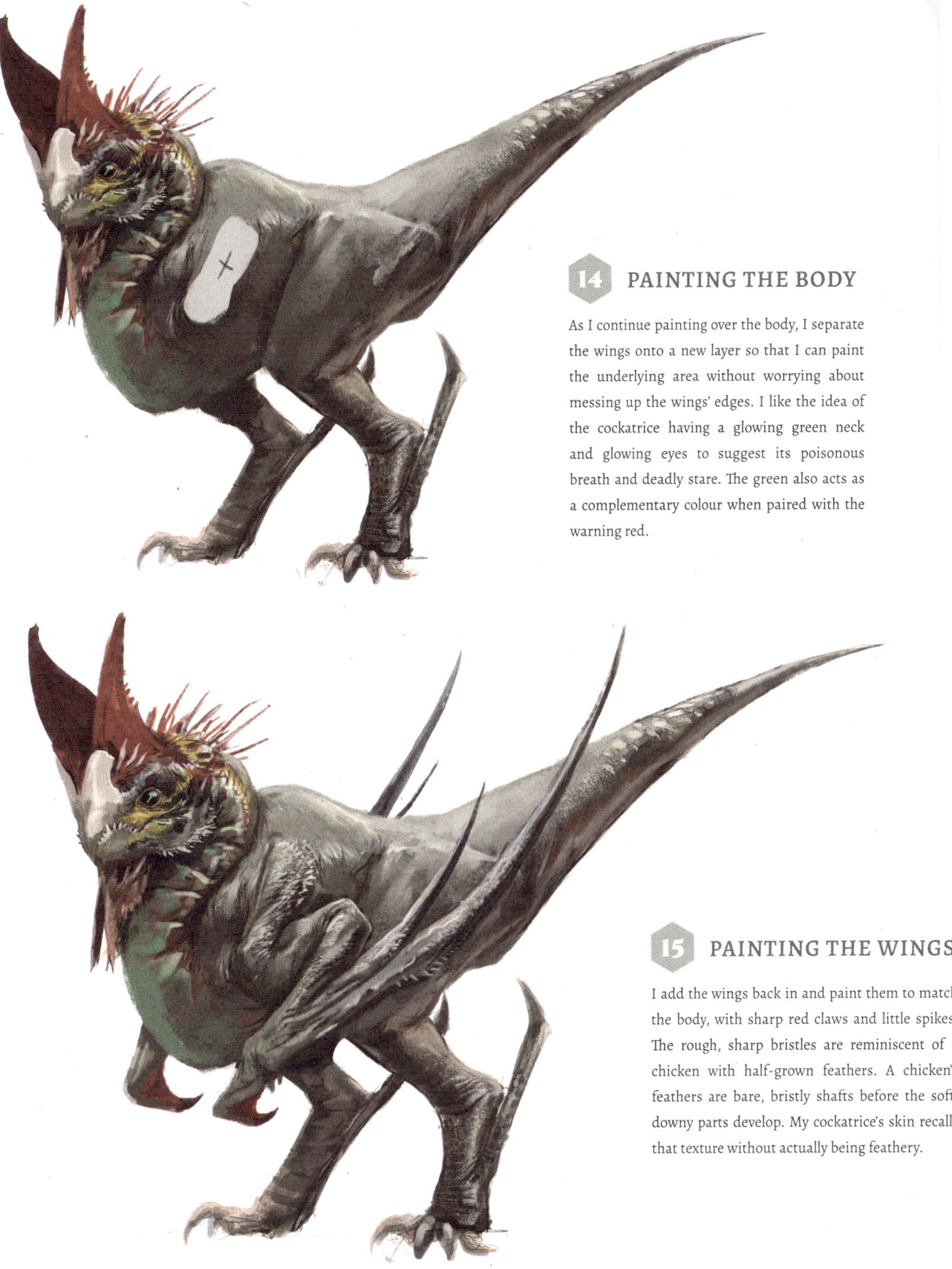

14 PAINTING THE BODY

As I continue painting over the body, I separate the wings onto a new layer so that I can paint the underlying area without worrying about messing up the wings' edges. I like the idea of the cockatrice having a glowing green neck and glowing eyes to suggest its poisonous breath and deadly stare. The green also acts as a complementary colour when paired with the warning red.

15 PAINTING THE WINGS

I add the wings back in and paint them to match the body, with sharp red claws and little spikes. The rough, sharp bristles are reminiscent of a chicken with half-grown feathers. A chicken's feathers are bare, bristly shafts before the soft, downy parts develop. My cockatrice's skin recalls that texture without actually being feathery.

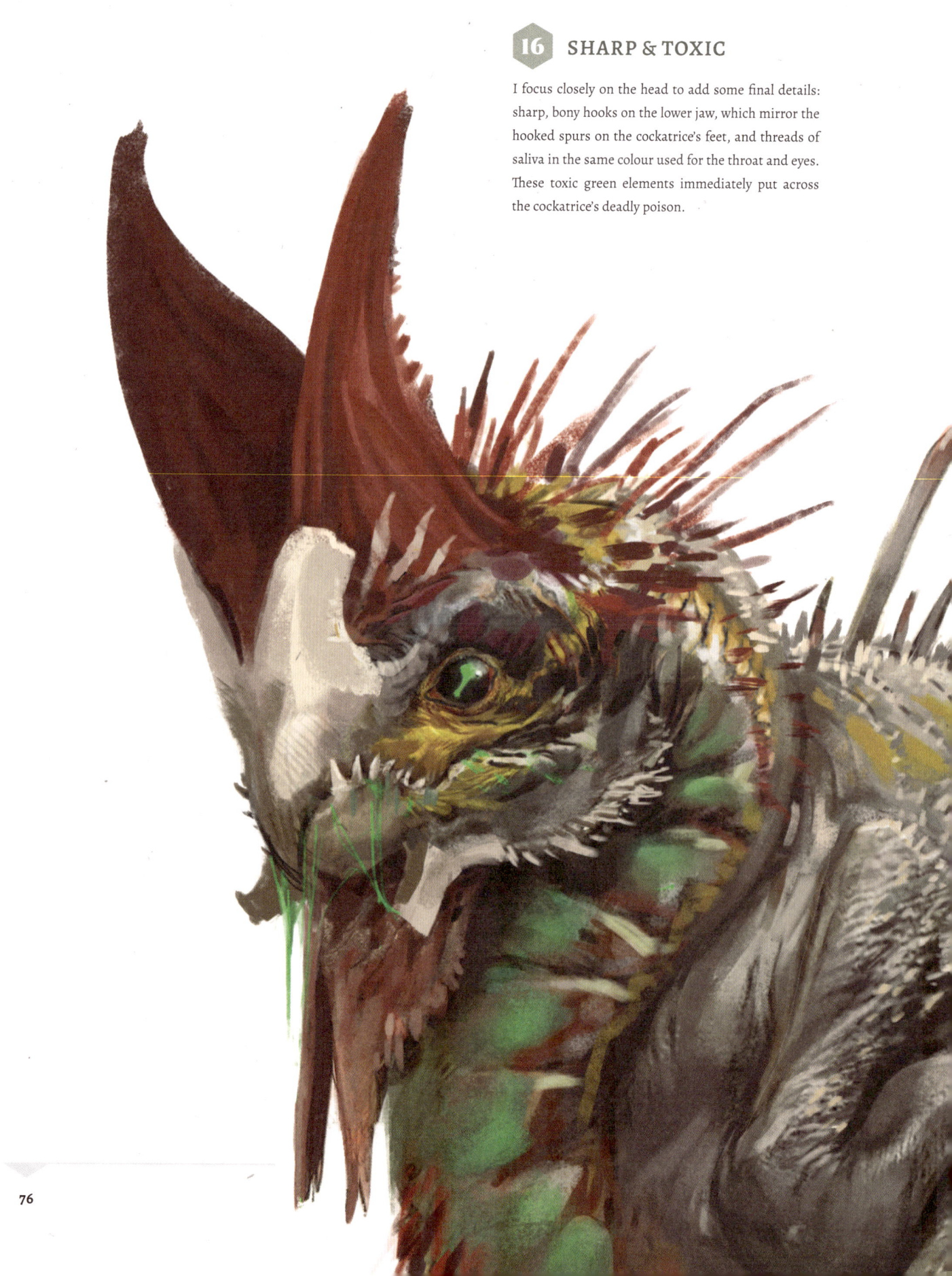

16 SHARP & TOXIC

I focus closely on the head to add some final details: sharp, bony hooks on the lower jaw, which mirror the hooked spurs on the cockatrice's feet, and threads of saliva in the same colour used for the throat and eyes. These toxic green elements immediately put across the cockatrice's deadly poison.

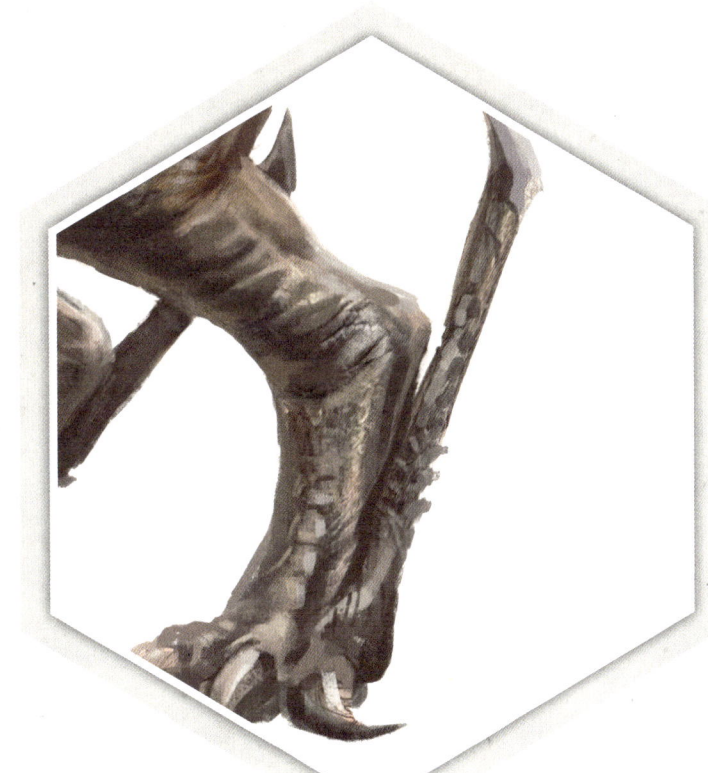

17 SPUR DETAILS

To finish off the feet, I sharpen up the shape of the talons and deadly spurs. As my take on the cockatrice does not have feathered wings for flying, it relies on its strong, muscular legs for mobility. These, along with the tail, are the most dinosaur-like elements remaining from those early sketch stages.

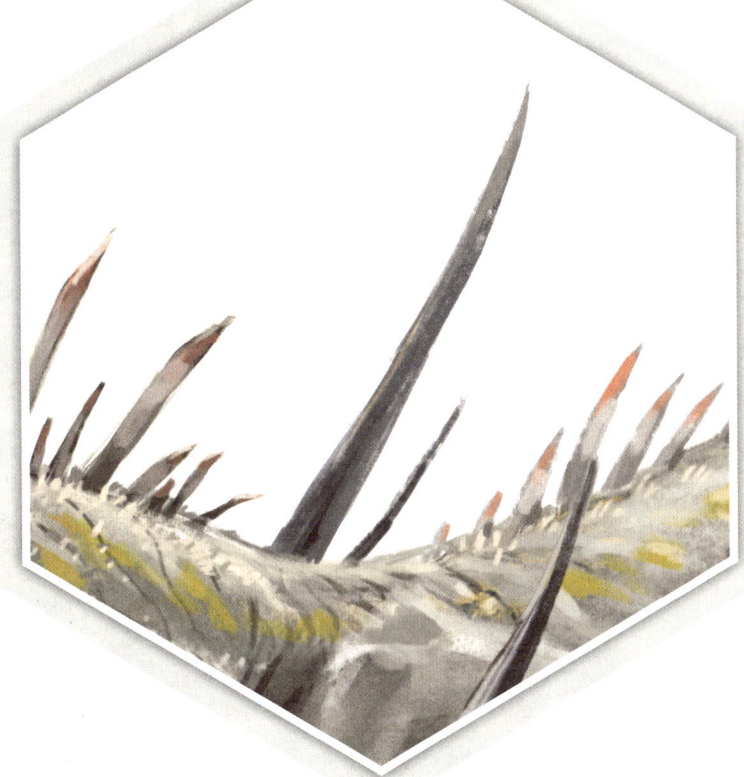

18 DORSAL SPIKES

I finalize the details on the rest of the body, painting in yellow spots, adding more sharp quills to the neck and chest, and extending bony spikes all the way down the spine and tail. This creates more balance and visual consistency across the cockatrice's design.

COCKATRICE

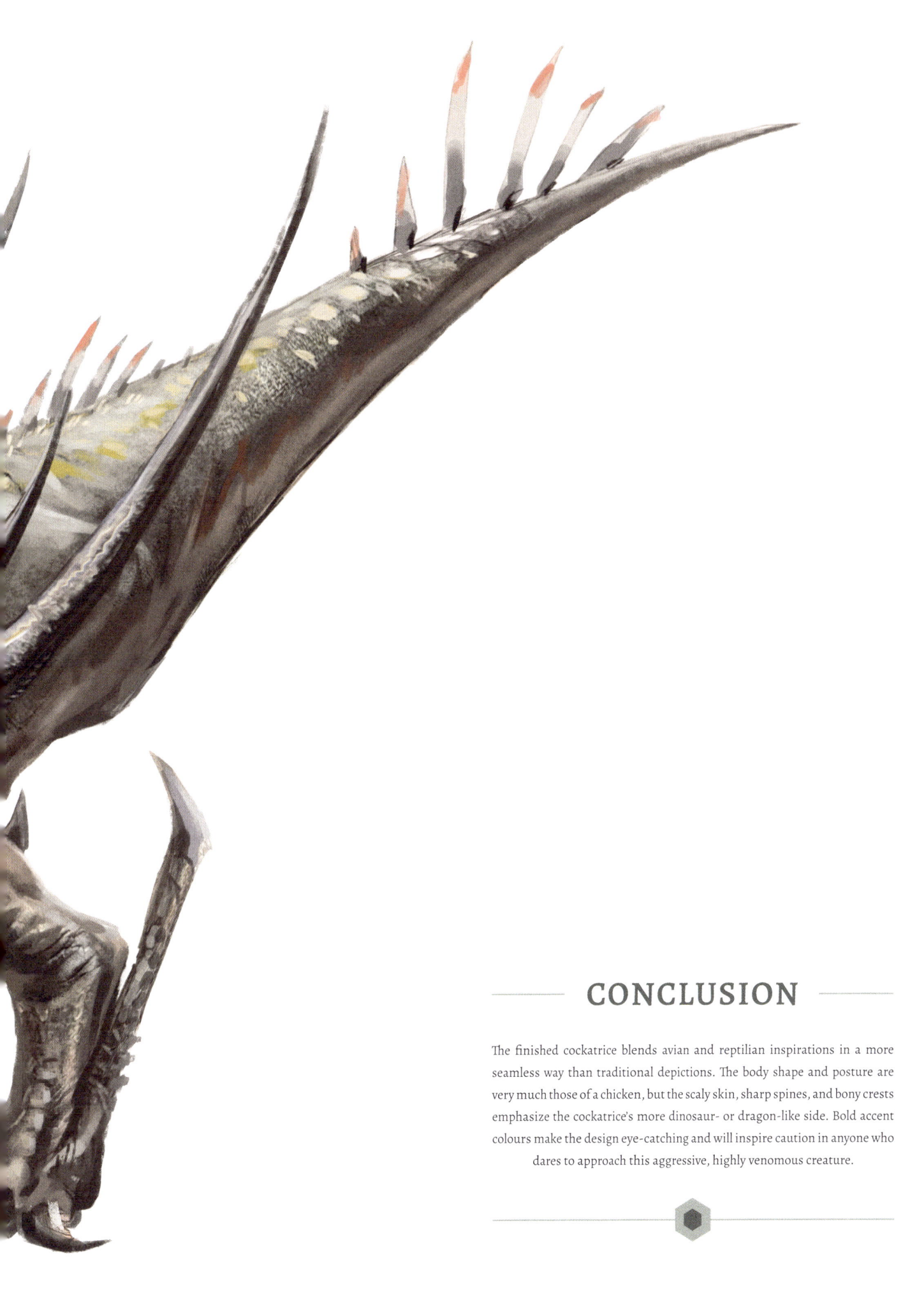

CONCLUSION

The finished cockatrice blends avian and reptilian inspirations in a more seamless way than traditional depictions. The body shape and posture are very much those of a chicken, but the scaly skin, sharp spines, and bony crests emphasize the cockatrice's more dinosaur- or dragon-like side. Bold accent colours make the design eye-catching and will inspire caution in anyone who dares to approach this aggressive, highly venomous creature.

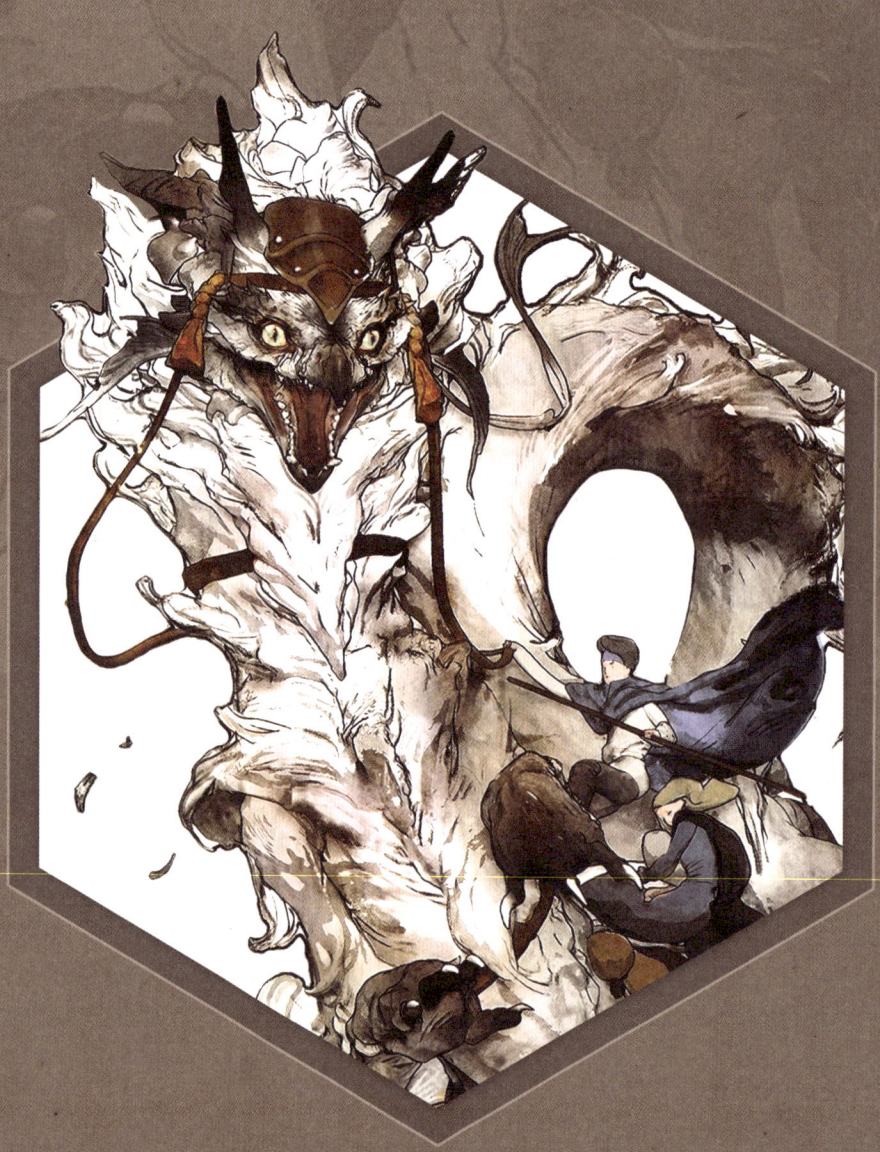

EAST ASIAN DRAGON

Dragons are a theme I frequently encounter in my work designing creatures. I have designed many variations on the theme of a long, Eastern dragon, and each time the challenge lies in how to introduce features I have not tried before, within the creature's limited range. The long, serpentine dragons of East Asian lore tend to feature more mammalian elements than typical European dragons, such as antlers and whiskers. Unlike their Western counterparts, they are usually benevolent figures, associated with good luck, prosperity, water, and weather. In this tutorial, I will elaborate on how I tackle such a creature design – from brainstorming and preliminary research to planning and producing a final illustration – in a way that combines classic features with new twists.

ENTEI RYU

Final image © Entei Ryu

01 PAST DESIGNS

Before starting a new dragon design, I recall the designs of other dragons I have worked on. I aim to avoid similar designs, to help myself stay curious and motivated during the creation process. Here are some sketches from my previous dragon-themed work:

- A dragon-shaped demon that stands on two legs like a human warrior, with well-developed muscles, wielding a sword.

- A small, flying dragon about the size of a human head, with four legs and two wings like a Western dragon, plus a slender tail and spiky features.

- A chubby, fluffy, family-carrying dragon, whose design is inspired by goats and moths.

- A bird-like terrestrial dragon with an ostrich's body and a deer's antlers.

With each of these dragons, I incorporated some unusual new motifs into my designs, and this time will be no exception.

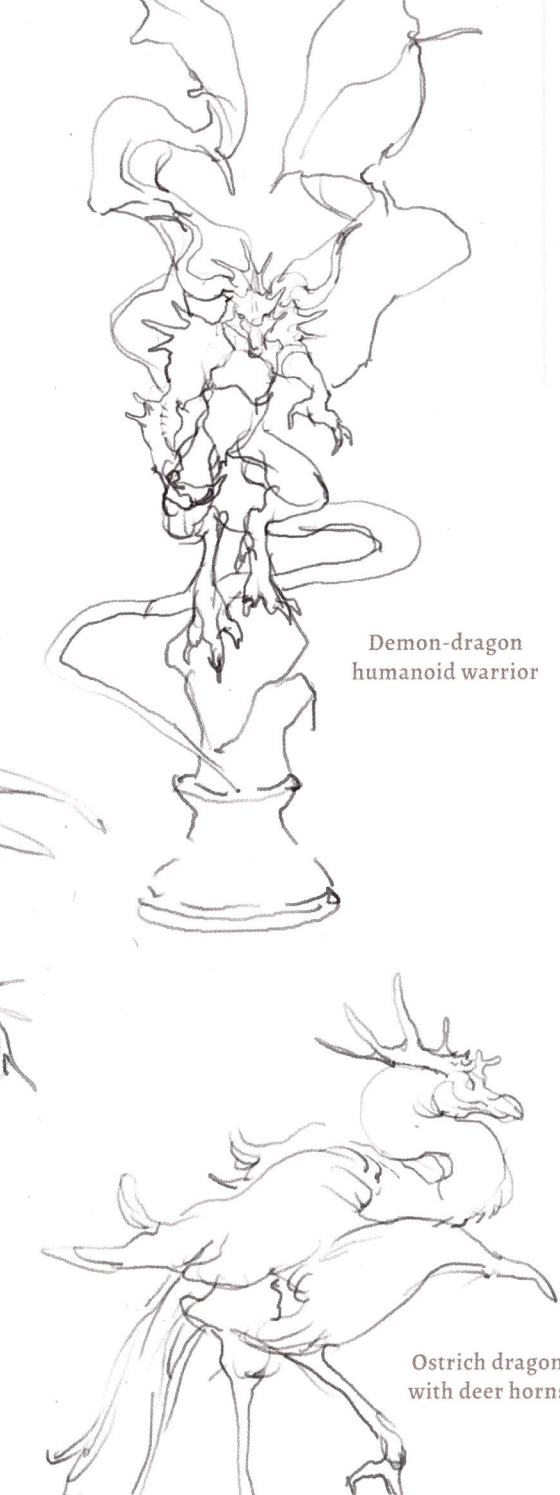

Demon-dragon
humanoid warrior

Small, long,
four-legged snake

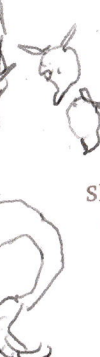

Sheep-moth dragon
with little babies

Ostrich dragon
with deer horns

During the brainstorming phase at the beginning of the creation process, I recommend using a mind map to organize your inspirations. I start by extracting the distinctive features of a typical East Asian dragon: the silhouette, antler-like horns, and long body. From there, I consider real animals that I could reference, such as cats, lions, birds, and owls. I distil the characteristics from each of these that I want to use in my design: the sharp gaze of a cat, the thick mane of a lion, the feathers of a bird, and the distinctive facial shape of an owl.

I also summarize the purpose that will shape these features in my dragon design. What style and personality should the dragon have? I want this creature to have a lively, sharp gaze, a majestic presence, and a divine appearance. Beyond physical traits, I also consider environmental and cultural aspects. These make me think about the creature's modes of movement and communication, which are also very important in creature design.

Although this preliminary thinking is all focused on text, it is the foundation for the subsequent development of the design.

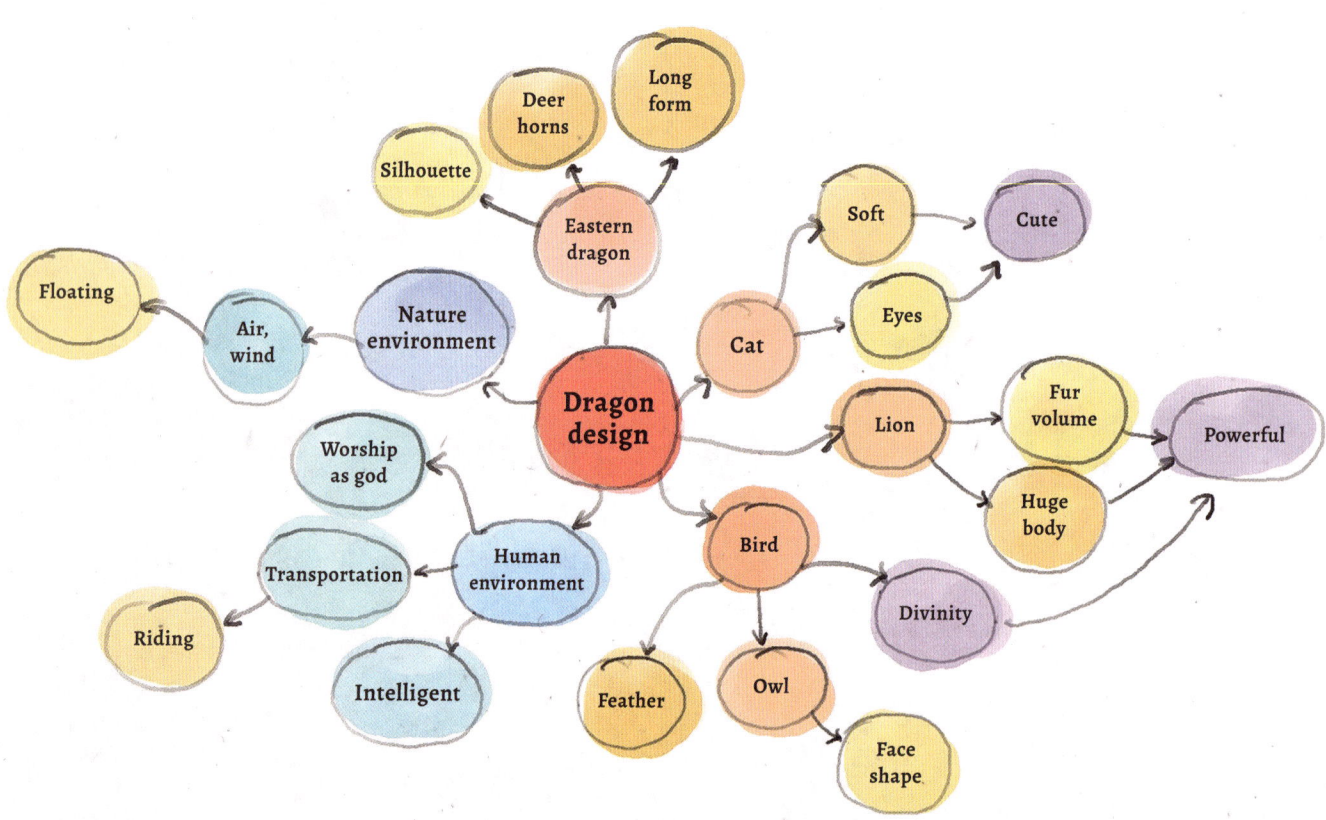

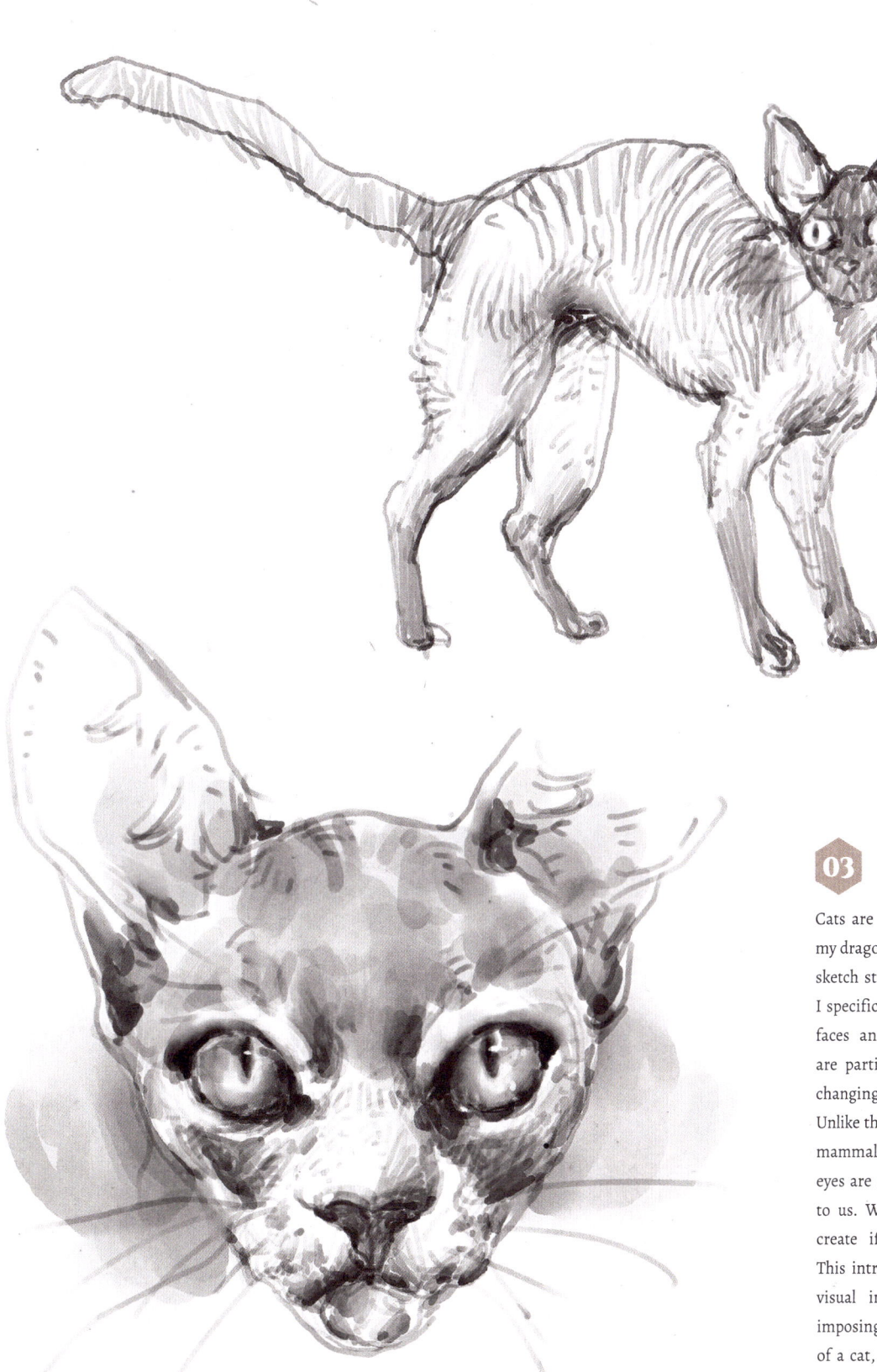

03 CAT STUDIES

Cats are one of the chosen references for my dragon design, so I conduct a few quick sketch studies to observe their soft forms. I specifically study cat breeds with thinner faces and large, round eyes. Cats' eyes are particularly beautiful and expressive, changing pupil size with variations in light. Unlike the gentle, drooping eyelids of giant mammals like whales and elephants, cat eyes are sharp and alert, but still adorable to us. What kind of contrast would this create if applied to a larger creature? This intriguing blend could add a unique visual impact, combining the dragon's imposing size with the distinct, lively eyes of a cat, potentially creating a compelling and unexpected trait in the design.

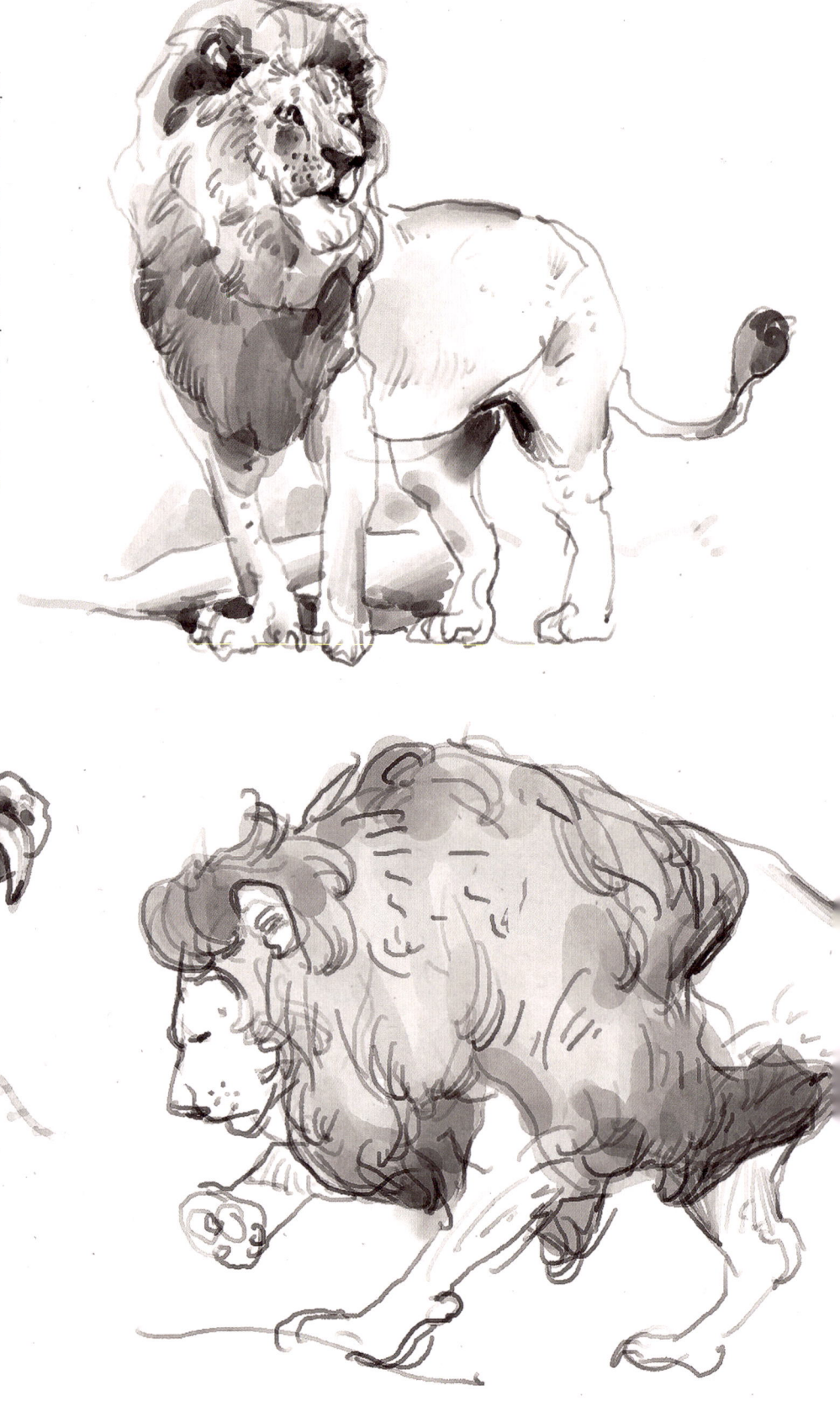

04 LION STUDIES

I also create sketch studies of lions, focusing primarily on the volumetric sense and flow of a male lion's mane, crafting the fur to give the creature a more majestic presence. I will also draw inspiration from lions' paws for the design of the dragon's claws, as they are structured to bear a lion's massive weight and are distinctly different from a domestic cat's paws. Since the dragon I'm designing is larger than a lion, I observe the relationships between parts of these two differently sized creatures to infer what the parts of my fantasy creature might look like. This approach will help ensure that the dragon's anatomy is not only impressive but also plausible, supporting its larger size with robust and appropriately scaled features.

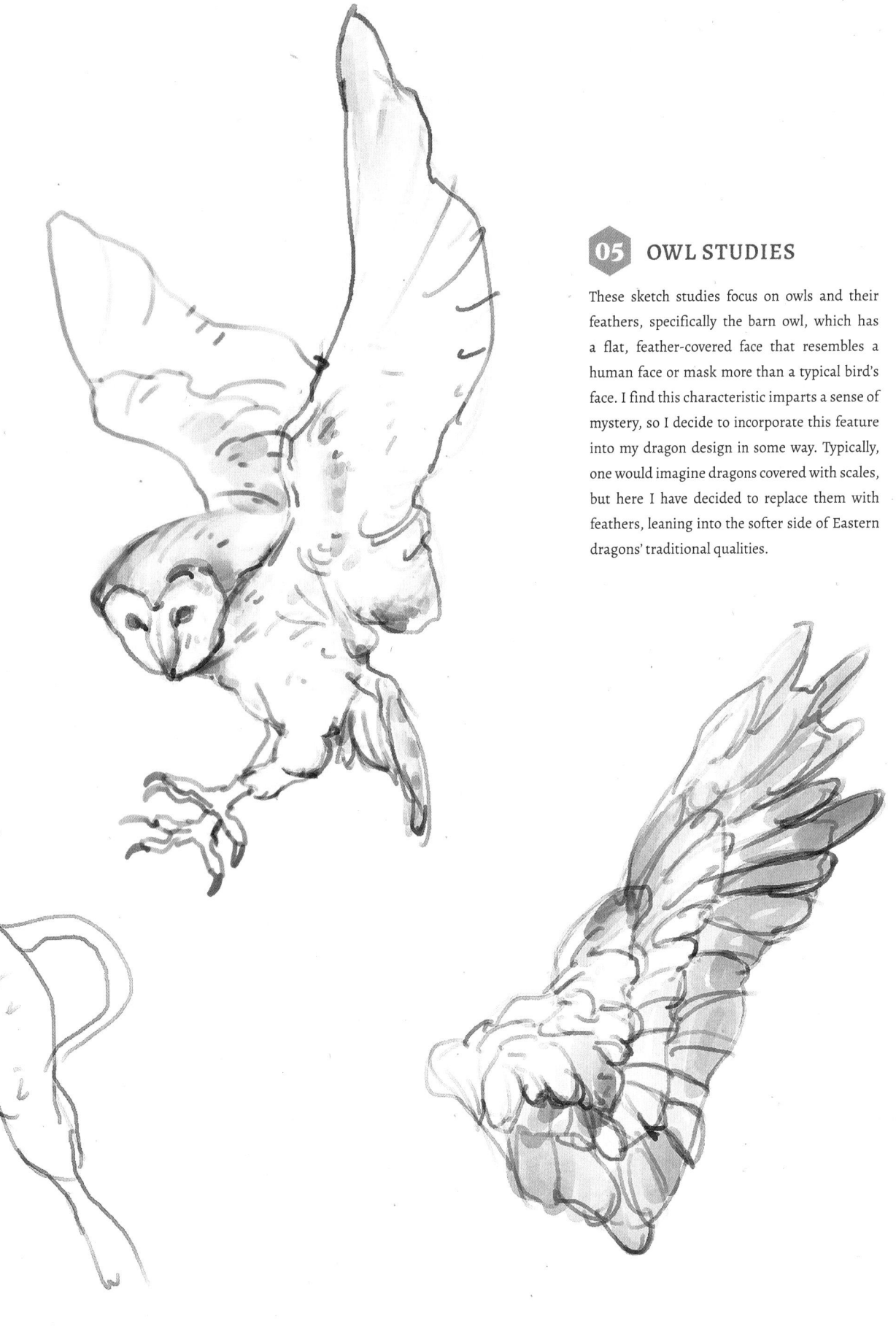

05 OWL STUDIES

These sketch studies focus on owls and their feathers, specifically the barn owl, which has a flat, feather-covered face that resembles a human face or mask more than a typical bird's face. I find this characteristic imparts a sense of mystery, so I decide to incorporate this feature into my dragon design in some way. Typically, one would imagine dragons covered with scales, but here I have decided to replace them with feathers, leaning into the softer side of Eastern dragons' traditional qualities.

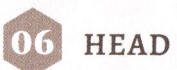

06 HEAD VARIATIONS

I draw three versions of the head, generally referencing the aforementioned animals. Here I experiment with different proportions, overall contours, the length of the fur, the shape of the mouth, and so on. Ultimately, I choose option A, which combines a lion's mane and bird's beak with the more classic features of antlers and long ears. In comparison, option B is more heavily feline, and option C is more traditional than the goal I have in mind.

A

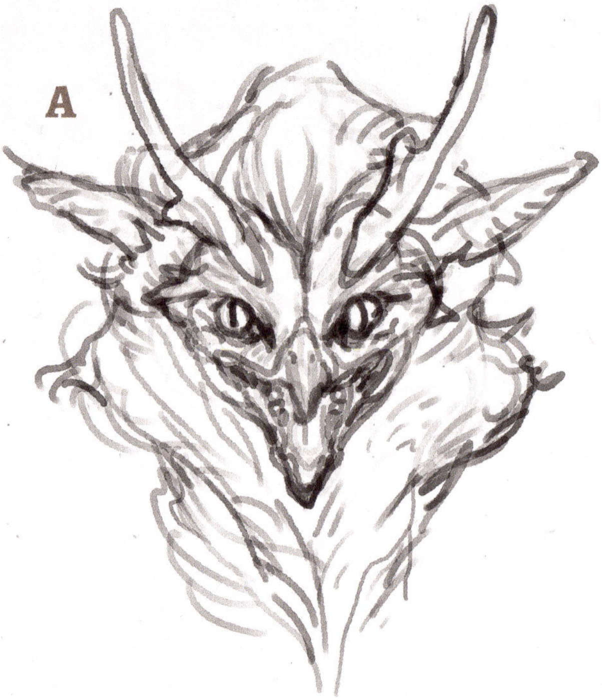

B

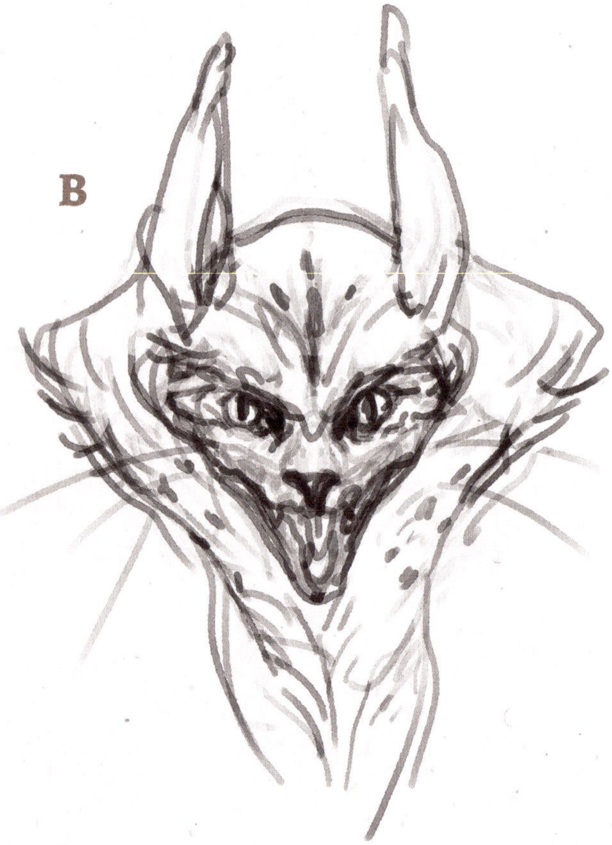

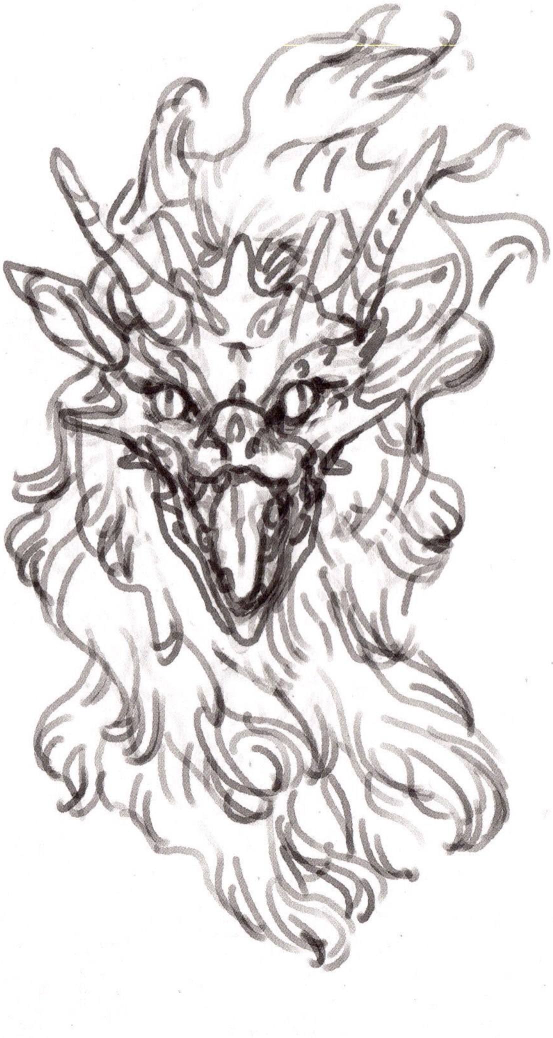

C

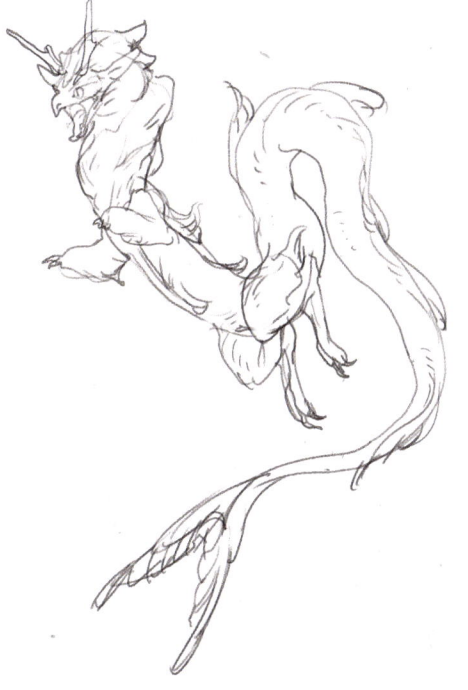

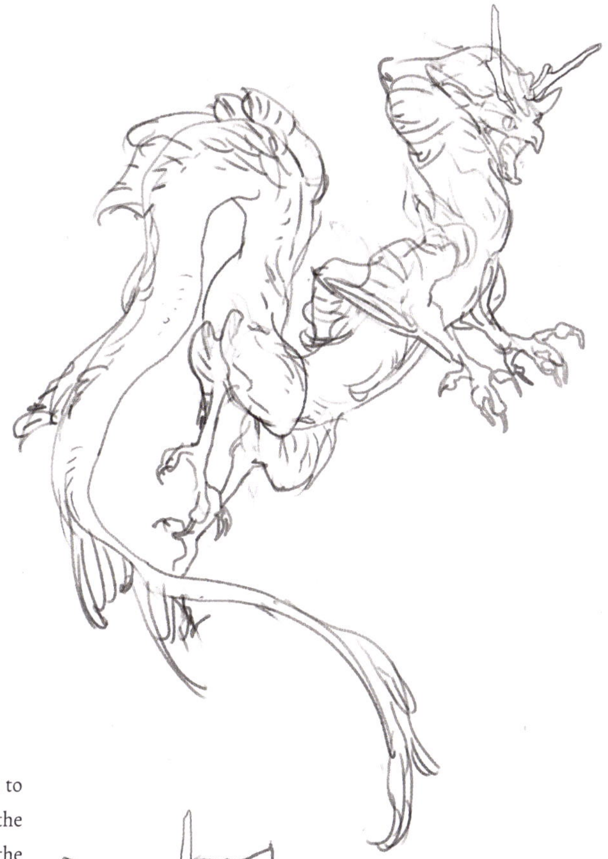

07 BODY VARIATIONS

Next I sketch some experiments with body features. Overall, I want to create a soft, elongated dragon, so the general proportions are set in the traditional serpentine style. Based on this, I try different shapes for the claws, such as those with more fur or a stronger skeletal feel. I also test shapes for the feathers and fur on the body. I lean towards the top-left option, which is moderately fluffy, with downy front talons like an owl.

SIMPLE SHAPES

Use simple, basic geometry in your sketches: spheres, triangles, and quadrilaterals. Classic geometry never goes out of style and simple shapes are more likely to attract the viewer's attention. What can you subtract from your design to make the shapes more powerful?

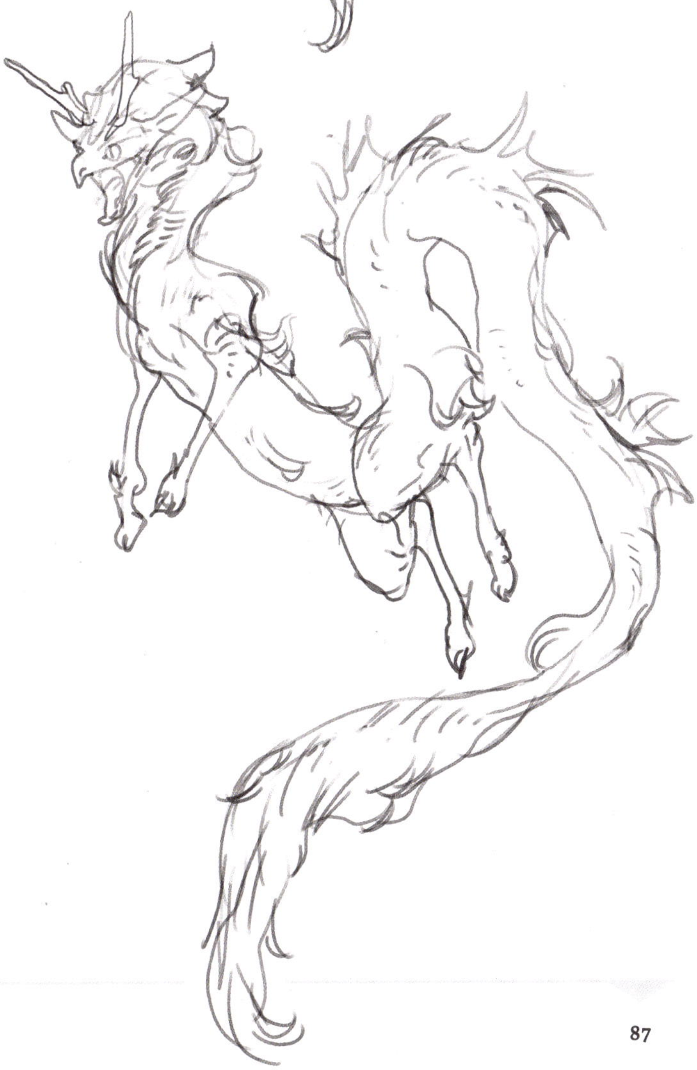

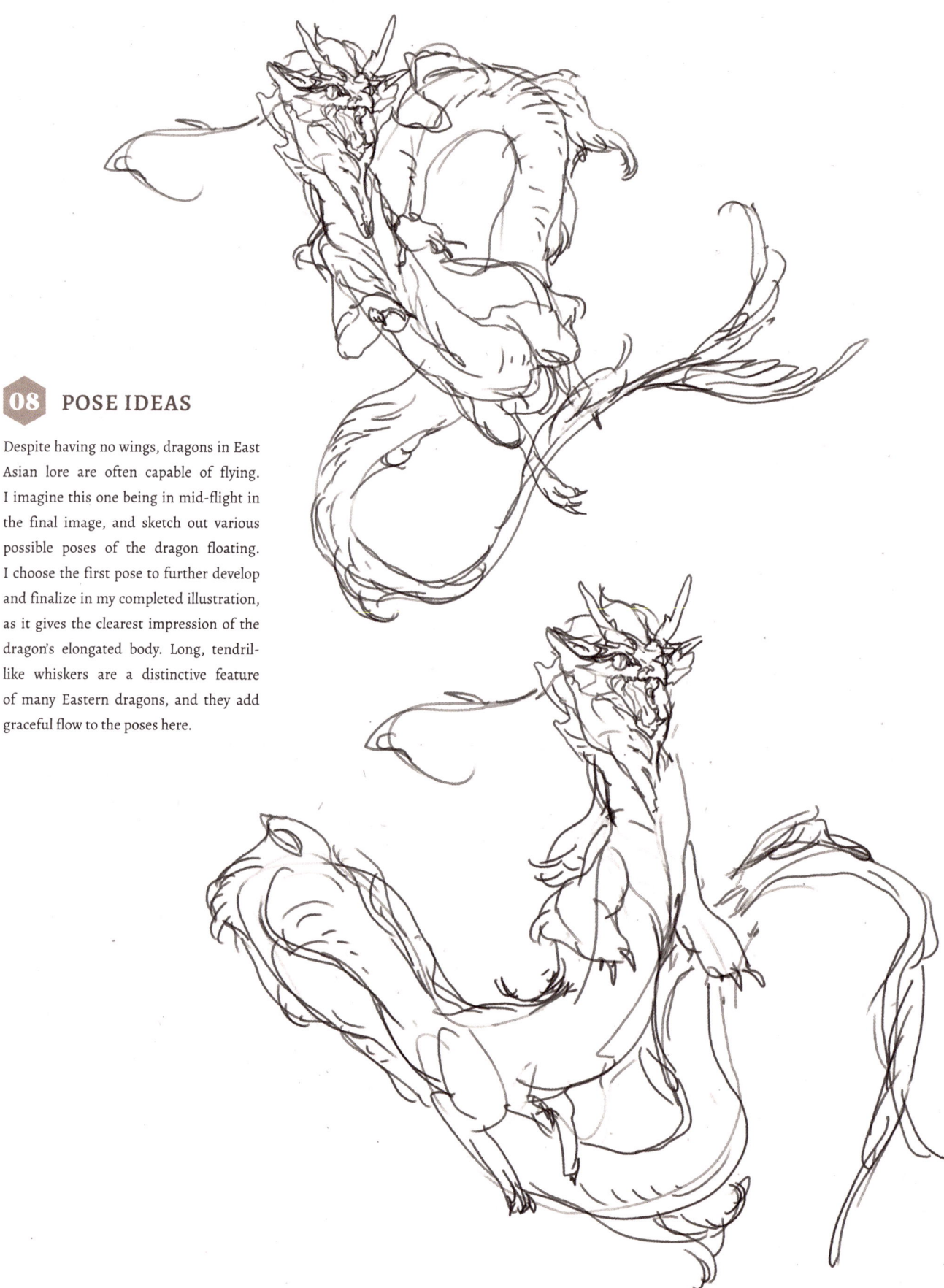

08 POSE IDEAS

Despite having no wings, dragons in East Asian lore are often capable of flying. I imagine this one being in mid-flight in the final image, and sketch out various possible poses of the dragon floating. I choose the first pose to further develop and finalize in my completed illustration, as it gives the clearest impression of the dragon's elongated body. Long, tendril-like whiskers are a distinctive feature of many Eastern dragons, and they add graceful flow to the poses here.

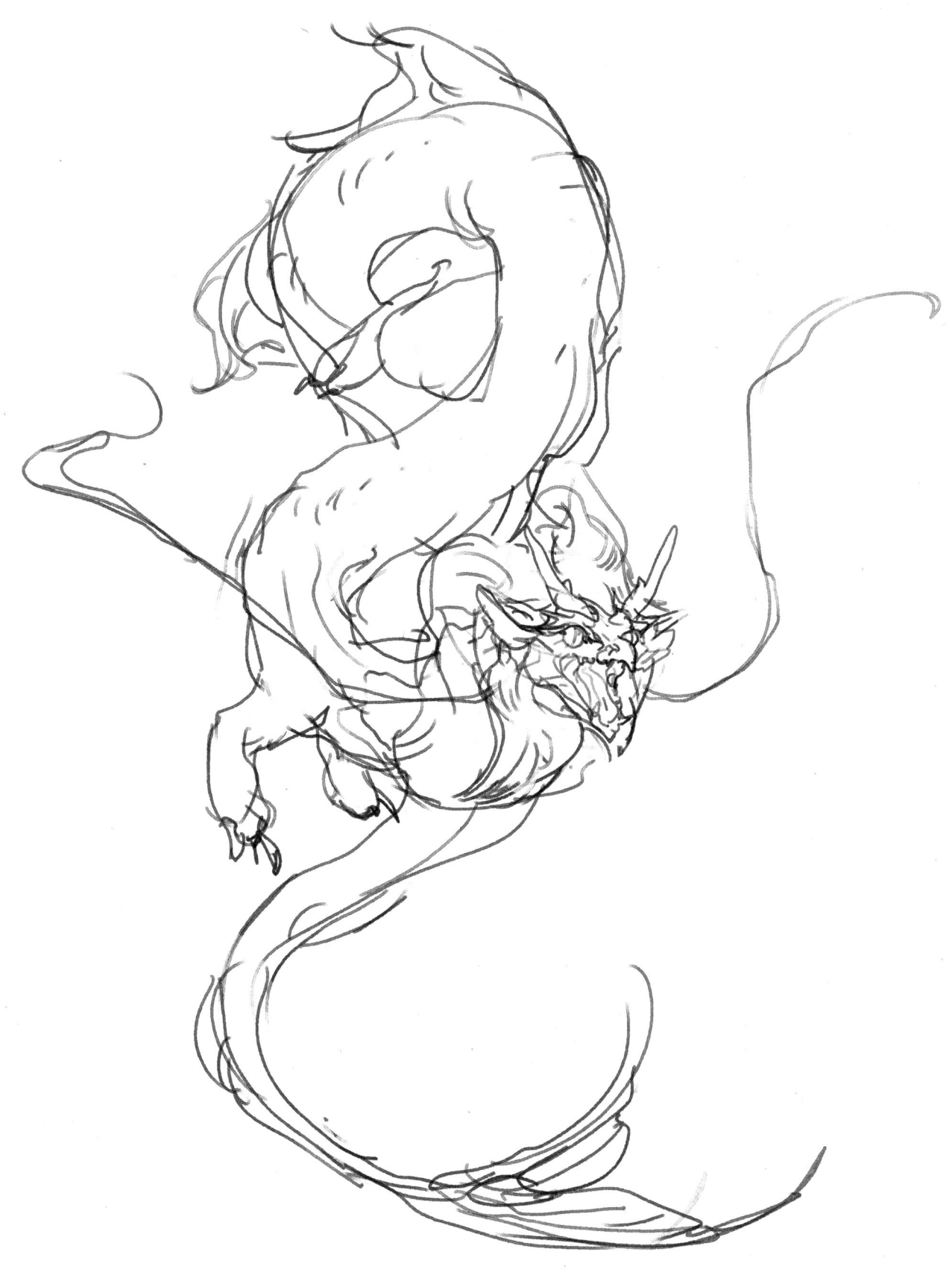

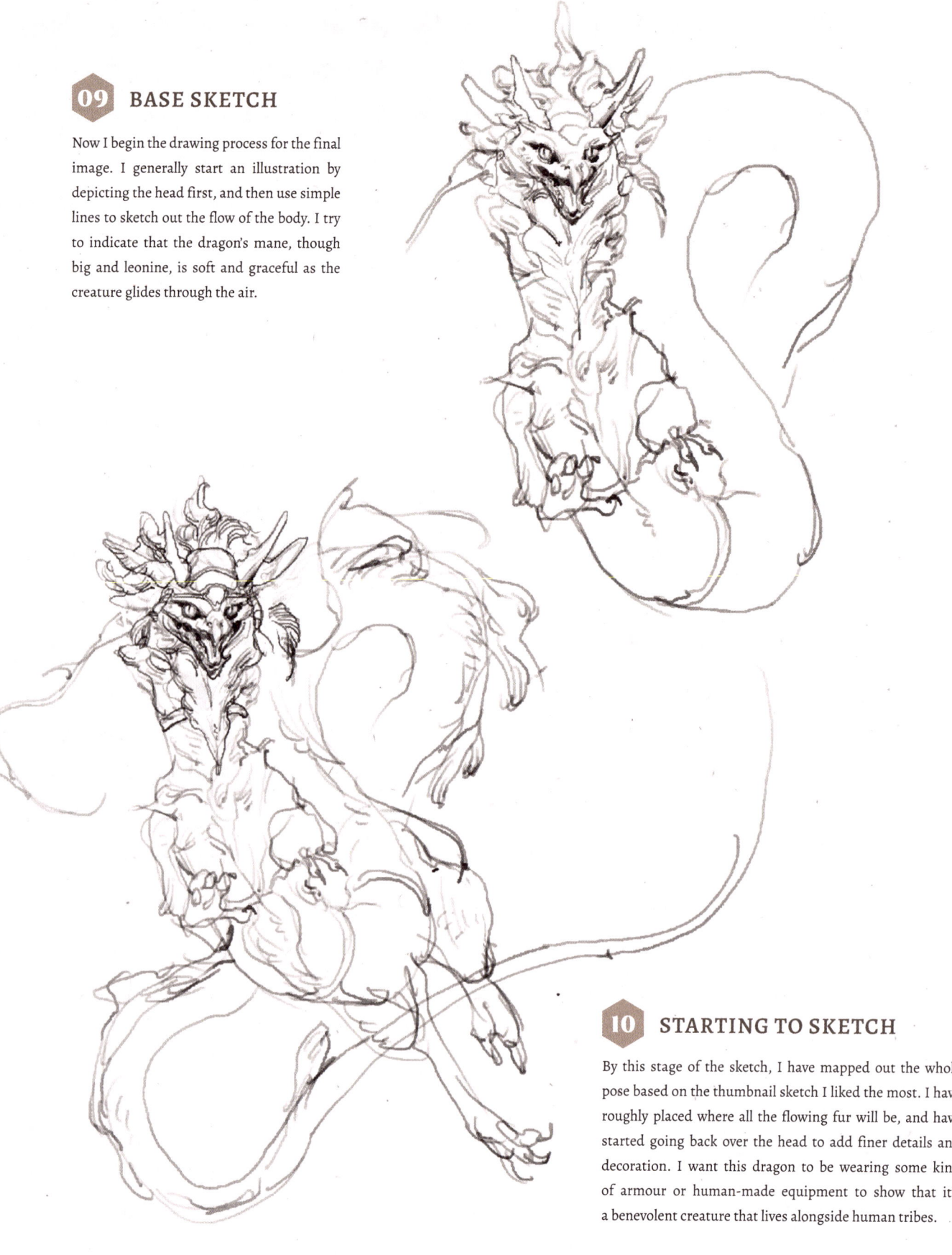

09 BASE SKETCH

Now I begin the drawing process for the final image. I generally start an illustration by depicting the head first, and then use simple lines to sketch out the flow of the body. I try to indicate that the dragon's mane, though big and leonine, is soft and graceful as the creature glides through the air.

10 STARTING TO SKETCH

By this stage of the sketch, I have mapped out the whole pose based on the thumbnail sketch I liked the most. I have roughly placed where all the flowing fur will be, and have started going back over the head to add finer details and decoration. I want this dragon to be wearing some kind of armour or human-made equipment to show that it's a benevolent creature that lives alongside human tribes.

FULL SKETCH

Here I have fully sketched the whole dragon, to a moderate level of detail, and have even added some tones and shading to indicate depth. I have added accessories on the dragon's back for riding, along with luggage and travellers. This benevolent dragon coexists with human settlements, serving as a means of transportation during migrations, and also as a deity they worship. Having the comparison with human bodies helps to convey the size of the creature.

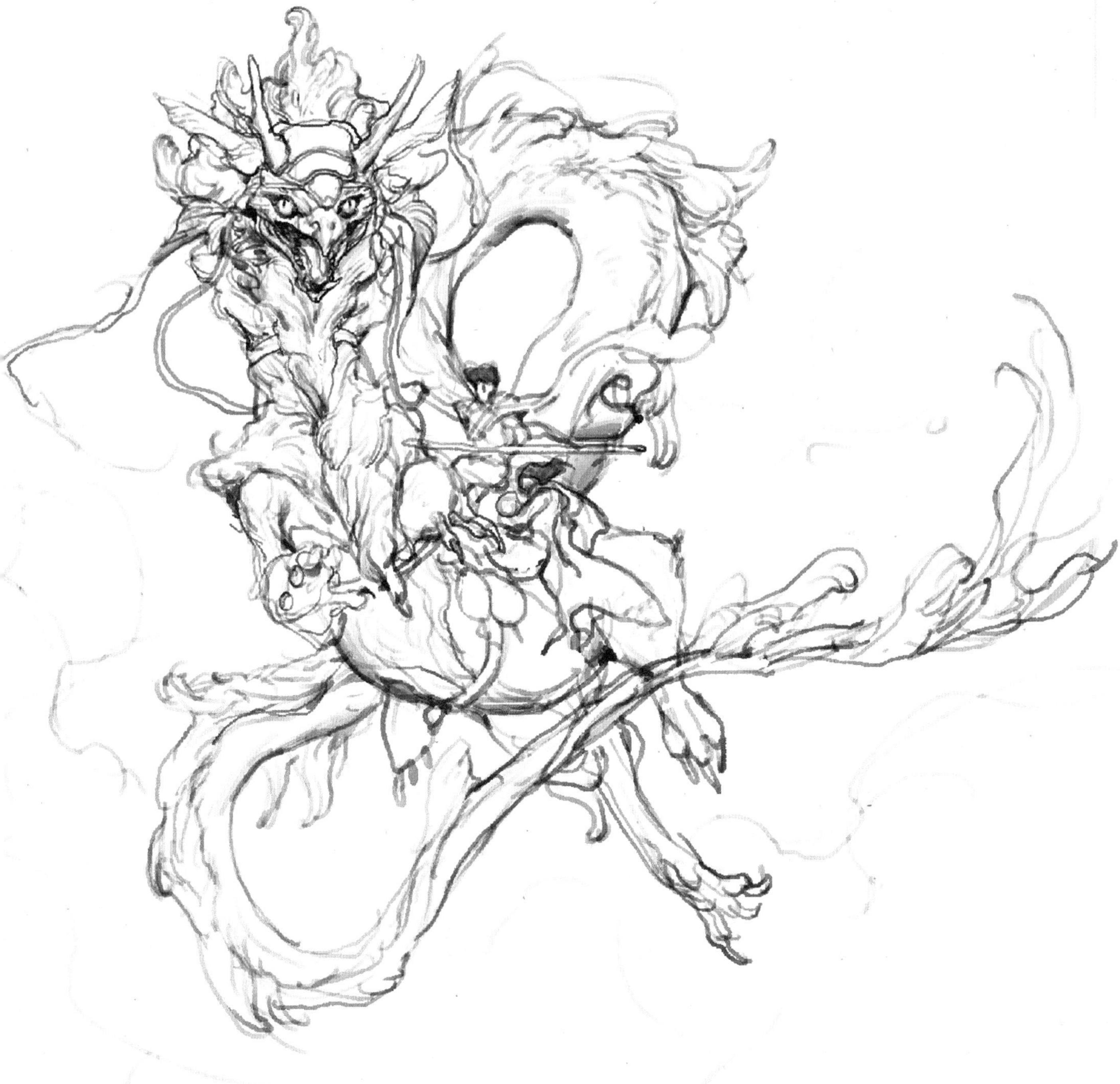

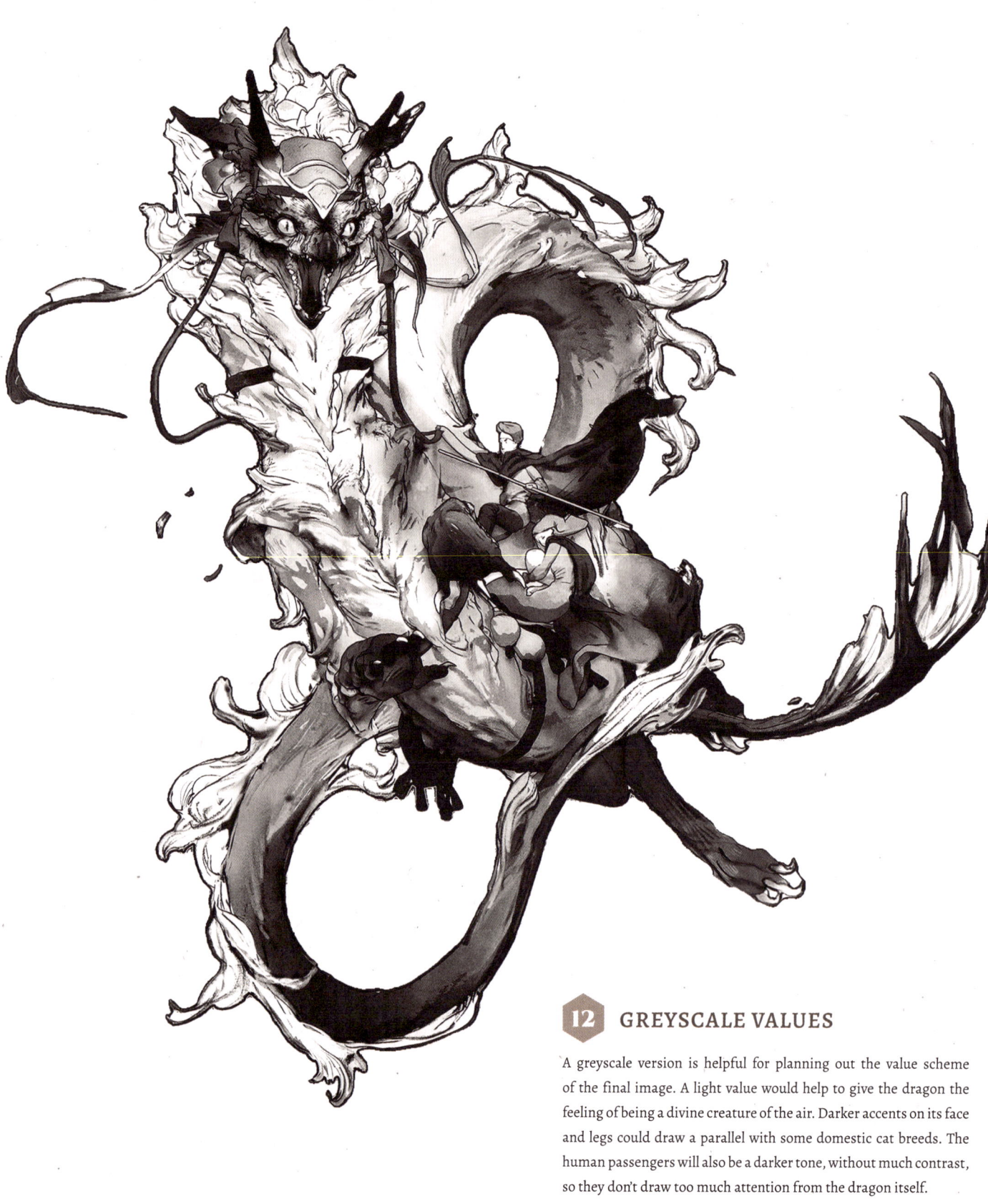

12 GREYSCALE VALUES

A greyscale version is helpful for planning out the value scheme of the final image. A light value would help to give the dragon the feeling of being a divine creature of the air. Darker accents on its face and legs could draw a parallel with some domestic cat breeds. The human passengers will also be a darker tone, without much contrast, so they don't draw too much attention from the dragon itself.

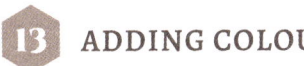 **ADDING COLOUR**

I begin adding colour to the greyscale image. Considering the characteristics of bird feathers, I could have opted for a wide and intense palette, but I want the dragon to be light-coloured, rendered in an almost ink-wash style. I decide on a soft cream colour, similar to the plumage of the barn owl. The armour is in brown leather, for a rustic look that harmonizes well with the dragon's natural colour.

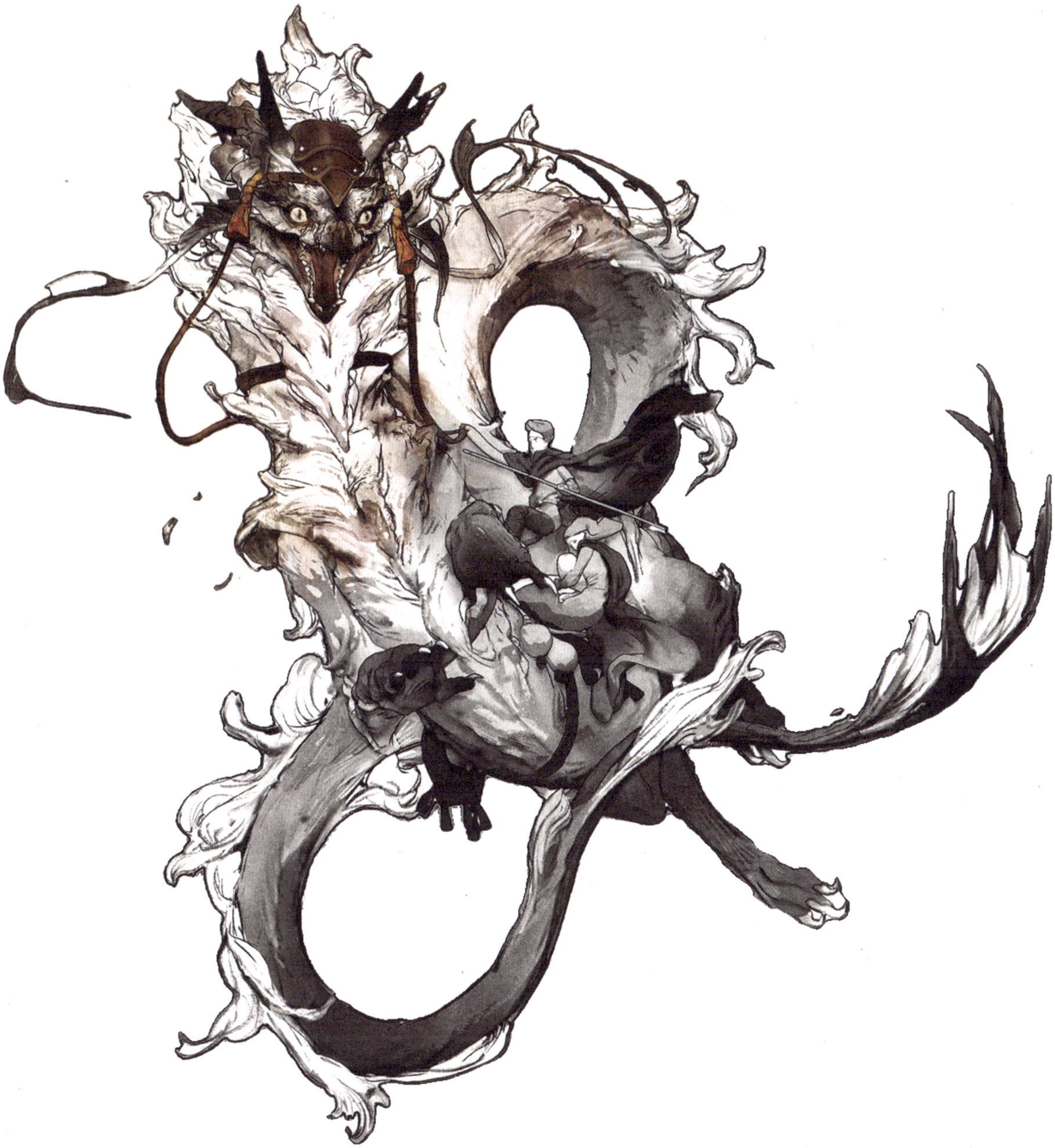

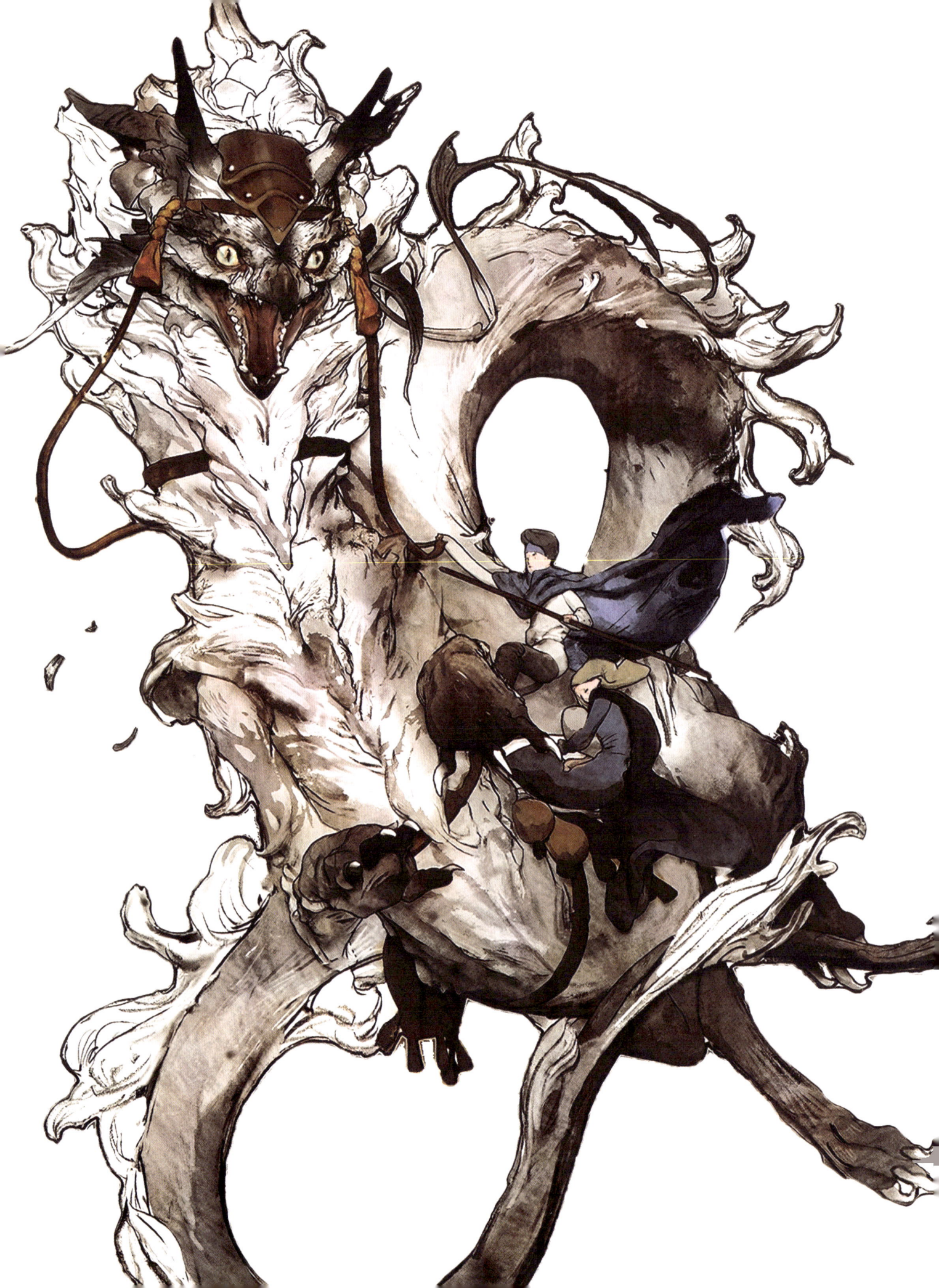

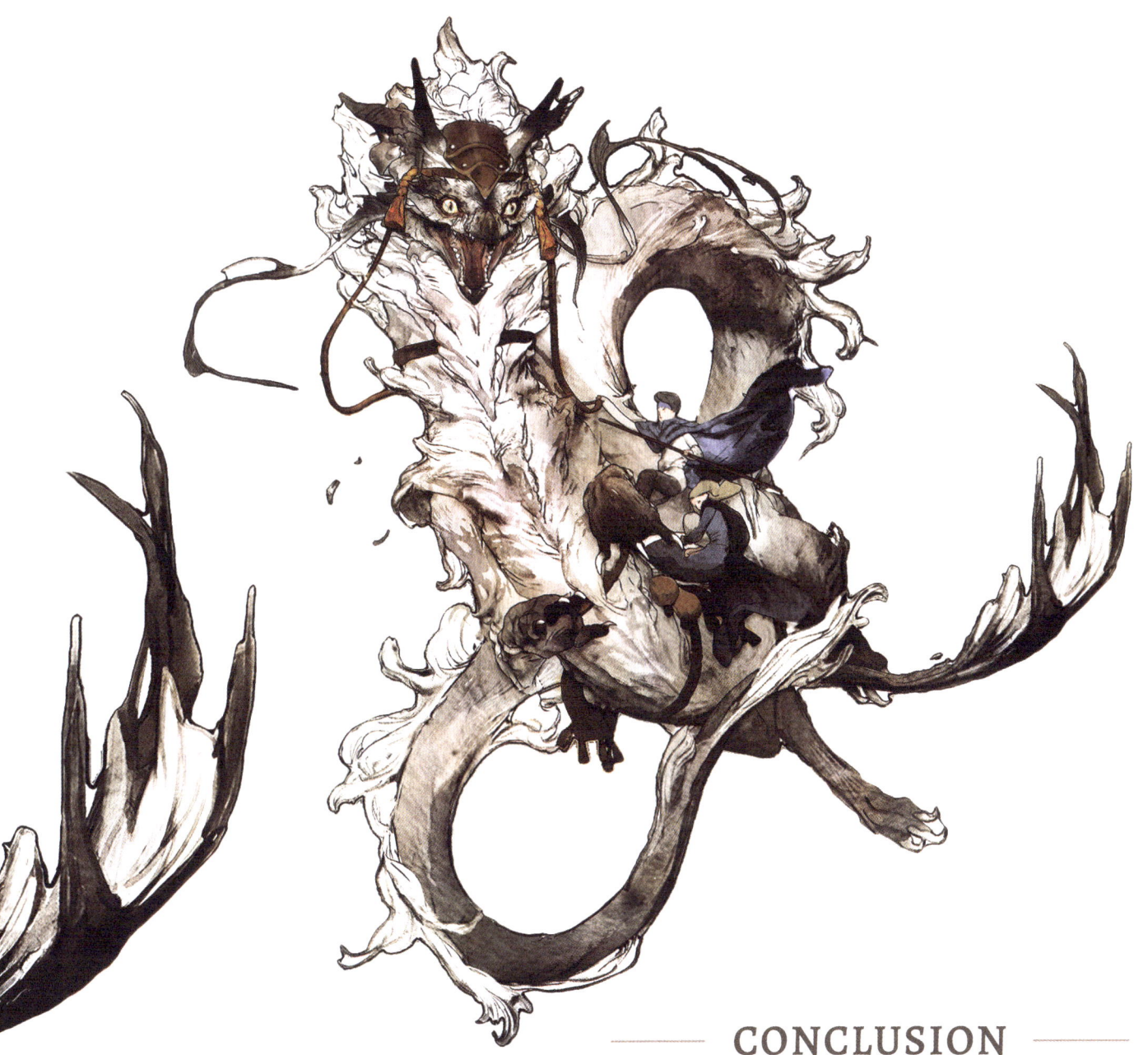

CONCLUSION

I really like this final design because, as I mentioned at the beginning, it allowed me to try many elements I had not experimented with before, making the project a journey in itself. The design has many classic qualities of an East Asian dragon, with a long, snake-like body, antlers, whiskers, and a mix of different animals' features. However, it also doesn't conform to the traditional look, incorporating cute creatures that capture my imagination, such as cats and birds. It's large but not gigantic in size, allowing it to coexist with the human inhabitants of a fantasy world.

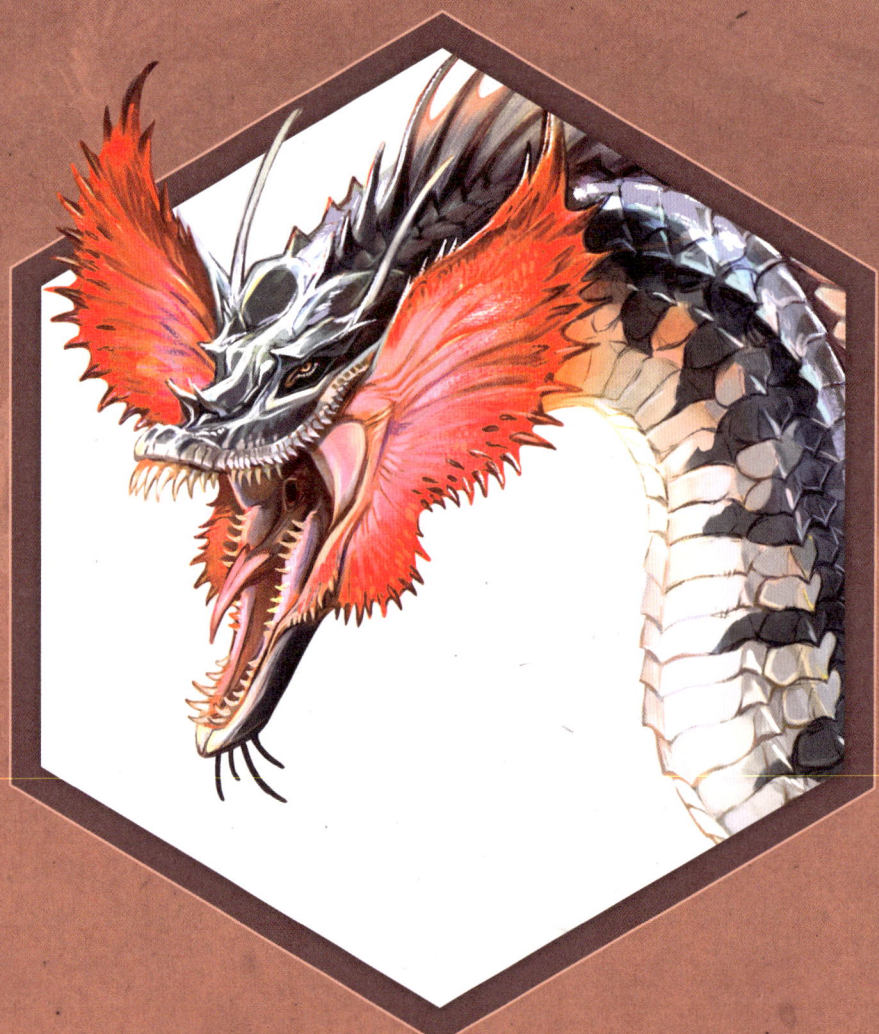

EUROPEAN DRAGON

European dragons, of all draconic creatures, may be the most diverse in visual representation throughout myth. Their narrative themes and personality (representations of chaotic nature, evil, and greed) tend to be more firmly established than their body shape. Traits like the number or presence of limbs, wings or no wings, and the extent of their magical powers are all amorphous, up to the imagination of folklore. Lately though, in modern media, one image has risen to the top when people think of *the* Western or European dragon, and that is of a flying, fire-breathing hexapodal (six-limbed) apex predator. A design as iconic and classic as it is tricky to pull off.

KATE PFEILSCHIEFTER

Final image © Kate Pfeilschiefter

01 WING COMPARISONS

The first problem to tackle for a European dragon is one of their most energetically demanding abilities: flight. This amazing form of locomotion is such a physically extreme activity that it leaves no part of the body unscathed by its demands, making real-world flying animals integral reference for any flying creature design. For this more classic dragon I'll skip studying invertebrates and stick to vertebrates, which leaves three groups that have attained true powered flight: bats, birds, and pterosaurs. Each has transformed their forelimbs or arms into wings – bats and pterosaurs with a patagium (skin) and birds with feathers. I'll be sticking closer to bats, as I'd like a more traditional dragon wing, but I will also add some pterosaur reference regarding the length of the hand bones.

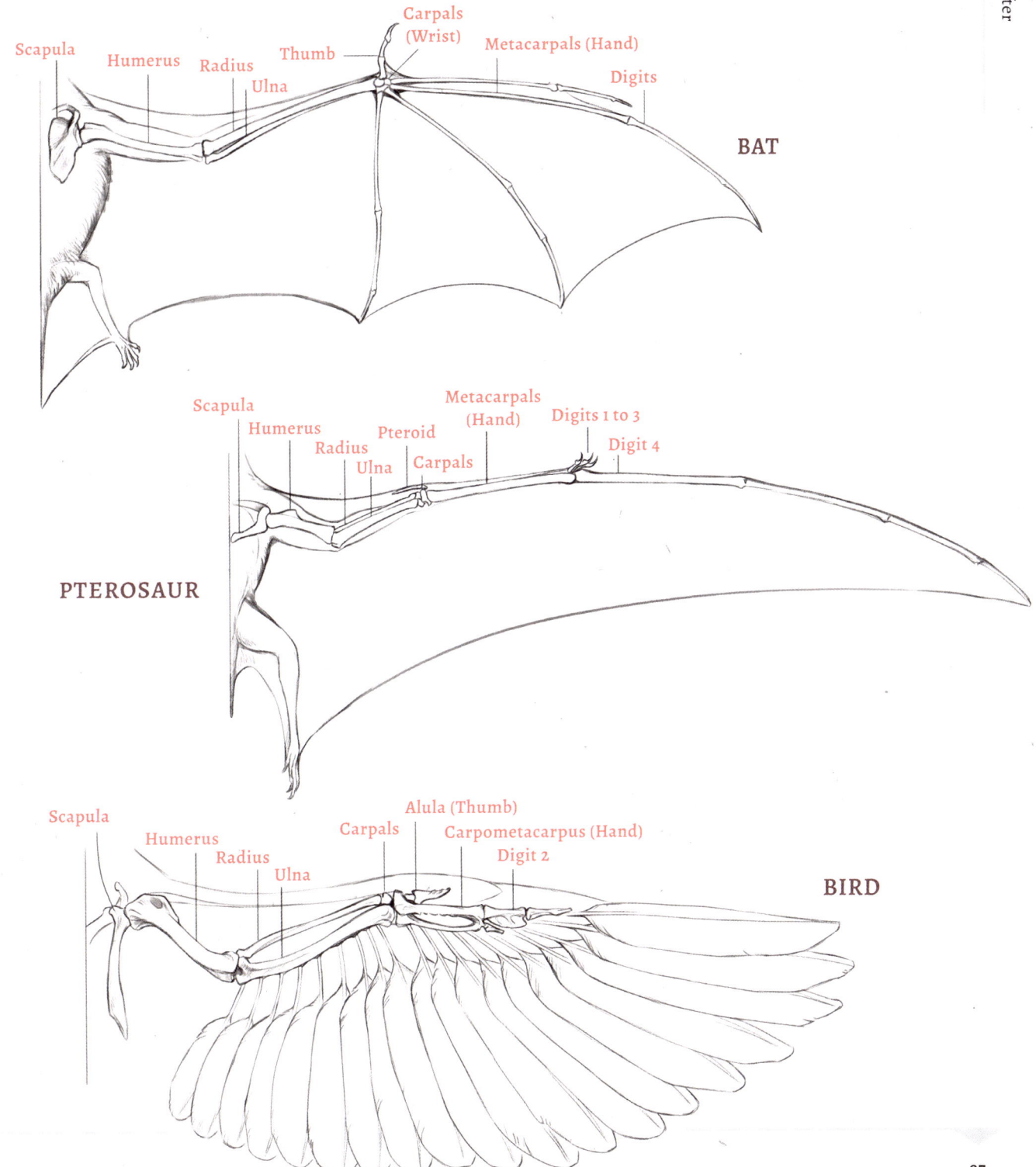

BODY COMPARISONS

Flight is not produced by wings alone – the entire body is bent towards its purpose. Adaptations include selective fusion of vertebrae to create a rigid aerodynamic trunk (the more rigid the body, the better for the stressors of flight); a shortened tail to reduce drag; a strong shoulder girdle with wings stabilized by a sturdy bone connected to the sternum (the coracoid in birds and pterosaurs, or clavicles in bats); and a broad-keeled sternum for supporting the huge pectoral muscles important for powered flight (the keel being larger in birds, as feathered wings are less efficient than membranous wings). I'll take liberties with my dragon by giving it a long tail and a less rigid torso, but it's important to know the rules before you break them.

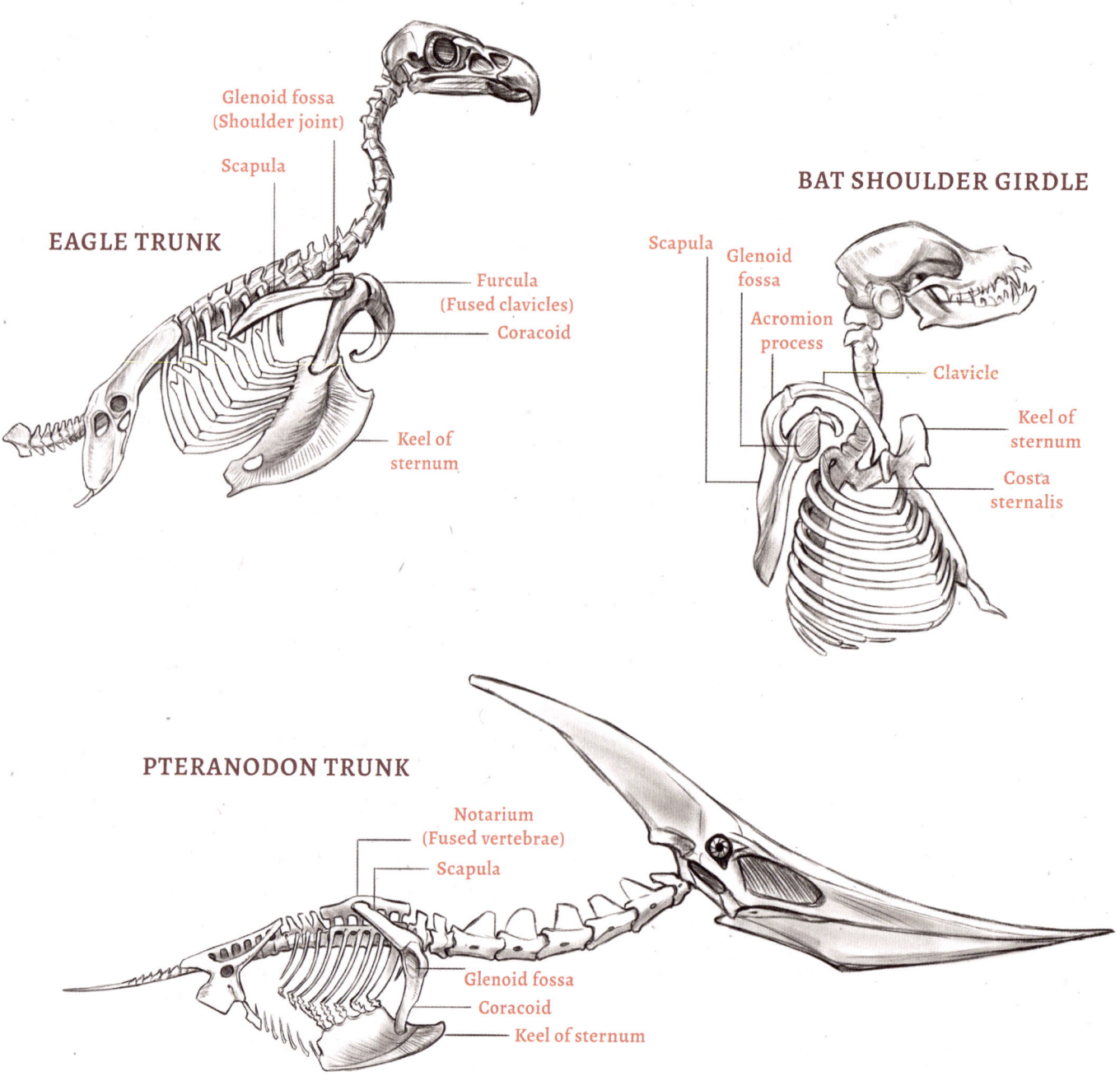

EAGLE TRUNK

Glenoid fossa
(Shoulder joint)

Scapula

Furcula
(Fused clavicles)

Coracoid

Keel of
sternum

BAT SHOULDER GIRDLE

Scapula

Glenoid
fossa

Acromion
process

Clavicle

Keel of
sternum

Costa
sternalis

PTERANODON TRUNK

Notarium
(Fused vertebrae)

Scapula

Glenoid fossa

Coracoid

Keel of sternum

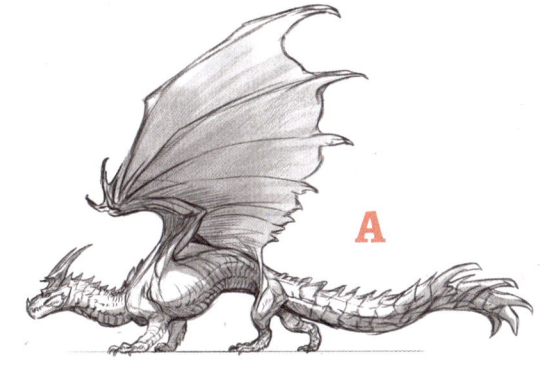

A

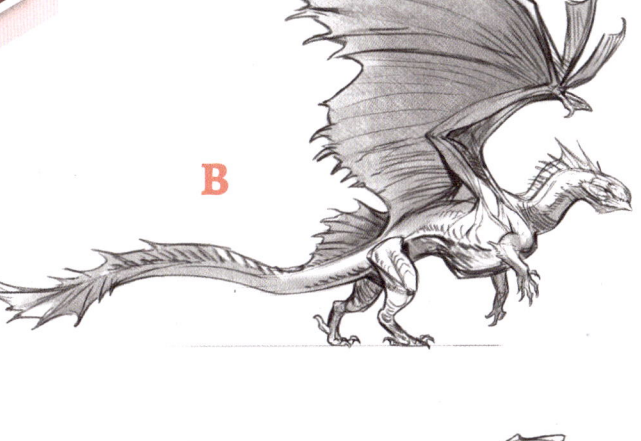

B

C

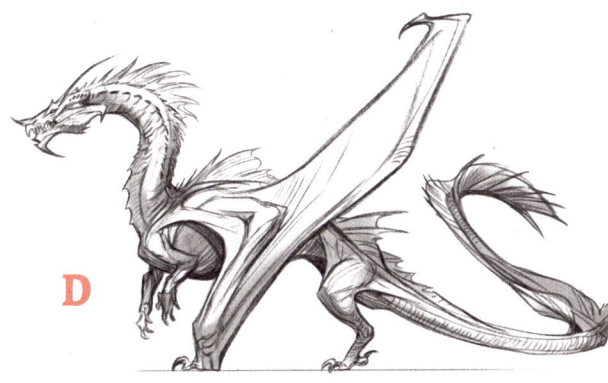

D

 03 BODY SHAPES

After considering the flight adaptations of our animal examples, I want to explore optional stances and body shapes with quick sketches. I know the mouth will be important, and I'm leaning towards an association with water, inspired by myths such as the Lambton Worm. I also want to consider how my dragon would launch itself into the air. For this, I like the ability to take on an upright stance suggested by sketches B and D. Sketch D shows off the ability to support itself with its wings like a pterosaur, which could help with take-off. Sketch B looks like its hind limbs are powerful enough to jump into flight, and the separate second and third wing-fingers offer interesting silhouette variety. Some of these sketches position the front legs in front of or behind the wings. Whatever I choose, I must be sure to leave room for the muscle attachments and scapula of each limb, and imagine where the coracoid and/or clavicles for bracing the wings might be.

TECHNICAL CHALLENGES

A creature with six limbs (four weight-bearing limbs and two wings) is a puzzle to design, as no real vertebrate animal living or extinct has such a body. No one has the one true answer to making a vertebrate hexapod that could work in the real world and still resemble a dragon! Here I also need to consider the rigours of flight and another unheard-of feature – exhaling deadly fire from the mouth. The aim of this particular design is to present a plausible, believable solution to all these puzzles, enough that it could work in a live-action film, but that will still visually read as a European dragon, while doing a couple of things differently to keep it fresh.

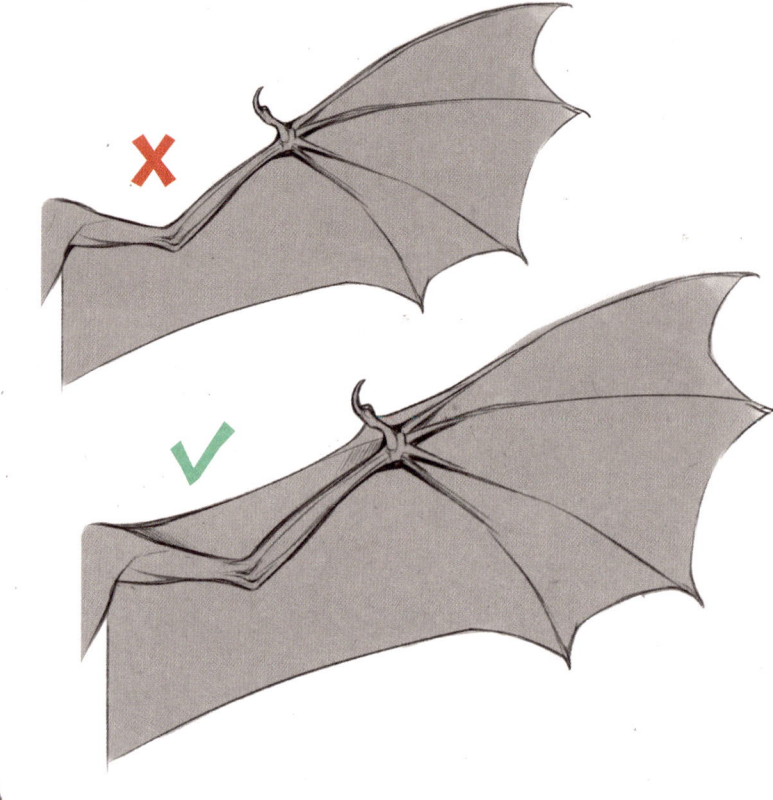

WE HAVE LIFT-OFF!

An easily overlooked but essential bit of flight anatomy is the skin and muscle spanning the gap between the shoulder and wrist on flying animals. Often forgotten, this leading edge is essential to creating the wing's airfoil shape and creating lift.

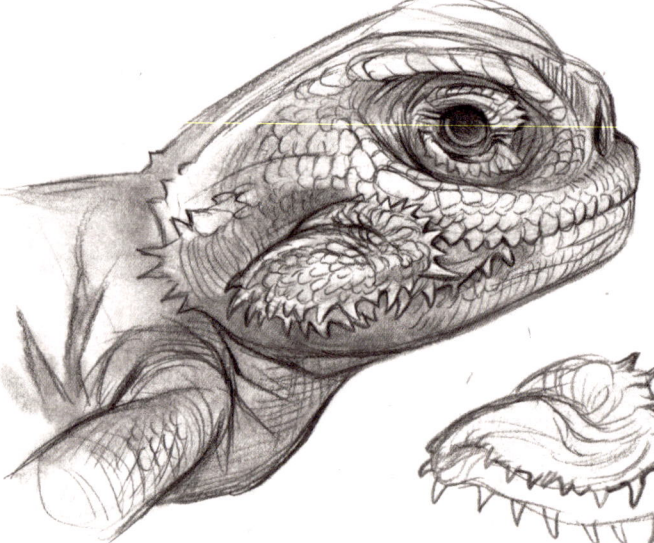

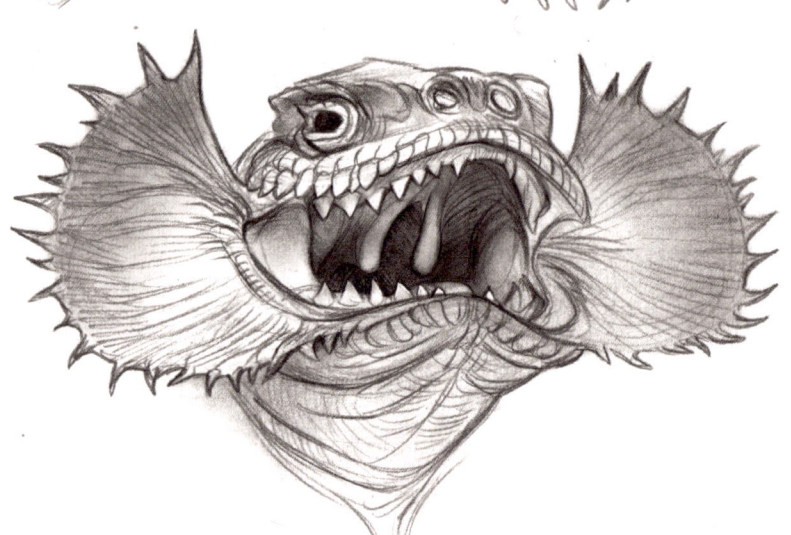

04 TOAD-HEADED AGAMA

Before proceeding too far with the body, I want to do some animal studies for the head. I want this dragon to have a warning display that foretells the fiery threat they pose to potential challengers. Many creatures with dangerous weapons, such as venom, warn of their capacity for harm by using sound or visuals (for example, the white mouth of a water moccasin, or a rattlesnake's rattle). Employing something similar would be fun and make sense for a fire-breather. As this mouth display is going to be one of the design's key traits, it's important to nail down how it will work. Toad-headed agama lizards are among the first real animals to come to mind. When studying the agama lizard, I pay close attention to how the cheek flaps fold away and unfurl.

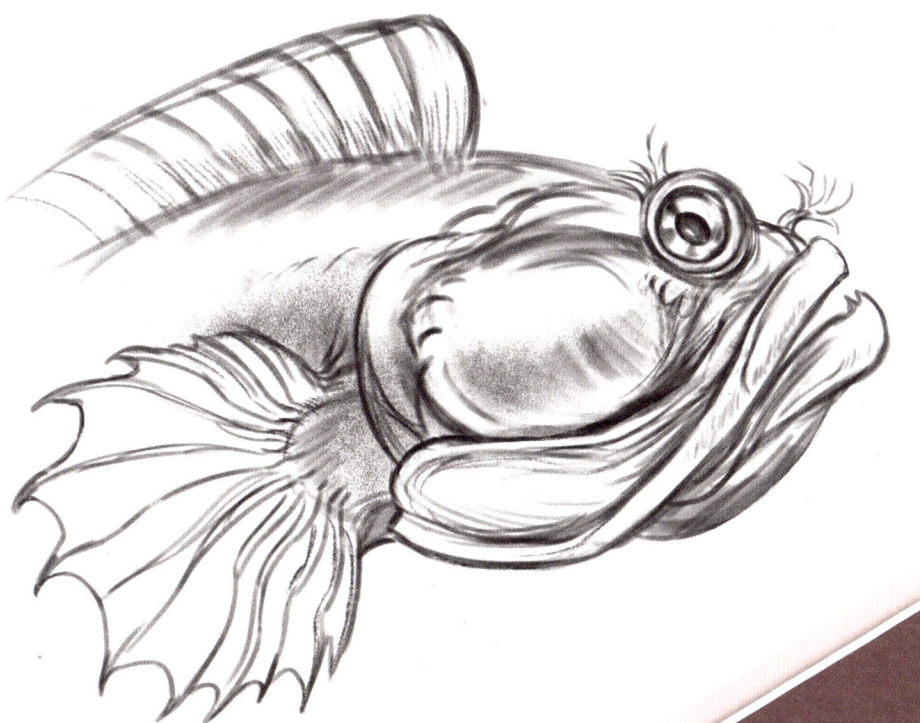

 SARCASTIC FRINGEHEAD

Another prominent example is a fish called the sarcastic fringehead. The agama lizard's display is restricted to cheek skin towards the back of the jaw, but the fringehead uses its entire mandible. The skulls of fishes are divided into more separate articulating parts than most mammal, reptile, and bird skulls, allowing them to project their maxilla (upper jaw) forwards to expand their gape even further than normal.

ANIMAL INSPIRATION

Researching new animals helps expand your visual library. The creatures in the natural world will always beat those from fiction, so fostering a love for real animals will ensure you are never lacking for reference ideas.

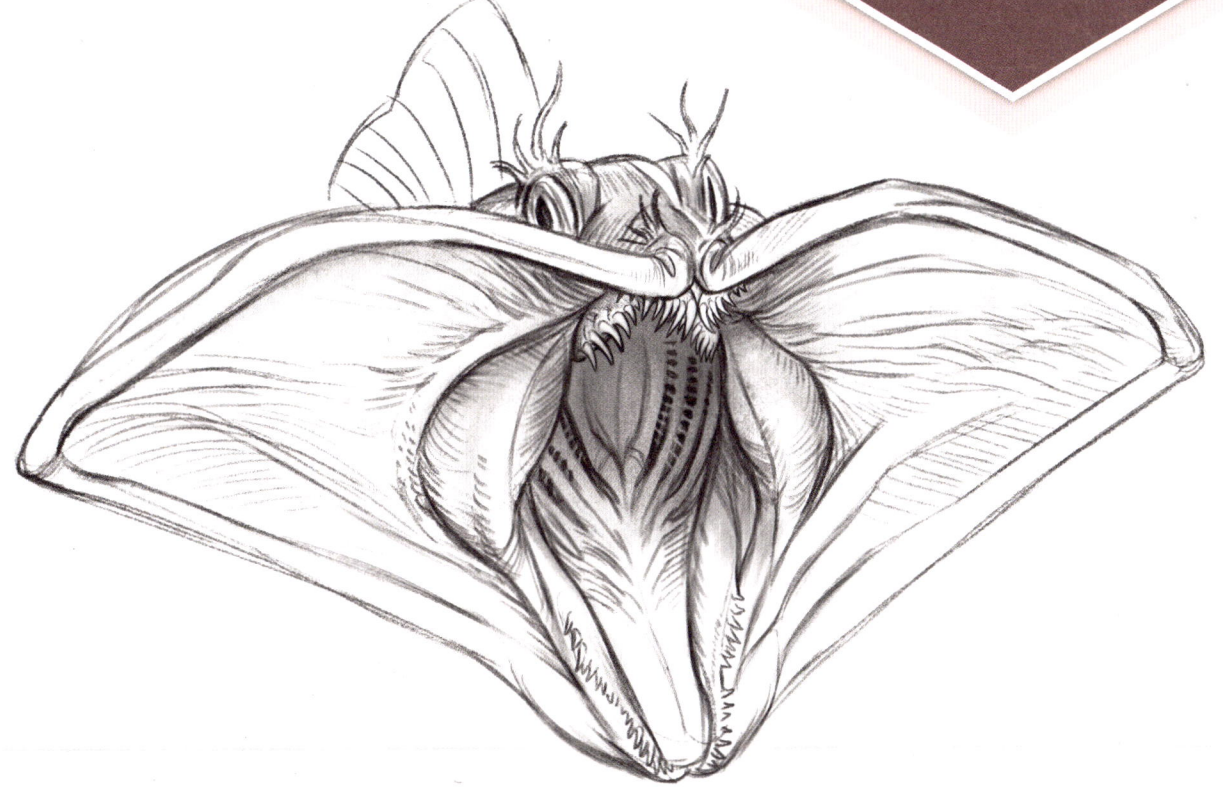

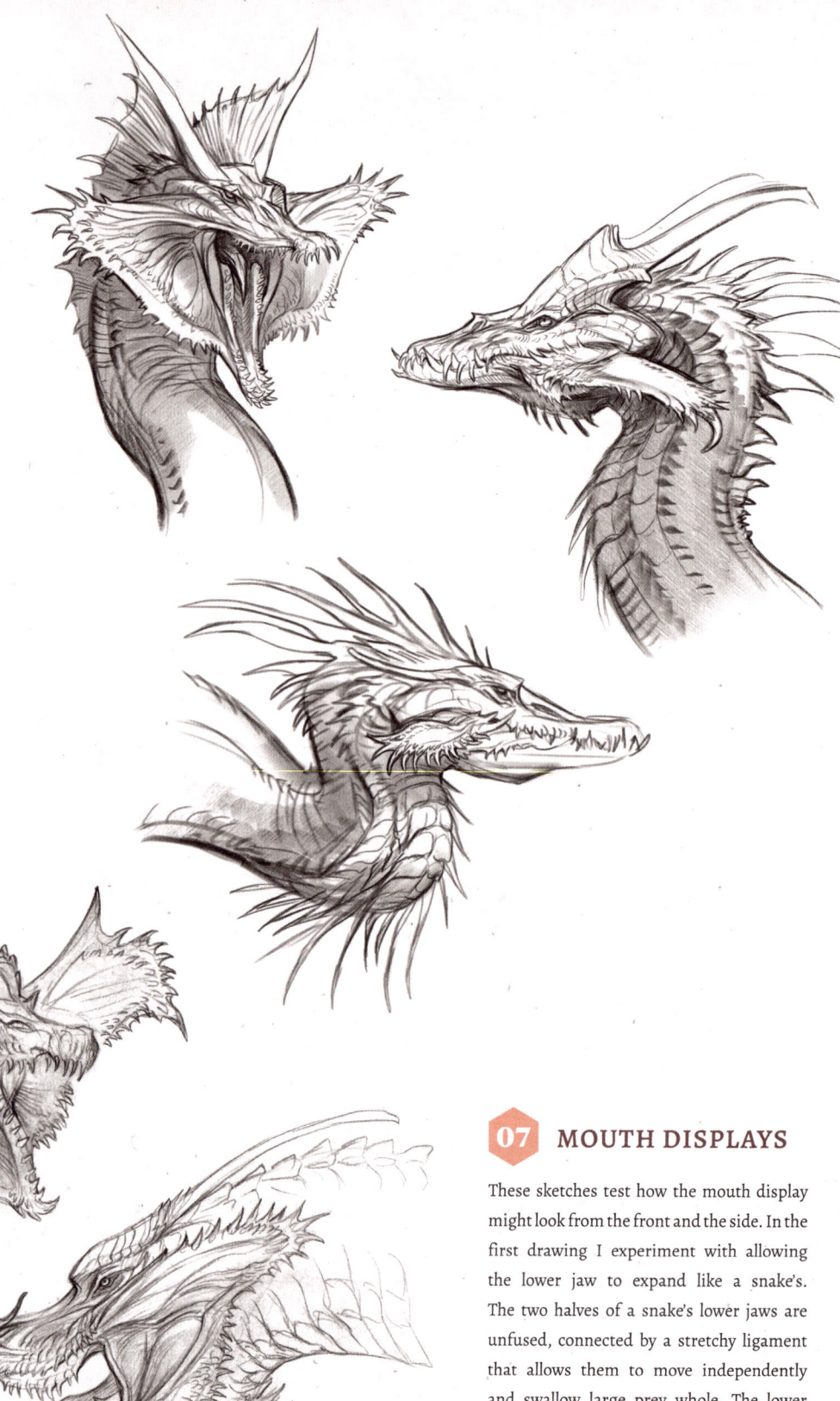

06 HEAD SKETCHES

Here the real work of figuring out the design begins. The head is key to getting the personality right and can tell you so much about a creature's lifestyle and behaviour. For these head sketches I'm using thinner hooked teeth to suggest a diet of slippery fish, and the nostrils are positioned further up on the skull to keep them out of the water. Having exposed teeth unscaled by lips – like a crocodile's – may also suggest an amphibious lifestyle, though that may be a step too far for a dragon that also flies.

07 MOUTH DISPLAYS

These sketches test how the mouth display might look from the front and the side. In the first drawing I experiment with allowing the lower jaw to expand like a snake's. The two halves of a snake's lower jaws are unfused, connected by a stretchy ligament that allows them to move independently and swallow large prey whole. The lower drawing experiments with lips that can curl back and expose the teeth for extra 'creep' factor, but the mouth flaps are too small and understated.

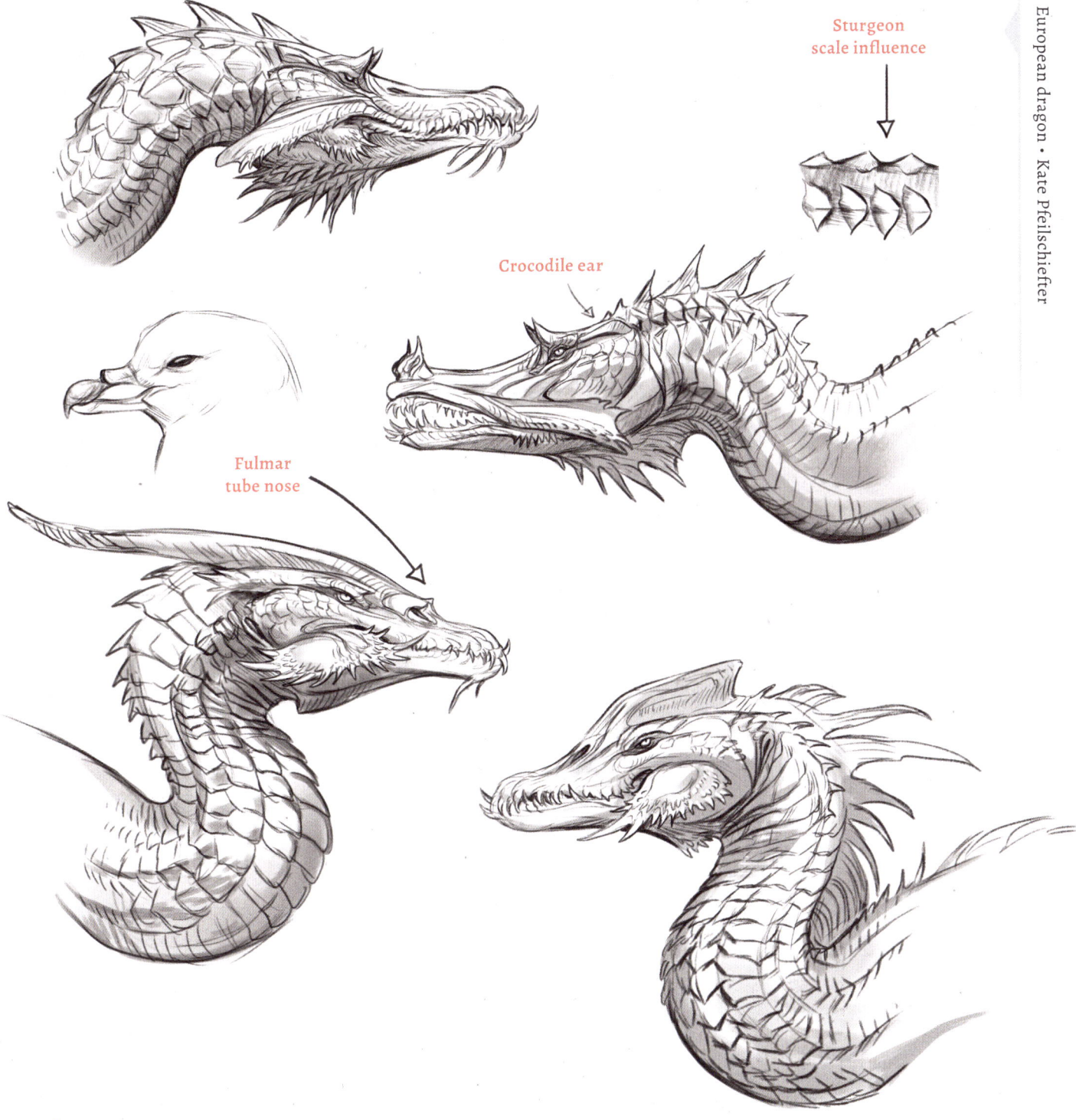

Sturgeon scale influence

Crocodile ear

Fulmar tube nose

08 FINESSING IDEAS

Now I'm closing in on the design. The chief decision lies between leaning more towards crocodiles or more towards birds. I'm trending towards bird-like influences because if I reference herons – another water specialist – that can reinforce the serpentine elements of the dragon's neck. I imagine this dragon as a hunter who's happy to lunge at prey whether it's in water or at the water's edge, so both herons and crocodiles have relevancy. I also experiment with using sturgeon scales and different nostril designs. A fulmar nose would provide the dragon with an excellent sense of smell and help them filter out saltwater should they venture into an estuary.

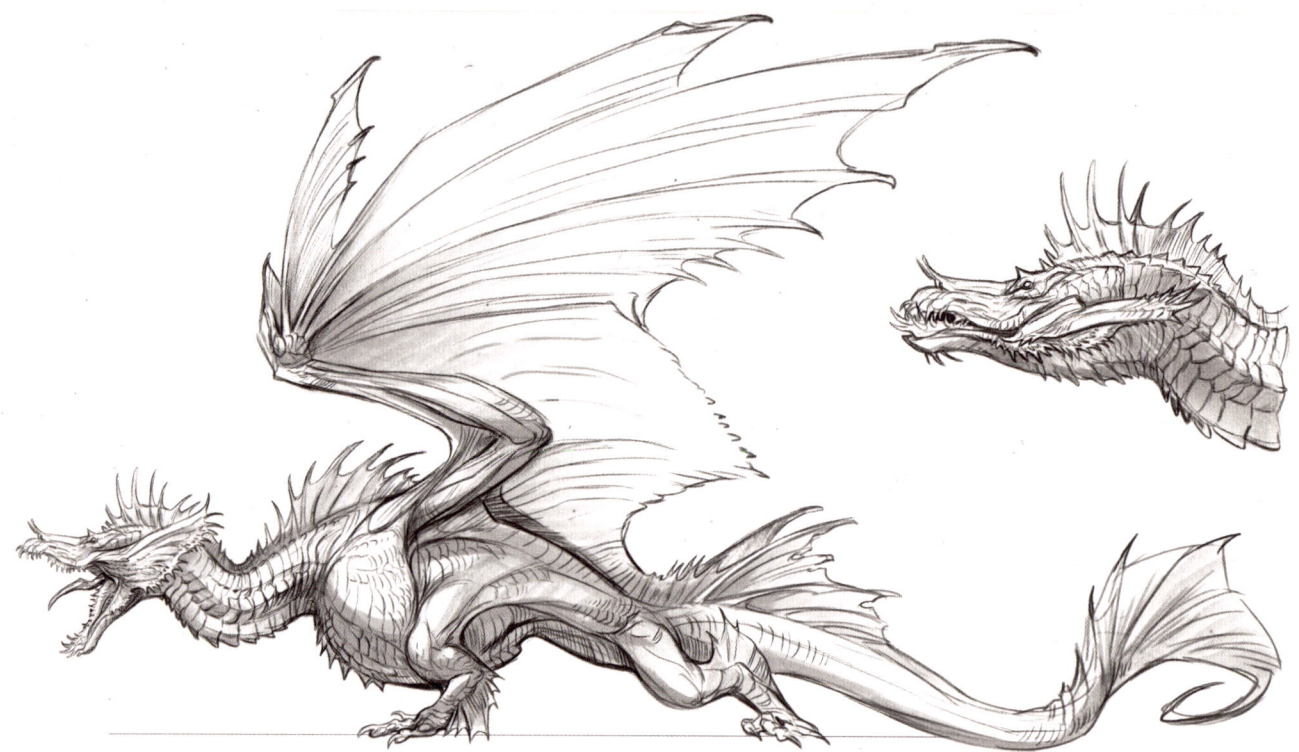

09 LOW & SHORT-LEGGED

Picking elements of my favourite heads from the previous drawings,
I start testing options for their full bodies. I keep the fulmar nose from
step 08 as I enjoy the odd, almost skeletal touch it adds. However, this
test is overall too close to a crocodilian's stature for my liking. It feels at
home in the water but too low-slung to the ground with too-short legs,
so I struggle to imagine how it would take off for flight.

10 UPRIGHT & MOBILE

The option below is closer to the heads in step 06. I'm continuing to use
fish elements for the scales and frills, since this supports the amphibious
theme, and decide to lose the horns as they compete for prominence
with the mouth display. During our earlier body exploration I liked the
more upright stance that suggested an ability to launch with the hind
legs, which I feature again here. The wings can also help by providing an
additional vaulting push as the dragon jumps into the air. I distinguish
the front arms by giving them extra membrane so they can help with
paddling, while leaving a few fingers free for mobility.

Scale studies

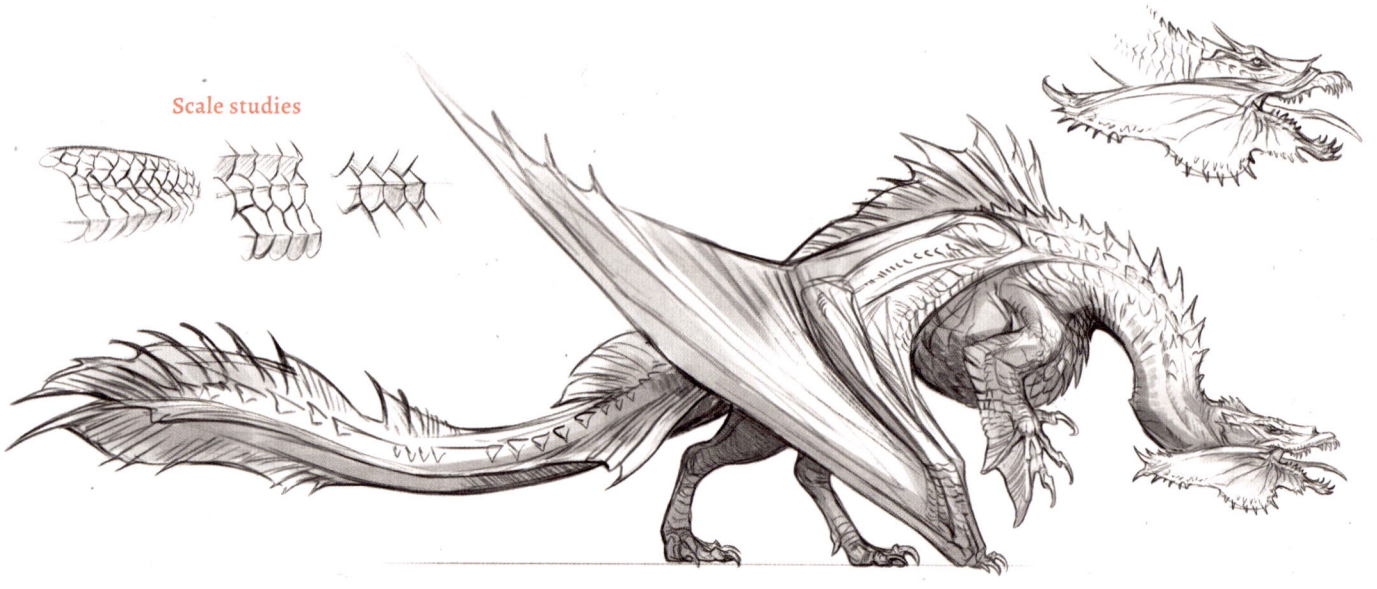

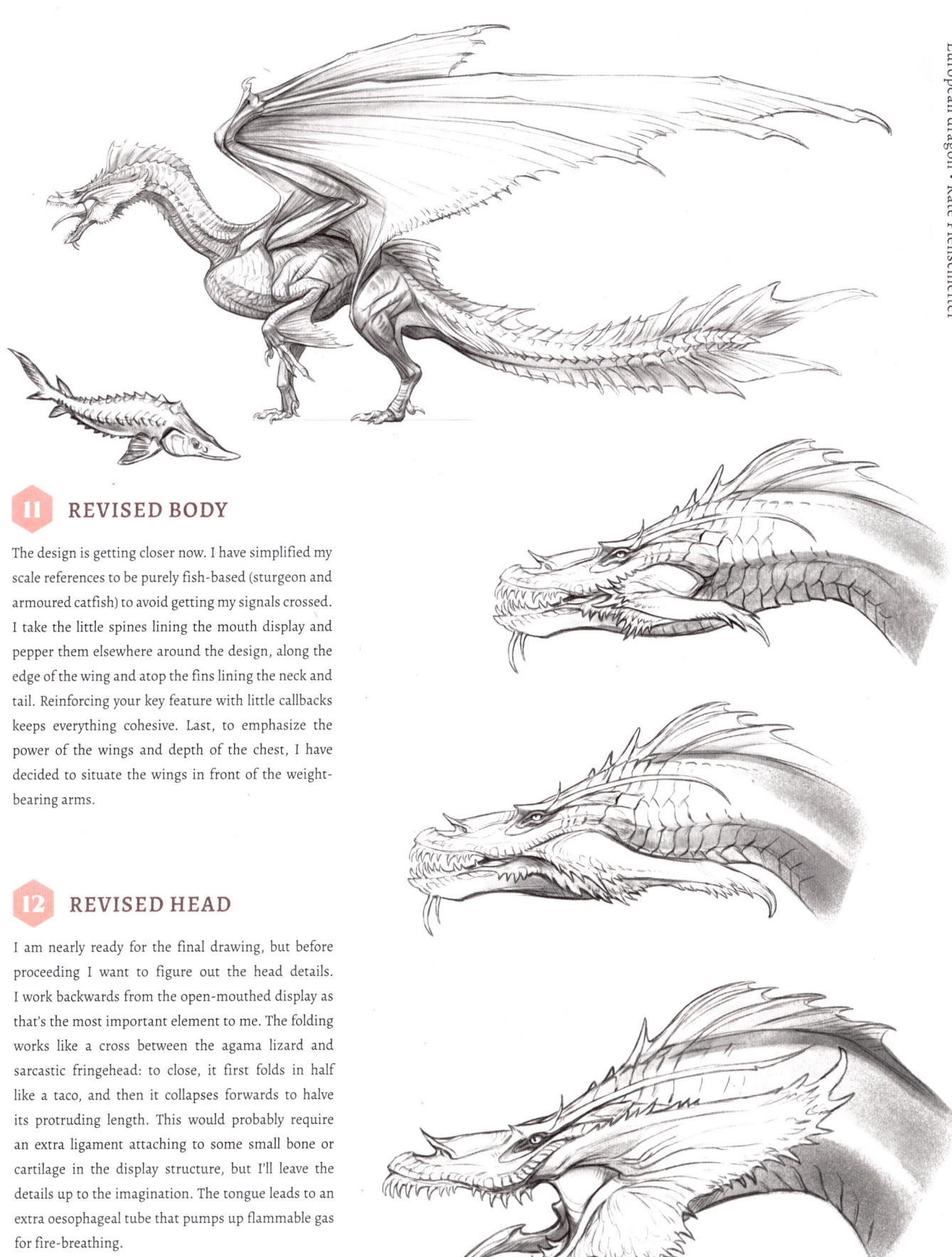

11 REVISED BODY

The design is getting closer now. I have simplified my scale references to be purely fish-based (sturgeon and armoured catfish) to avoid getting my signals crossed. I take the little spines lining the mouth display and pepper them elsewhere around the design, along the edge of the wing and atop the fins lining the neck and tail. Reinforcing your key feature with little callbacks keeps everything cohesive. Last, to emphasize the power of the wings and depth of the chest, I have decided to situate the wings in front of the weight-bearing arms.

12 REVISED HEAD

I am nearly ready for the final drawing, but before proceeding I want to figure out the head details. I work backwards from the open-mouthed display as that's the most important element to me. The folding works like a cross between the agama lizard and sarcastic fringehead: to close, it first folds in half like a taco, and then it collapses forwards to halve its protruding length. This would probably require an extra ligament attaching to some small bone or cartilage in the display structure, but I'll leave the details up to the imagination. The tongue leads to an extra oesophageal tube that pumps up flammable gas for fire-breathing.

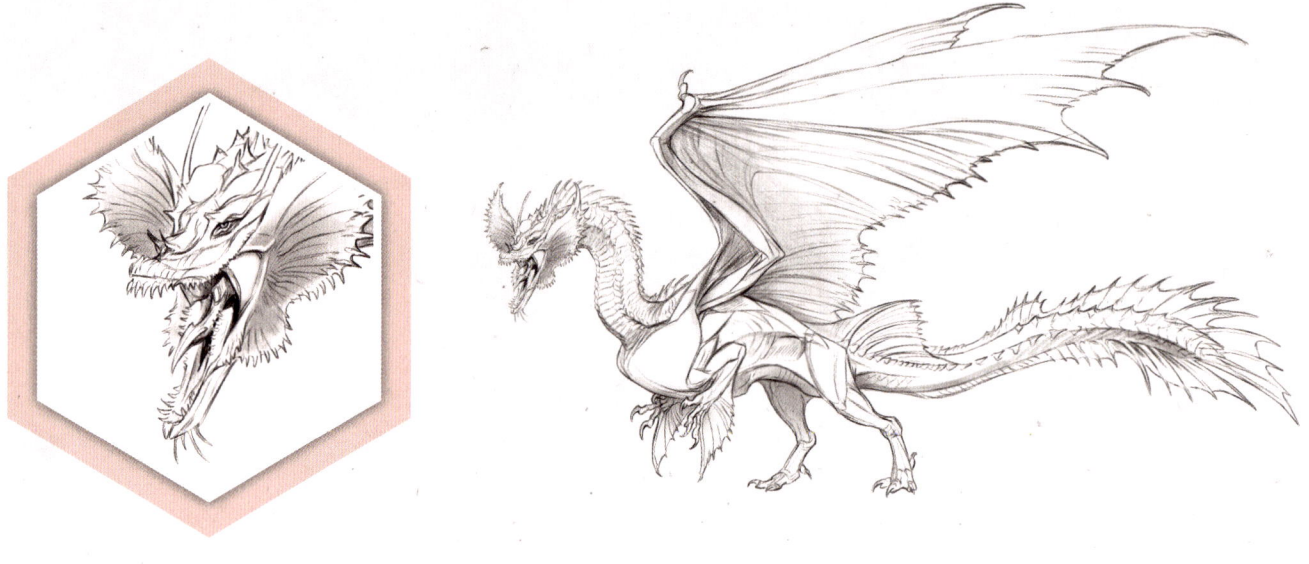

13 FINAL SKETCH

Now I begin the underlying sketch for the illustration and make my final design tweaks. I swap the bat-like connection of the wing membrane from the lower thighs to the back to be more like the first body test. This will allow the legs to be held under the body in flight like a bird, supporting the overall heron-like posture I'm imagining for this dragon. The added fan at the base of the tail can provide the extra lift support and steering that the old leg connection would have done. The pose is chosen to showcase the mouth display, the versatility of the arms, and the ability to become bipedal for take-off.

14 FINAL LINE ART

Next I clean up stray lines and figure out my scale patterns, mixing together the sturgeon and armoured-catfish traits. Deciding the pattern now rather than later in the painting stage saves time. A useful tip before beginning is to draw lines following the flow you'd like the scales to take across the body. These scales all have a slight keel (triangular raised edge) along their midpoint that helps me imagine where the lines should go. In general, it helps mobility if scales become smaller around areas of articulation, such as the bases of limbs, tails, or necks.

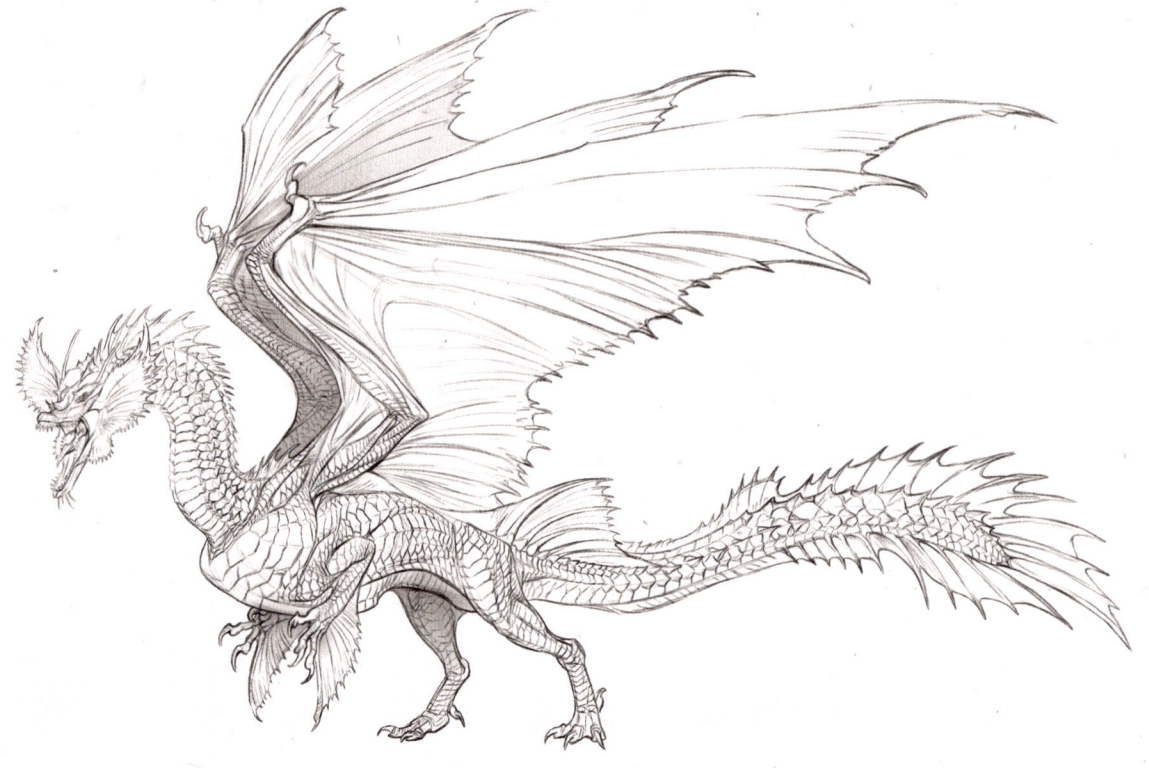

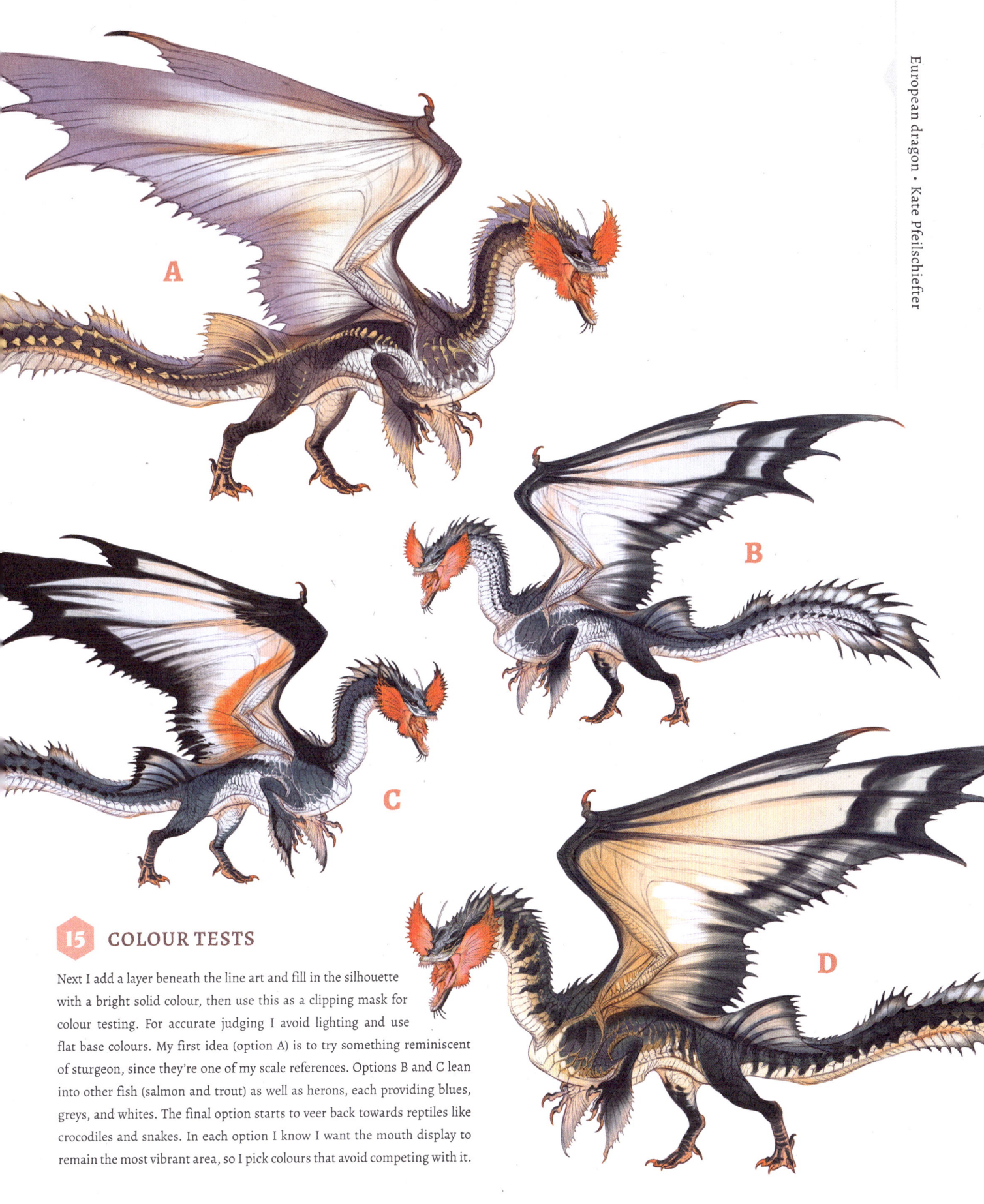

⬡15 COLOUR TESTS

Next I add a layer beneath the line art and fill in the silhouette with a bright solid colour, then use this as a clipping mask for colour testing. For accurate judging I avoid lighting and use flat base colours. My first idea (option A) is to try something reminiscent of sturgeon, since they're one of my scale references. Options B and C lean into other fish (salmon and trout) as well as herons, each providing blues, greys, and whites. The final option starts to veer back towards reptiles like crocodiles and snakes. In each option I know I want the mouth display to remain the most vibrant area, so I pick colours that avoid competing with it.

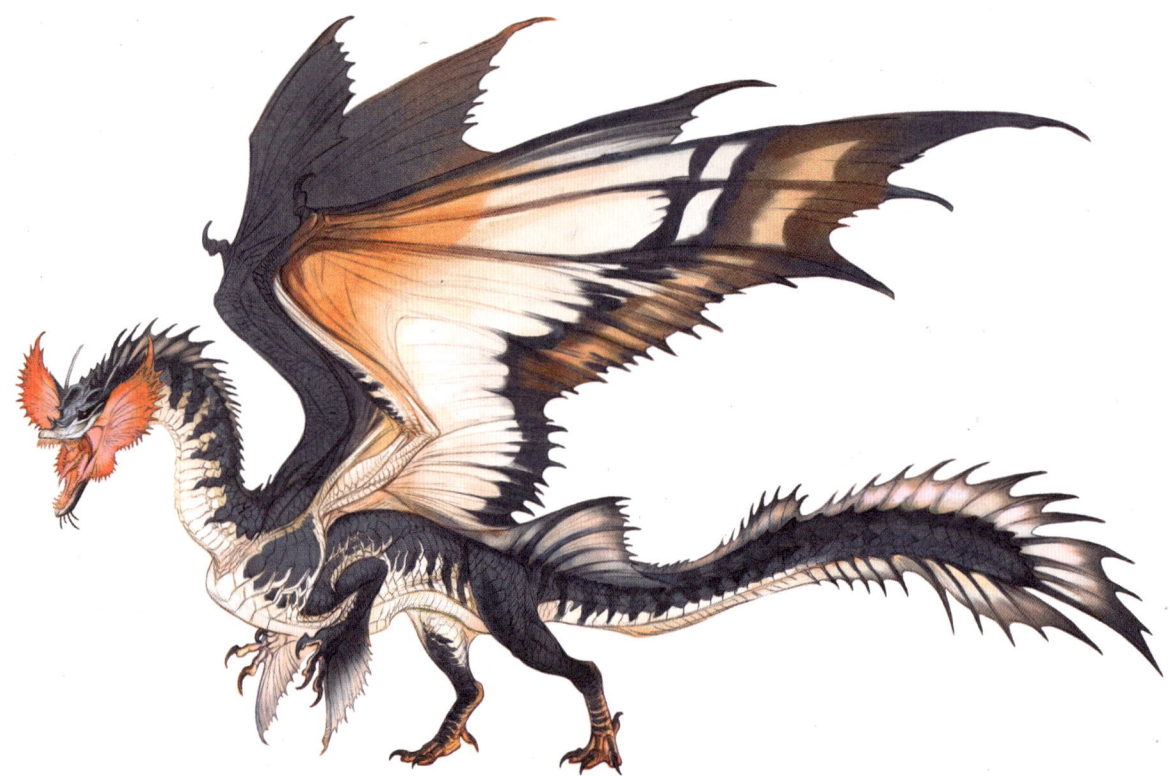

16 CHOSEN PALETTE

My final flat colours are a variation on colour option D, chosen because it felt the most threatening. I desaturate the blues to appear more grey-black, and reduce some of the extra warm tones, as the warm-to-cool ratio started to feel too evenly distributed. I want my warm tones to pop against the cools, and being more selective with them helps to keep the mouth display from falling out of focus. Less is more when it comes to your accent colours.

17 ADDING SHADOWS

Taking the flat colour I used to fill in the silhouette, I then use a Multiply layer to determine my lighting direction by painting shadows. Later I'll add a little backlighting, as if there's some sunlight glowing through the frills and wings, which will splash warm colours around the scene as the light passes through blood vessels. The wings are going to cast a large shadow across the body, but I'll lighten it up with a lot of bounce lighting.

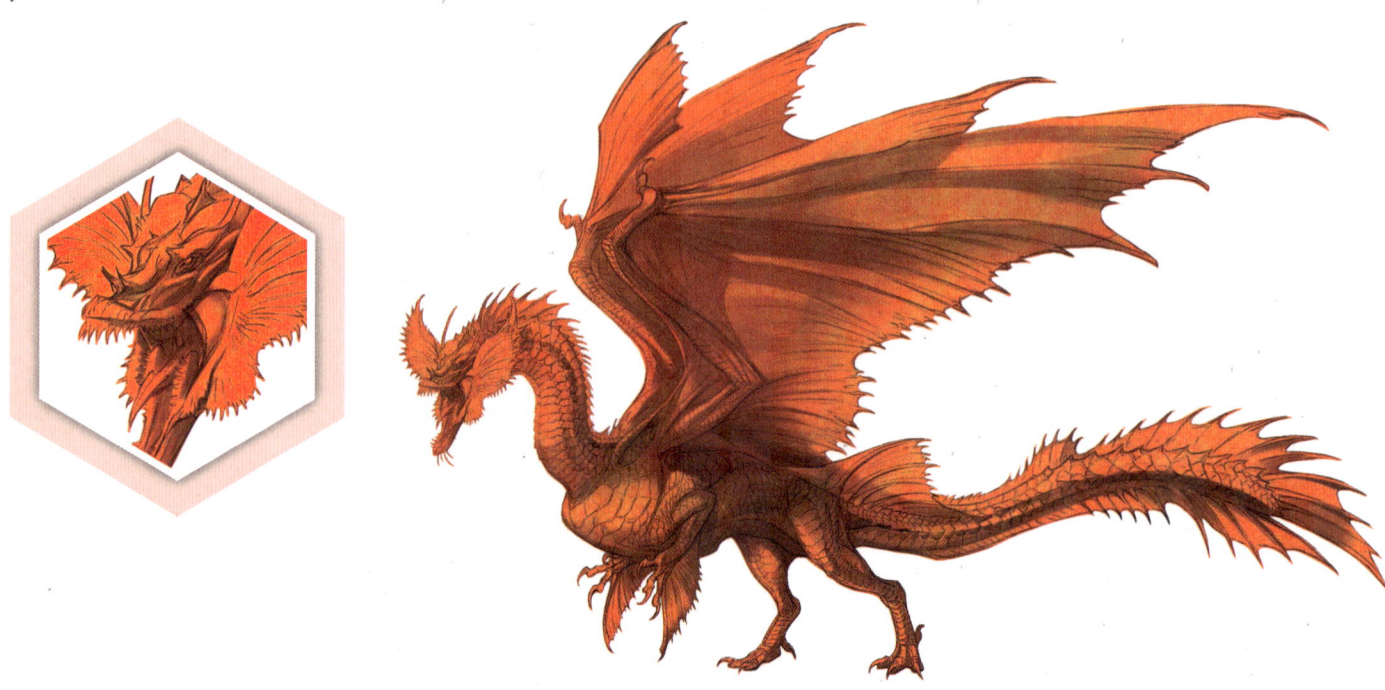

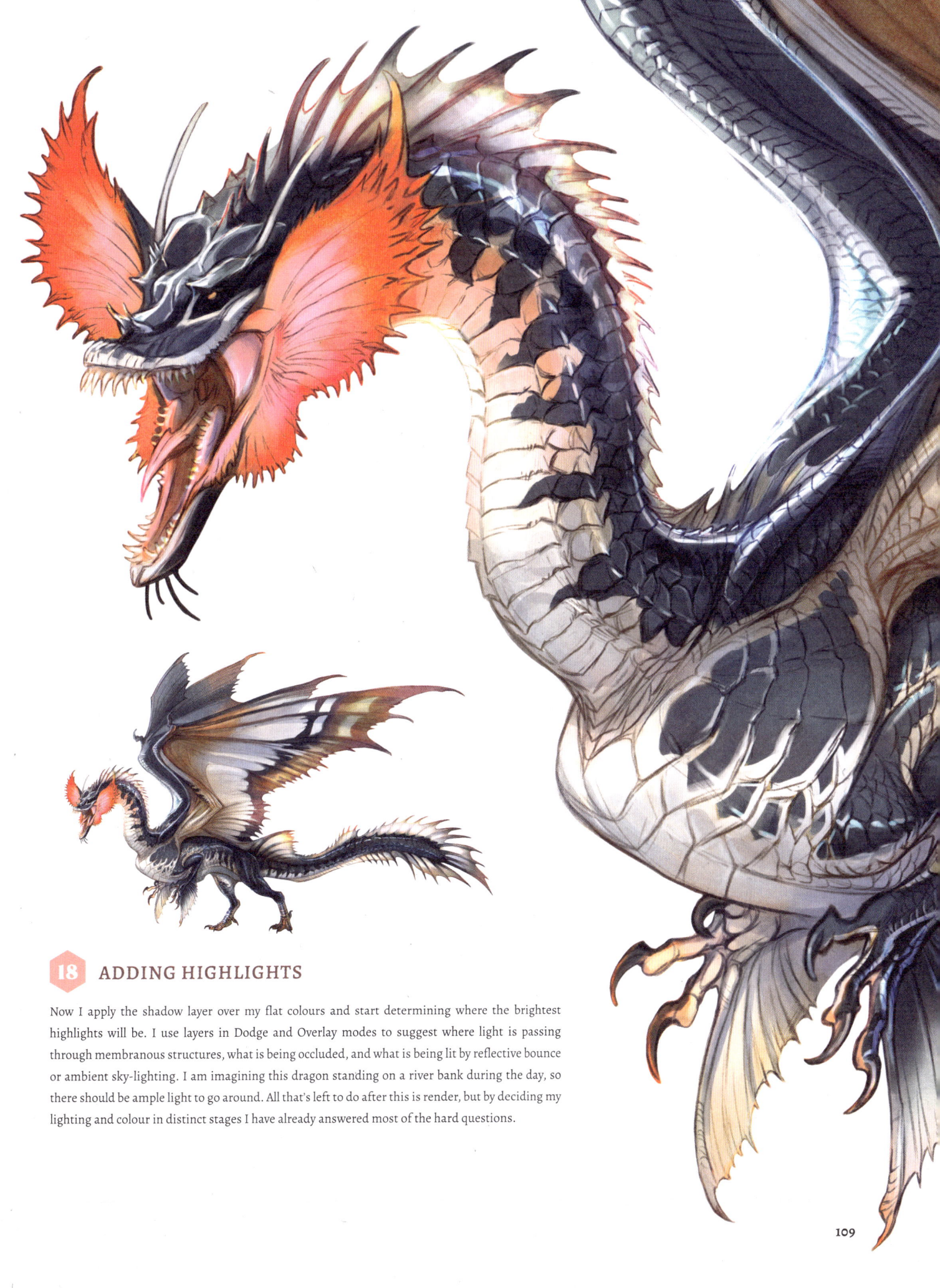

18 ADDING HIGHLIGHTS

Now I apply the shadow layer over my flat colours and start determining where the brightest highlights will be. I use layers in Dodge and Overlay modes to suggest where light is passing through membranous structures, what is being occluded, and what is being lit by reflective bounce or ambient sky-lighting. I am imagining this dragon standing on a river bank during the day, so there should be ample light to go around. All that's left to do after this is render, but by deciding my lighting and colour in distinct stages I have already answered most of the hard questions.

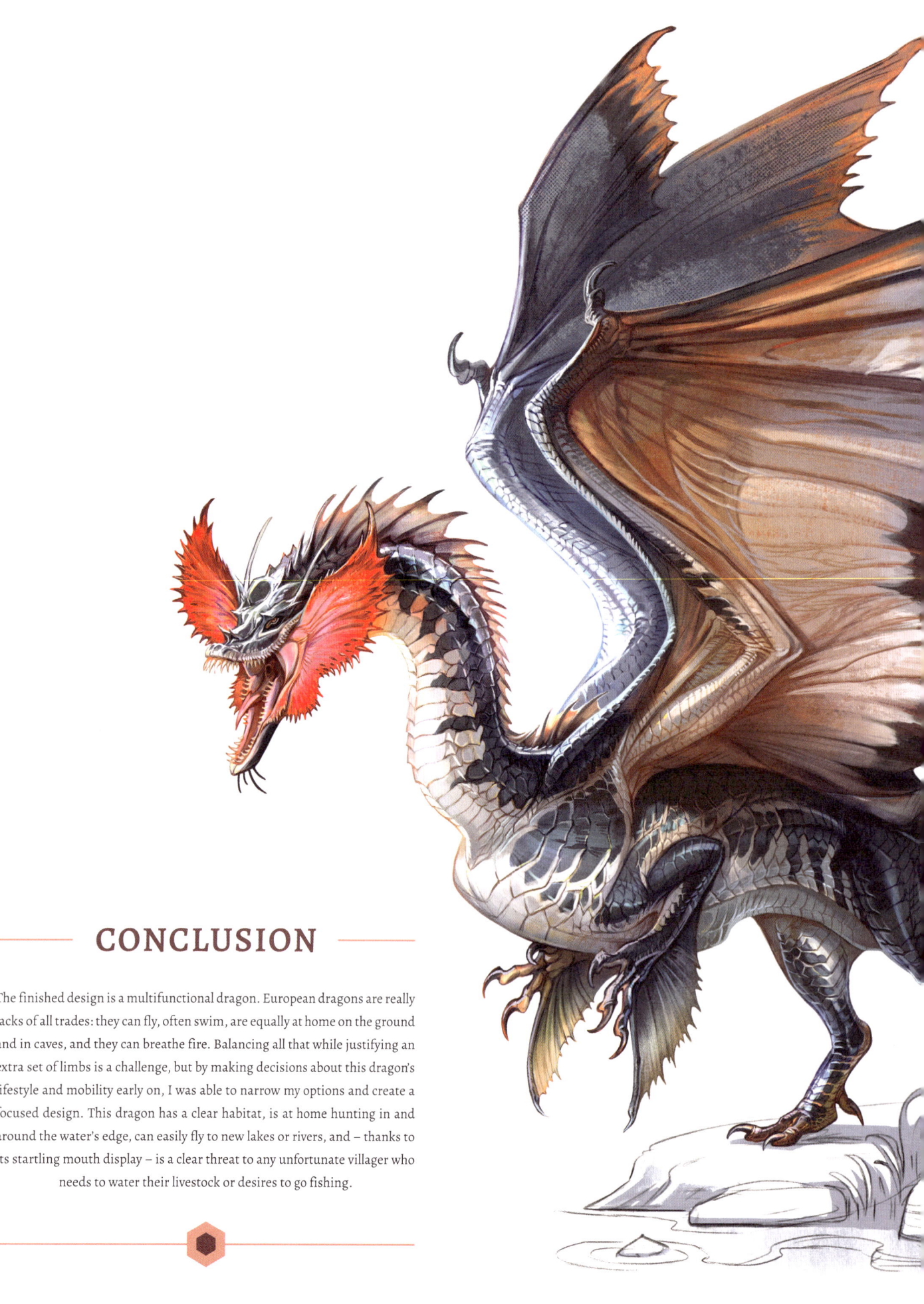

CONCLUSION

The finished design is a multifunctional dragon. European dragons are really jacks of all trades: they can fly, often swim, are equally at home on the ground and in caves, and they can breathe fire. Balancing all that while justifying an extra set of limbs is a challenge, but by making decisions about this dragon's lifestyle and mobility early on, I was able to narrow my options and create a focused design. This dragon has a clear habitat, is at home hunting in and around the water's edge, can easily fly to new lakes or rivers, and – thanks to its startling mouth display – is a clear threat to any unfortunate villager who needs to water their livestock or desires to go fishing.

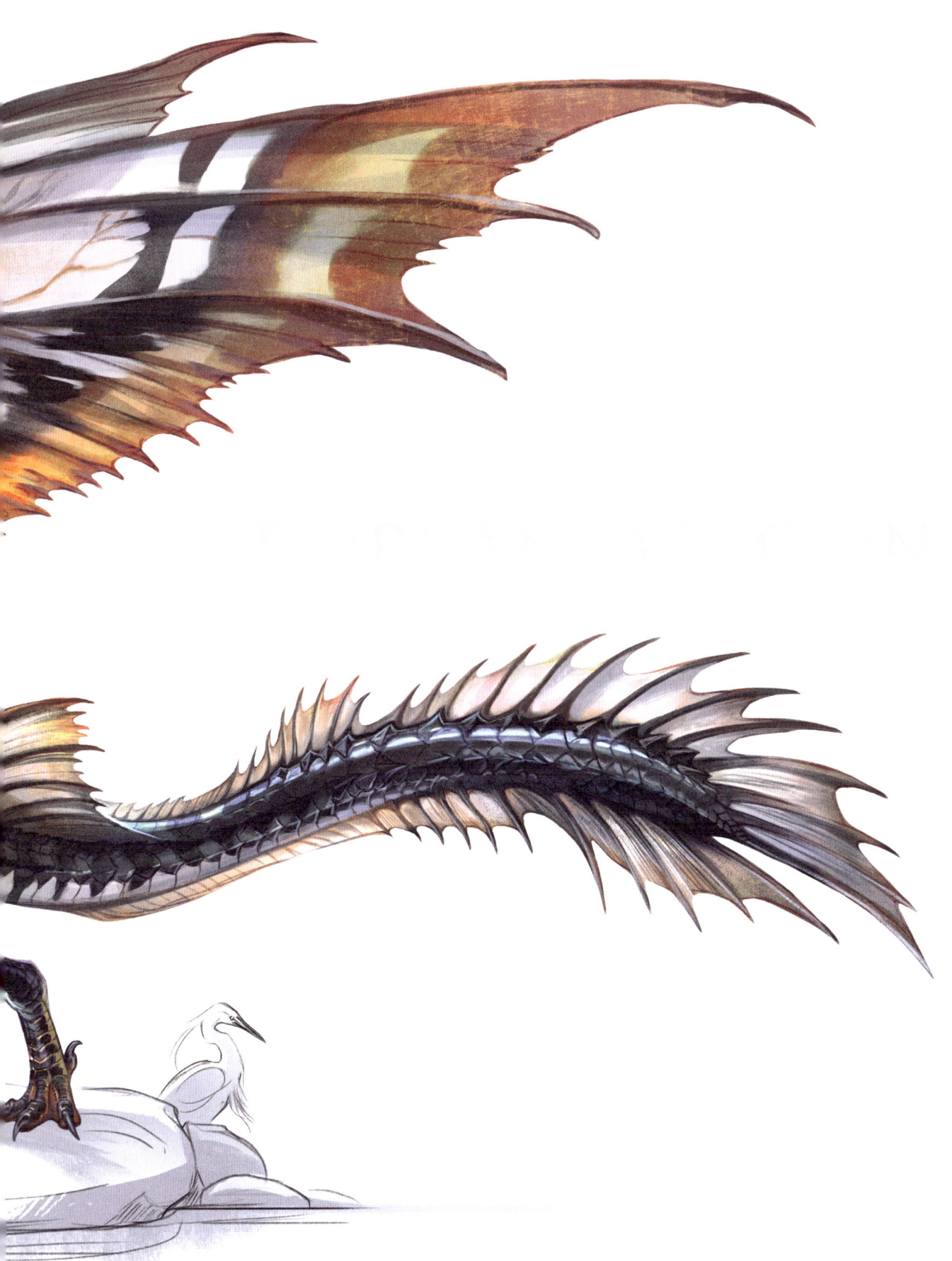

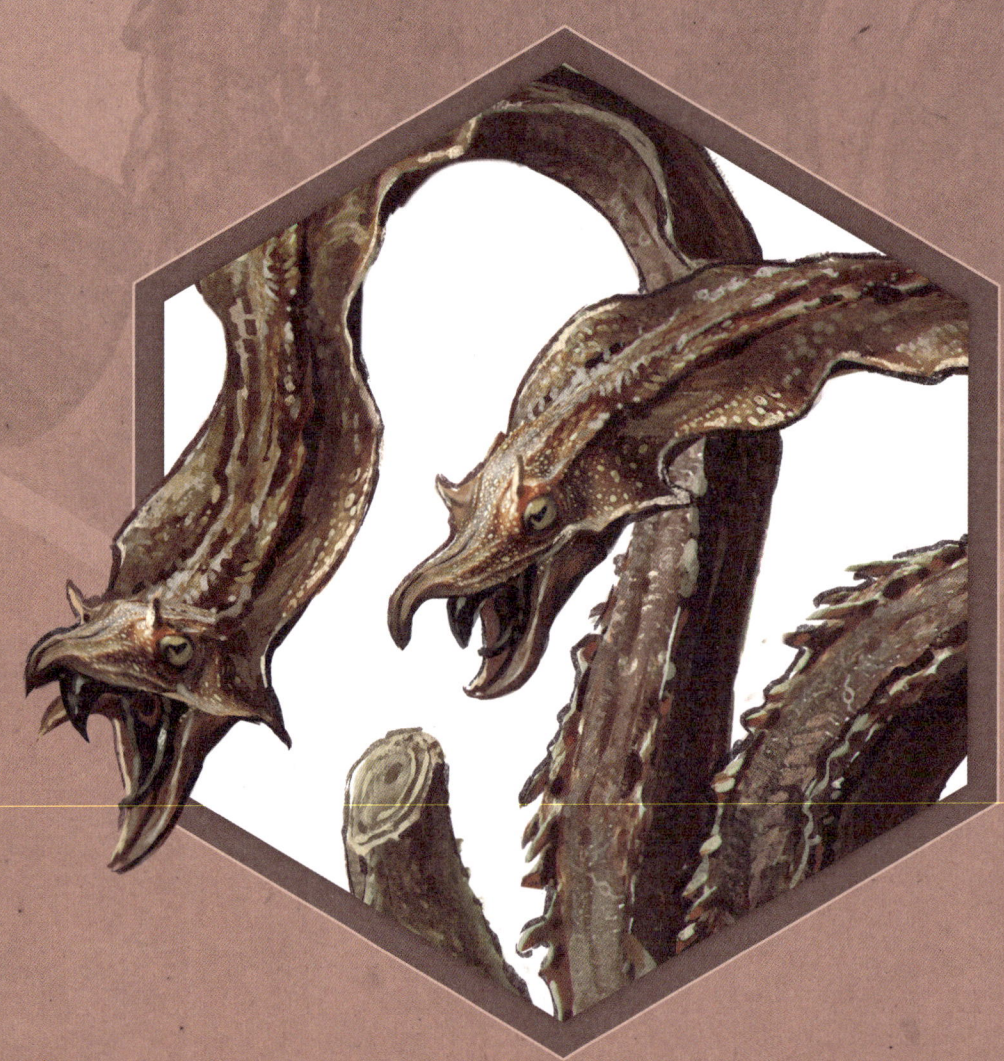

HYDRA

In this chapter, I have the pleasure of designing the Hydra, the many-headed serpent from Greek mythology. What fascinates me most about the Hydra is imagining how its multiple heads might function in the real world. How and why could such a creature evolve? This question opens up many design challenges and possibilities. I'll walk you through my creative process, showing how insights from the biology of regeneration, nervous systems, and cephalopods shape my final concept.

ANNA PODEDWORNA

Final image © Anna Podedworna

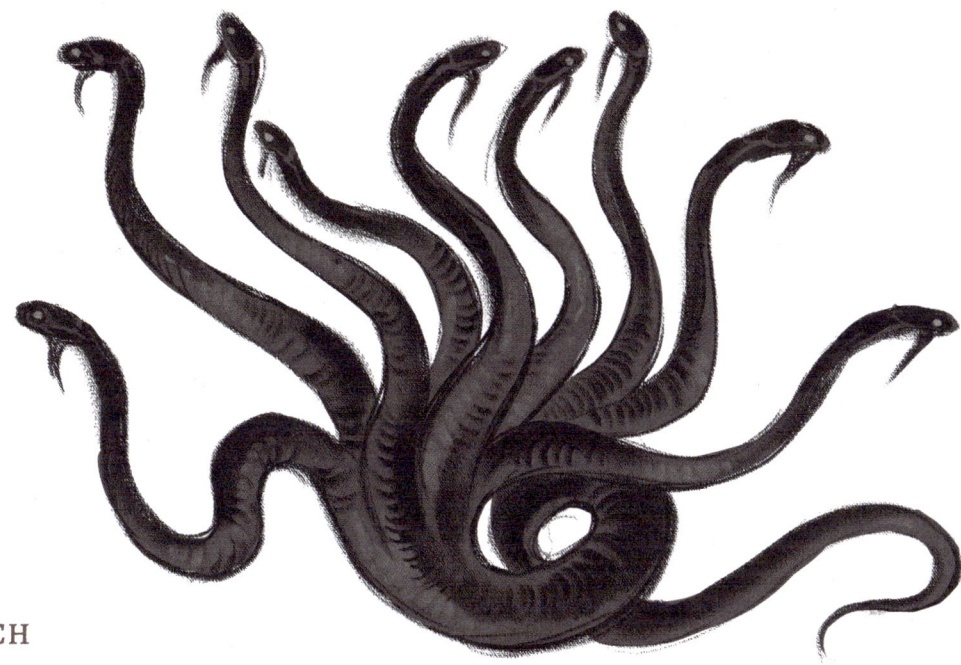

01 RESEARCH

I begin by researching how the Hydra is traditionally represented. The Lernaean Hydra is a lake-dwelling serpent from Greek and Roman mythology that guards the entrance to the underworld. Known for its deadly poisonous breath and blood, even the Hydra's scent is said to be lethal. Descriptions of the Hydra vary depending on the source, but it often has seven to nine heads. Each time a head is cut off, two more grow in its place. Initially, the Hydra was depicted as a many-headed serpent, but modern interpretations often show it with a dragon-like body and limbs.

REGENERATION

Dragons are typically an amalgamation of powerful predatory animals, such as snakes, crocodiles, birds of prey, and big cats. However, since the Hydra's defining feature isn't its sheer strength but its multiple regenerating heads, I choose a different primary inspiration: animals capable of regenerating large parts of their bodies. For example, axolotls and tadpoles can regrow limbs, and many lizards can drop and regrow their tails. Most fascinating to me, however, are octopuses and cuttlefish, which can regenerate their nervous systems, tentacles, and even parts of their eyes.

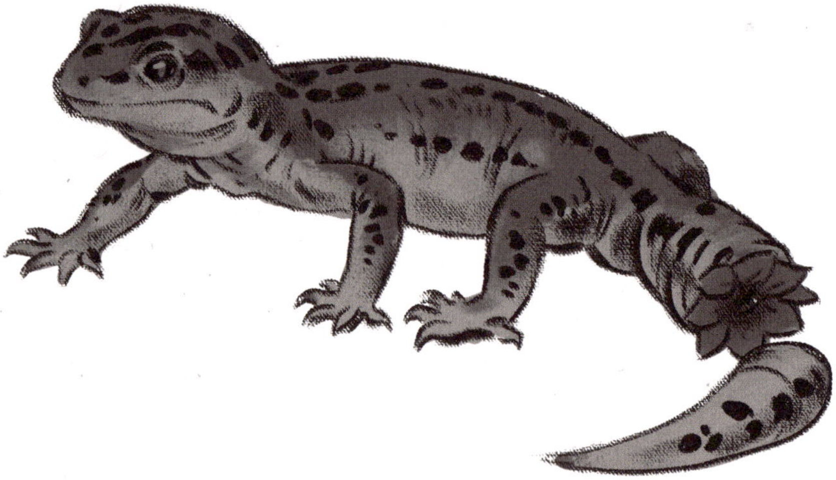

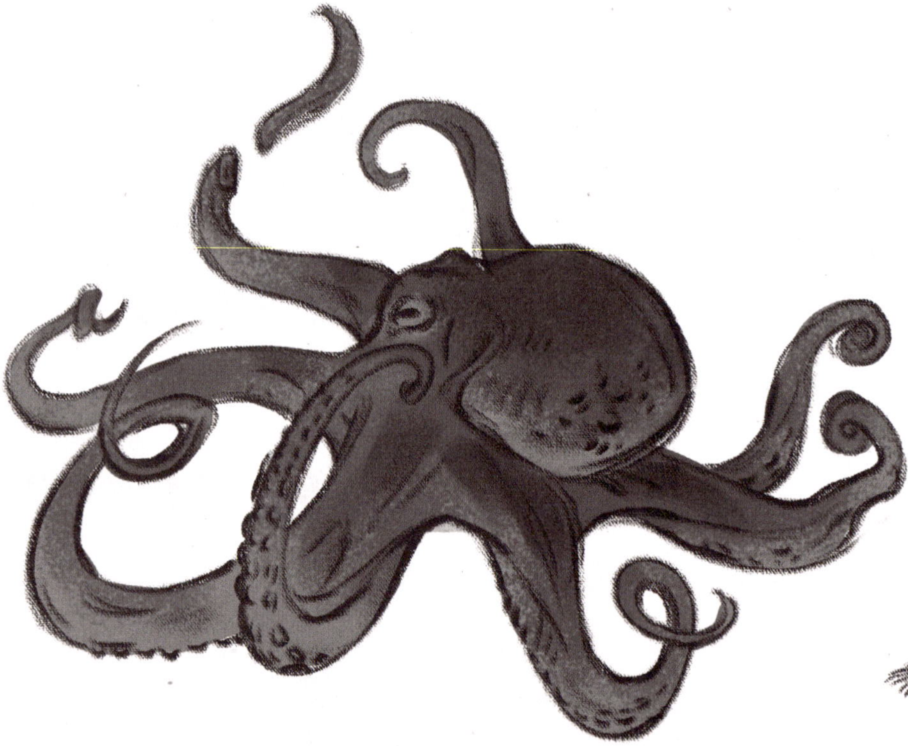

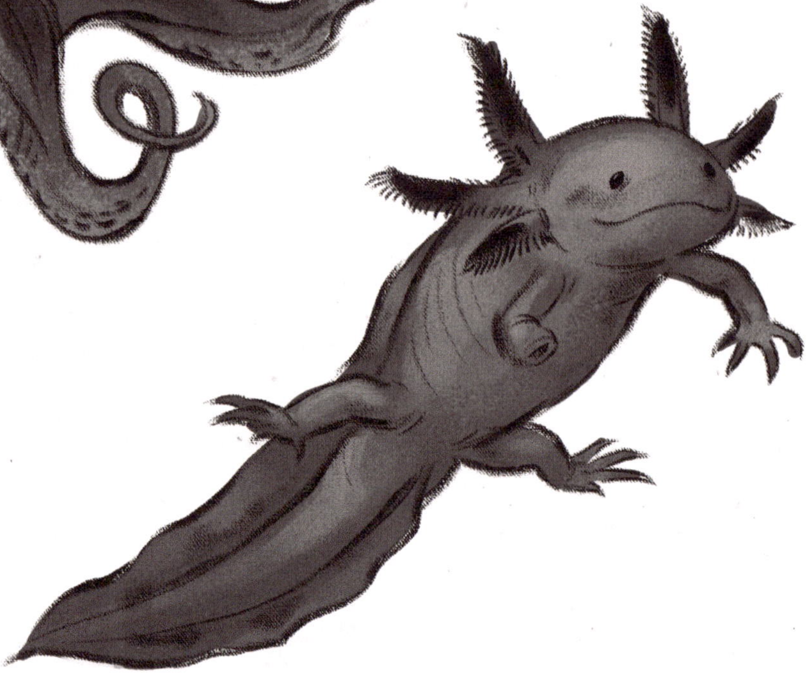

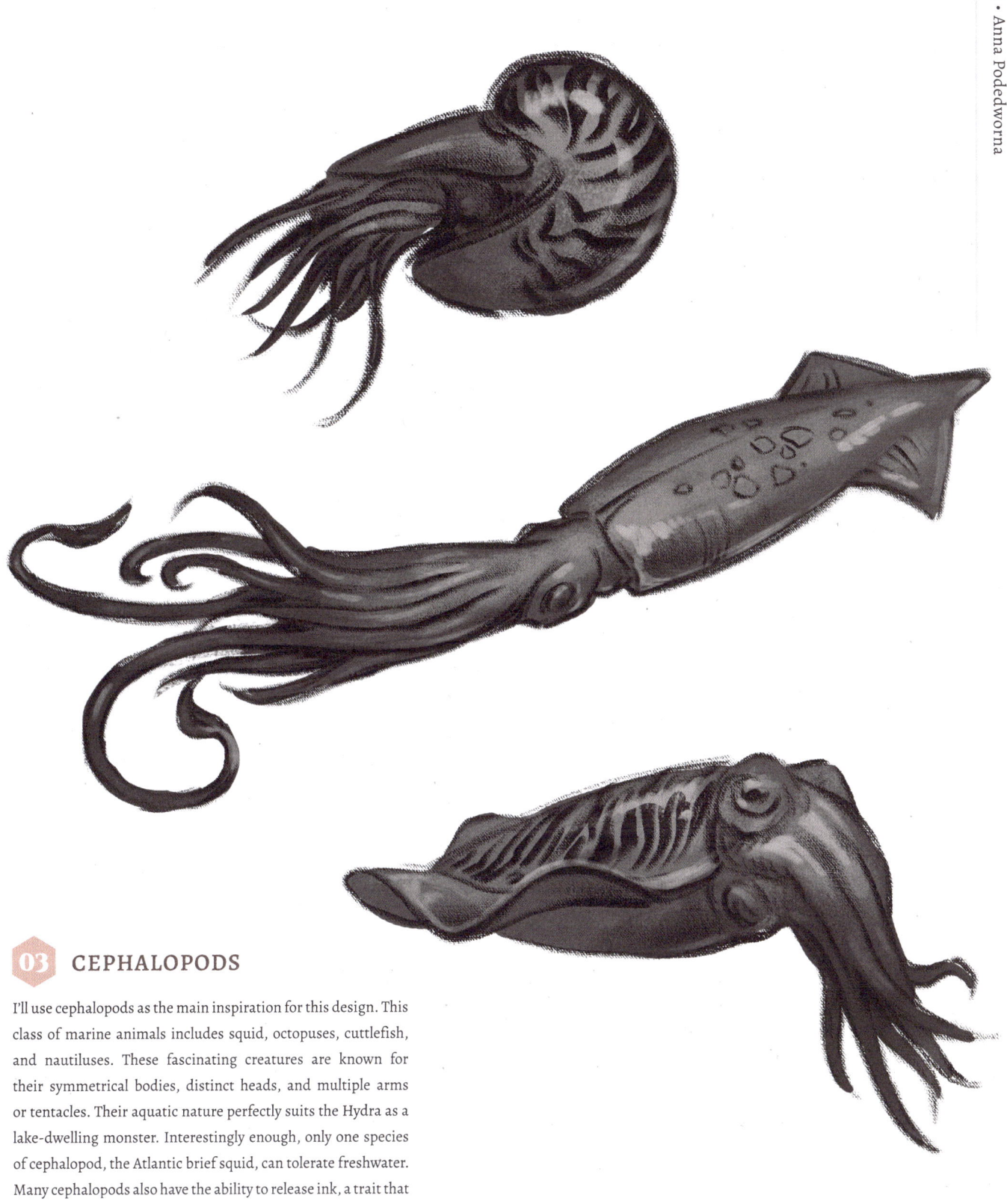

03 CEPHALOPODS

I'll use cephalopods as the main inspiration for this design. This class of marine animals includes squid, octopuses, cuttlefish, and nautiluses. These fascinating creatures are known for their symmetrical bodies, distinct heads, and multiple arms or tentacles. Their aquatic nature perfectly suits the Hydra as a lake-dwelling monster. Interestingly enough, only one species of cephalopod, the Atlantic brief squid, can tolerate freshwater. Many cephalopods also have the ability to release ink, a trait that could be adapted to represent the Hydra's poisonous breath.

04 HYDROSTATIC LIMBS

Cephalopod limbs are fascinating structures. Octopuses have eight arms, while squid and cuttlefish have eight arms with two distinctive longer tentacles. Their limbs function as muscular hydrostats – structures composed primarily of muscle without any skeletal support. Similar examples of hydrostatic structures include the human tongue, manatee's snout, or elephant's trunk. Cephalopod limbs also feature numerous suckers along their undersides. When a sucker makes contact with a surface, it flattens and moulds to fit, forming a seal. Suckers can also smell and taste.

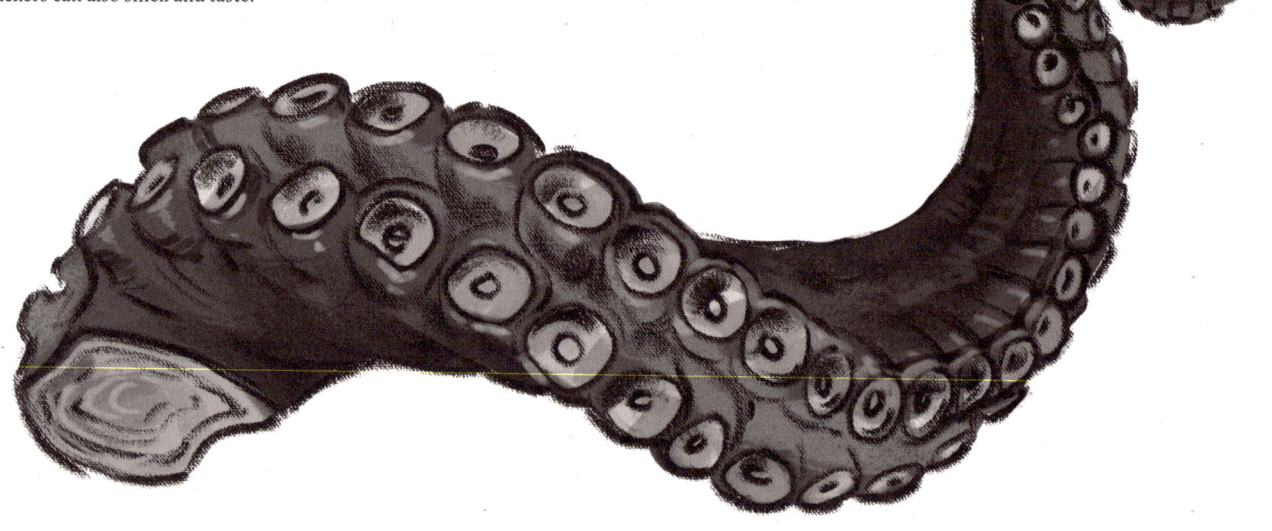

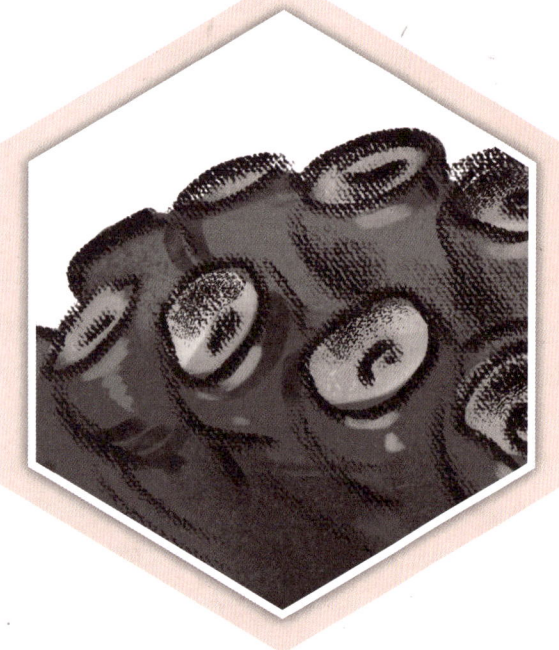

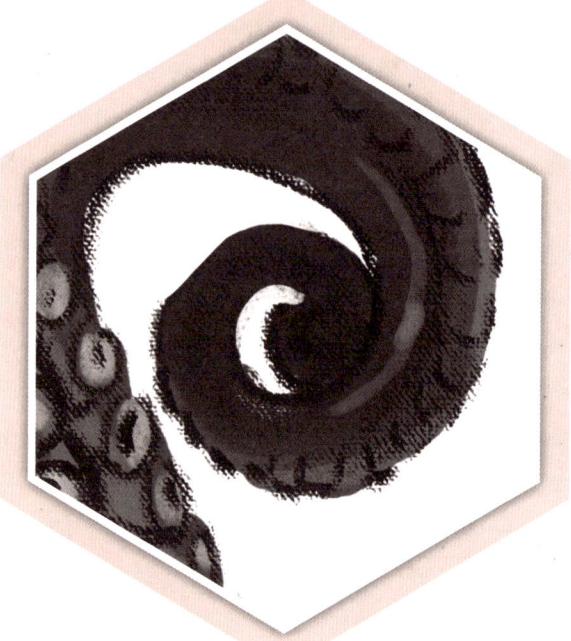

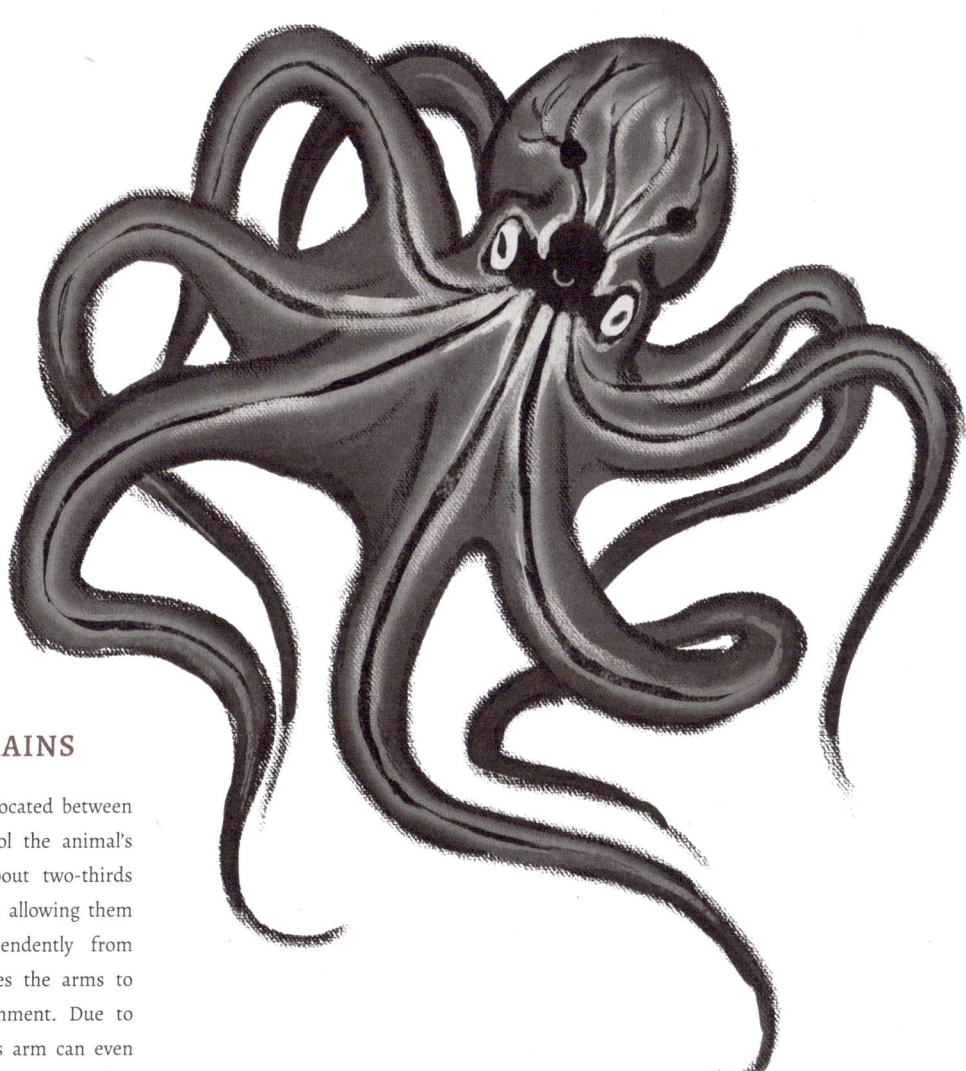

05 OCTOPUS BRAINS

An octopus's central brain is located between its eyes, but it doesn't control the animal's every movement. In fact, about two-thirds of its neurons are in its arms, allowing them to operate somewhat independently from the central brain. This enables the arms to react quickly to their environment. Due to this independence, an octopus arm can even continue to grasp objects for a short time after being severed. This concept translates perfectly to the head-regenerating Hydra.

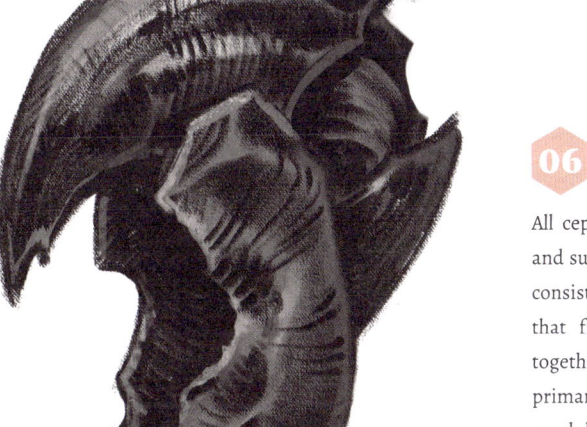

06 CEPHALOPOD BEAK

All cephalopods have a beak located centrally and surrounded by their appendages. The beak consists of two parts, with an upper mandible that fits into the lower mandible, working together in a scissor-like motion. Composed primarily of chitin, the beak is strong enough to crush bones. This is in contrast to birds' beaks, which are made of two bony forms covered with a thin epidermis.

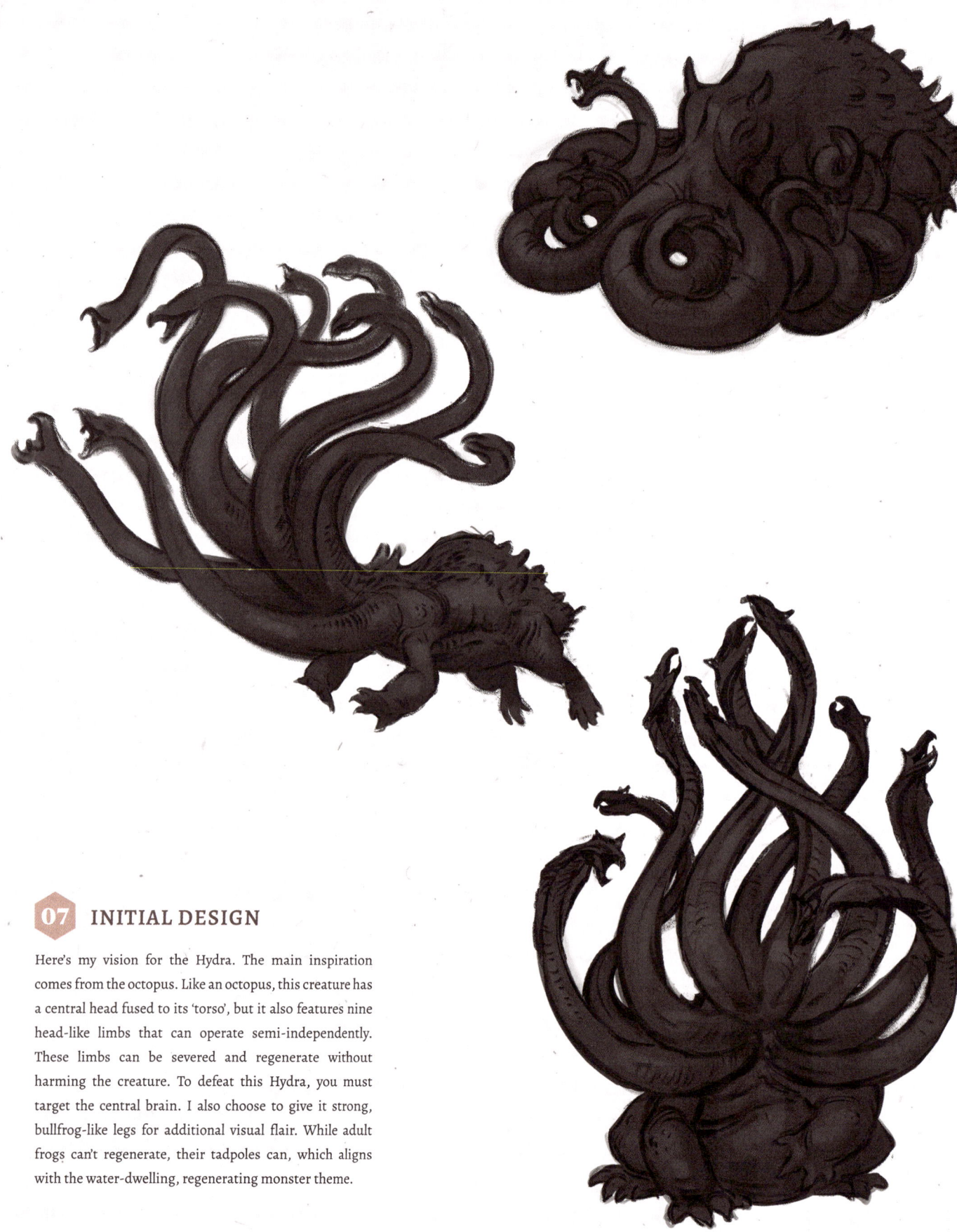

07 INITIAL DESIGN

Here's my vision for the Hydra. The main inspiration comes from the octopus. Like an octopus, this creature has a central head fused to its 'torso', but it also features nine head-like limbs that can operate semi-independently. These limbs can be severed and regenerate without harming the creature. To defeat this Hydra, you must target the central brain. I also choose to give it strong, bullfrog-like legs for additional visual flair. While adult frogs can't regenerate, their tadpoles can, which aligns with the water-dwelling, regenerating monster theme.

08 HEAD EXPLORATIONS

The body plan of my Hydra is fairly simple, so I focus on designing the heads next. I want to maintain a dragon-like silhouette for the head but take a more unconventional approach with the details. After a few attempts, I decide against adding teeth. Instead, I choose an octopus beak (see right), so that when the mouth is closed, the head resembles the end of a tentacle.

HYDROSTATIC HEADS

As mentioned earlier, tentacles are muscular hydrostats, and so are the Hydra heads in my design. There's no spine or skull; the only rigid structure is the beak. This soft, flexible design allows real-life octopuses to squeeze through tight spaces, and I envision the Hydra having similar abilities. It could slip into narrow crevices, ambushing unsuspecting travellers, with its tentacle-like heads following prey into even tighter spots. It's a monster that's hard to evade.

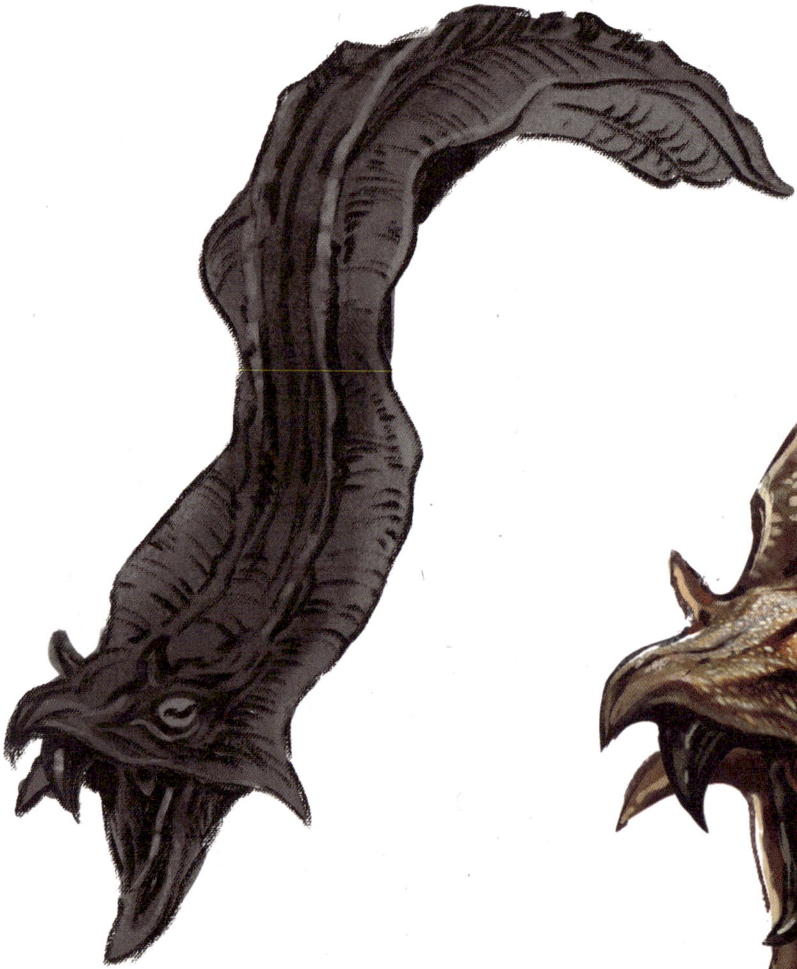

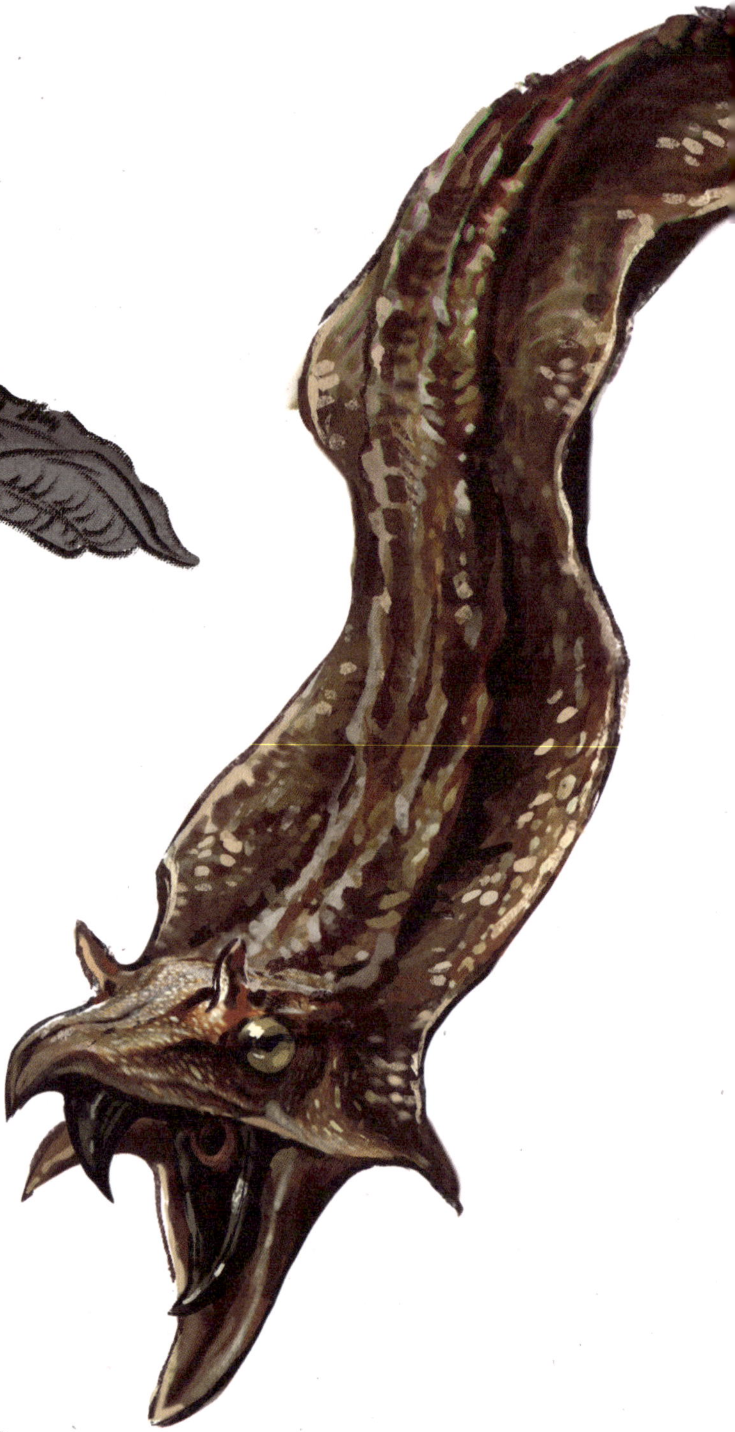

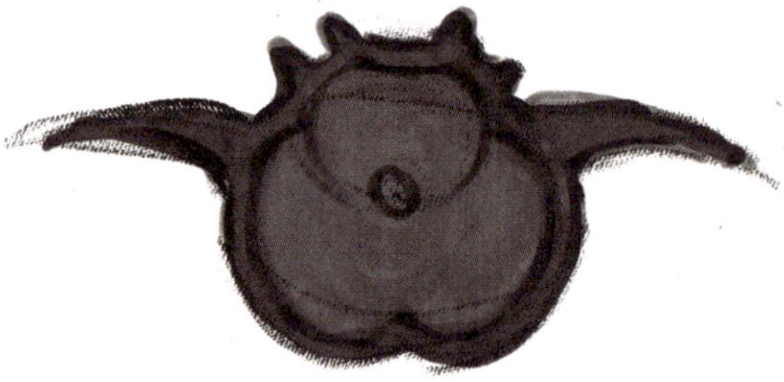

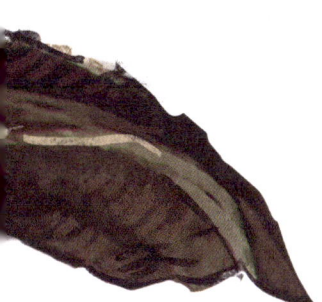

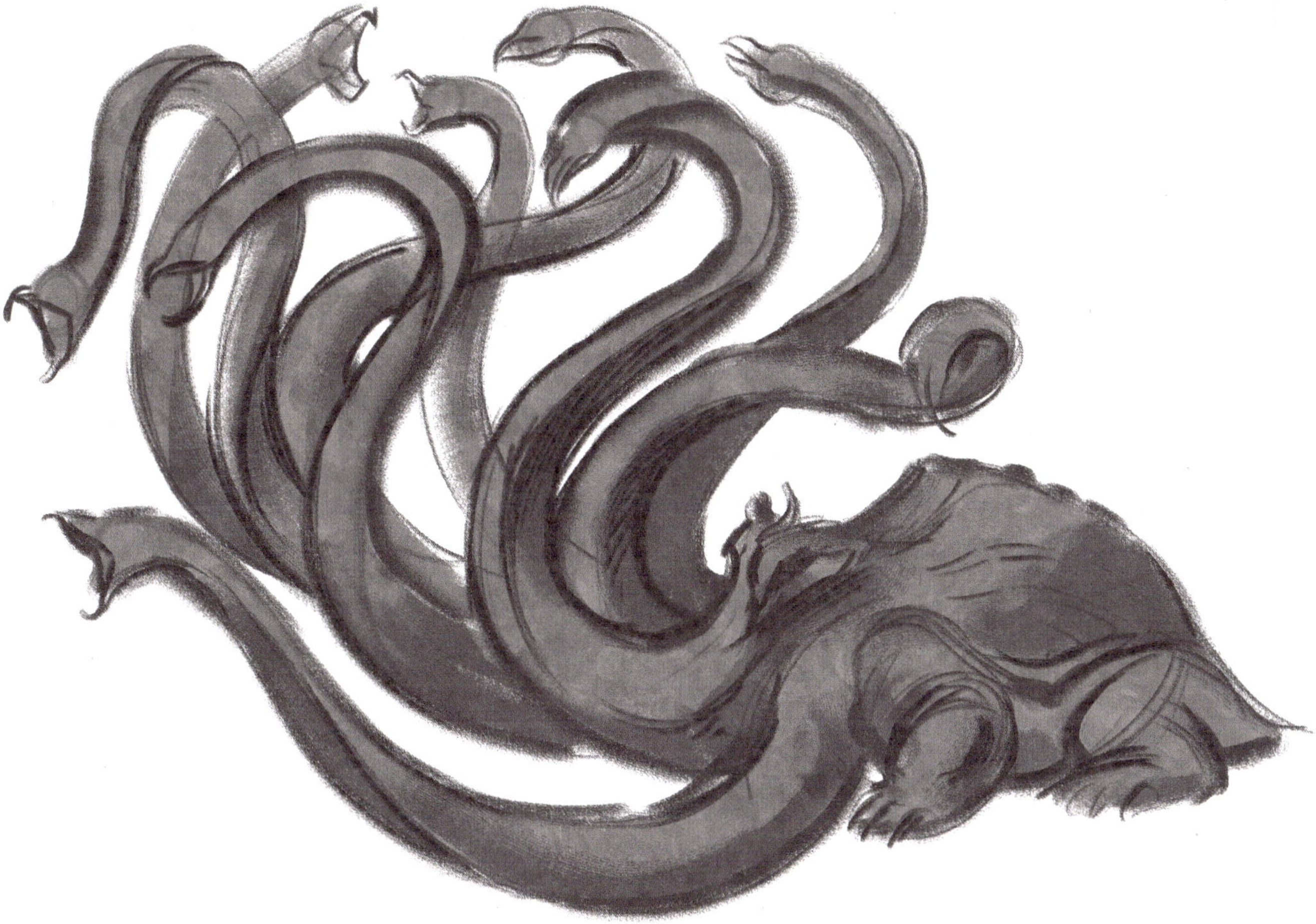

10   SKETCHING THE FINAL

Now I can begin to focus on the final image. I select a pose that clearly conveys the design. In concept art, clarity and readability take precedence over dynamic or illustrative style. Since the design is complex with many small details, I choose a simple semi-side view to keep it clear and readable while showcasing all the key elements effectively.

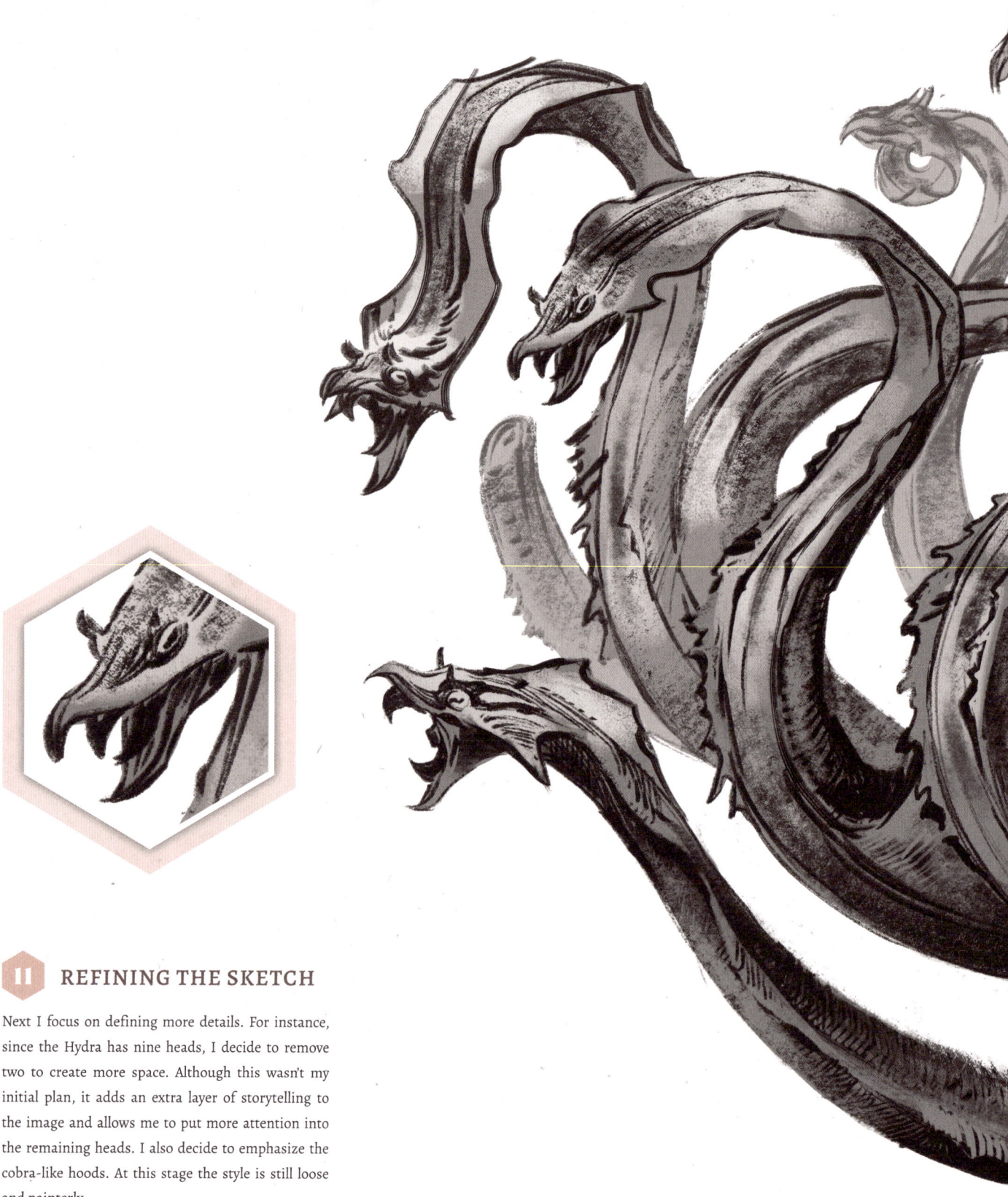

11 REFINING THE SKETCH

Next I focus on defining more details. For instance, since the Hydra has nine heads, I decide to remove two to create more space. Although this wasn't my initial plan, it adds an extra layer of storytelling to the image and allows me to put more attention into the remaining heads. I also decide to emphasize the cobra-like hoods. At this stage the style is still loose and painterly.

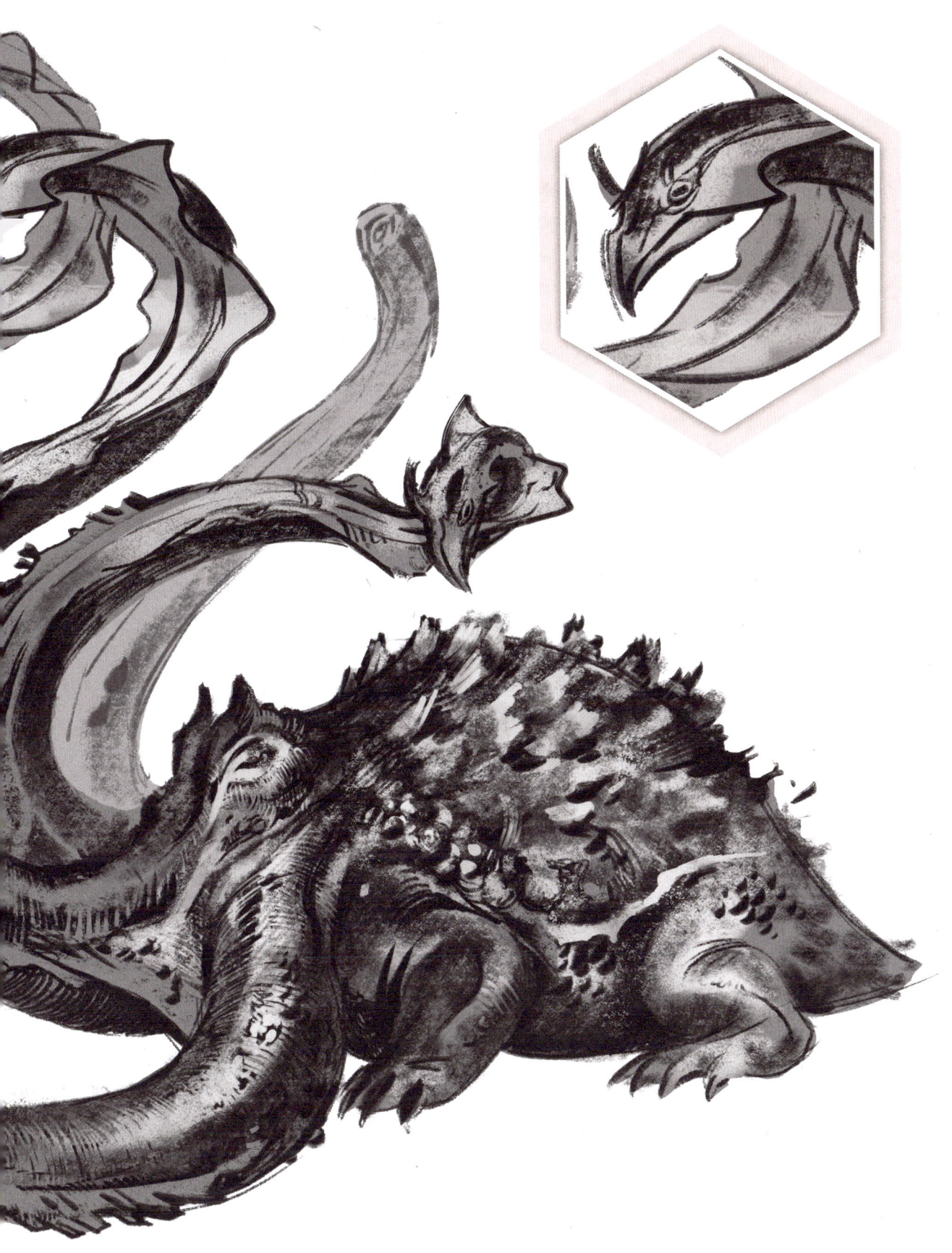

At the black-and-white stage, it's time to lock in the details. I begin using photo textures and loose brushstrokes to fill in the design and add visual noise. This is when I decide on the skin texture. I choose a mix of toad and octopus skin. The texture is rough and bumpy, with a warty appearance that gives it an uneven look. I also integrate octopus-like papillae, which allow the skin to change texture, appearing even more rough or spiky when needed.

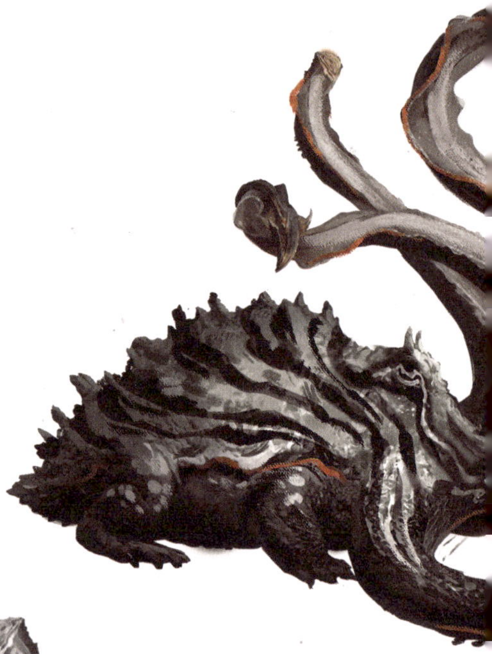

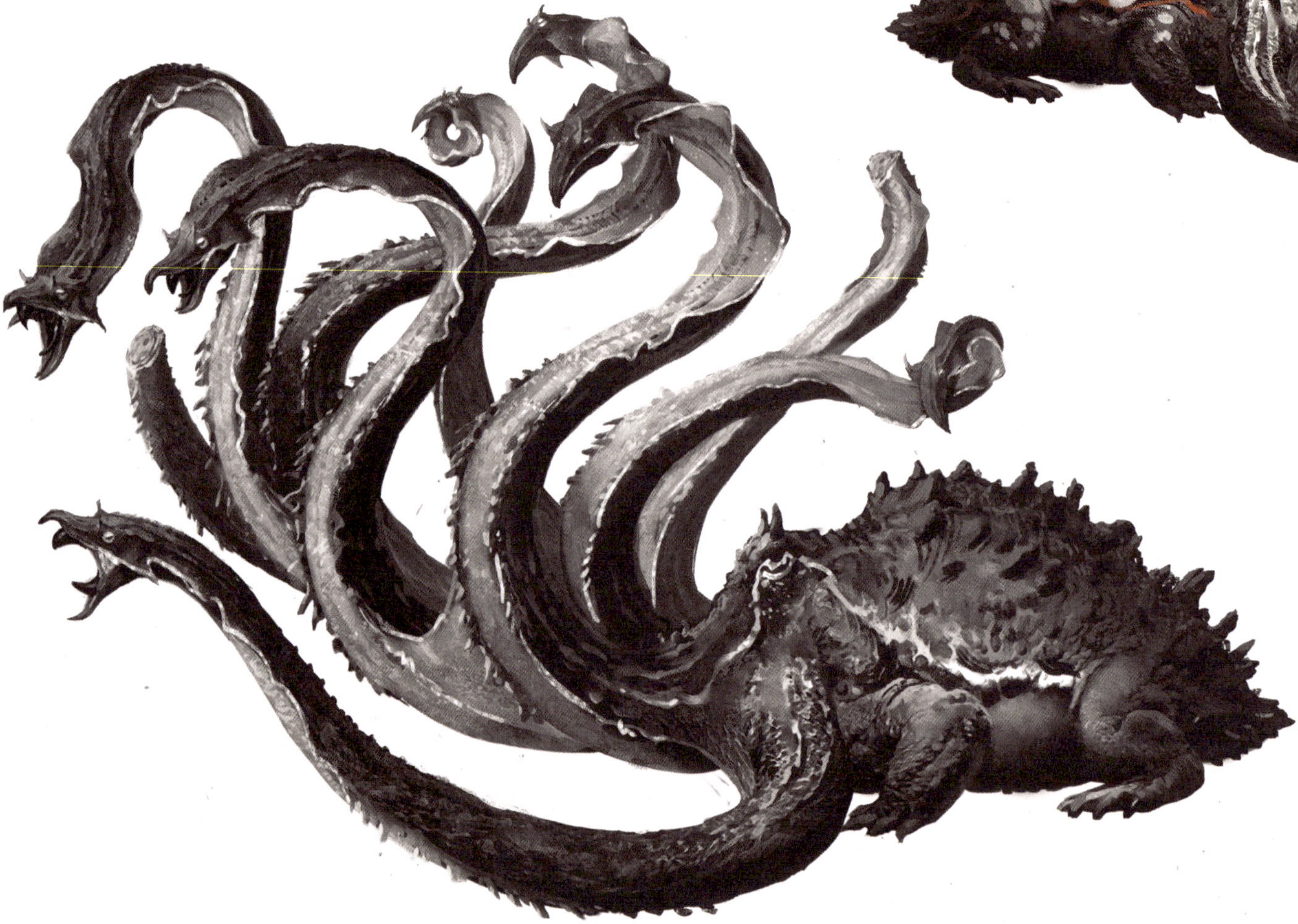

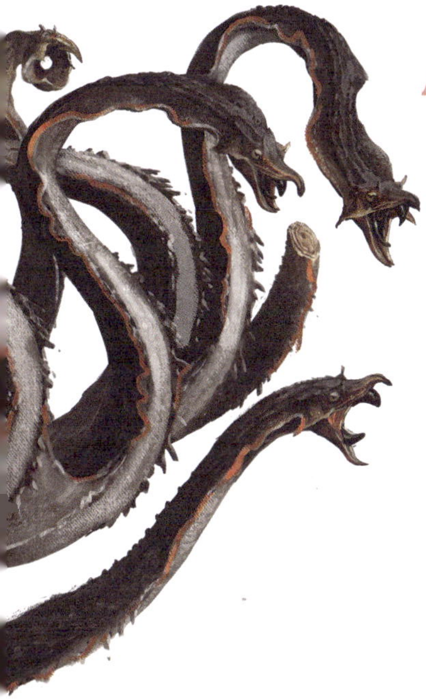

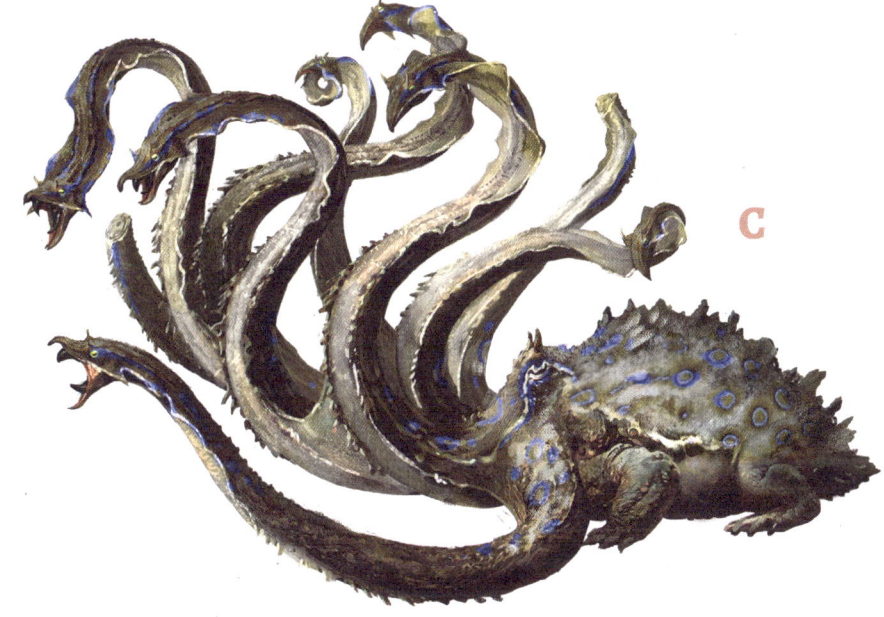

A

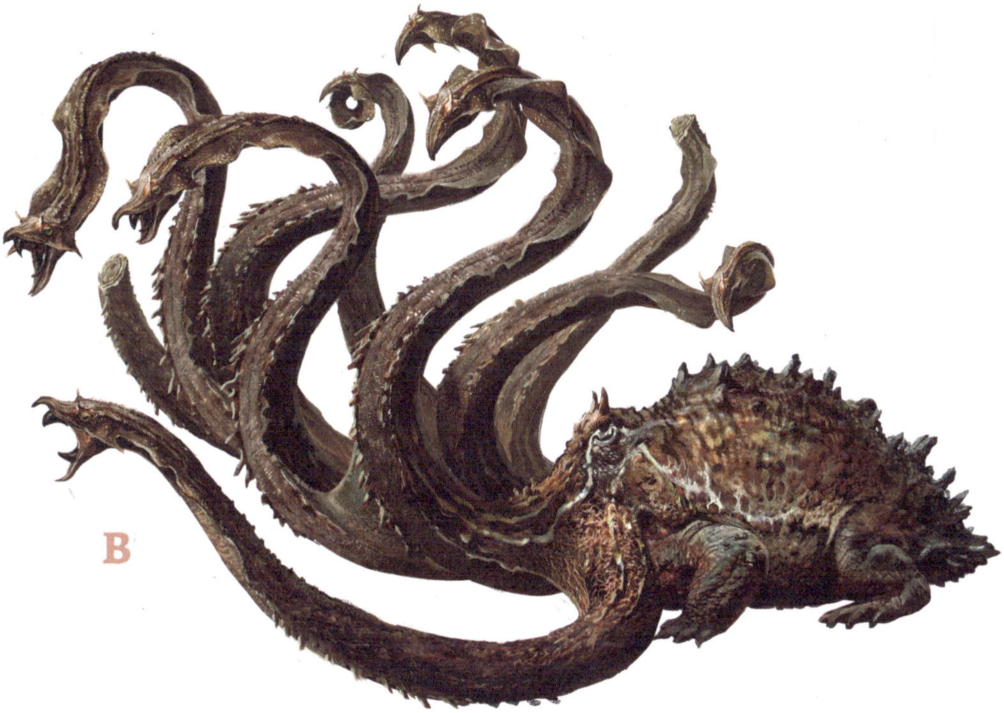

B

C

13 COLOUR PALETTE

Picking colours is always a fun stage. For this design, I draw inspiration from three real-life cephalopods: the Pacific striped octopus (A), the giant Pacific octopus mixed with stripes from cuttlefish (B), and the blue-ringed octopus (C). I want the eyes of the main head to blend seamlessly into the body. Eyespot mimicry is a common feature in which patterns on an animal resemble eyes, either to deter predators or to redirect their attention from more vulnerable body parts. My primary inspiration here is the foureye butterflyfish, whose real eye is hidden by a striped body pattern, while the fake eye near its tail misdirects potential threats.

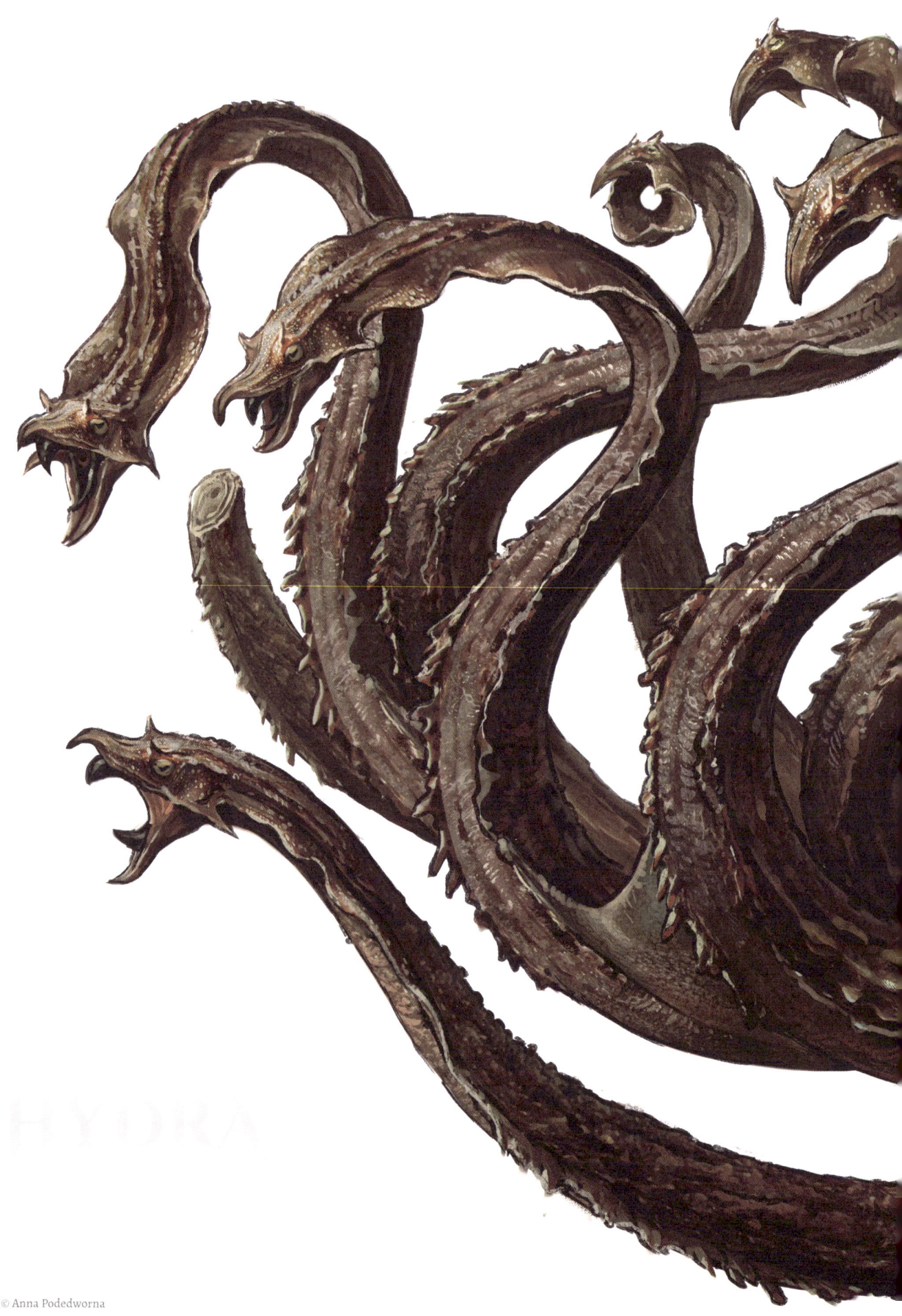

HYDRA

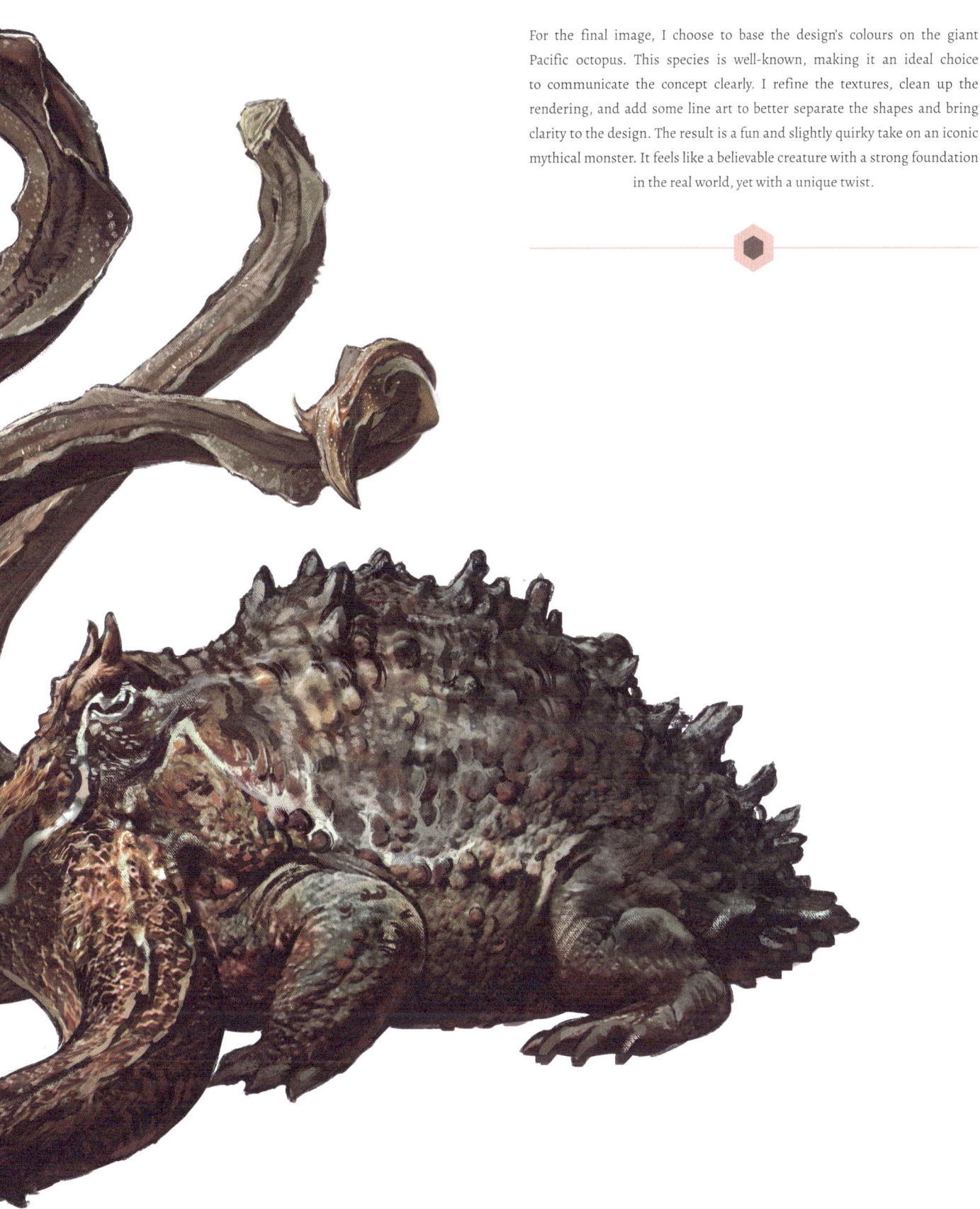

CONCLUSION

For the final image, I choose to base the design's colours on the giant Pacific octopus. This species is well-known, making it an ideal choice to communicate the concept clearly. I refine the textures, clean up the rendering, and add some line art to better separate the shapes and bring clarity to the design. The result is a fun and slightly quirky take on an iconic mythical monster. It feels like a believable creature with a strong foundation in the real world, yet with a unique twist.

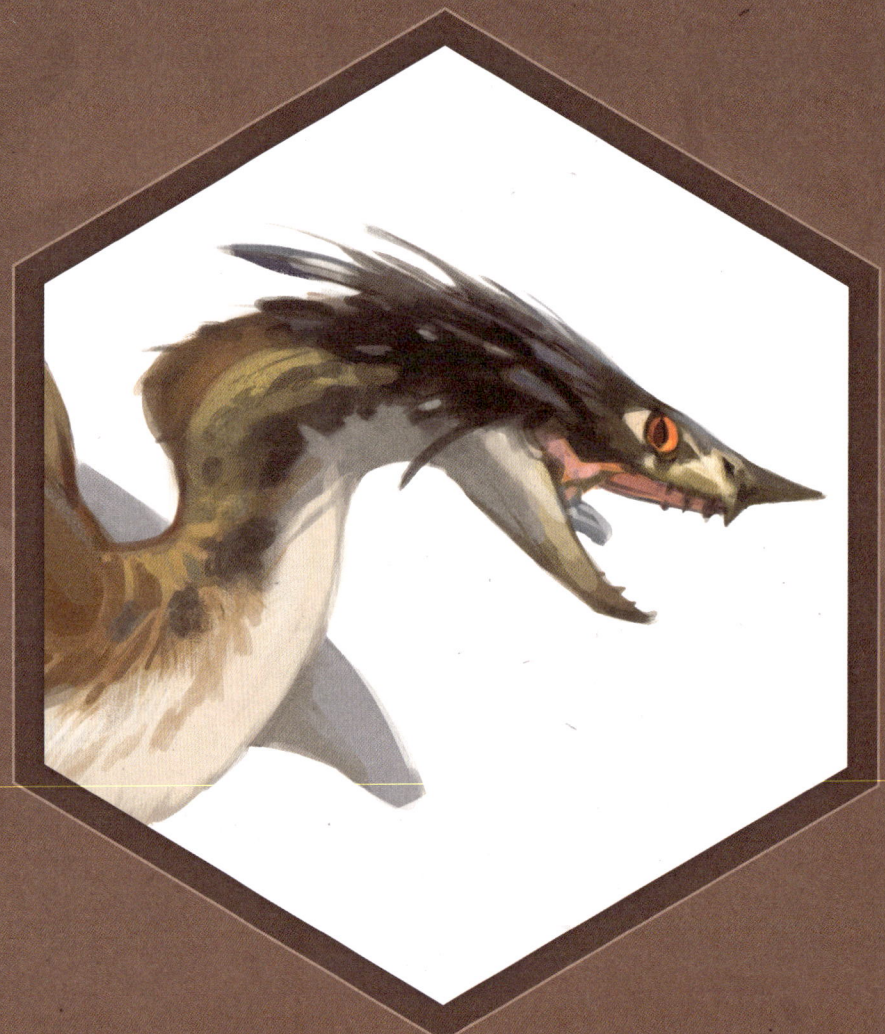

JACULUS

In this tutorial I will be designing the jaculus, which is also known as the javelin snake – a small arboreal dragon from Greek mythology. I plan to go over my process, from research to final painting, and my thinking along the way. I don't believe there is any one correct way to create, so this is not intended to be a strict guide. My hope is that the reader might find pieces of information to take from this and incorporate into their own unique process. Let's get into it!

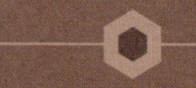

ALLIE IRWIN

Final image © Allie Irwin

01 ARBOREAL SNAKES

Before doing any designing, I start with research. The mythology tells us a few important things. First, we know the jaculus is arboreal, meaning it lives in trees. It is said that it would descend from the branches to attack those passing below. We also know that it's fast, for at least a short burst, and strong enough to inflict damage. The name 'javelin snake' also implies that it has a hardened skull or horn to attack with. With all that knowledge, I can start researching animals that could have comparable traits. An obvious place to start is snakes, so I research snakes that can glide, snakes that have sharper spear-like heads, and just about any snake that I find interesting.

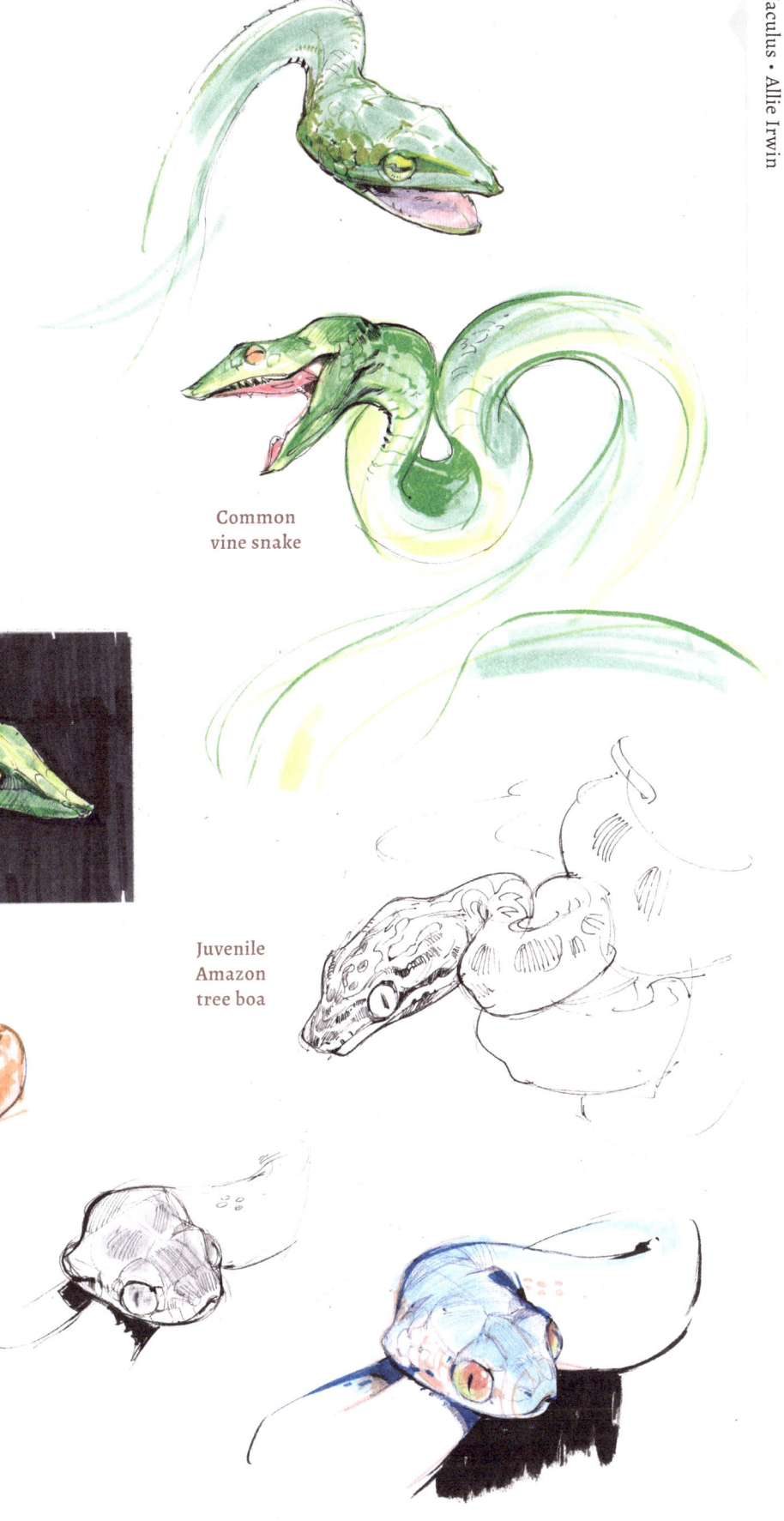

Common
vine snake

Juvenile
Amazon
tree boa

Brown
tree snake

02 ARBOREAL LIZARDS

I research lizard species next. I'm personally always drawn to geckos and all the interesting patterns and shapes that they have. Tree monitors also seem like a good candidate due to them already being a little dragon-shaped. The list of arboreal lizards goes on, but I mainly look at geckos, chameleons, and monitor lizards. I choose these specifically because they each move and hold branches in their own unique way.

All the studies shown here were done traditionally with a combination of pencil and markers.

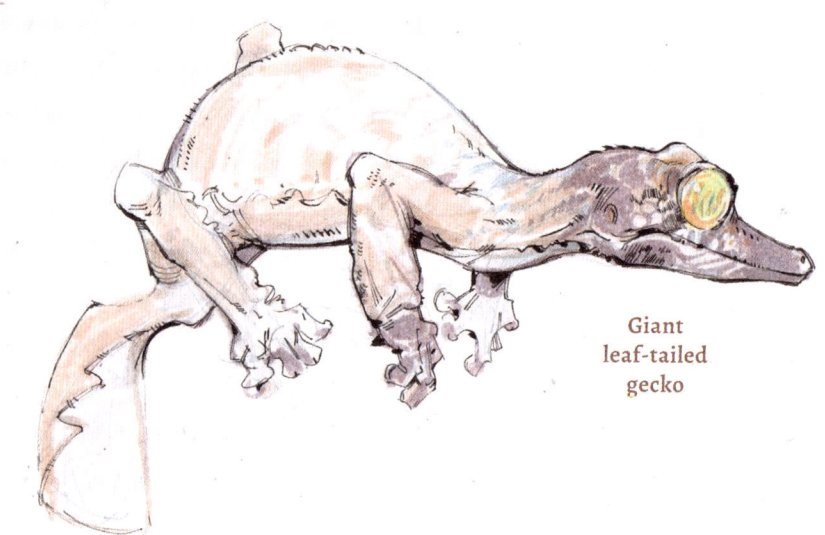

Giant leaf-tailed gecko

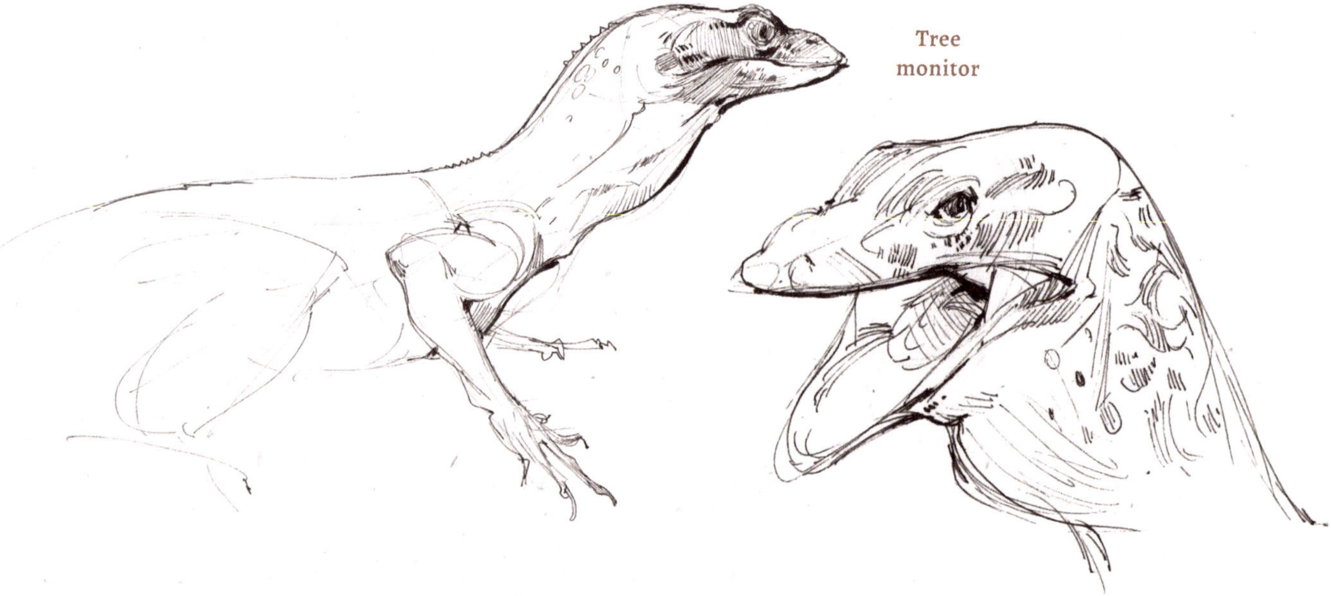

Tree monitor

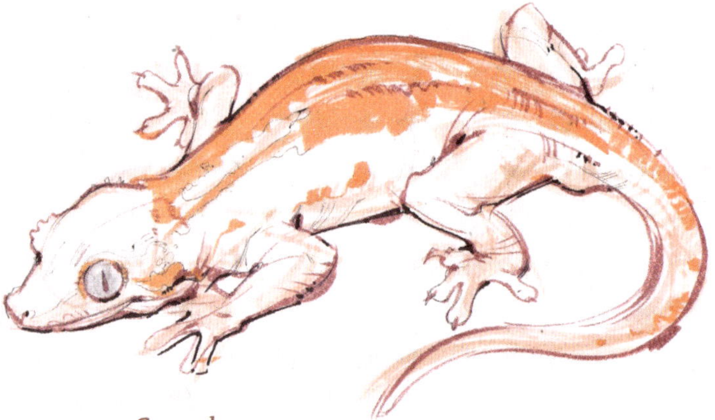

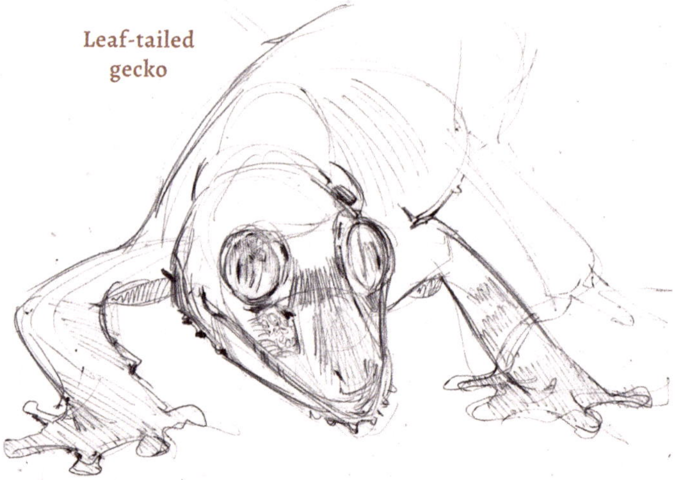

Leaf-tailed gecko

Gargoyle gecko

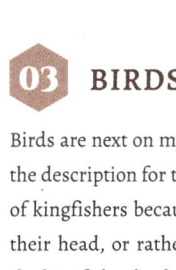

03 BIRDS

Birds are next on my list to explore. When I first read the description for the jaculus, I immediately thought of kingfishers because they also dive at prey and use their head, or rather beak, as a javelin. Researching the kingfisher leads me to explore other diving birds, such as cormorants and something called an Oriental darter. Oriental darters have very long, almost snake-like necks that I find interesting.

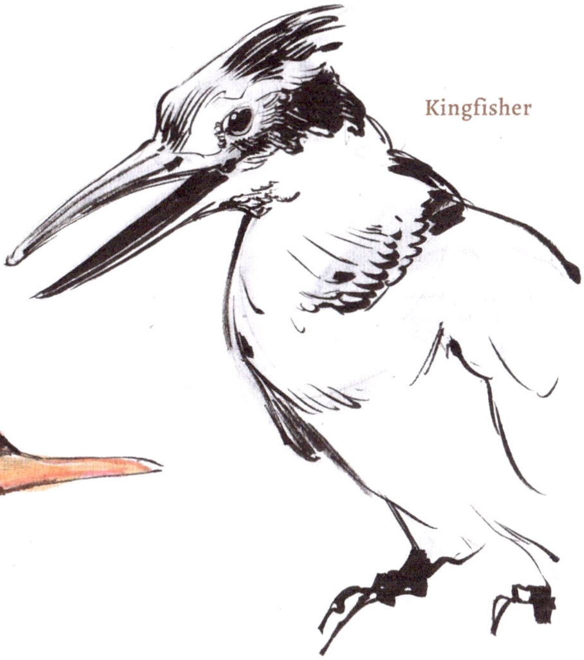

Kingfisher

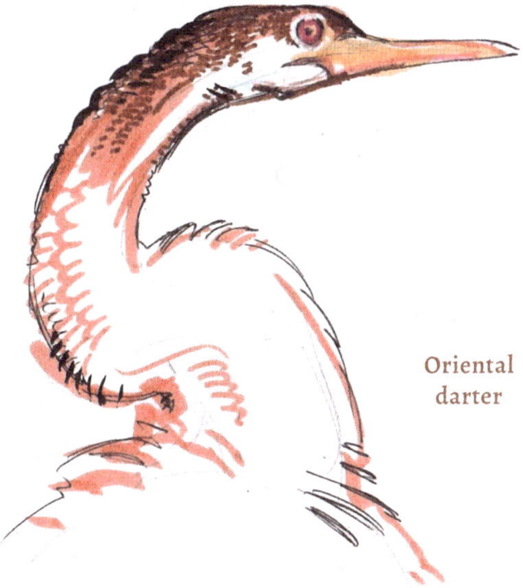

Oriental darter

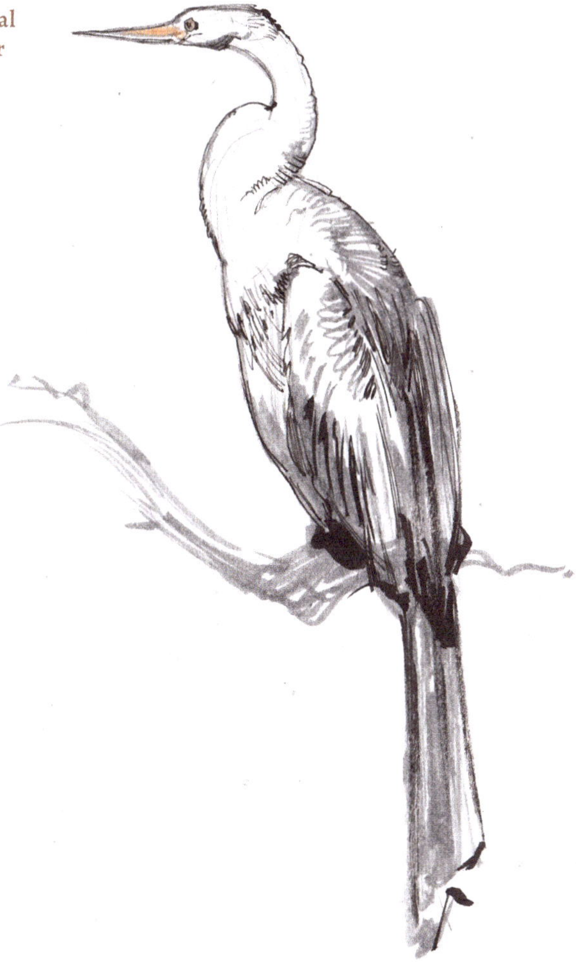

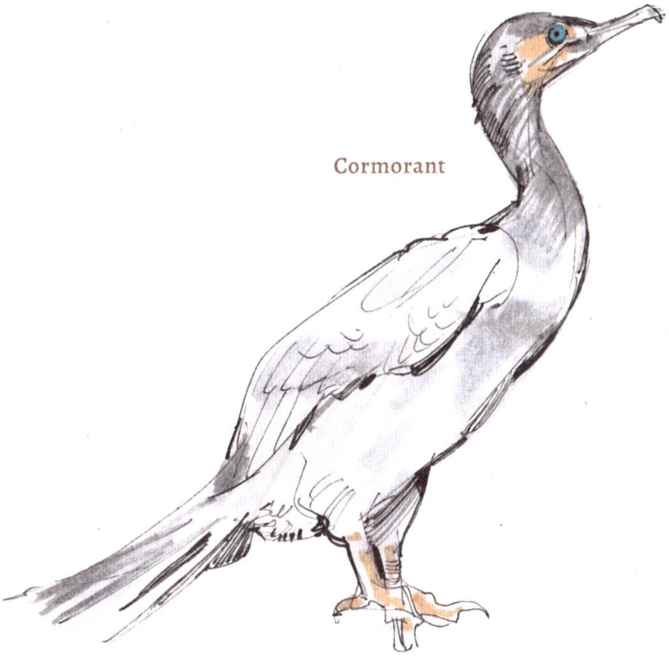

Cormorant

04 ARBOREAL MAMMALS

To me, one of the most distinct characteristics of a dragon is how they are often described as being a mix of reptile, mammal, and bird. The first tree-dwelling mammal that comes to my mind is a squirrel. Pine martens also seem like a good candidate because they have longer bodies that could meld well with reptilian features. While both of these examples are quick and agile, I also want to reference some mammals on the opposite end of the spectrum. Prehensile-tailed porcupines are interesting because they approach movement in trees very differently, using their tail to hold branches and stay balanced.

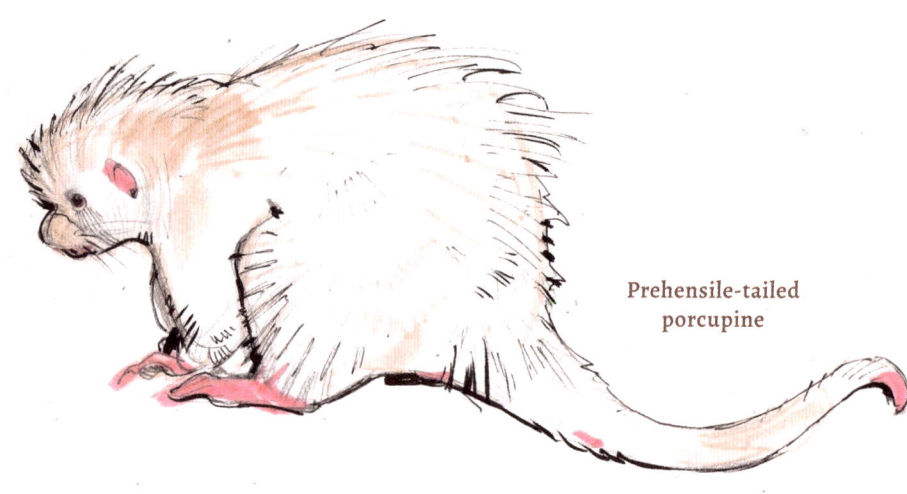

Prehensile-tailed porcupine

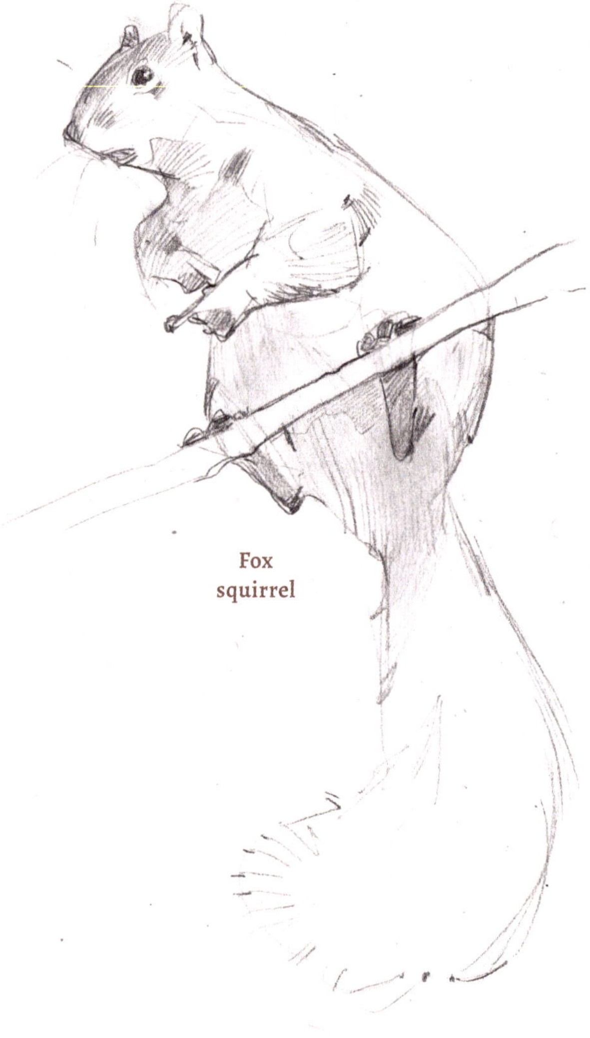

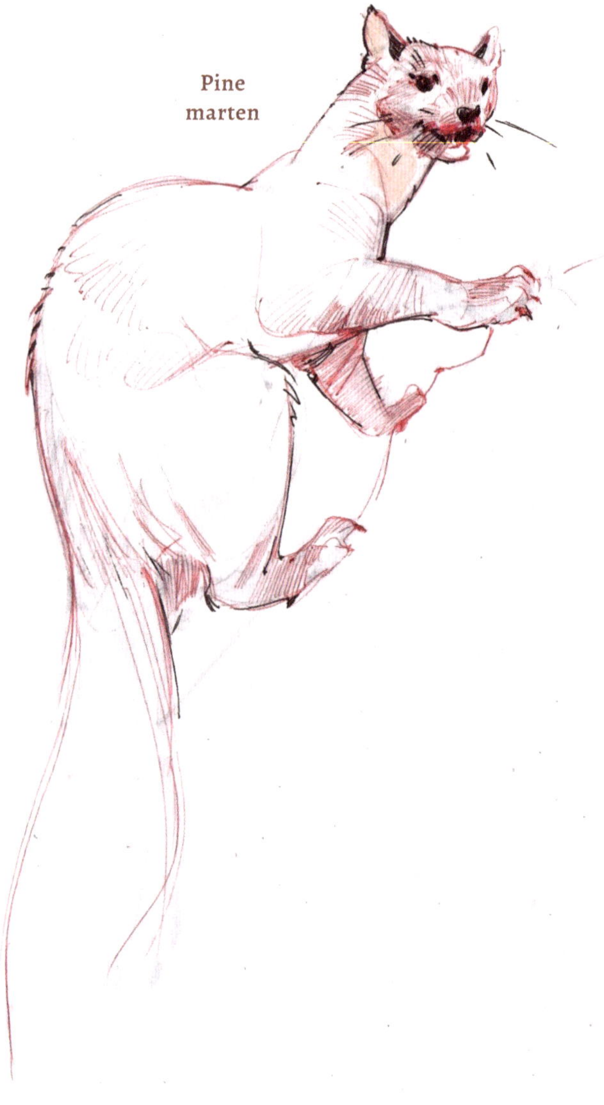

Pine marten

Fox squirrel

05 ## HORNS & NOSES

Next, I want to research some possibilities for the spine or horn of the jaculus. I think of the thorny devil lizards of Australia, Jackson's chameleons with their rhino-like horn placement, and the previously mentioned kingfishers for their piercing beaks. I also think that softshell turtles could be useful because, despite not having horns, they do have a nose that protrudes above the mouth in a unique way. I could see it hardening into something adjacent to a narwhal horn.

Softshell turtle

Thorny devil

Jackson's chameleon

06 EYE STUDIES

Throughout the research process, I always keep note of any interesting eyes I find. There is such a wide array of eye colours and pupil shapes in animals, especially within reptiles. I also love the eye areas of certain birds that have a difference in skin colour and texture around the head, such as roosters or macaws. I have a section of my reference board with eyes from various geckos, a northern gannet, a vine snake, a skink, and a cormorant, to name just a few.

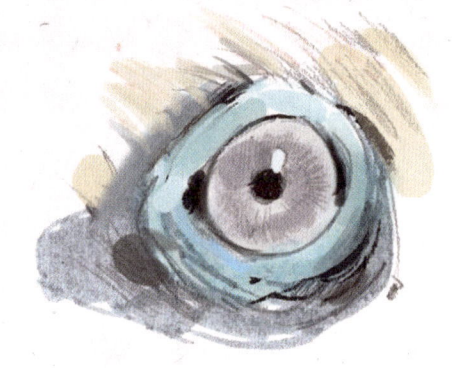

Gannet

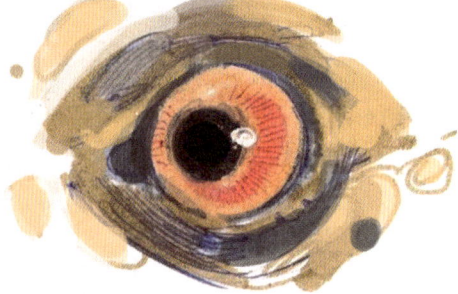

Skink

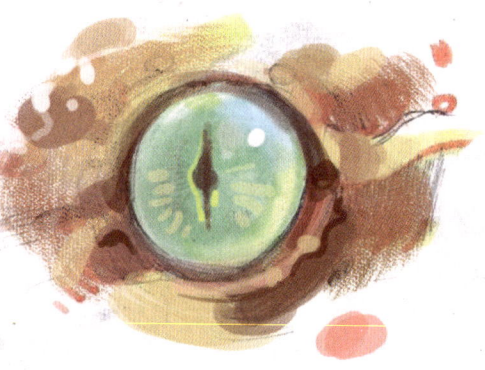

Gecko

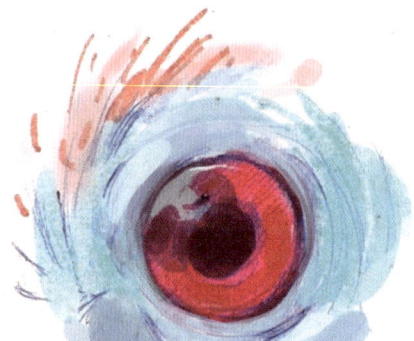

Hoatzin

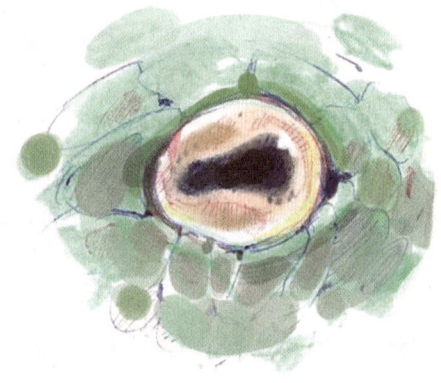

Vine snake

- Super pattern heavy pointed edges, low body

- Prehensile tail, Big claws, almost sloth-like

- Short neck, Big Horn.

- Long neck, Vine snake head, Long tail.

- Long neck, Big back limbs and short front, Big wings

07 WRITING RECIPES

Now that I have enough reference to draw on, I'm almost ready to start on some thumbnails. However, before I start drawing at all, I like to write down some 'recipes'. These just serve as a way for me to organize my ideas and jot down what traits from my research I think might go well together. I never stick to them exactly, but I do find it useful to have something to look back on when feeling stuck and out of ideas.

08 THUMBNAILS

When sketching the first round of thumbnails, I usually try to stay as loose as possible. I find that starting on paper helps me think through my drawings more efficiently. When you work digitally, it gives you the ability to go back and revise your drawing endlessly, which is great, but it also allows you to get bogged down in making one thumbnail perfect while there are still other ideas to explore. When I do want to go back and refine a thumbnail further, I just scan the page and bring it into Photoshop.

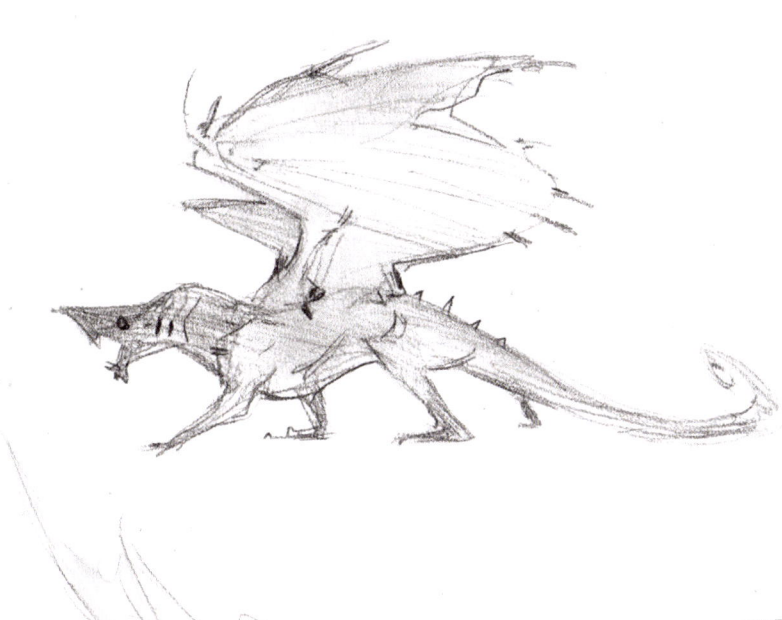

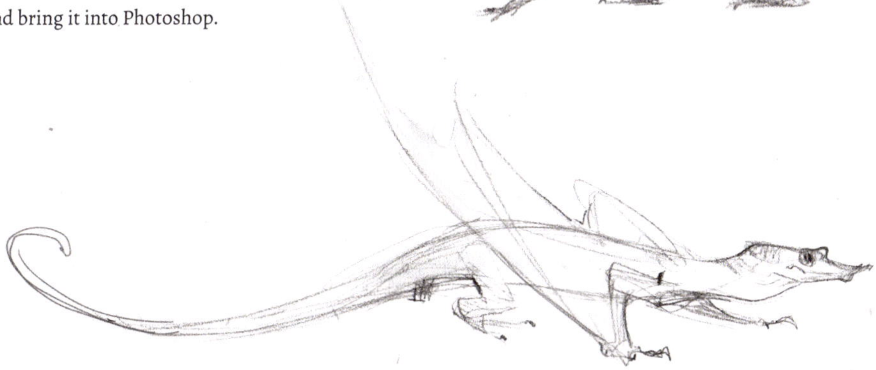

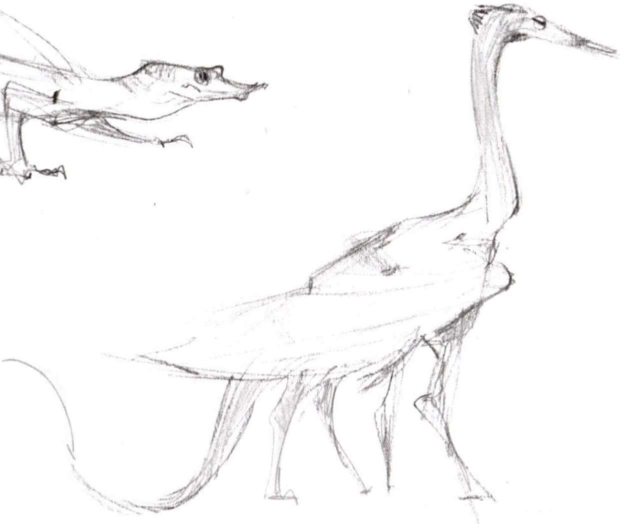

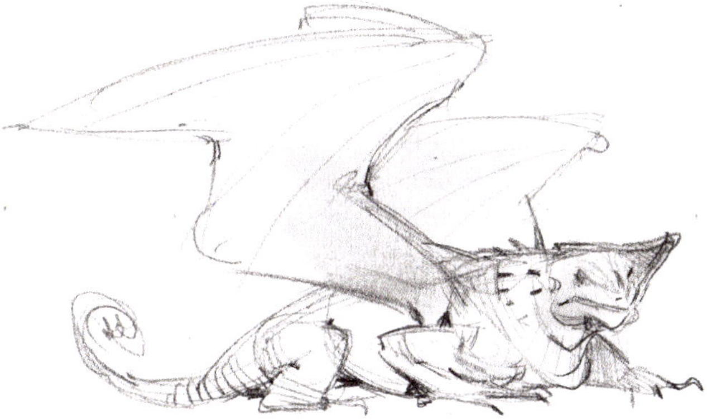

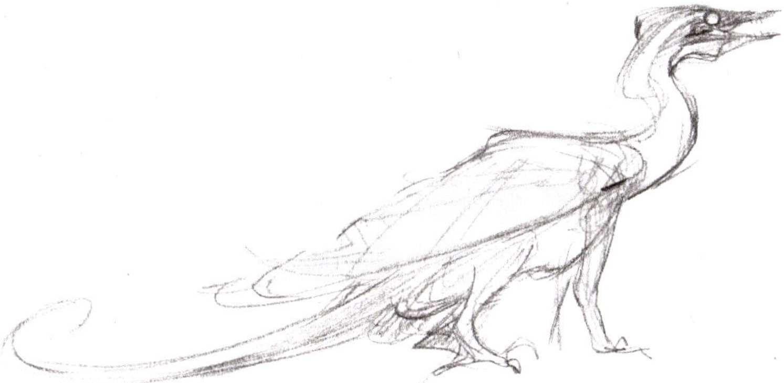

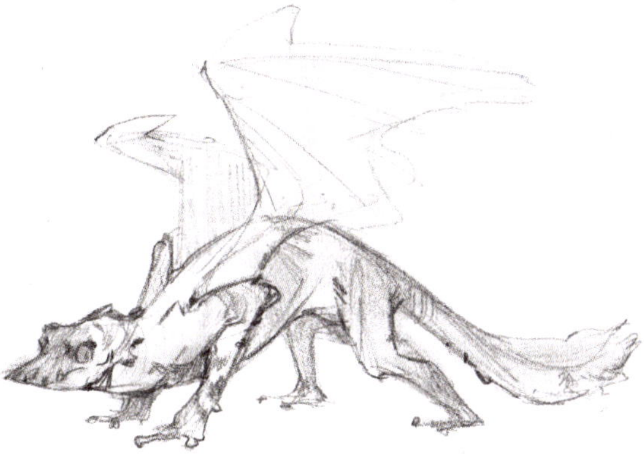

09 HEAD IDEAS

Now I start exploring the head in more detail. I try to think of ways to incorporate the spear/horn aspect. I want to explore some heads that lean more reptilian, some that lean more avian, and some that feel like an even mix of the two. I like the idea of fur or feathers protruding from scales, or even from under the frill of something like a crested gecko. I have found that focusing on just the head can help to develop my ideas for the direction of the entire creature.

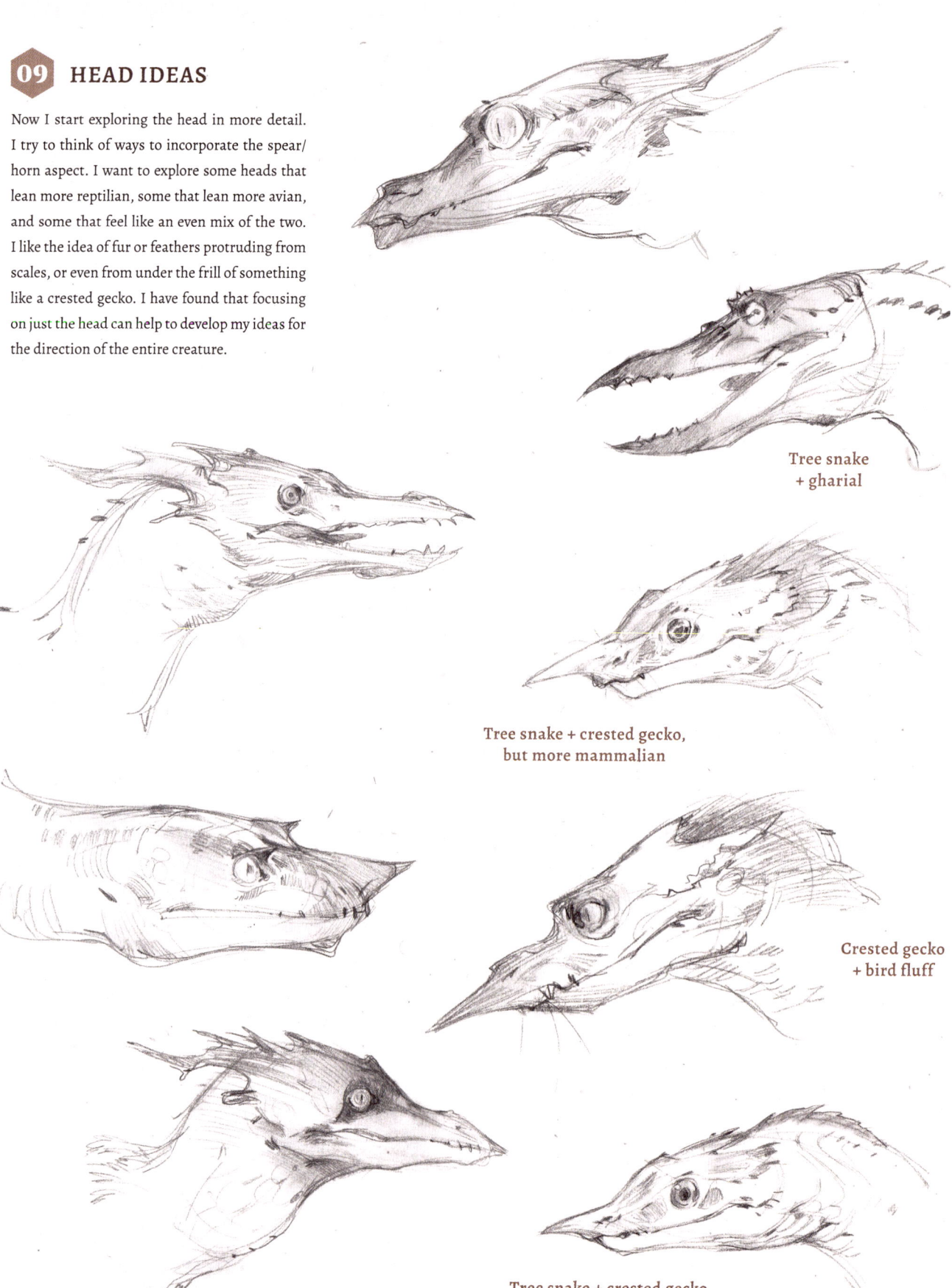

Tree snake + gharial

Tree snake + crested gecko, but more mammalian

Crested gecko + bird fluff

Tree snake + crested gecko, but less mammalian

10 HOGNOSE SNAKE

I briefly explore adding a transformative element to the head. In my research, I came across a video of a hognose snake in a defensive display. This snake can puff out and flatten its head and neck to make itself appear bigger. There might be something interesting there that could relate to the javelin detail from mythology. Maybe the jaculus puffs out its head to become a sharper spear shape. I decide not to move forward with this, but it's still fun to think about.

 11 STRONG PREDATOR

Now that I've thought through my ideas at the thumbnail phase, I feel confident in moving on to some more in-depth sketching. Here I explore a version of the jaculus that feels more slow and powerful. I imagine it creeping along a branch, using its prehensile tail to hold on, stalking prey. The wings are smaller because it's adapted to crawl and glide between trees rather than fly quickly.

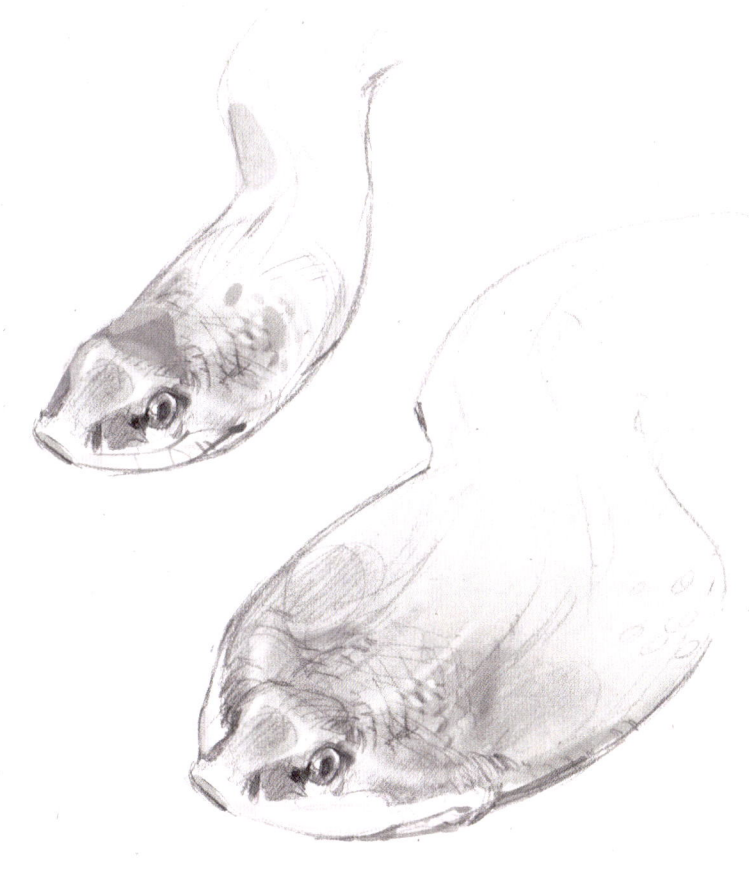

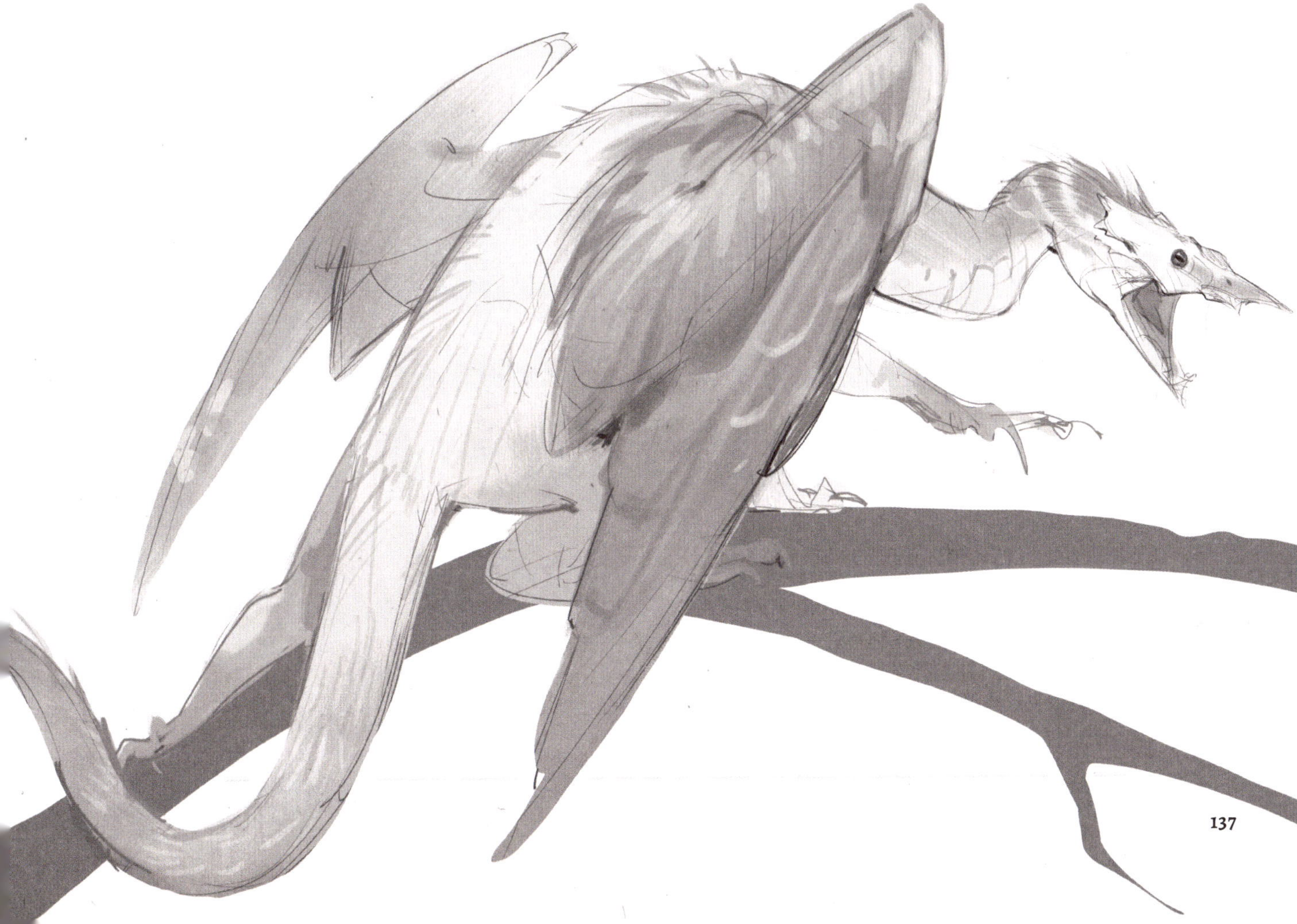

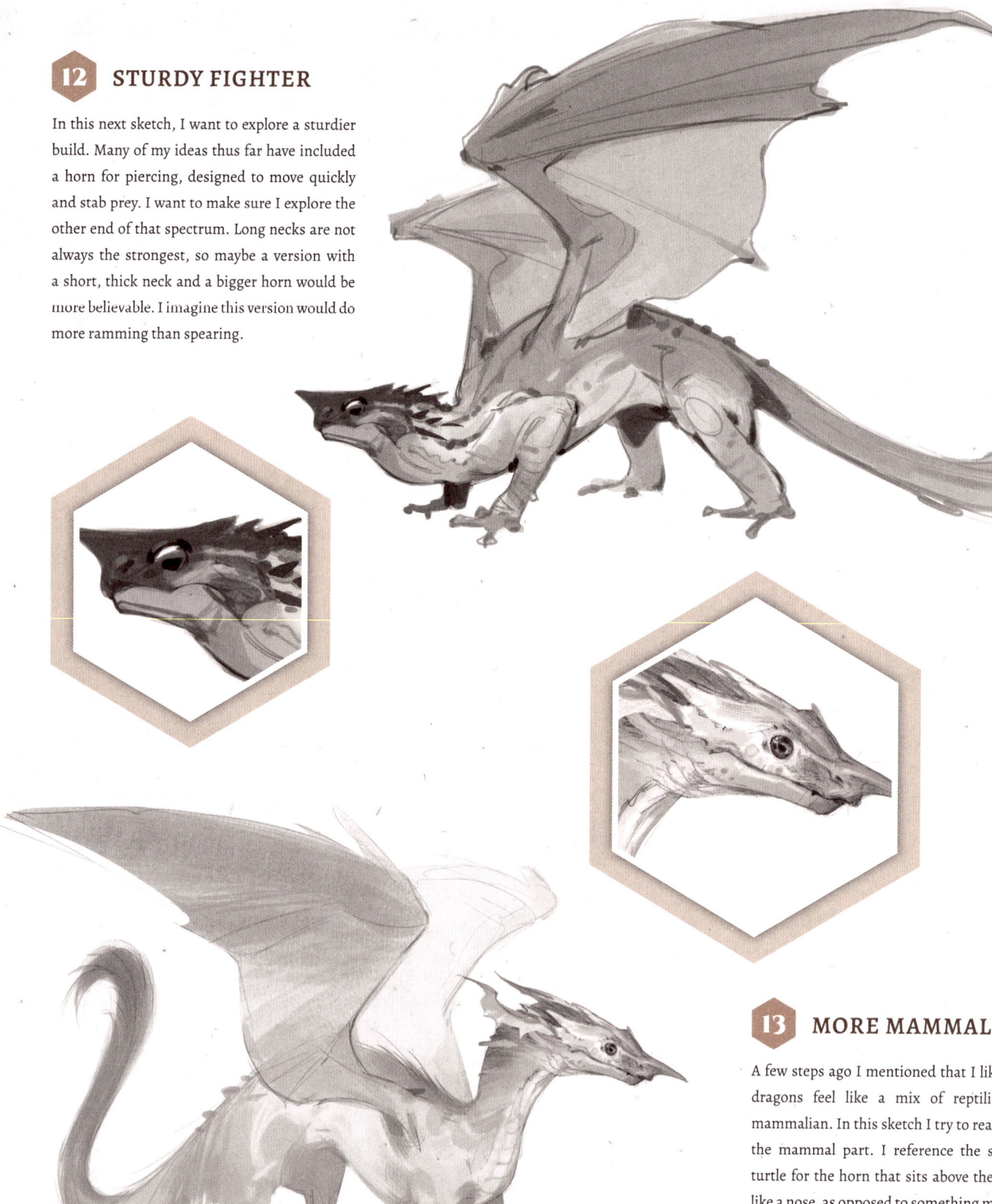

12 STURDY FIGHTER

In this next sketch, I want to explore a sturdier build. Many of my ideas thus far have included a horn for piercing, designed to move quickly and stab prey. I want to make sure I explore the other end of that spectrum. Long necks are not always the strongest, so maybe a version with a short, thick neck and a bigger horn would be more believable. I imagine this version would do more ramming than spearing.

13 MORE MAMMALIAN

A few steps ago I mentioned that I like when dragons feel like a mix of reptilian and mammalian. In this sketch I try to really push the mammal part. I reference the softshell turtle for the horn that sits above the mouth like a nose, as opposed to something more like a rhino horn. I also try adding a more upright tail position like that of a squirrel. The aim is to help the design read as more arboreal and just a little more unusual.

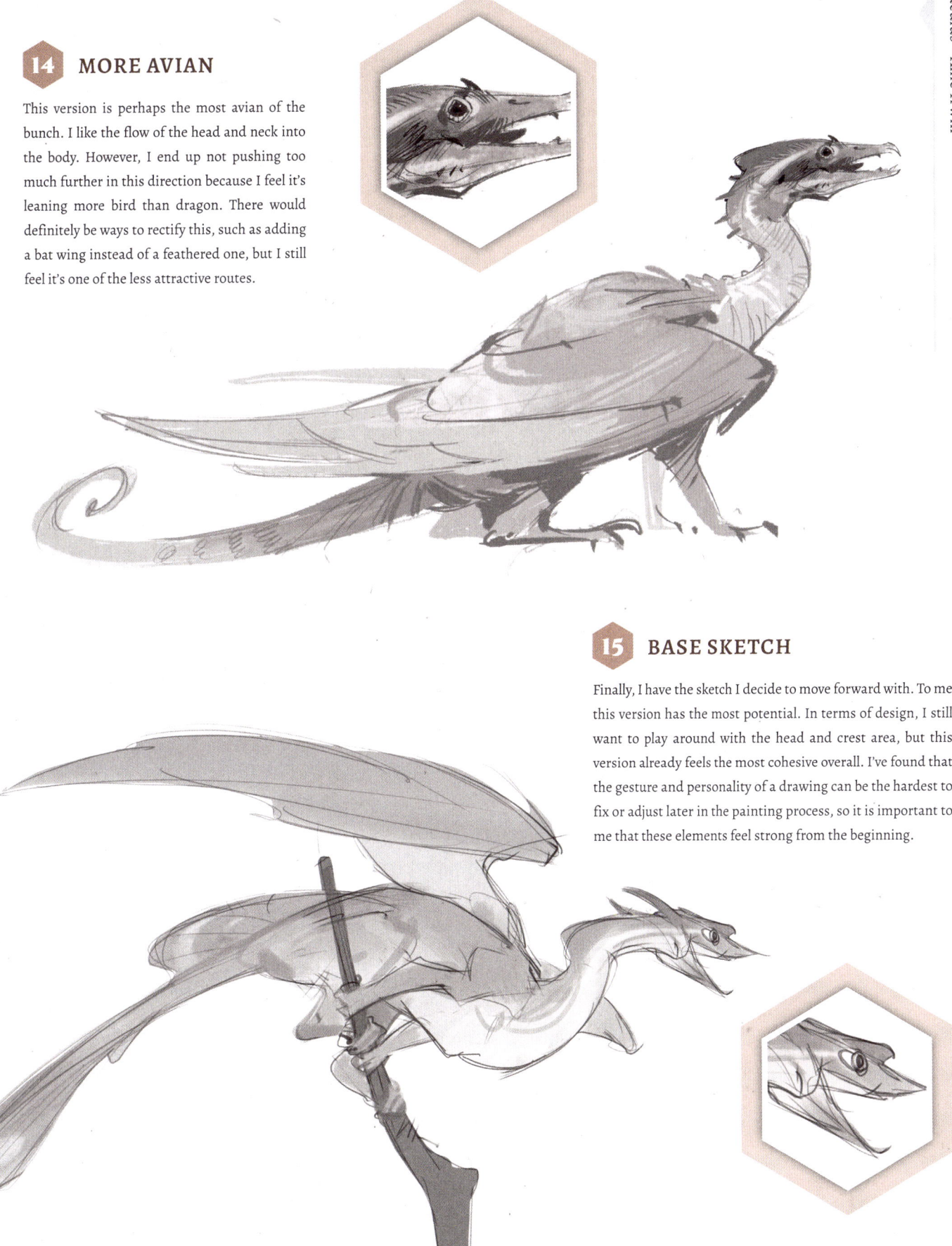

14 MORE AVIAN

This version is perhaps the most avian of the bunch. I like the flow of the head and neck into the body. However, I end up not pushing too much further in this direction because I feel it's leaning more bird than dragon. There would definitely be ways to rectify this, such as adding a bat wing instead of a feathered one, but I still feel it's one of the less attractive routes.

15 BASE SKETCH

Finally, I have the sketch I decide to move forward with. To me this version has the most potential. In terms of design, I still want to play around with the head and crest area, but this version already feels the most cohesive overall. I've found that the gesture and personality of a drawing can be the hardest to fix or adjust later in the painting process, so it is important to me that these elements feel strong from the beginning.

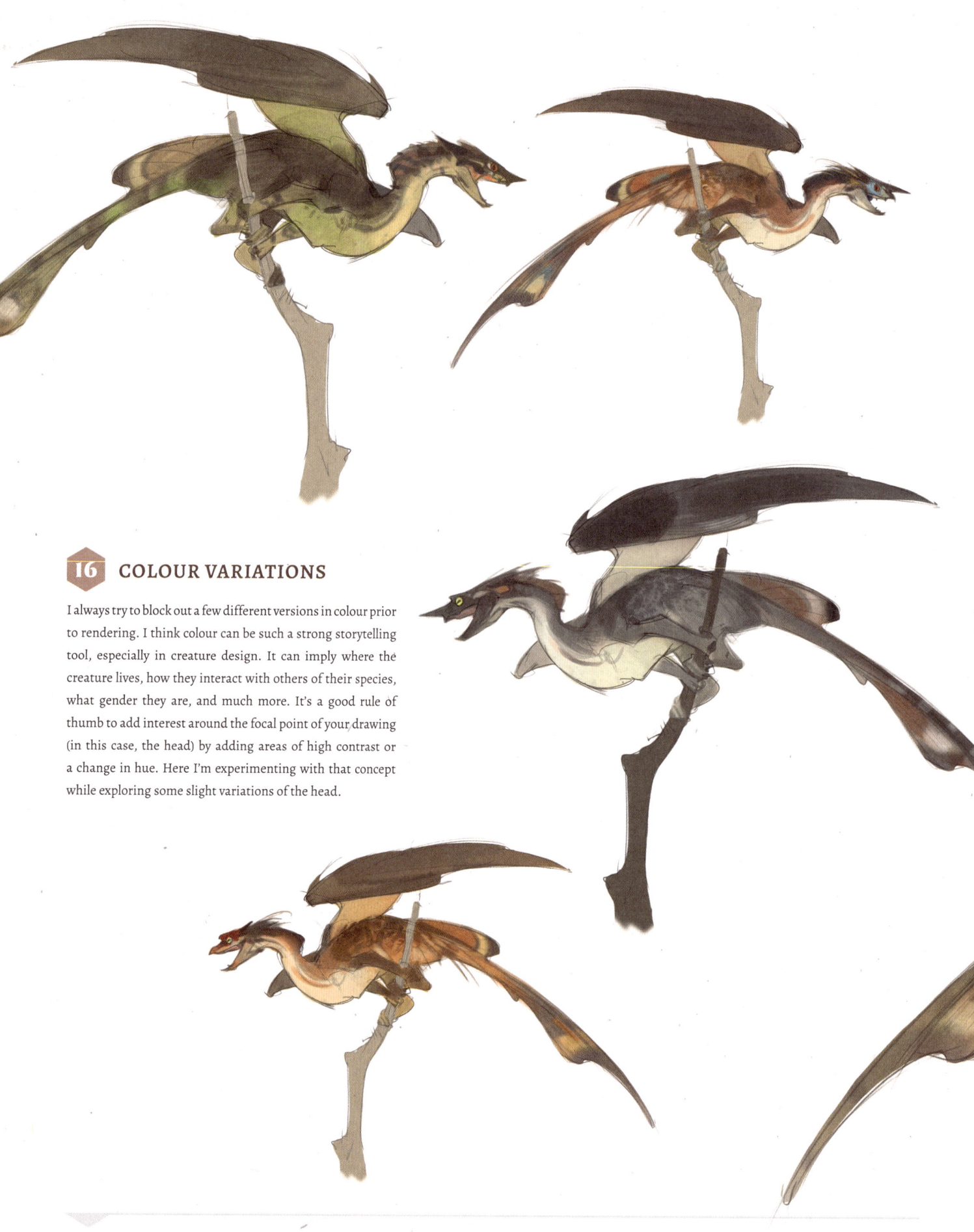

16   COLOUR VARIATIONS

I always try to block out a few different versions in colour prior to rendering. I think colour can be such a strong storytelling tool, especially in creature design. It can imply where the creature lives, how they interact with others of their species, what gender they are, and much more. It's a good rule of thumb to add interest around the focal point of your drawing (in this case, the head) by adding areas of high contrast or a change in hue. Here I'm experimenting with that concept while exploring some slight variations of the head.

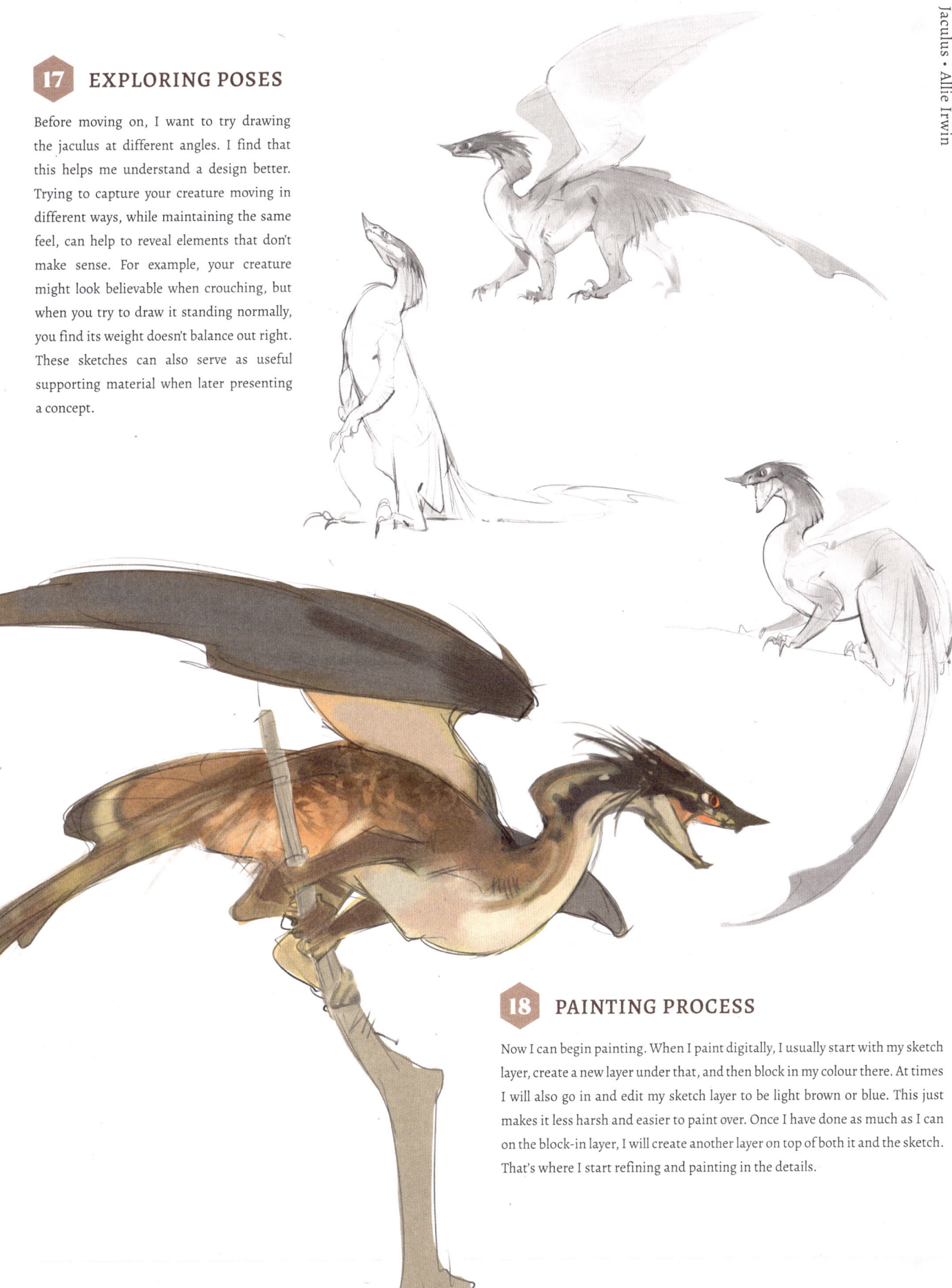

17 EXPLORING POSES

Before moving on, I want to try drawing the jaculus at different angles. I find that this helps me understand a design better. Trying to capture your creature moving in different ways, while maintaining the same feel, can help to reveal elements that don't make sense. For example, your creature might look believable when crouching, but when you try to draw it standing normally, you find its weight doesn't balance out right. These sketches can also serve as useful supporting material when later presenting a concept.

18 PAINTING PROCESS

Now I can begin painting. When I paint digitally, I usually start with my sketch layer, create a new layer under that, and then block in my colour there. At times I will also go in and edit my sketch layer to be light brown or blue. This just makes it less harsh and easier to paint over. Once I have done as much as I can on the block-in layer, I will create another layer on top of both it and the sketch. That's where I start refining and painting in the details.

141

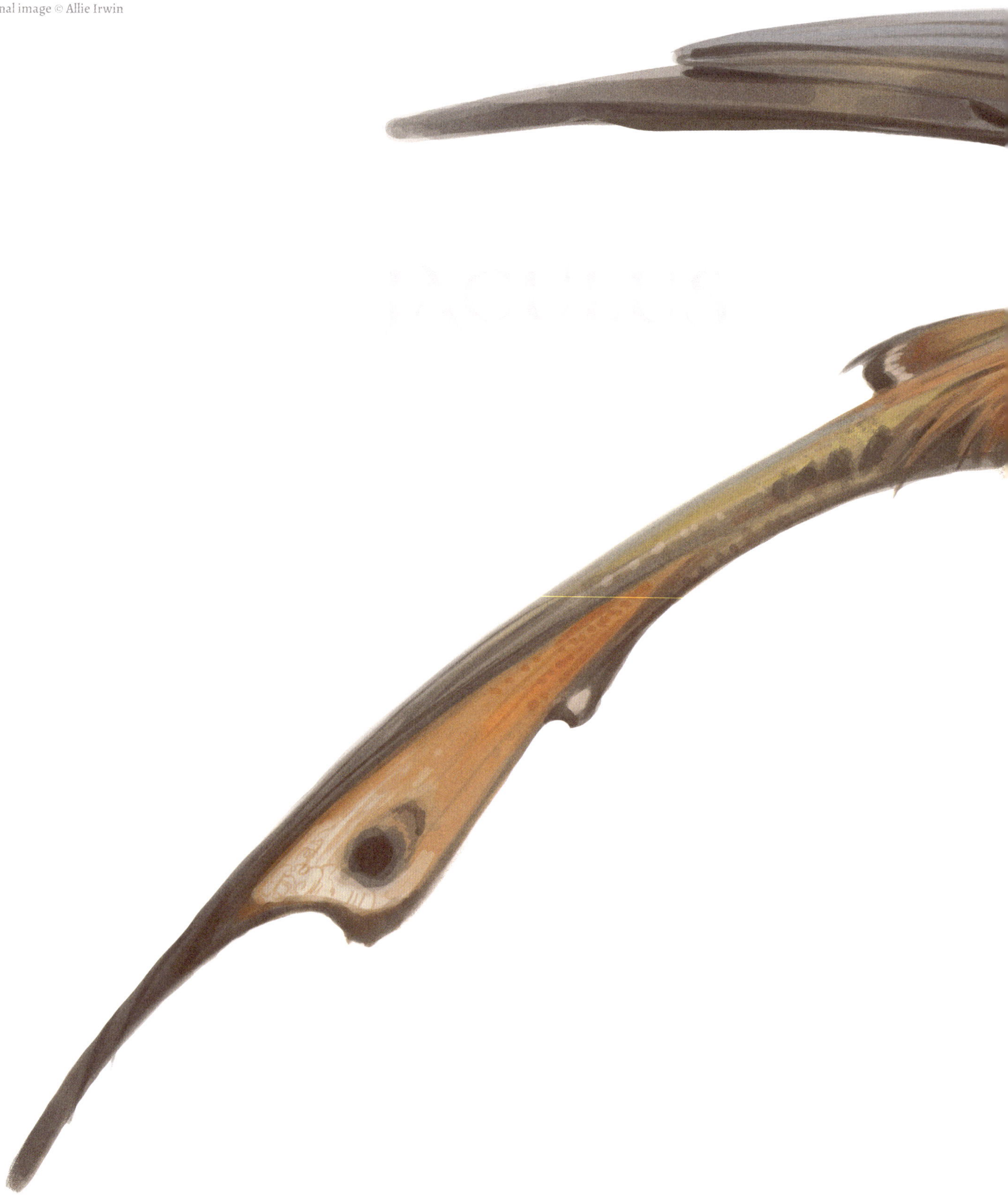

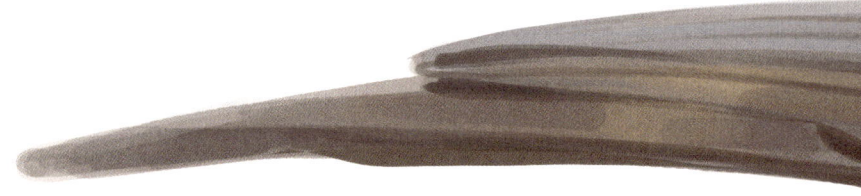

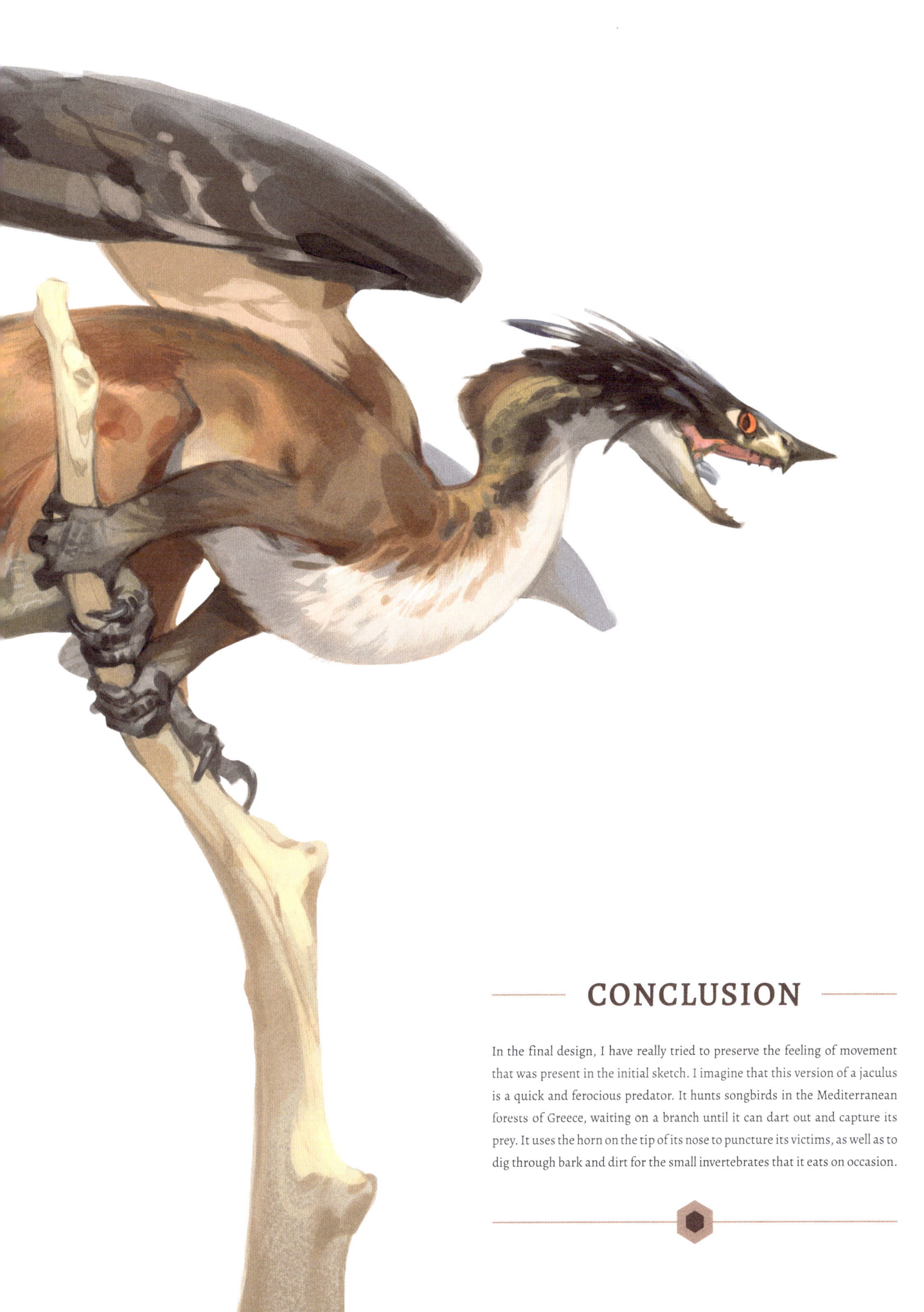

CONCLUSION

In the final design, I have really tried to preserve the feeling of movement that was present in the initial sketch. I imagine that this version of a jaculus is a quick and ferocious predator. It hunts songbirds in the Mediterranean forests of Greece, waiting on a branch until it can dart out and capture its prey. It uses the horn on the tip of its nose to puncture its victims, as well as to dig through bark and dirt for the small invertebrates that it eats on occasion.

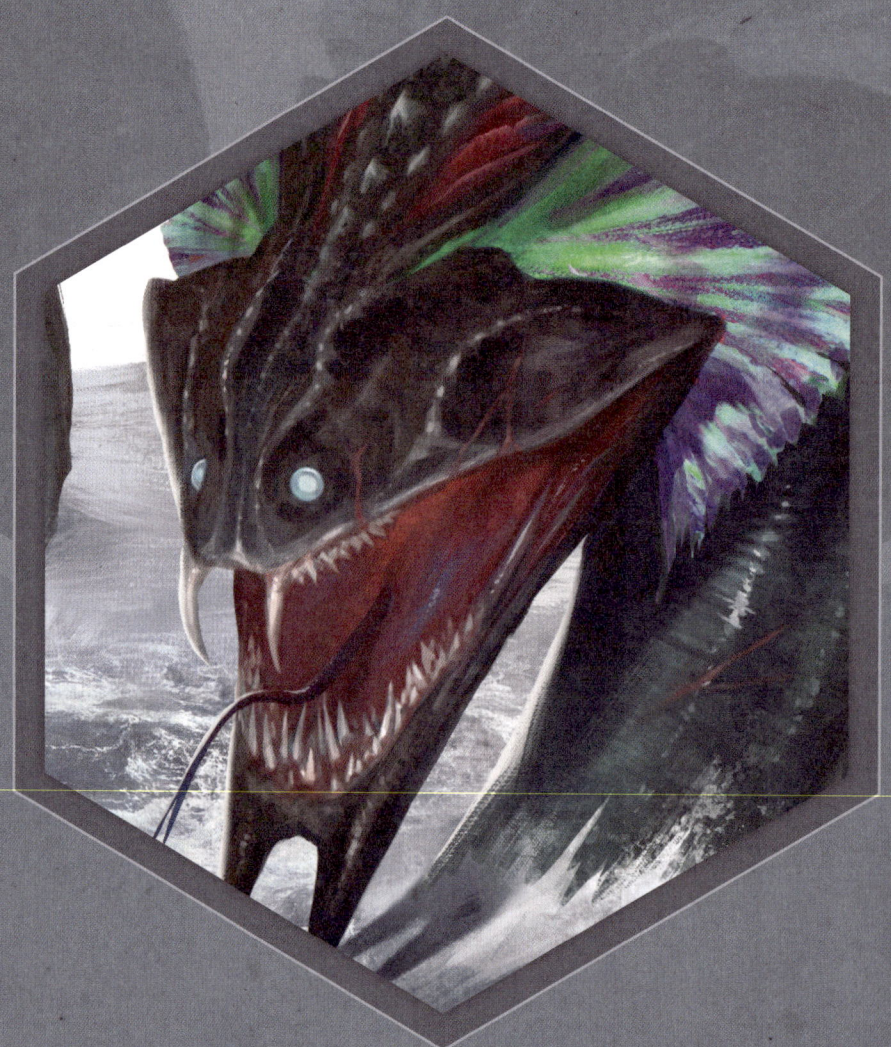

JÖRMUNGANDR

Also known as the Midgard Serpent, Jörmungandr is an enormous sea serpent from Norse mythology, an offspring of Loki cast into the ocean by Odin. Lying underneath the waves, he surrounds the Earth with his body and holds his tail in his mouth, and is the subject of multiple encounters with Thor, who tries to fish or lift him from the ocean. Jörmungandr eventually releases his tail for Ragnarök, the great battle at the end of the world. During this cataclysmic conflict between gods and jötnar, Jörmungandr is slain by Thor, but not before fatally wounding the god with his poison.

GIOVANNI LAZZARI

Final image © Giovanni Lazzari

SKETCHBOOK

I start with sketches in my sketchbook, just exploring different ideas for aquatic creatures. It's important to find a broad array of options beyond just a generic 'giant snake'. Exploring more widely will help me find a more unique design that still fits the brief and the function of this creature. Could Jörmungandr resemble a crocodile, an eel, or some kind of plesiosaur?

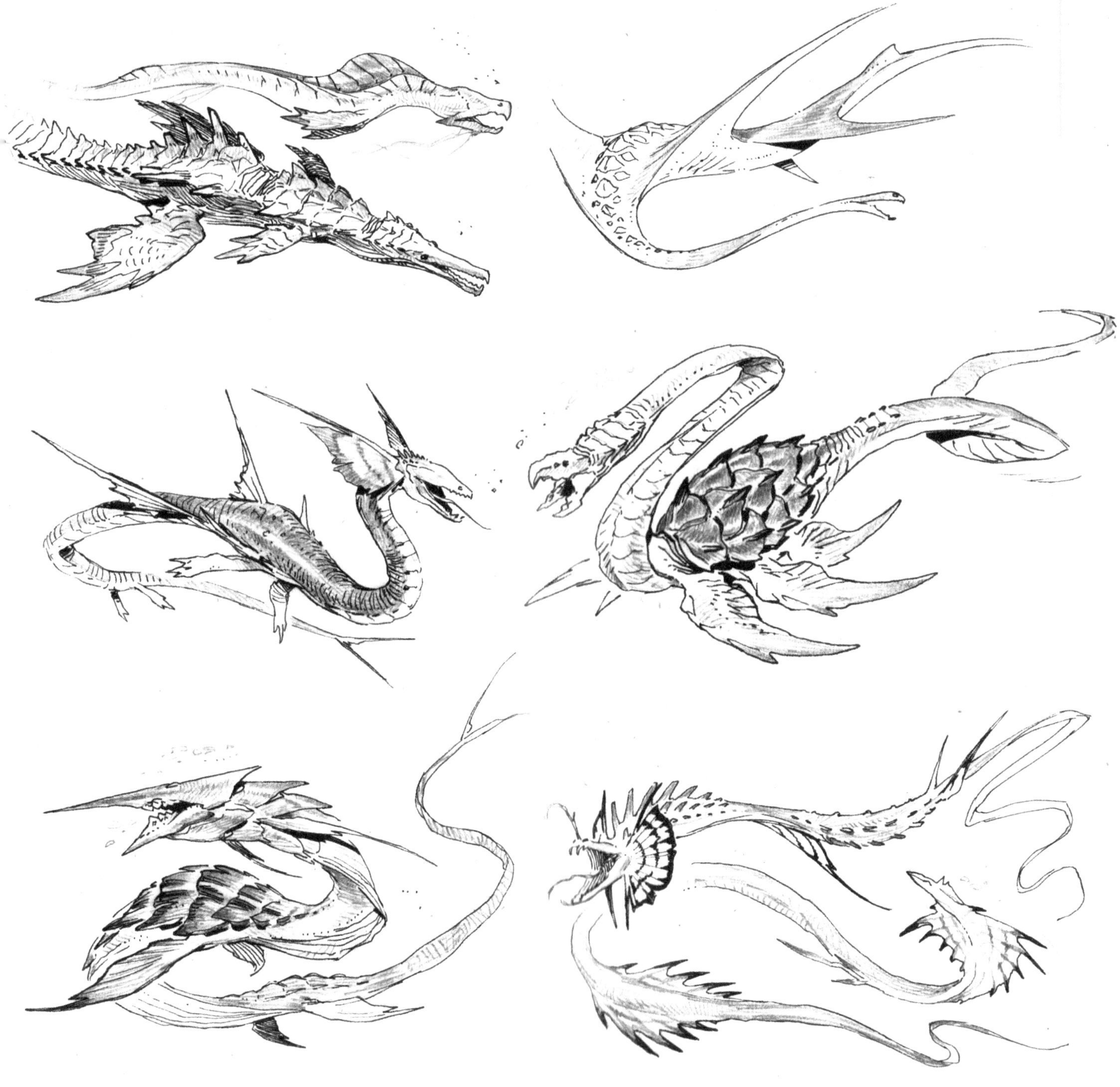

02 HEAD SKETCHES

I make separate pages of head sketches, exploring different options inspired by a range of reptiles and deep-sea fish. This stage is important because a character or creature's head is the first place the audience will look. It's often a good idea to design it separately like this, focusing purely on this part of the design.

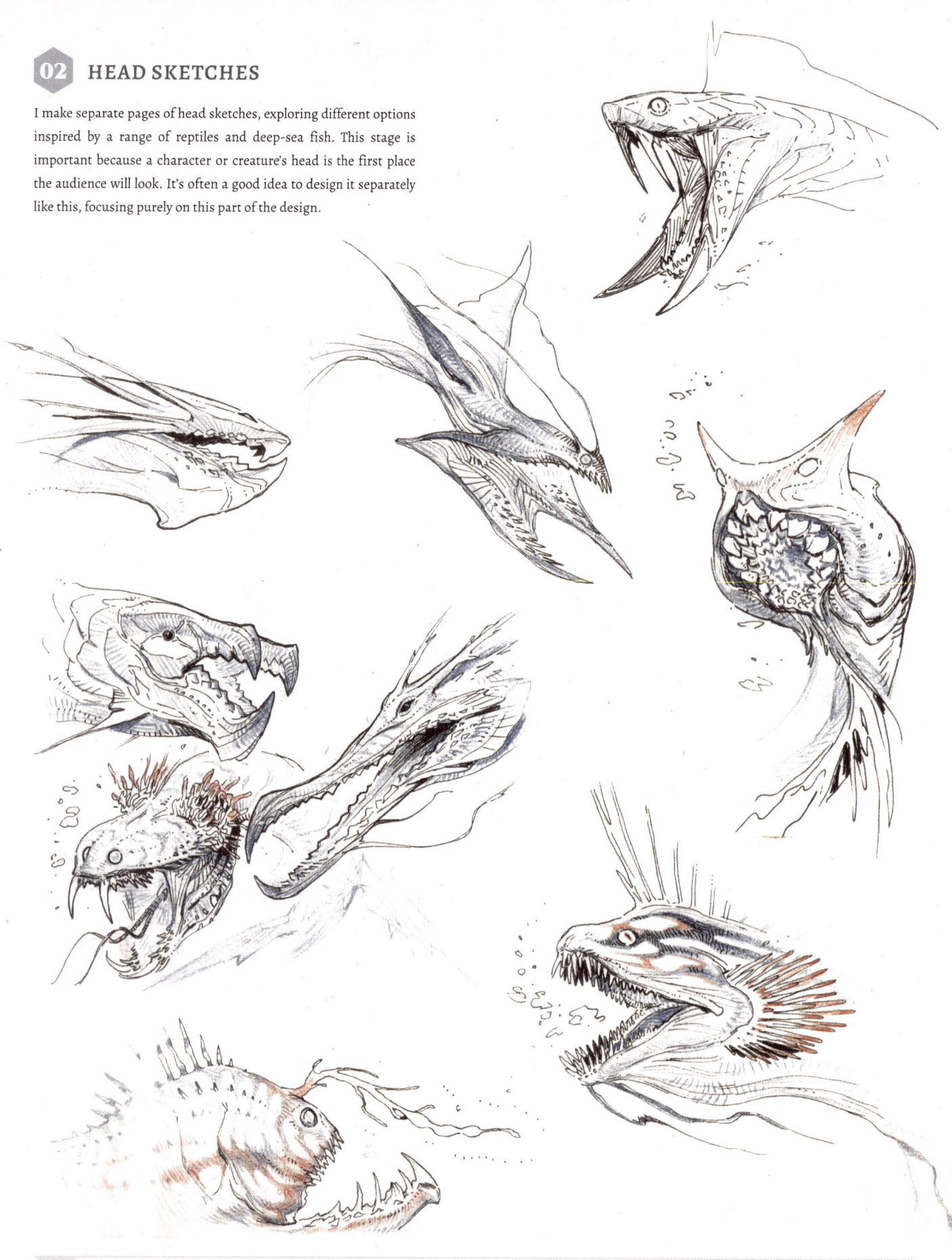

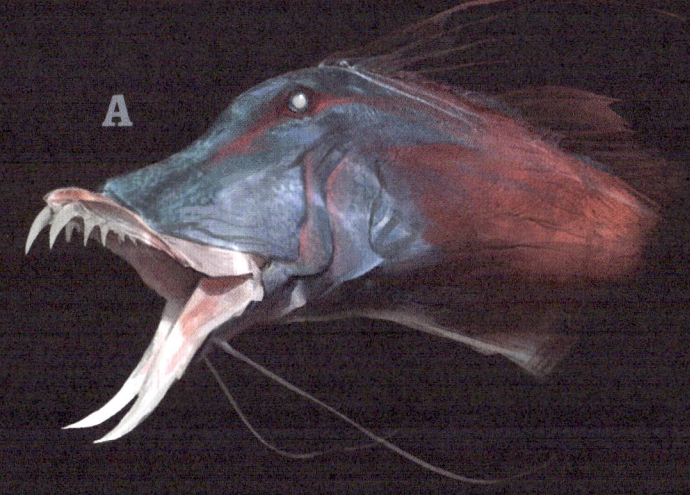

A

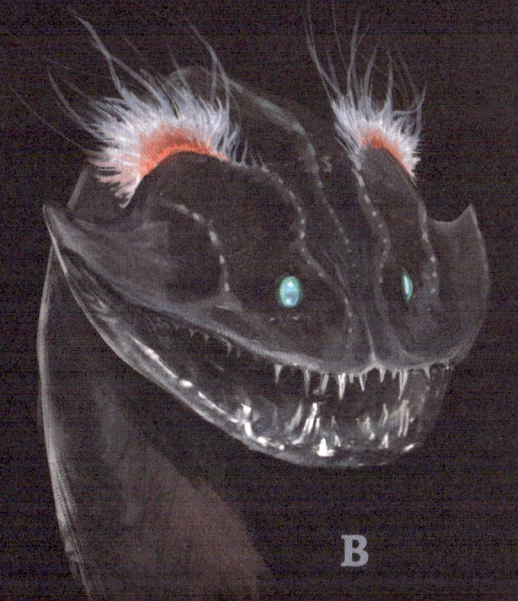

B

03 HEAD CONCEPTS

Moving into digital software, I paint a few head sketches testing different forms, colours, and textures. I want to continue leaning away from just designing a giant snake, so I go for more unorthodox interpretations based on deep-sea fish, crocodiles, and various aquatic creatures. Option B is similar to a dragonfish, with a black body, small eyes, and needle-like teeth, and feels like something ancient that lives deep in the ocean. The orca-inspired option C could feel really massive and weighty, while option D's crocodilian look is more classically like a dragon.

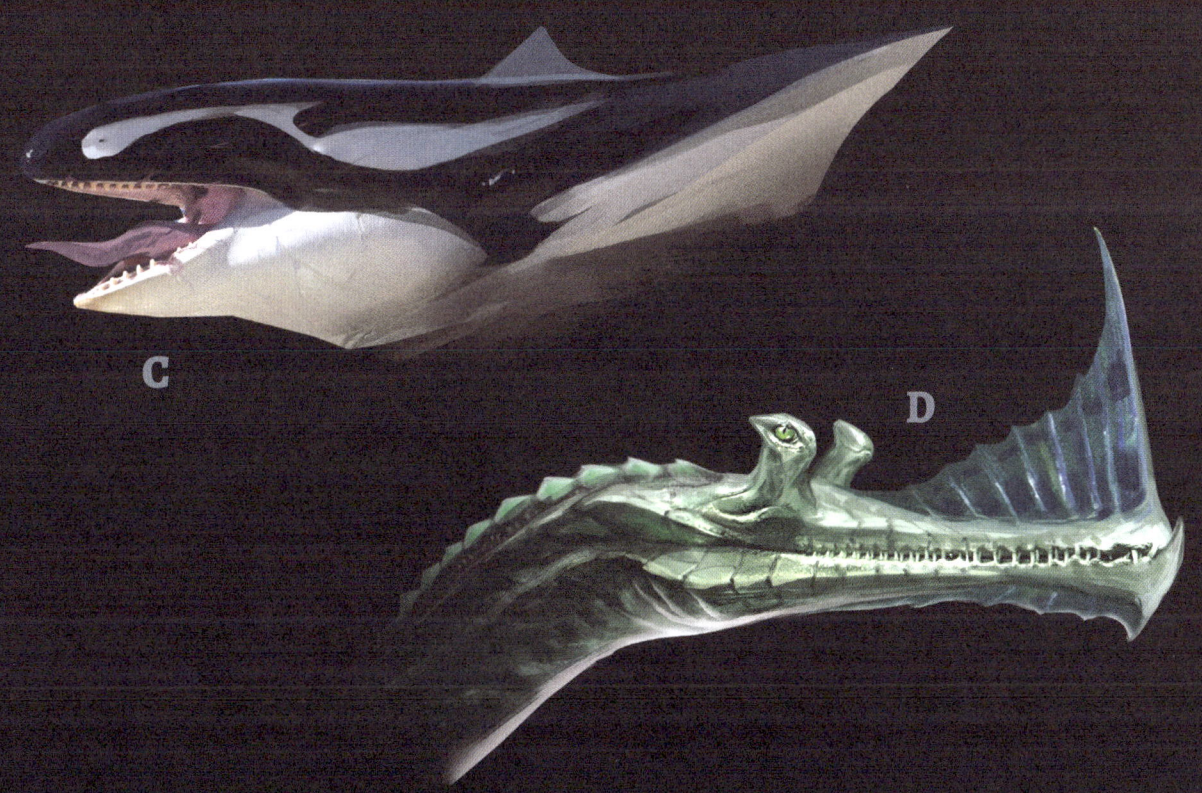

C

D

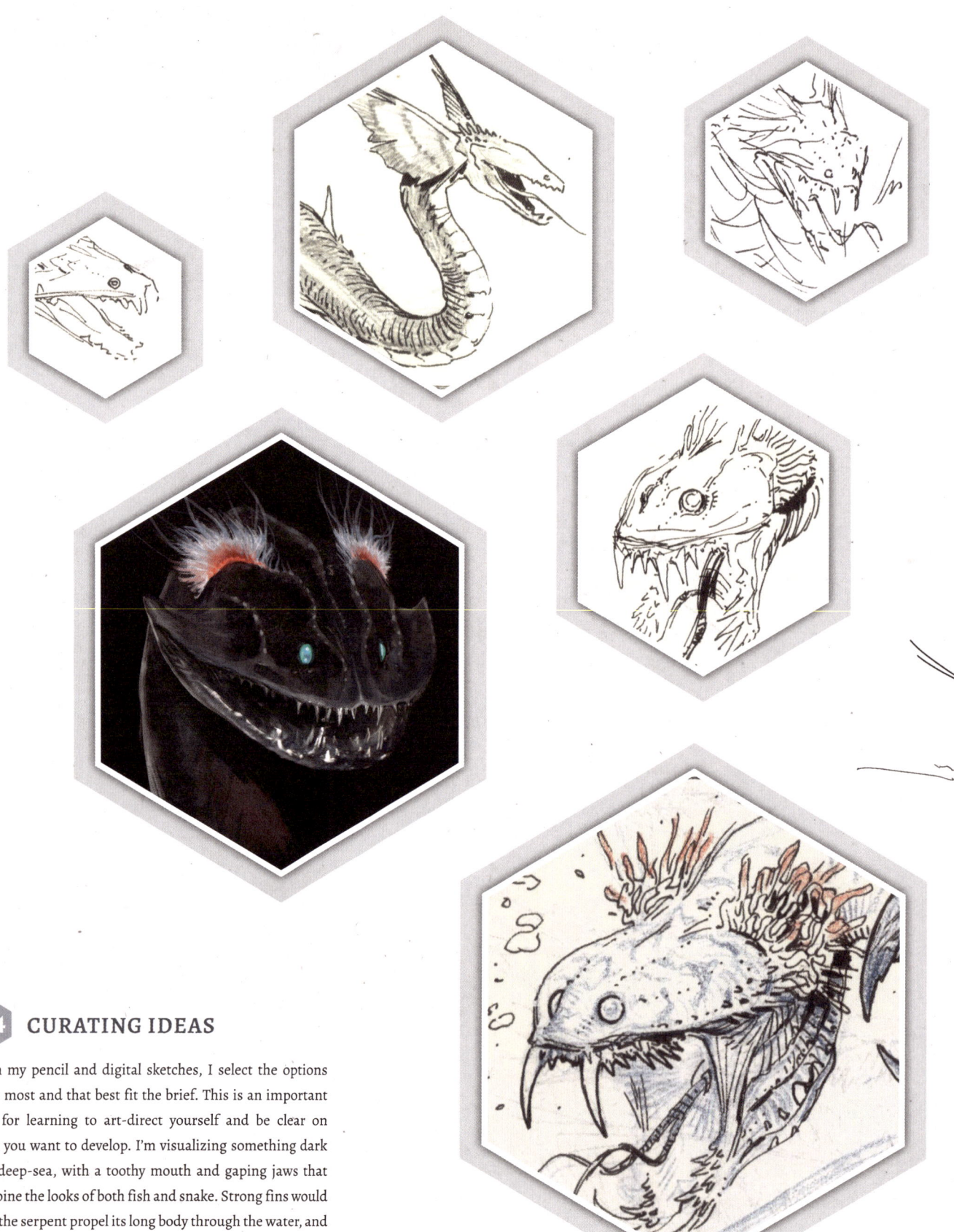

04 CURATING IDEAS

From my pencil and digital sketches, I select the options I like most and that best fit the brief. This is an important step for learning to art-direct yourself and be clear on what you want to develop. I'm visualizing something dark and deep-sea, with a toothy mouth and gaping jaws that combine the looks of both fish and snake. Strong fins would help the serpent propel its long body through the water, and create a fearsome display when it breaks the surface.

SKETCHBOOK TO DIGITAL

I take one of the small pencil thumbnails and roughly elaborate on it in my drawing software, fleshing out an idea for a pose and composition. I want to include the ocean's surface in my final presentation of the creature, but still show its design clearly, not hiding the underwater portions of its body. A half-submerged 'cutaway' view seems like a good way to achieve that.

06 BASE SKETCH

This is when I begin to establish the final design. I make another sketch over my thumbnail, cleaner but still rough, focusing on establishing a dynamic pose and clarifying the elements of the design. My Jörmungandr has a wide, gaping mouth like a deep-sea predator. The poisonous fangs and forked tongue of a snake keep a reptilian 'serpent' aspect, and sharp fins add direction and a more dangerous look to the design. I fill the sketch with greyscale tones to help create masks and selections during the colouring stages.

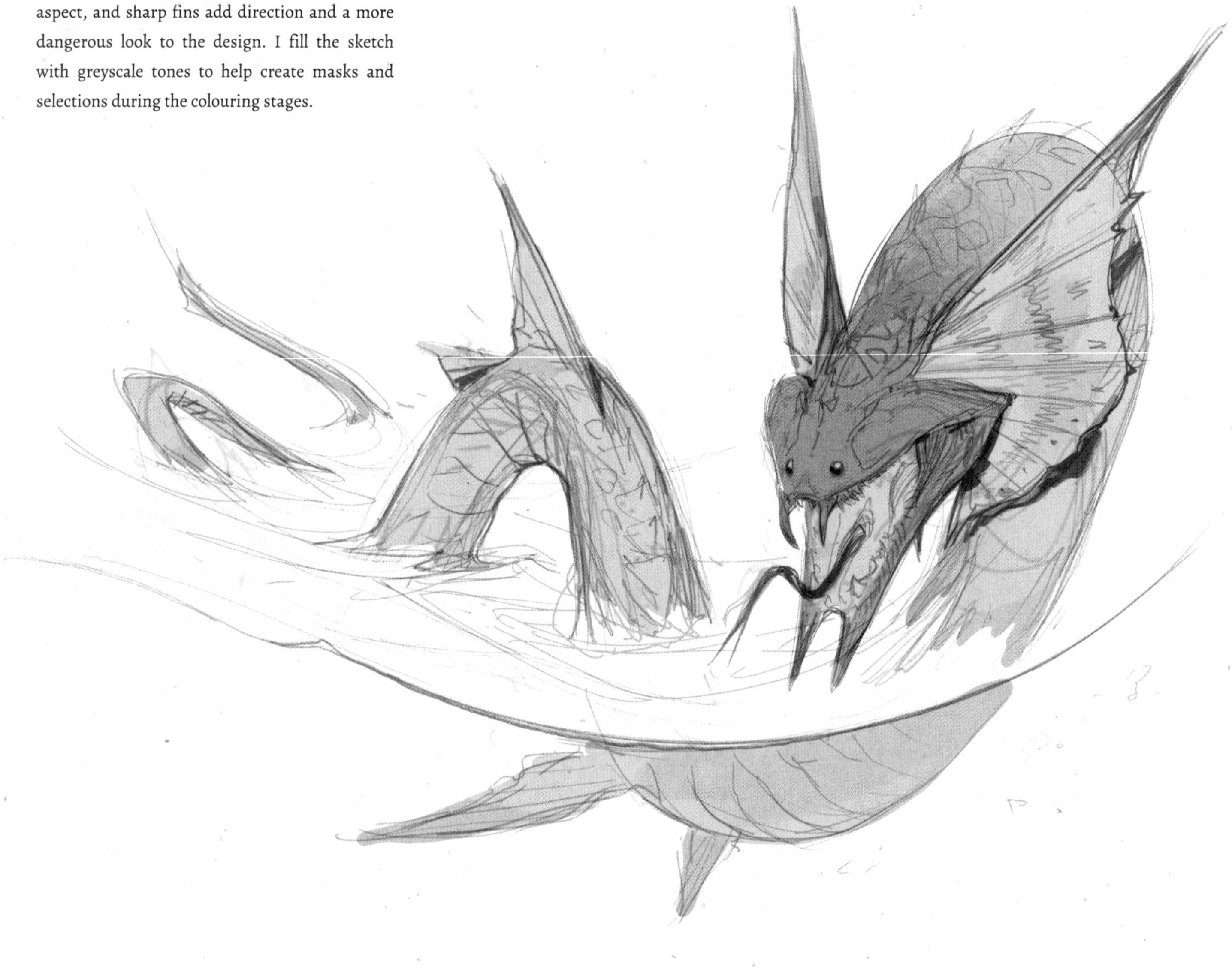

07 TEXTURE & COLOUR

I fill out the base shape of the creature with a combination of textures and rough painting – just enough to create a realistic base for painting in Photoshop, with no lighting details or environment yet. I want the serpent to have dark, fish-like scales – ridges of bony scutes to add structure and detail to the body, and brighter colours on the fins and frills.

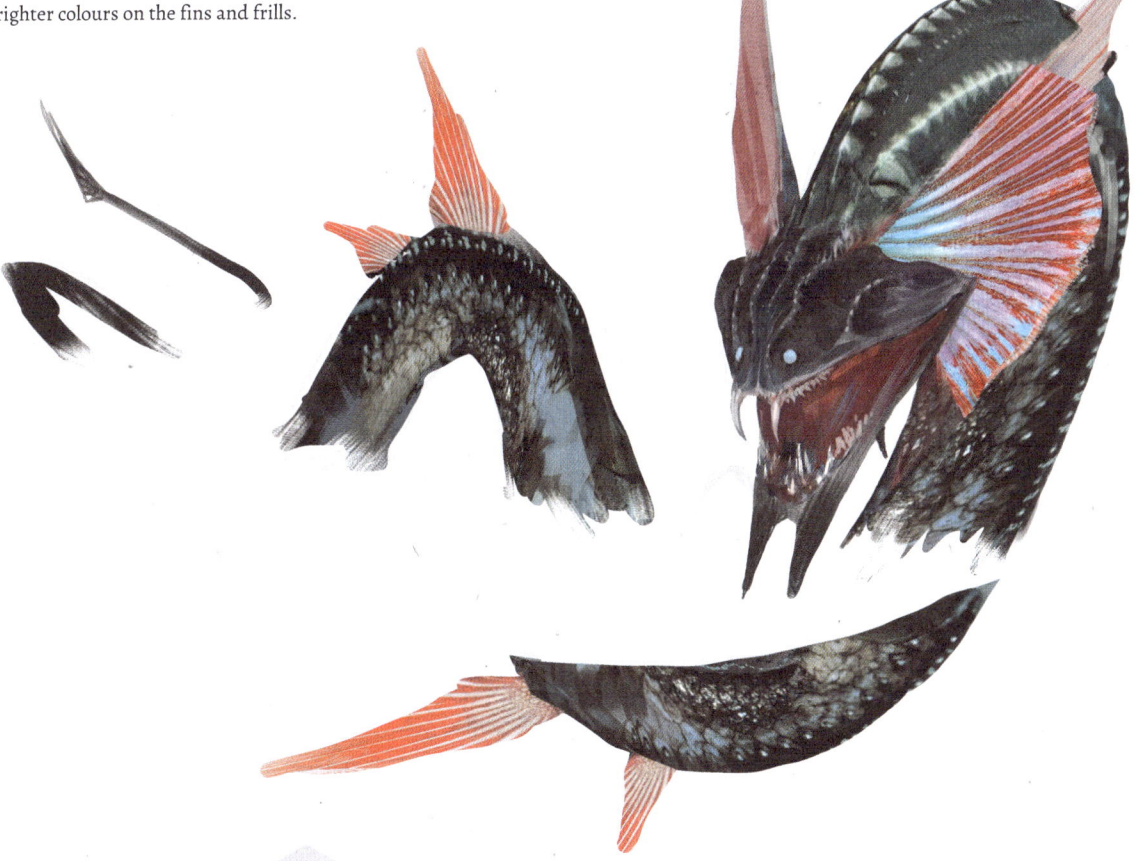

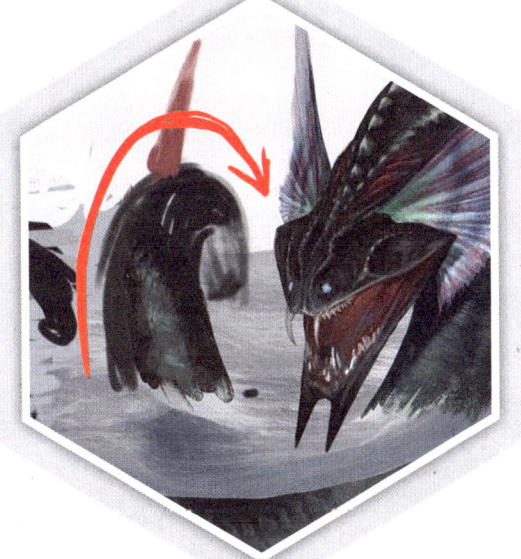

08 'HEY, HOW ABOUT THIS?'

I make a start on painting the creature, but pause to ask my friend Gabe (featured elsewhere in this book, on page 66) for feedback on the piece so far, as it's very important to get another opinion. An outsider will see things you cannot, and may even suggest new ideas that you would never have considered. In this case, Gabe sends me a paintover suggesting a more dynamic twisting pose, which adds more length to the serpent and depth to the whole scene.

STARTING TO RENDER

I continue to render the creature, cleaning up, altering, and adding to the base. As I paint in the details and surface textures, I go for a smoother look with smaller, less-visible scales, to emphasize Jörmungandr's great size and slippery aquatic look. The bright red fins are toned down to a green and purple palette, which looks more harmonious but still has an element of vibrant, poisonous colour. Red gills echo the colour of the serpent's open mouth and highlight its fish-based nature.

 ADDING WATER

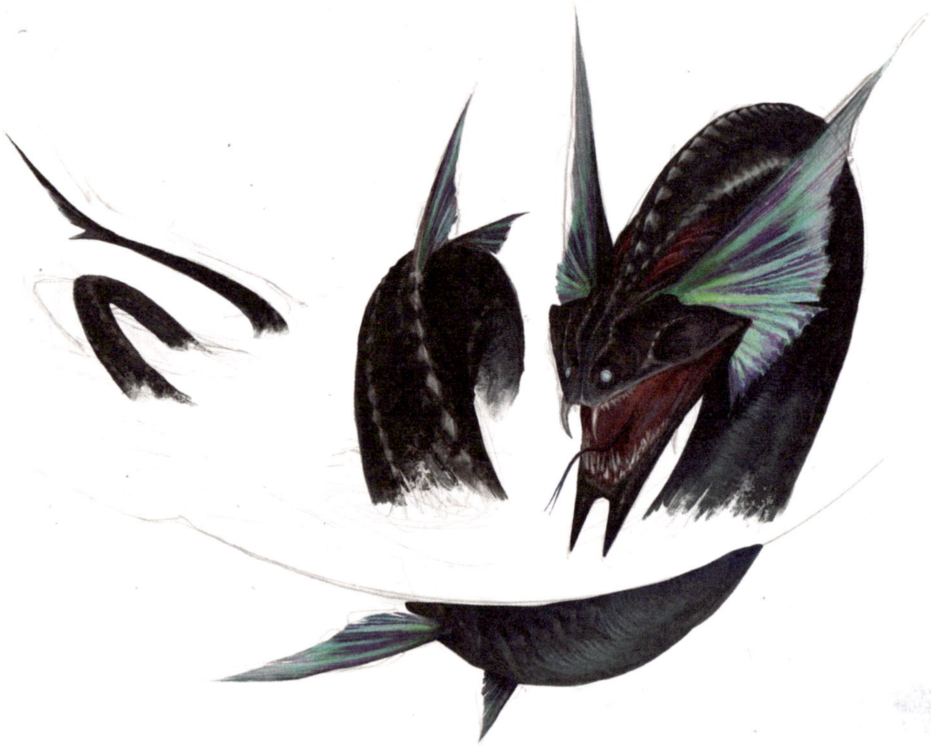

I paint the surface of the water for context, trying to create the impression of large, crashing ocean waves for scale. The sides and distant background dissolve into brushstrokes that will give the final image a painterly finish. At this stage, the design is now developed enough that I can hide the rough sketch layer.

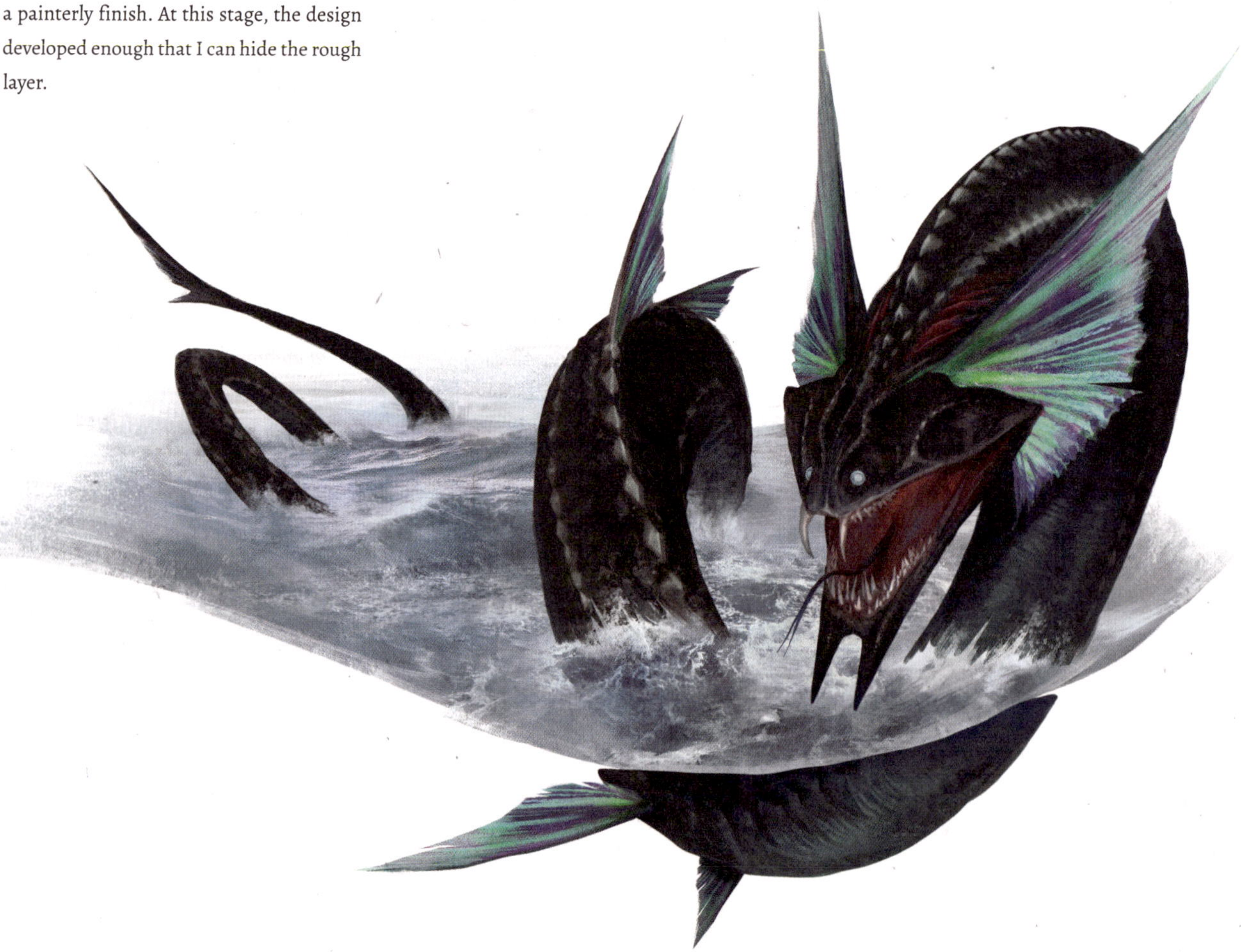

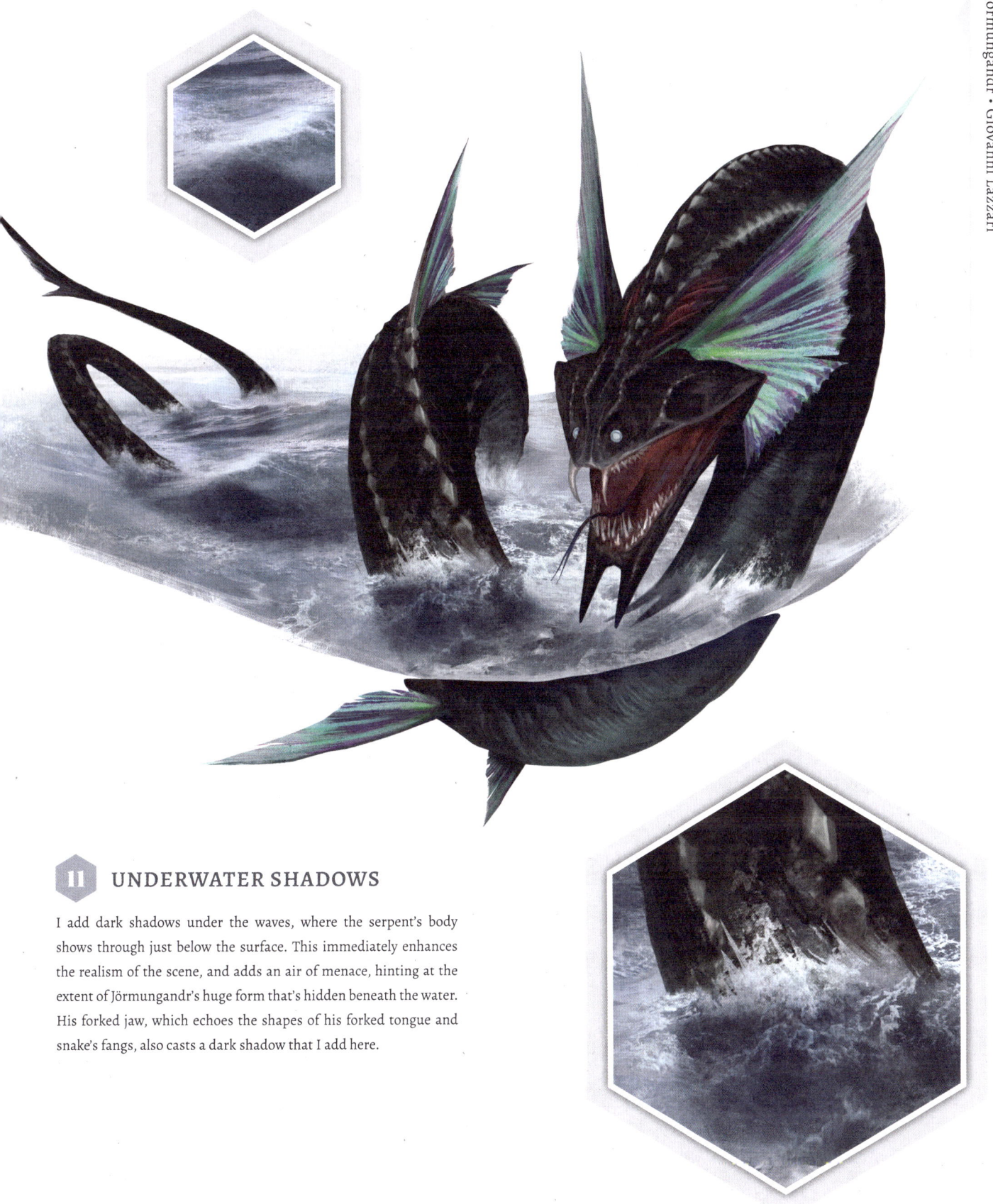

11 UNDERWATER SHADOWS

I add dark shadows under the waves, where the serpent's body shows through just below the surface. This immediately enhances the realism of the scene, and adds an air of menace, hinting at the extent of Jörmungandr's huge form that's hidden beneath the water. His forked jaw, which echoes the shapes of his forked tongue and snake's fangs, also casts a dark shadow that I add here.

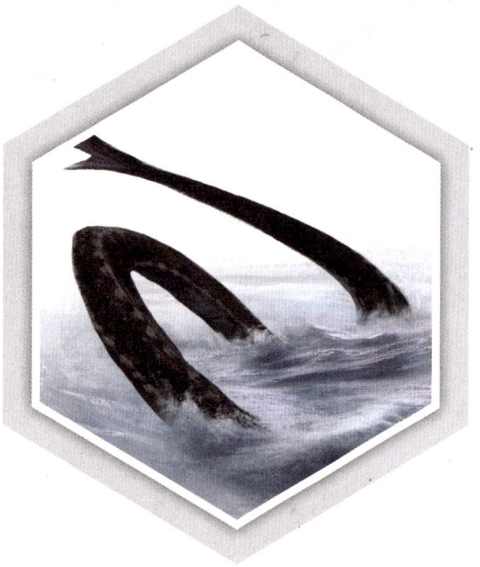

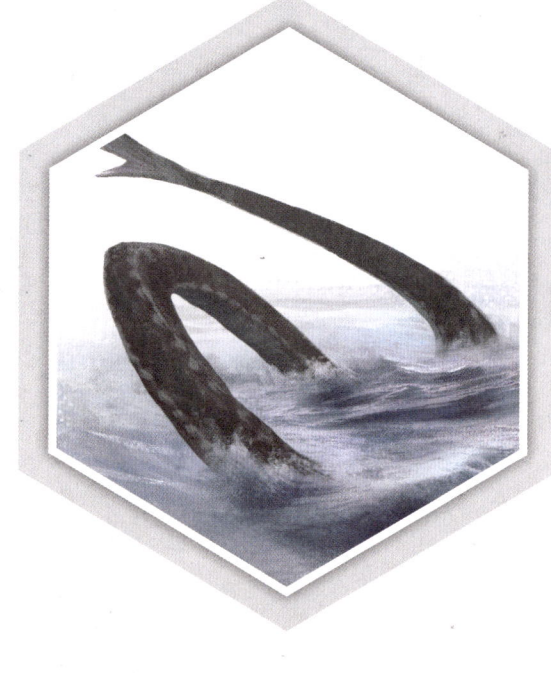

 ## ATMOSPHERIC FOG

A subtle volumetric fog helps to suggest the large scale of the creature – its huge body is literally fading into the fog, the same way a distant environment would. It's a very simple addition, but tells the viewer so much about the size of the creature, as well as adding a more realistic atmosphere to the scene. This massive creature rising violently from the water would cause spray and particles to fill the air, creating a misty effect.

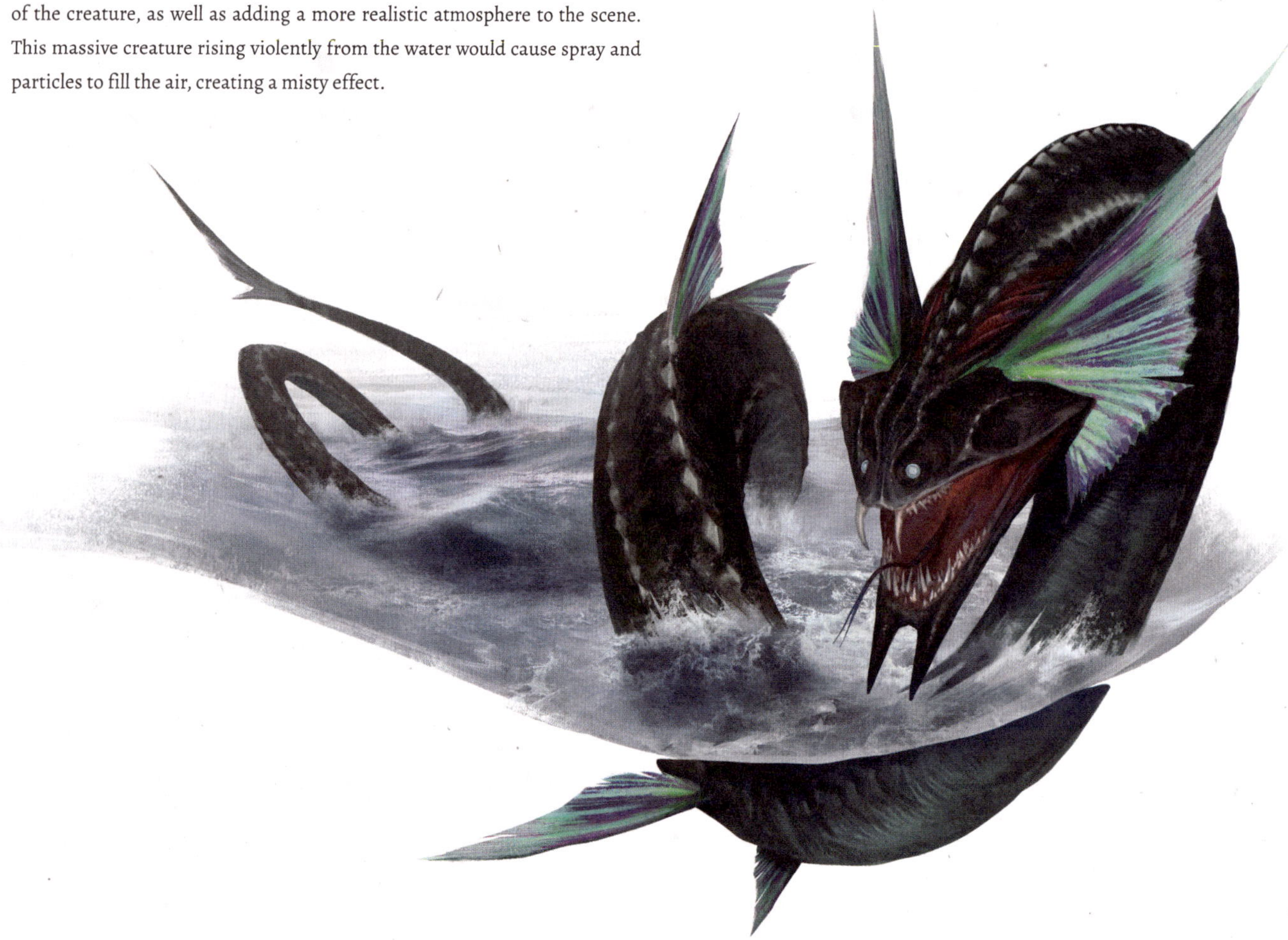

RIM LIGHTING

I add a subtle rim light on some areas of the serpent, helping its curved body and head to stand out from the environment. Like the fog, this is a small and subtle detail but makes a design much more believable and at home in the lighting, depth, and atmosphere of its surroundings. Use rim lighting in moderation, though, or your design will lose its sense of form.

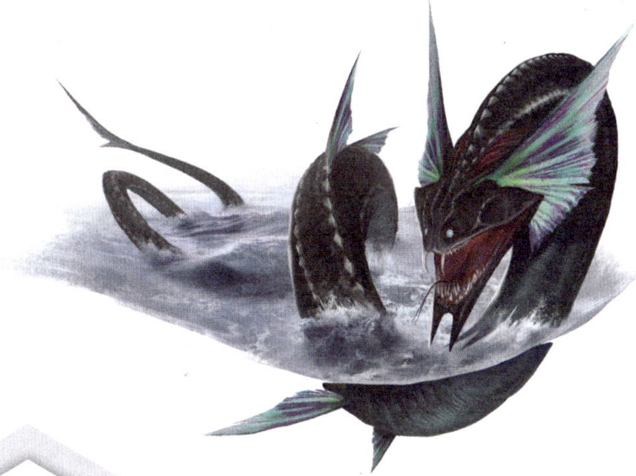

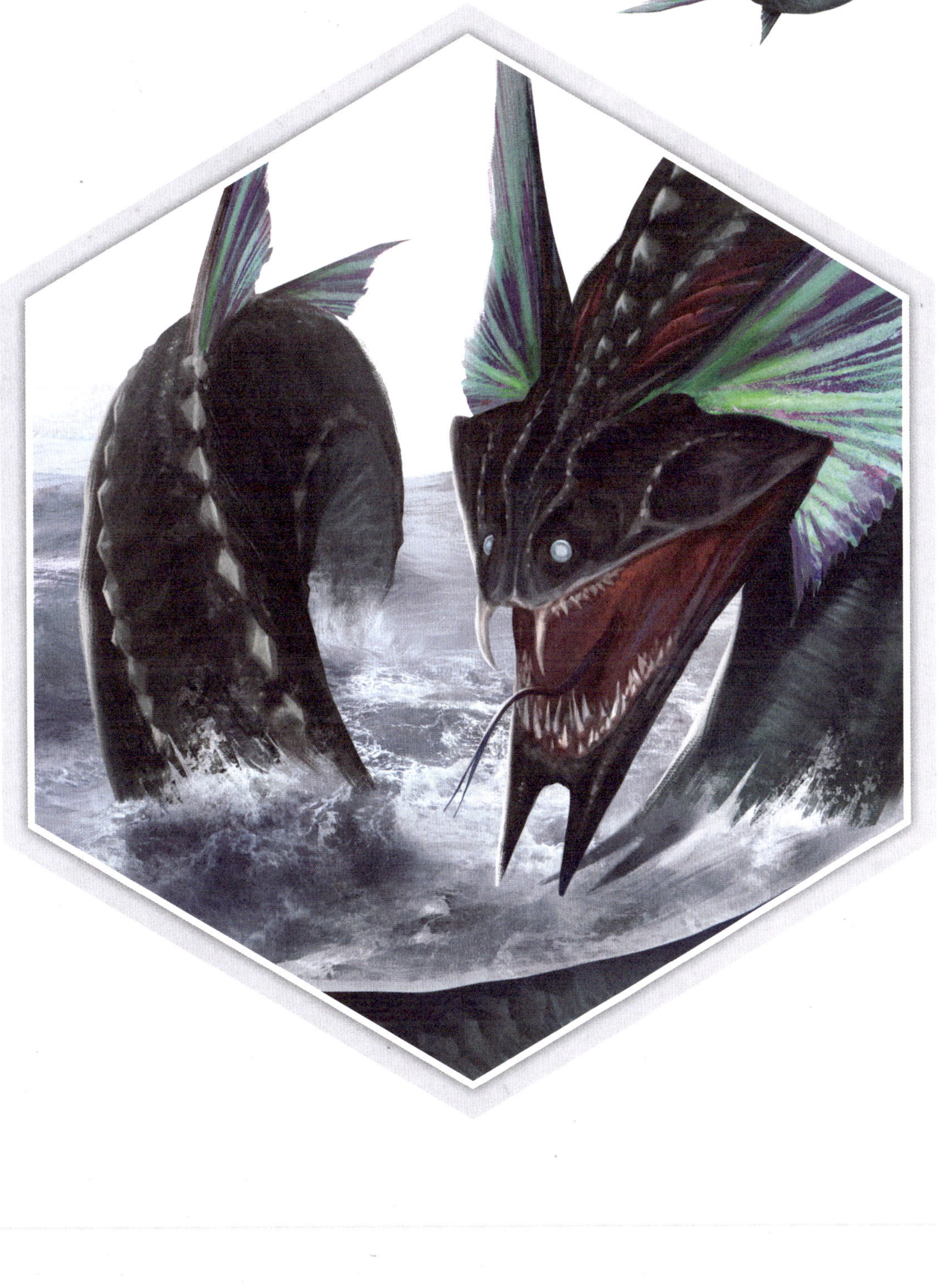

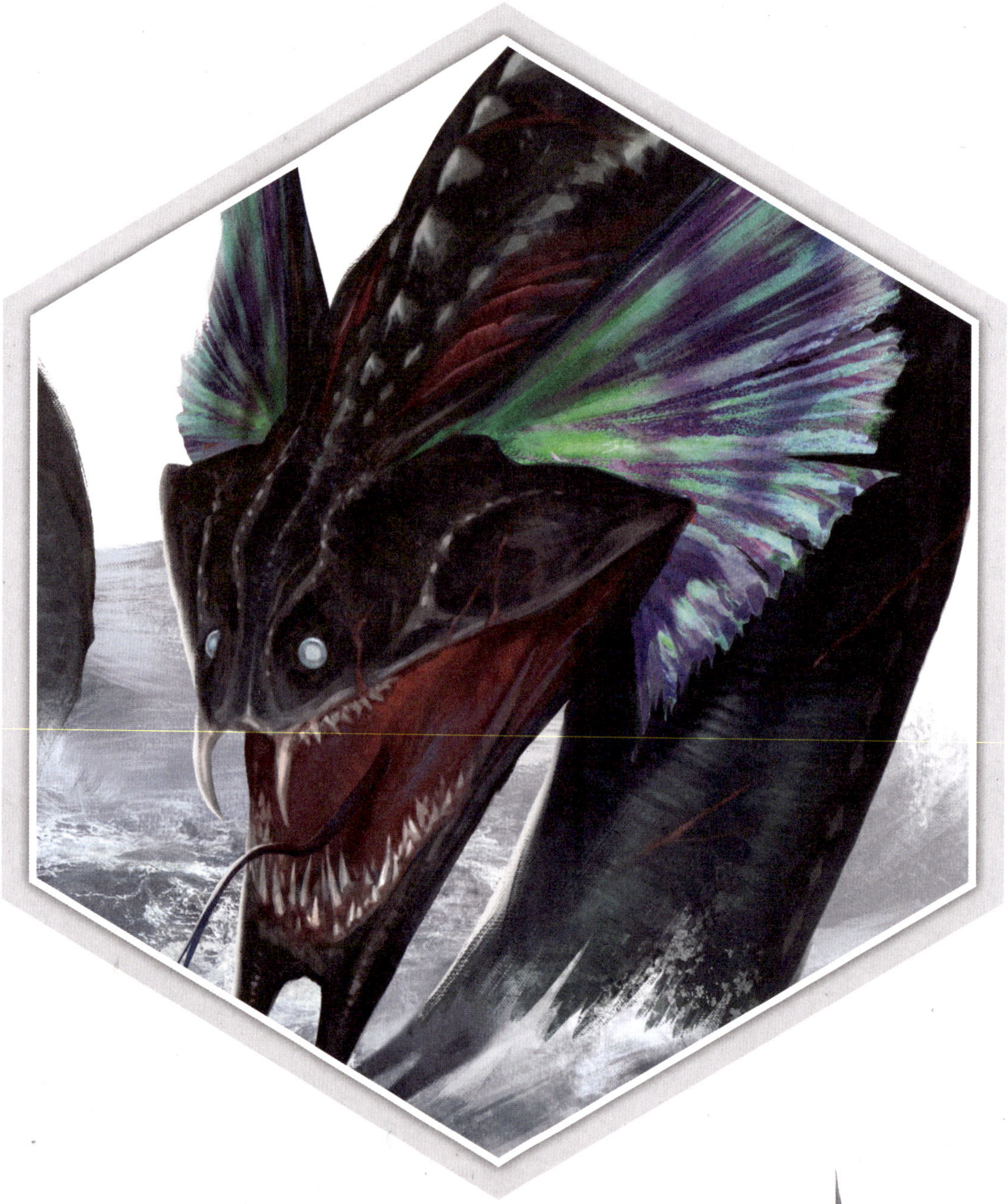

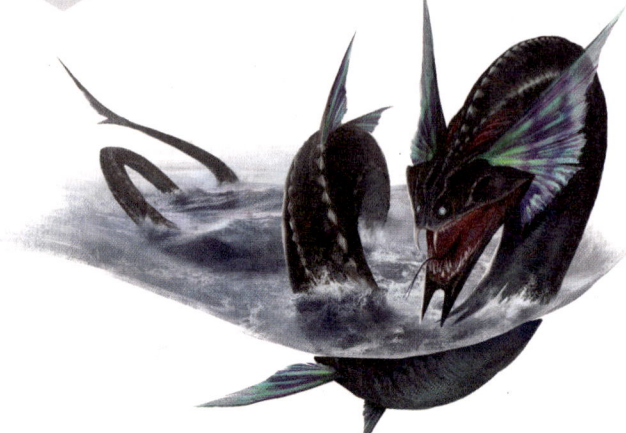

FINER DETAILS

Now I add more detail to the fins and various other small features, such as scars, that enhance the realism of the creature, making it less perfect and more worn. When designing a specific single creature such as Jörmungandr, details like these help to show its individual qualities, such as its age and reminders of past conflicts.

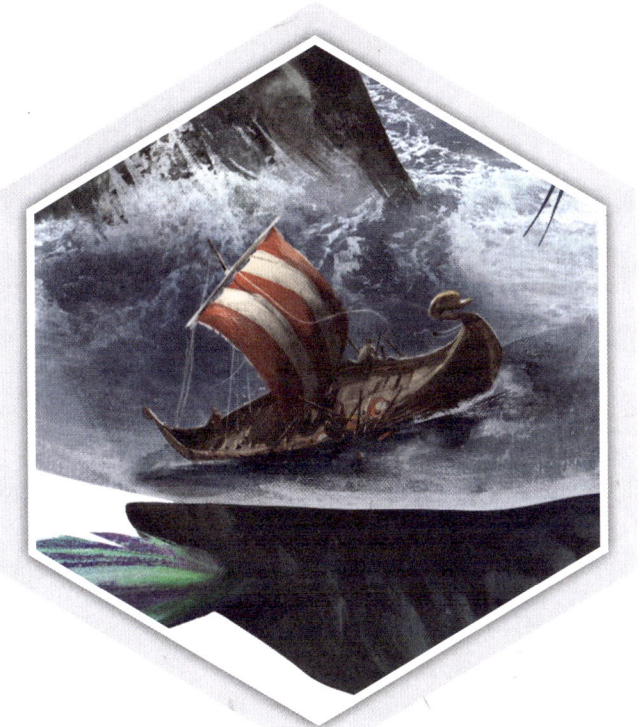

15 SHIP IN PERIL

I add a Viking longship, both for scale and to show a clear connection to Norse mythology. The human crew and wooden ship are tiny and fragile as they're dwarfed by Jörmungandr and the crashing waves raised by his body. This addition elevates the final design by bringing in an element of narrative to which the viewer can connect.

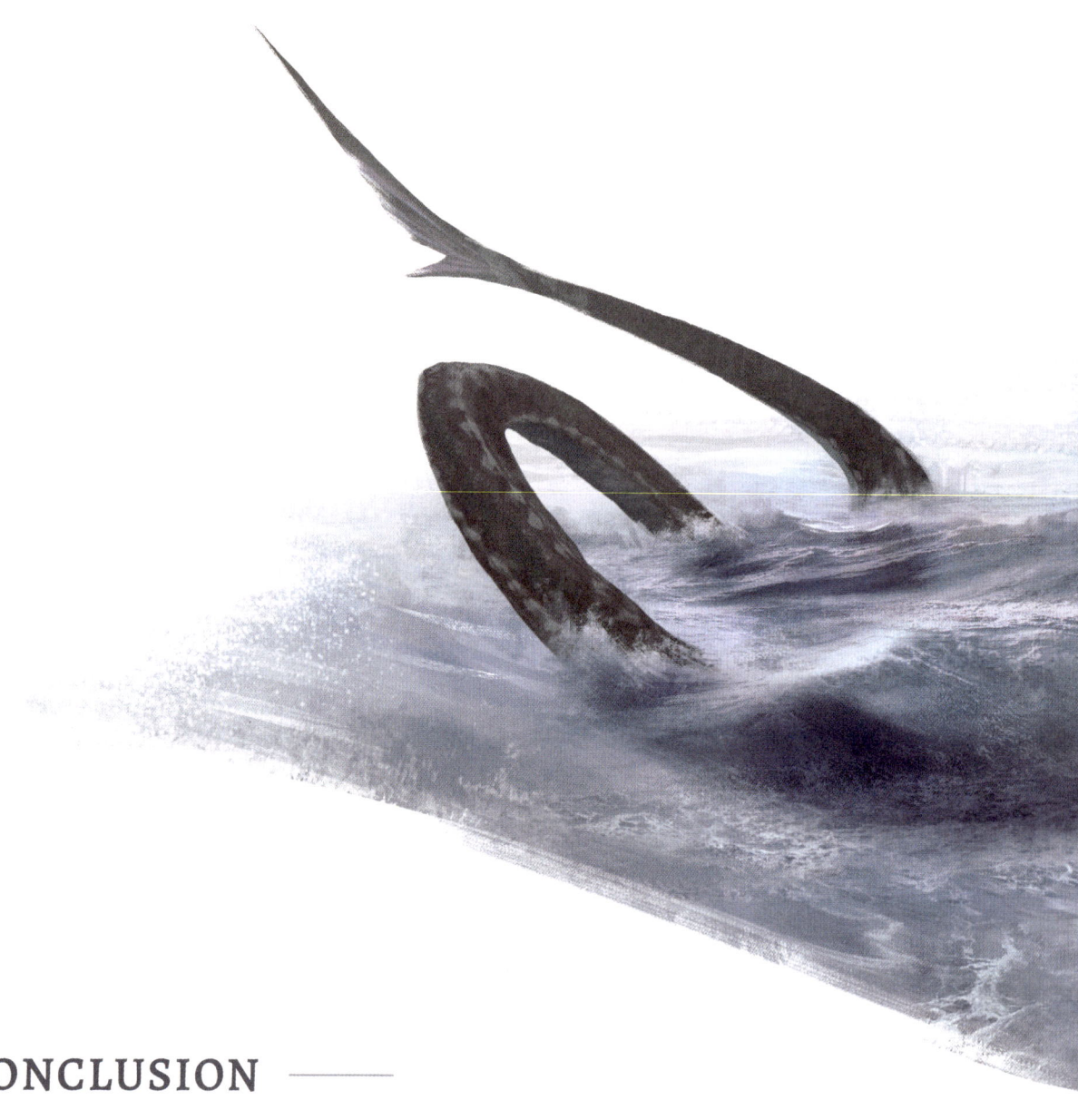

CONCLUSION

The final touch is adding highlights to make the serpent's skin seem shiny and wet from the water, and to add extra definition to its bony skull and thick coils. And with that, Jörmungandr is complete. The finished design looks the part of an ancient, primordial sea monster that could battle a Norse god, while also bringing in some more unusual inspirations and features that put my own twist on the myth.

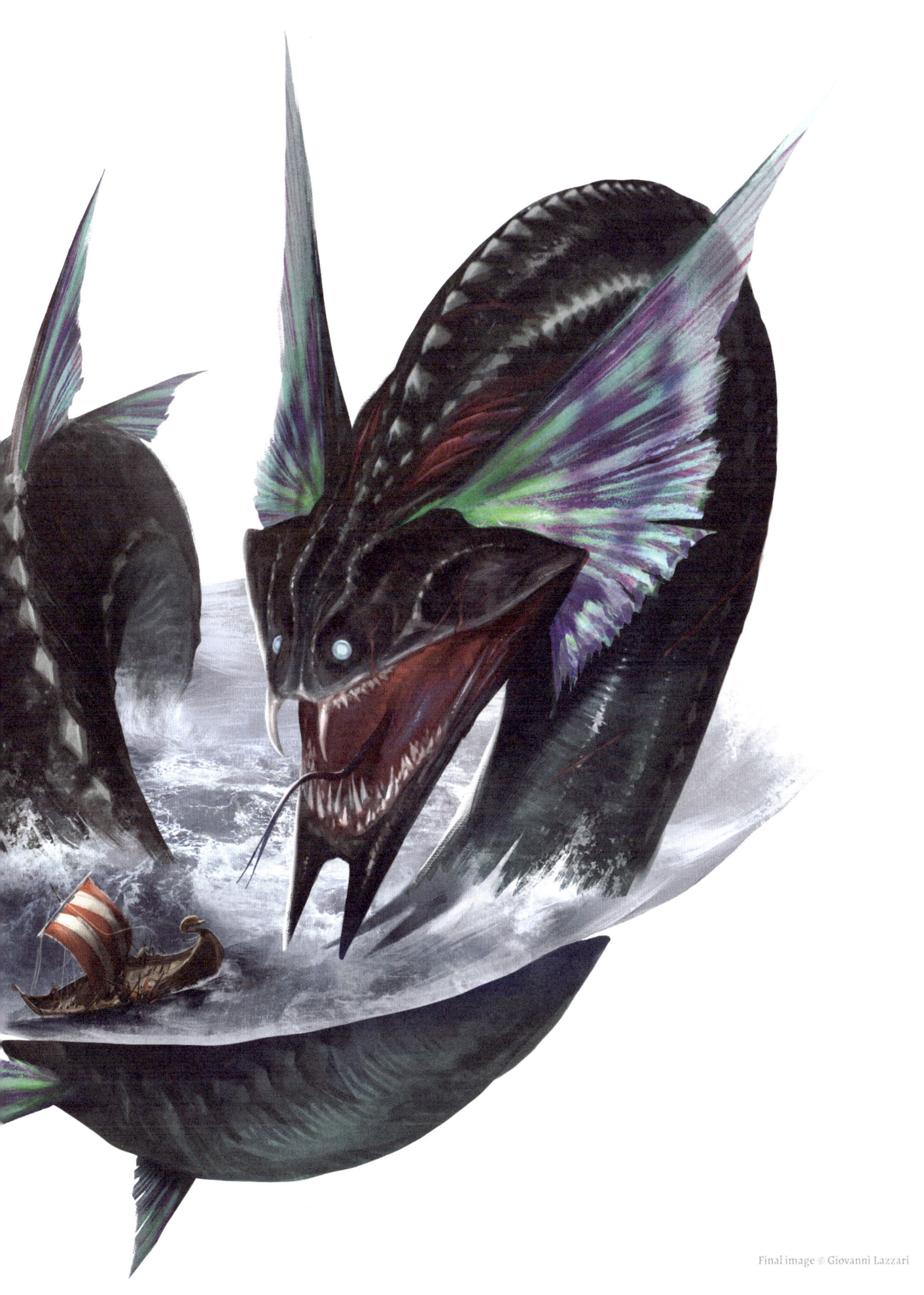

Final image © Giovanni Lazzari

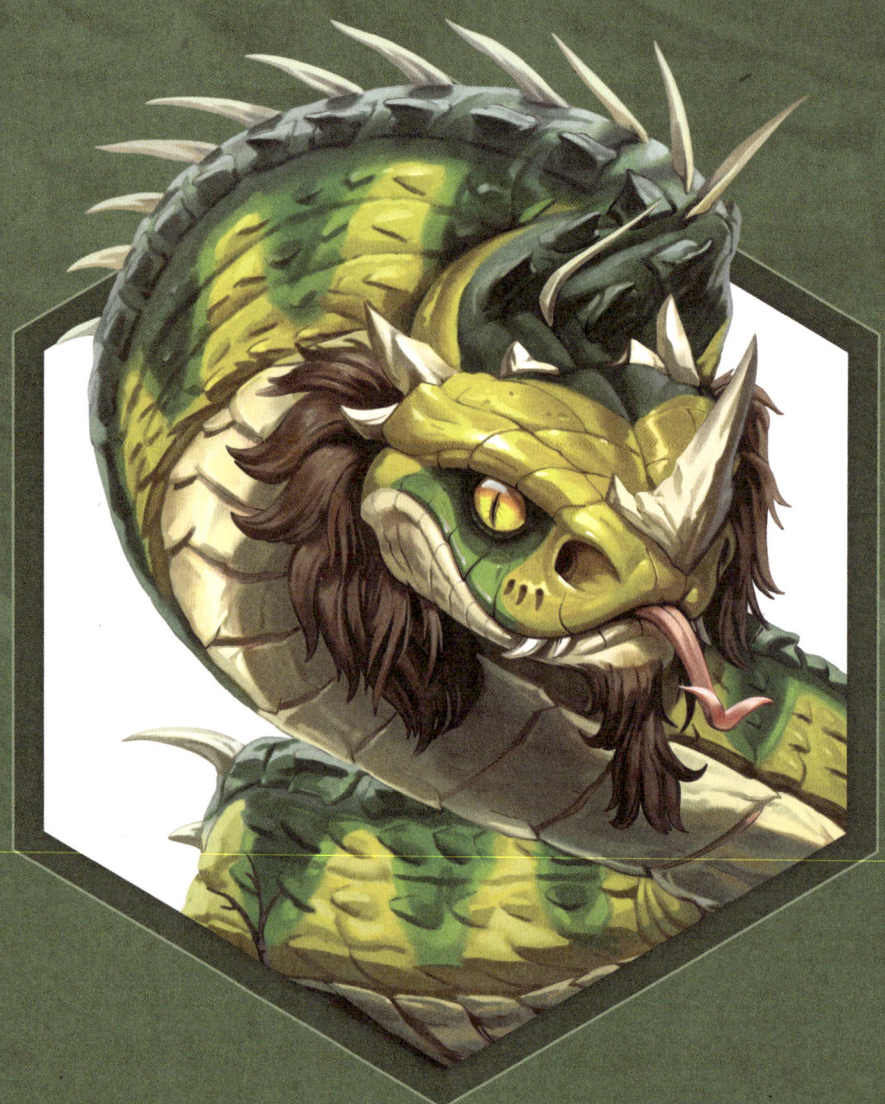

LINDWORM

The Lindworm is an old mythical dragon, often depicted as a serpent-like creature that is said to feed on unwary humans in the forests of Europe. For this tutorial, I'll be focusing on how to take the idea of a simple mythical creature and create something unique, despite the limitation of having few detailed descriptions or dragon-like features to work from.

DAMIEN MAMMOLITI

Final image © Damien Mammoliti

RESEARCH

In researching for the Lindworm, the biggest surprise to me is the lack of artistic representation of it from historical fables. It's often described as a long, serpent-like creature, sometimes thought to have two arms, but no wings. It is often called the 'wheel snake' because of its preference to bite its tail and roll after humans, with some old Nordic depictions of dragons also showing the coils and biting of the tail. I focus on this idea to come up with some depictions for this dragon that is otherwise plainly described.

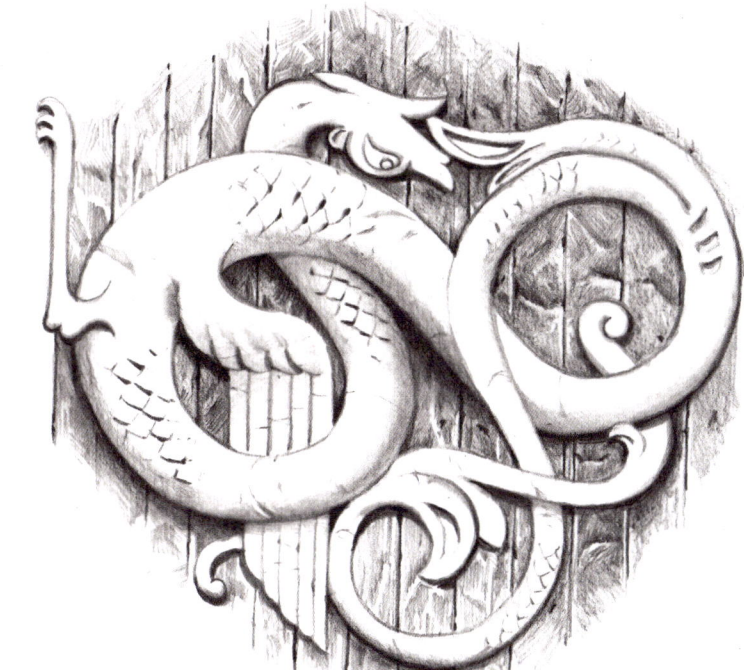

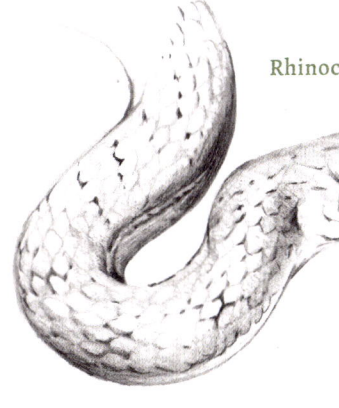

Rhinoceros ratsnake

Musk ox

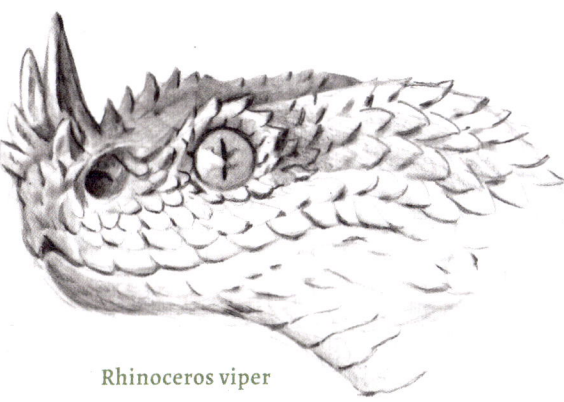

Rhinoceros viper

 ## ANIMAL EXPLORATIONS

Exploring descriptions of the Lindworm, it seems to be described as a combination of a snake with some kind of mane and a reptilian face. In researching what animals to focus on, I think of the musk ox, which could be a good reference for the mane of the creature, as it is an animal seen in northern Europe. The dragon has also been depicted in statue form, which was based on the remains of a woolly rhinoceros. This gives me a great idea: my design can take after real-world snakes that often have rhinoceros-like horns on their noses!

Crocodile skink

03 SCALE EXPLORATIONS

Going further into my referencing, I want to test out some scale patterns and types to see what could work best for the Lindworm. I'm enamoured with the crocodile skink's unique scale palette, with a softer side and sharpened spikes along the back. The plated skink's back would be a great reference for a dragon that likes to wheel around the forest! Taking that idea even further, the blue crested lizard's spines would be a great look for a dragon that could use the additional traction along its back.

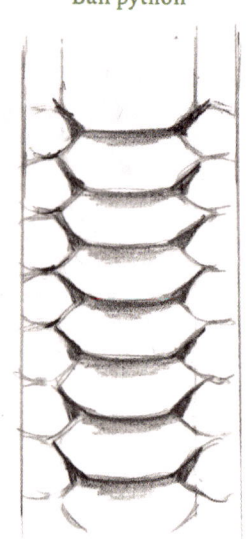

Ball python

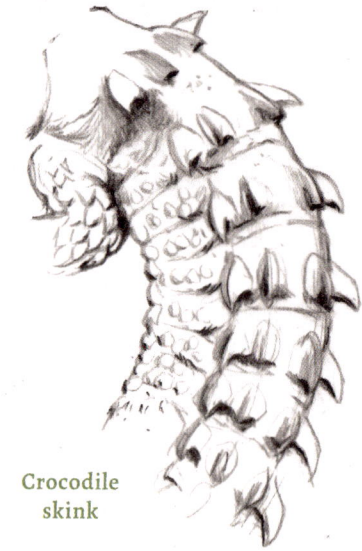

Crocodile skink

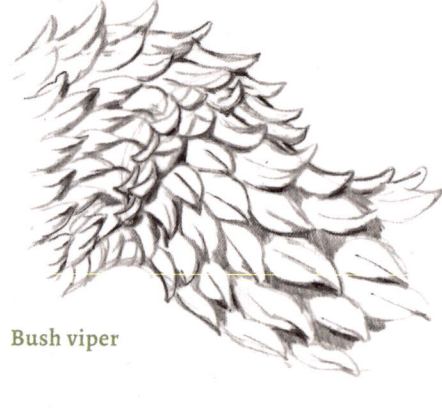

Bush viper

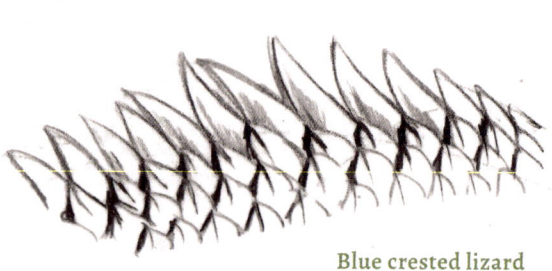

Blue crested lizard

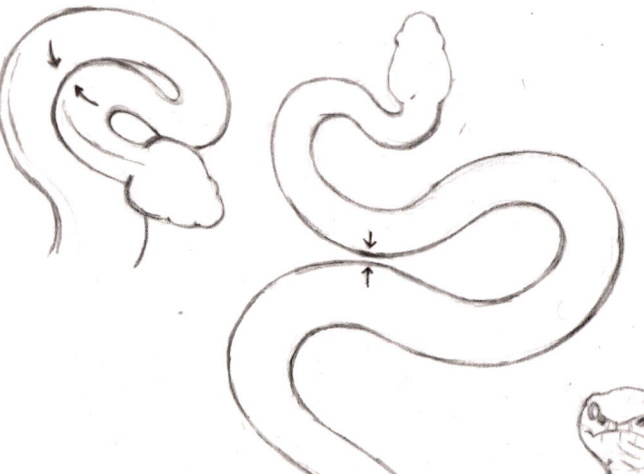

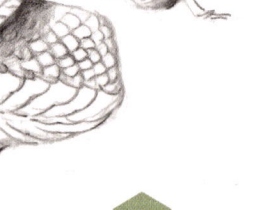

04 SNAKE BEHAVIOUR

Since the Lindworm's main form in stories is that of a serpent, I want to spend some time focusing on the body language of snakes. This will make sure that my depiction of the creature will not only look accurate but *feel* accurate to how a snake would prepare itself to strike. In my research, I note that a snake often likes to touch various parts of its own body, resting coils upon coils to wind itself up like a spring.

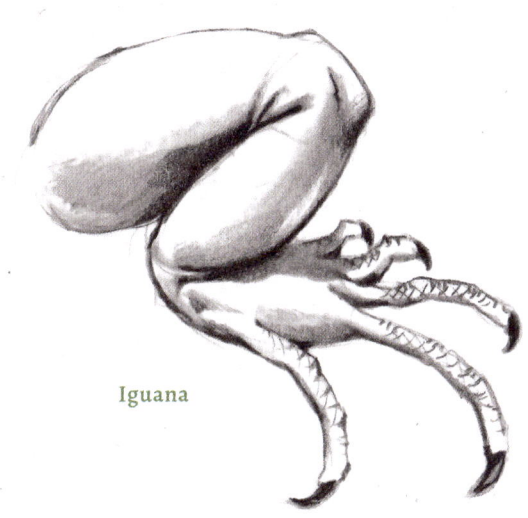

Iguana

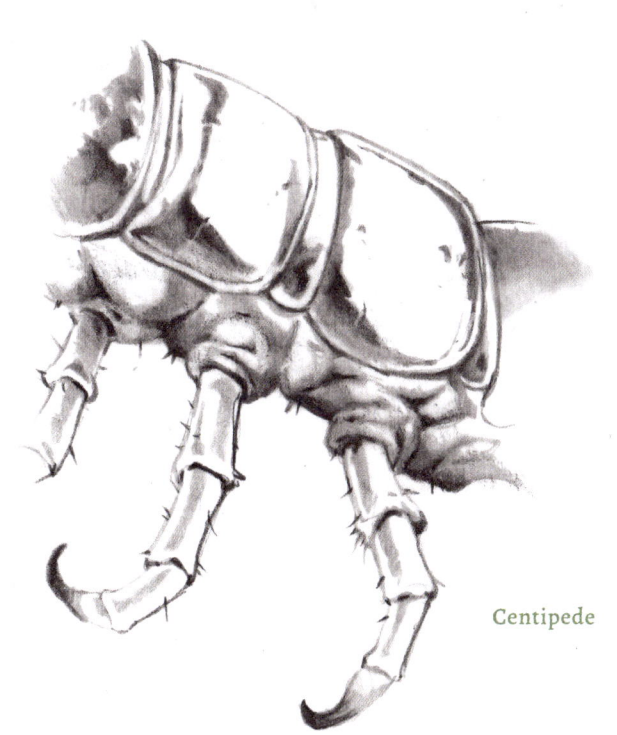

Centipede

05 LEG EXPLORATIONS

Mythological dragons are often depicted as chimeric creatures that take parts of animals from different groups (such as reptiles, bats, or other mammals), so I want to do some explorations on the legs that the dragon is suggested to have. However, in researching, it's unclear if the creature is meant to have legs at all! I consider taking an idea from another type of animal: a centipede. Perhaps the reason people disagree about the legs is because they are hard to see? It's a curious option, and one I have never tried before.

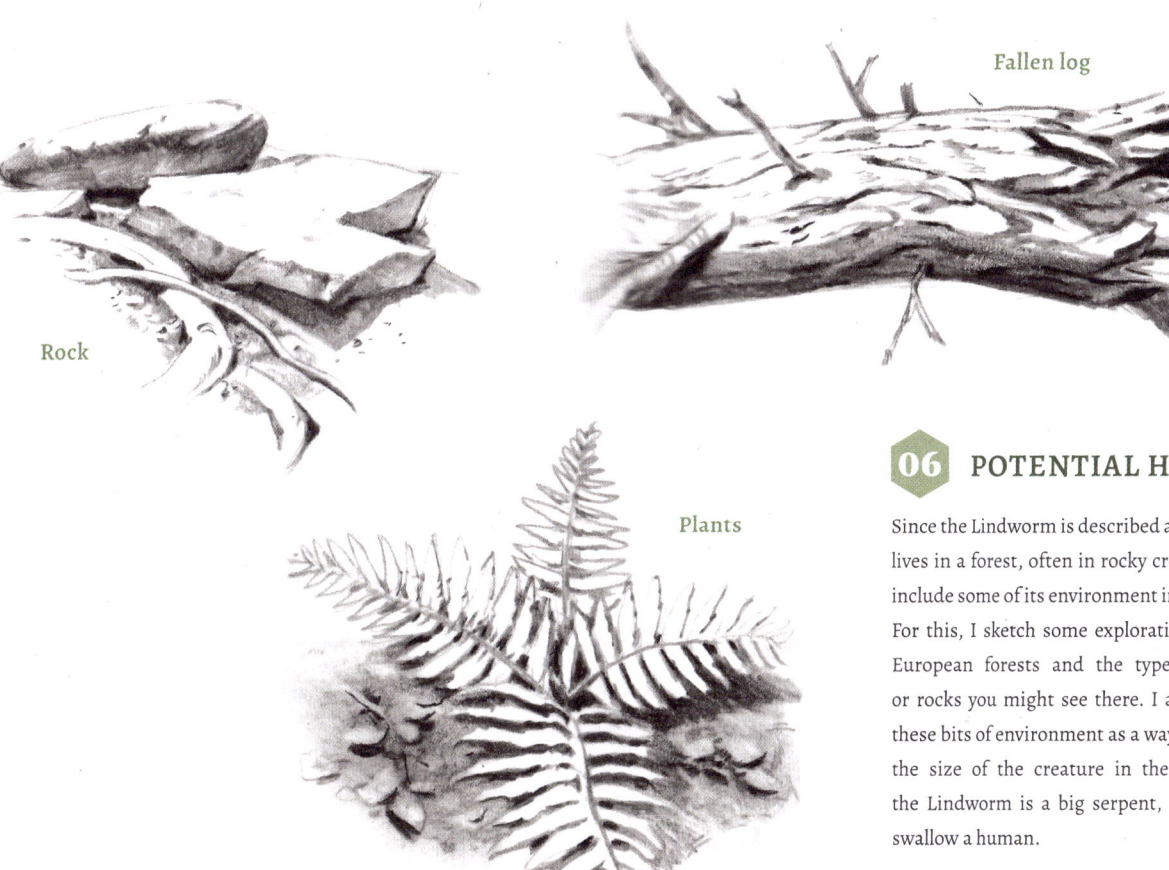

Fallen log

Rock

Plants

06 POTENTIAL HABITATS

Since the Lindworm is described as a creature that lives in a forest, often in rocky crevices, I want to include some of its environment in the final scene. For this, I sketch some explorations of northern European forests and the types of shrubbery or rocks you might see there. I also want to use these bits of environment as a way to help suggest the size of the creature in the illustration, as the Lindworm is a big serpent, large enough to swallow a human.

The Lindworm is said to have the ability to bite its own tail, roll around like a wheel, swallow a human, and perhaps even spit a milk-like substance. It's also suggested that the dragon might be a creature of luck, often sitting on a hoard of treasure. So, in designing it, I want to explore some of these capabilities. What might the Lindworm's tail look like, if it were to bite it? What could help it roll fast enough to catch a human? And would a beard help the dragon appear luckier?

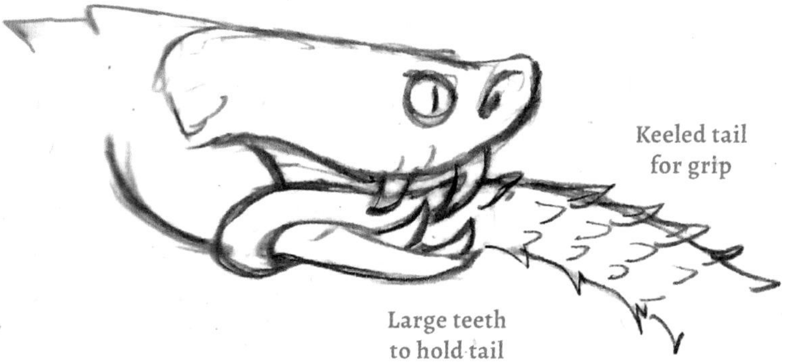

Keeled tail for grip

Large teeth to hold tail

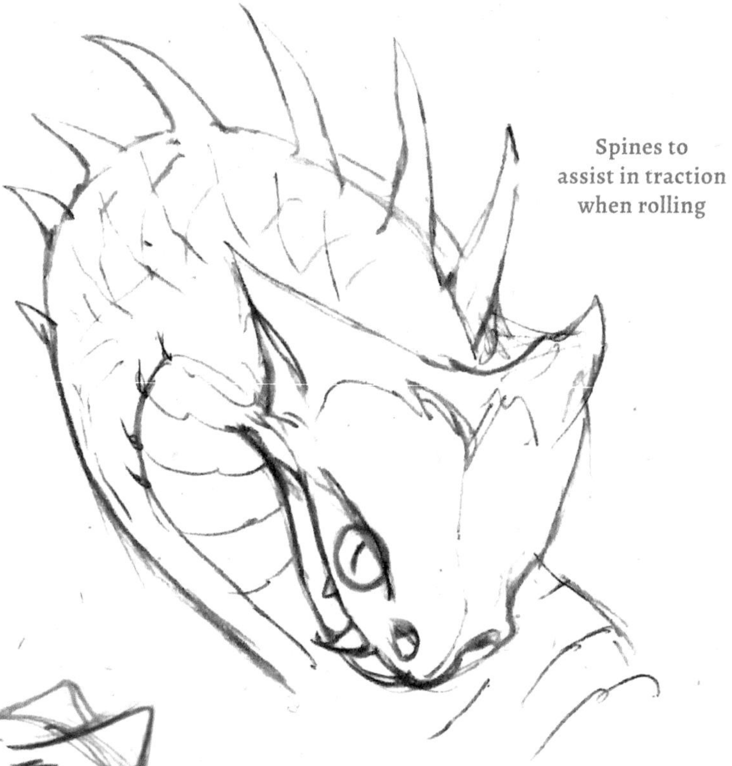

Spines to assist in traction when rolling

Wide head to swallow a human

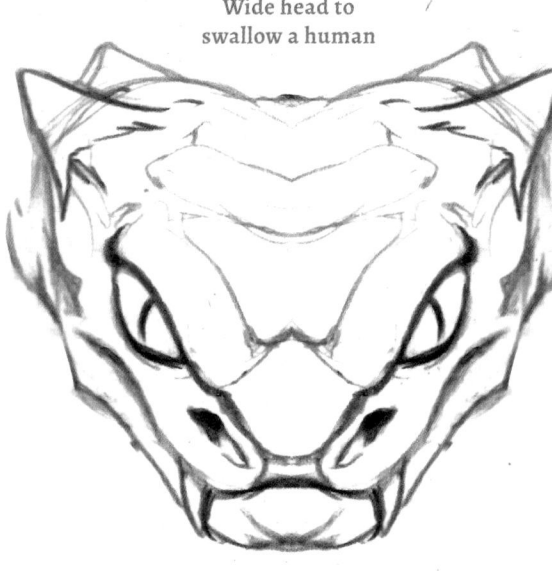

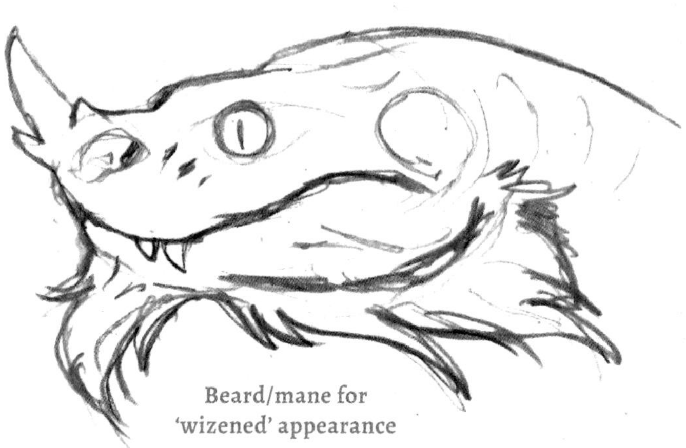

Beard/mane for 'wizened' appearance

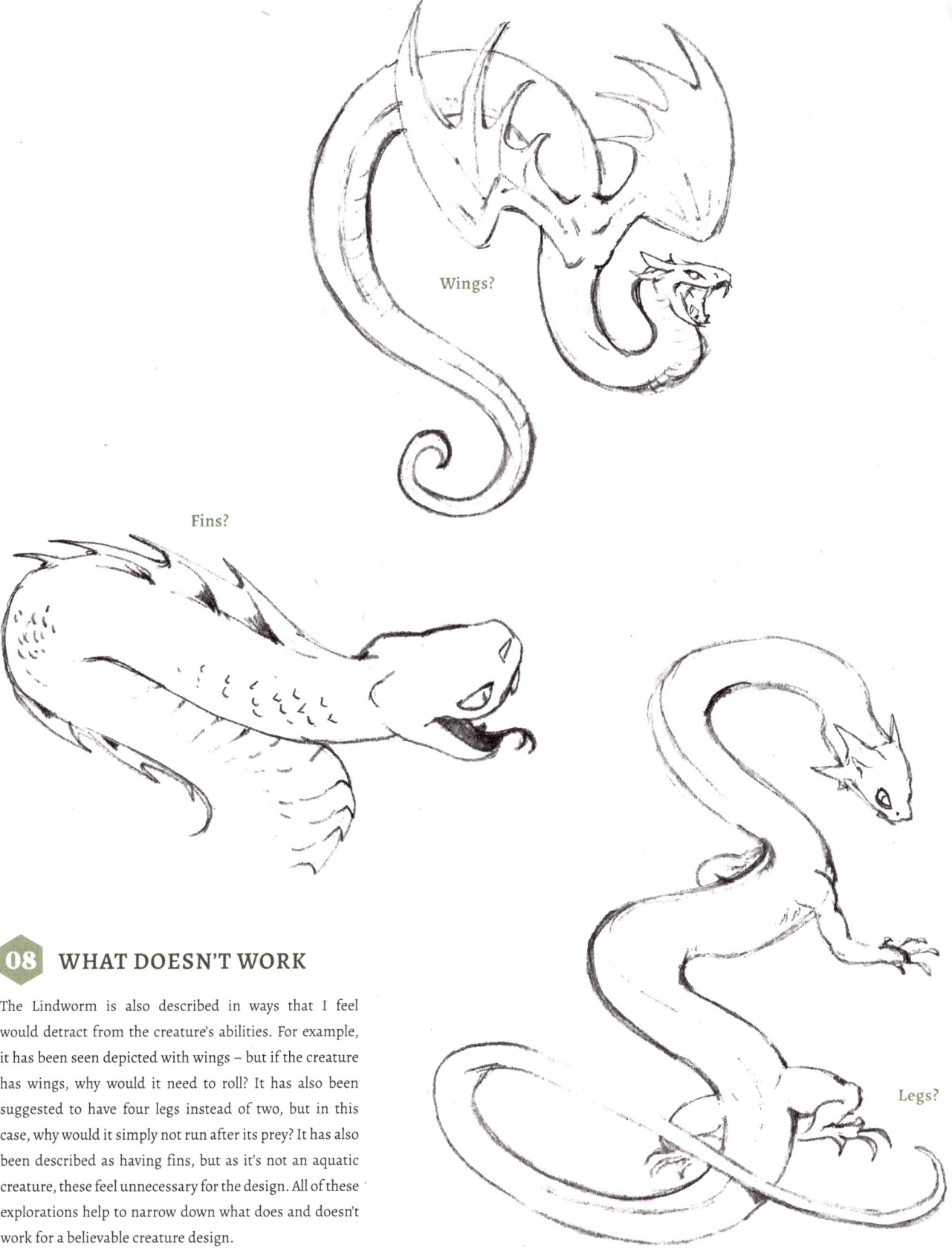

Wings?

Fins?

Legs?

08 WHAT DOESN'T WORK

The Lindworm is also described in ways that I feel would detract from the creature's abilities. For example, it has been seen depicted with wings – but if the creature has wings, why would it need to roll? It has also been suggested to have four legs instead of two, but in this case, why would it simply not run after its prey? It has also been described as having fins, but as it's not an aquatic creature, these feel unnecessary for the design. All of these explorations help to narrow down what does and doesn't work for a believable creature design.

09 HEAD VARIATIONS

When designing any dragon, the best part is exploring the head, as it has a lot of capacity to suggest personality and even the creature's hunting instinct. In the Lindworm's case, you could simply put a snake's head on a snake's body, but in doing so you'd be robbed of an opportunity to include a lot of those chimeric qualities that make a dragon unique. So, for this, I carry out some exploration on shape, parts, what to include, and what to keep out of the design for the dragon's head.

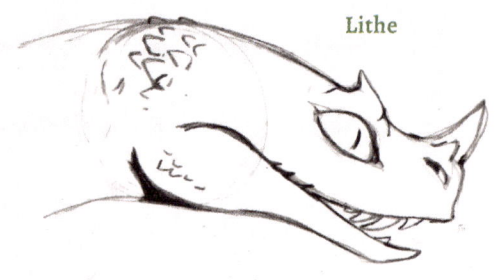

Lithe

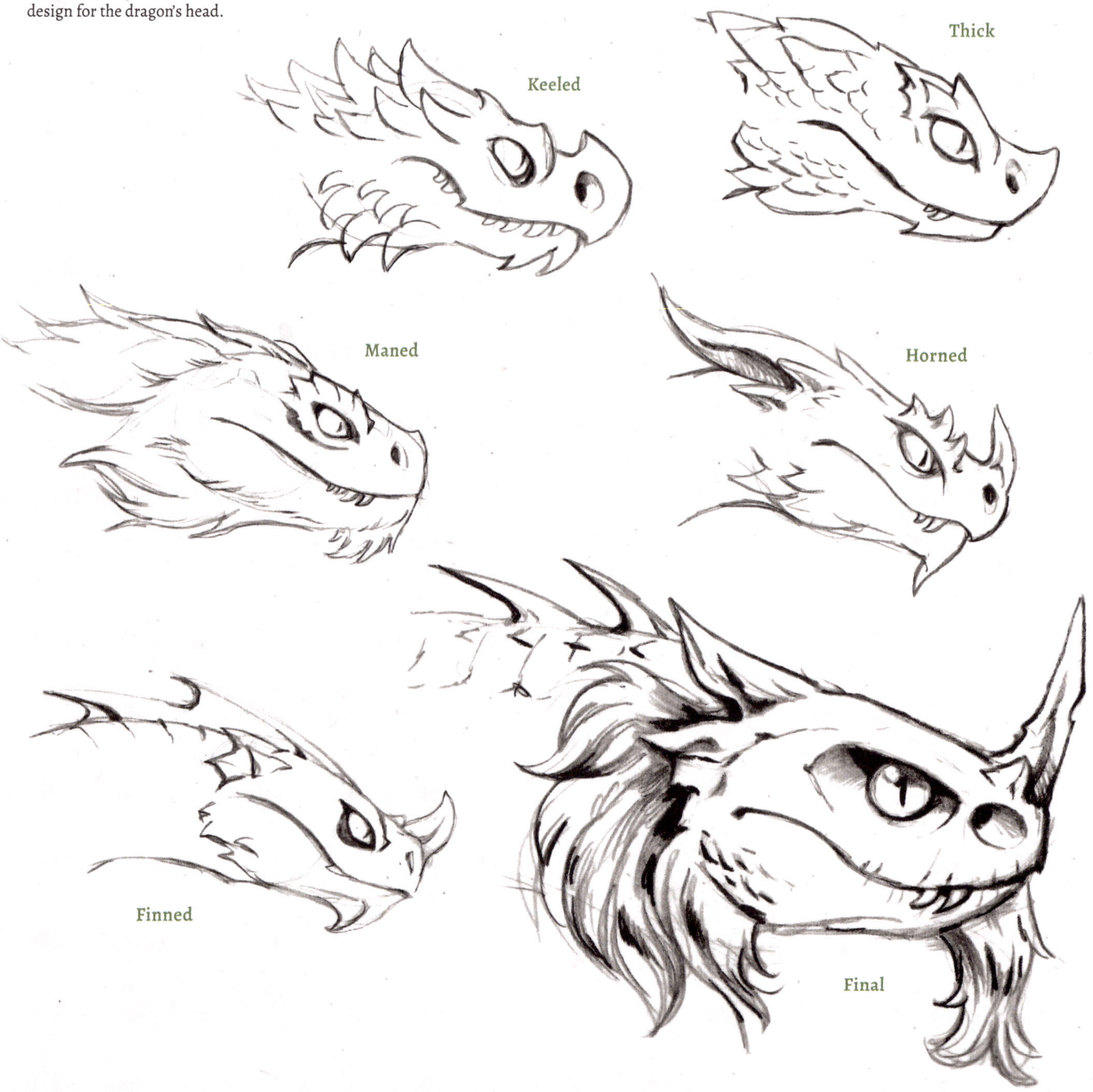

Keeled

Thick

Maned

Horned

Finned

Final

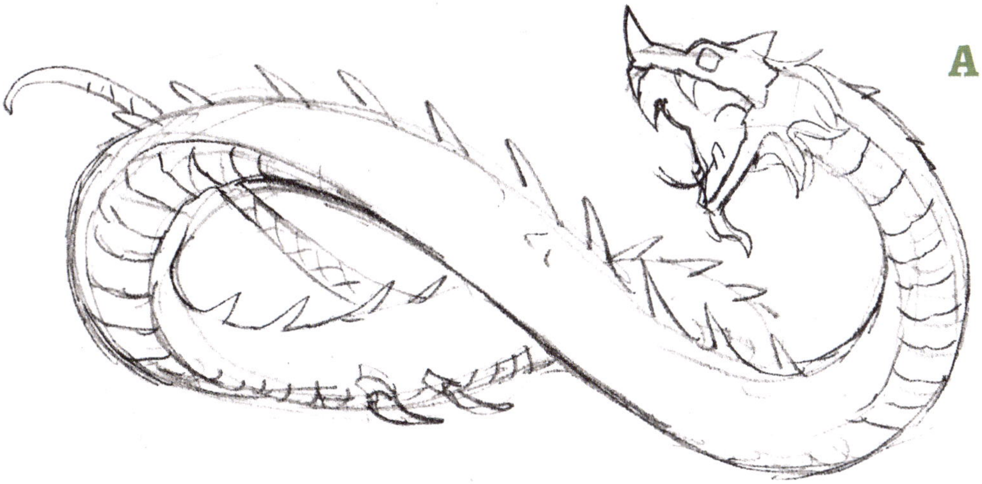

A

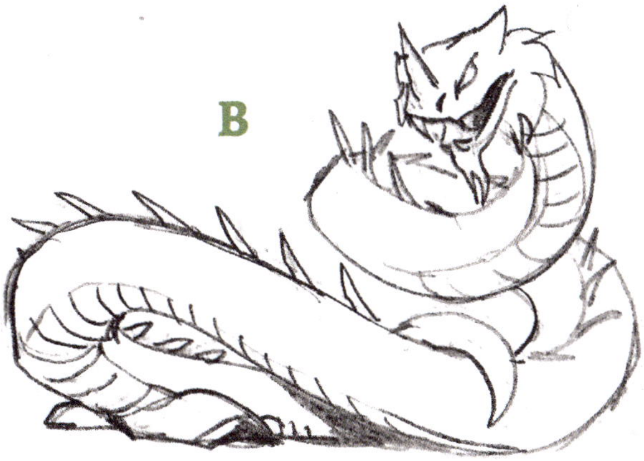

B

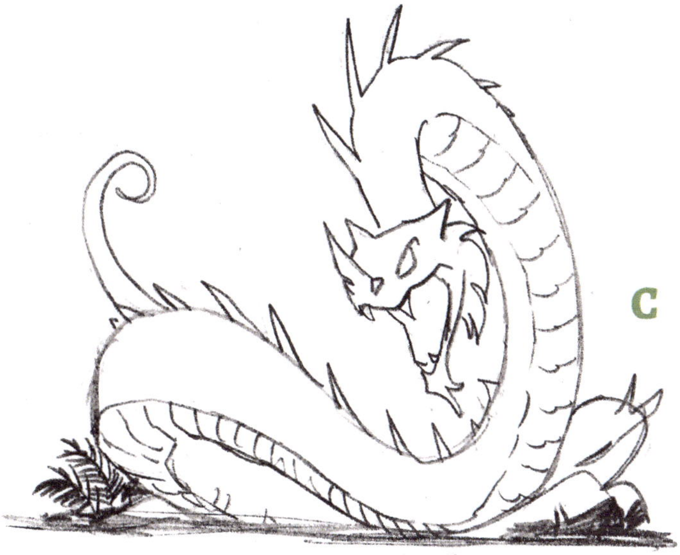

C

⬡10 POSE THUMBNAILS

Posing the Lindworm has its limitations, considering that the dragon is mostly a snake, with little else to emphasize in a silhouette. However, there are some poses that are unnatural and don't suit the realistic depiction of what a snake might move and act like.

I sketch out some possible poses, but some are too aggressive (C), some are unnatural (B), and others simply have weak composition when considering that the focus of the animal should almost always be its head or upper body (A).

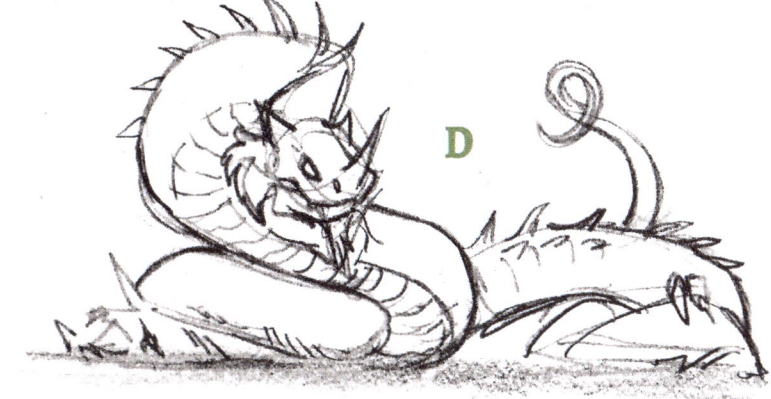

D

FULL SKETCH

Finally, after a lot of research and contemplation, I sketch out my Lindworm. Most of what I have researched goes into this dragon: a wide, imposing head, long spines down an armoured back, and a coiled tail to suggest the wheel-like nature of the dragon. And I've even included the centipede legs! They are subtle enough that they could be missed, which was my intention. The Lindworm has come to life.

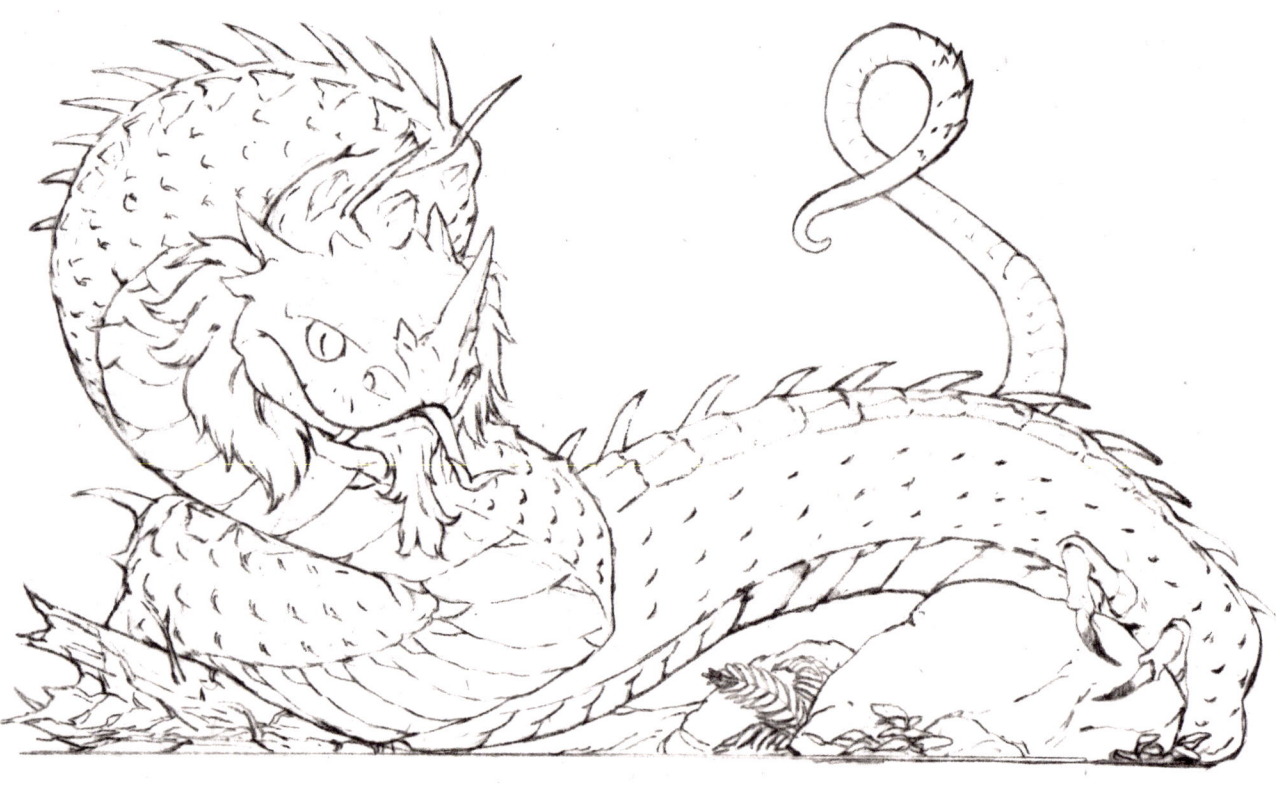

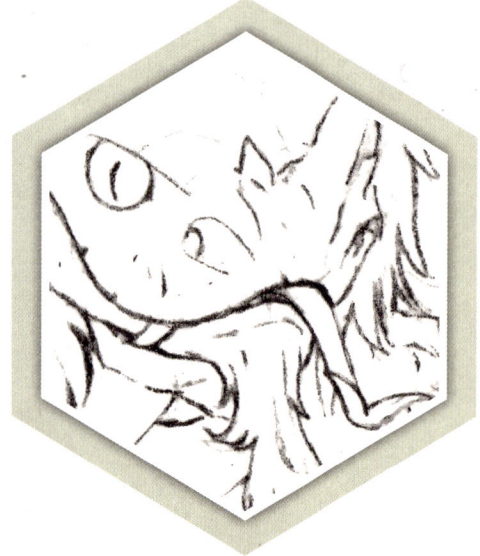

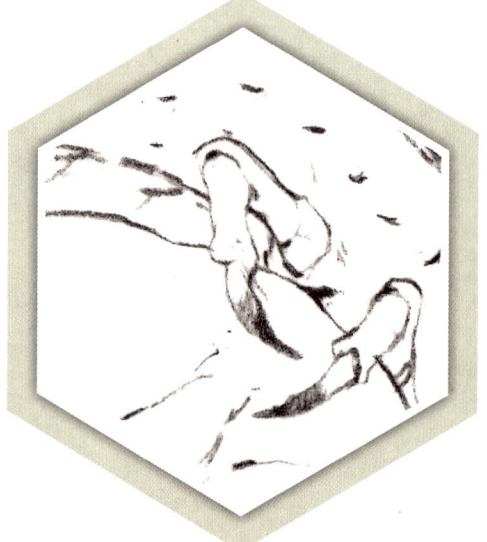

⬡12 COLOUR ROUGHS

Now that I have my sketch, I can head into exploring colours for the creature. My main focus for the Lindworm is to create a colourful snake, with 'a dark body and light-coloured belly', as the fables go. The green and cream version (A) is a very traditional snake's colour palette. White and brown (B), while unique, might be too unique for a forest setting. Similar concerns arise with the blue-green and white palette (C). The pairing of green-yellow and cream (D) still maintains a natural-looking palette, but also suggests the creature is gold-coloured, which helps with the mythology of a lucky dragon with a hoard of treasure.

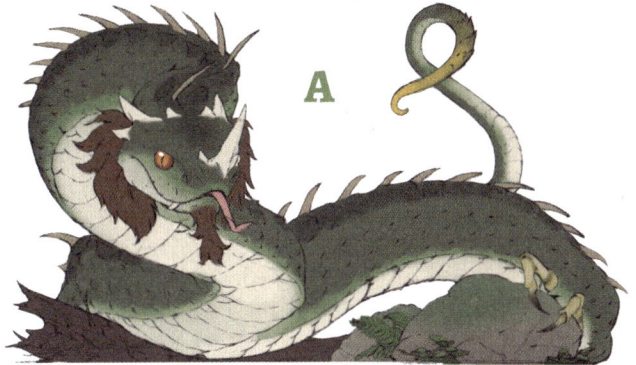

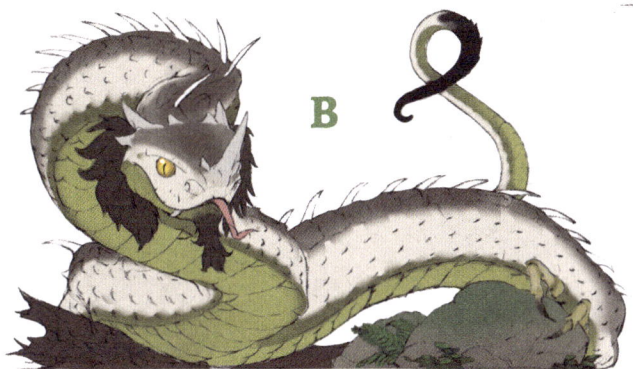

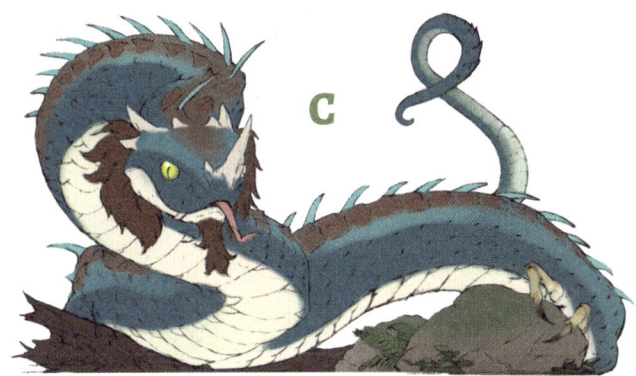

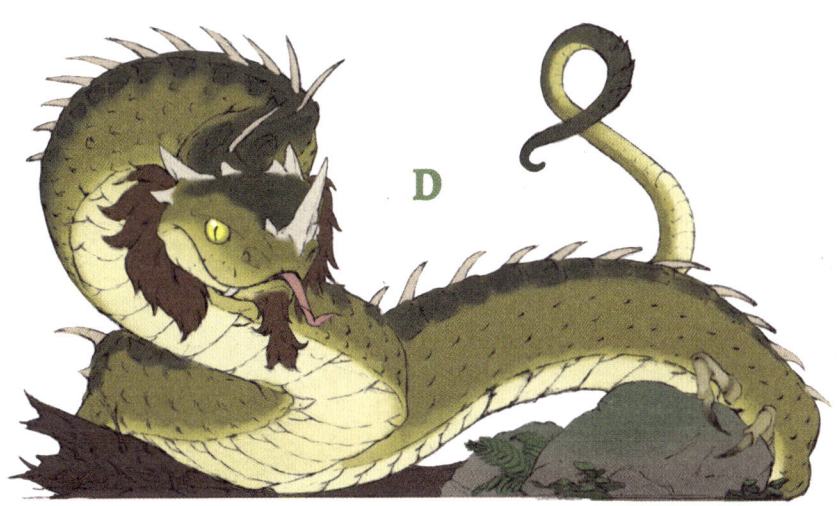

Along with a colour palette, reptiles often have a pattern as well. Here I explore a uniform option (A), as well as banded (B), striped (C), or spotted (D) patterns. Most of these versions could work well, but I end up preferring the banded, as I imagine a ground serpent might need the dappled texture on its scales to hide better under a canopy of trees. It's not a dragon that hides below leaf-litter, so having too cryptic of a pattern wouldn't make sense, either. I also like the idea of the banded pattern as it would spin when the serpent is rolling around in the forest.

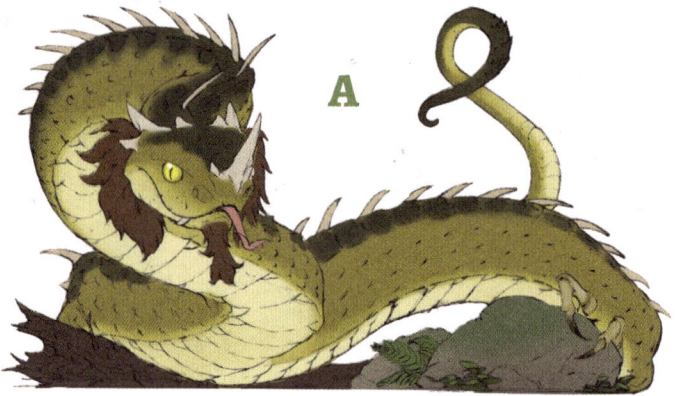

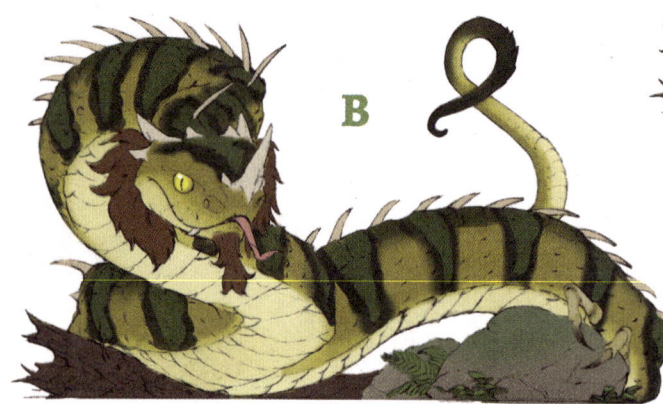

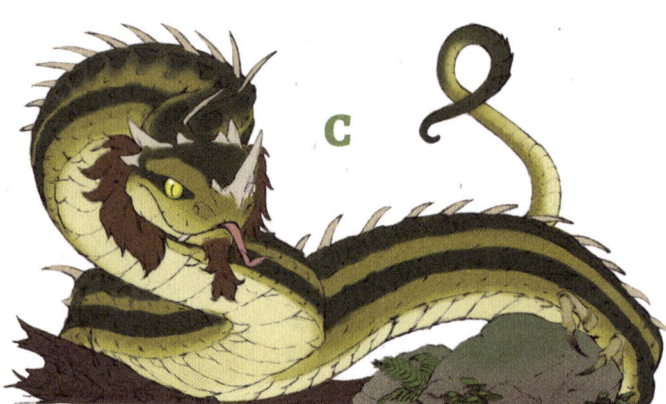

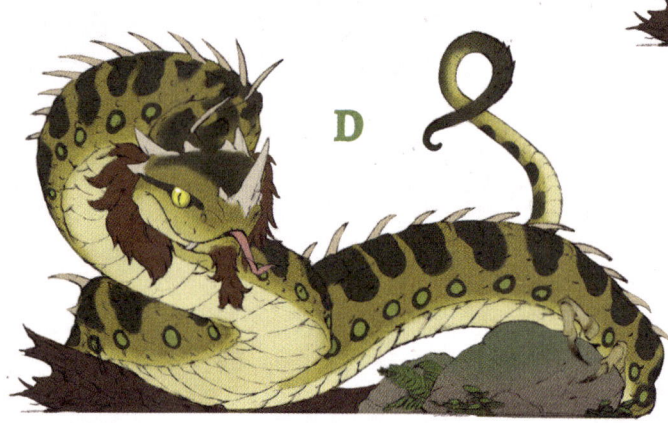

14 FINAL COLOURS

After tweaking the pattern, and adding a bit of colour around the eyes, here's the colour rough over my sketch. The dragon feels cohesive, despite being a creature of many parts, and might be something ancient Europeans might flee from in a dark forest (or perhaps, if they're brave, ask for a bit of good luck). From here, I can take my original sketch and start building up my final illustration.

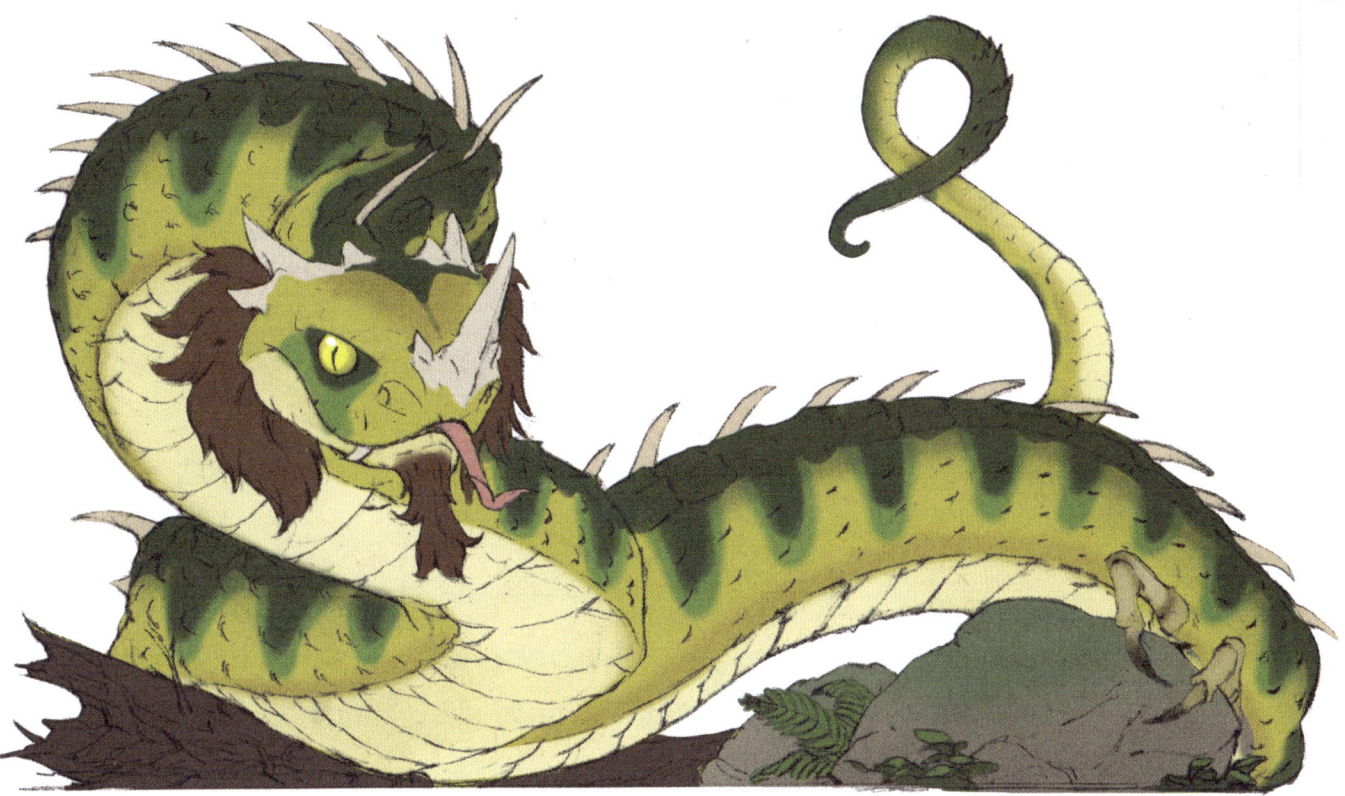

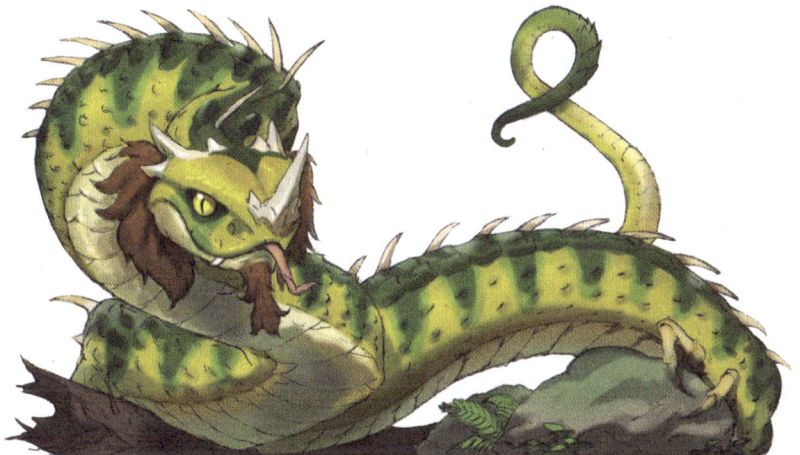

15 LIGHTING ROUGH

Before I start rendering and cleaning up my illustration, I want to be sure of the pattern and colours by laying some basic lighting over the Lindworm. I really want to emphasize the three-dimensional aspect of the snake-like body as it seemingly leans out towards the viewer. It's important to test out the lighting and see if I can emphasize the coil of the neck and upper body with a top-down light source.

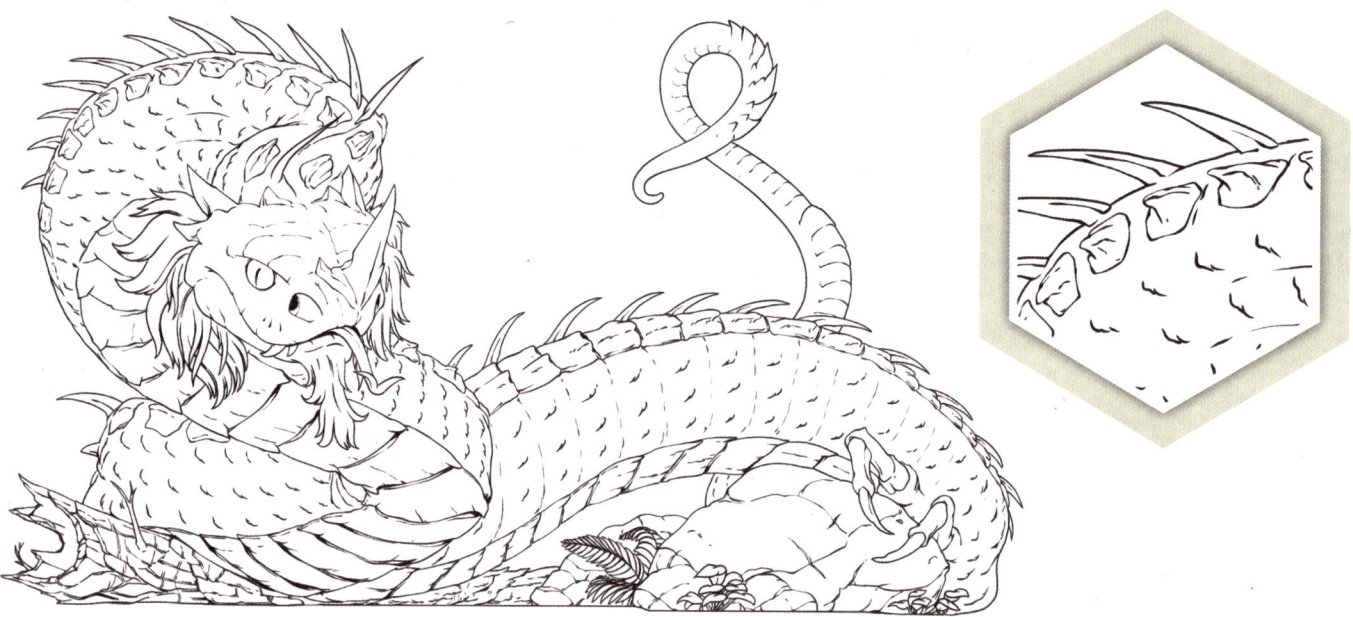

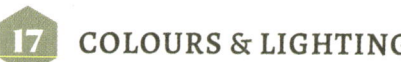

16 LINE ART

From there, I take my original sketch and clean everything up with a basic digital 'ink' layer to refine the anatomy, loosely lay out the scale pattern, and plan for my eventual colour layers. I want to convey the weight of the serpent's body leaning on the tree stump, with a heaviness that makes it feel more tactile and real to the viewer. You can imagine yourself being pinned by such a large creature as it rolls over you!

17 COLOURS & LIGHTING

I place the flat colours beneath my ink layer, so that I can work out the pattern, clean it up, and refresh the lighting and local colours to help bring out the details in the design. I emphasize more reds and pinks to match with the browns, and warm up parts of the body to make the creature feel more alive. Now I'm ready to take everything one step further and render out the details.

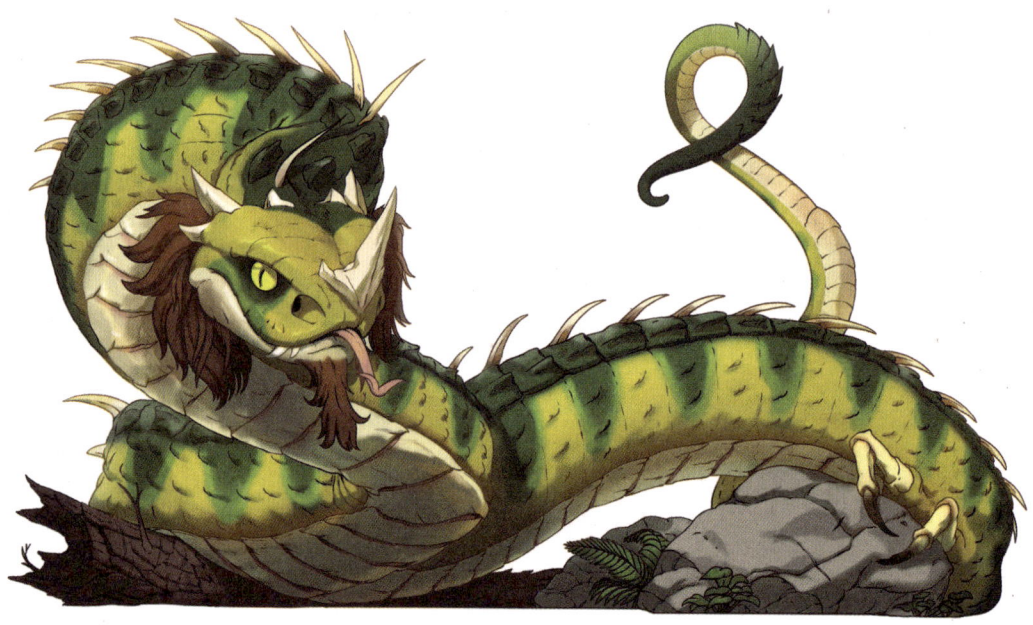

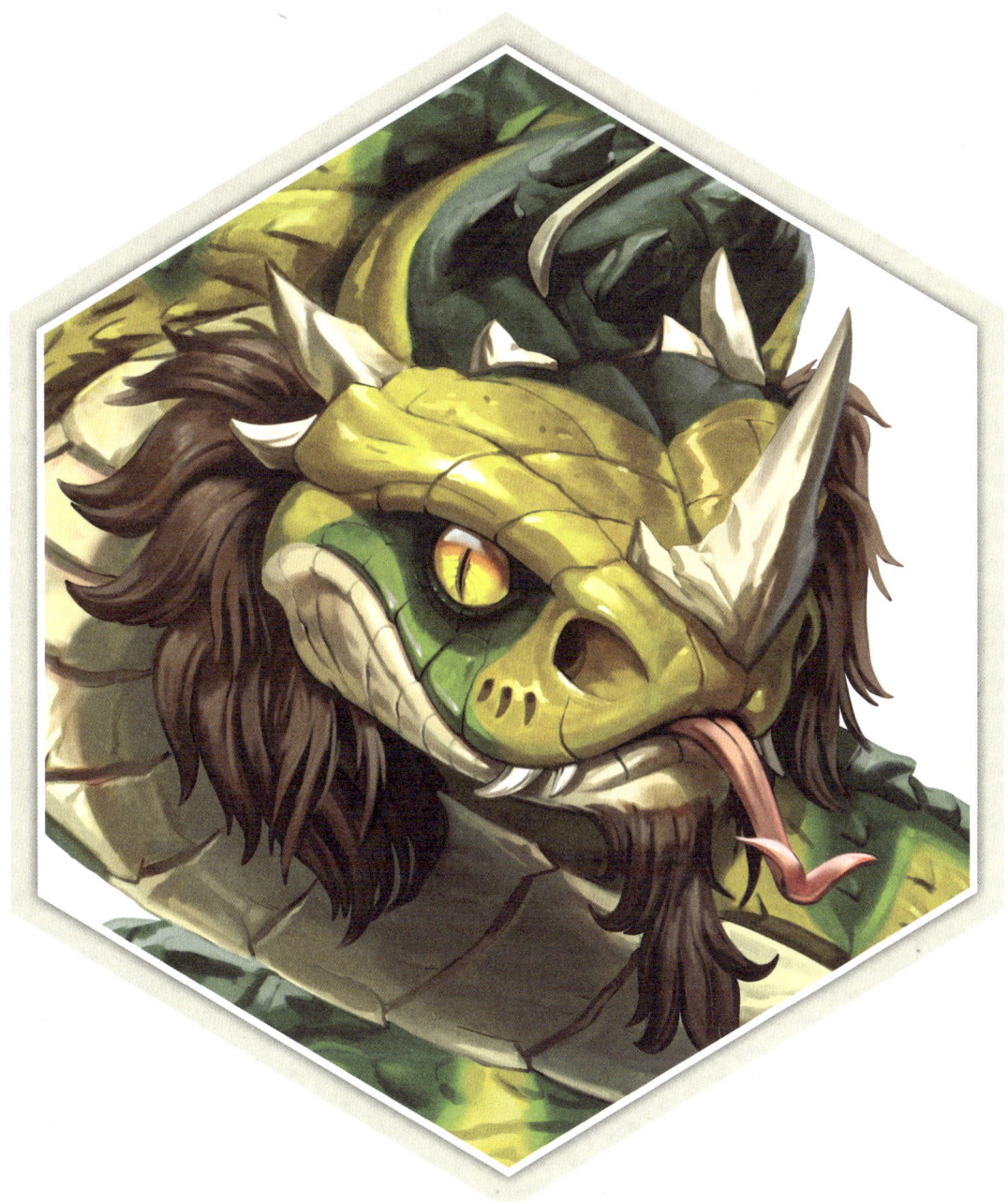

18 RENDERING

Whenever rendering any creature, I pay special attention to the head and face area, as it's the focus of my design. The rest of the dragon's body may be less detailed overall compared to the head, but I am sure to add specific details that matter, such as small scars on the tail from biting itself too much. I also pay attention to borrowing colours from all over the creature's body; this ensures my colours don't stray too far from the established palette, and everything about the dragon's look stays consistent.

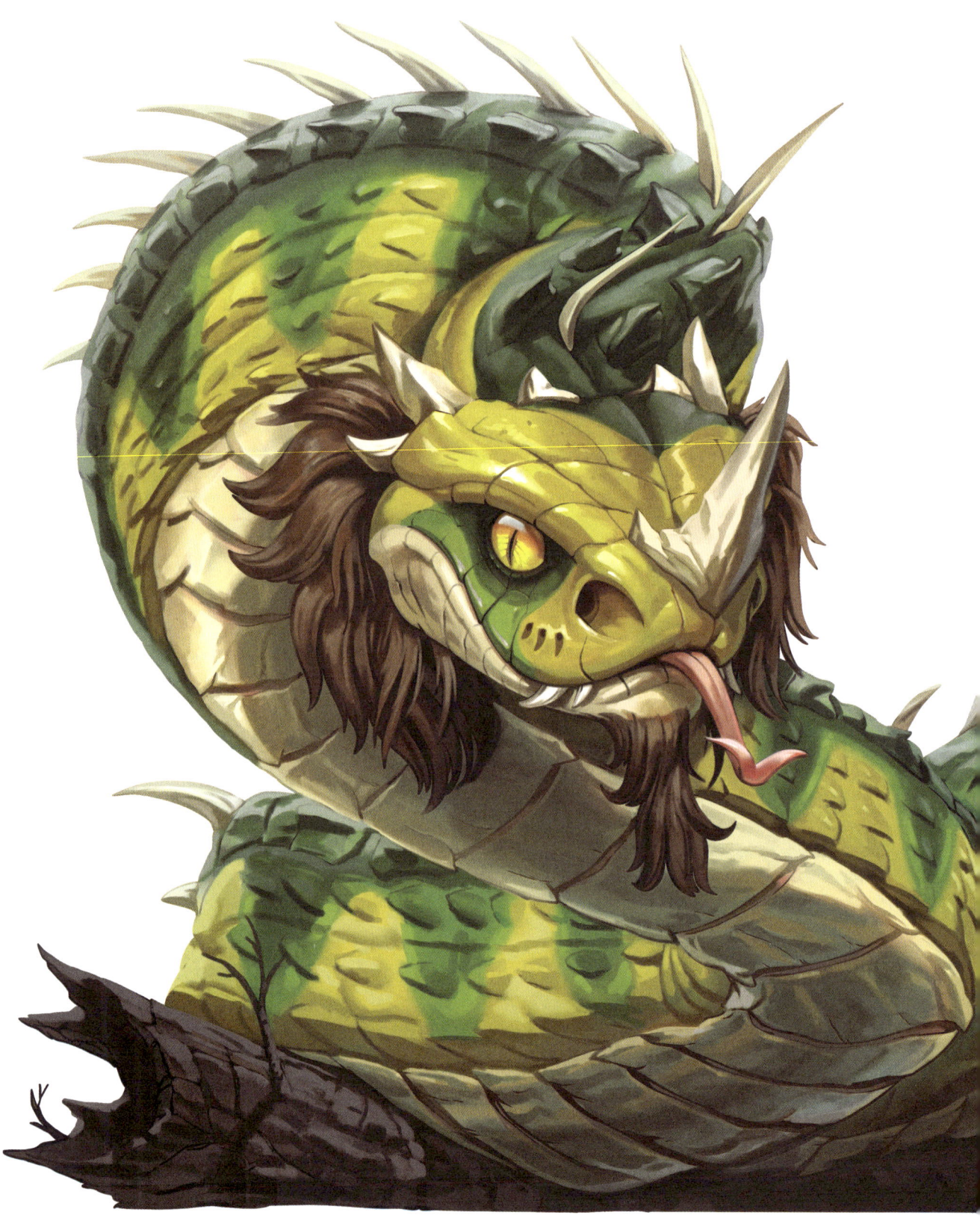

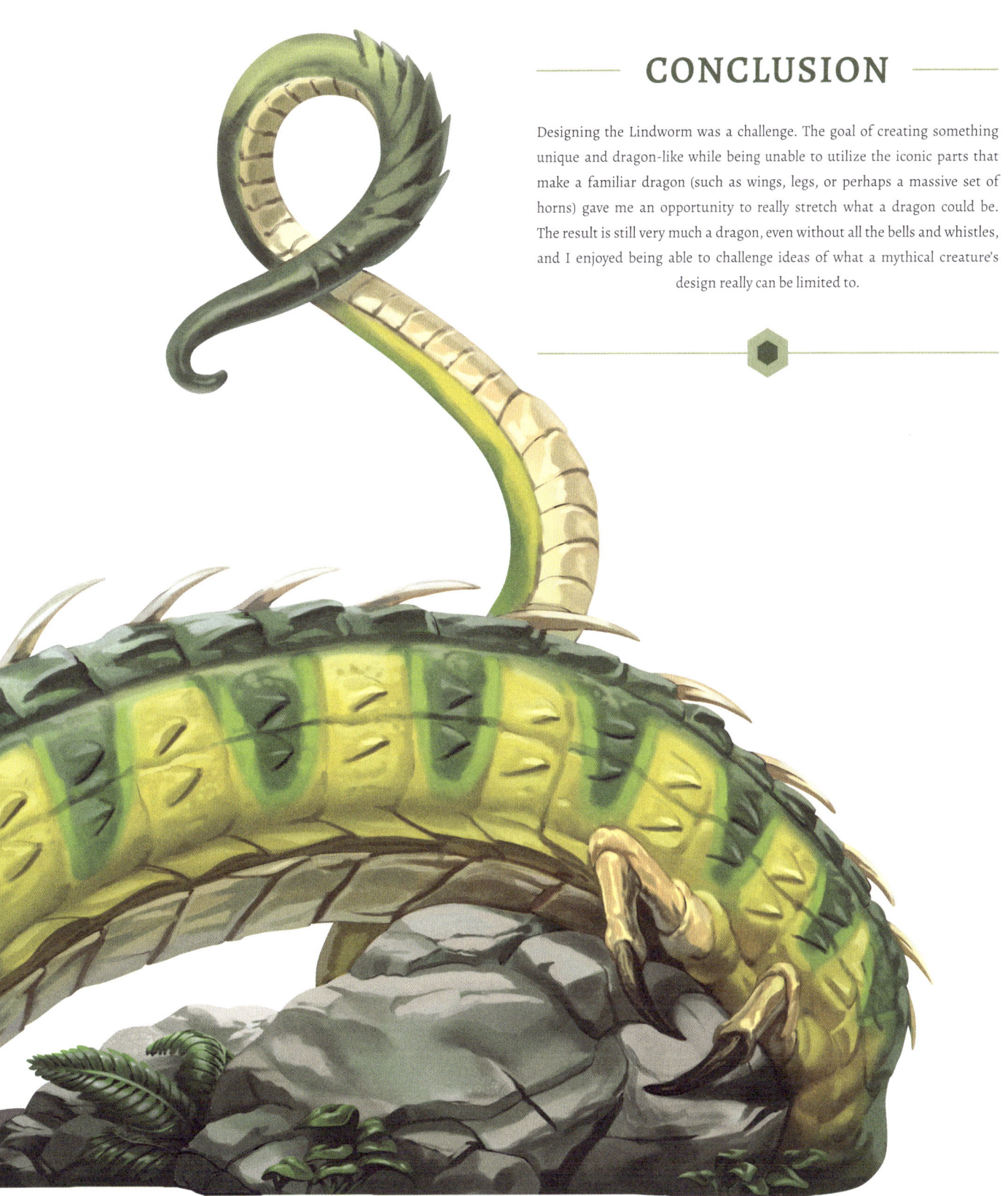

CONCLUSION

Designing the Lindworm was a challenge. The goal of creating something unique and dragon-like while being unable to utilize the iconic parts that make a familiar dragon (such as wings, legs, or perhaps a massive set of horns) gave me an opportunity to really stretch what a dragon could be. The result is still very much a dragon, even without all the bells and whistles, and I enjoyed being able to challenge ideas of what a mythical creature's design really can be limited to.

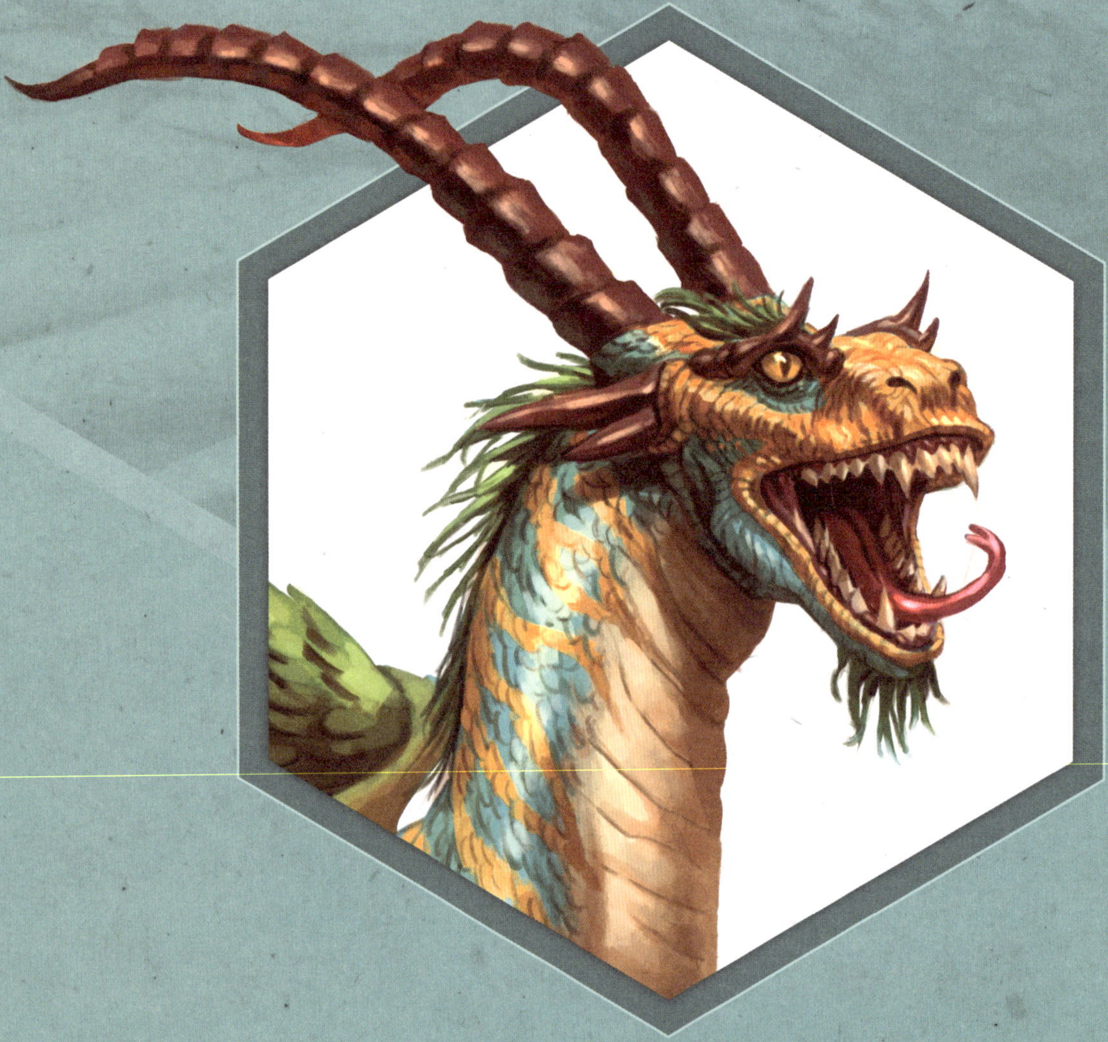

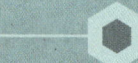

MUŠḪUŠŠU

Mušḫuššu is the regal and fearsome beast that prowled the edges of our earliest attempts at civilization, in the fertile valleys and mountains of ancient Mesopotamia. Regarded as a sacred animal and the servant of the Babylonian god-king Marduk and his son, the scribe god Nabu, this creature graces the Ishtar Gate and many other artefacts from the bygone days of Iraq. In this tutorial I will try to find the truth behind this long-gone dragon of Babylon, trying to recreate what it might have truly looked like, for few mortals would have chanced upon a creature of the gods.

HAZEM AMEEN

Final image © Hazem Ameen

HISTORICAL SOURCES

The first order of business is to actually read up on what our sources tell us about Mušḫuššu: a strange dragon with the wings and hind legs of an eagle, the head and neck of a horned snake, and the forelimbs and torso of a lion. The animal was clearly important to the ancient Mesopotamians, representing divine favour, kingship, and justice. I begin by studying what they tell us about Mušḫuššu, studying the carvings on vases and mud-brick walls. This step is the foundation for everything to come.

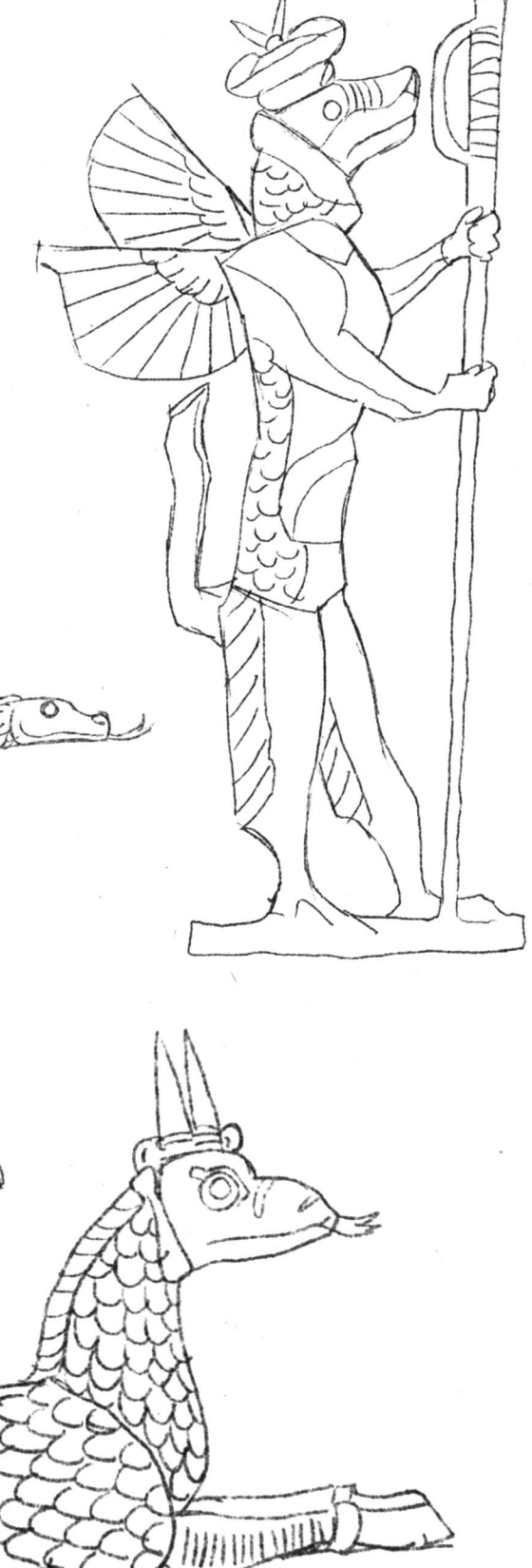

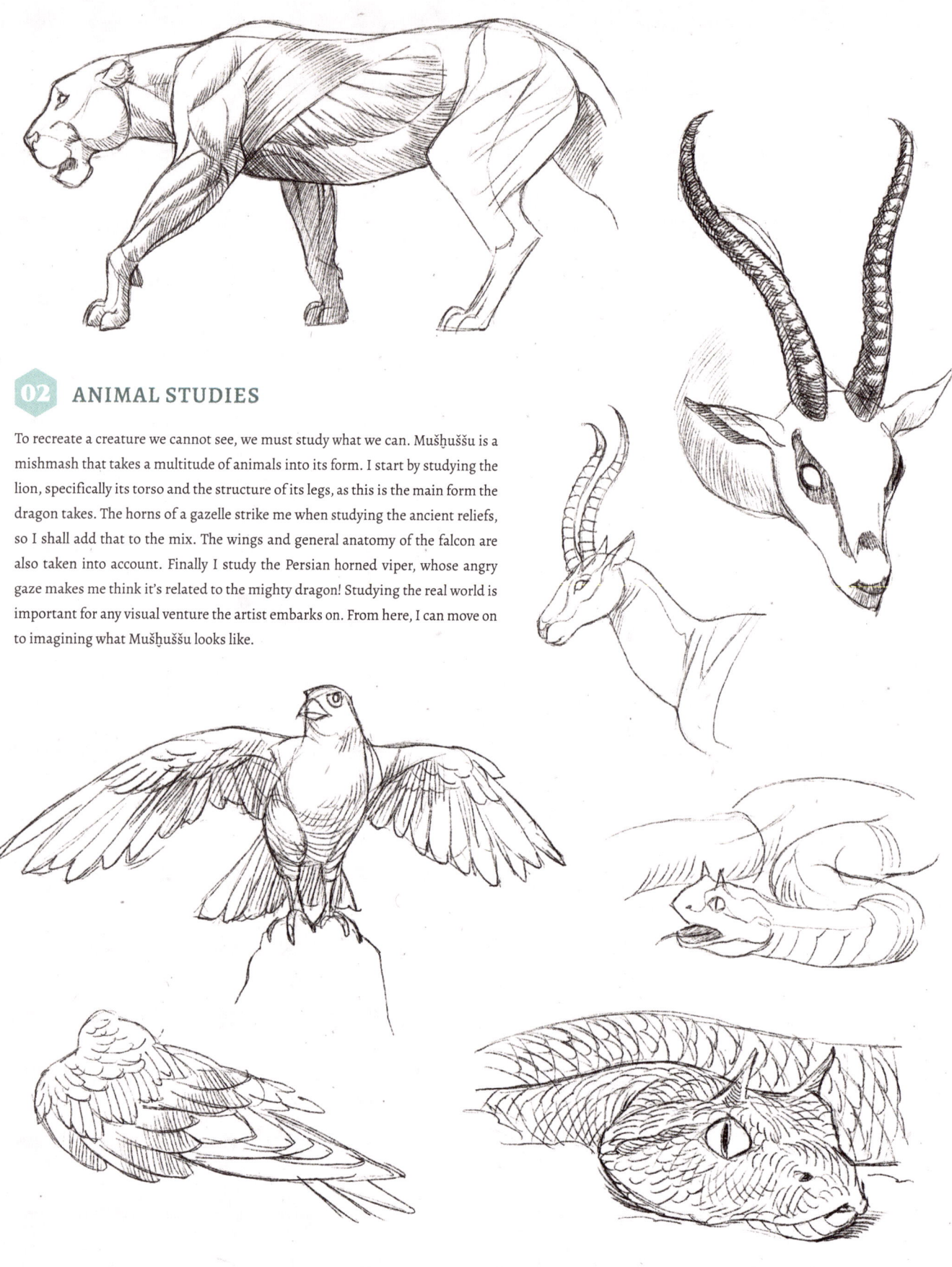

02 ANIMAL STUDIES

To recreate a creature we cannot see, we must study what we can. Mušḫuššu is a mishmash that takes a multitude of animals into its form. I start by studying the lion, specifically its torso and the structure of its legs, as this is the main form the dragon takes. The horns of a gazelle strike me when studying the ancient reliefs, so I shall add that to the mix. The wings and general anatomy of the falcon are also taken into account. Finally I study the Persian horned viper, whose angry gaze makes me think it's related to the mighty dragon! Studying the real world is important for any visual venture the artist embarks on. From here, I can move on to imagining what Mušḫuššu looks like.

03 INITIAL IDEAS

I sketch a few explorations of Mušḫuššu. The idea that the ancients who carved the dragon into their frescoes were not fully aware of what it looked like, and might have only caught glimpses of creatures or heard tell of stories from legends, is one that I like. To keep Mušḫuššu from seeming like a hodgepodge of animals slapped together, it's best to choose one dominant animal – in this case, the Asiatic lion. The subordinate animal here is the snake, after which I add other elements, such as the falcon's wings or horns from various animals.

I'll take the most appealing aspects of the drawings here and decide on what to add to my dragon. The wings, the leaner body, and the gazelle horns seem to work the best.

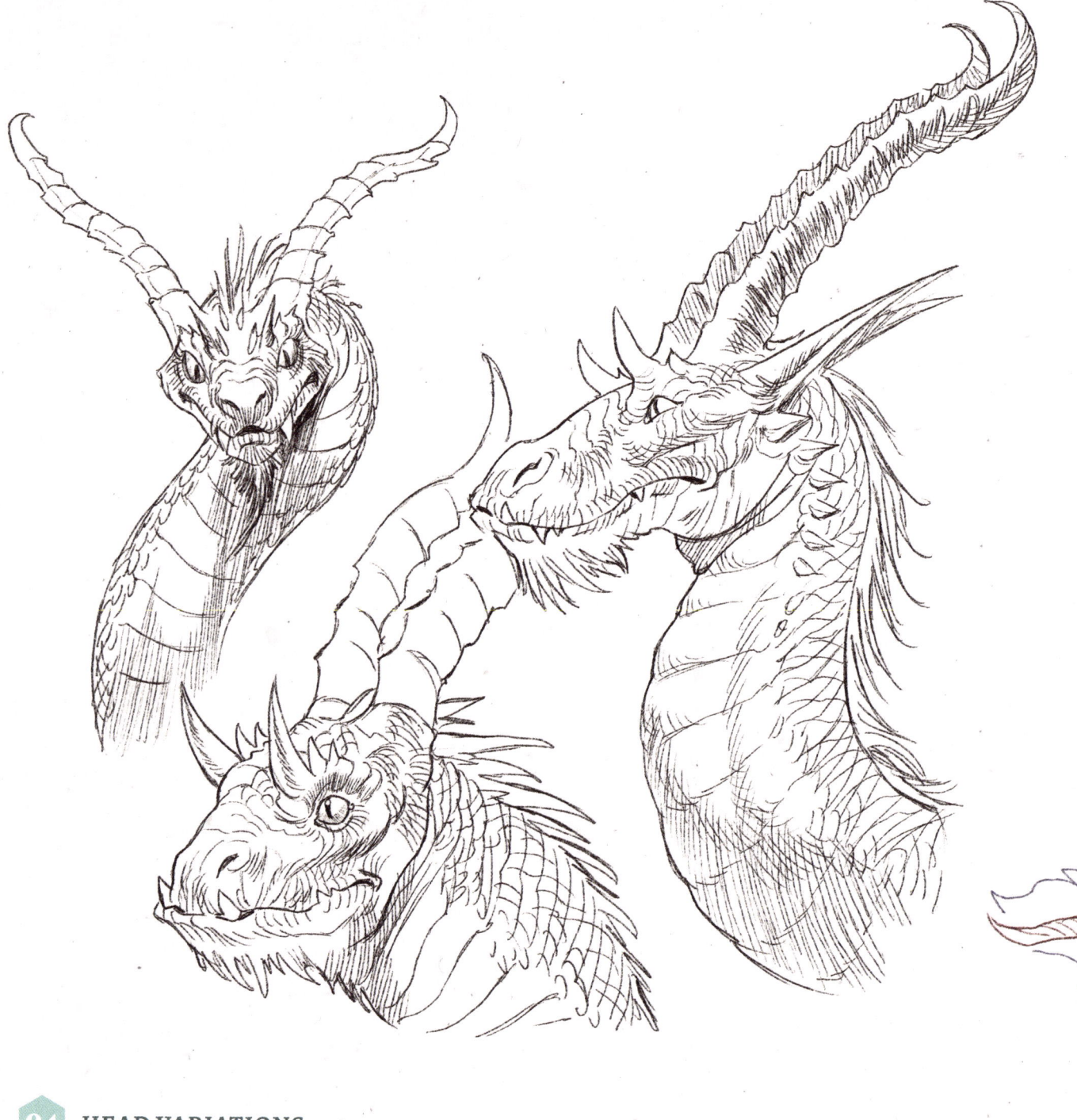

04 HEAD VARIATIONS

Next, I continue to explore head designs, aiming to nail the look that will crown this mighty dragon. The left head harkens back to the serpentine nature of Mušḫuššu. The right one looks like a more conventional dragon, with a canine or equine snout. The bottom one feels like more of an ancient reptile with some personality, with the gazelle horns giving a unique look to the Babylonian beast, so that is what I will be proceeding with.

05 SCALE & STRUCTURE

While drawing any subject, it helps to know the foundational structure underneath, whether it be from humans, lions, birds, or any other creature. Learning how muscles and bones work for one creature will help in drawing many others, as many animals share anatomy through their evolutionary ancestry. Here I'm trying to construct the anatomy of Mušḫuššu and her size relative to humans at the time. The base structure is that of a feline, built upon with all the other ingredients from the animal kingdom that make up this dragon. Having the foundations figured out, I can now really think about how the dragon will look to the naked eye.

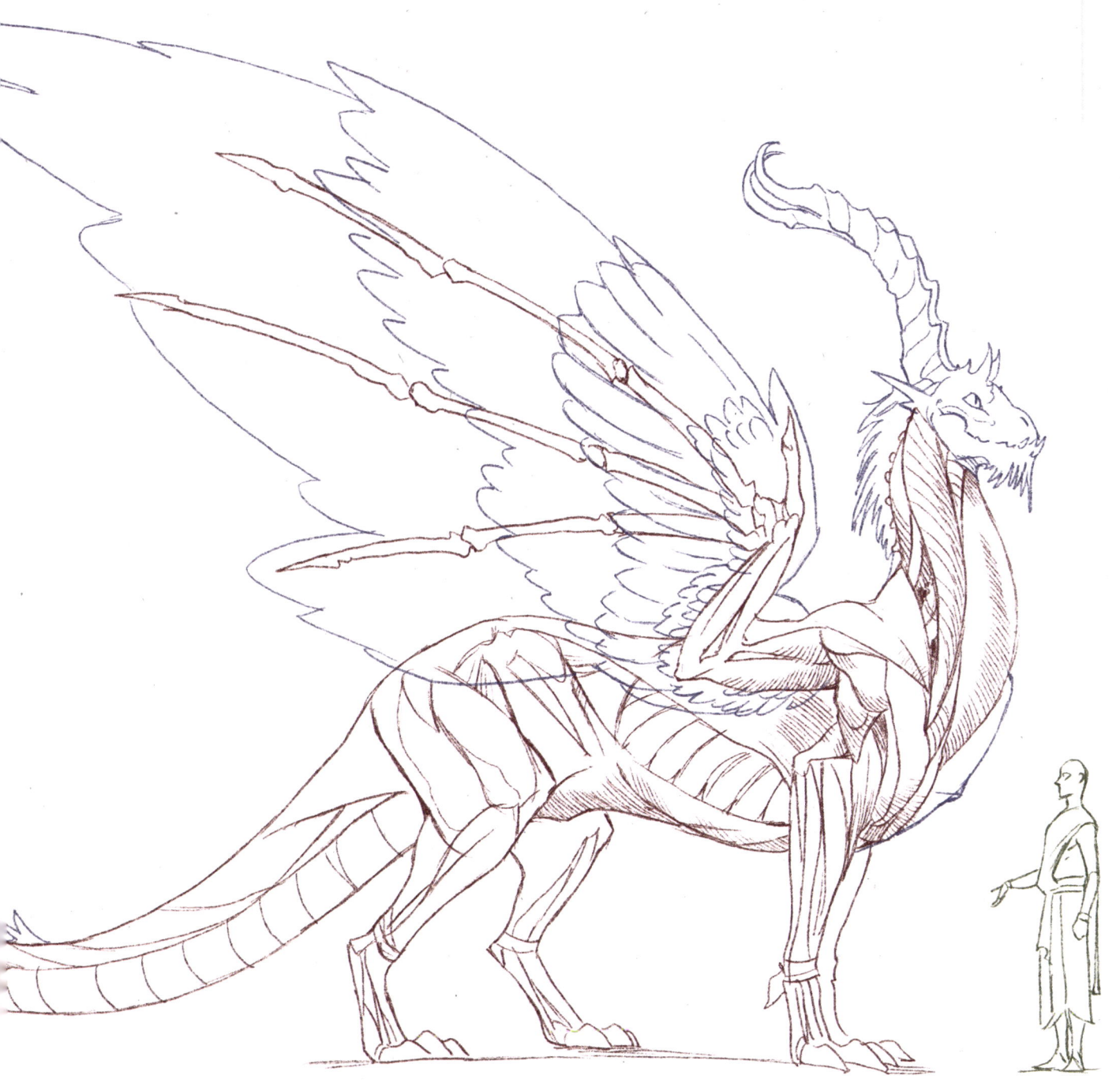

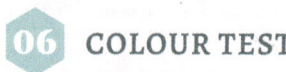

06 COLOUR TESTS

Now I can bring this delightful Bronze-Age beast into the realm of colour. I try out three variations here, all of which could suit various breeds of Mušḫuššu living out in the wilderness of Mesopotamia (which wasn't all desert, despite what people may think). A maroon, ochre, and cyan colour scheme could work well in different ecosystems, but, personally, the sapphire of the blue dragon reminds me of the lapis lazuli that decorates much of what we've found from ancient Babylon. I choose to proceed with that.

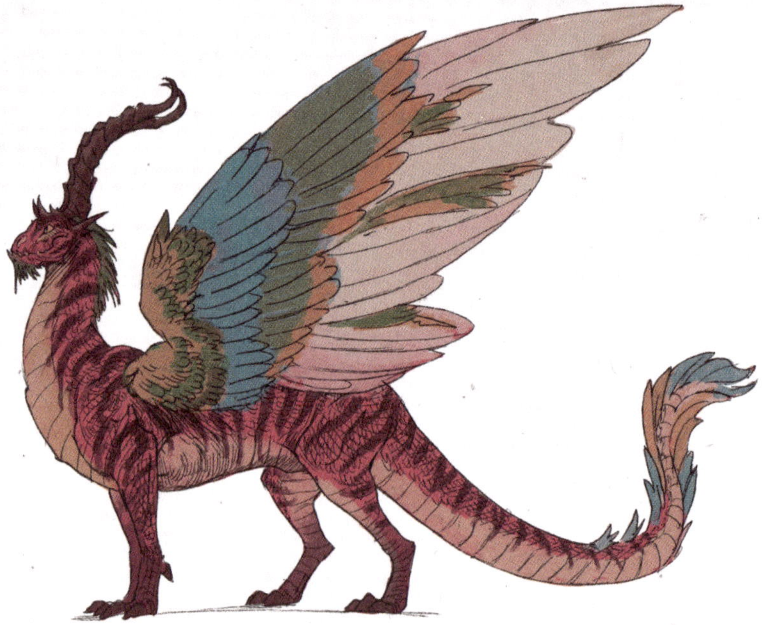

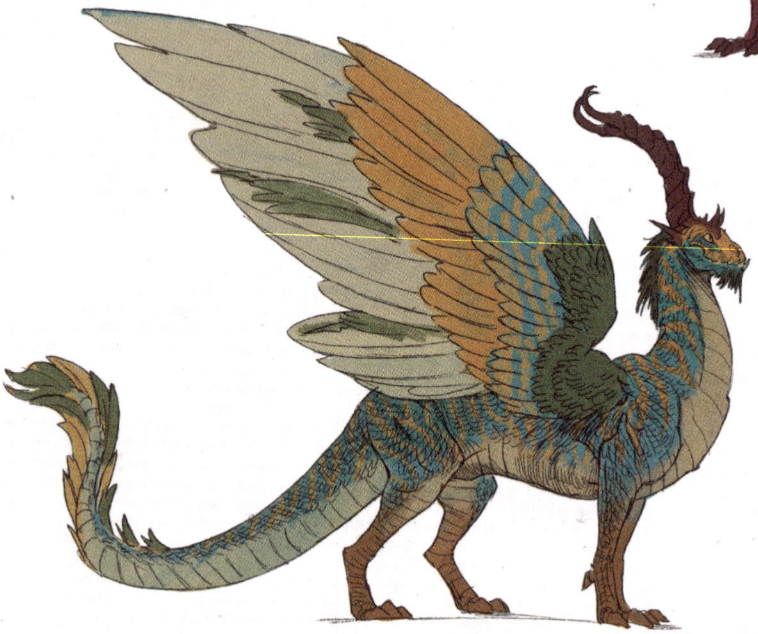

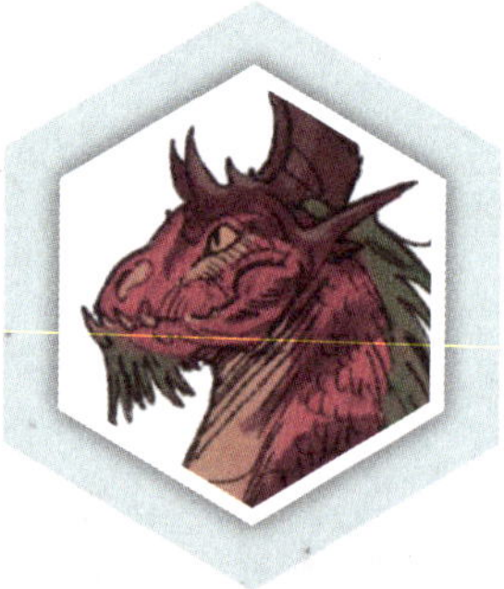

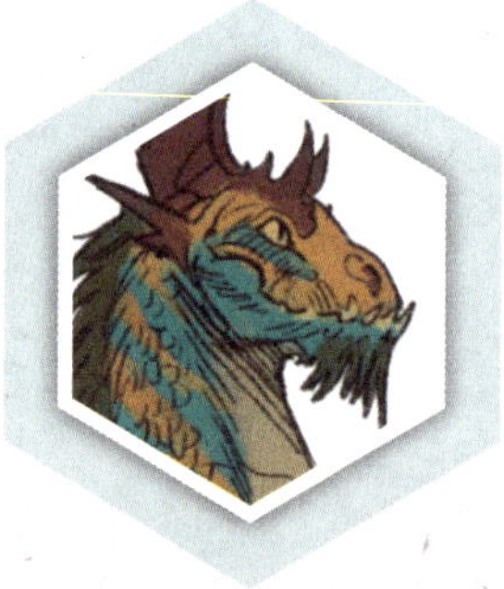

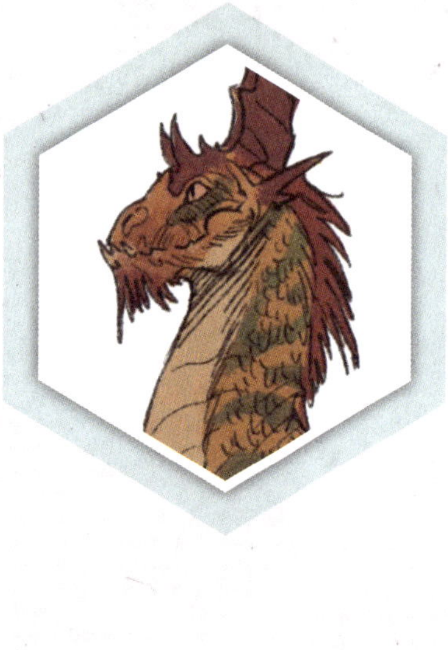

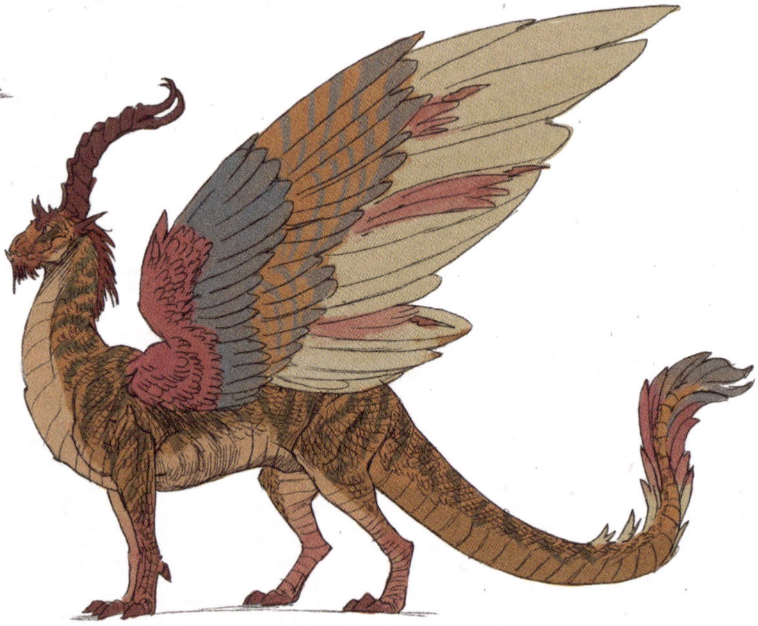

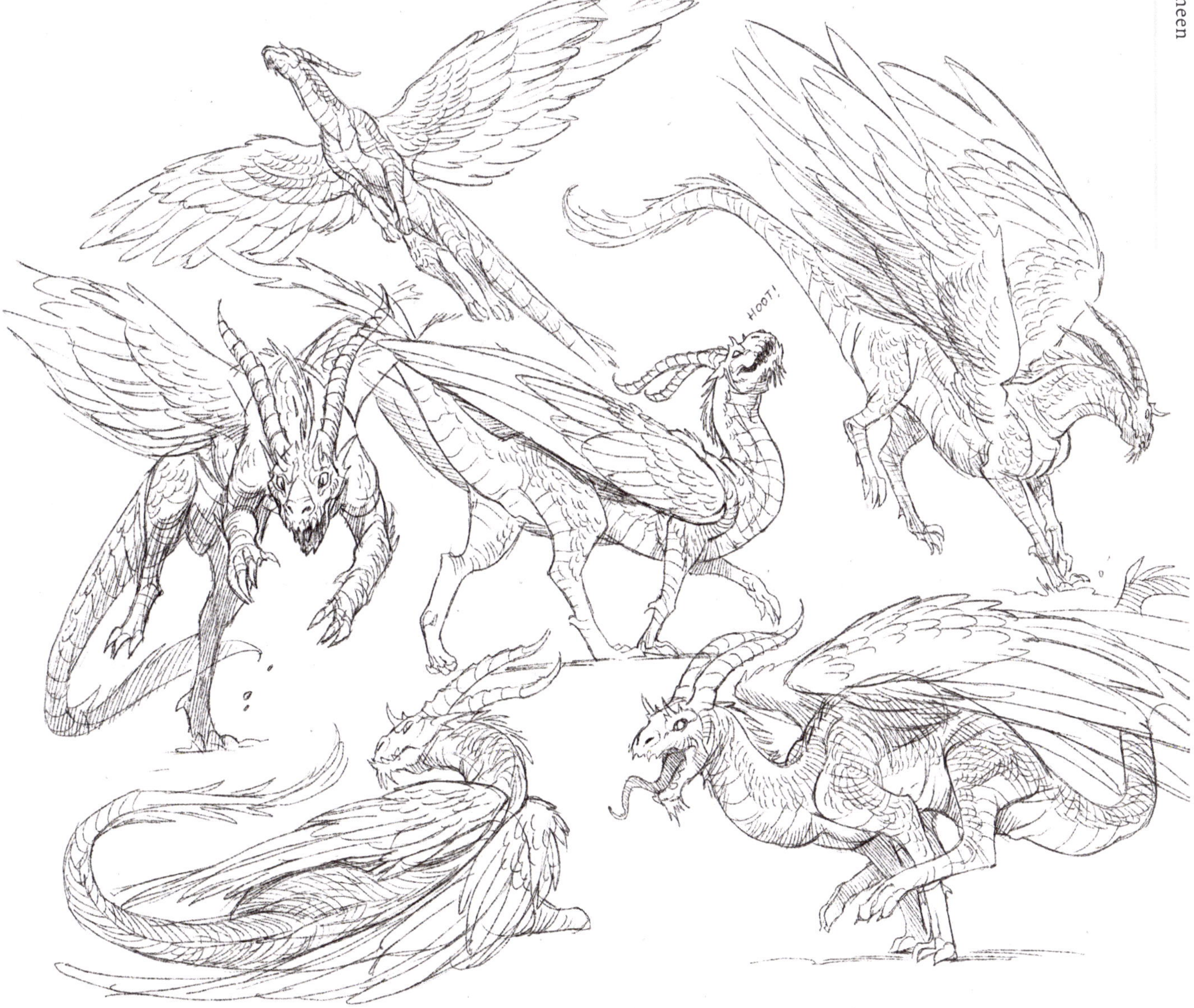

HOOT!

07   POSE & ACTION

Next I try to visualize the dragon performing various actions. Mušḫuššu was probably a lively and curious beast, flying and gliding from rock to grassland, leaping to capture any unfortunate prey. It may have been playful around its brethren and vicious towards its foes or food, but I can also imagine it lazing around or performing elaborate winged dances in its mating rituals. Sketching around like this is an easy way to bring such a concept out and inject some much-needed life into an idea.

183

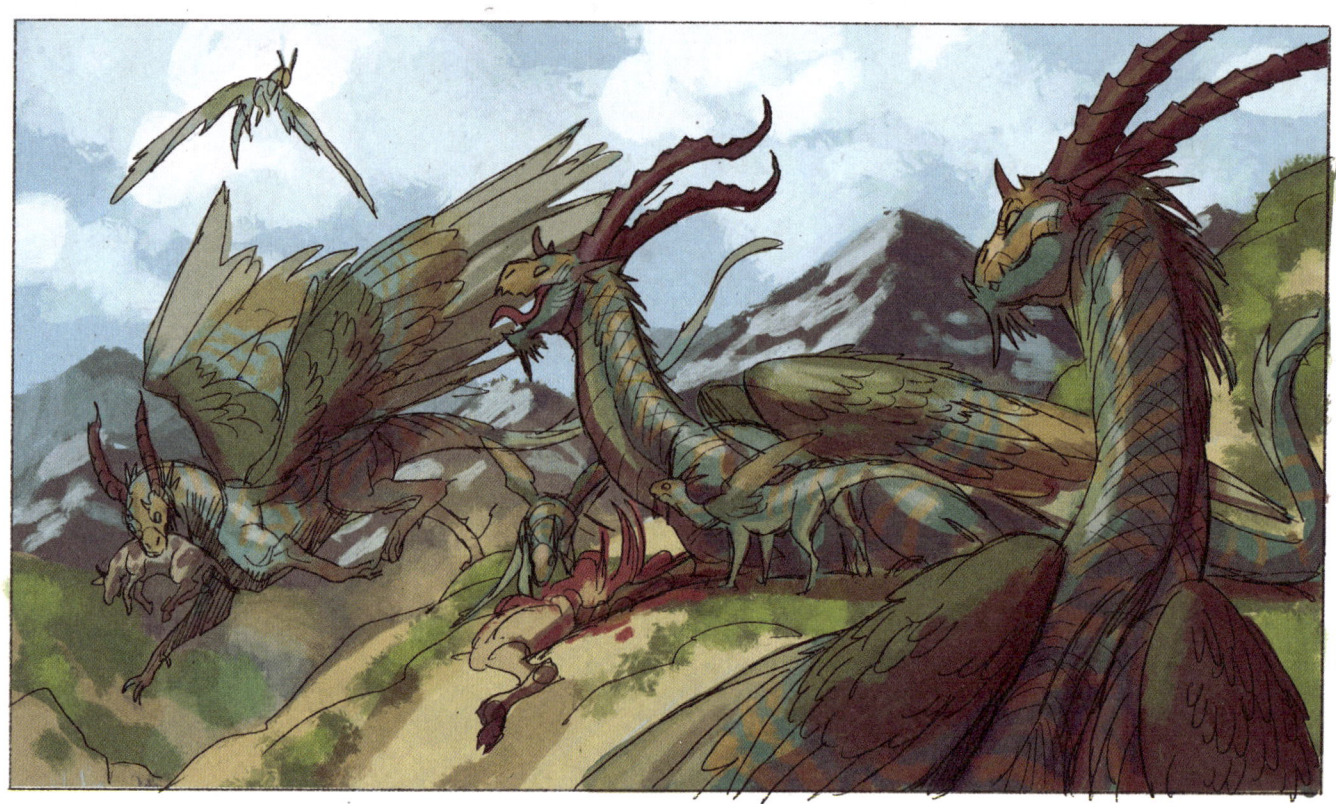

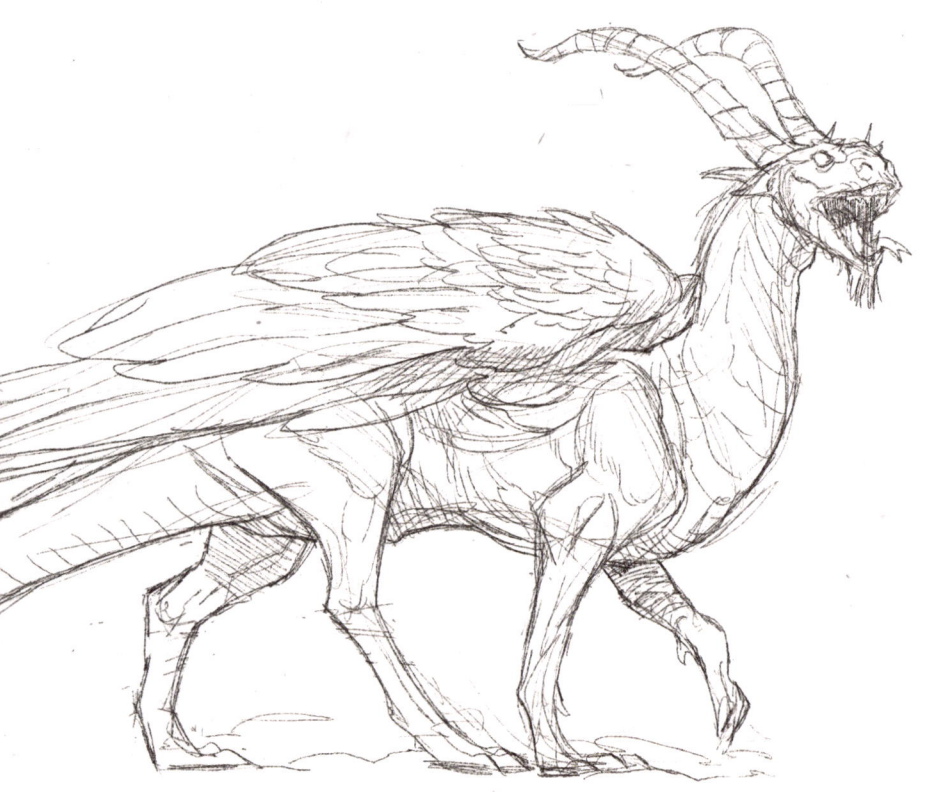

ENVIRONMENT

What about locale? Where did the Babylonian beast live before it reached the famed ancient city? I imagine it gliding and hunting on the green and ice-capped Zagros Mountains, which range across the land between Iran and Iraq. Here I depict a family of dragons devouring livestock stolen from some unfortunate Bronze-Age cowherd. The Mušḫuššu I imagine here to be fiercely protective of their loved ones, but solitary in their old age, like many felines behave today.

ROUGH SKETCH

I move on to the final vision of my dragon, starting with a sketch of Mušḫuššu. Having visualized her beforehand and drawn the beast in multiple poses, creating a naturalistic pose comes easily. At this stage, anatomy isn't at the forefront of my mind, but rather gesture and form. This rough sketch is the blueprint upon which I will build the rest of the painting.

10 ANATOMY CHECK

Within the sketch, it is important to establish structure. I have explored Mušḫuššu's anatomy beforehand, but will reiterate it here. I emphasize the underlying skeleton in this sketch, as anything built on a poor foundation is sure to crumble. This step might not be necessary if you're more experienced in the craft, but having it in the back of your mind, or using it as practice to better understand the forms you draw, will always yield results.

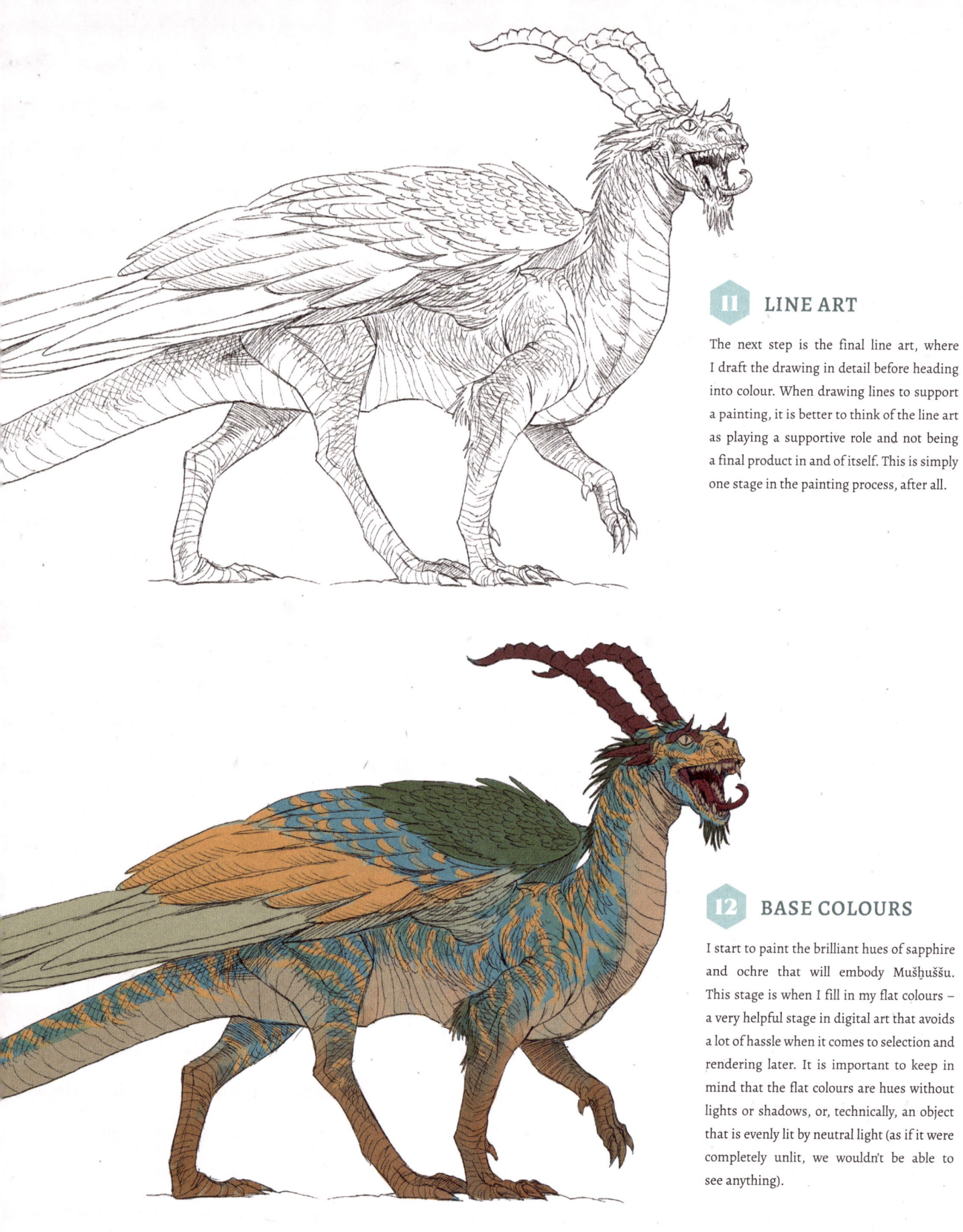

11 LINE ART

The next step is the final line art, where I draft the drawing in detail before heading into colour. When drawing lines to support a painting, it is better to think of the line art as playing a supportive role and not being a final product in and of itself. This is simply one stage in the painting process, after all.

12 BASE COLOURS

I start to paint the brilliant hues of sapphire and ochre that will embody Mušḫuššu. This stage is when I fill in my flat colours – a very helpful stage in digital art that avoids a lot of hassle when it comes to selection and rendering later. It is important to keep in mind that the flat colours are hues without lights or shadows, or, technically, an object that is evenly lit by neutral light (as if it were completely unlit, we wouldn't be able to see anything).

ROUGH LIGHTING

As I apply light, shade, reflective light that bounces back, and highlights created by the light source, the dragon slowly comes to life. At this stage, I think about other stages of hue, such as how various materials – horns, scales, and skin – reflect colour and light. For example, the hard, shiny scales and horns have a brighter sheen than the feathery wings. Generally, the main focus at this stage is planning the visual clarity of the final image.

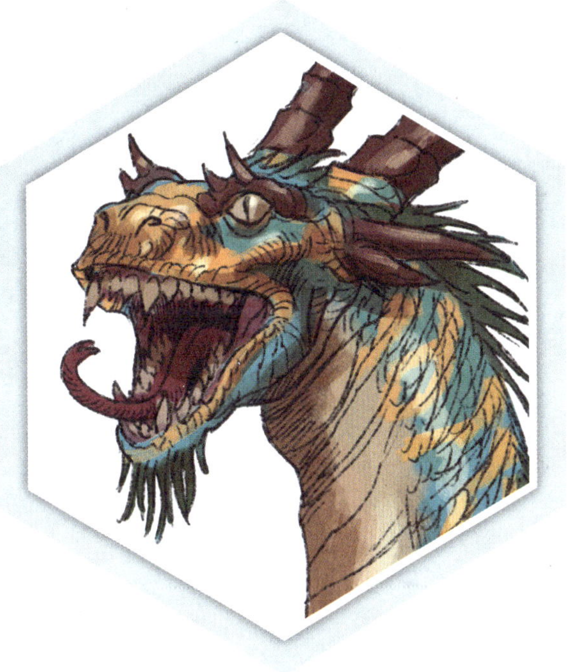

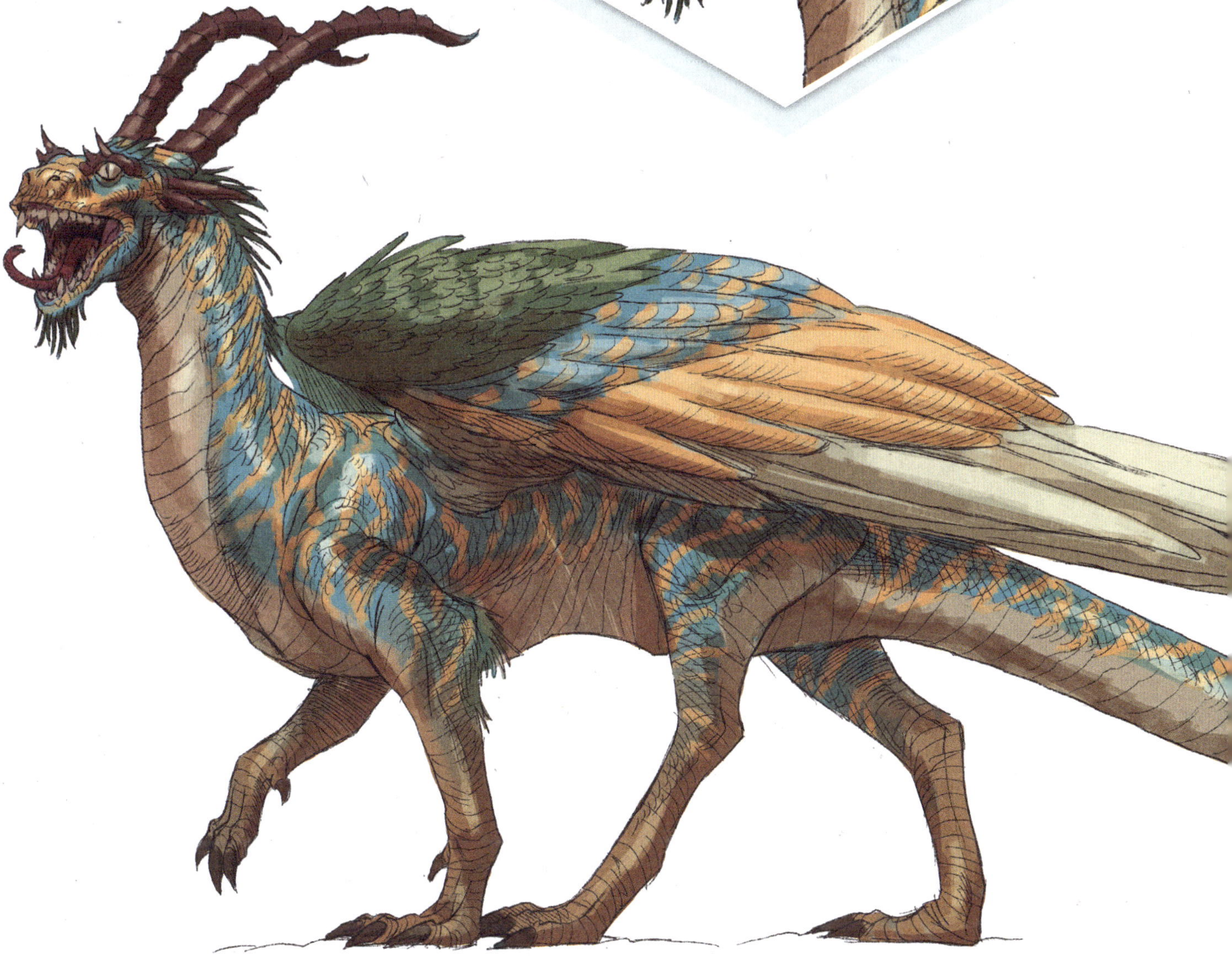

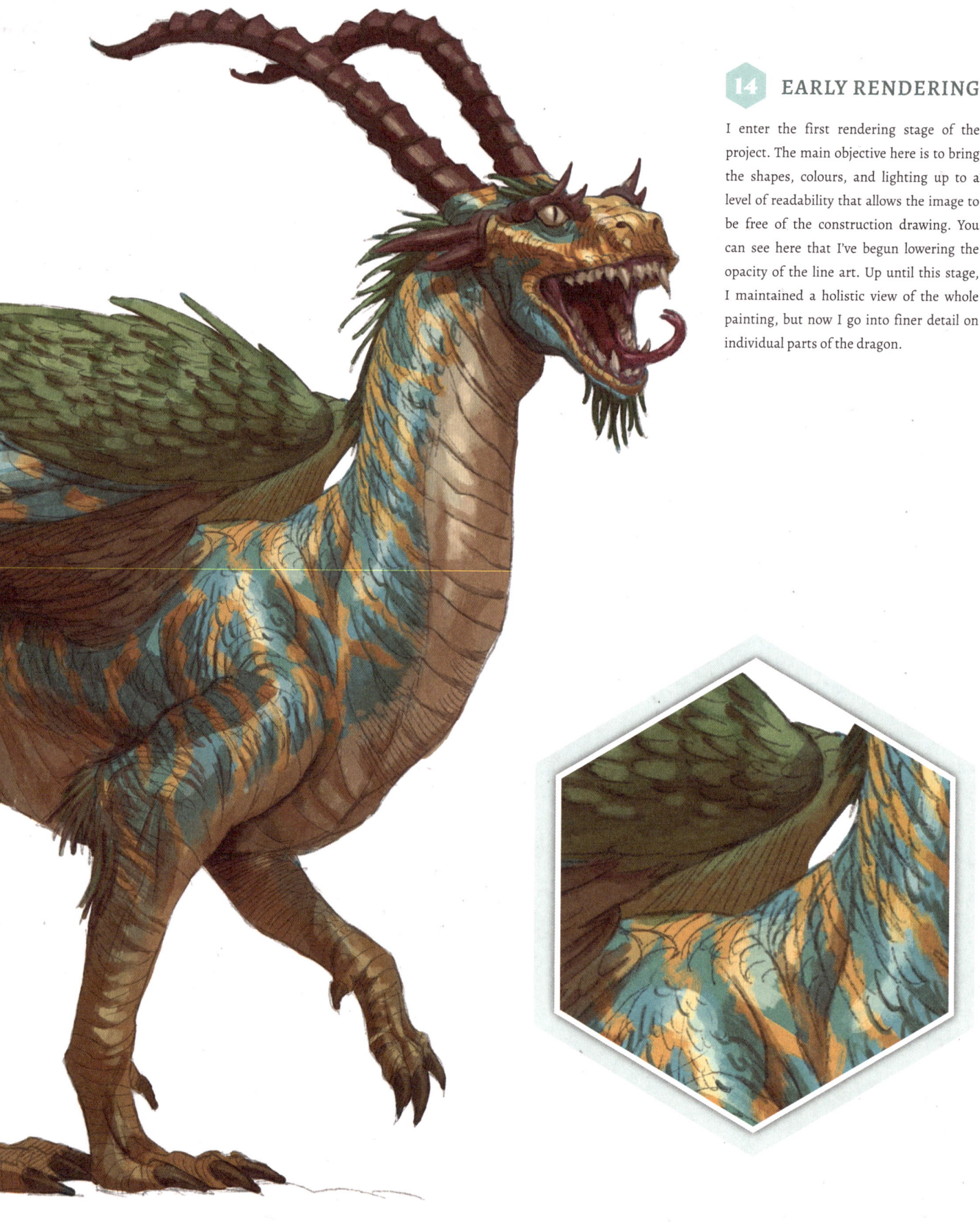

I enter the first rendering stage of the project. The main objective here is to bring the shapes, colours, and lighting up to a level of readability that allows the image to be free of the construction drawing. You can see here that I've begun lowering the opacity of the line art. Up until this stage, I maintained a holistic view of the whole painting, but now I go into finer detail on individual parts of the dragon.

15 REMOVING LINE ART

In the second stage of rendering, I continue on the journey of creating a polished image, pushing and pulling out the various forms and materials until I can turn off the line art completely. In this stage, it is easy to fall down a rabbit hole of endless rendering, lovingly detailing individual parts of the painting while forgetting the image as whole. It's best to take a step back once in a while to objectively examine your process.

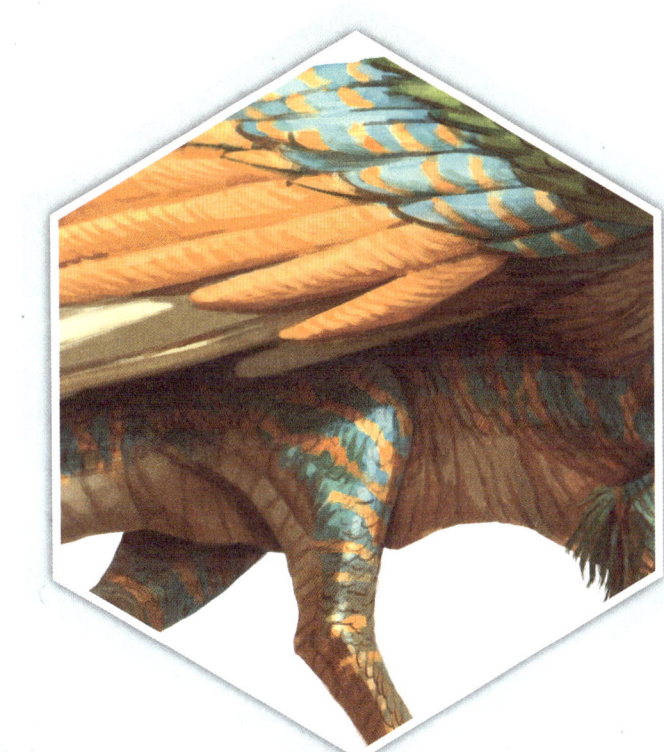

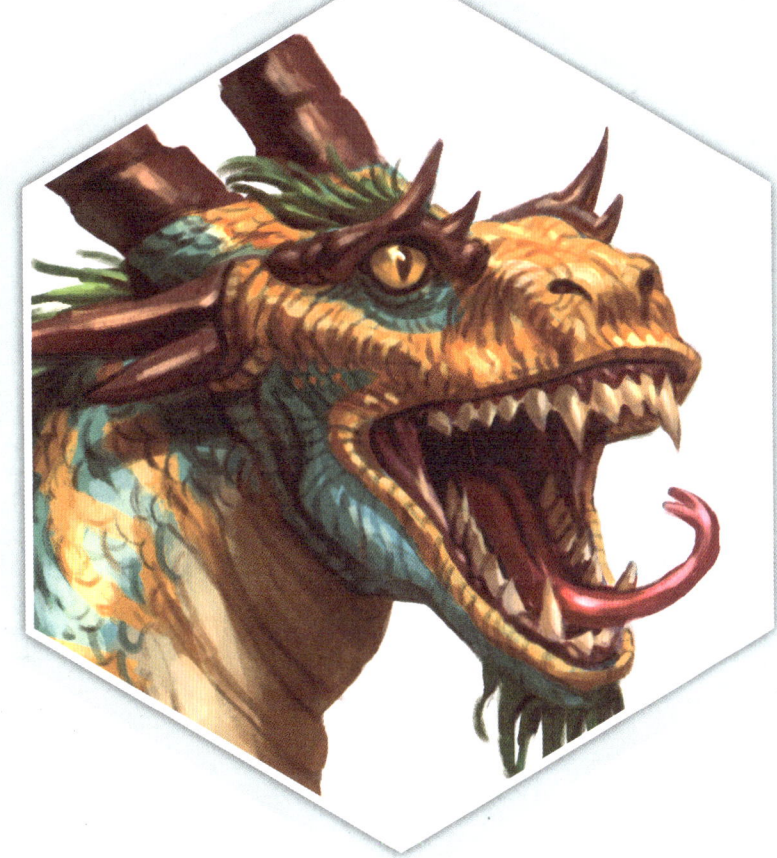

16 FINAL DETAILS

In the final stage of rendering, I detail out the focal point of the image, which in most creatures and characters will be the face. These final touches include specular highlights, such as the bright highlight on the eyeball and facial ridges, and dark occlusions, such as the shadowed insides of the dragon's mouth and lips. It's small flourishes like these that bring the painting to a finish.

CONCLUSION

The final painting showcases the majesty and ferocity of an early dragon that emerged from the Middle East. Mušḫuššu here seems familiar – many of us will have seen her shape depicted on archaeological finds – and yet different from the way she is interpreted in the ancient reliefs of Babylon. For a dragon so unknown, that balance makes sense to me, and seems a good rule of thumb for creature design. The colours reflect the richness of Mesopotamian civilization and the feline movement of the beast reflects her ingenuity and might. Perhaps the great Babylonian god Marduk would look upon this dragon and recognize her as his own.

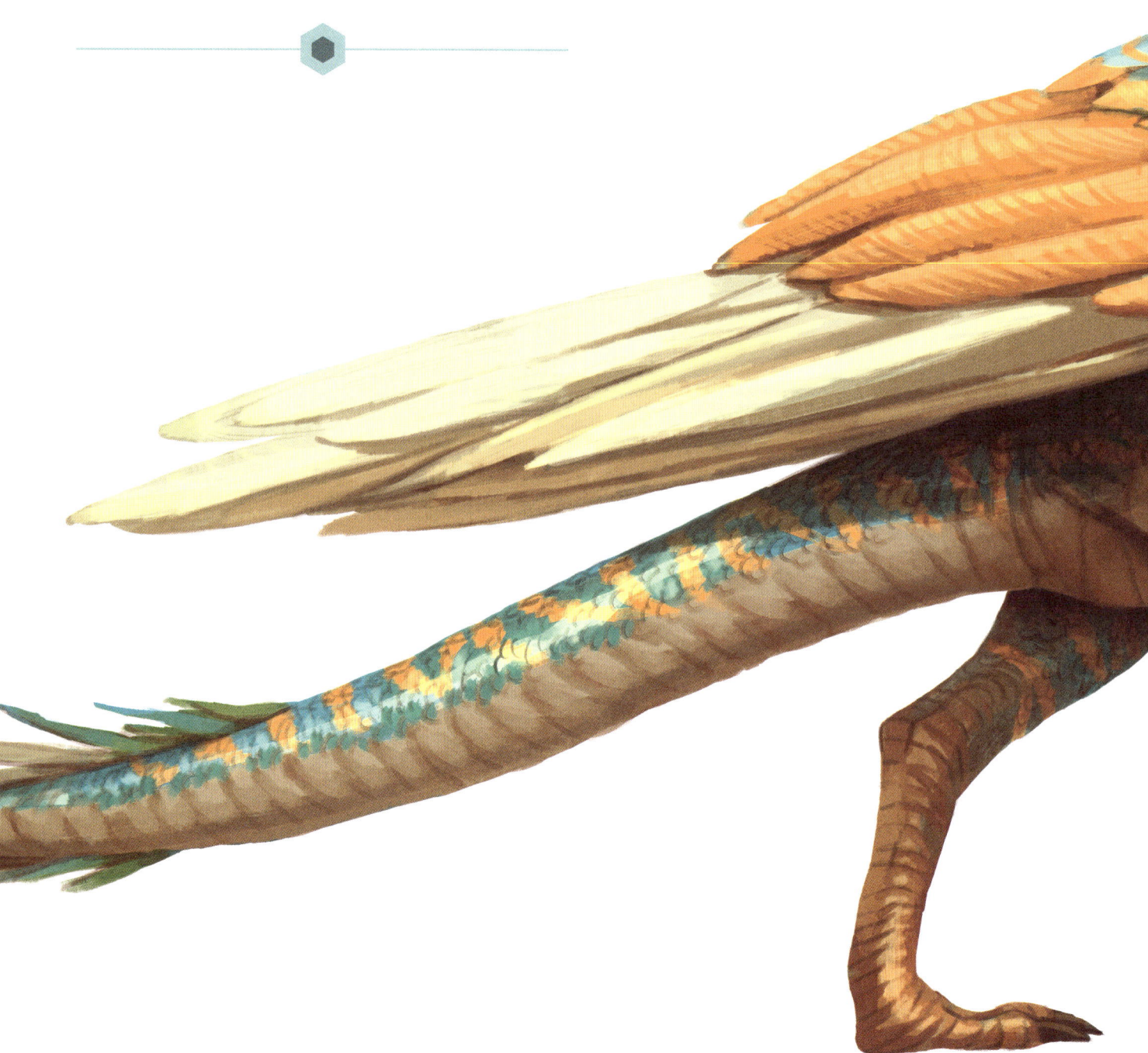

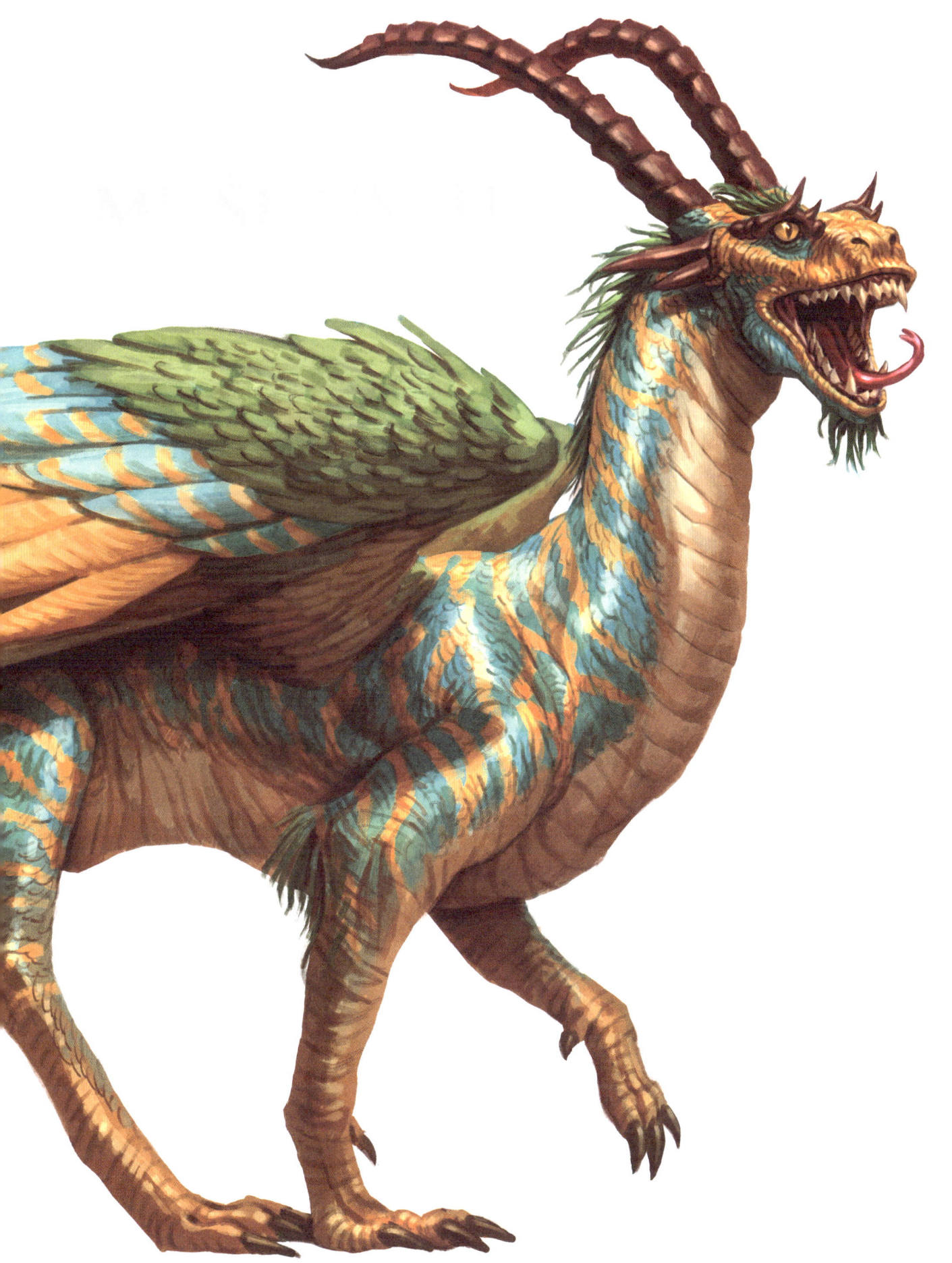

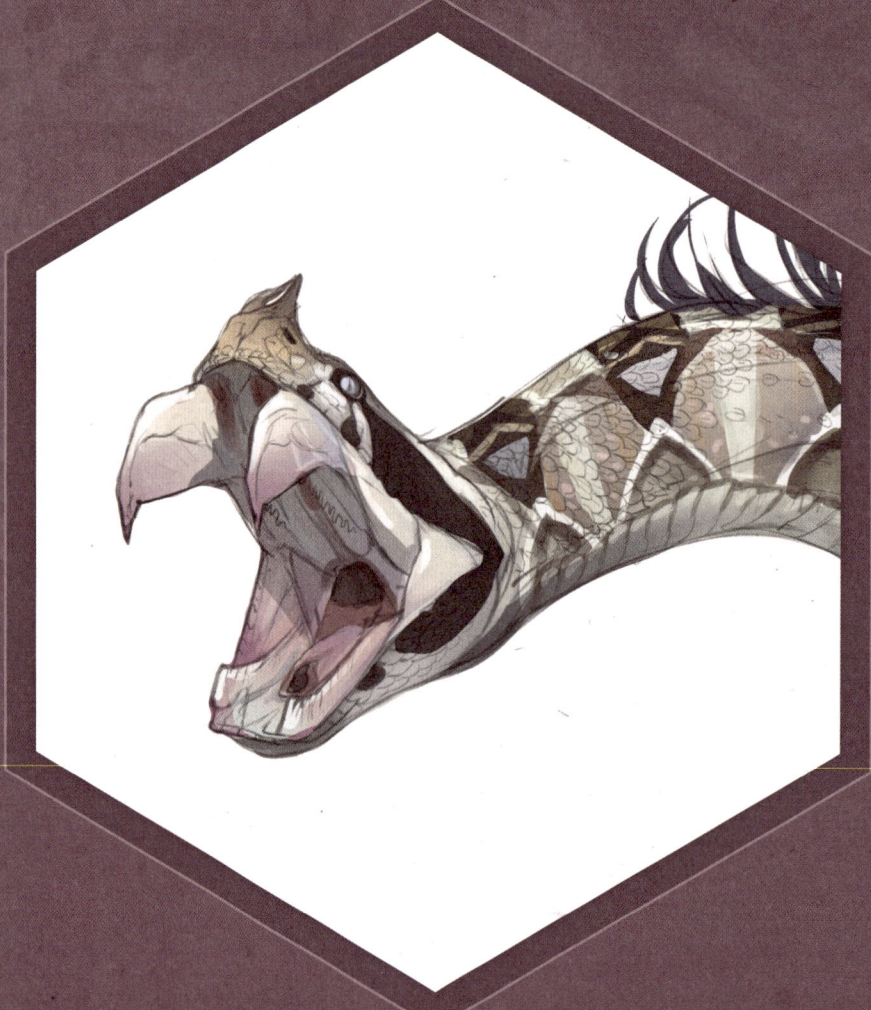

THE QUESTING BEAST

This tutorial will walk you through my thought processes as I design the Questing Beast. This creature is a mythical chimera from Arthurian legend, often described as having the head of a snake, the body of a leopard, the feet of a deer, and the tail of a lion: *'the strangest beast that ever [King Arthur] saw or heard of.'*

ALLISON THEUS

Final image © Allison Theus

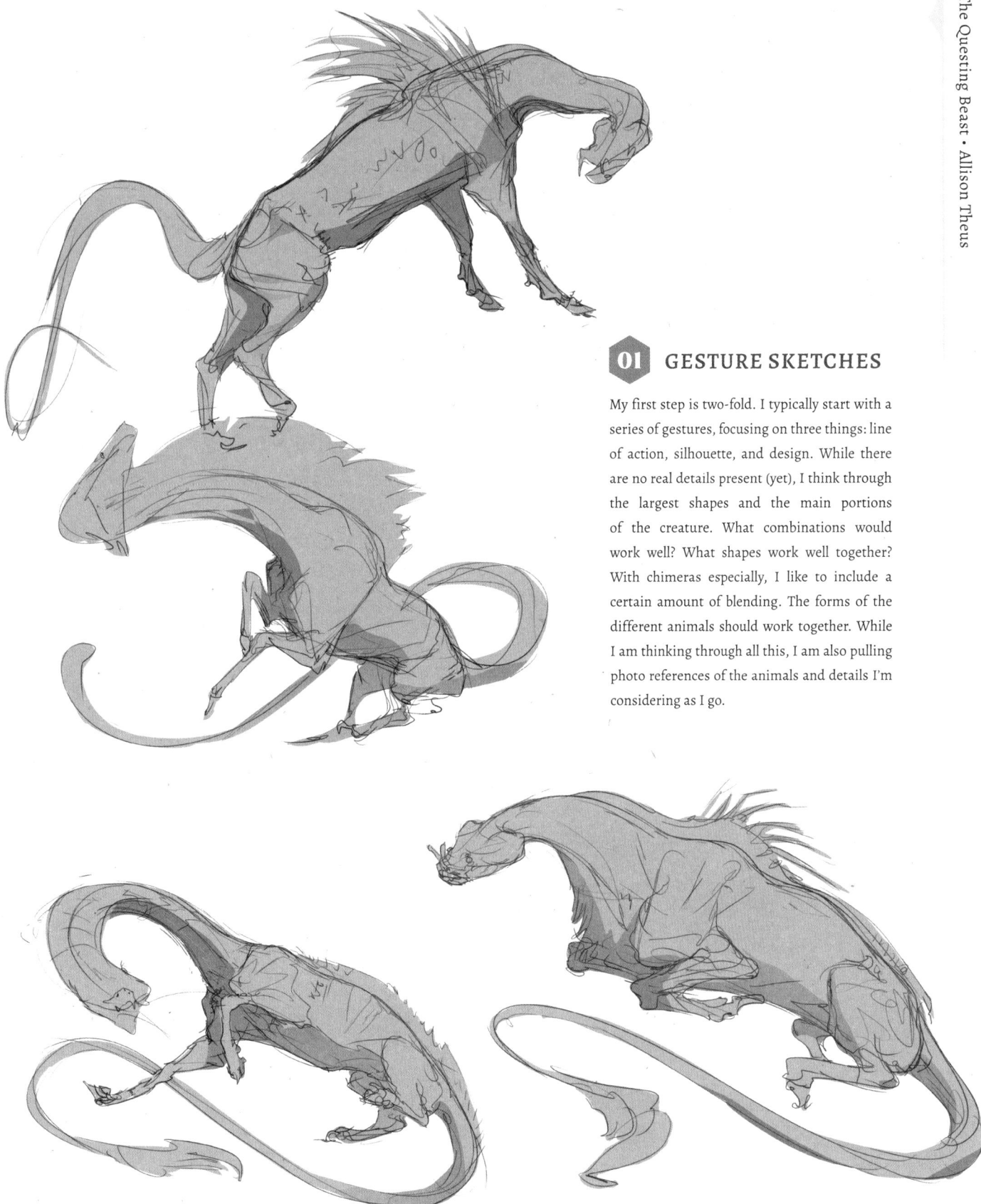

01 GESTURE SKETCHES

My first step is two-fold. I typically start with a series of gestures, focusing on three things: line of action, silhouette, and design. While there are no real details present (yet), I think through the largest shapes and the main portions of the creature. What combinations would work well? What shapes work well together? With chimeras especially, I like to include a certain amount of blending. The forms of the different animals should work together. While I am thinking through all this, I am also pulling photo references of the animals and details I'm considering as I go.

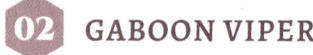 02 GABOON VIPER

Given that the general description of this creature very strongly resembles a giraffe, and because of the mention of a leopard, I'm going to create context for this animal and place it in Africa. The other main piece of the chimera is a snake, and fortunately, there are so many gorgeous species to pick from! It is easy to gloss over snakes if you have not been exposed to them in some way, but snakes bring an incredible wealth of visual information to the table. My immediate go-to is the Gaboon viper, a thick and powerful ambush predator with an iconic head and fabulous pattern.

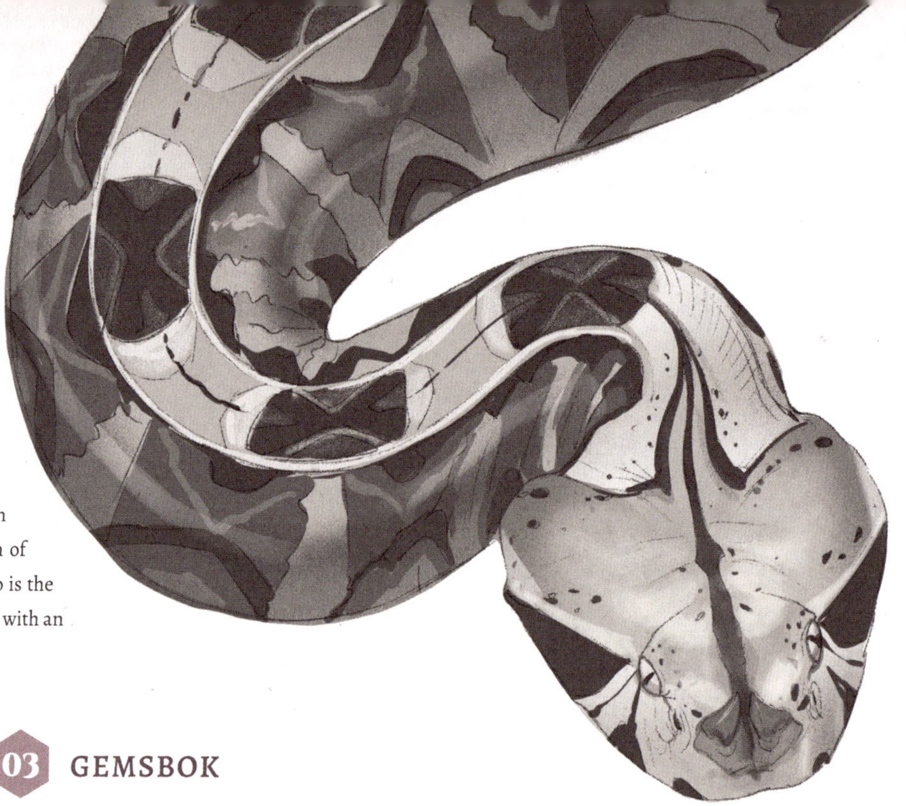

03 GEMSBOK

While there is a native species of deer in North Africa, I desire far more variety in my design. I decide to switch the deer portion for various antelope. The gemsbok is one of my favourites and may be a good match for the Gaboon viper. It is a little thicker and heftier than other antelope, and I like its bold markings. It might be a good match for the leopard part as well, and the shapes may flow together a little easier.

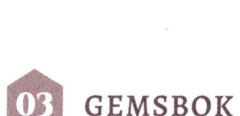

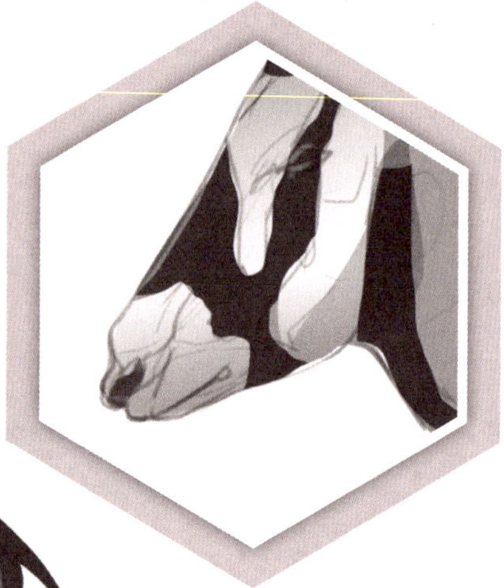

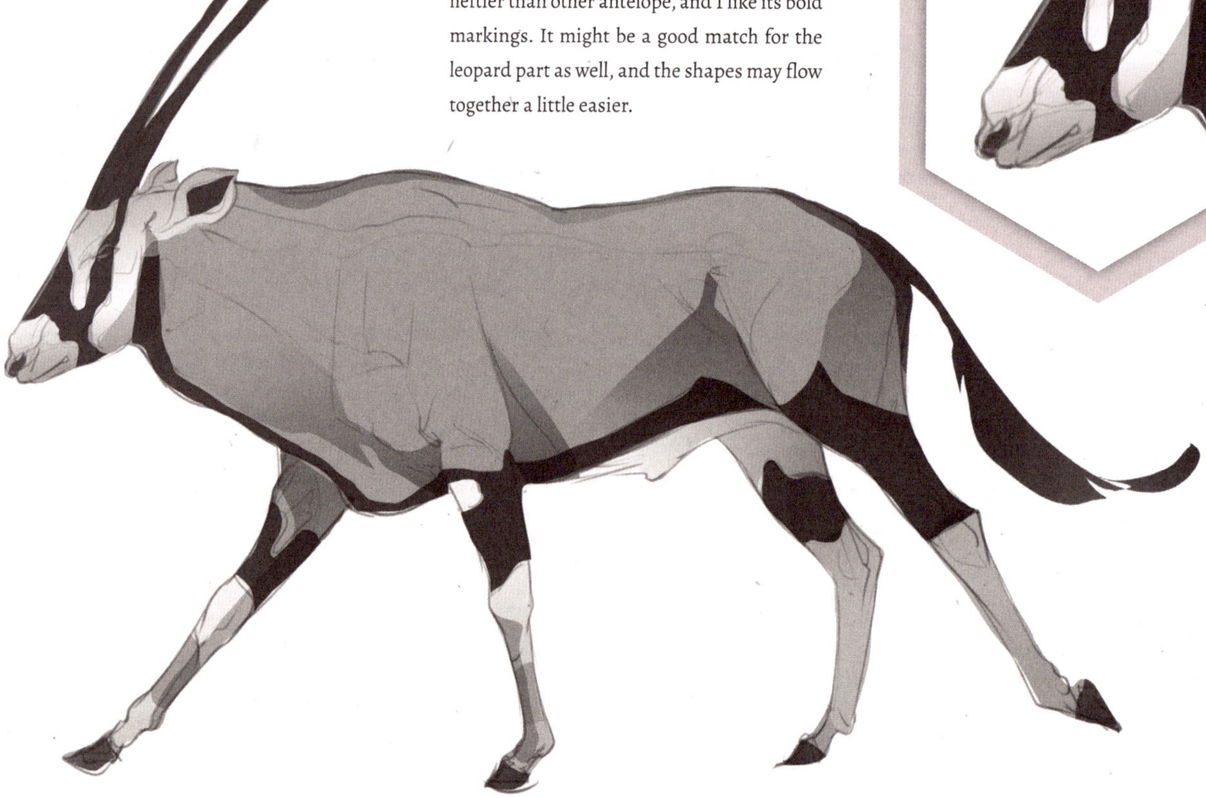

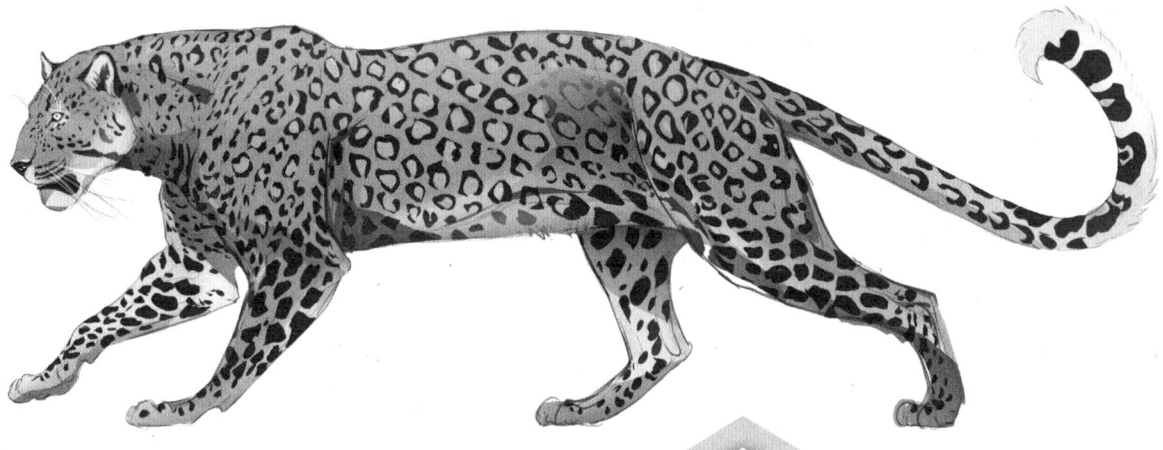

04 LEOPARD

Leopards are supple and powerful, able to ambush with great ferocity. Combining the suppleness of a leopard's body with the antelope body (which is flexible in a different way), is going to be a challenge. I will likely have to pick one direction or the other, and that's something that was at the forefront of my mind as I completed the initial gestures. To make a cohesive design, the shapes need to work together somewhat seamlessly to provide the illusion that this creature could exist.

05 GABOON-GEMSBOK MIX

I take that first rough gesture from page 193 and start to clarify it. I think the triangular head of the Gaboon viper and the thickened neck could do well with a heavier-set body. I toy briefly with trying to blend antelope and leopard legs, but then go more antelope for this version. For interest, I add porcupine quills and hair to the creature. They bring a pleasing busyness that could be used to help one pattern transition into another. The design is not exactly what I am looking for, but I feel it has great promise.

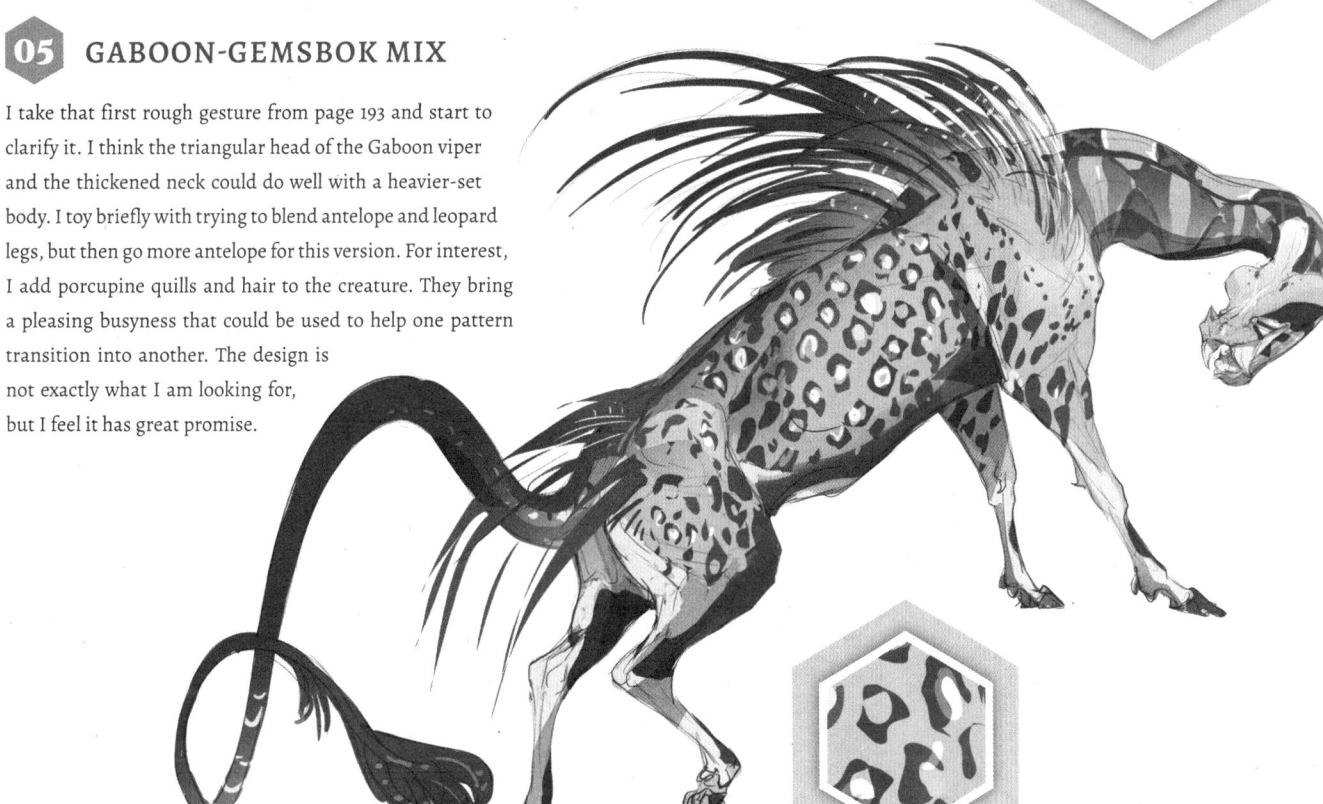

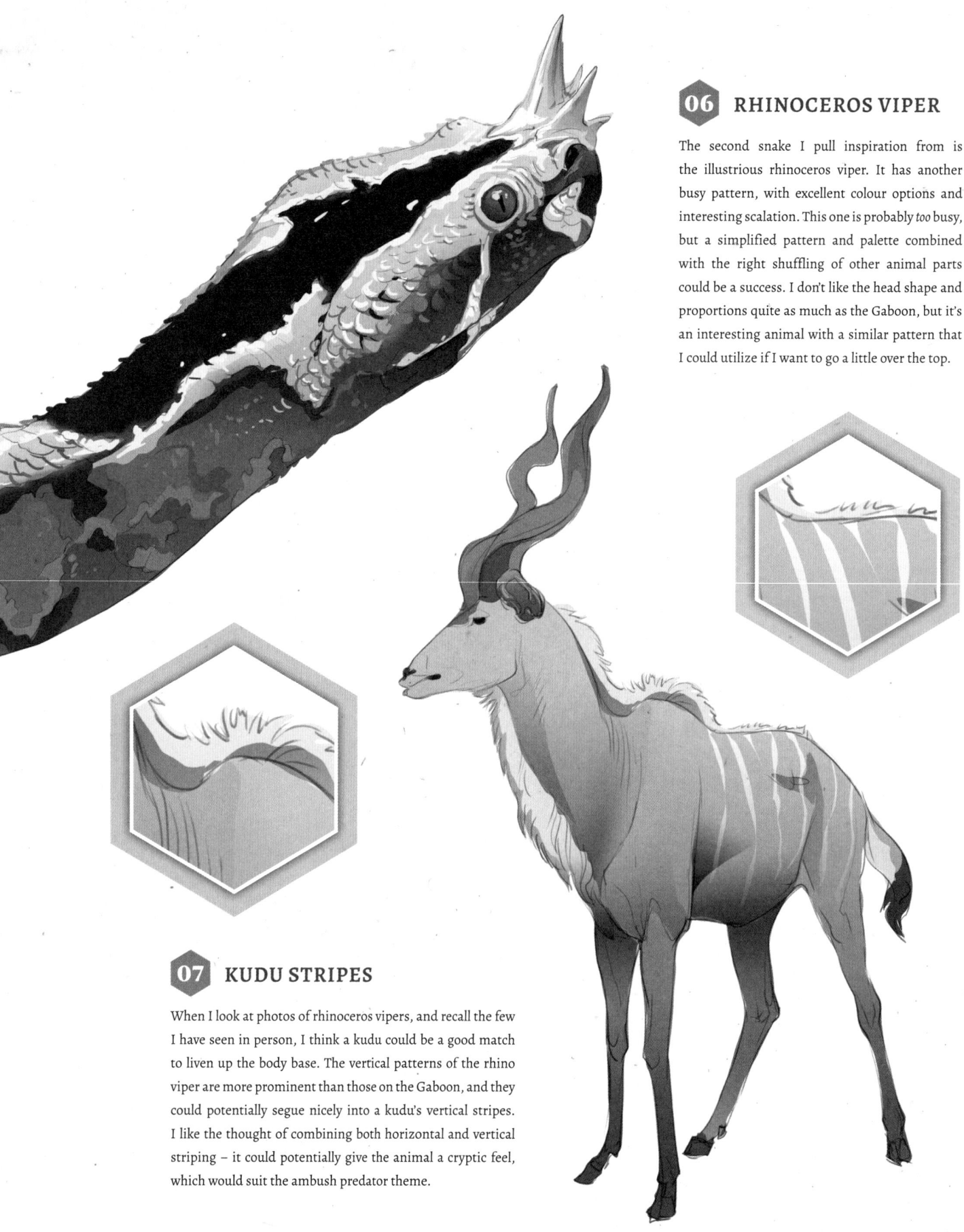

06 RHINOCEROS VIPER

The second snake I pull inspiration from is the illustrious rhinoceros viper. It has another busy pattern, with excellent colour options and interesting scalation. This one is probably *too* busy, but a simplified pattern and palette combined with the right shuffling of other animal parts could be a success. I don't like the head shape and proportions quite as much as the Gaboon, but it's an interesting animal with a similar pattern that I could utilize if I want to go a little over the top.

07 KUDU STRIPES

When I look at photos of rhinoceros vipers, and recall the few I have seen in person, I think a kudu could be a good match to liven up the body base. The vertical patterns of the rhino viper are more prominent than those on the Gaboon, and they could potentially segue nicely into a kudu's vertical stripes. I like the thought of combining both horizontal and vertical striping – it could potentially give the animal a cryptic feel, which would suit the ambush predator theme.

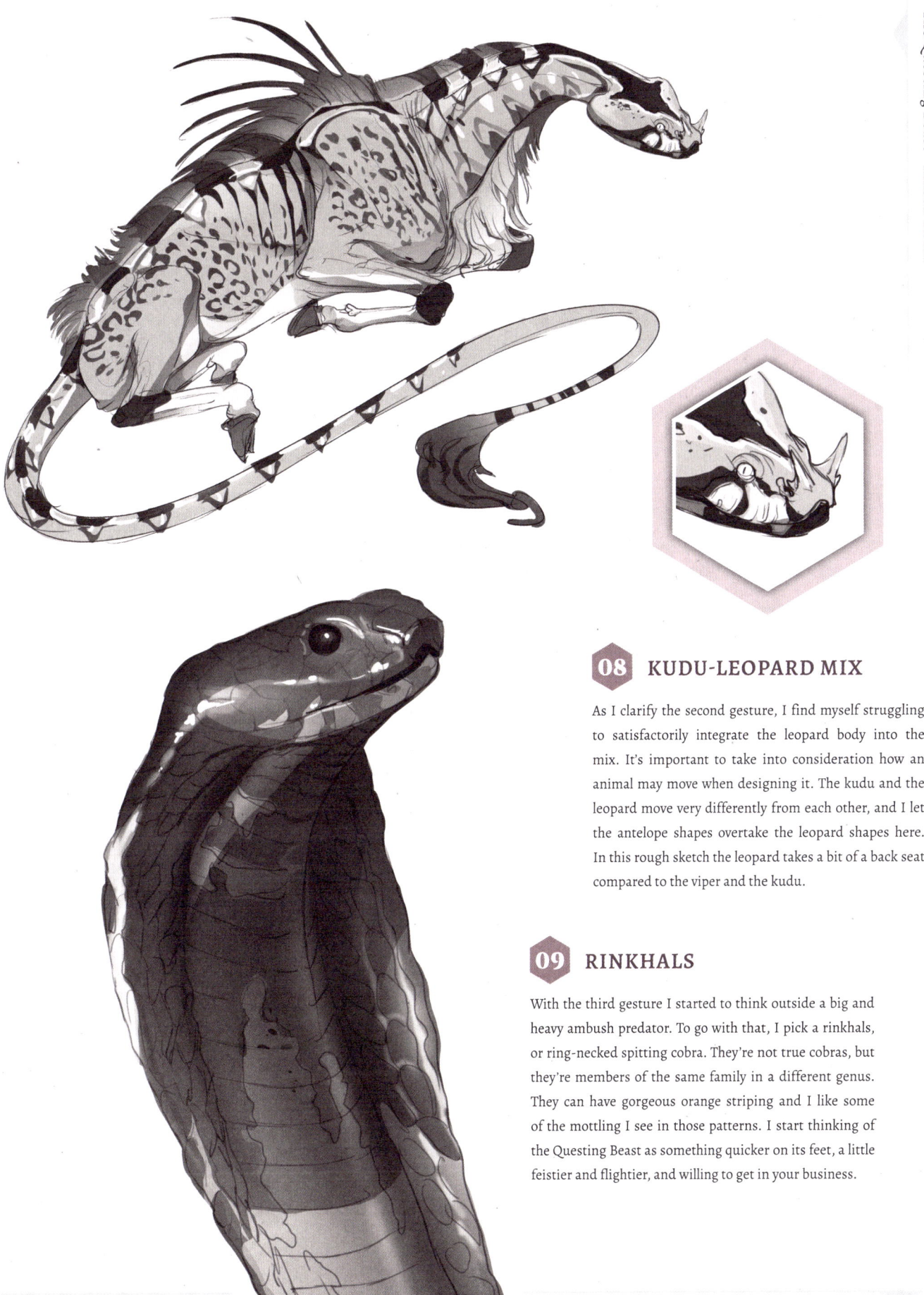

08 KUDU-LEOPARD MIX

As I clarify the second gesture, I find myself struggling to satisfactorily integrate the leopard body into the mix. It's important to take into consideration how an animal may move when designing it. The kudu and the leopard move very differently from each other, and I let the antelope shapes overtake the leopard shapes here. In this rough sketch the leopard takes a bit of a back seat compared to the viper and the kudu.

09 RINKHALS

With the third gesture I started to think outside a big and heavy ambush predator. To go with that, I pick a rinkhals, or ring-necked spitting cobra. They're not true cobras, but they're members of the same family in a different genus. They can have gorgeous orange striping and I like some of the mottling I see in those patterns. I start thinking of the Questing Beast as something quicker on its feet, a little feistier and flightier, and willing to get in your business.

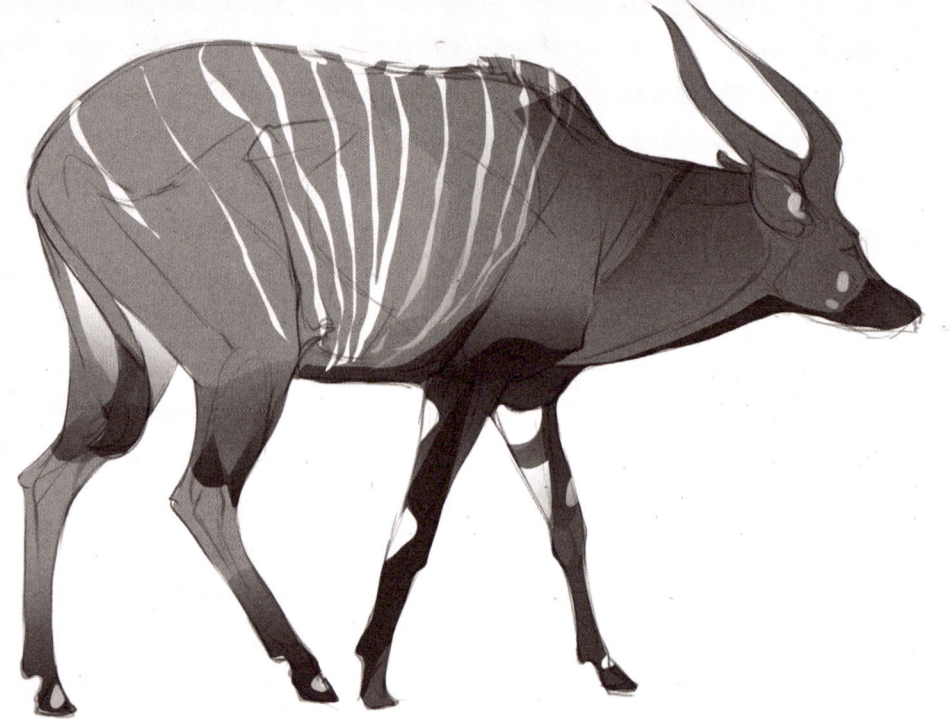

Next I start thinking about bongos. While they're still up there in size, as far as heavy antelopes go, their rounded backs and oval shapes could really work well with this next sketch. The bongo's vertical stripes are also a boon, as well as some of the subtle markings. I'm curious to bounce those shapes off those of the rinkhals.

11 RINKHALS-BONGO MIX

This rough has promise but is much less satisfying than the other two. The head and the antelope feet work, but I push too far into leopard territory for the rest of it and lose the cohesive feeling I am going for. I include feline back legs instead of antelope just to see how it would read. It's good to keep rough sketches quick so you can figure out what works and what doesn't in a decent time frame. This one is not working, but there are elements that could absolutely be repurposed for future designs.

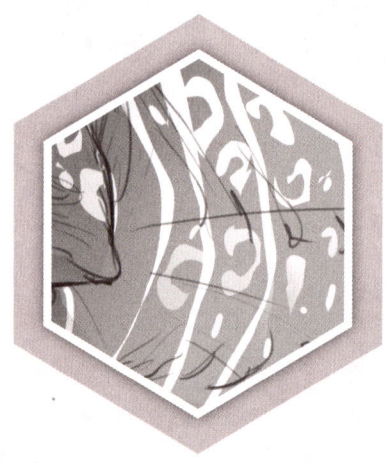

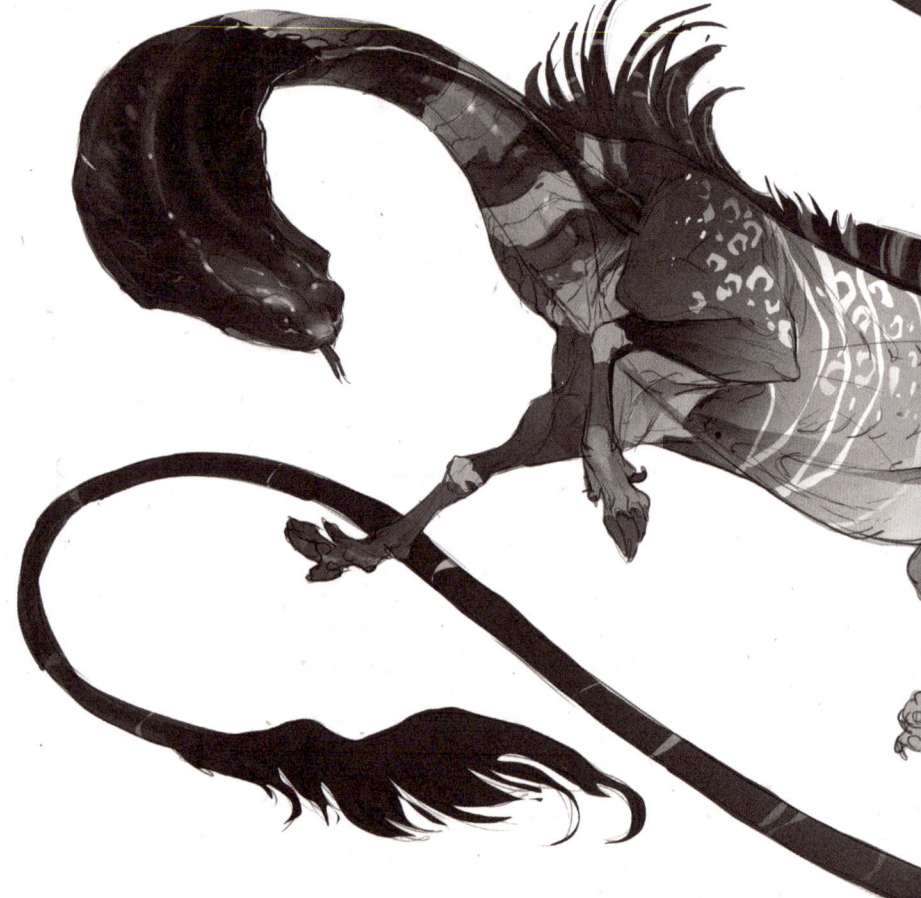

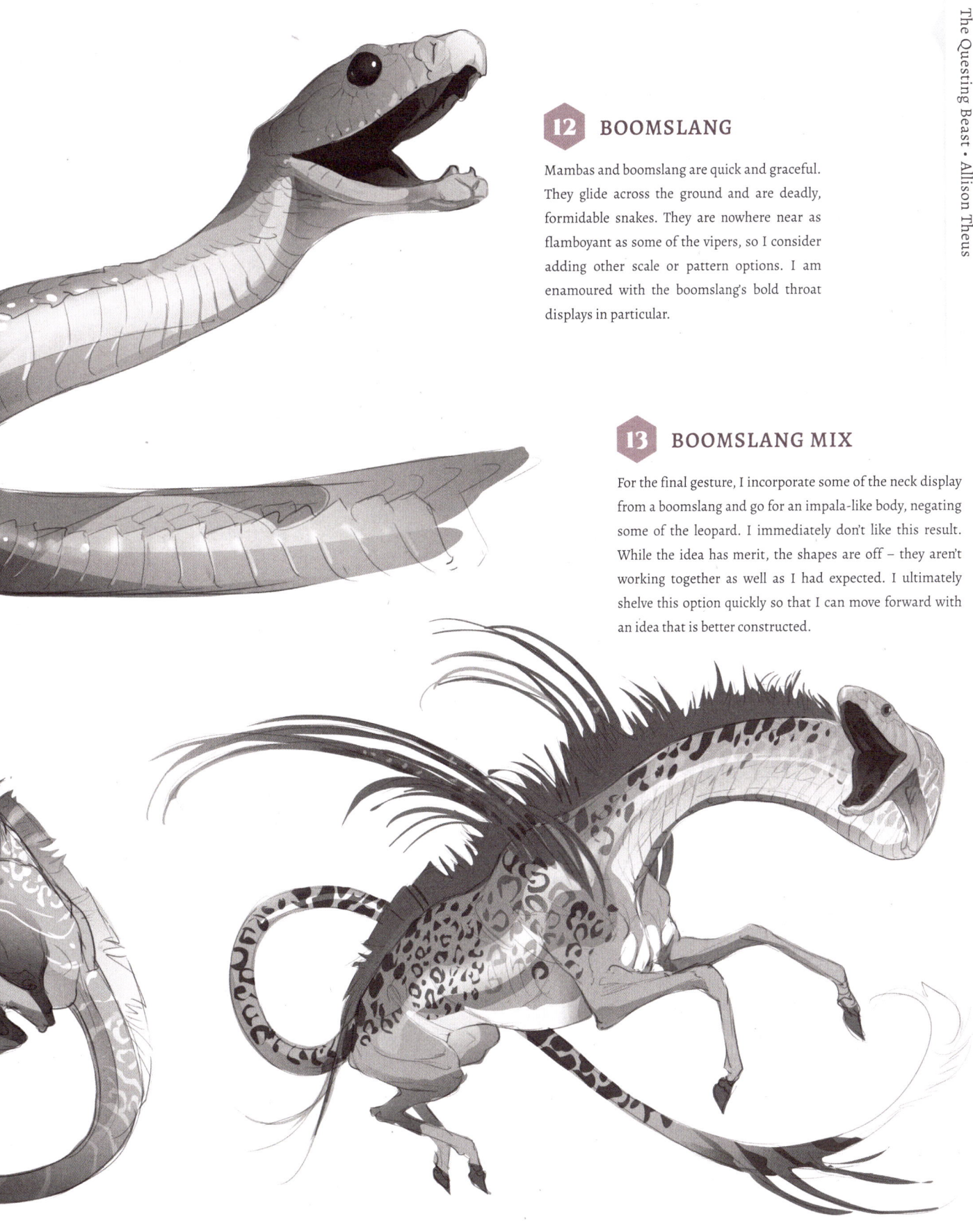

⬡12 BOOMSLANG

Mambas and boomslang are quick and graceful. They glide across the ground and are deadly, formidable snakes. They are nowhere near as flamboyant as some of the vipers, so I consider adding other scale or pattern options. I am enamoured with the boomslang's bold throat displays in particular.

⬡13 BOOMSLANG MIX

For the final gesture, I incorporate some of the neck display from a boomslang and go for an impala-like body, negating some of the leopard. I immediately don't like this result. While the idea has merit, the shapes are off – they aren't working together as well as I had expected. I ultimately shelve this option quickly so that I can move forward with an idea that is better constructed.

HEAD EXPLORATIONS

Out of curiosity, because I have been blending everything else, I make a few sketches blending antelope heads with snake heads. The two animals are constructed somewhat oppositely. A snake's eyes are close to its snout, versus an antelope's eyes, which are far from its snout. The snake's skull is wide while the antelope's is tall. It is a good exercise in attempting to balance forms, and while it is doable to an extent, the results are unsatisfactory. I decide I would rather move forward with just a snake's head to give the design more breathing room.

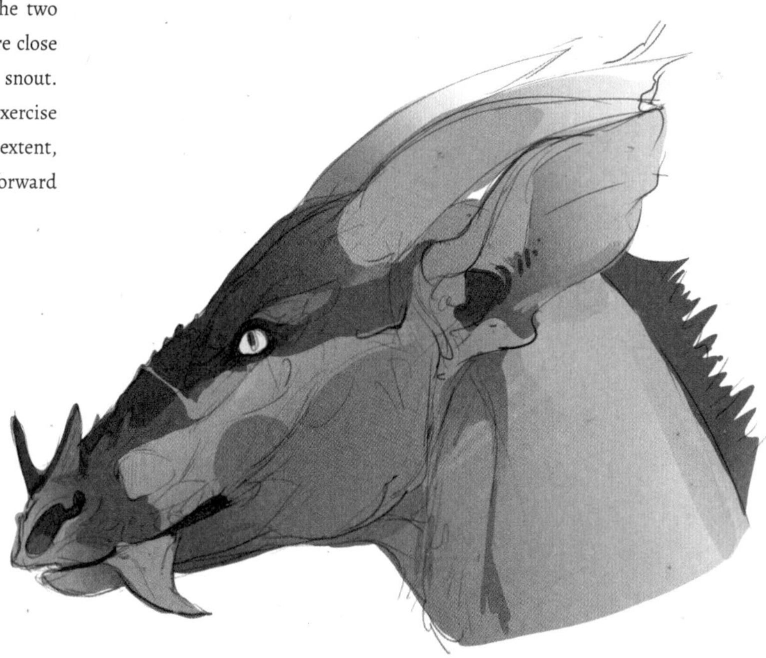

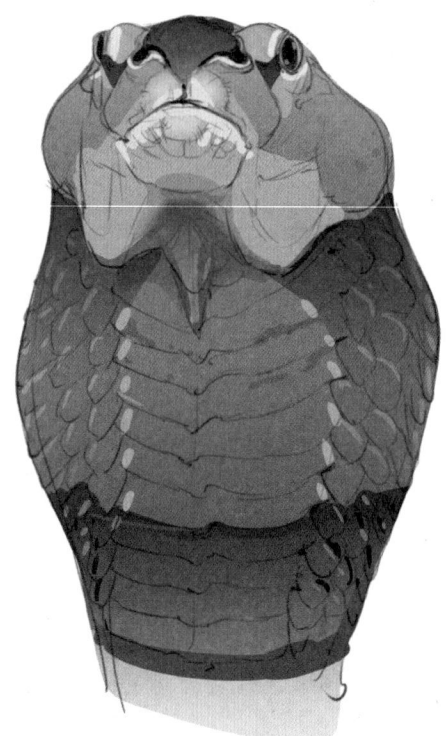

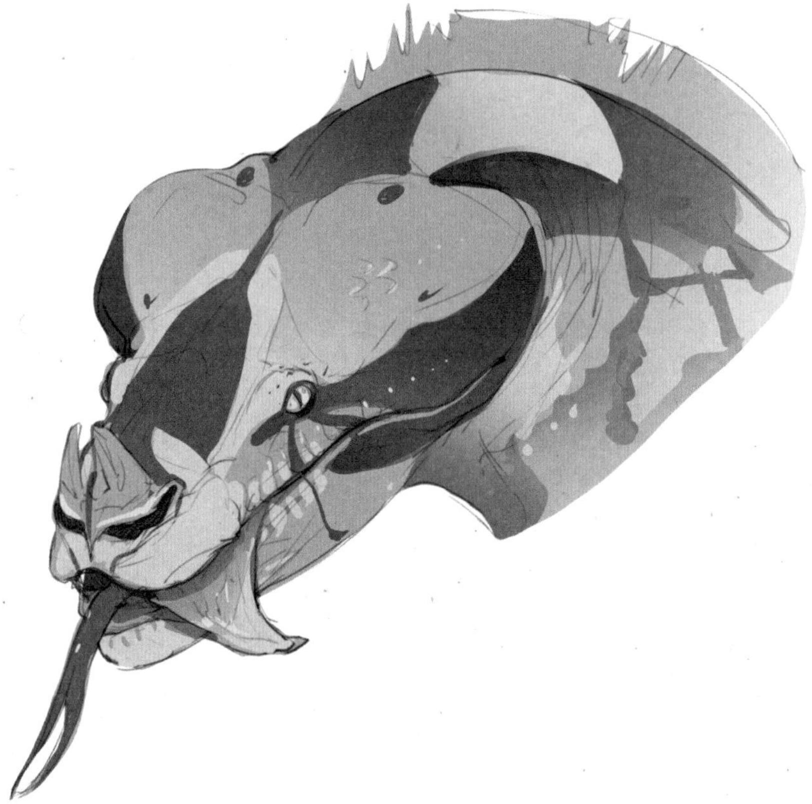

15 FINAL DESIGN GESTURE

After the initial rough passes I decide I want to focus on something more leopard-like. I want a powerful and supple design, with the option to combine both leopard and antelope legs. The initial gesture for the final is very energetic. I enjoy pushing poses in gestures to test-drive ideas early – it saves a lot of hassle. I add dewclaws to the design, as well as bringing back the porcupine quills, to help keep interest. I also split up the fur masses on the tail to better balance everything.

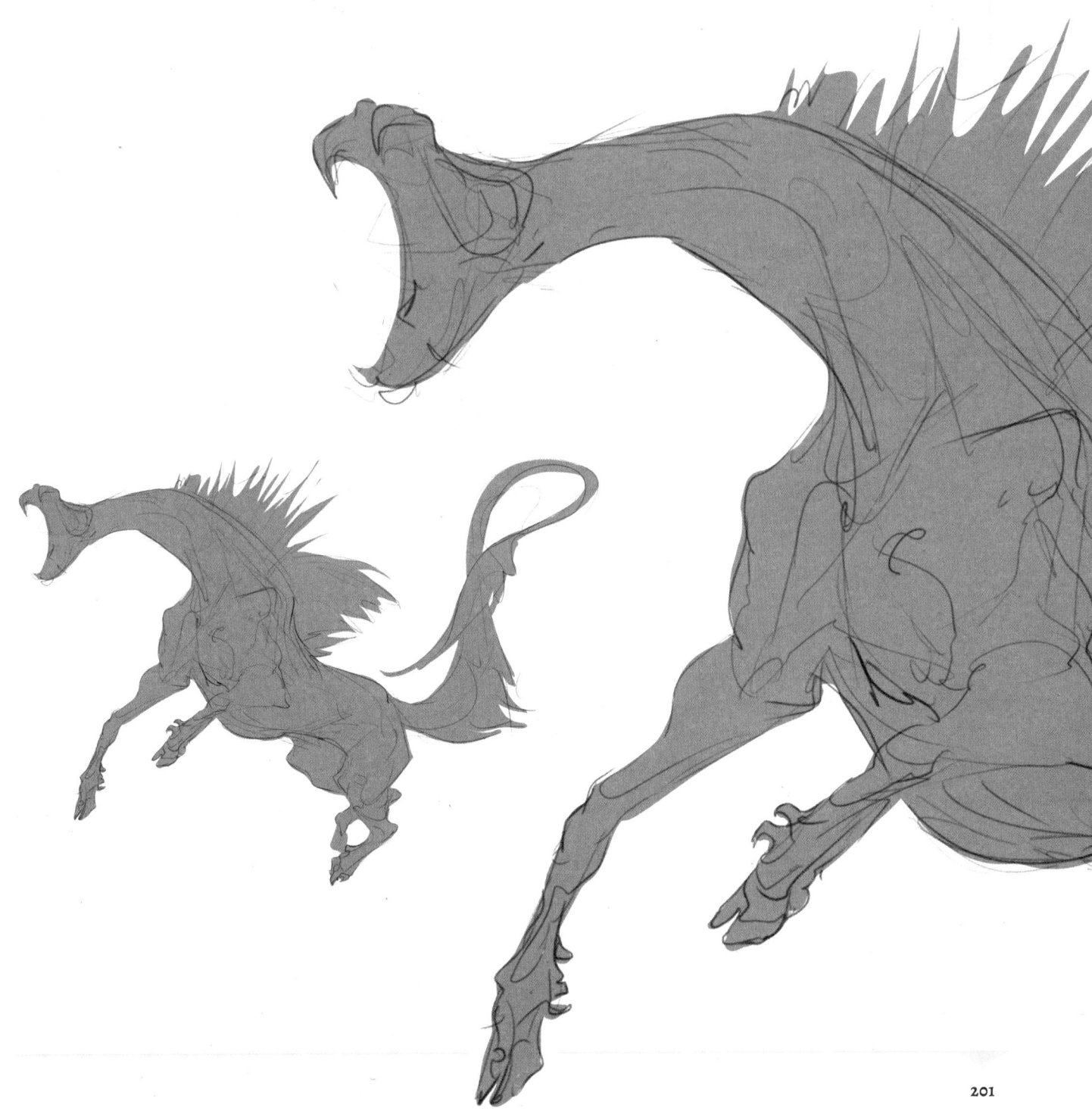

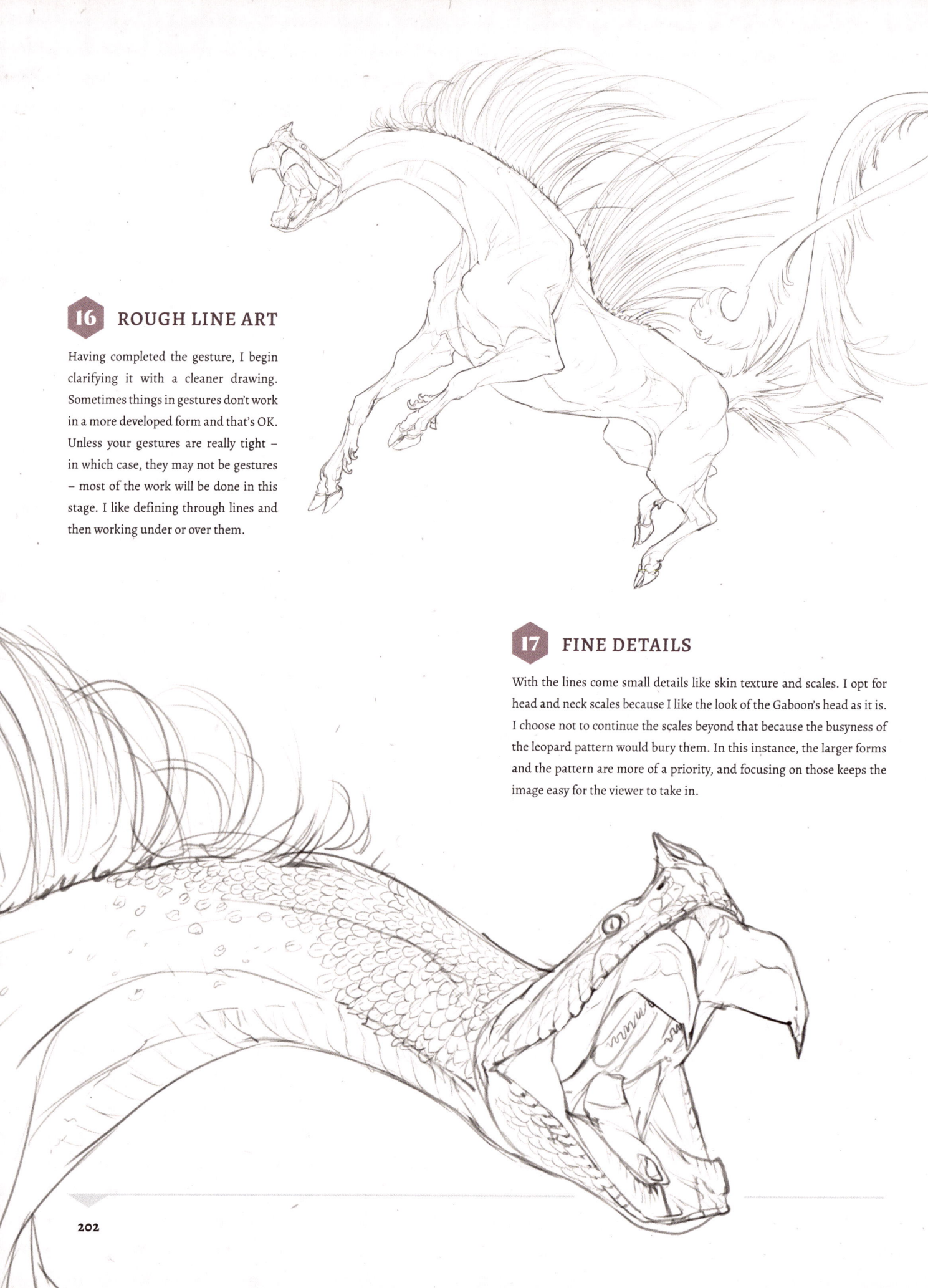

16 ROUGH LINE ART

Having completed the gesture, I begin clarifying it with a cleaner drawing. Sometimes things in gestures don't work in a more developed form and that's OK. Unless your gestures are really tight – in which case, they may not be gestures – most of the work will be done in this stage. I like defining through lines and then working under or over them.

17 FINE DETAILS

With the lines come small details like skin texture and scales. I opt for head and neck scales because I like the look of the Gaboon's head as it is. I choose not to continue the scales beyond that because the busyness of the leopard pattern would bury them. In this instance, the larger forms and the pattern are more of a priority, and focusing on those keeps the image easy for the viewer to take in.

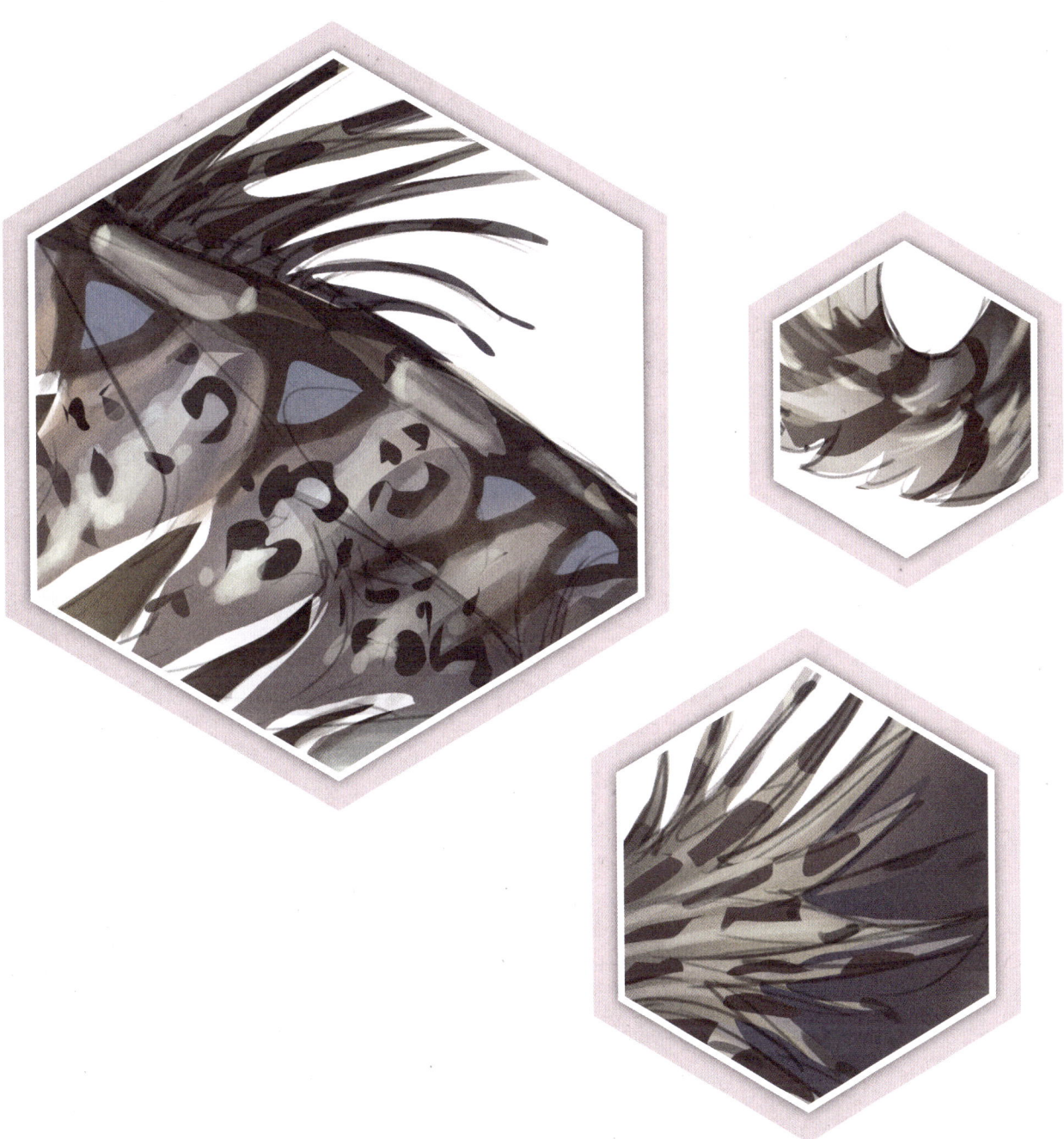

18 | COLOURATION

Patterns are important. Some designs are able to get away with subtle markings, but this is one of those instances where I think, 'The more, the better!' It's a little more work to finalize complicated patterns, but the end result is almost always worth it. As I contemplate the patterns I am using, I think of how Questing Beasts from other continents might look. An Argentine boa and a jaguar could be an interesting combination. If I could find an excuse to work a Mangshan viper in there, I would – or a blue viper, or a temple viper... There are so many good options!

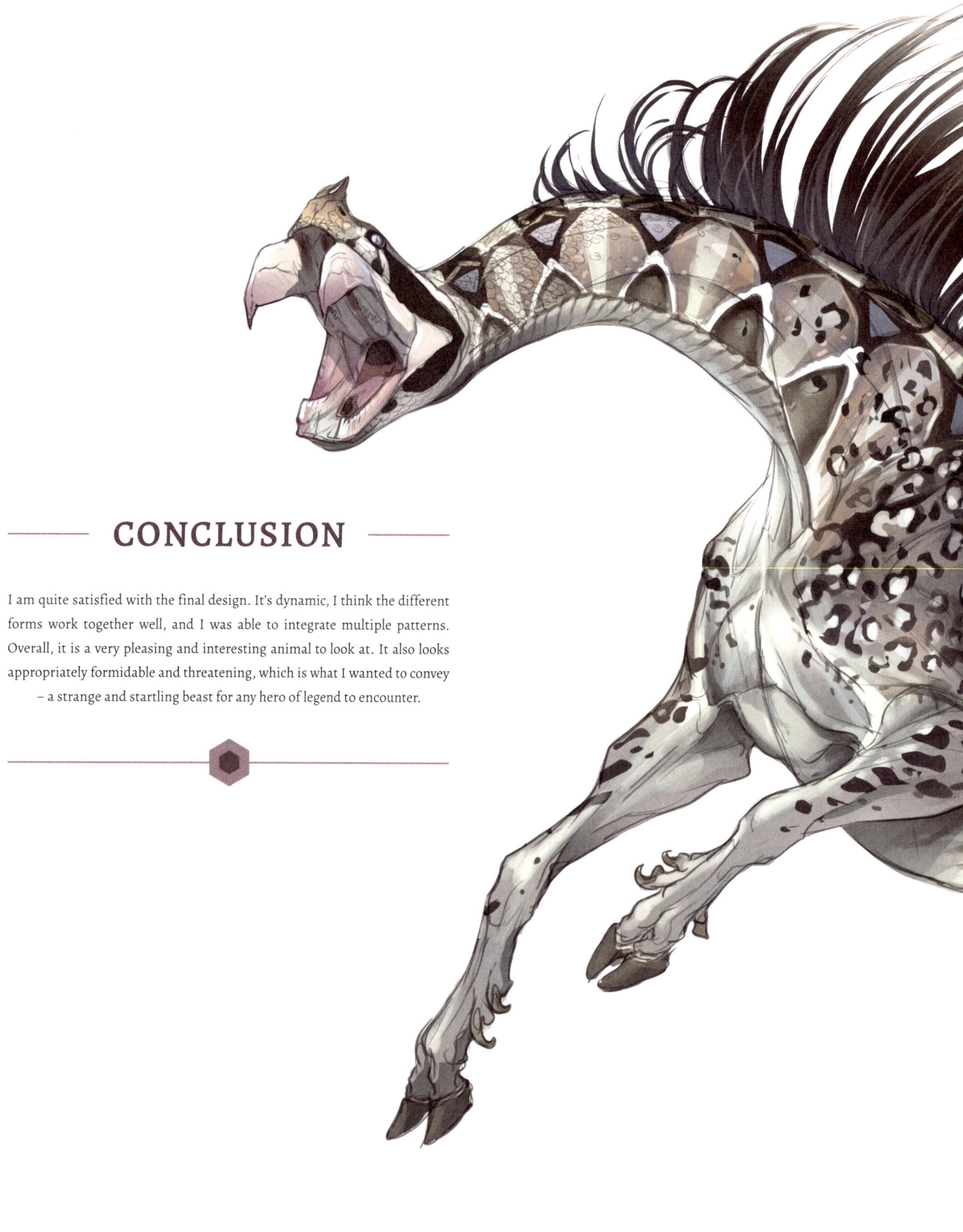

CONCLUSION

I am quite satisfied with the final design. It's dynamic, I think the different forms work together well, and I was able to integrate multiple patterns. Overall, it is a very pleasing and interesting animal to look at. It also looks appropriately formidable and threatening, which is what I wanted to convey – a strange and startling beast for any hero of legend to encounter.

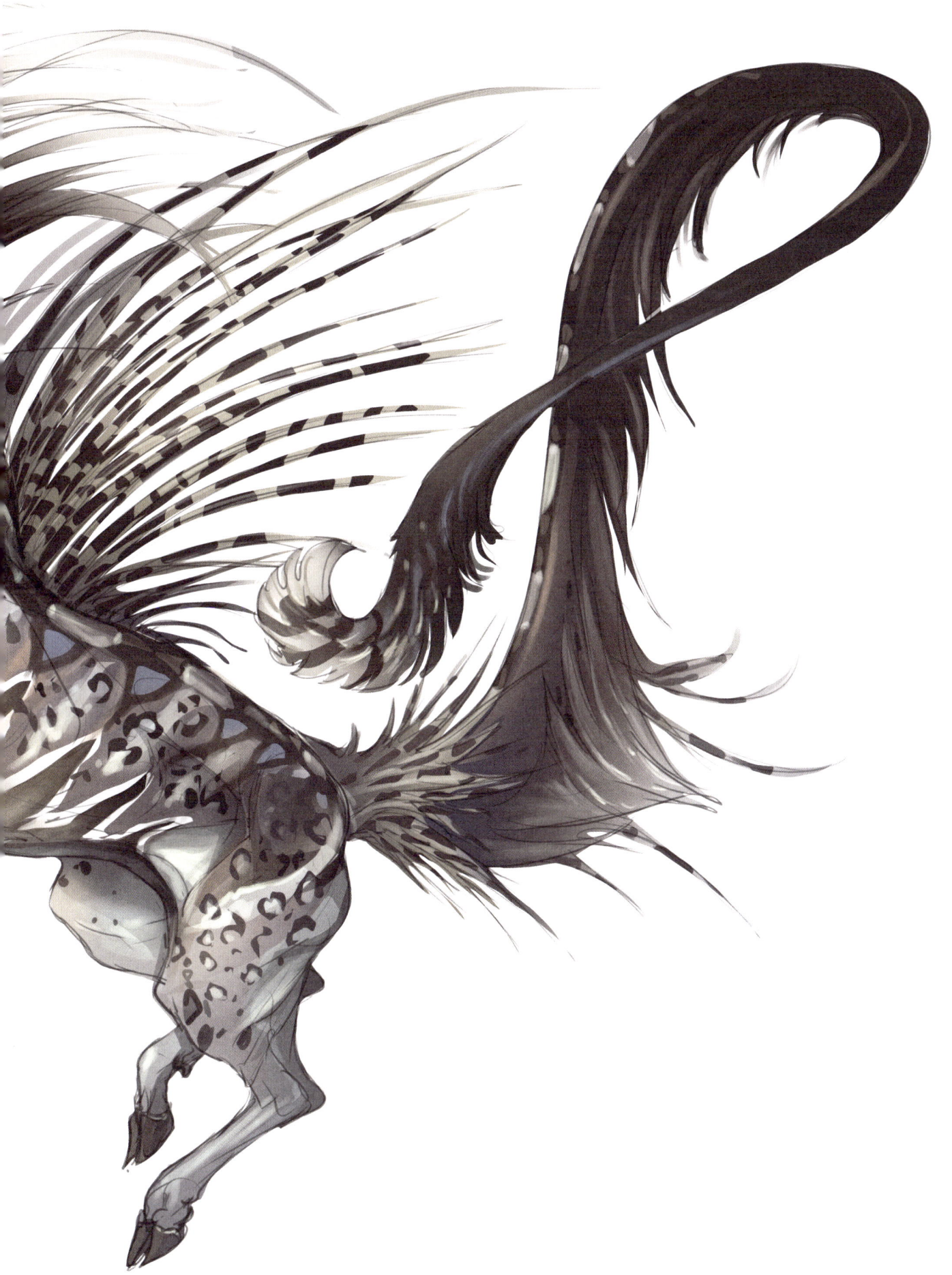

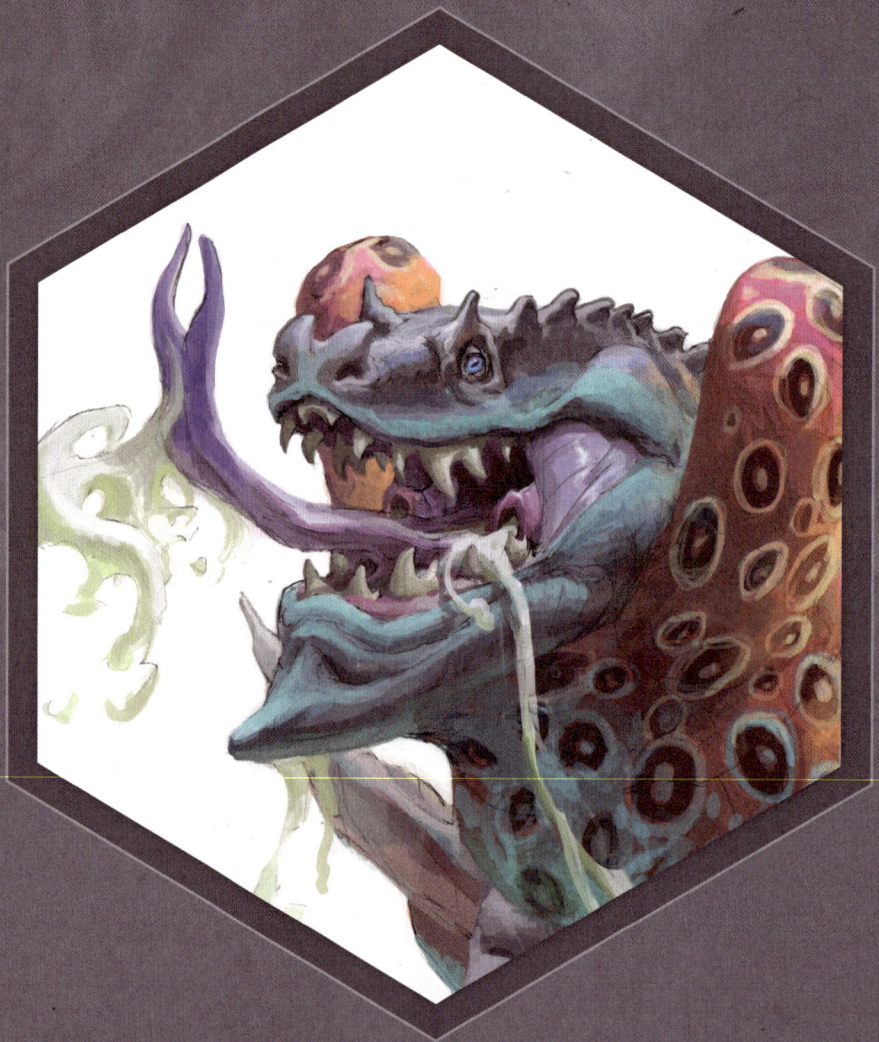

SALAMANDER

The salamander is a four-legged, lizard-like creature that is immune to fire and is capable of contaminating water and wells with its poisonous body. The challenge for this brief will be to create a convincing, naturalistic animal that is equally as comfortable in water as in fire. I also want to make sure that despite the creature's name, this dragon ends up looking very 'dragon-y', and not just like another earthly amphibian or reptile. I'll describe how I think about all the elements mentioned above, including the dragon's ability to extinguish fires, swim in wells, and produce toxic froth. Then through a series of exploratory sketches and colour studies, I'll show you how I arrive at a final design.

JORDAN K. WALKER

Final image © Jordan K. Walker

01 GILA MONSTER

I'm going to begin my design process by taking inspiration from the natural world. The writer Jonathan Swift described the salamander's 'gaudy coat' and 'loathsome spots', how it 'spews a filthy froth' that spreads leprosy and baldness to the unlucky person it touches, and how its body is cold enough to extinguish flames. The first animal that comes to mind is the Gila monster of the Sonoran Desert. These remarkable animals thrive in blistering heat just like the dragon, and are some of the world's only venomous lizards. Their bodies are also covered in striking bands of orange and black – a warning to predators that evokes the salamander's 'gaudy coat'.

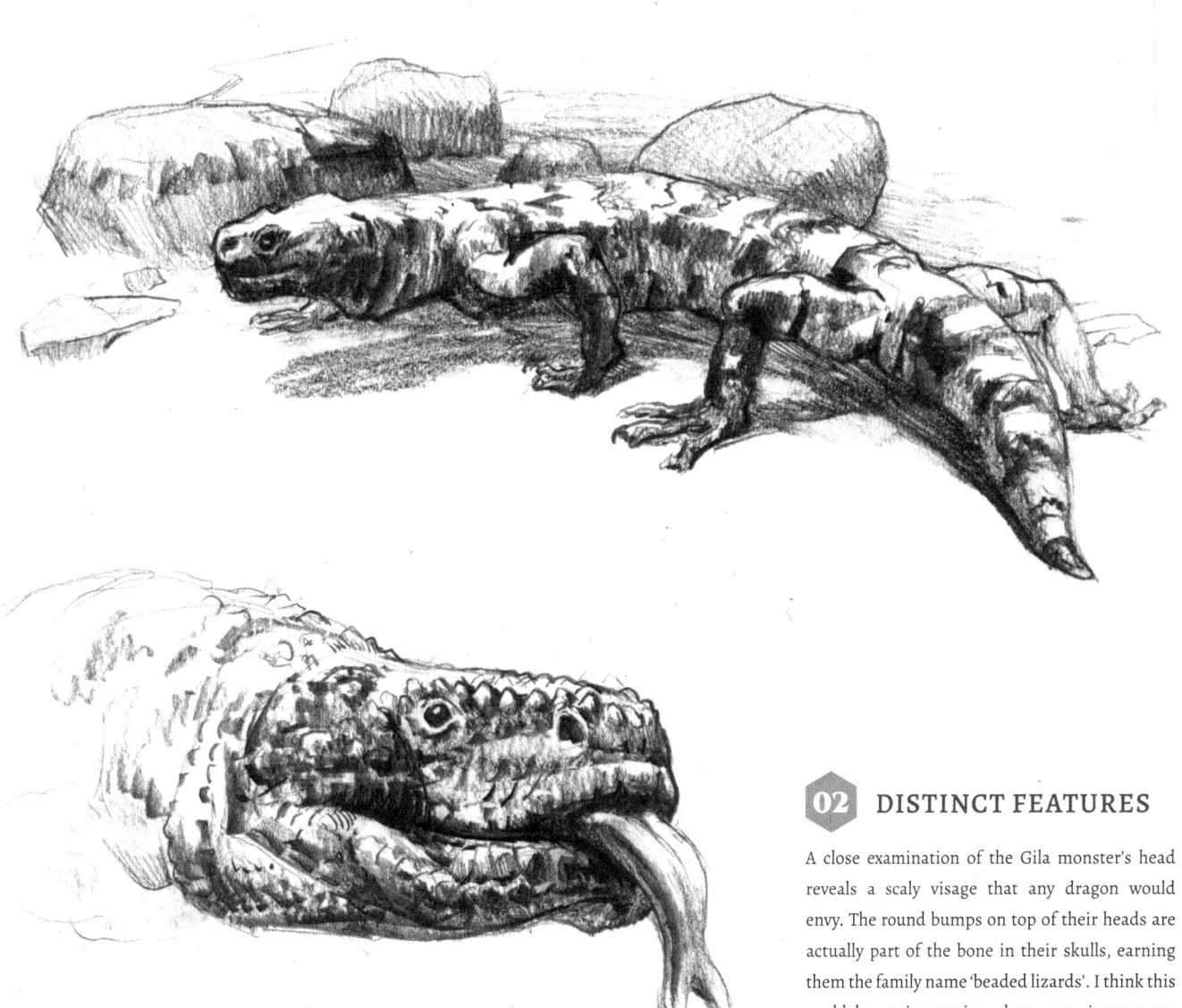

02 DISTINCT FEATURES

A close examination of the Gila monster's head reveals a scaly visage that any dragon would envy. The round bumps on top of their heads are actually part of the bone in their skulls, earning them the family name 'beaded lizards'. I think this could be an interesting element to incorporate into my design. The wide, muscular tongue of the Gila monster is not only visually distinct, but I could also see something similar being a means by which my dragon could fling poisonous froth from its mouth.

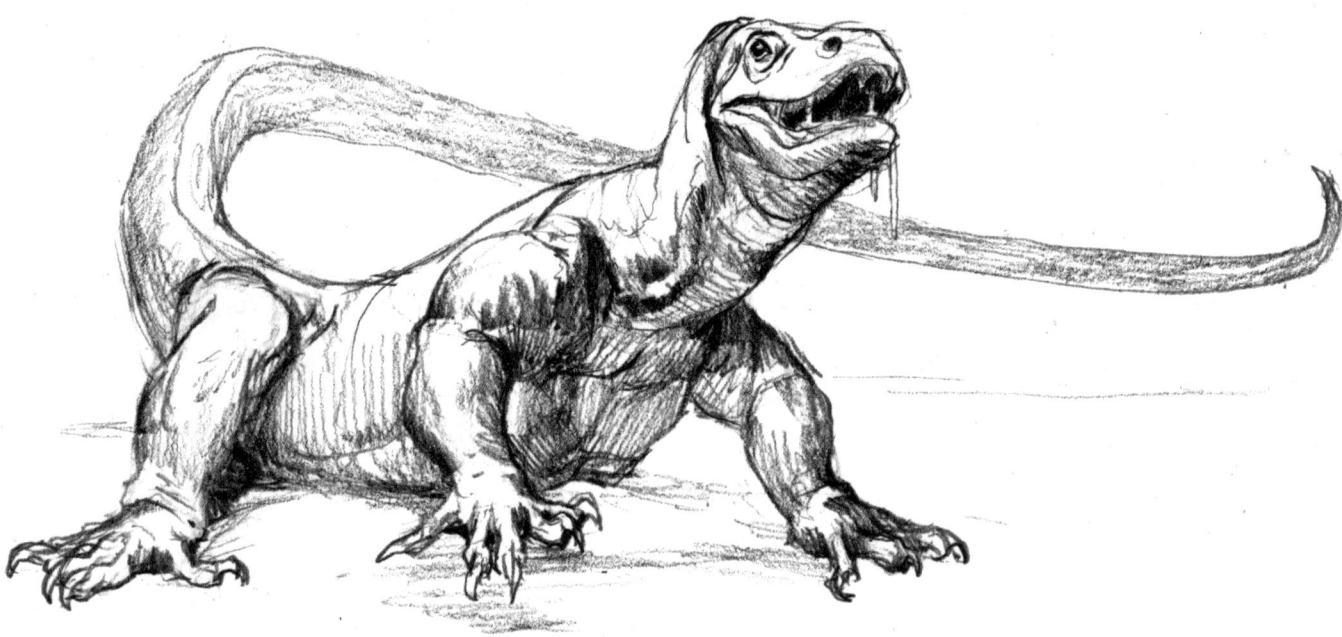

 KOMODO DRAGON

Another formidable lizard I'll draw inspiration from is the Komodo dragon. These enormous monitor lizards are the largest in the world, and are infamous for their deadly bite. Komodo dragons are another rare example of a venomous lizard. They have a gland in their lower jaw that secretes an anti-clotting toxin, which often causes their prey to bleed to death. If that weren't enough, they also harbour deadly bacteria in their saliva, which is constantly dripping from their gaping maws. Perhaps my salamander will use a similar strategy to produce its 'filthy froth'.

ECOLOGICAL CONTEXT

Even if a creature has magical properties, it's still an animal and exists as part of a larger ecosystem. In this instance, I'm wondering what the salamander's described behaviours say about its ecological niche. Does it swim into rivers and wells in search of prey such as fish and crayfish? Why does it extinguish fires? What are the natural predators that it has such formidable protections against? It's important to ask questions like this, as they will help to inform your design.

04 CANE TOAD

Another toxic animal on my list of inspirations is the cane toad. These amphibians are native to South America, but have rapidly taken over Australia and the southern United States due to ill-advised human intervention. Notable for the enormous poison-producing glands behind their eyes, these amphibians have no natural predators outside their native range. They are one of the world's most successful invasive species, and an uncontrollable nuisance in many aquatic and terrestrial habitats – including urban areas. My salamander could employ similar poison-producing structures. I also think that the cane toad's insatiable and problematic behaviour could be echoed by my well-hopping, fire-extinguishing little dragon.

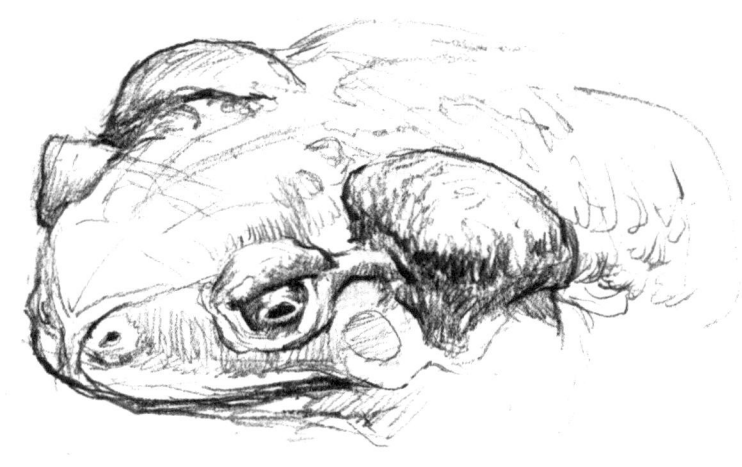

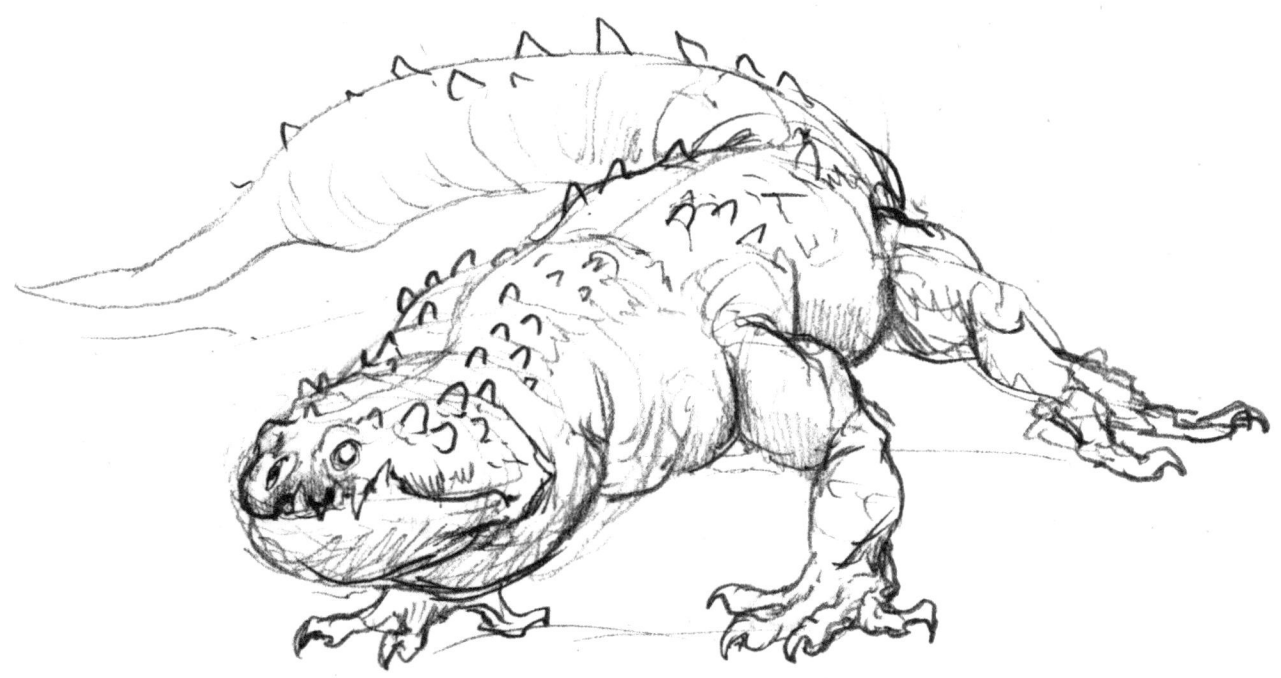

05 FIRST IDEA

Now that I've drawn some inspiration from the natural world, I'll begin a series of thumbnail drawings to explore some design possibilities for my salamander. These quick drawings are not meant to be finished – they allow me to experiment with different combinations of features, shapes, and proportions before I settle on a final design. My first attempts will often miss the mark. It's important to get the bad ideas out of the way first and build towards something better. In this case, I like the dragon's bulky head, but its skinny legs seem too weak to support the chunky body, and it looks too much like a regular lizard.

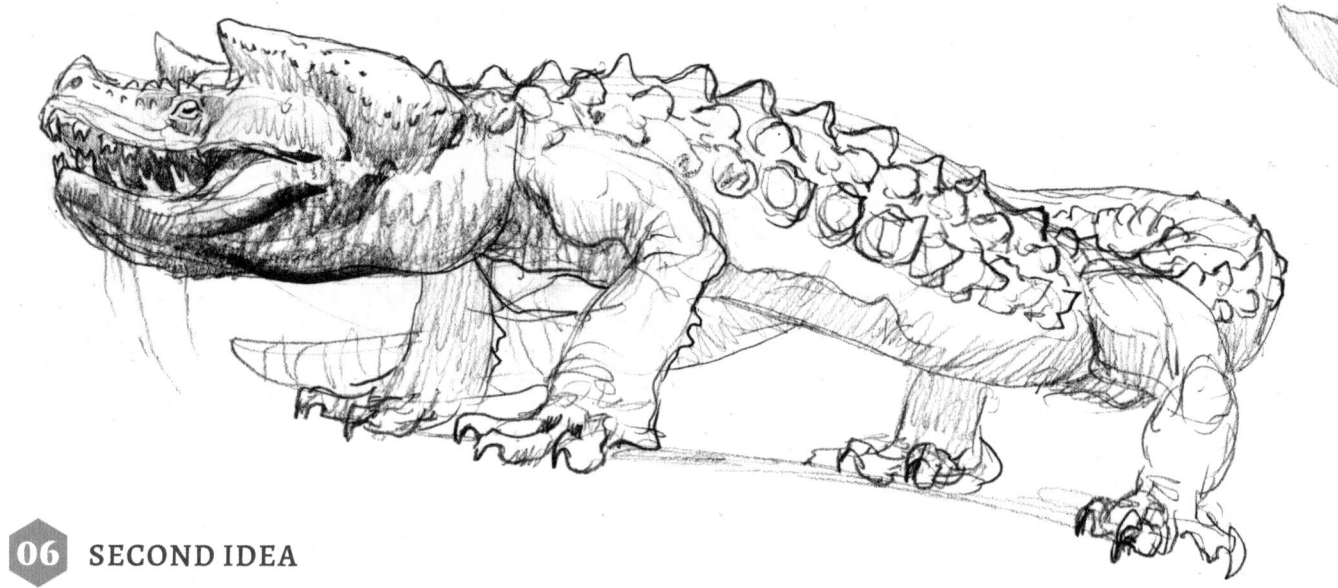

06 SECOND IDEA

This design incorporates some more features I am excited about, such as
the distinctive dorsal 'beads' evoking a Gila monster, and some poison-
producing glands above and behind the dragon's jaws. I'm thinking
about the creature's size at this point, and it seems that in order to
inhabit wells and exist in human spaces it might need to be fairly small –
perhaps no larger than an otter or a mid-sized dog. Structures like these
beads could provide additional protection against potential predators
(such as bigger dragons). Once again, however, I find that this design
looks too 'lizard-y'. I need my salamander to be distinct from some more
traditional dragons, but it still must feel like it belongs among them.

07 THIRD IDEA

Here I experiment with the salamander's proportions, featuring a wide,
toad-like head and an distinctive double tail. I also incorporate some tiny
vestigial wing spurs where the front limbs join with the body, hinting at
a distant evolutionary connection to wyverns. I don't like how short the
body is in comparison to the length of the tail, as this causes the creature
to look stiff and inflexible. I also need to focus on the dragon's ability to
swim, which doesn't seem plausible with this design.

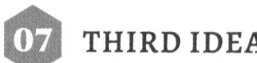

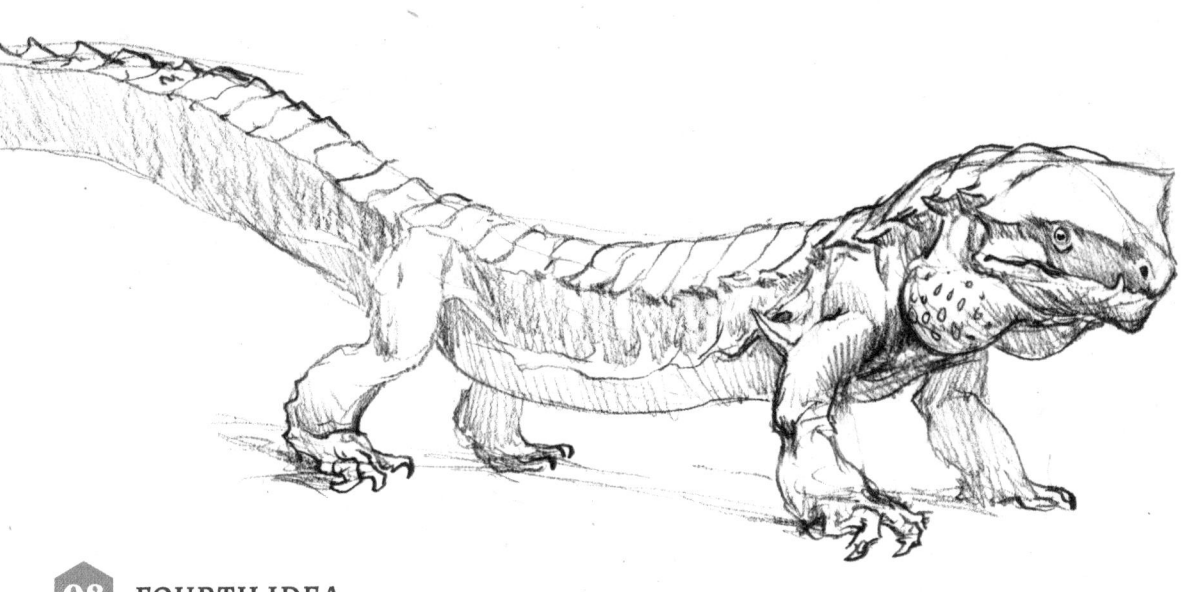

08 FOURTH IDEA

With this concept, I briefly abandon the dorsal beads in favour of smooth, hydrodynamic plating reminiscent of crocodilians. The long, flexible body, paddle-like tail, and wide limbs all point to a creature at home in water as much as on land. In this instance, I shift the poison-producing glands below the dragon's jaw. I draw a lot of inspiration from aquatic lizards and real world salamanders for this one, and though this design is very pleasing and naturalistic, I think it still requires some more fantastical elements.

09 STRONGEST IDEA

This design incorporates some of my favourite elements, such as the dorsal bumps and poison-producing glands, as well as a flexible body and tail. The limbs seem good for walking as well as swimming, and the pointed chin on the creature's lower jaw adds a more 'dragon-y' flavour. I'm also beginning to think about how this creature manages to be immune to fire. Perhaps in addition to the natural 'coldness' described, it also has layers of fatty tissue on its limbs, underside, and tail for protection as it walks through flames. There is still much work to do before I arrive at a final design, but this general body plan will be my blueprint for further iterations.

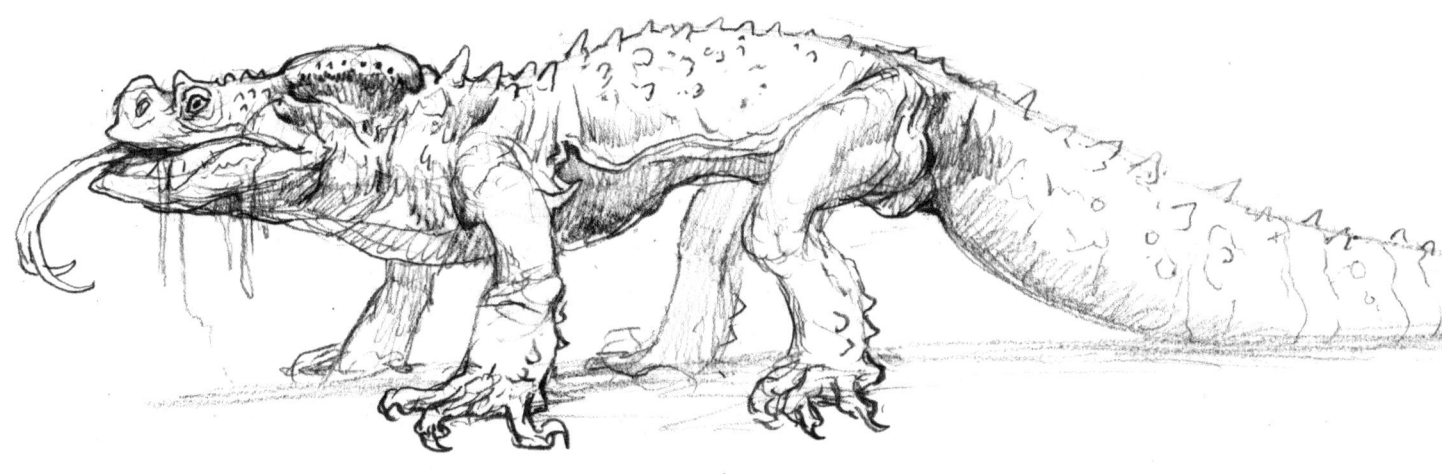

10 POISON IDEAS

Now that I've figured out a rough idea of this creature's body plan, I will home in on some of the critical design elements. Most important on this list are the salamander's head and poison-producing glands. My goal here is to develop a unique and easily recognizable silhouette. I am also interested in figuring out the mechanics of how the poison glands might connect to the creature's jaw. This first iteration proposes an upper and lower gland on each side, and a serrated keratin beak instead of teeth. I like the concept, but the silhouette isn't very strong.

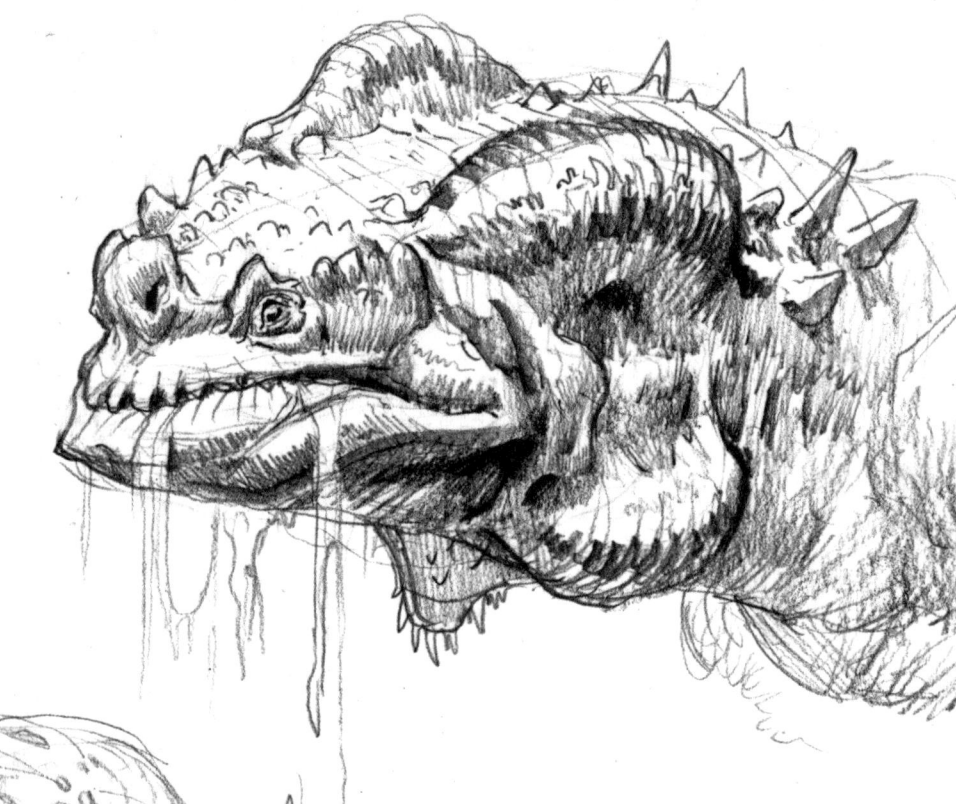

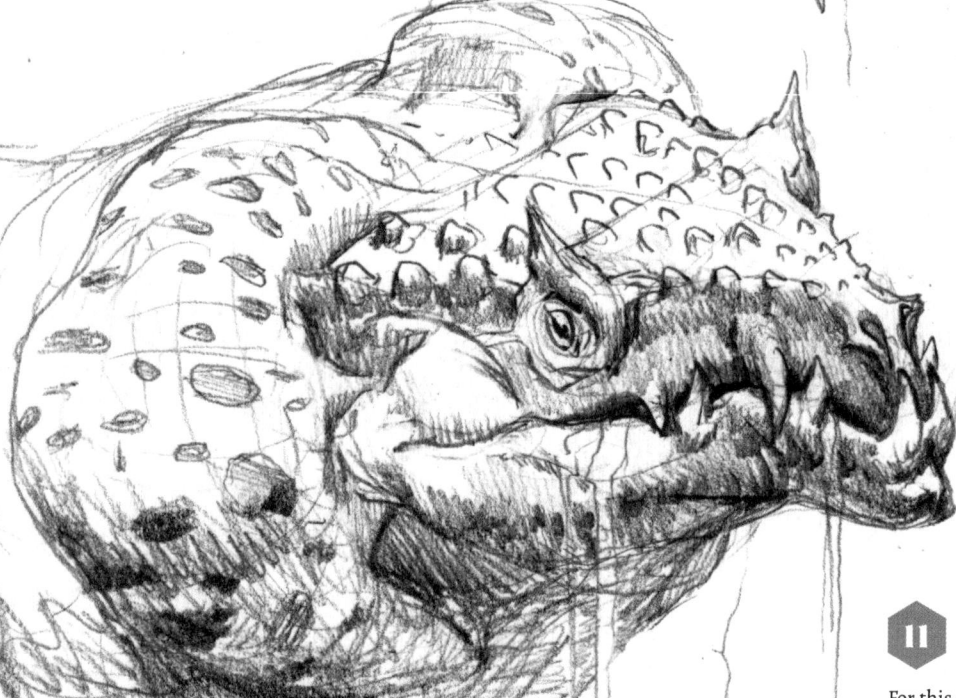

11 THROAT POUCH

For this second head study, I think it might be interesting if the salamander's poison glands are contained inside a large inflatable throat pouch. This pouch could expand as more poison froth is produced, to be expelled in a huge explosion out of the creature's mouth to deter predators. The head in this design is very distinctive, with exposed, interlocking teeth and pronounced eye-ridges. The overall effect might be too angular and pointy for what I am looking for, but it's still worth exploring some more options.

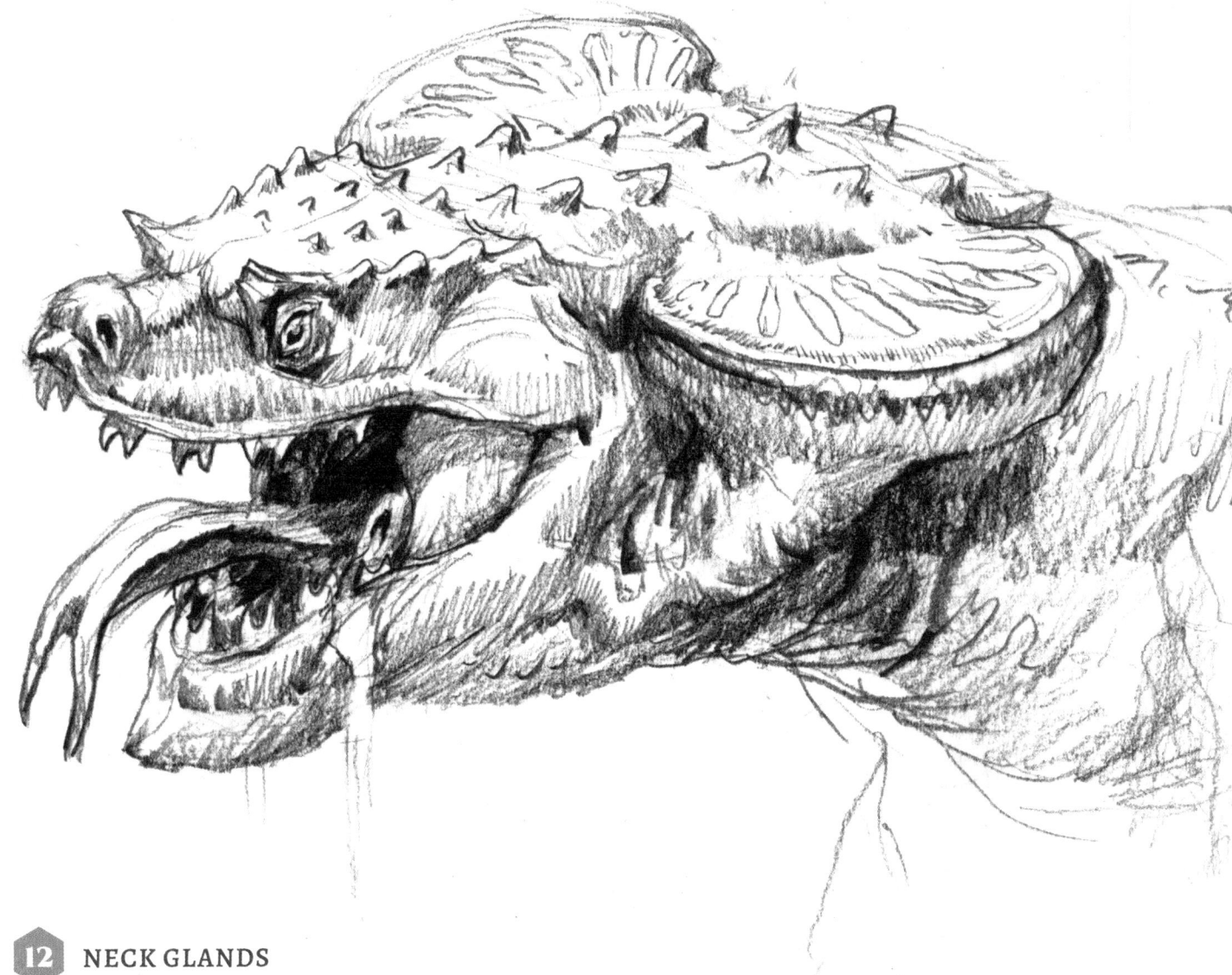

12 NECK GLANDS

This head design features a more naturalistic jaw with lips covering
unusual teeth. The poison glands in this instance are built into an
interesting 'bellows' structure, which can be depressed via muscles
in the neck to push toxic fluid out of orifices in the creature's mouth.
Though this gland structure might be a bit overwrought, I'm much
happier with the shape of the face in this design.

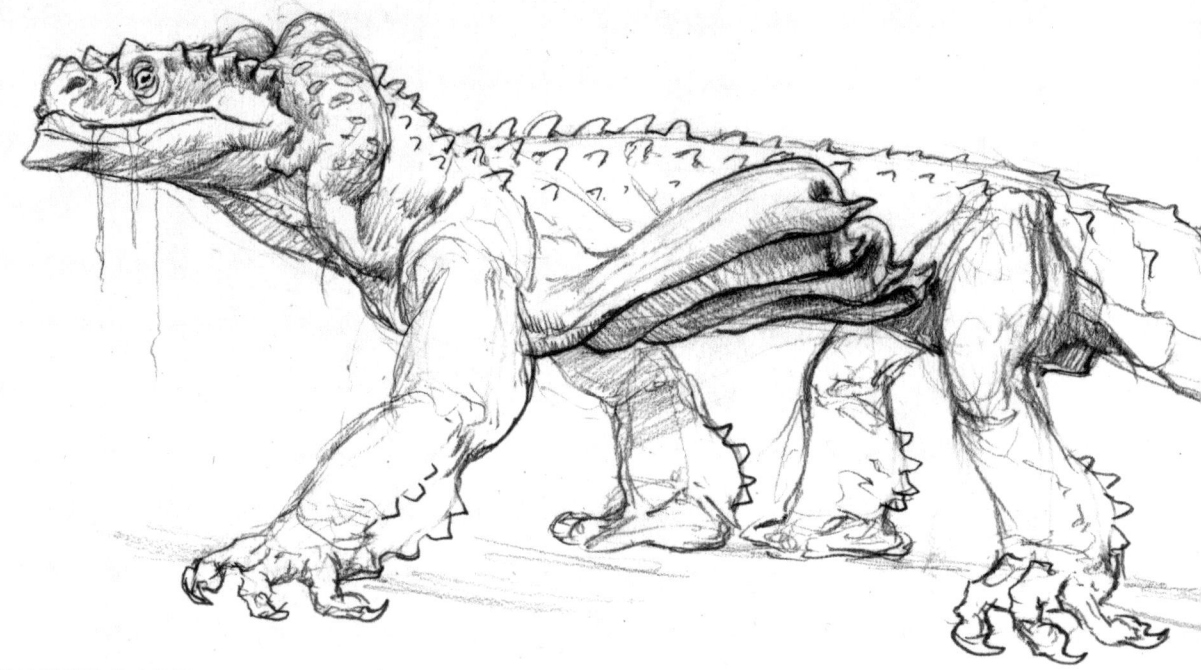

13 REVISING THE BODY

Taking cues from my round of head studies, I approach the creature's body plan again with some new ideas. The salamander is known to have an inherently low body temperature, and maybe it extinguishes fires intentionally in order to absorb heat. Many ectothermic reptiles sprawl on hot stones in order to achieve this goal. My salamander could do the same thing on burning coals, with an increased heat-absorbing surface area provided by flexible, elongated ribs (similar to those of the Southeast Asian flying lizard) that it can fold against the sides of its body when not in use.

14 CHOSEN DESIGN

This thumbnail drawing represents my final design for the salamander. It has abundant fatty tissue on its limbs, rib membranes, and a wide, paddle-like tail with a flat underside, all of which help insulate its internal organs from flames while it absorbs heat. The tail, along with webbed feet inspired by aquatic turtles, aids it in swimming. I combined elements of the second and third head studies, and enlarged the throat pouch and poison glands to develop an interesting silhouette. The webbed rib structure is reminiscent of the wings of better-known dragons, and I'm pleased with the overall effect of the design.

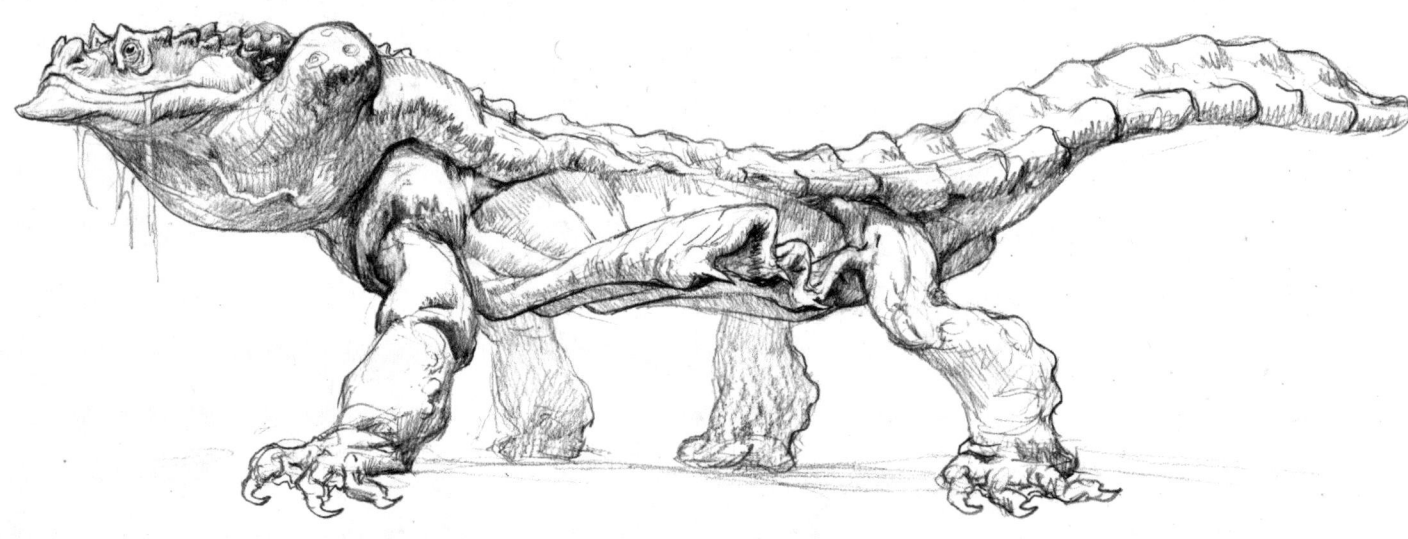

EXTINGUISHING FIRE

Now that I've settled on the dragon's design, I want to show off its ability to extinguish fires. Here we see a salamander basking on the burning embers of someone's hearth, with its rib membranes and limbs fully extended. In its attempt to absorb heat, the salamander acts like a blanket smothering the fire and starving it of oxygen. This behaviour, coupled with their penchant for poisoning wells and other bodies of water while they hunt for prey, would mark these little dragons as a major nuisance in human settlements.

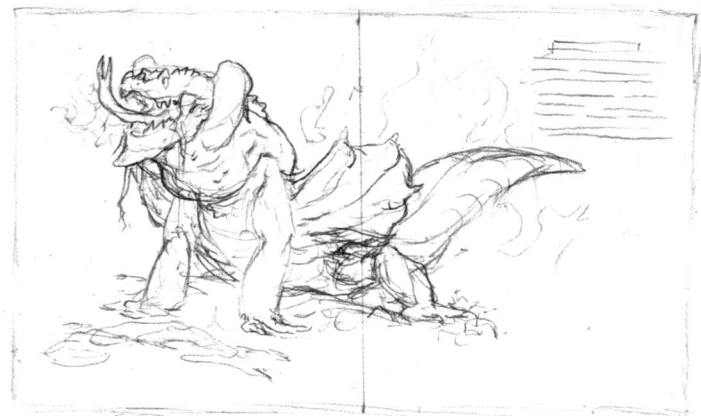

 16 COMPOSITION PLAN

Before I get into designing the colours on the 'gaudy coat' of the salamander, I want to figure out the composition for my final painting. This very rough thumbnail drawing of the salamander in full threat display takes into account the general placement of text and the central gutter that will appear on the final pages of this chapter. It's important to consider these elements as an illustrator; even the best painting in the world can look terrible in a printed book if a head or other important element is stuck in the seam between pages!

 17 FINAL SKETCH

Using the previous compositional thumbnail as a guide, I create this full-scale drawing as the framework for my final painting. Here we see a salamander reared up in a threat display. This pose features all of the most interesting elements of the design. The dragon's mouth is wide open, displaying rows of teeth and a long tongue flinging toxic froth. The throat pouch and poison glands are prominent, as are the creature's extended rib membranes. The wide tail is visible and raised slightly, as the salamander's spine is curved into an arc that implies movement and aggression.

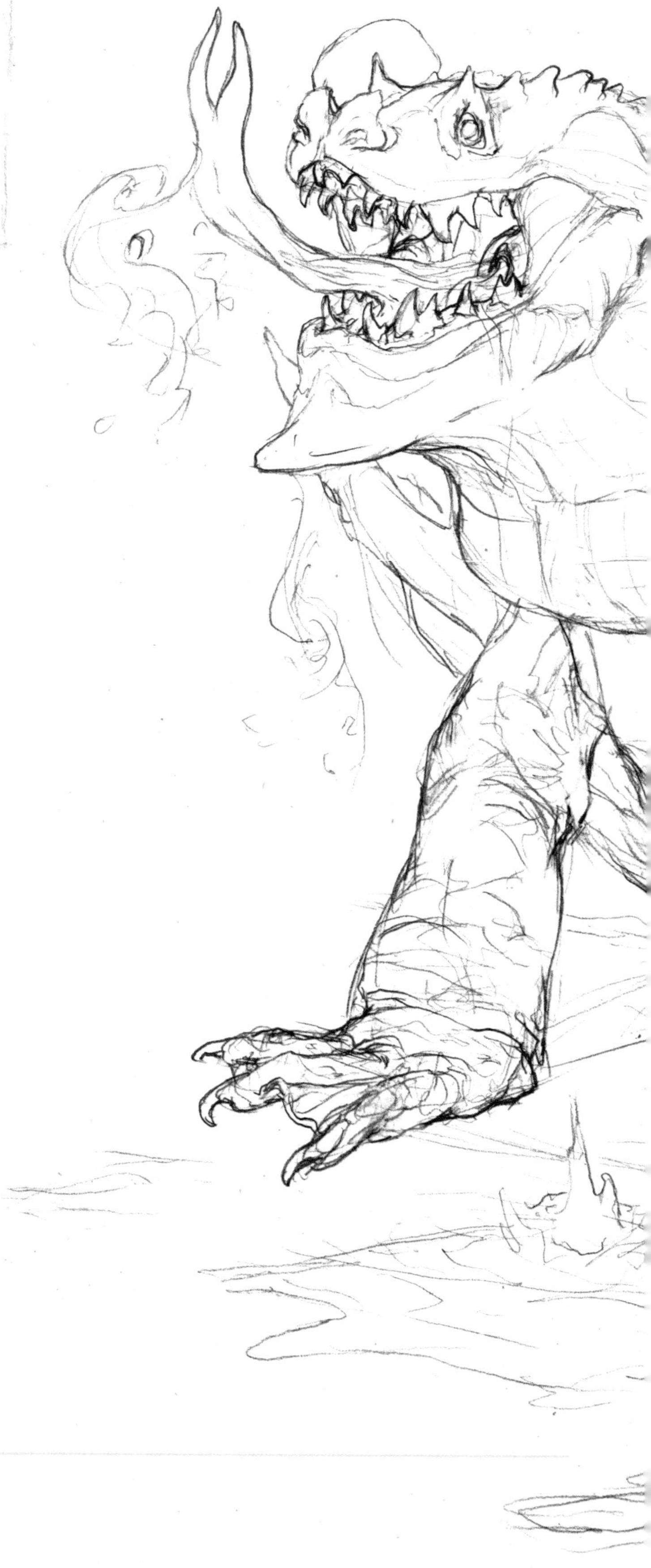

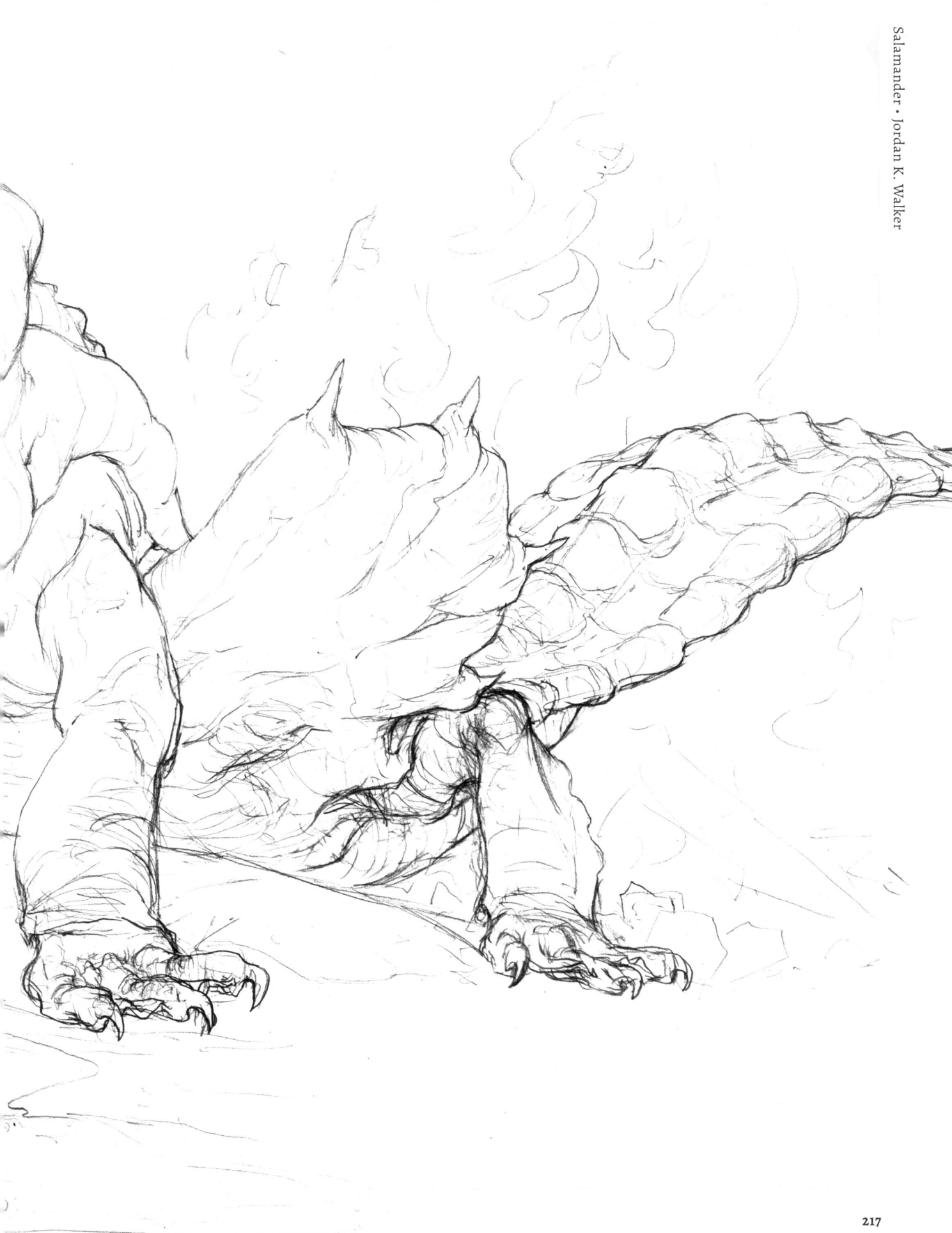

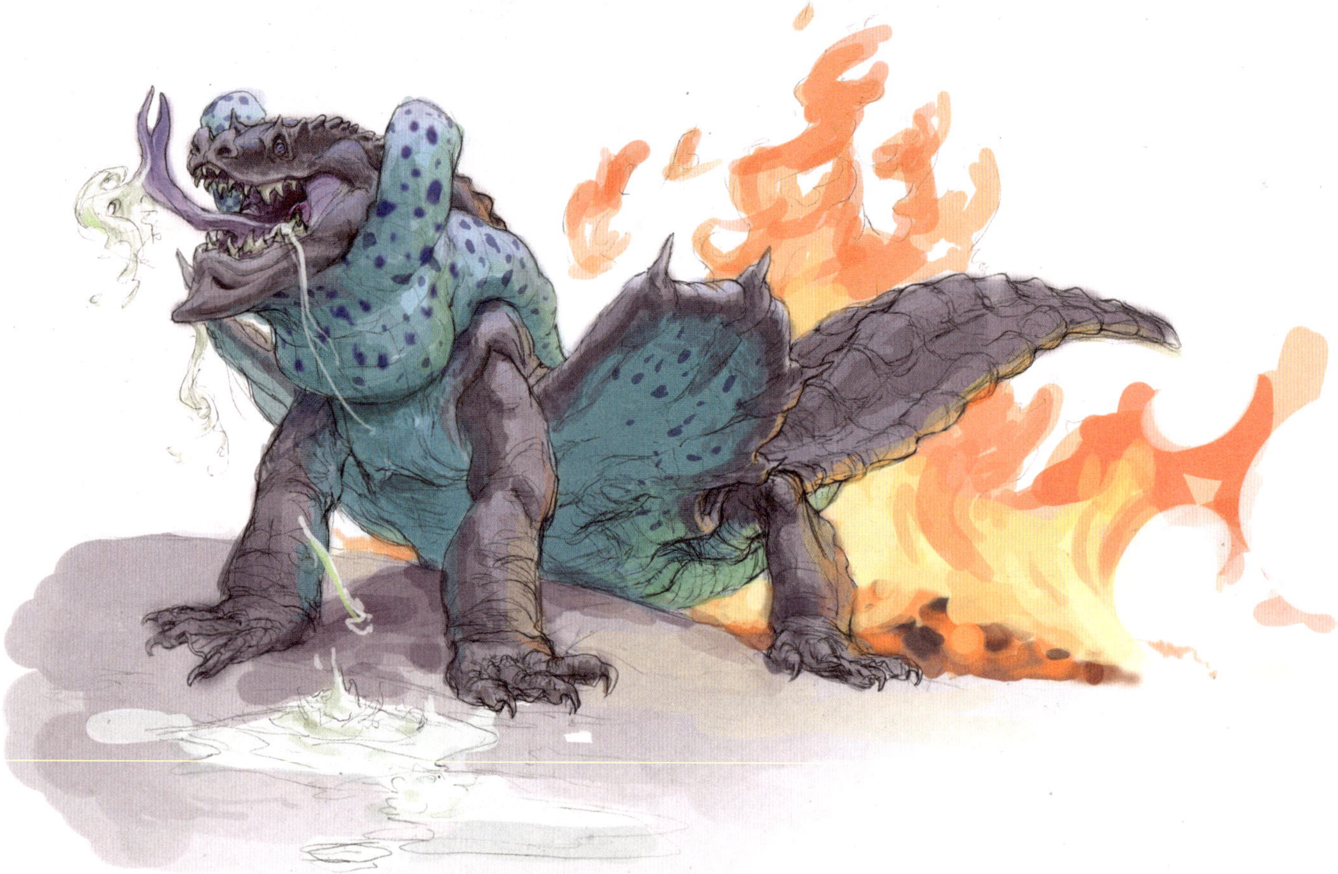

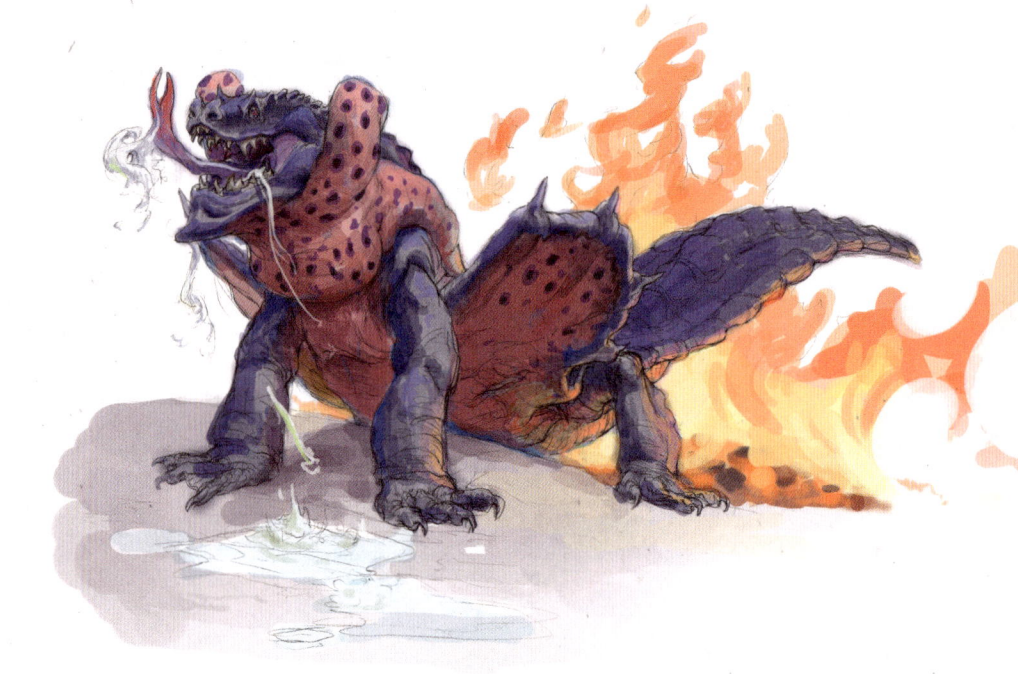

18 COLOUR ROUGHS

While working on this design I have been thinking about where to place the salamander's 'loathsome spots', as they are a key feature in the description. Drawing inspiration from poisonous animals such as Gila monsters and poison dart frogs, I experiment with a few iterations featuring vibrant colours and strong contrasts between light and dark. I want to concentrate the most striking patterns on the salamander's throat pouch and the undersides of its rib membranes. These features are most dramatically featured in the threat display, and would help ward off predators.

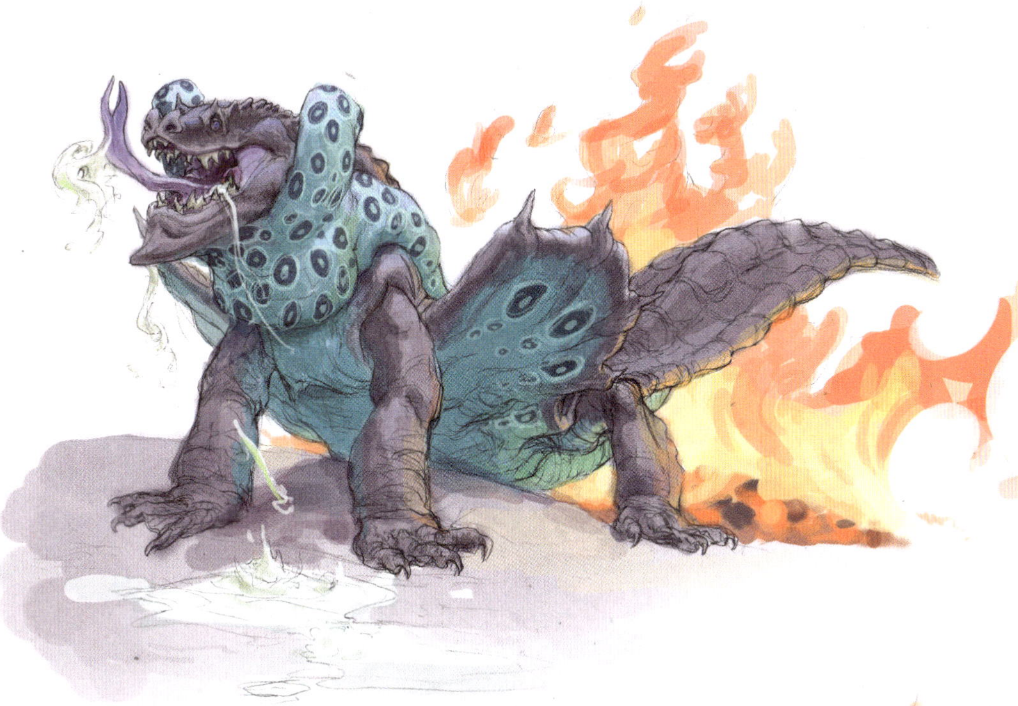

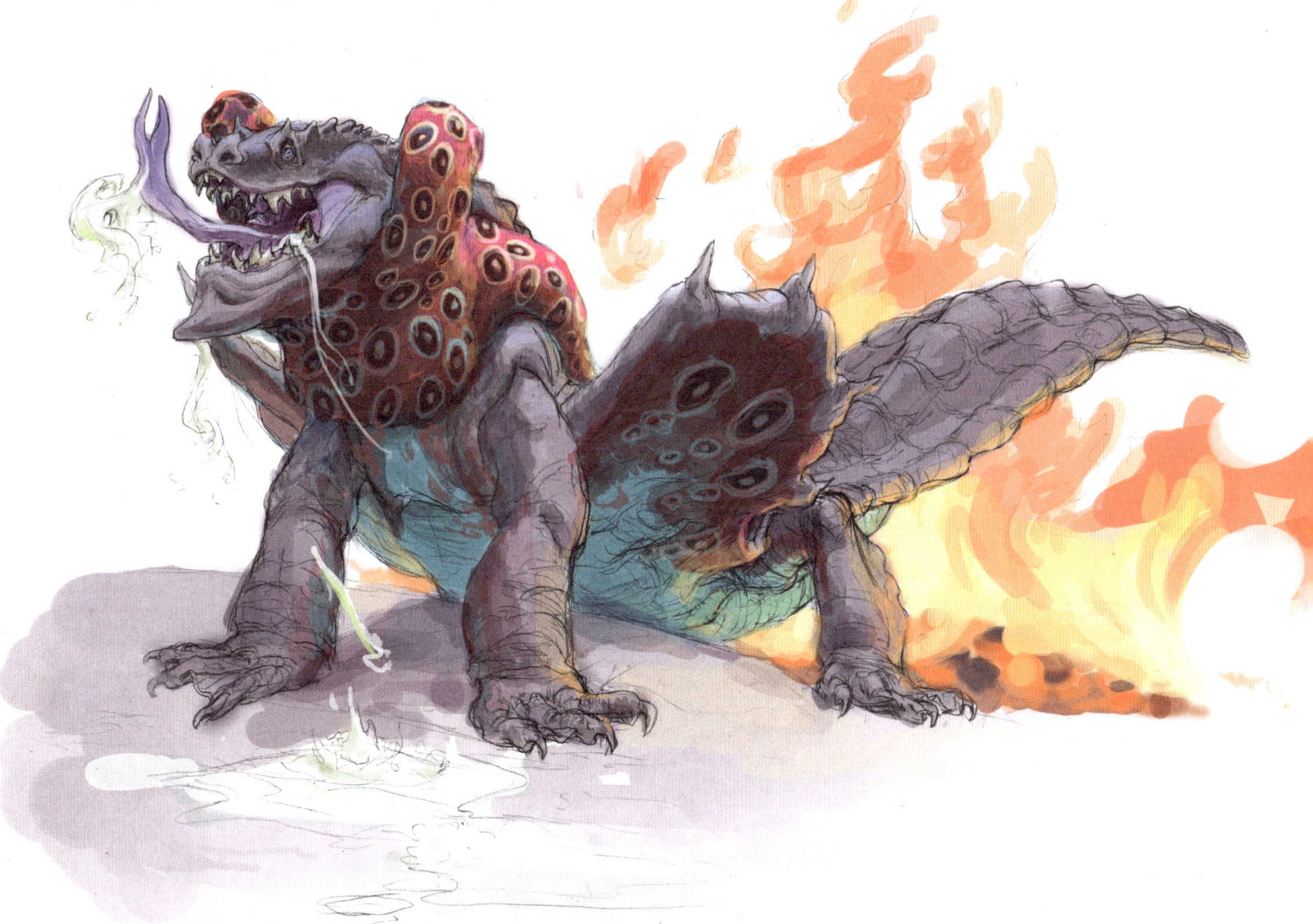

Salamander • Jordan K. Walker

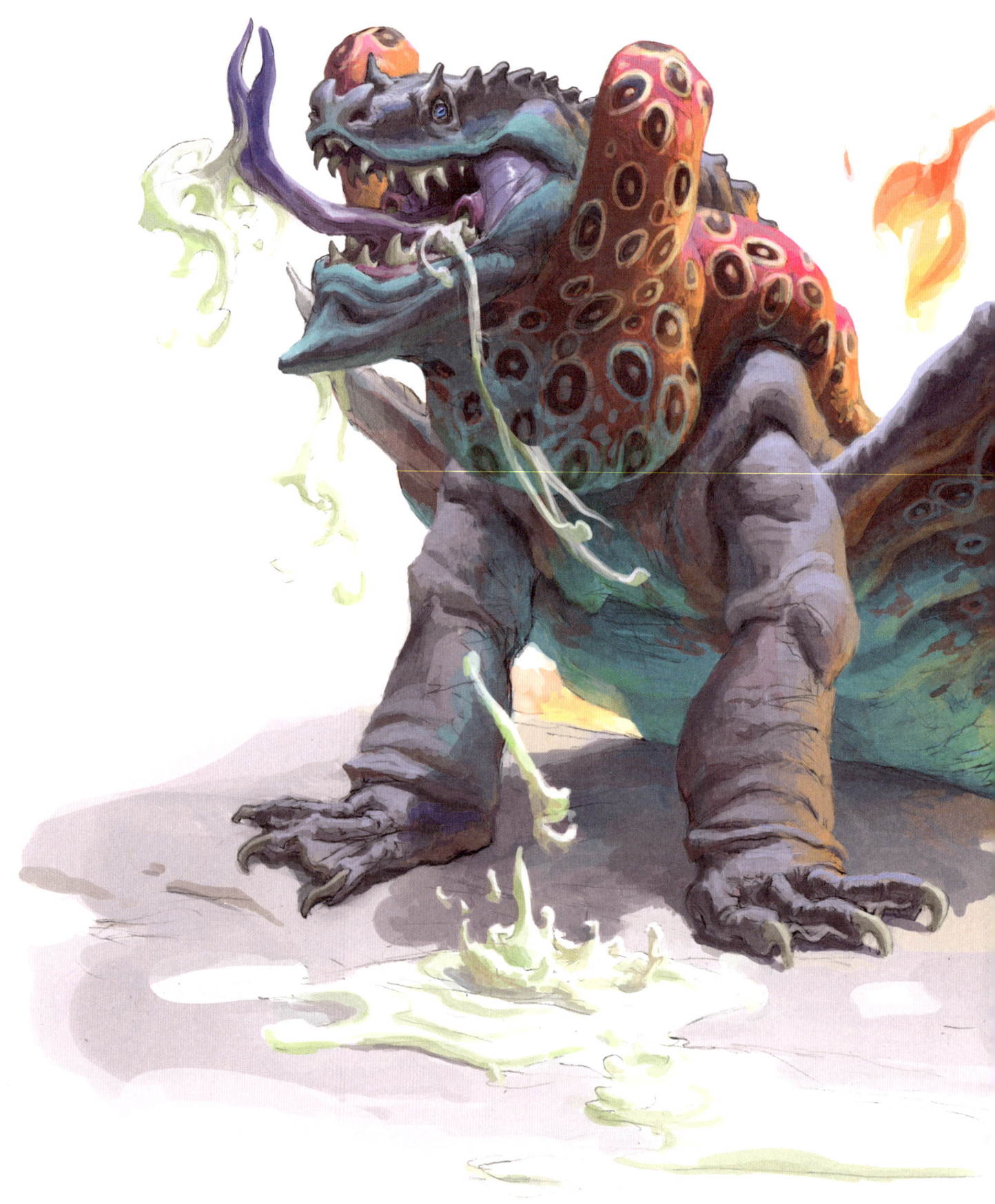

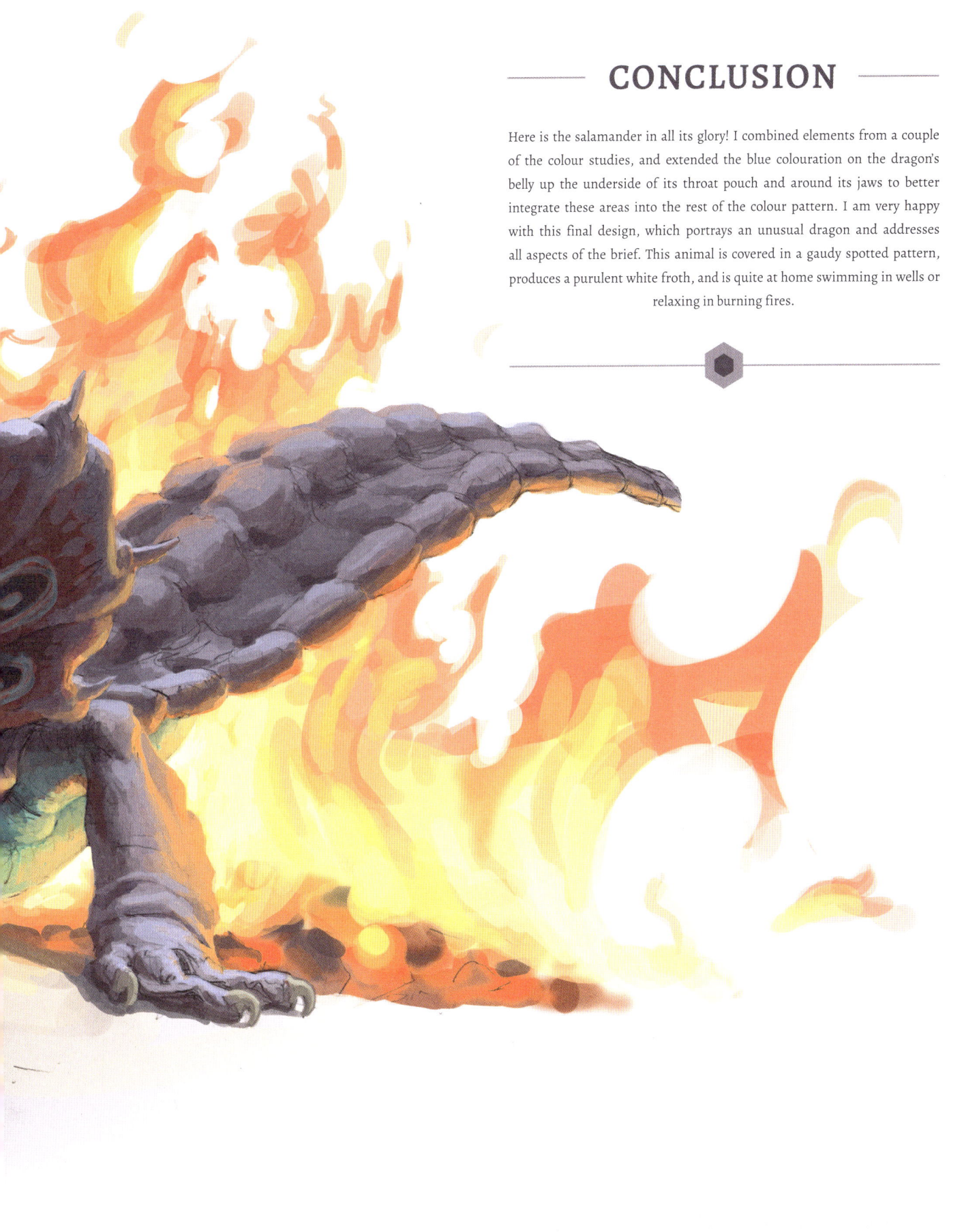

CONCLUSION

Here is the salamander in all its glory! I combined elements from a couple of the colour studies, and extended the blue colouration on the dragon's belly up the underside of its throat pouch and around its jaws to better integrate these areas into the rest of the colour pattern. I am very happy with this final design, which portrays an unusual dragon and addresses all aspects of the brief. This animal is covered in a gaudy spotted pattern, produces a purulent white froth, and is quite at home swimming in wells or relaxing in burning fires.

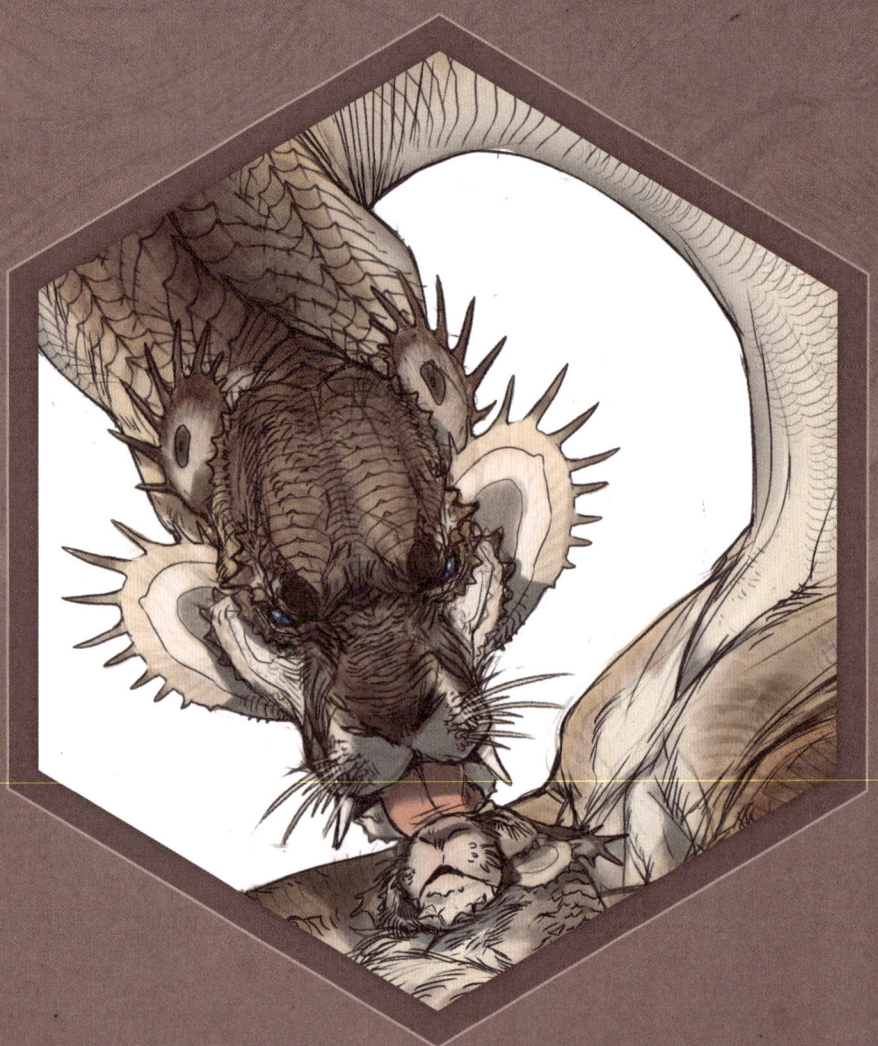

TATZELWURM

In the following steps, I will take you through my design process for the tatzelwurm, a feline-dragon hybrid from Germanic folklore. Also known as the Stollenwurm ('dragon of the mine-tunnels') these dragons are long and thin, with feline features, a venomous bite, poisonous breath, and a nasty, high-pitched hiss. In addition to the creature itself, I will also be looking at how the dragon's environment shapes the way it looks, using real-world examples of animals suited to living in mountains, tunnelling and hunting their prey underground, and how to combine these references with the strange and fantastical.

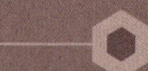

APRIL PRIME

Final image © April Prime

01 FELIFORMIA

I start by identifying which animals I can use as inspiration for a realistic tatzelwurm. Historical art of the tatzelwurm depicts it with a long and powerful body, front (and sometimes back) legs, claws, and a cat-like face. The long, thin body is perfect for worming down burrows and chasing prey, and the enormous claws would be ideal for making dens. I sketch a few studies of marbled polecats, civets, and banded linsangs to help myself understand a very long body. While they are not close direct relatives, all these animals fall under *Feliformia*, meaning they are cat-like.

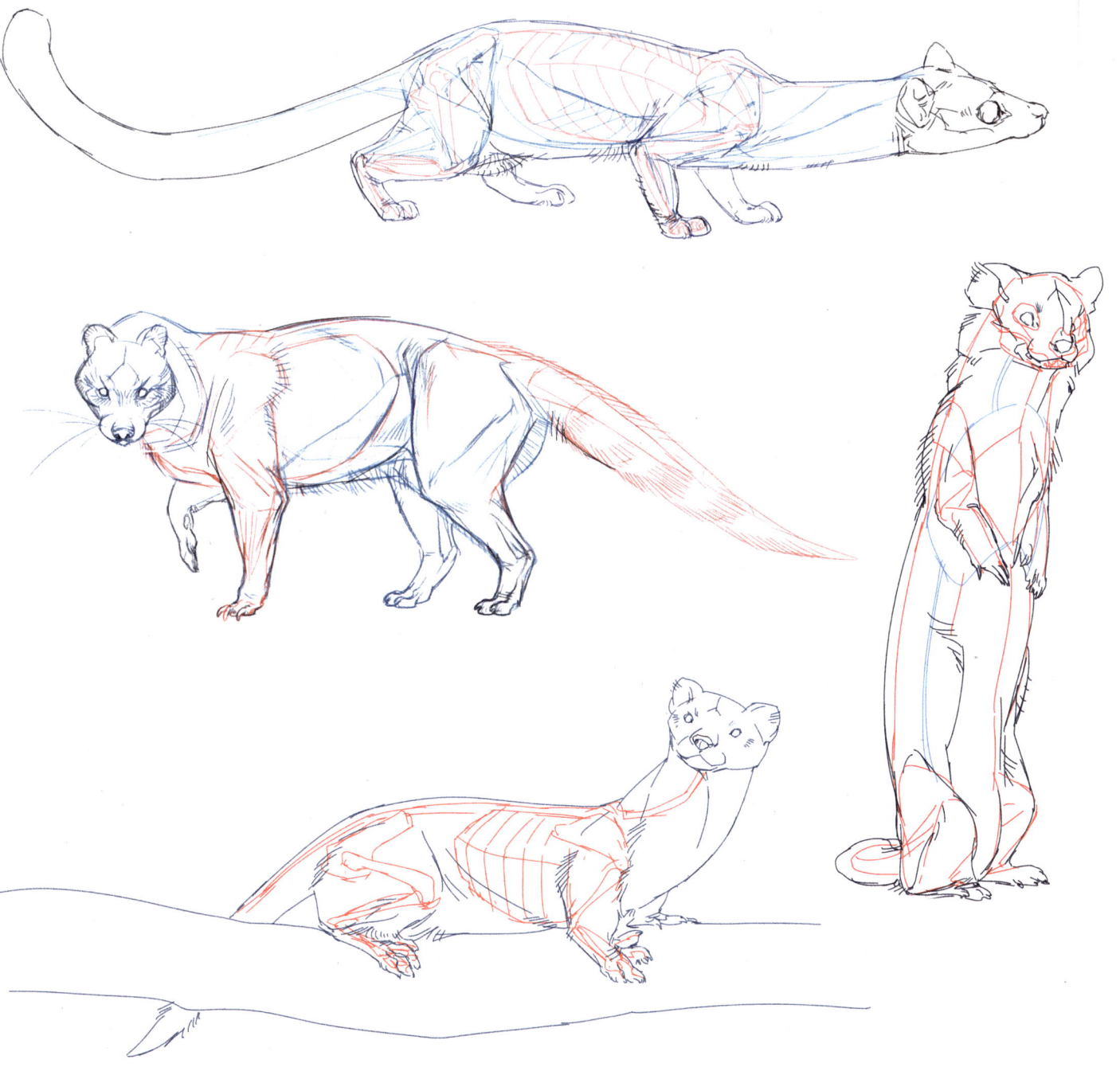

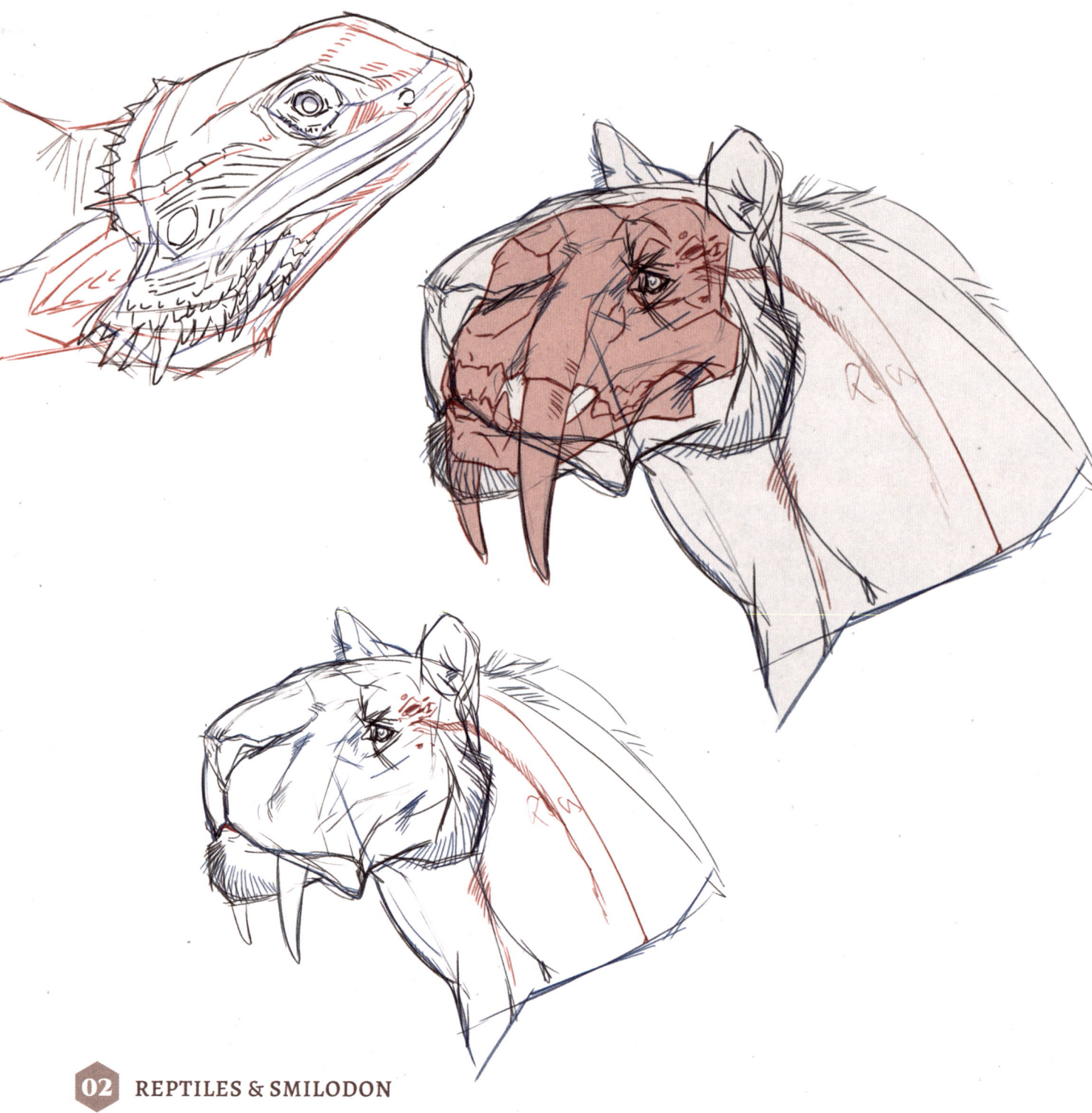

02 REPTILES & SMILODON

I take a look at some reptiles next, as the tatzelwurm is a dragon, after all. Bearded dragons and horned toads are a favourite source of inspiration for me – I love their spiky necks and thick collars of large scales. In addition, I'm going to bring some prehistoric life into the mix with *Smilodon fatalis*, a species of sabre-toothed cat. Using prehistoric animals is a fantastic way to give your designs a primal and ferocious edge. I sketch some quick form studies of a bearded dragon, trying to get a feel for the flow of the animal's head and larger scales. Alongside that is my own interpretation of a sabre-toothed cat, which I build up around a skull. Try your hand at reconstructing an animal from a skull – it's a great way to learn the ins and outs of how bones affect the surface form.

GENERAL KNOWLEDGE

Understanding what you're studying is important. In many of my drawings here, you can see the animal as well as its basic muscle groups and a rough block-in of its bones. Many quadrupeds share similar enough anatomy that once you become familiar with it, it's not too hard to wrap your head around new animals. You don't need to know the name of every muscle and bone – you just need to aim for an understanding of the basic shapes and attachment points. I always try my best to learn a little bit more each time I do a study or sketch of an animal and its anatomy.

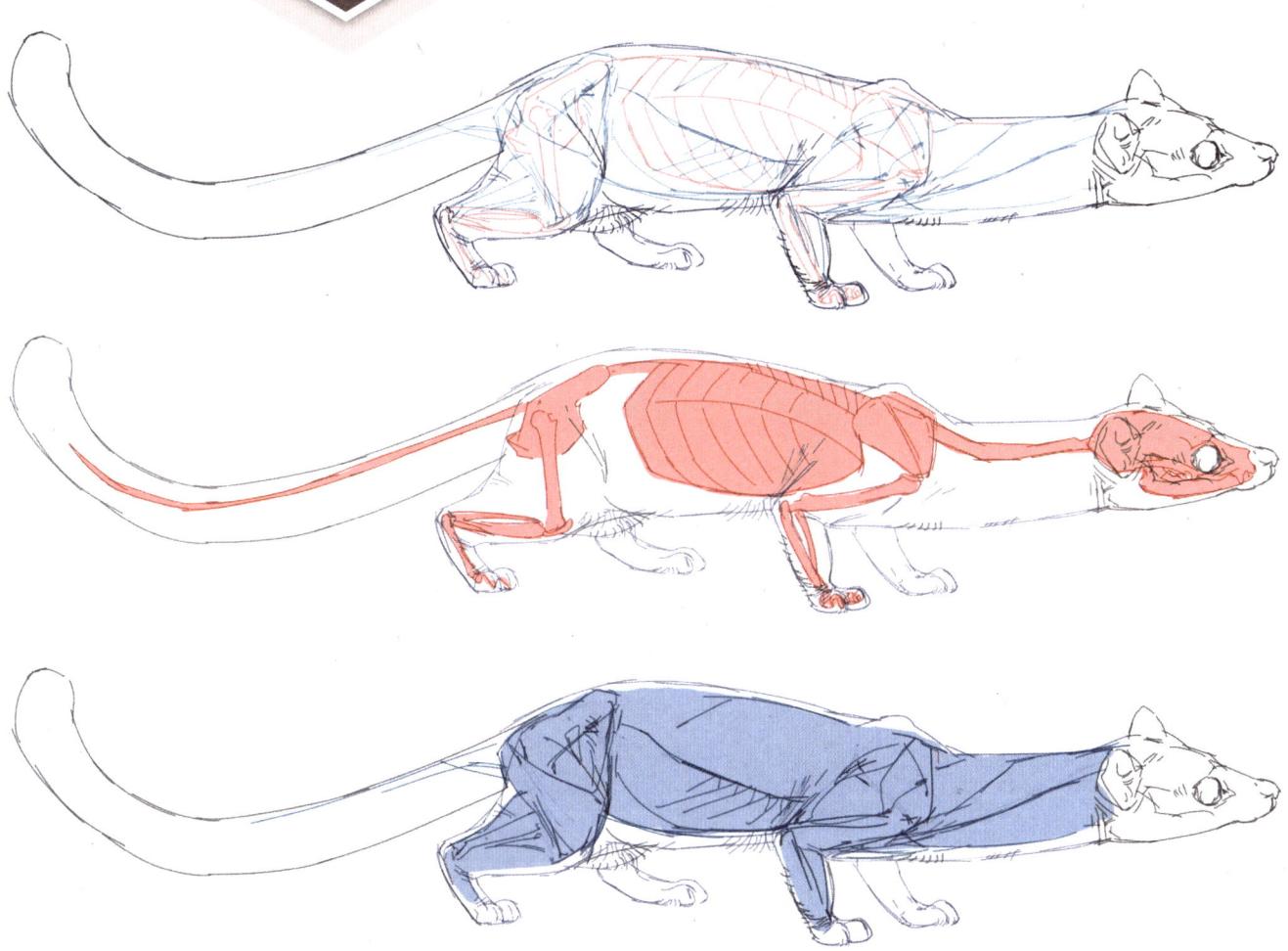

03 HEAD SKETCH

Now I can bring all my animal references together and work out how the head of the tatzelwurm could look. While sketching, I had the idea of the tatzelwurm being a type of dragon that is easily mistaken for a feline relative from a distance. This has happened many times in human history, with travellers mistaking manatees for mermaids and oarfish for sea serpents. This first pass of the dragon's head also features horns, though I may remove them later. I don't often add horns to my dragons, as I prefer a sleek look.

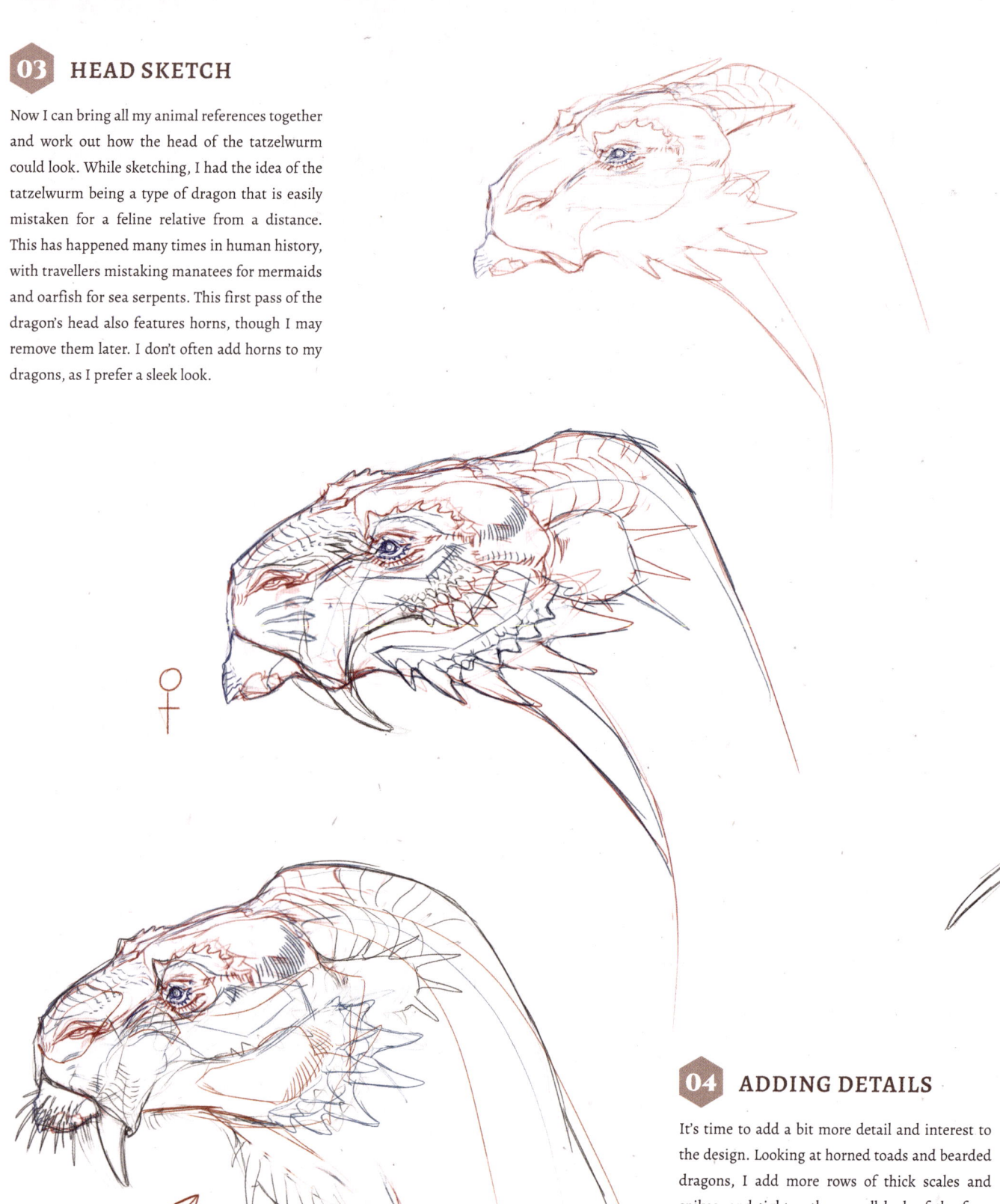

04 ADDING DETAILS

It's time to add a bit more detail and interest to the design. Looking at horned toads and bearded dragons, I add more rows of thick scales and spikes, and tighten the overall look of the face. Taking inspiration from the teeth of *S. fatalis*, I add tusks, which I picture them using for digging, grooming, and fighting with rival males.

DON'T BE AFRAID TO TRACE

Tracing is often considered taboo by inexperienced artists, but it's not. Of course, don't trace someone's work and then claim it as your own, but tracing photographs of a research subject, such as animals, is a great way to study. Use it to strengthen your hand-eye coordination, add to your visual library, get a better understanding of form, and forge those neural pathways!

 ## 05 BODY IDEAS

Here, I'm considering the body of the tatzelwurm. Despite me saying this is a true dragon, the overall body is very cat-like, or mammalian in general. This is a personal preference of mine when it comes to dragons, just because I love big cats most of all! The wings are vestigial, meaning they no longer serve a function. I picture the tatzelwurm's ancestors being more typical-looking dragons, but over time their mountainous habitat and preference for ground-dwelling has resulted in a loss of flight.

I decide I prefer the body of the bottom image. The idea here is that even the back legs of the tatzelwurm are beginning to become useless, as they prefer to burrow and slide around on their stomachs.

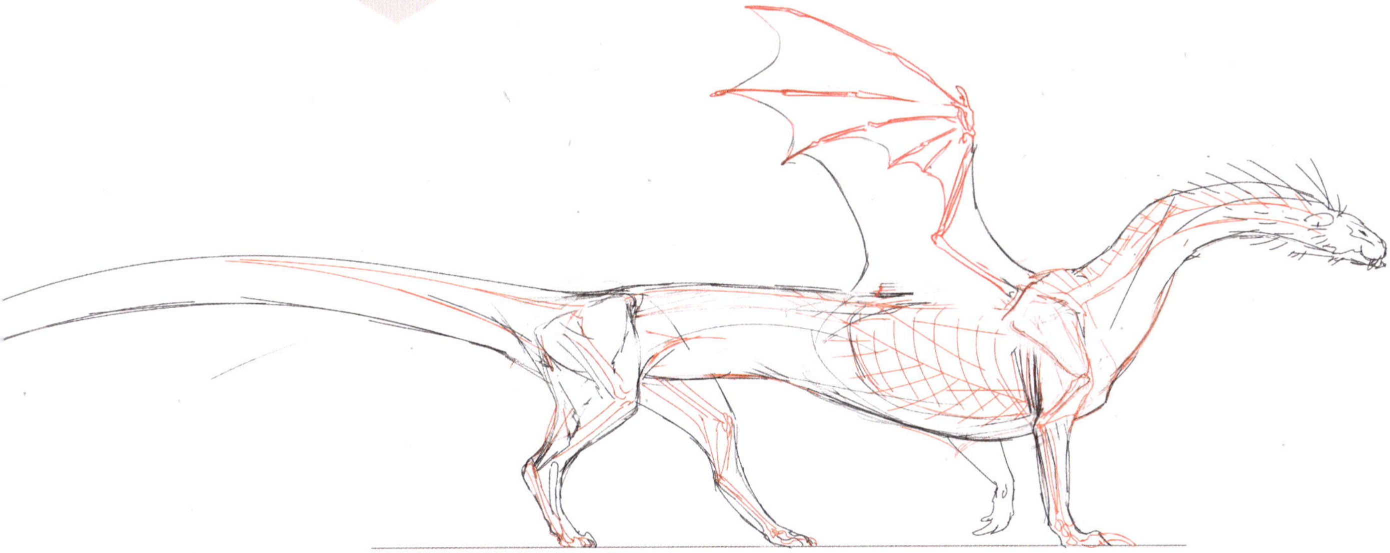

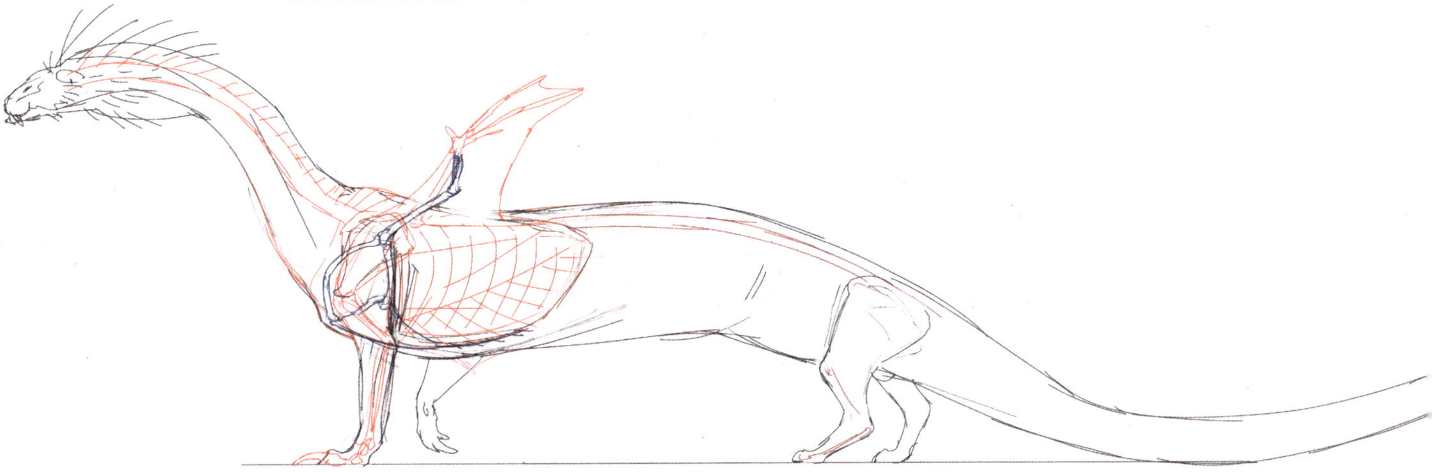

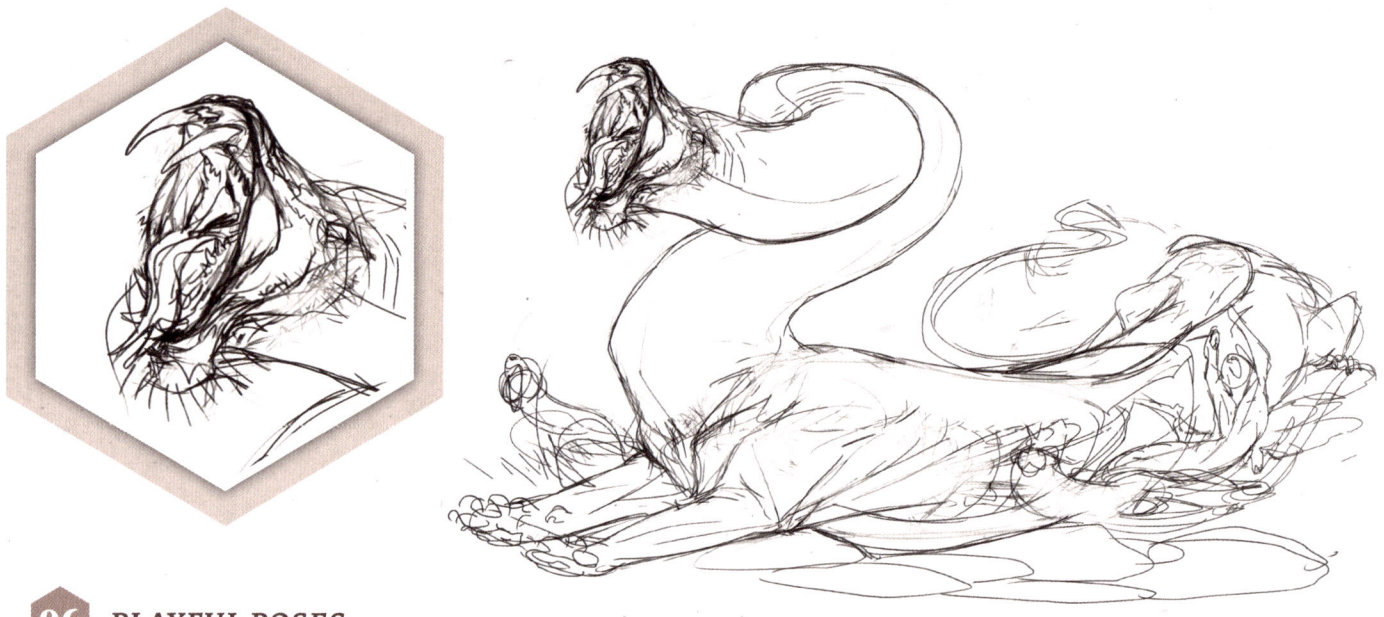

06 PLAYFUL POSES

Next I look into some rough poses and thumbnails for the tatzelwurm. When it comes to concept art, I generally do a lot of the designing on the fly, constantly drawing and redrawing over the same image. If I am drawing or designing fantastical creatures with a heavy basis in biology or real-world animals, I like to pose them doing very ordinary things. Sleeping, playing, perhaps eating a meal – things that real animals do. Fancy poses are dramatic and exciting, but I prefer to save them for big 'hero' paintings. In this idea, a male tatzelwurm yawns and stretches while his cubs play nearby.

07 THE FAMILY

While I like the pose of the previous idea, I decide I want to try more of a side view, to show off the long body and elegant shape of the tatzelwurm. I like the idea of portraying an entire family, with an adult male and female and several cubs. This second sketch shows the female in the front, grooming one of her cubs, while the rest of her litter cuddle up against her soft stomach fur. Her mate yawns behind her, wings outstretched. In this version I also trial the idea of their wings being very paw-like, which I'll end up using in the final design and illustration.

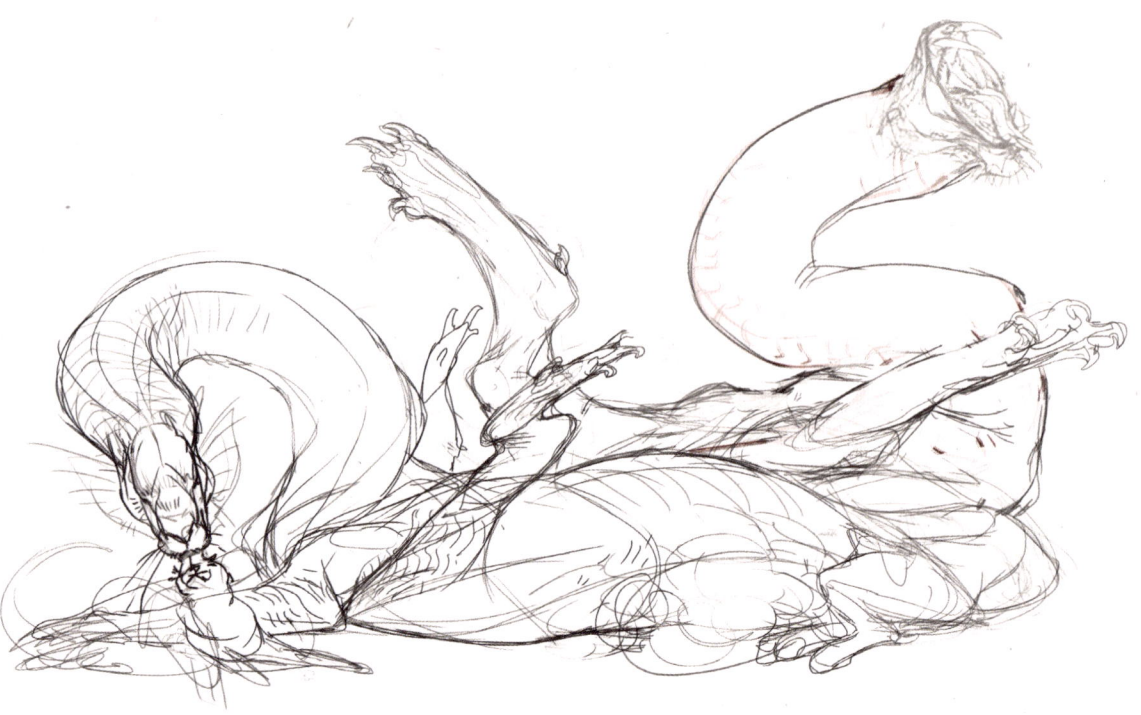

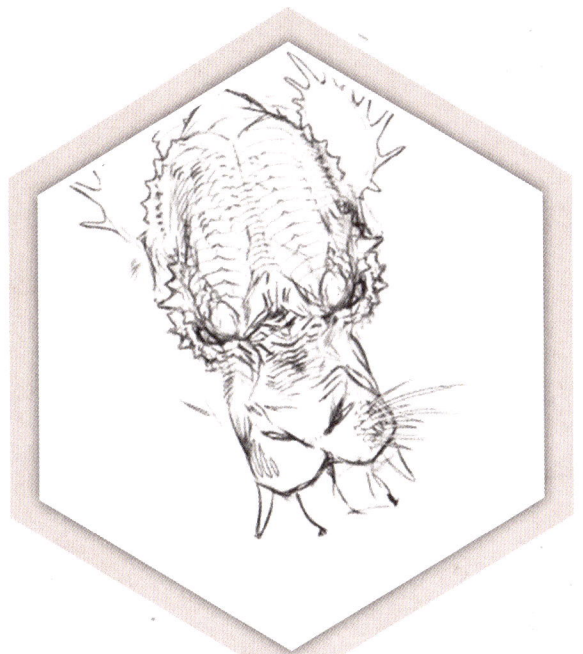

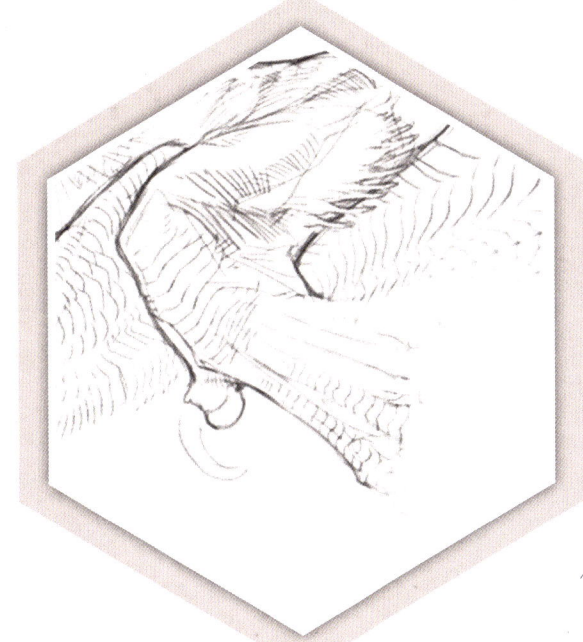

08 STARTING THE LINE ART

Now that I have a rough sketch I like, it's time to start the process of cleaning up. My base sketches tend to be very simple, as I prefer to develop the finer details as I go along. I'll be doing somewhat tight line art for this piece, as I want it to have more of a scientific feel as opposed to something painterly. I have my sketch on one layer, lightened to about 10% opacity. I then proceed to draw on a new layer over the top – a pretty standard process for creating line art.

09 DEVELOPING LINE ART

A small jump later, you can see how much the line art has changed from my rough sketch. I even got a bit carried away and started colouring a leg! My approach here is not to make very clean line art, more of a very tight sketch. The male was taking too much attention away from the scene, so I removed him. In his place, I roughly sketch a leaping tatzelwurm cub, so I can show off the wings and chest. This pose is inspired by watching my own two cats chasing insects.

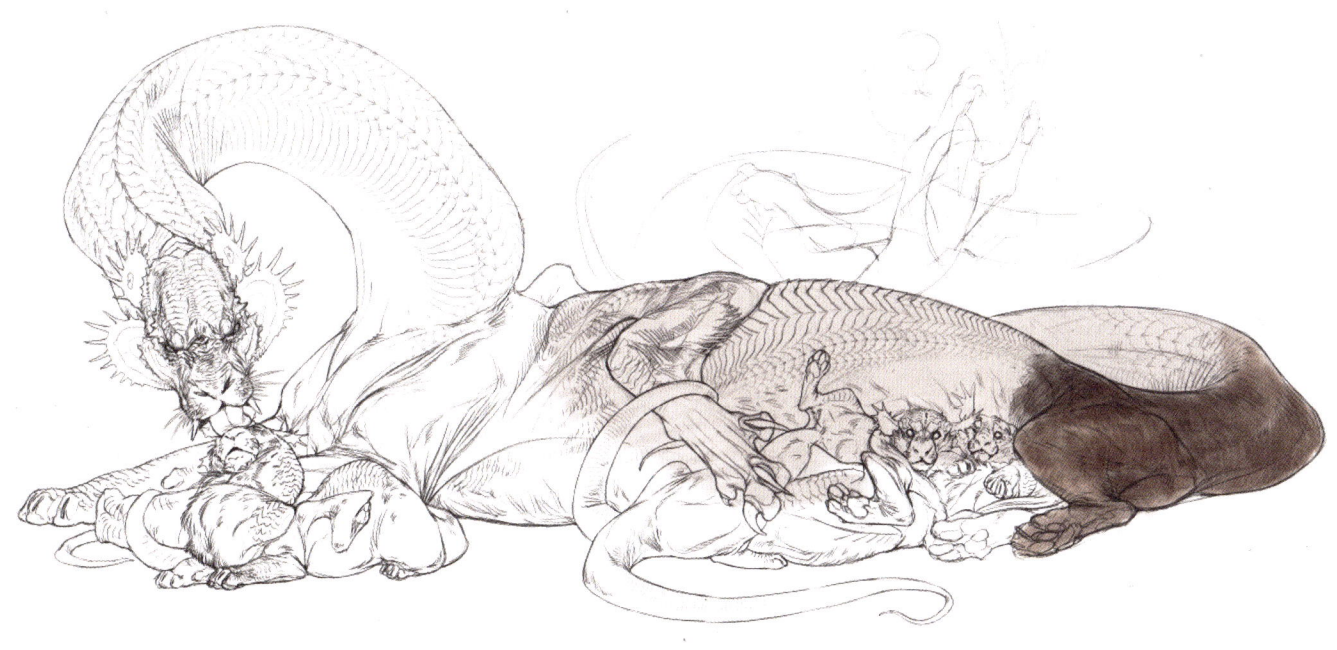

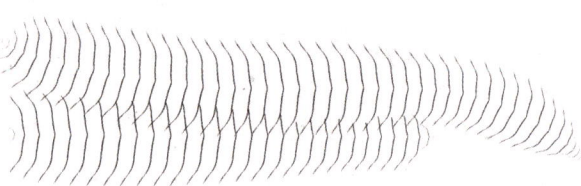

MAKE A SCALE BRUSH

Scales are time-consuming, and their layout can be hard to draw. Making a custom scale brush in Photoshop can help – it's as simple as drawing a single scale, going to **Edit > Define Brush Preset**, and then playing around with options such as spacing and flow. To make the scales follow the brush's direction, open the brush settings and go to **Shape Dynamics > Angle Jitter > Direction**.

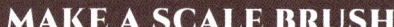

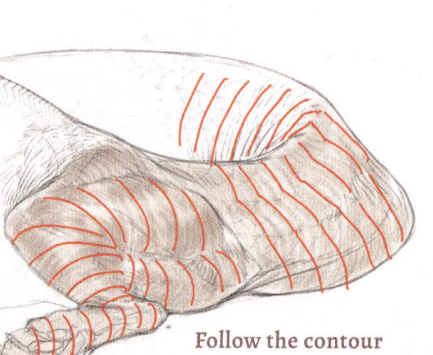

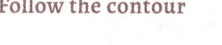
Follow the contour

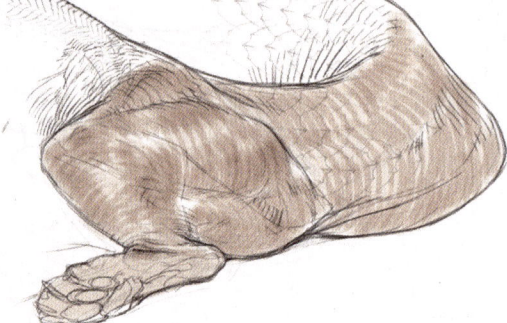

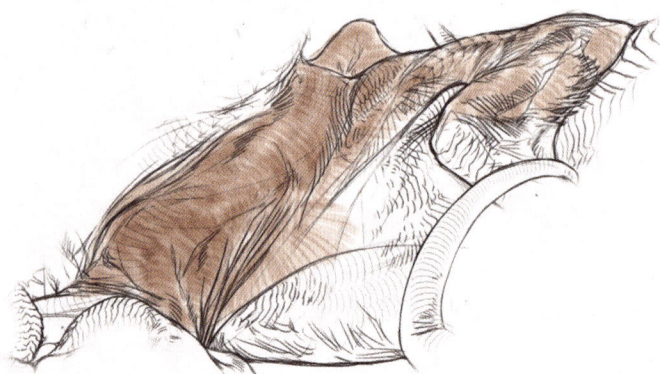

10 **FOLLOWING FORM**

This is a good opportunity to talk about how I colour sketches. My approach is a little different to how I would approach a full painting, like something I would do for *Magic: The Gathering*, but it's how I colour much of my concept work. I typically use the regular round brush, but lately I've been enjoying Eilert Janßen's marker brushes for Photoshop, which you can find for free on Gumroad. I love Copic markers, and these brushes are a fun digital alternative. The key to colouring here is to follow the form and contour of the muscles. Here's where knowledge of underlying musculature is essential. You can see how sculptural the result is, which I find very visually appealing.

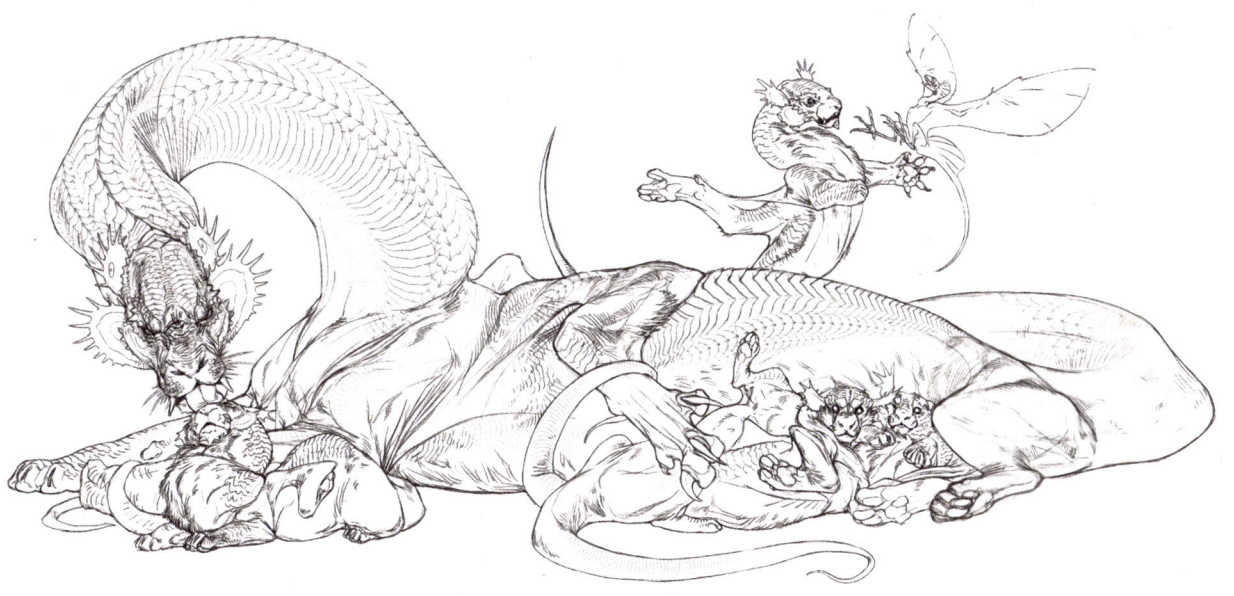

 FINAL LINE ART

Here's the final tight sketch for this mother tatzelwurm and her four cubs. I set this layer to Multiply mode, which will enable me to colour underneath it. I will be applying colour both underneath and above the lines, as well as some colouring directly onto the line-art layer.

 STORY MOMENTS

'Charm' and 'whimsy' are the two descriptors I get most often when people describe my work, and I love it. I find a lot of the charm comes from 'story moments' or the little stories playing out all over the image as a whole. There are a few narrative elements here: there's the sweet, almost comical moment that the mother wurm shares with her cub as she grooms him; the other is the tired mother trying to wrangle her unruly children as they play, using her 'wing' to steady them; the last is the largest of the cubs leaping to try to catch a curious little wyvern who got too close!

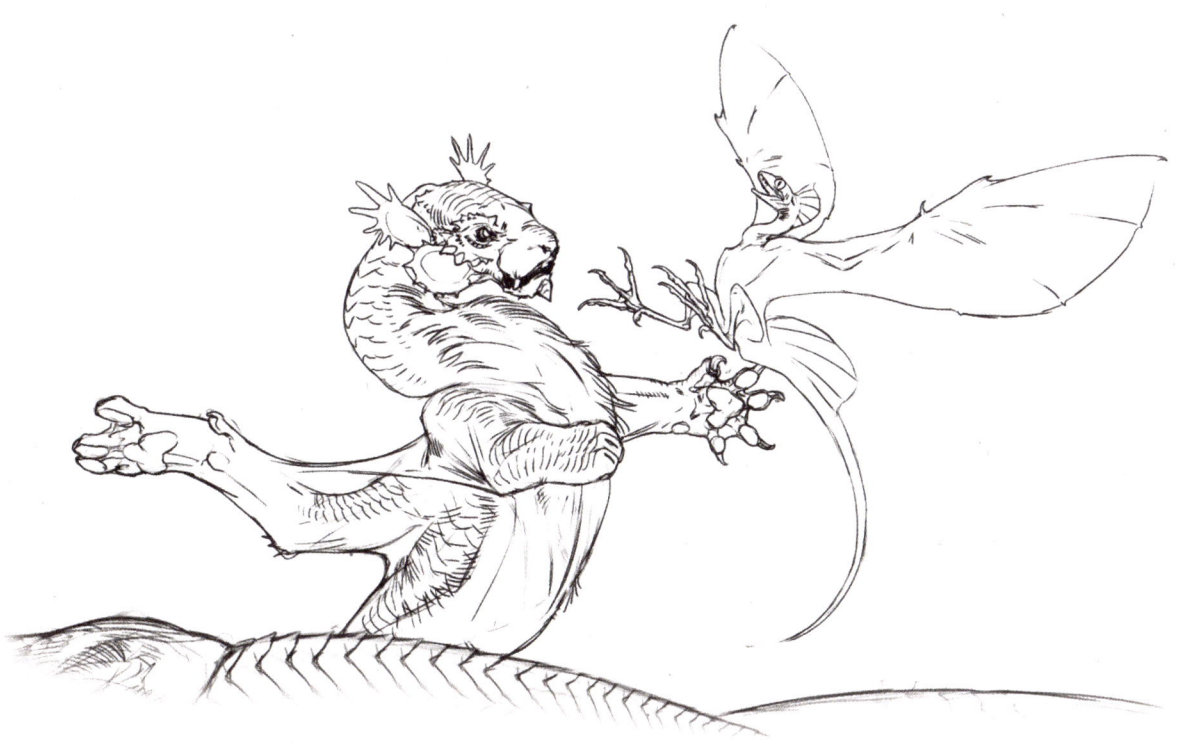

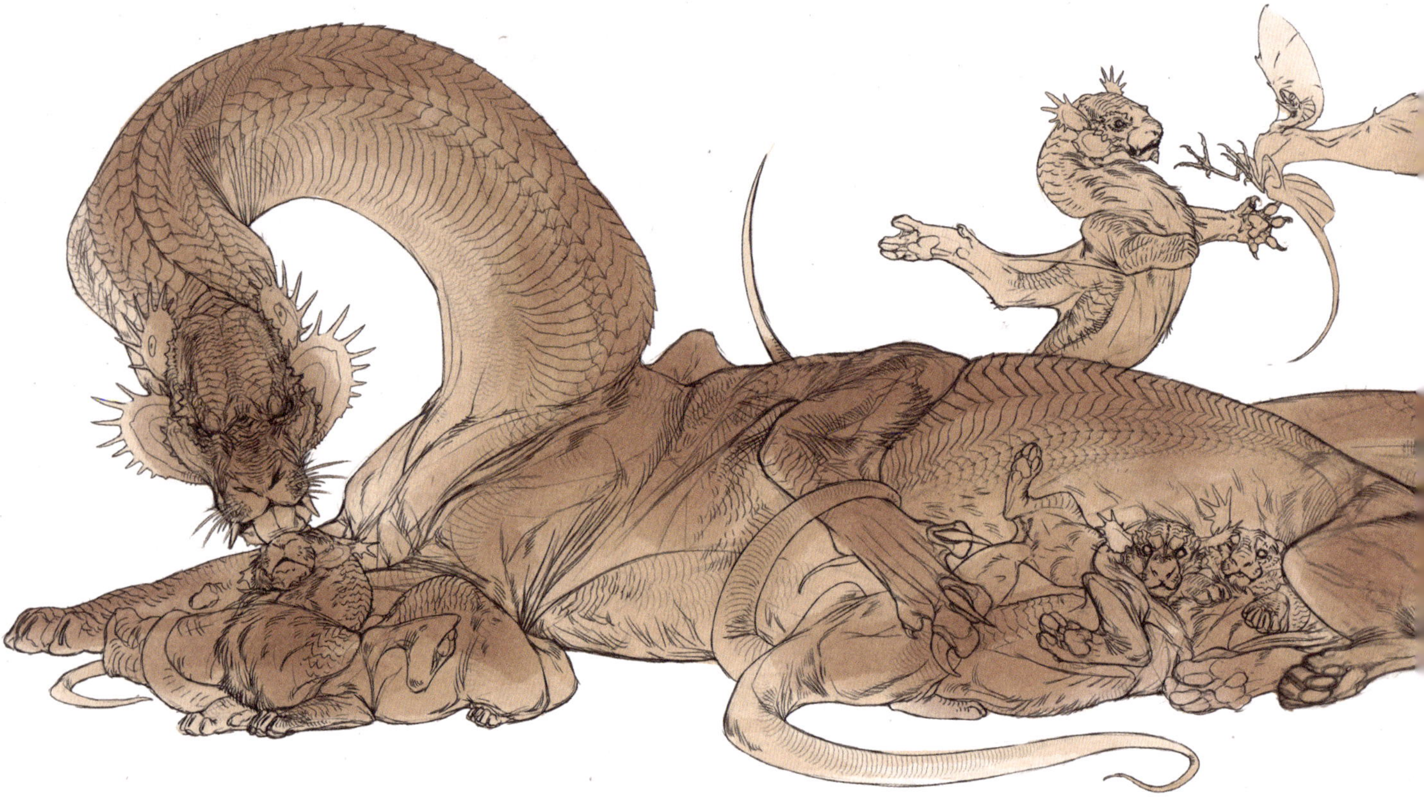

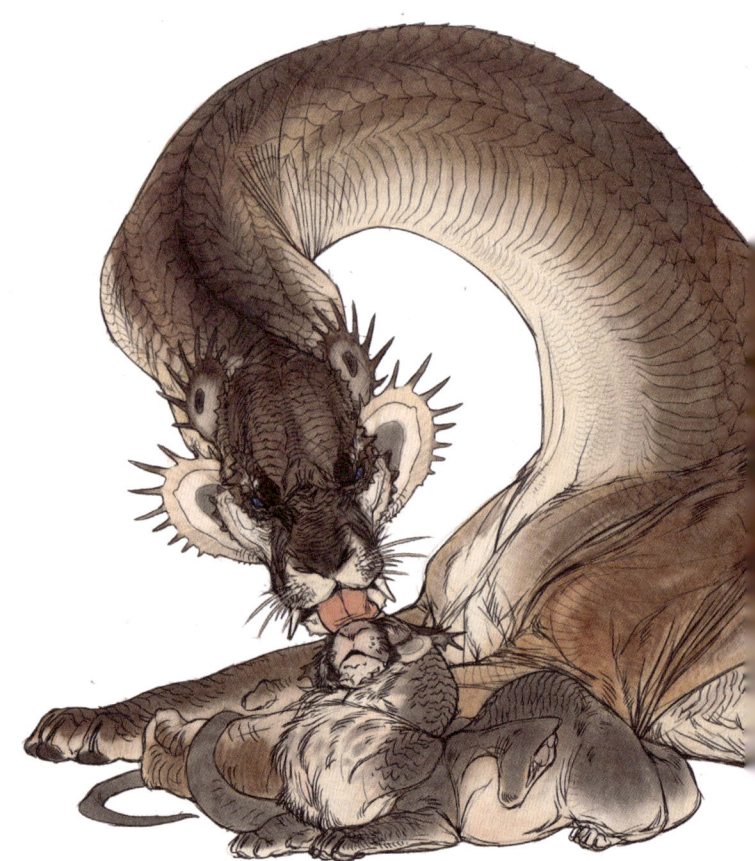

13 BASE COLOURS

Next up is laying the flat colour. I usually like to auto-select the negative space around my image, then invert the selection – it makes laying down flat colour much easier. I block in some very basic colours for the tatzelwurm: a warm brown to a lighter yellow stomach. The variation in the opacity and the light texture of the marker brush I'm using really help with adding subtle visual interest and texture.

14 COLOUR VARIATION

Now I can add some interest and variation to the flat colours and define the look of each individual creature. The cubs of many species of large cats have spots or stripes for camouflage, which typically fade as they reach adulthood. The tatzelwurm cubs are a duller brown compared to their rusty-coloured mother, so they can blend in with snow-covered rocks. The dark markings around their eyes help them to avoid becoming snow-blind, similar to the dark markings around the eyes of meerkats, which cut down the glare from the sun.

TAKE BREAKS

The most important thing is to look after your health. I pushed myself far too hard in my twenties, and I'm paying the price with intermittent wrist pain and regular visits to the physiotherapist. Do your wrist stretches and try to get good sleep. I recommend weightlifting for a strong body, mind, and soul. It's also a great way to learn about human muscle anatomy – you're art in motion!

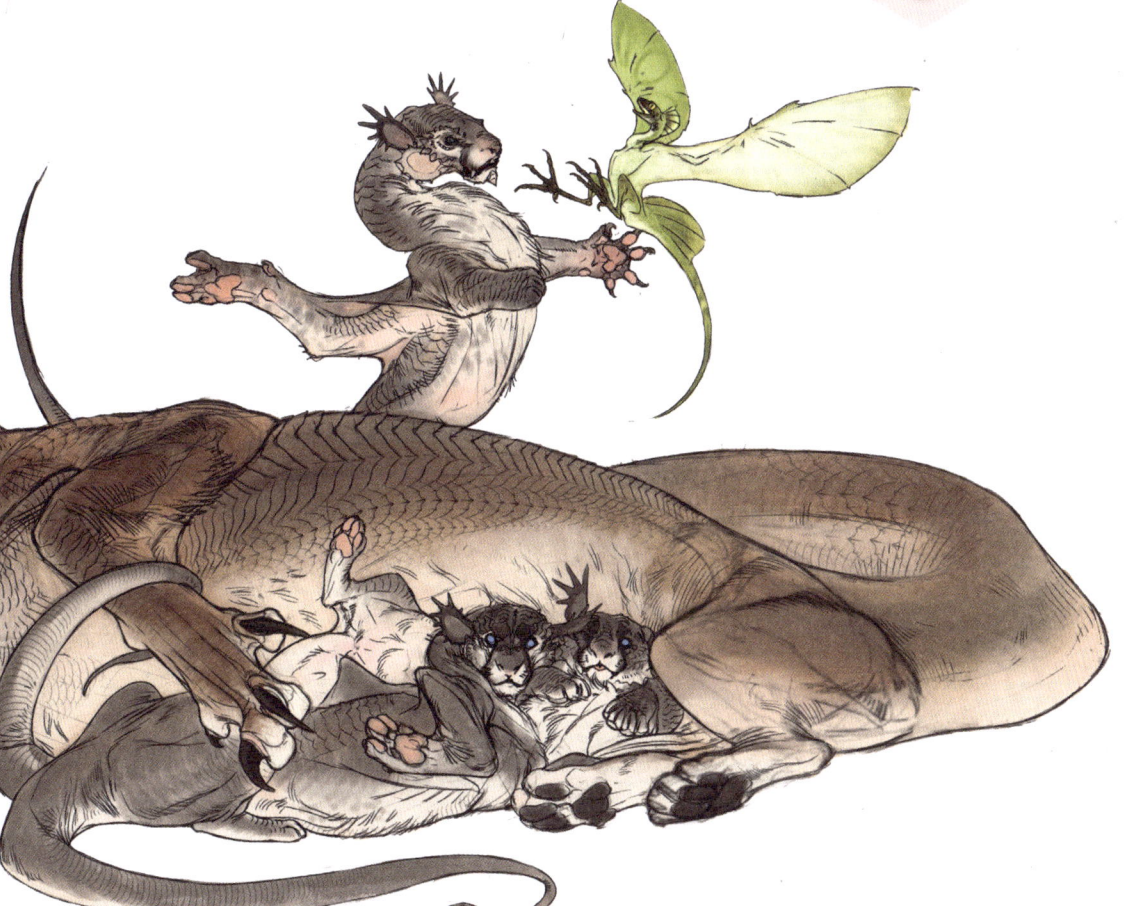

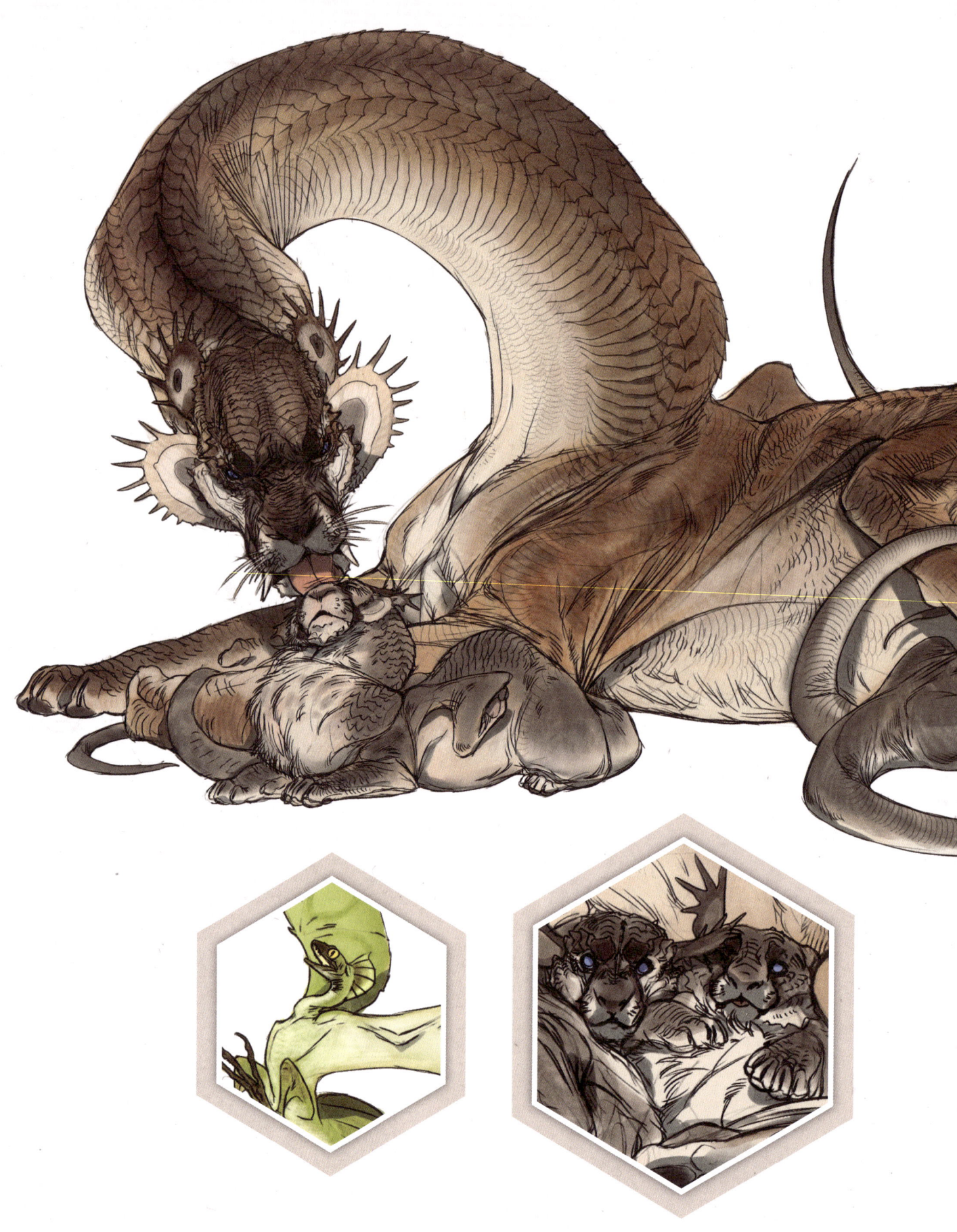

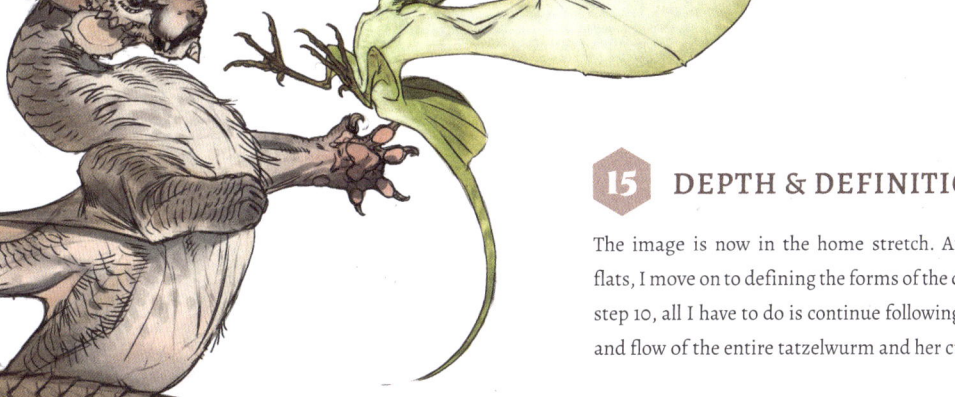

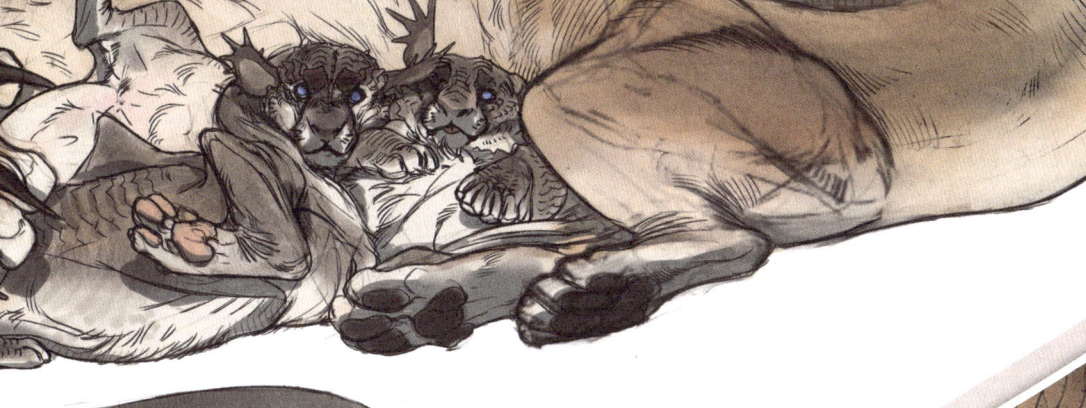

15 DEPTH & DEFINITION

The image is now in the home stretch. After finishing the flats, I move on to defining the forms of the dragon. As I did in step 10, all I have to do is continue following the musculature and flow of the entire tatzelwurm and her cubs.

16 FINE DETAILS

With a little bit more shading with a large soft brush, and a few shadows under the scales, the image is nearing completion. Look at the difference the edge shadows can make! They really give a sense of curvature and form to the 2D image.

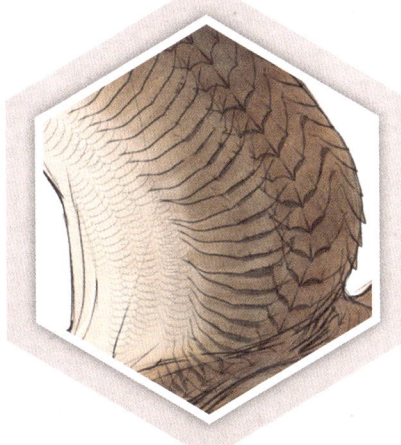

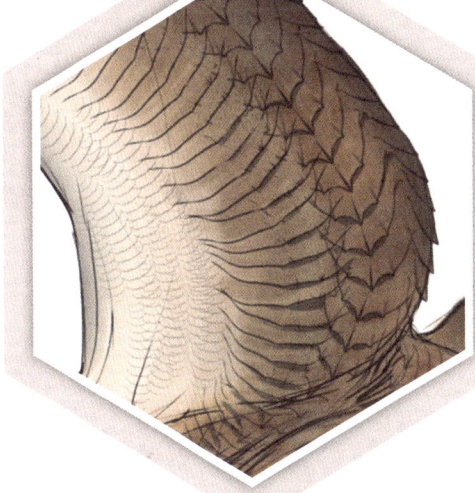

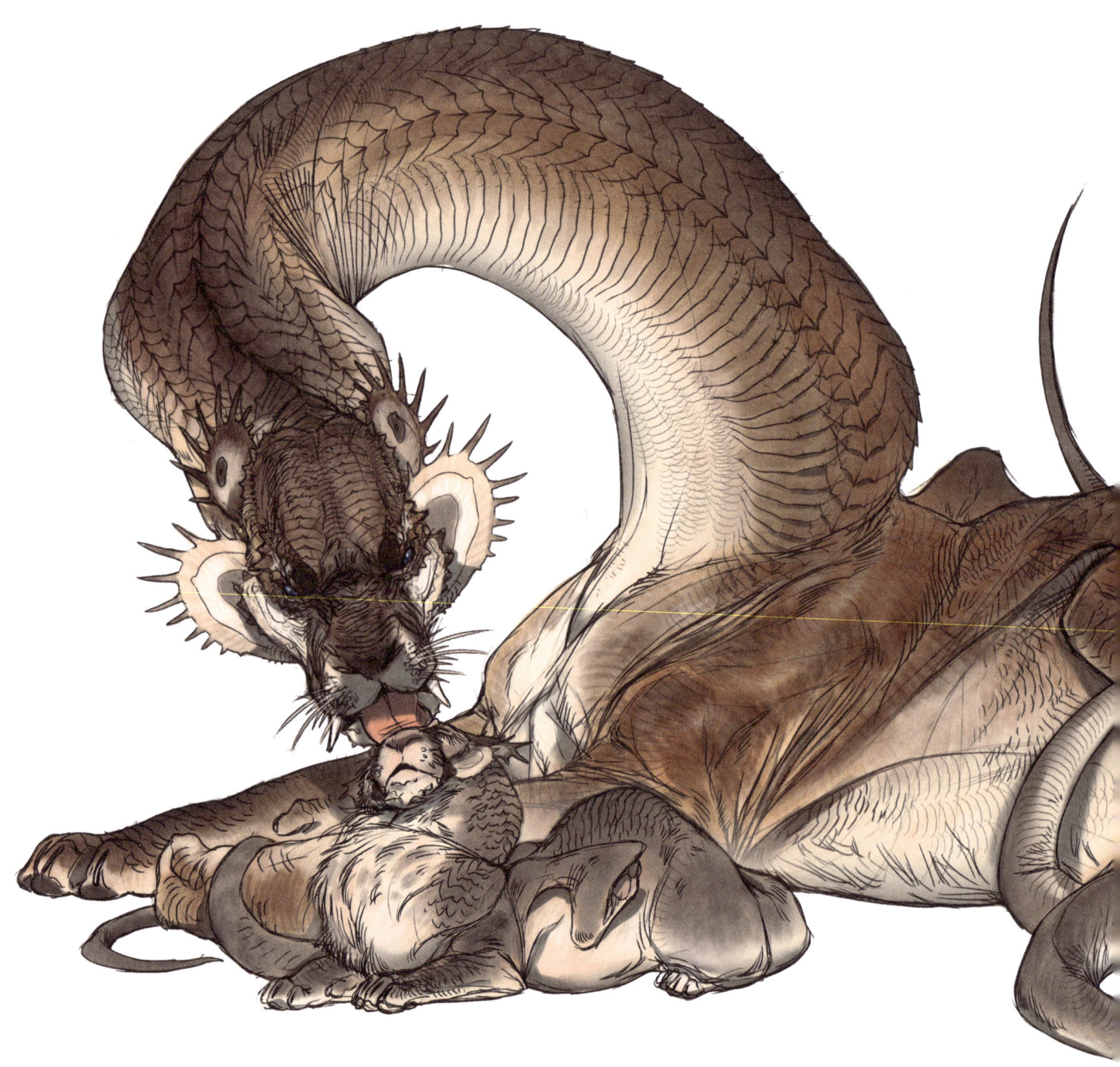

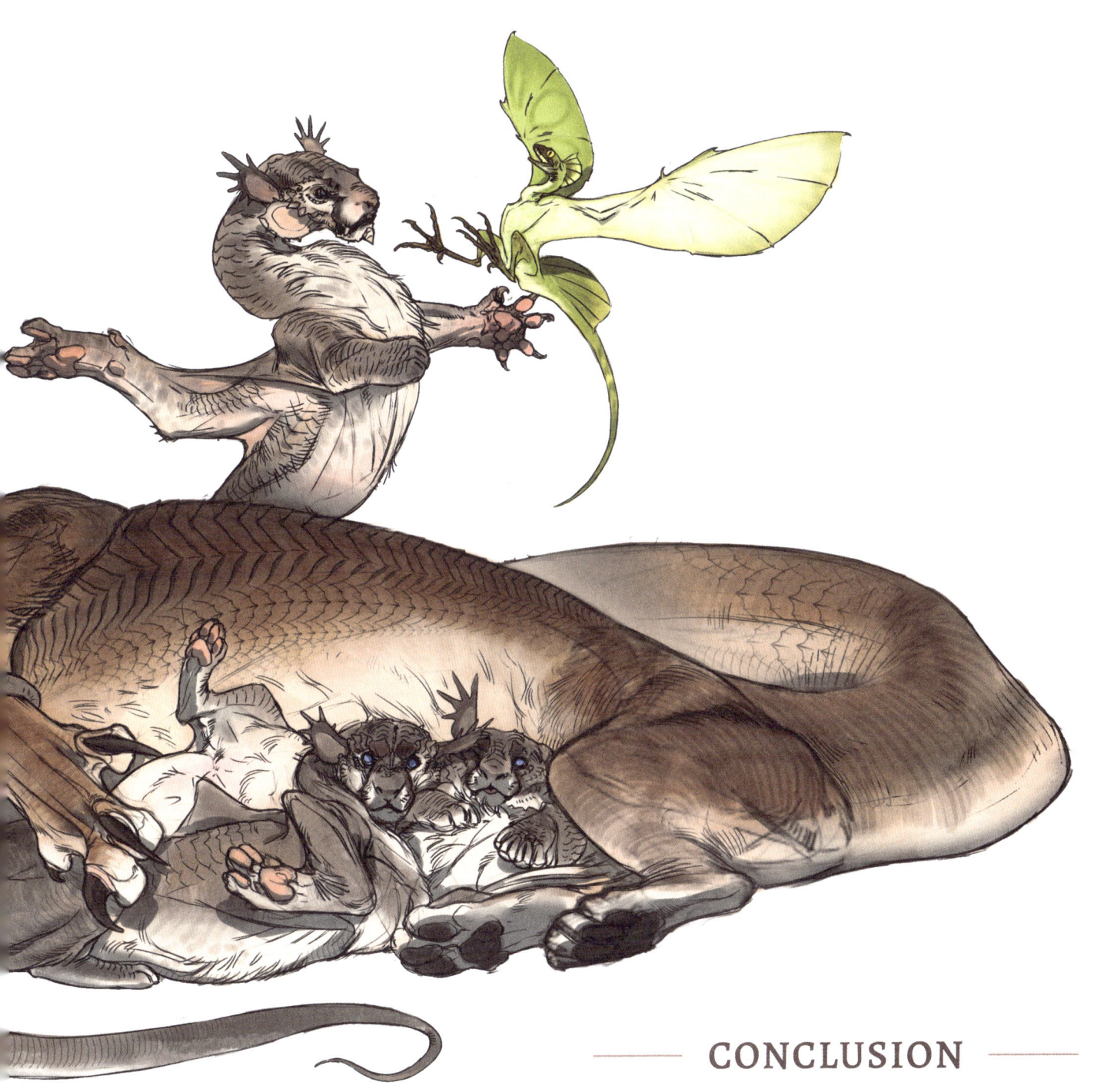

CONCLUSION

The final design is my take on a semi-realistic tatzelwurm. I'm happy with it, especially with how the 'ears' turned out – tympanic scales that resemble the ears of a mountain lion are a fun, appealing idea, and I love how they add so much expression to the cubs. As opposed to being a wacky hybrid creature, this tatzelwurm feels grounded in reality. This isn't a weird cat-lizard monster, just a dragon with a case of mistaken identity! The anatomy feels smooth and well integrated, and overall the design is quite simple, with a strong silhouette and cohesive colours, which make it a success in my view.

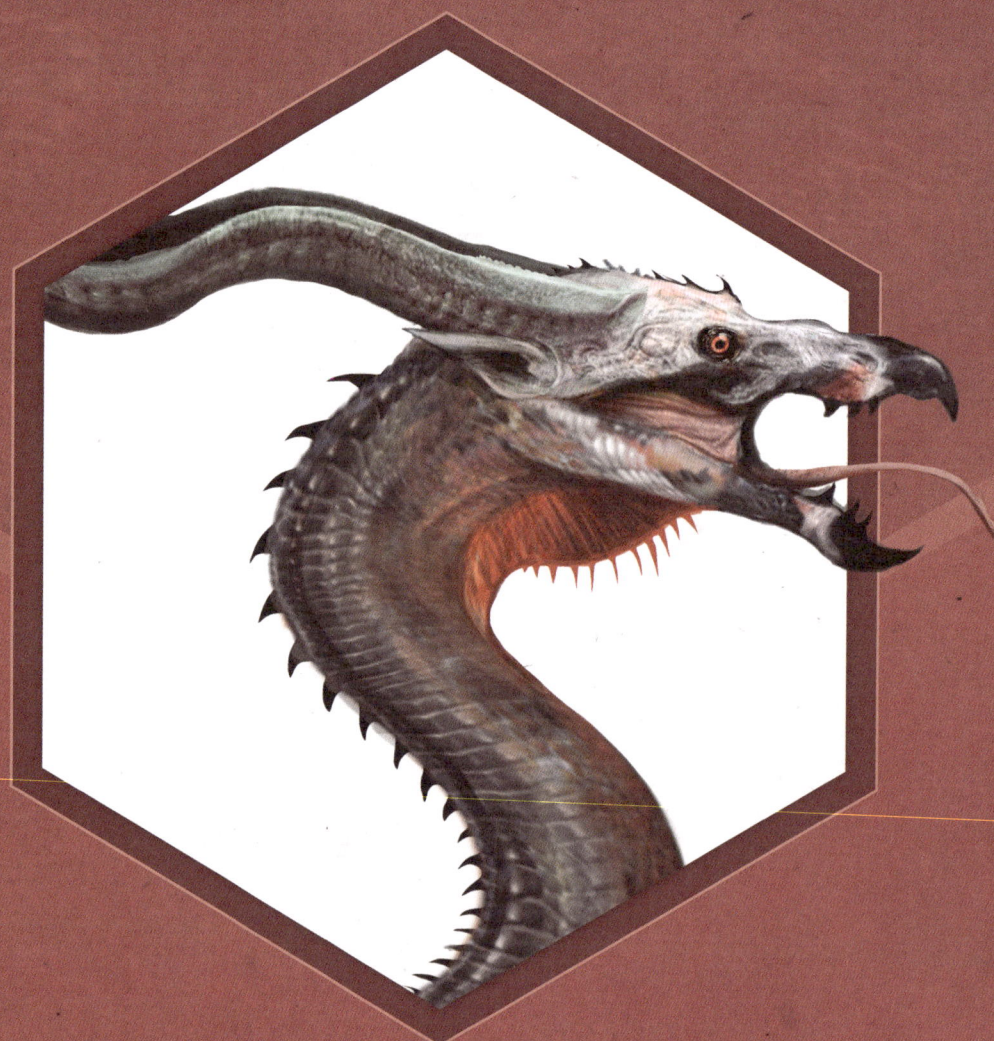

WYVERN

The creature catalogued in this chapter is the wyvern. This well-known dragon notably has two legs and two wings, unlike its cousins that have four legs or none. In medieval heraldry, it often appears standing bipedal on sharp talons, with its barbed tongue and pointed tail on display. Those historical depictions will form the basis for my interpretation of this fabled beast.

VINCENT COVIELLO

Final image © Vincent Coviello

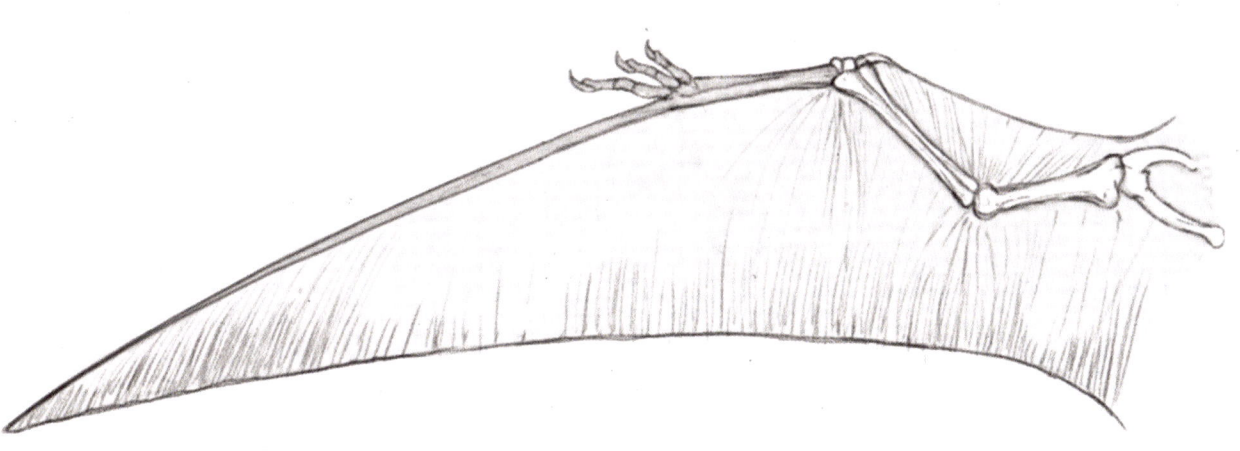

01 PTEROSAUR WING

Before sketching any ideas for a dragon, I start by researching animals that could inform my design. The wings are a key feature of the wyvern, so I begin my explorations there. Pterosaurs are a great place to pull inspiration for a dragon, in particular their wings, as the wyvern could have evolved for flight in a convergent way. Pterosaur wings have a very long 'finger' that gives the wing membrane its distinctive shape.

02 BAT WING

Like the pterosaur, bats are also a great reference for possible wing anatomy. Bat wings have long been a source of inspiration for the leathery wings of dragons, and they also offer an interesting option for finger anatomy and claws. A bat's wing has long fingers with membranes of skin stretched between them.

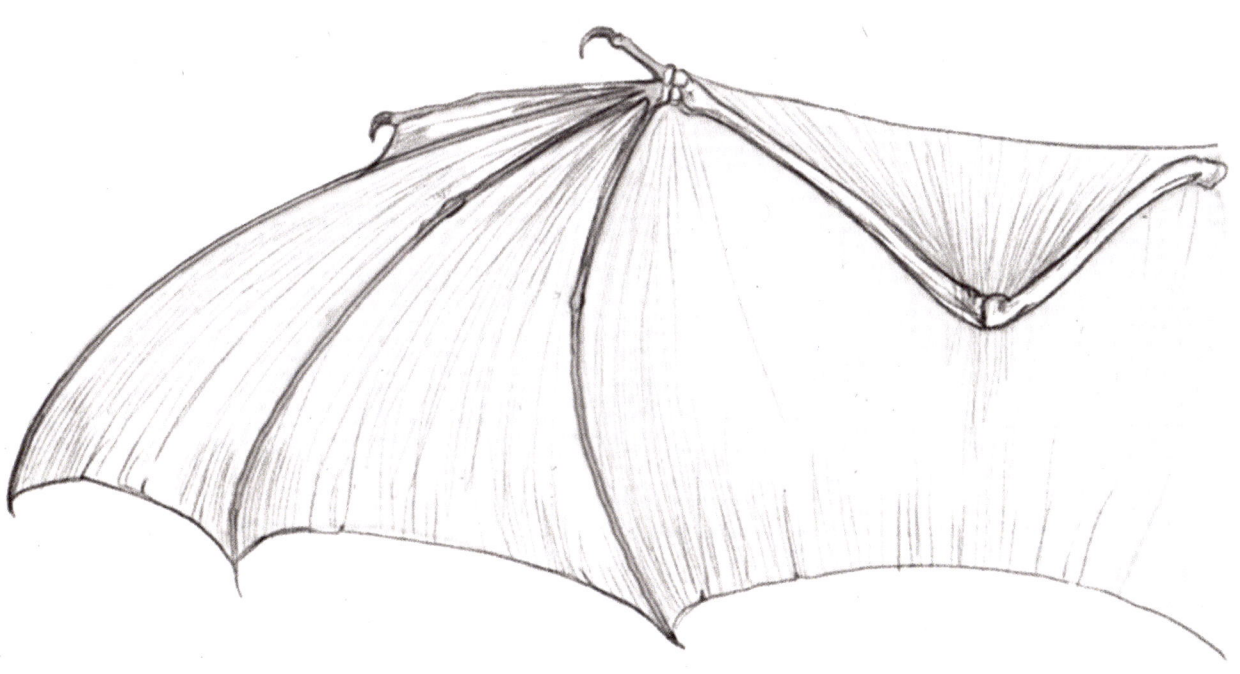

03 BIRD WING

While not as common as a reference point, bird wings could also be an interesting choice of feature for a wyvern. While wyverns are typically reptilian in their appearance, there is nothing to say a feathered one couldn't exist. Birds share common ancestry with many reptiles, so a wyvern with feathered wings could work well as a design.

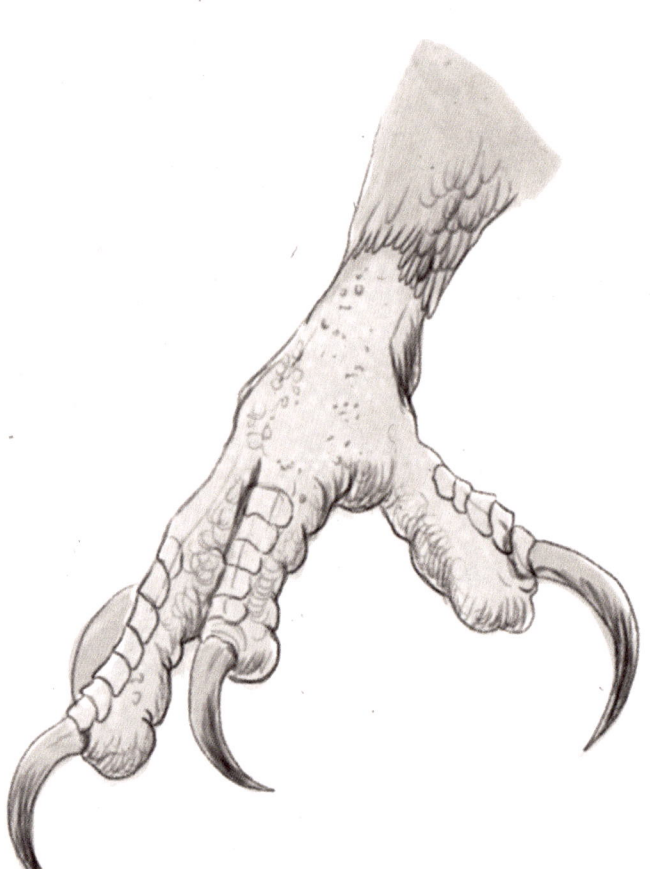

04 EAGLE FOOT

Eagles' talons are a great reference to pull from when thinking about the predatory nature of a wyvern. These large birds of prey have a powerful grip, with talons capable of tearing through flesh. This could inform the wyvern's eating habits. Eagles have anisodactyl feet, meaning they have three toes at the front and one at the back – the most common type of foot among birds.

05 OSPREY FOOT

Much like the eagle's talons, the osprey's foot is also informative and functional, built for catching slippery fish. With zygodactyl feet – feet with two claws at the front and two at the back – the wyvern could pluck its prey from the sky or from bodies of water. Animal adaptations such as these are an ecological wonderland to draw upon for a dragon.

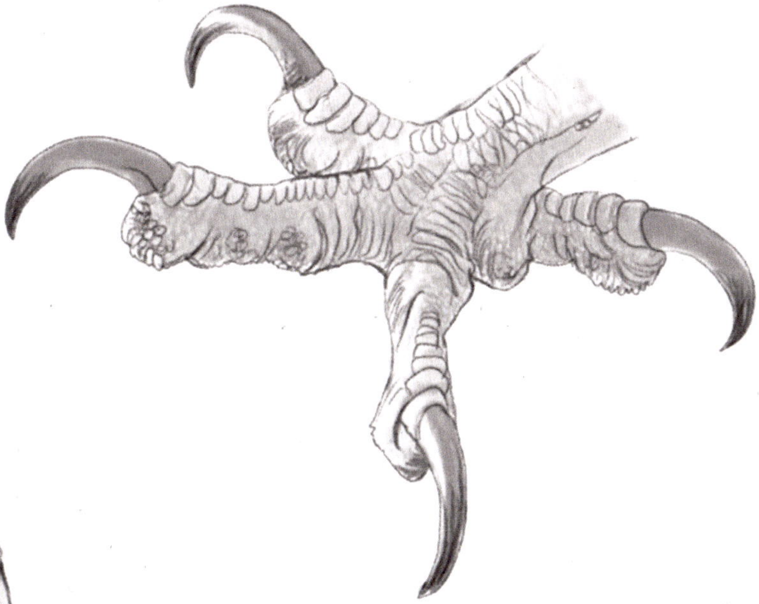

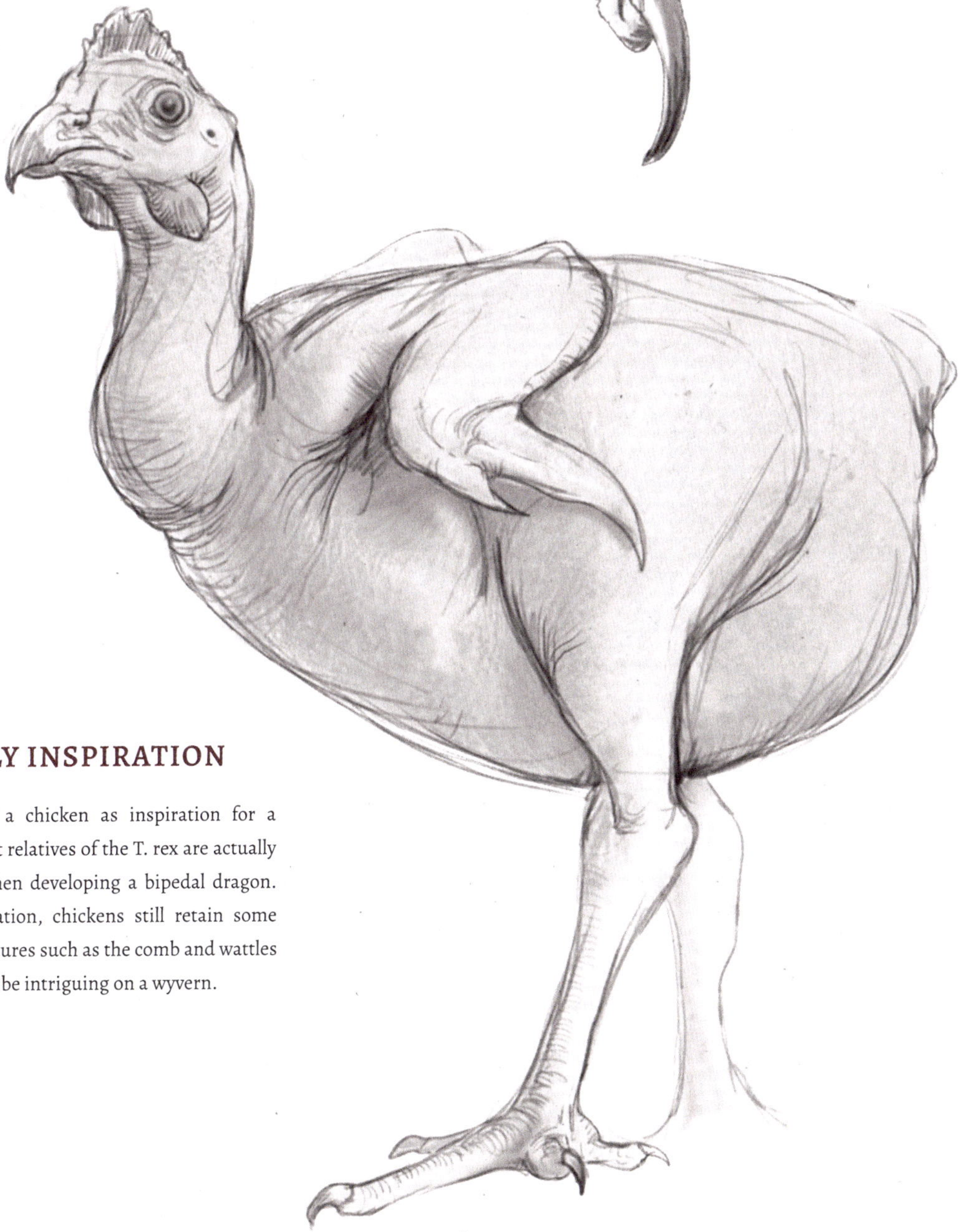

06 UNLIKELY INSPIRATION

One wouldn't think of a chicken as inspiration for a dragon, but these distant relatives of the T. rex are actually a great place to look when developing a bipedal dragon. Despite their domestication, chickens still retain some prehistoric attitude. Features such as the comb and wattles of a chicken's head could be intriguing on a wyvern.

07 MORAY EEL

Though this wyvern will probably not be an aquatic creature, there's no reason one can't look to the ocean for further inspiration. With their sinuous but muscular anatomy, an eel could be an interesting creature to refer to when developing the wyvern's look. Here I'm thinking specifically of the eel's muscular neck.

08 BAT ANATOMY

I find myself returning to the bat, arguably the most referenced animal when developing dragons. Its unique body structure and overall anatomy lends itself perfectly to the subject. A good place to look, besides their wings, is their face anatomy, which features nearly fantastical facial structures and growths that aid in hunting.

09 SAILFIN LIZARD

Like the bat, reptiles are a must when developing dragons. Sailfin lizards in particular have such interesting tail anatomy, with prominent dorsal 'sails' that give them their name. When developing my design, I'll pull from this to give my wyvern a rudder of sorts in flight, as well as a unique way to communicate.

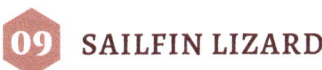

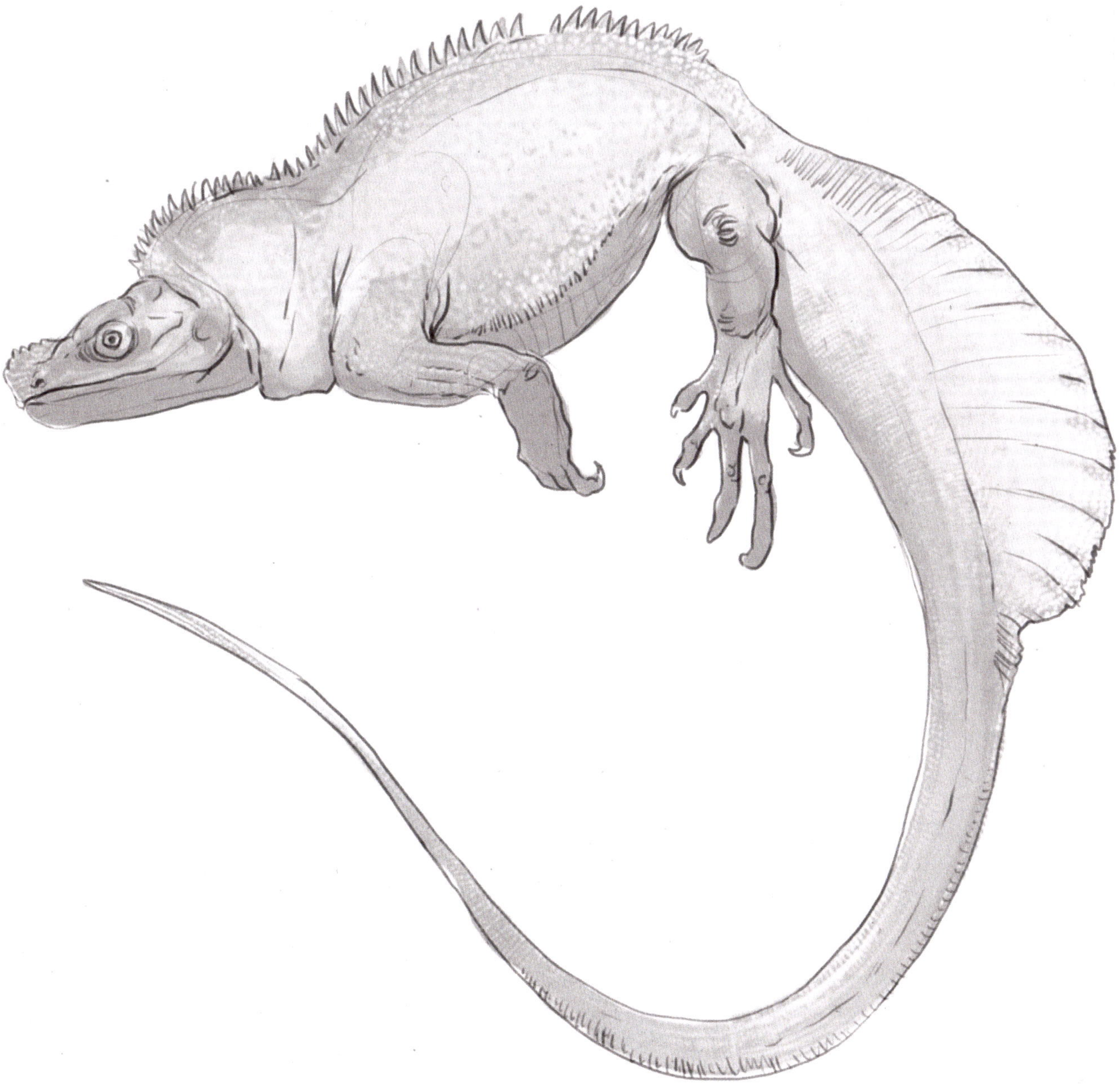

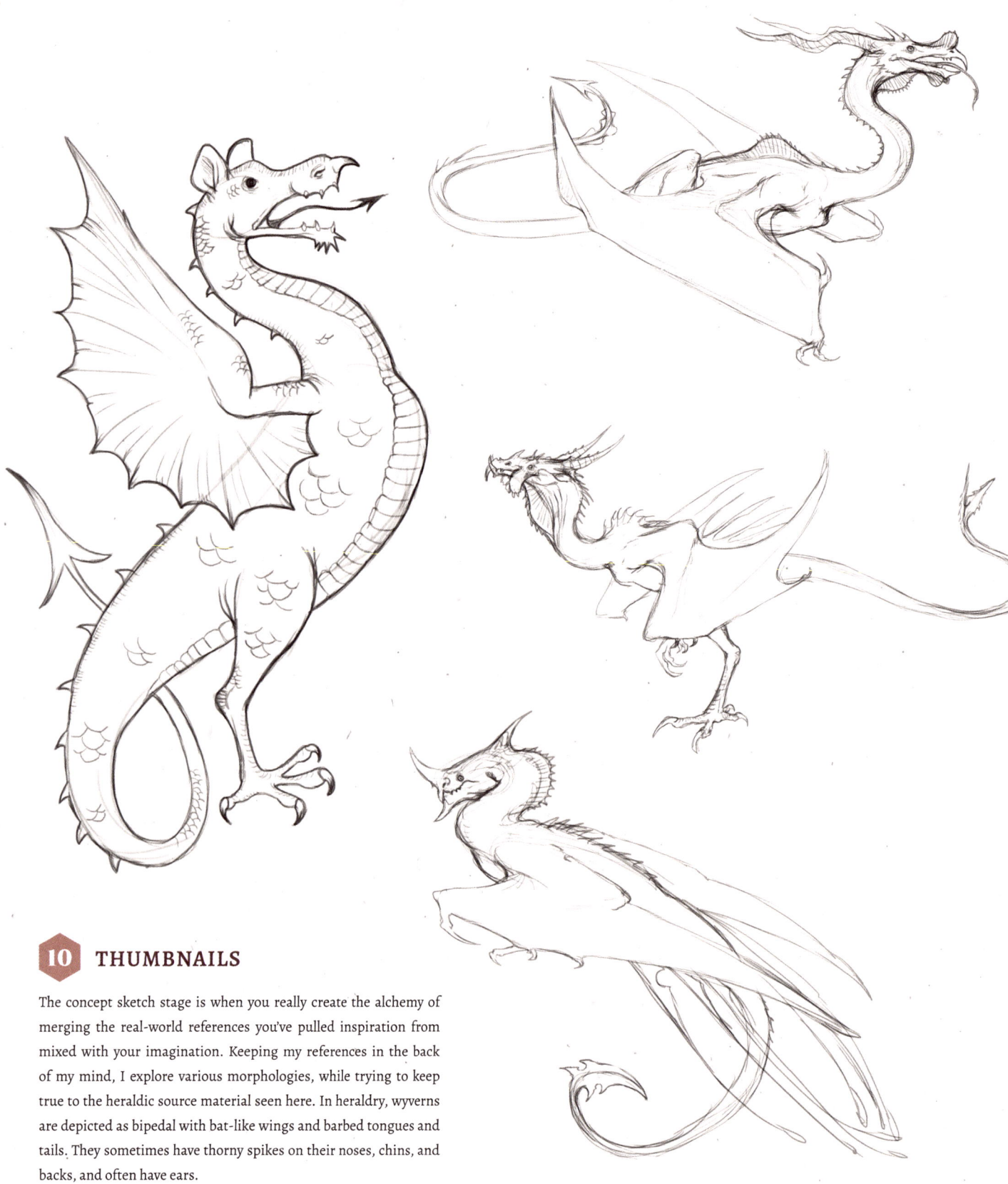

THUMBNAILS

The concept sketch stage is when you really create the alchemy of merging the real-world references you've pulled inspiration from mixed with your imagination. Keeping my references in the back of my mind, I explore various morphologies, while trying to keep true to the heraldic source material seen here. In heraldry, wyverns are depicted as bipedal with bat-like wings and barbed tongues and tails. They sometimes have thorny spikes on their noses, chins, and backs, and often have ears.

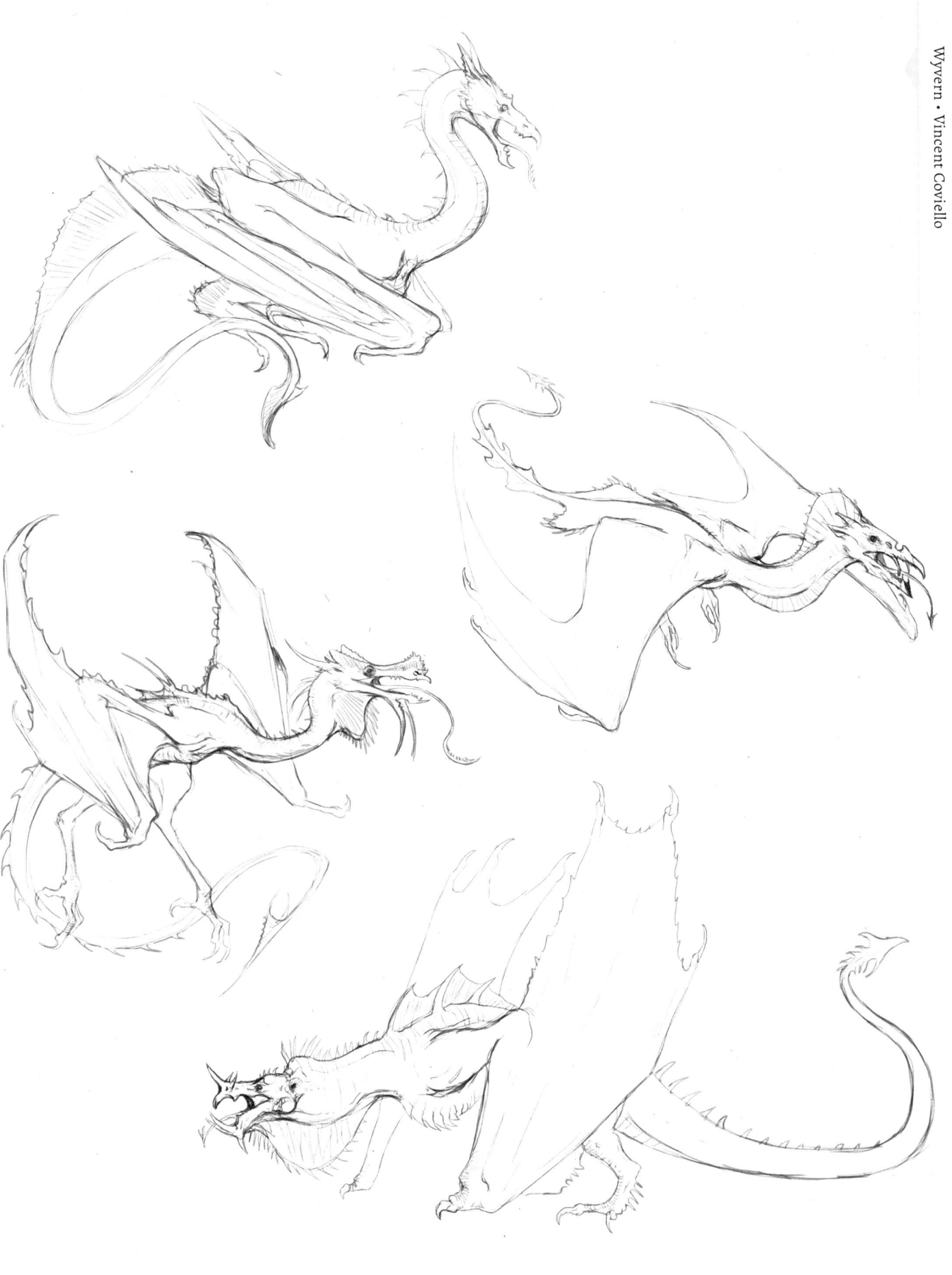

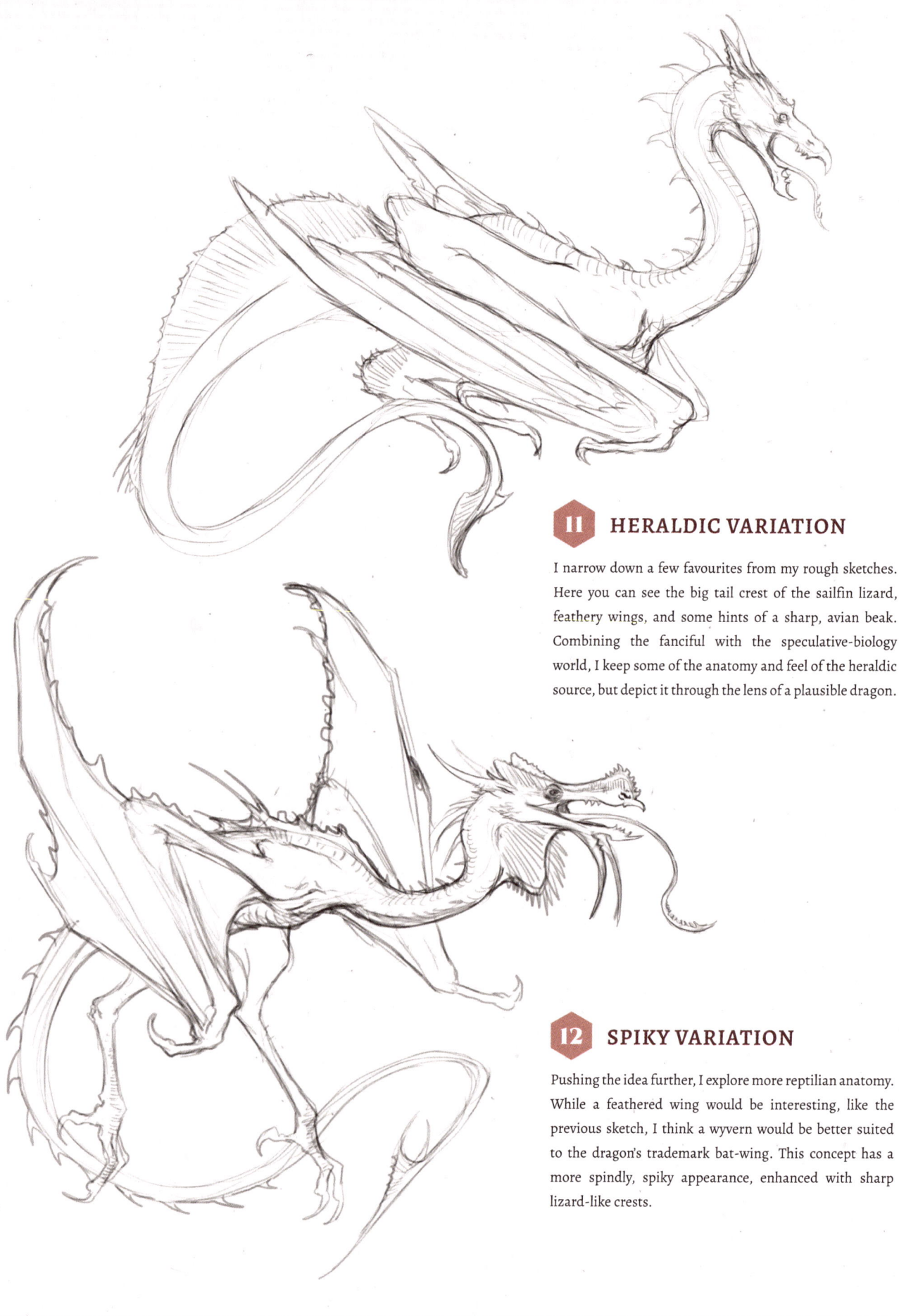

11 HERALDIC VARIATION

I narrow down a few favourites from my rough sketches. Here you can see the big tail crest of the sailfin lizard, feathery wings, and some hints of a sharp, avian beak. Combining the fanciful with the speculative-biology world, I keep some of the anatomy and feel of the heraldic source, but depict it through the lens of a plausible dragon.

12 SPIKY VARIATION

Pushing the idea further, I explore more reptilian anatomy. While a feathered wing would be interesting, like the previous sketch, I think a wyvern would be better suited to the dragon's trademark bat-wing. This concept has a more spindly, spiky appearance, enhanced with sharp lizard-like crests.

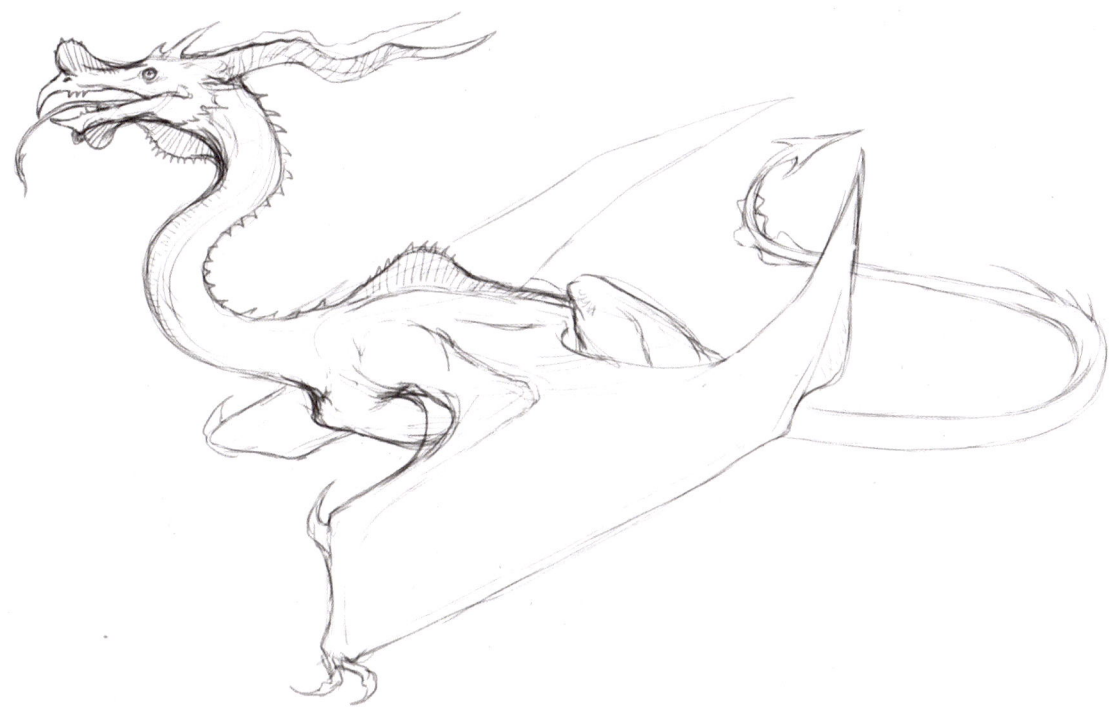

13 PTEROSAUR VARIATION

Looking back at the references, I'm inspired to use a pterosaur wing for this third option. This brings me to the idea of having prominent horns. Pterosaurs were capable of flight even with massive head crests, so this more fantasy-based feature could still work in the real world. The concept continues drawing inspiration from sailfin lizards, even combined with chicken-like details for the wyvern's head.

14 COMBINING IDEAS

This is the Frankenstein stage of development, where I synthesize the strongest design from elements of different sketches. In many cases you might like a wing from this concept, the head of that, the horns of another. By combining my favourite elements, I reach this final concept, which is a good meld of all three while still keeping somewhat true to the source.

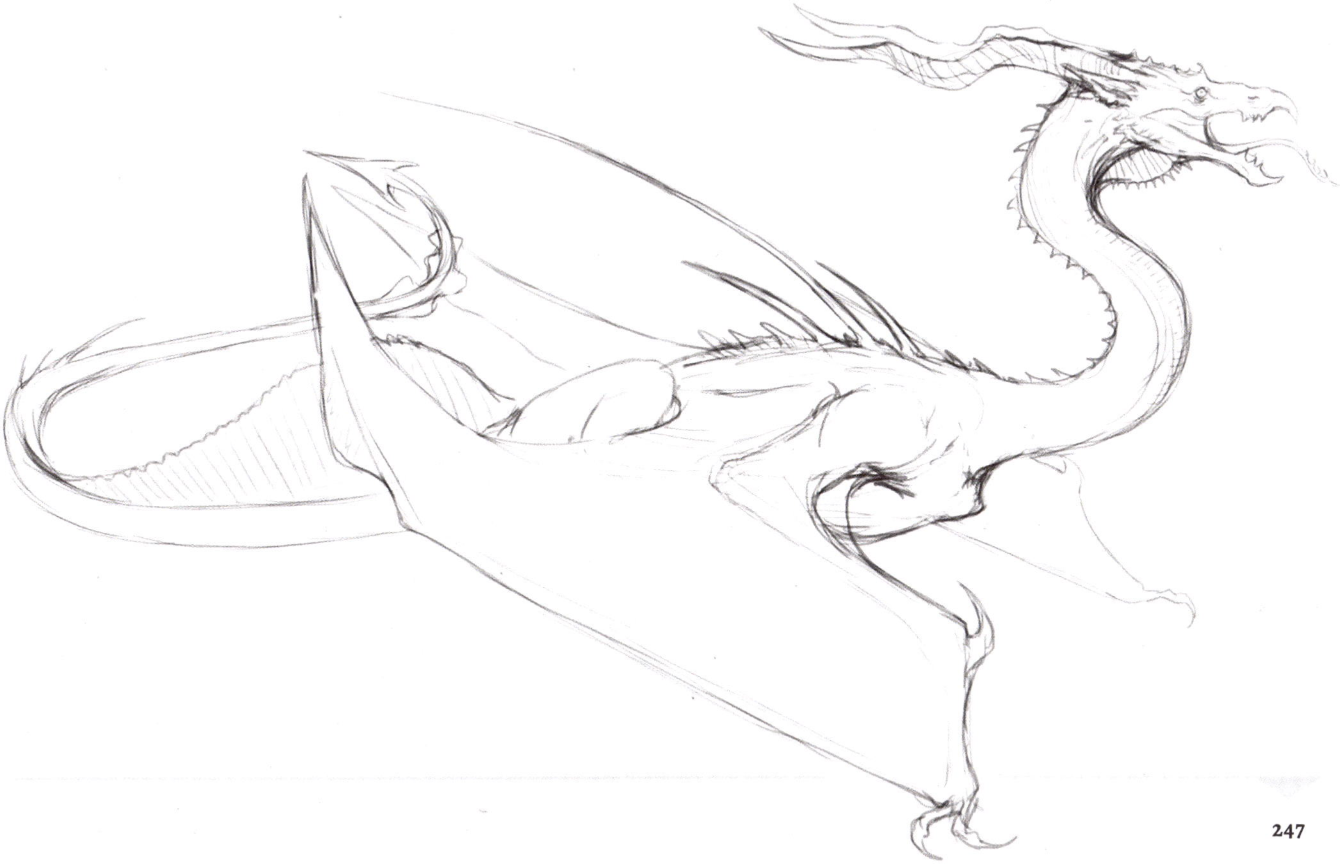

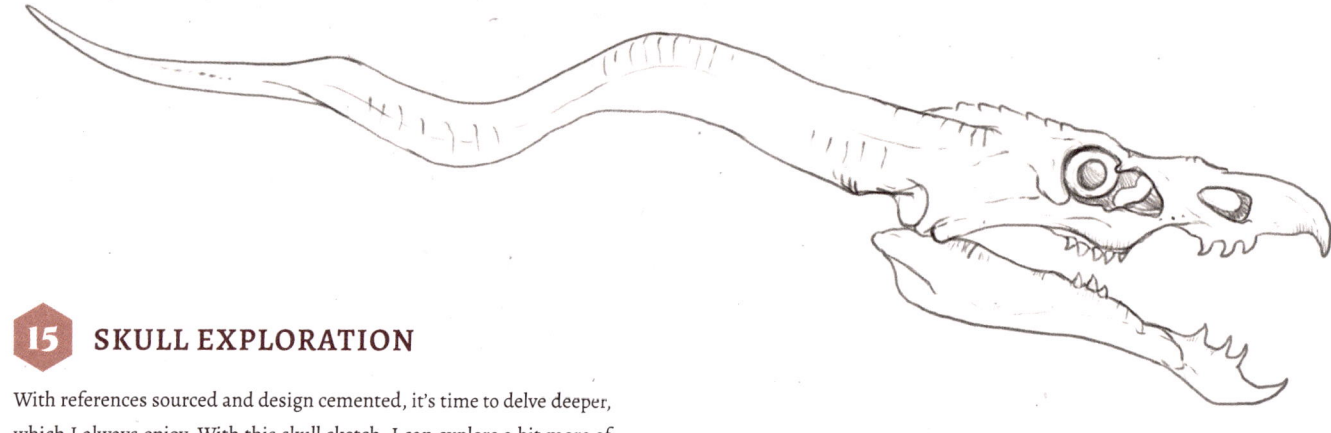

15 SKULL EXPLORATION

With references sourced and design cemented, it's time to delve deeper, which I always enjoy. With this skull sketch, I can explore a bit more of the dragon's internal anatomy. With a razor-sharp bill and a jaw lined with sharp teeth, you can clearly see the wyvern is an apex predator. The large horns add an element that's more heraldic and fantastical, but still in keeping with the shape and flow of the overall design.

16 FULL-BODY PLAN

Much like the skull sketch, drawing a full-body schematic or poses of your creature can help flesh out your overall design and imagine what it would be like in its habitat. Here you can more clearly see the full wingspan of the wyvern, and the sails and ridges on its tail in motion. In the final image it will be on all fours in a pterosaur-like crouch, but here you can also see the extent of its long limbs and sharp talons.

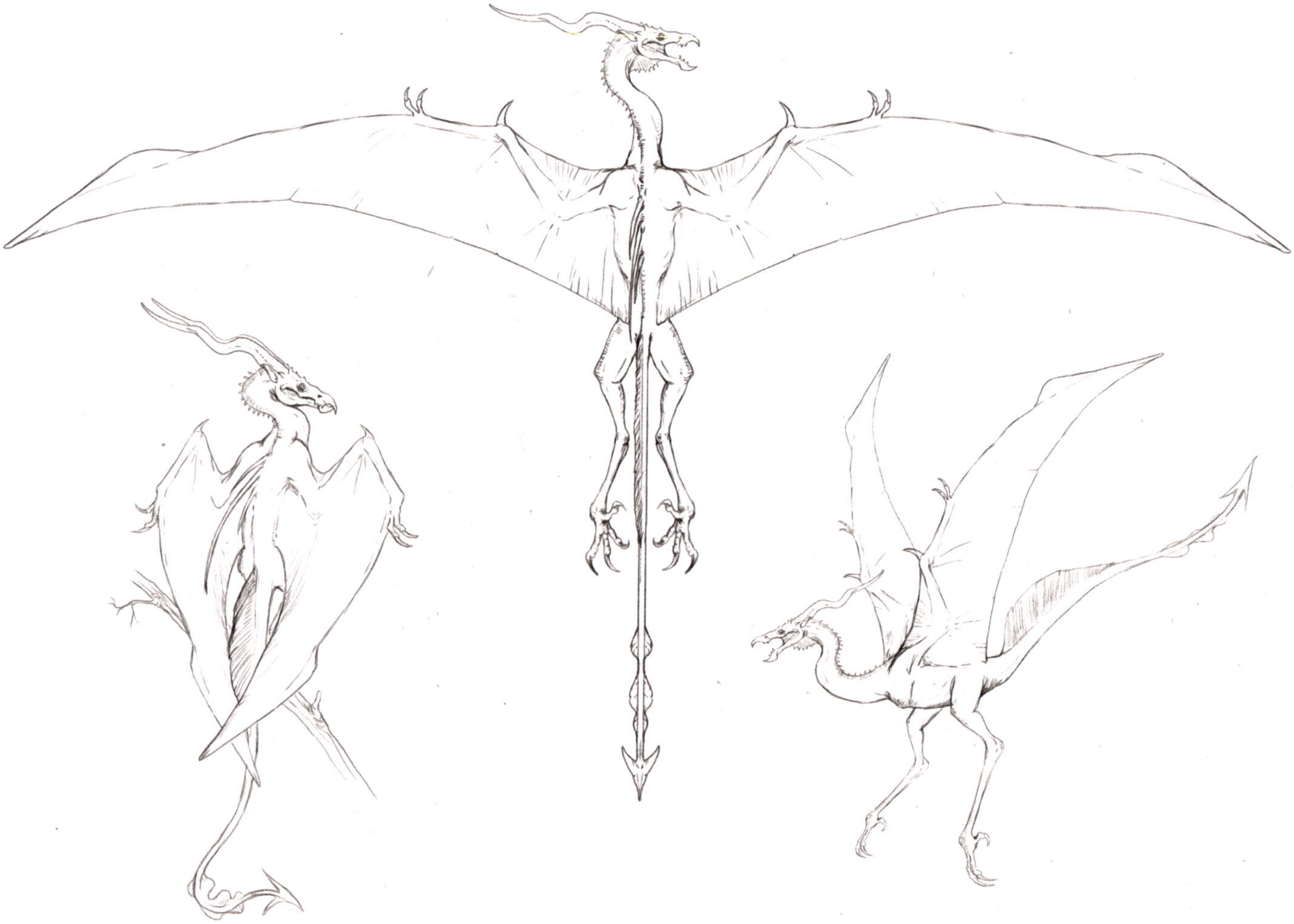

17 YELLOW PALETTE

When exploring colour, I want to keep the wyvern's palette naturalistic. I want to avoid anything too bright, remembering that this is an apex predator – less showy is best. My first attempt is very lizard-like, with a dark main colour accented with yellow-green crests. It's a good start but I feel it needs a bit more flare.

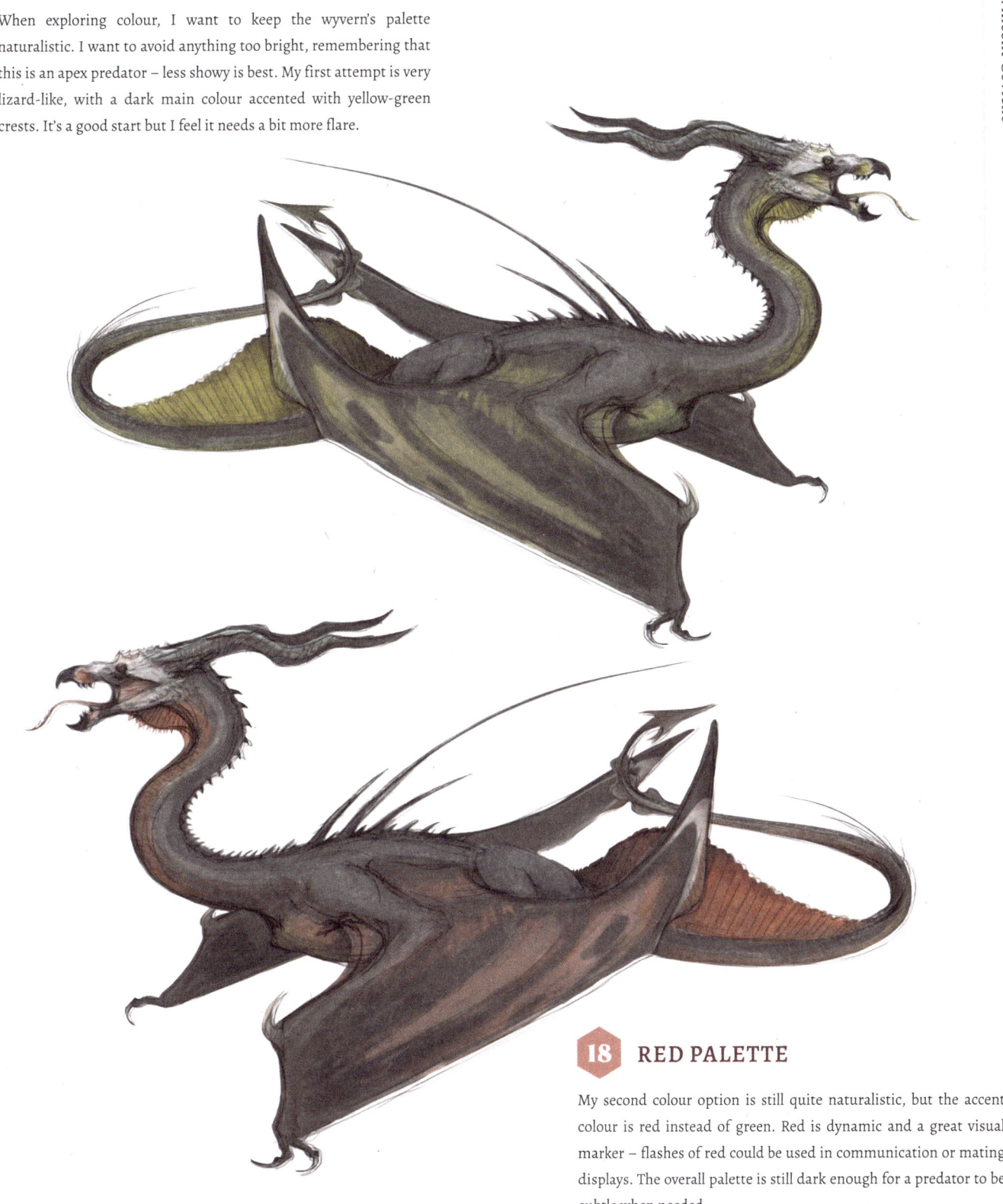

18 RED PALETTE

My second colour option is still quite naturalistic, but the accent colour is red instead of green. Red is dynamic and a great visual marker – flashes of red could be used in communication or mating displays. The overall palette is still dark enough for a predator to be subtle when needed.

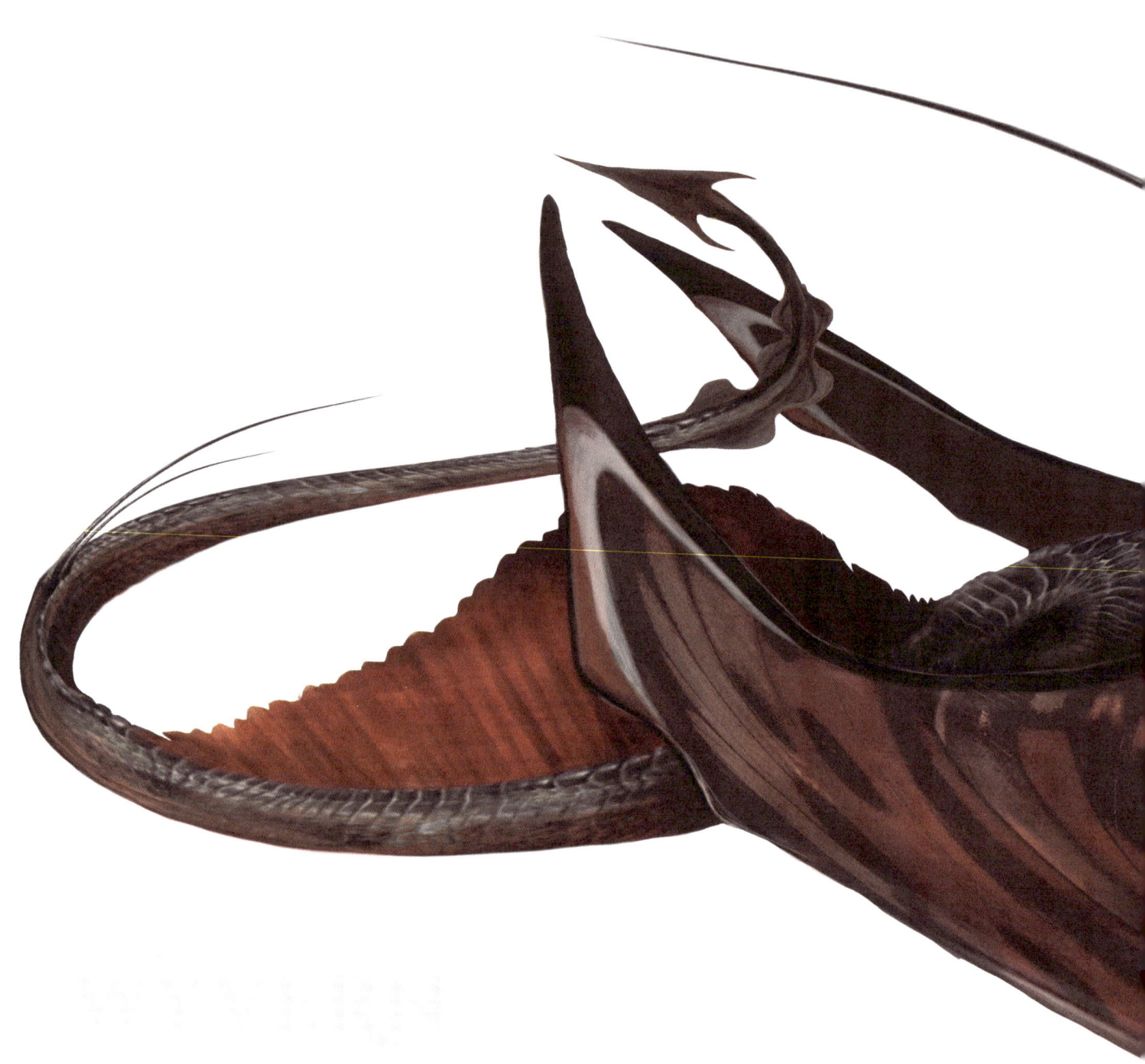

CONCLUSION

The final design manages to hold true to the wyvern's depiction in heraldry – a winged, bipedal beast combining elements of reptile and bird – while filtering it through the lens of speculative biology. By drawing inspirations from and parallels with real creatures, I am able to bring a fantasy creature into the real world and imagine how it's able to function within it.

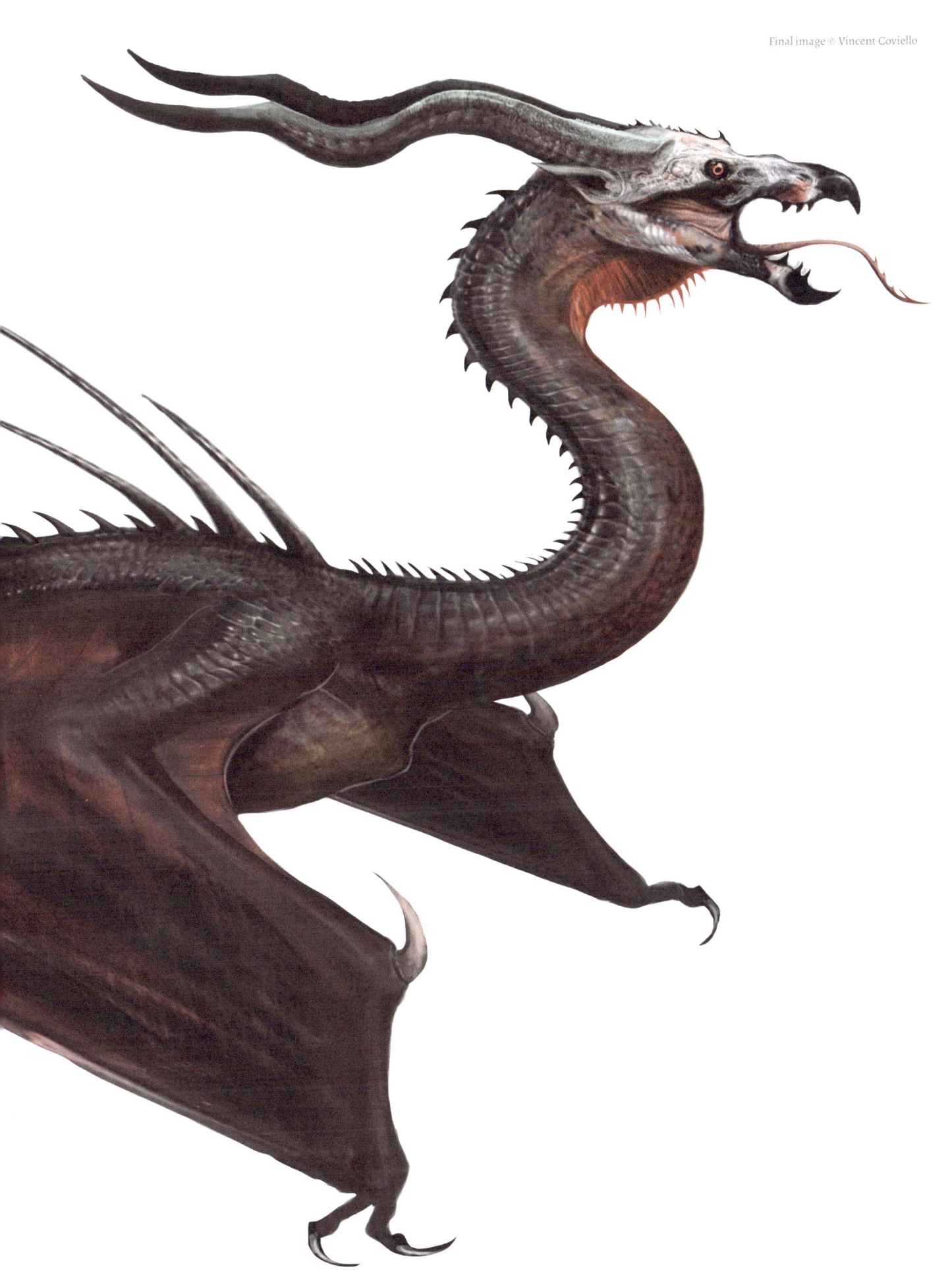

THE GALLERY

On these pages you will find an inspiring variety of dragons from the
portfolios and sketchbooks of four talented concept artists and illustrators,
along with insights into their passion for creature design.

◆

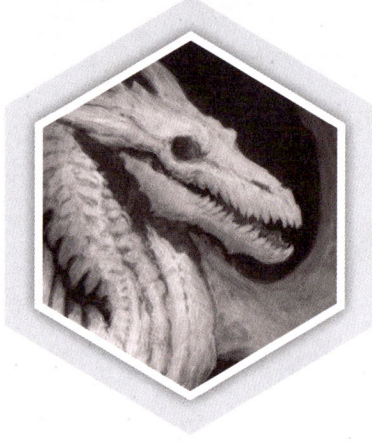

JOHN TEDRICK

Dragons have been a favourite subject of mine since I was very little, watching movies like *The Hobbit* (1977) and *Dragonheart*, and my love for them as a concept has only gotten stronger over time. Now they're part of my profession, and it's incredible getting to make dragons as a living! The following is a selection of dragons I've made in the past few years, for Smaugust (an online event where you draw a dragon a day throughout August) and for fun.

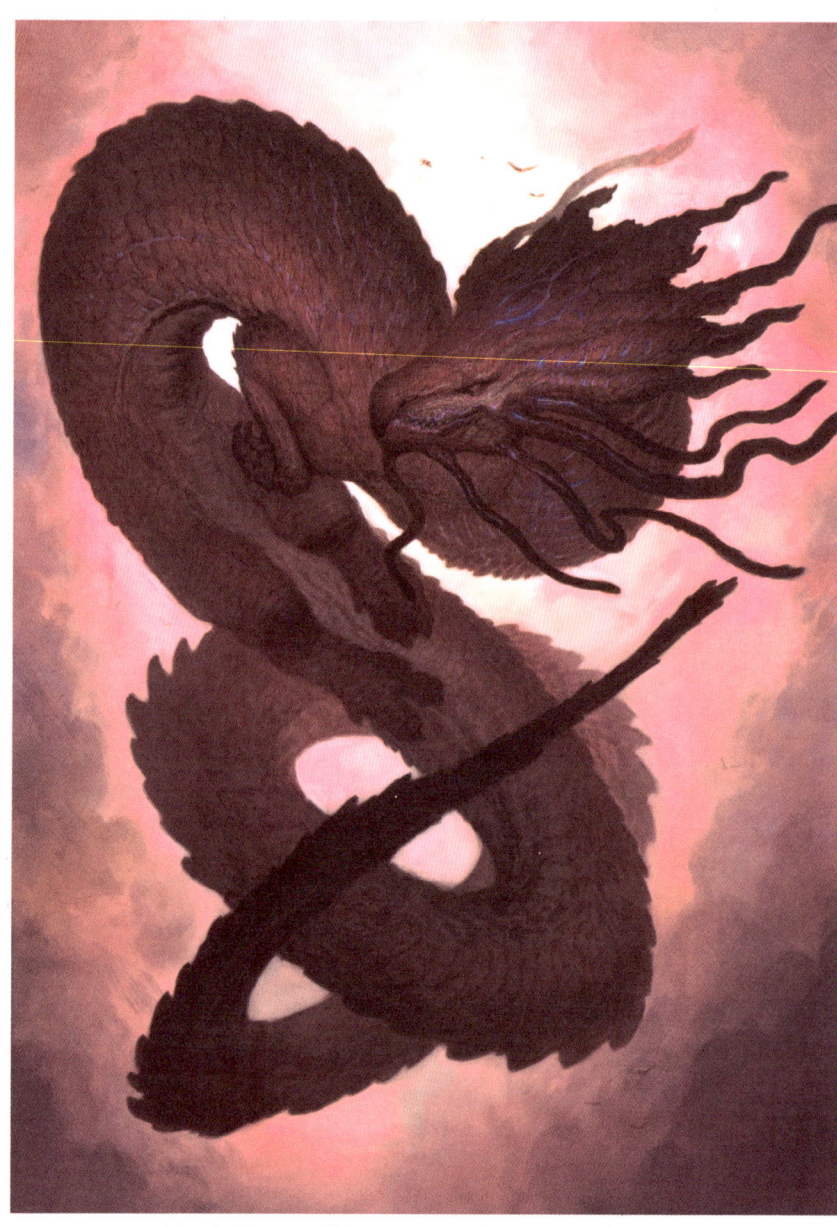

Rahastra, the Sunset Wind
A personal piece that had a brief stint in my portfolio. It's a serpentine design I'm still happy with, and I'll most likely do another painting of him in the future.

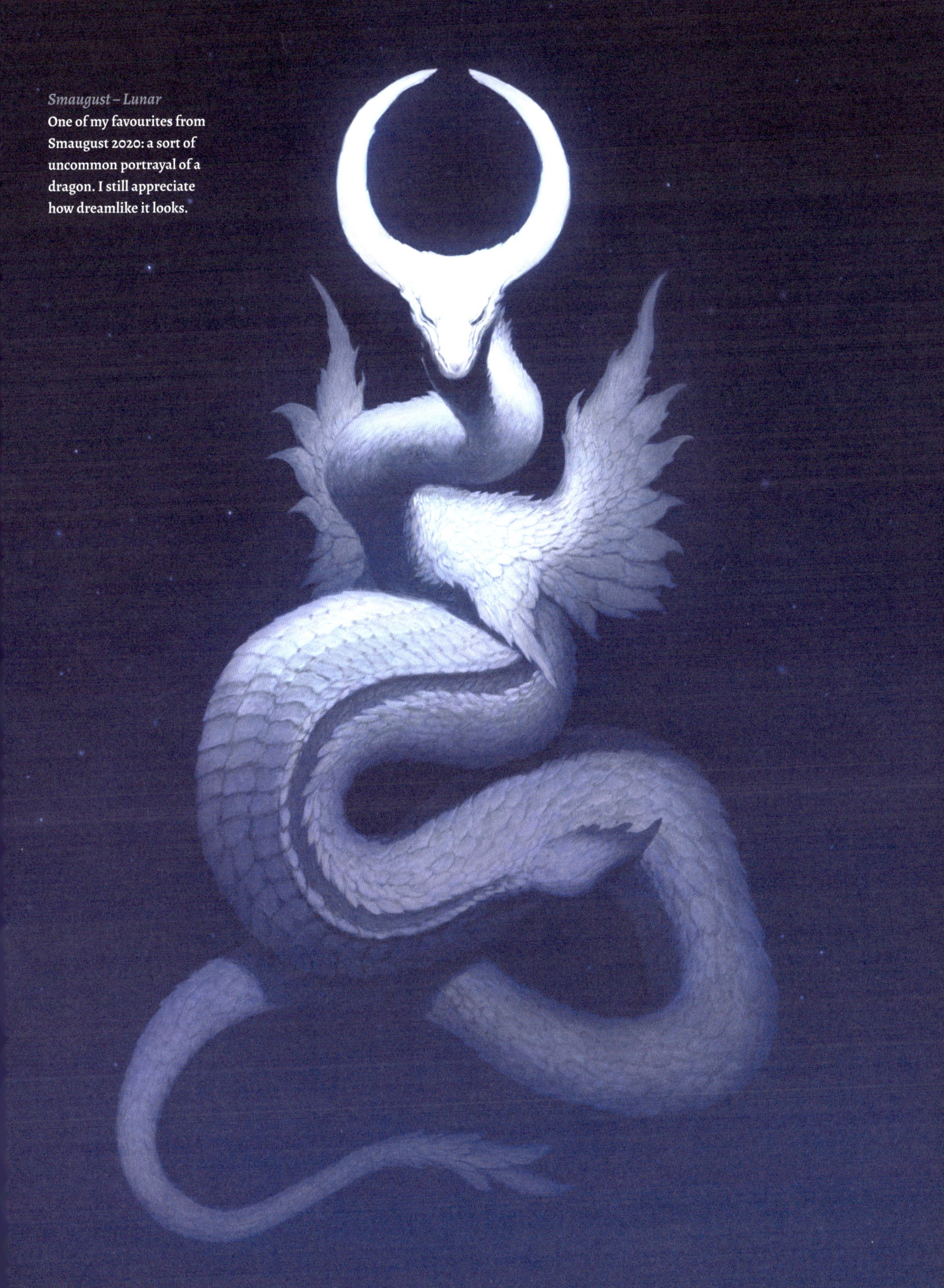

Smaugust – Lunar

One of my favourites from Smaugust 2020: a sort of uncommon portrayal of a dragon. I still appreciate how dreamlike it looks.

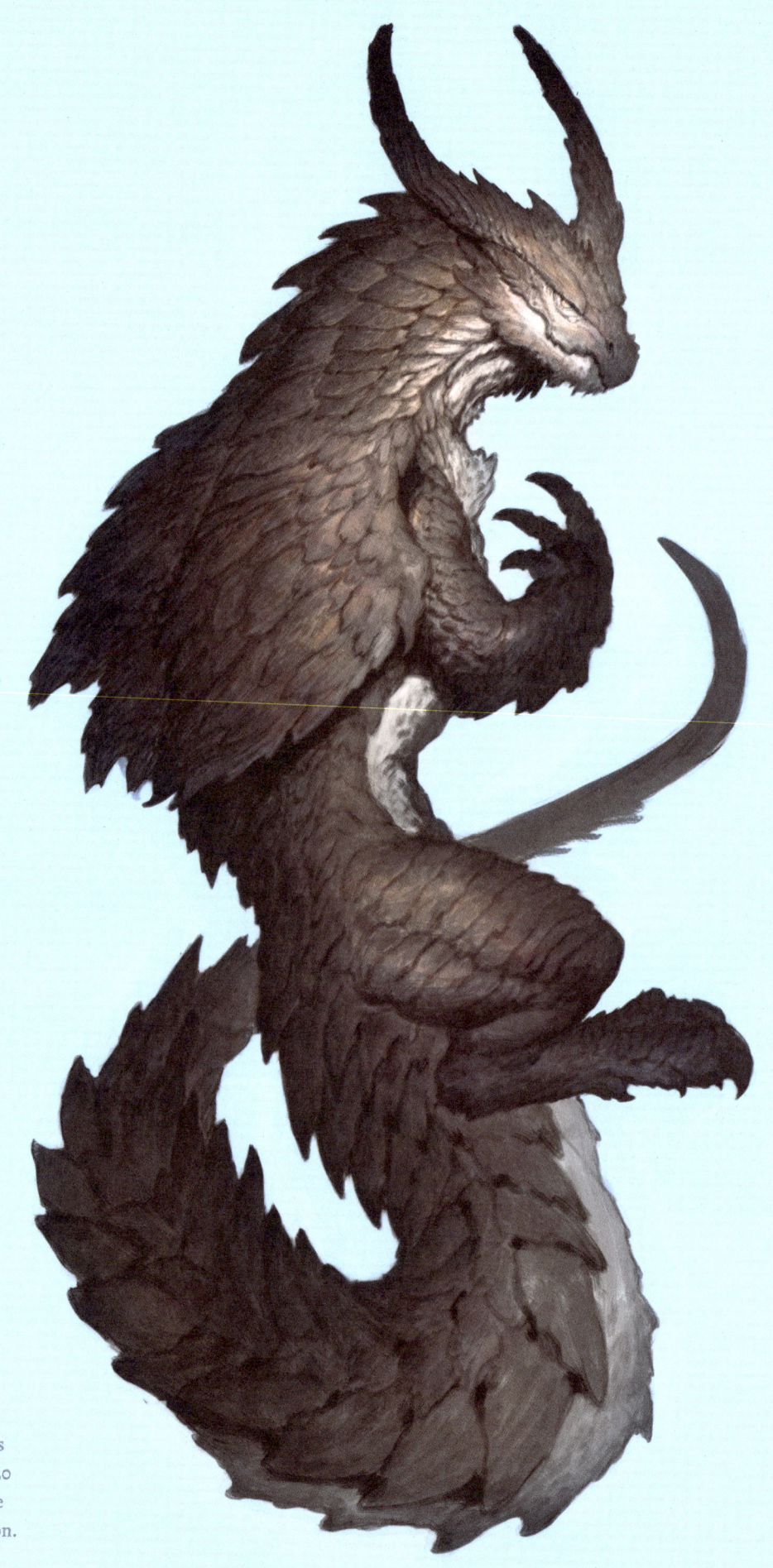

Smaugust – Ancient
One of the few dragons
I did for Smaugust 2020
that's fairly close to the
'classic' look of a dragon.

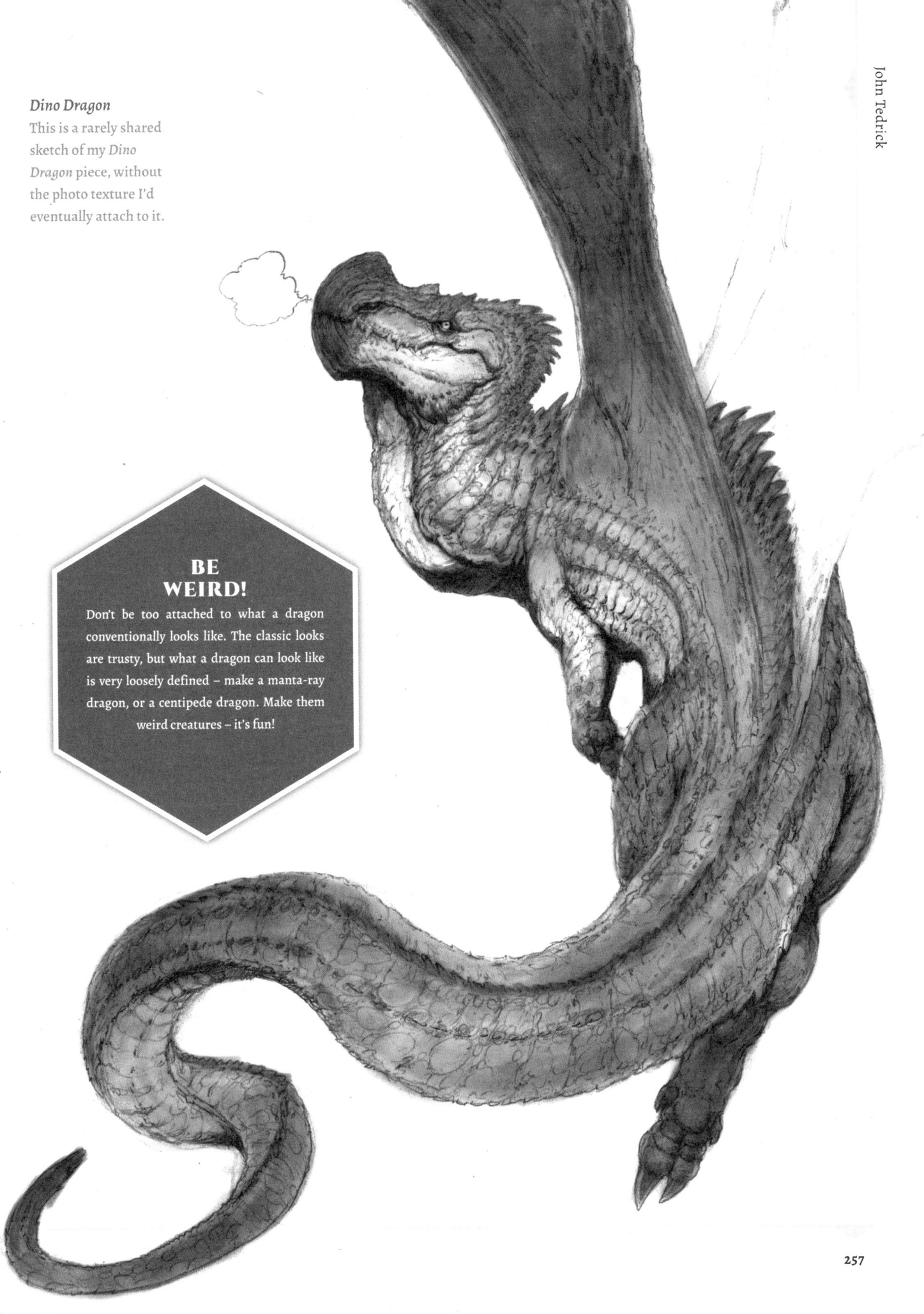

Dino Dragon
This is a rarely shared sketch of my *Dino Dragon* piece, without the photo texture I'd eventually attach to it.

BE WEIRD!

Don't be too attached to what a dragon conventionally looks like. The classic looks are trusty, but what a dragon can look like is very loosely defined – make a manta-ray dragon, or a centipede dragon. Make them weird creatures – it's fun!

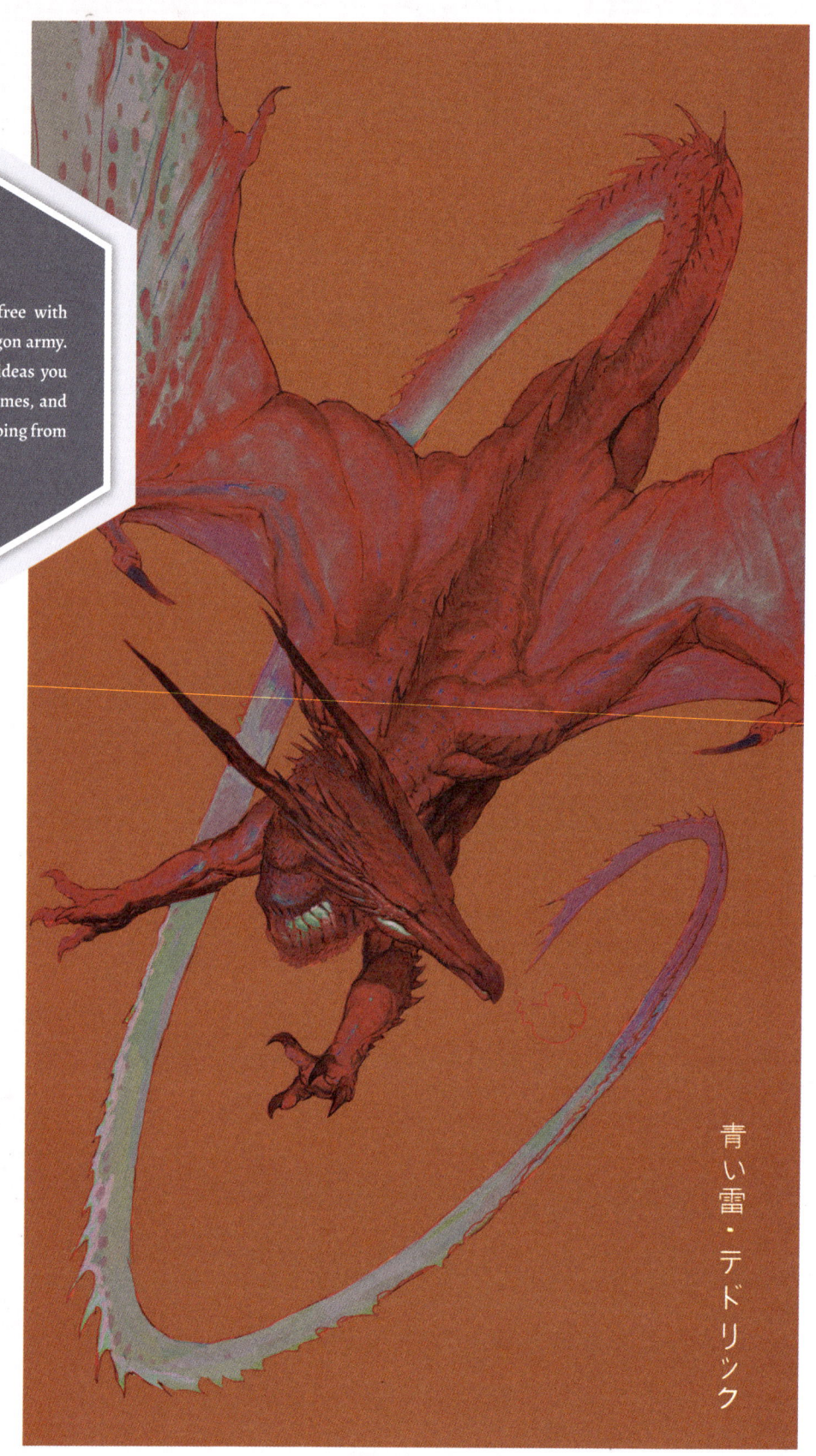

MAKE AN ARMY

Make a lot of dragons, and be free with your ideas as you fill out your dragon army. This can help you get to the big ideas you might feel are eluding you sometimes, and is generally a good practice for keeping from blocks or hang-ups.

Blue Lightning (Red Version)
An old sketchbook piece with a confusing title (the original was, indeed, blue). I was trying more graphical or inked looks at the time.

青い雷・テドリック

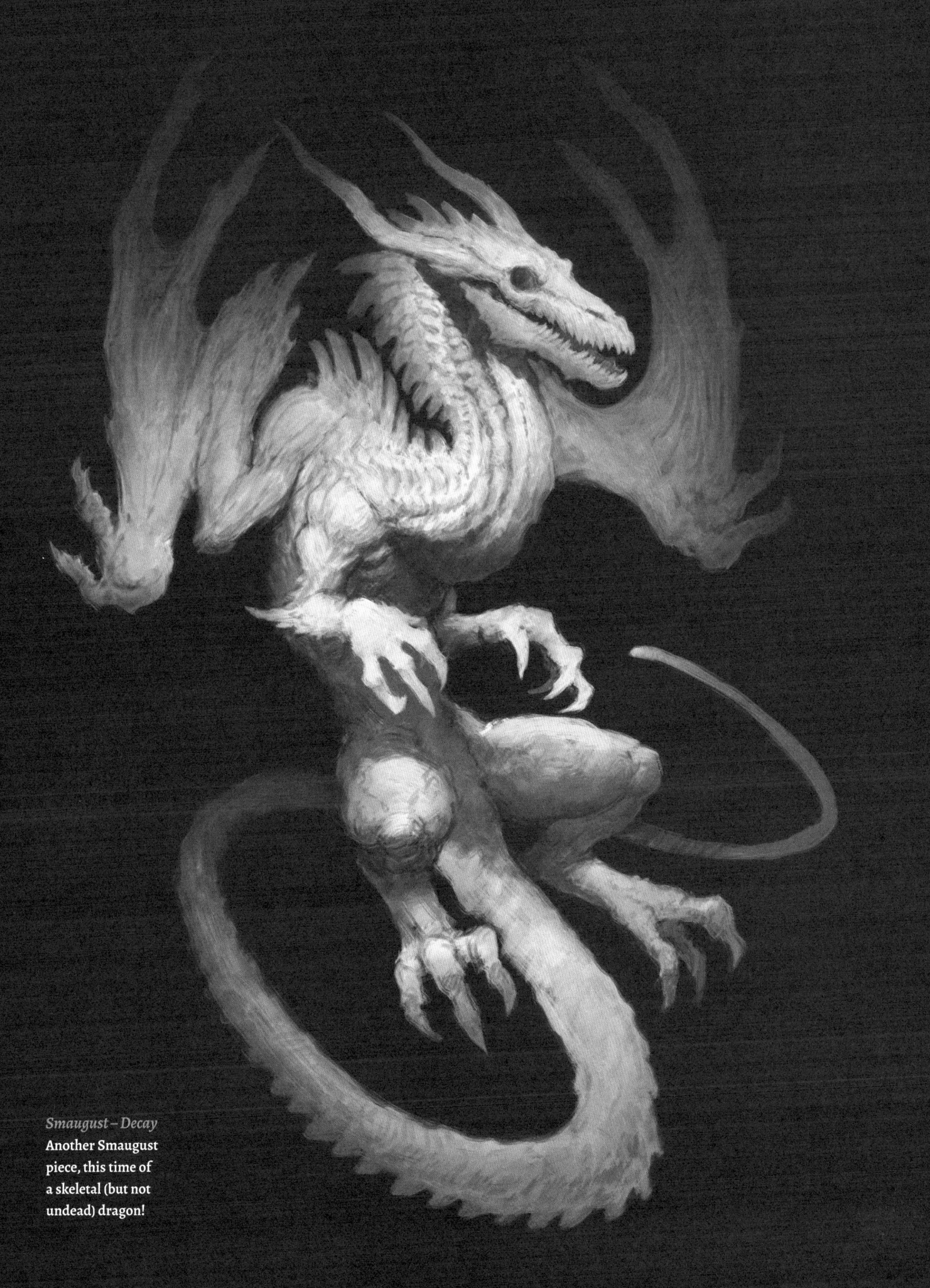

Smaugust – Decay
Another Smaugust piece, this time of a skeletal (but not undead) dragon!

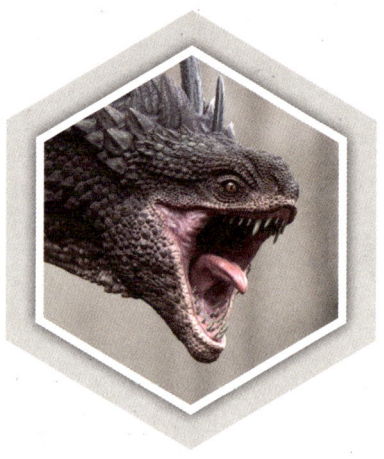

ROBIN BOONACKER

Dragons have captivated me since childhood. I remember watching countless movies and TV shows featuring these mythical creatures, with *How to Train Your Dragon* being a particular favourite. Beyond dragons, I'm deeply inspired by nature and animals. I combine this fascination with design principles to create unique and believable creatures that fit within the context of their respective worlds and environments. I enjoy spending time outdoors and use photography to gather reference material for my designs. Understanding how nature works is essential to my creative process.

I always try to push myself to create authentic and unique designs. In order to achieve that goal I have spent a lot of time studying human and animal anatomy, shapes, line work, and textures in order to achieve a certain balance, harmony, and movement in my work. In addition, I combine both 2D and 3D in my work to create balanced concepts, and to present my final work in the best possible way. But, most importantly, I try to have fun in designing my creatures – especially dragons!

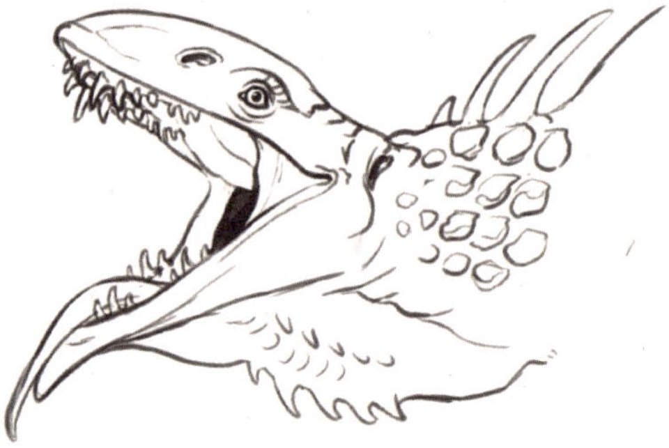

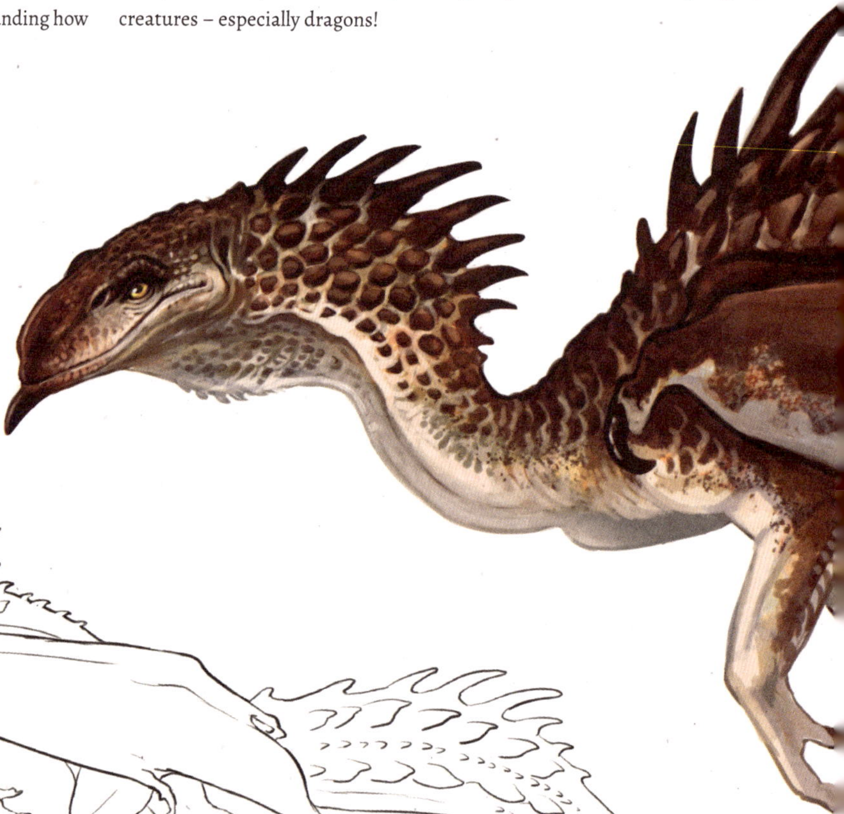

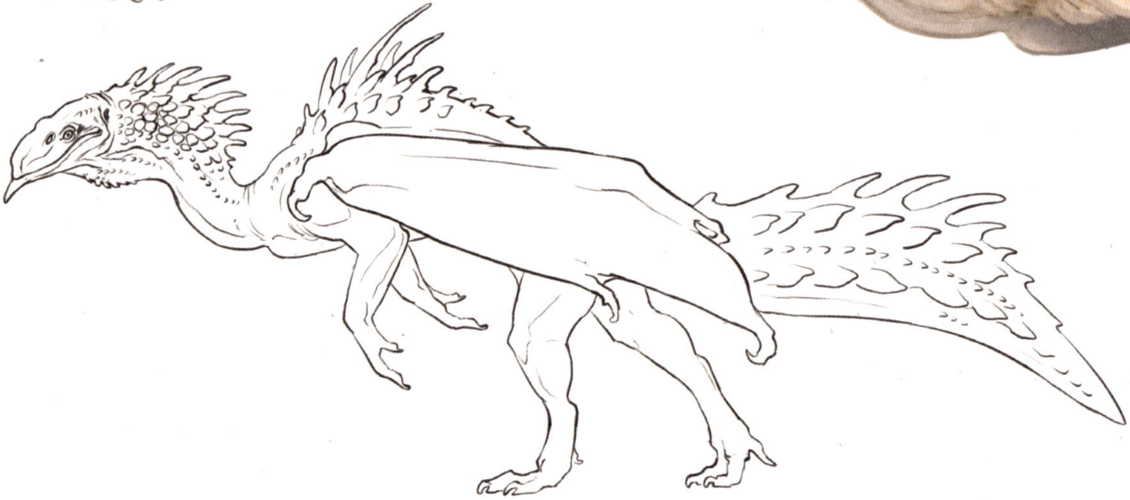

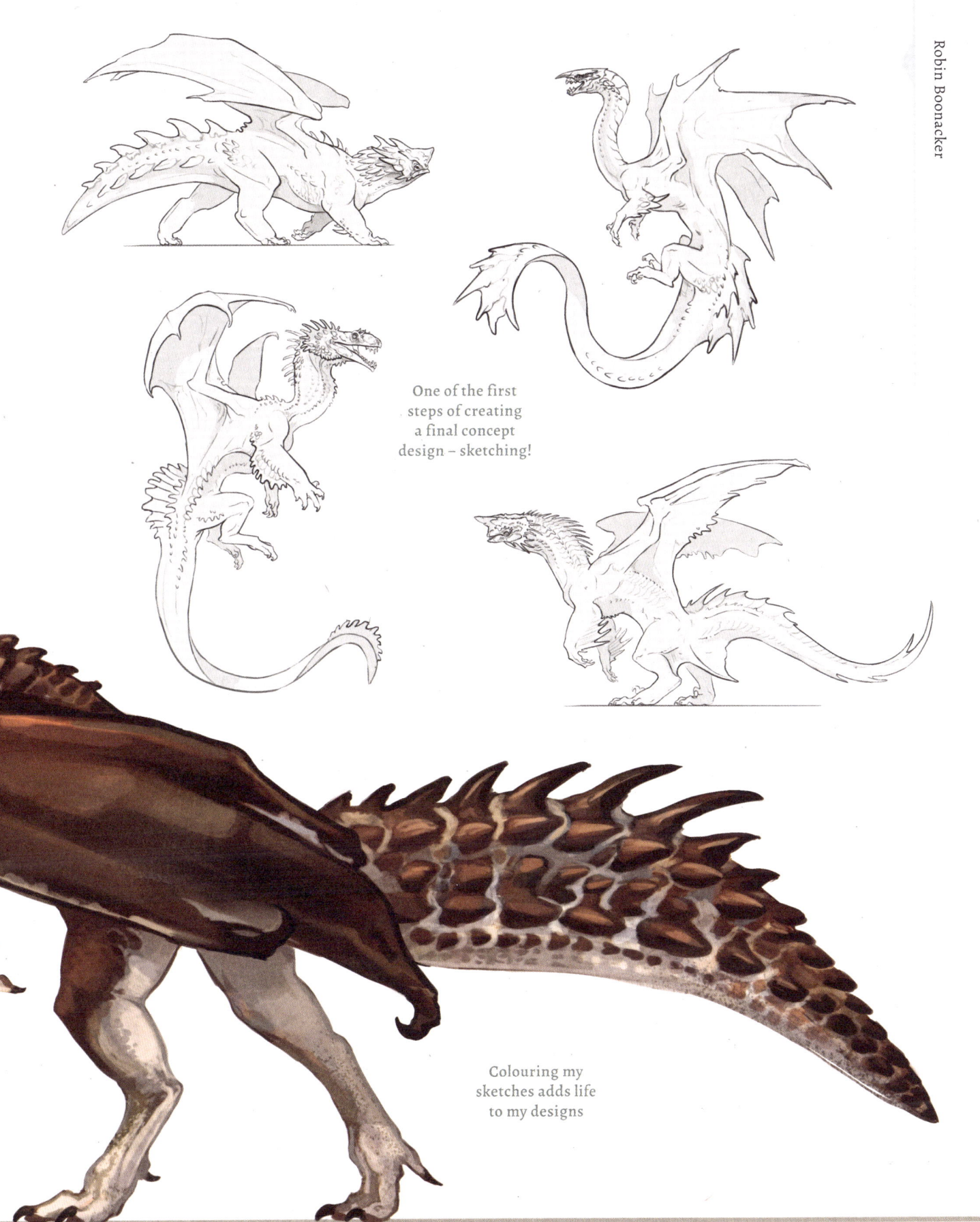

One of the first
steps of creating
a final concept
design – sketching!

Colouring my
sketches adds life
to my designs

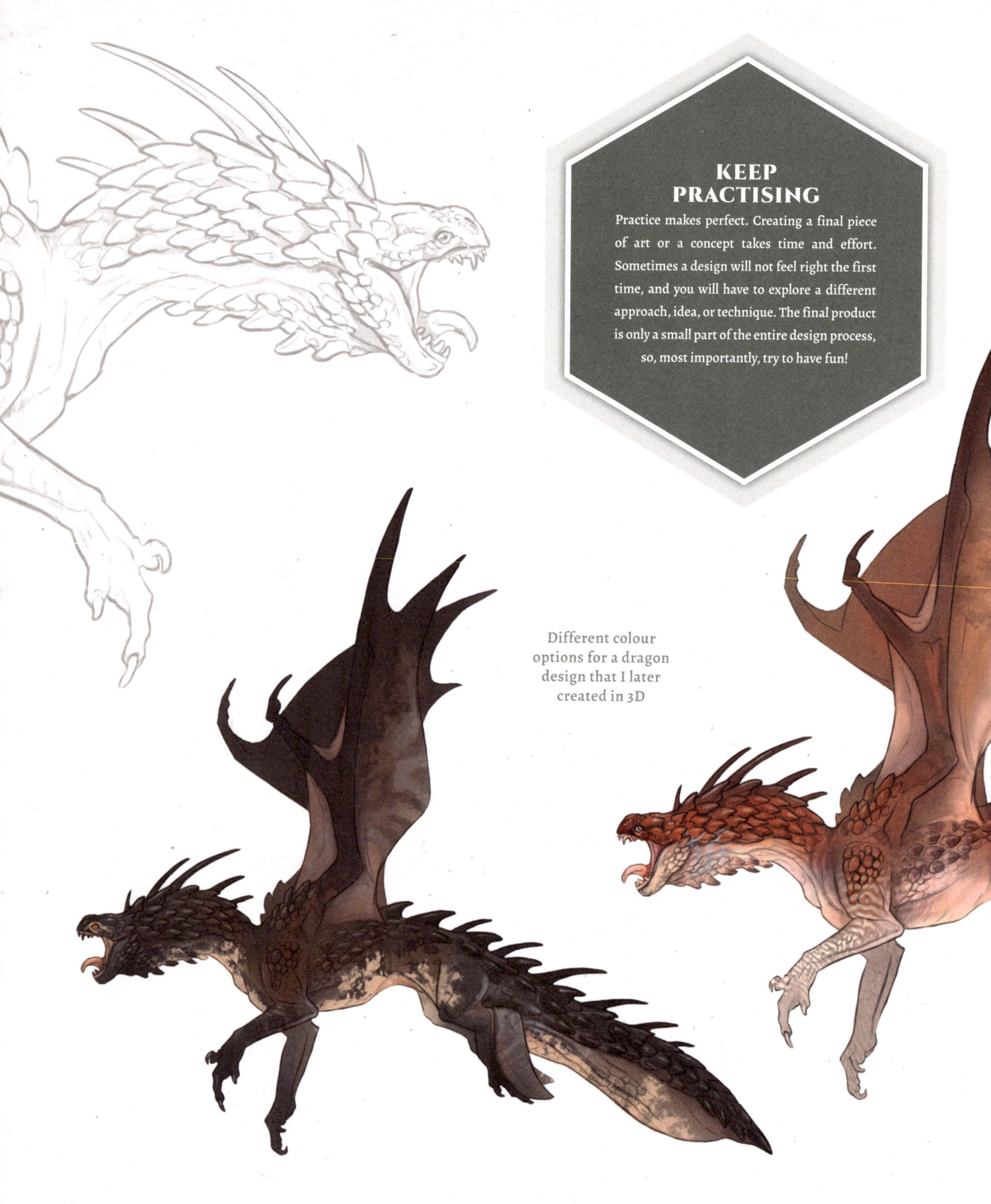

Different colour options for a dragon design that I later created in 3D

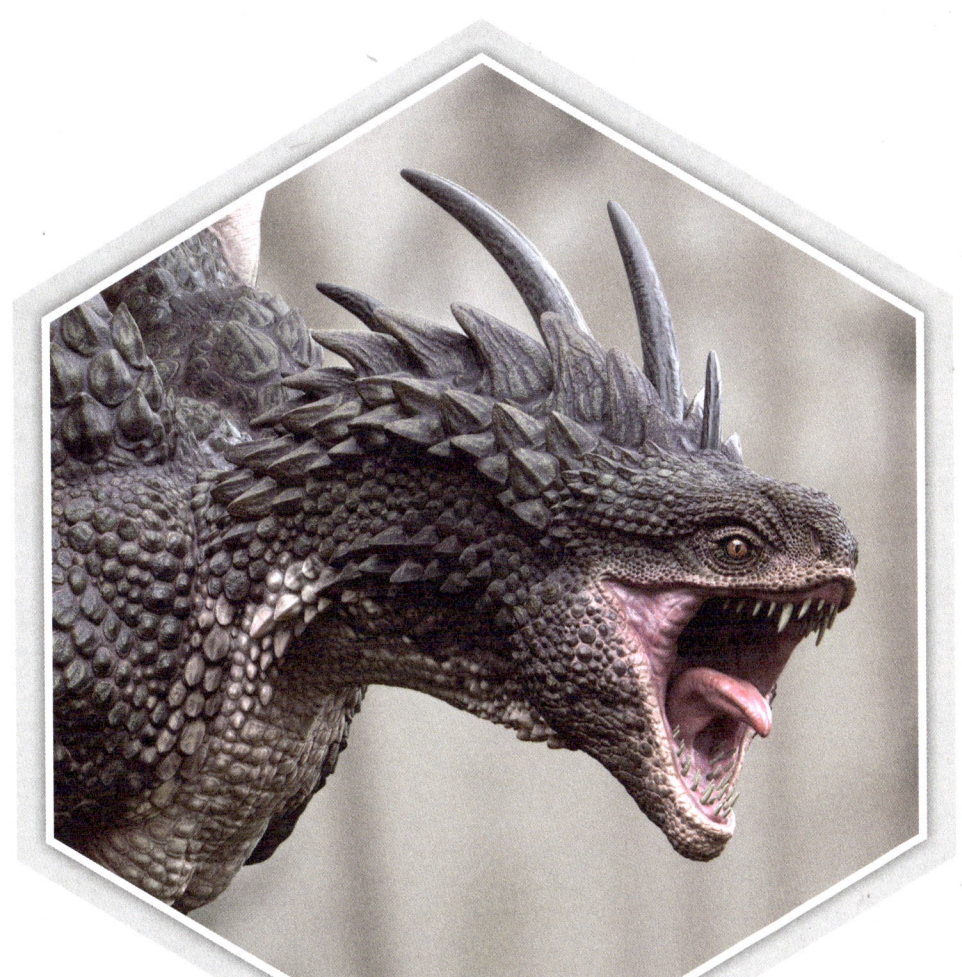

The final 3D version
of the spotted
brown dragon

CONTINUE LEARNING

Want to take your drawing skills to the next level? Consider doing a mentorship course with experienced professionals. While online tutorials and books can provide valuable guidance, personalized feedback from a mentor can be invaluable. They can offer personalized advice, identify areas for improvement, and help you develop your unique artistic style. Doing mentorships really helped me improve my art skills.

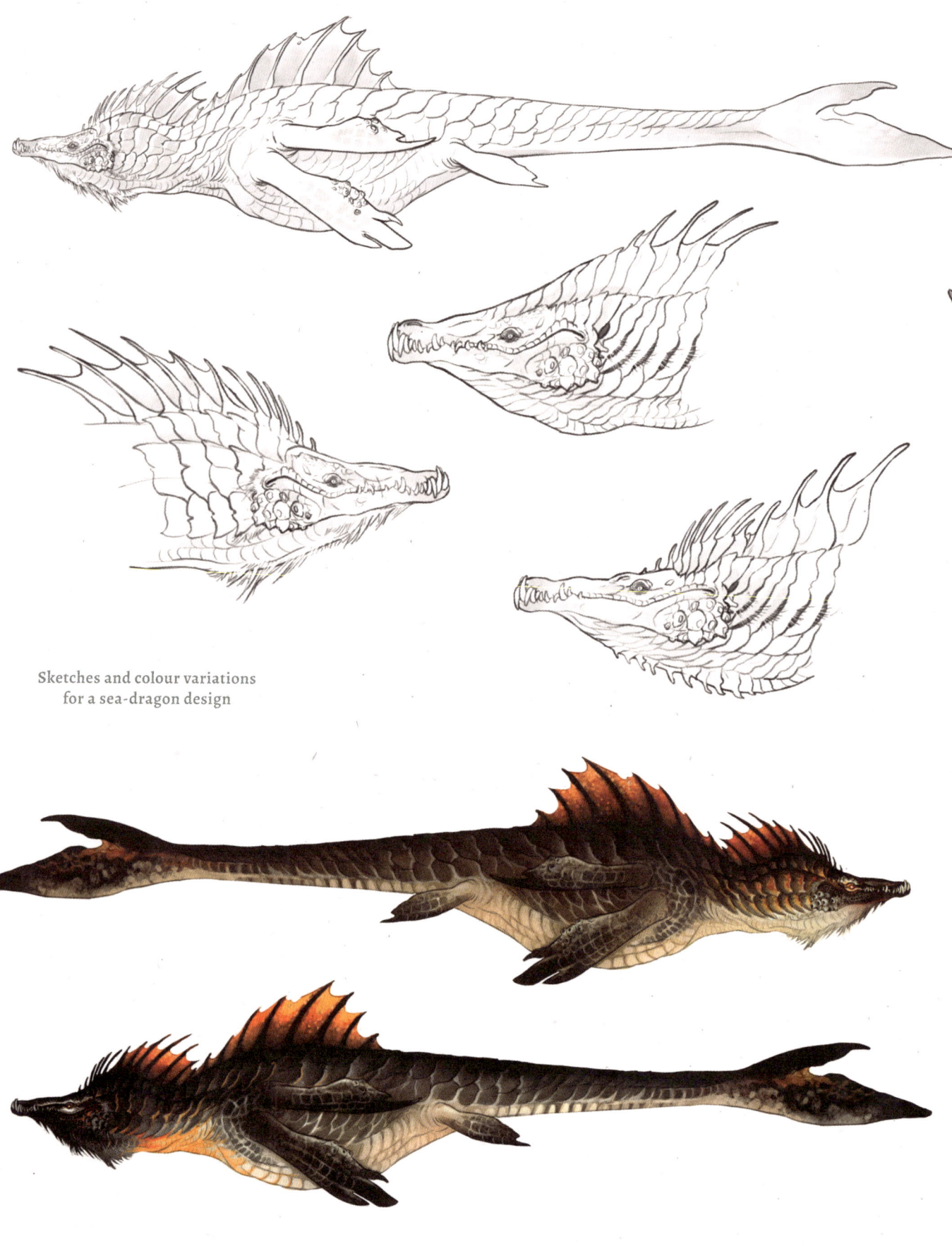

Sketches and colour variations
for a sea-dragon design

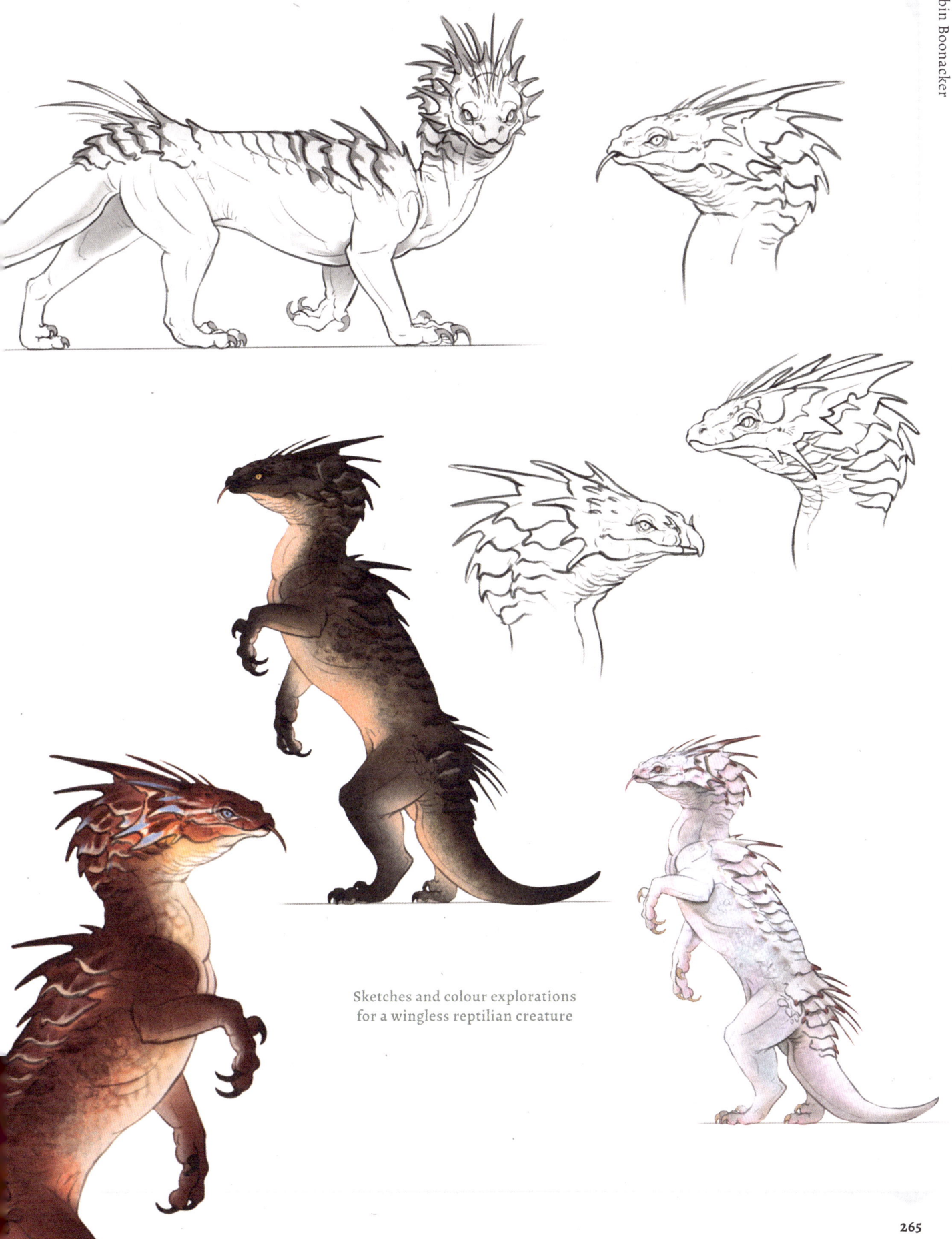

Sketches and colour explorations
for a wingless reptilian creature

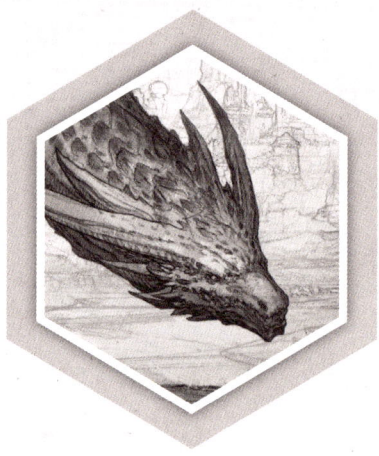

DIBUJANTE NOCTURNO
(FRAN GARCÉS)

It is wonderful for me to be able to participate in a book about dragons. Drawing these creatures has been very important to me in my life – I did it when I was a child and I still do it now. As you go through my sketchbooks, you can see what my artistic progress has been through my dragons. They are a safe haven to return to whenever I feel insecure.

In the past couple of years I have seriously taken up drawing dragons again, really trying to understand their shapes and draw them better. This excites me a lot. If, as a child, I had seen the dragons I draw today, what would I have thought?

I have learned to see dragons in many animals. Now I see their shapes in the anatomy of my pets and I'm able to draw them from there, sketching with pen in my sketchbook in a very loose way, in dynamic and stylized poses. Years ago I was only able to draw dragons in profile, but now I look for more complex perspectives. I like them to look powerful and dark, but always elegant. I enjoy learning to draw, and now I also enjoy teaching my students how to create these beautiful creatures.

Strength

When sketching I try to find interesting and dynamic poses. I imagine my dragons as powerful creatures – the thickness of the neck, the texture, the shadows on the face. I'm always looking for visual strength.

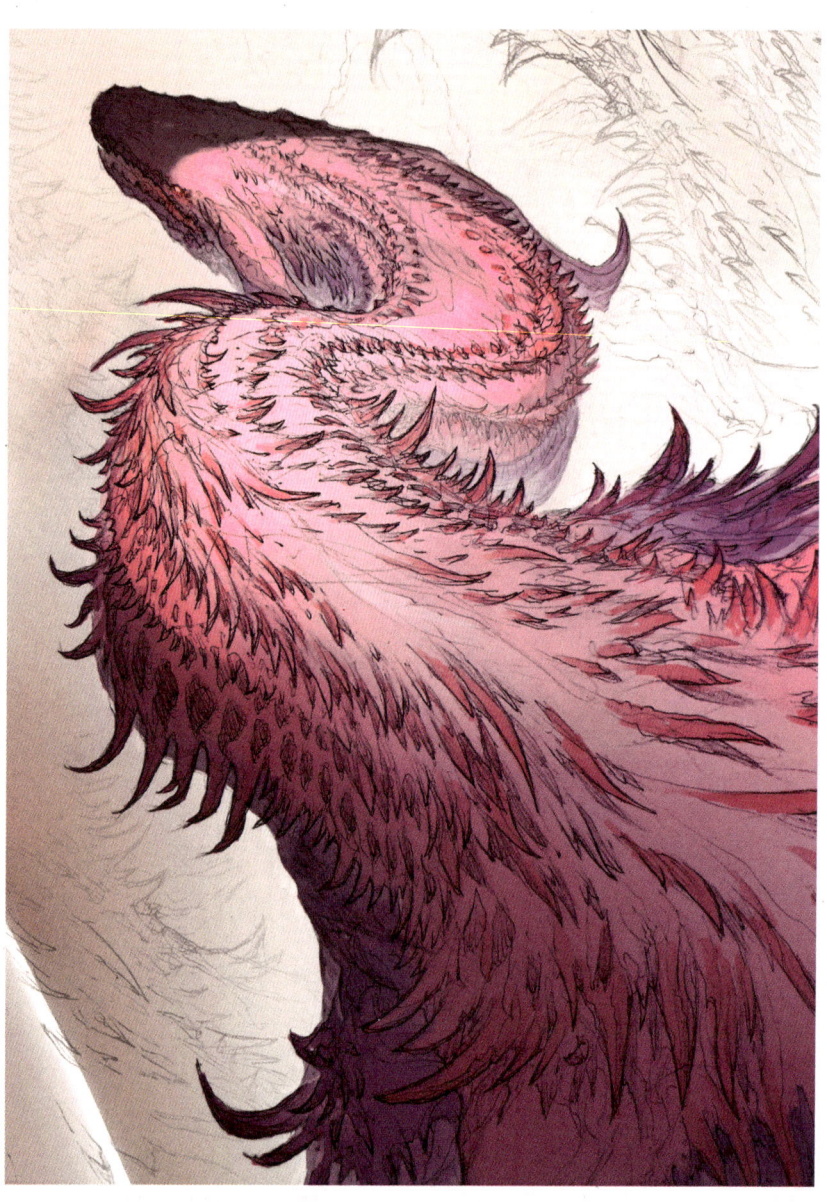

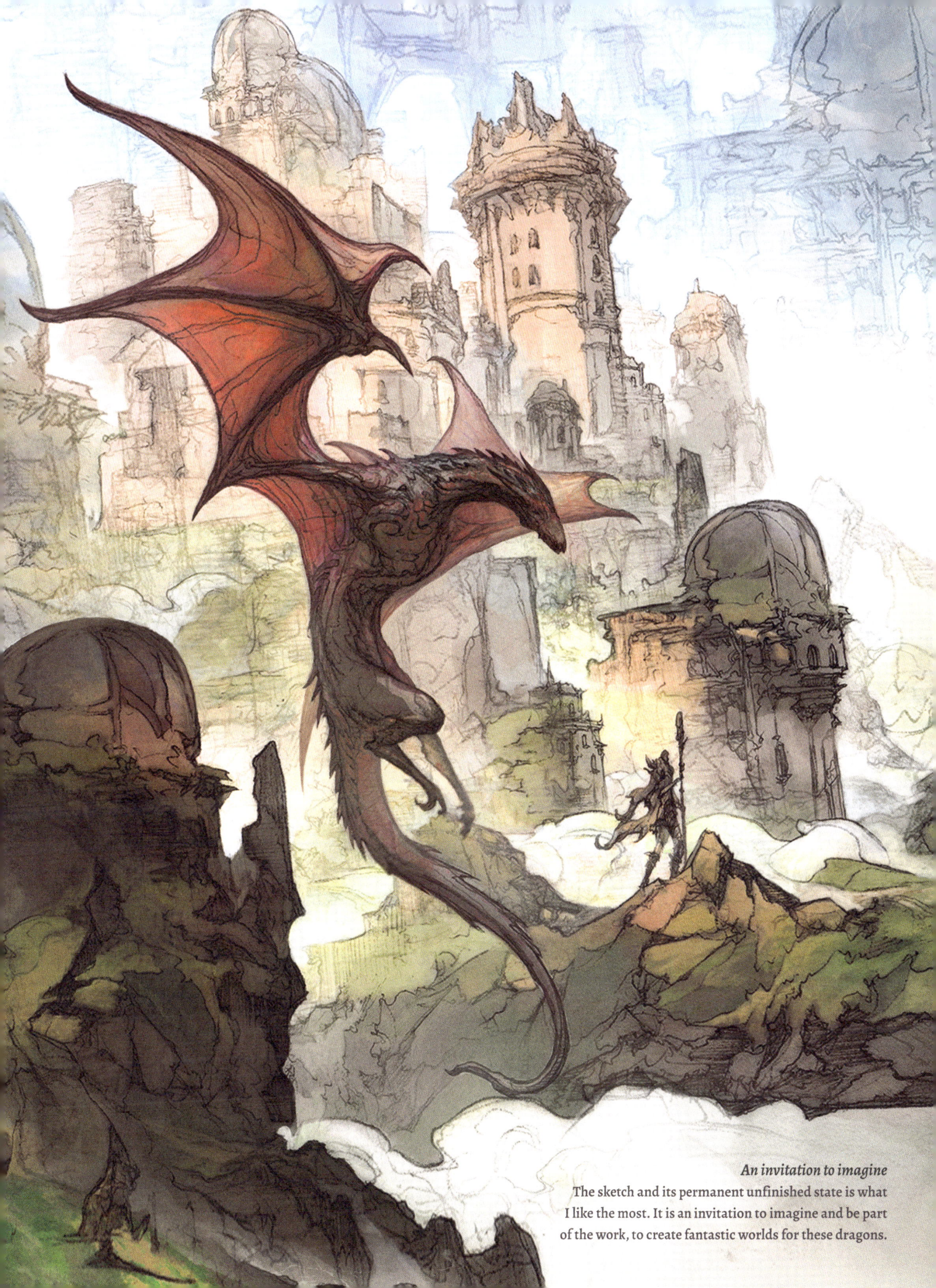

An invitation to imagine
The sketch and its permanent unfinished state is what
I like the most. It is an invitation to imagine and be part
of the work, to create fantastic worlds for these dragons.

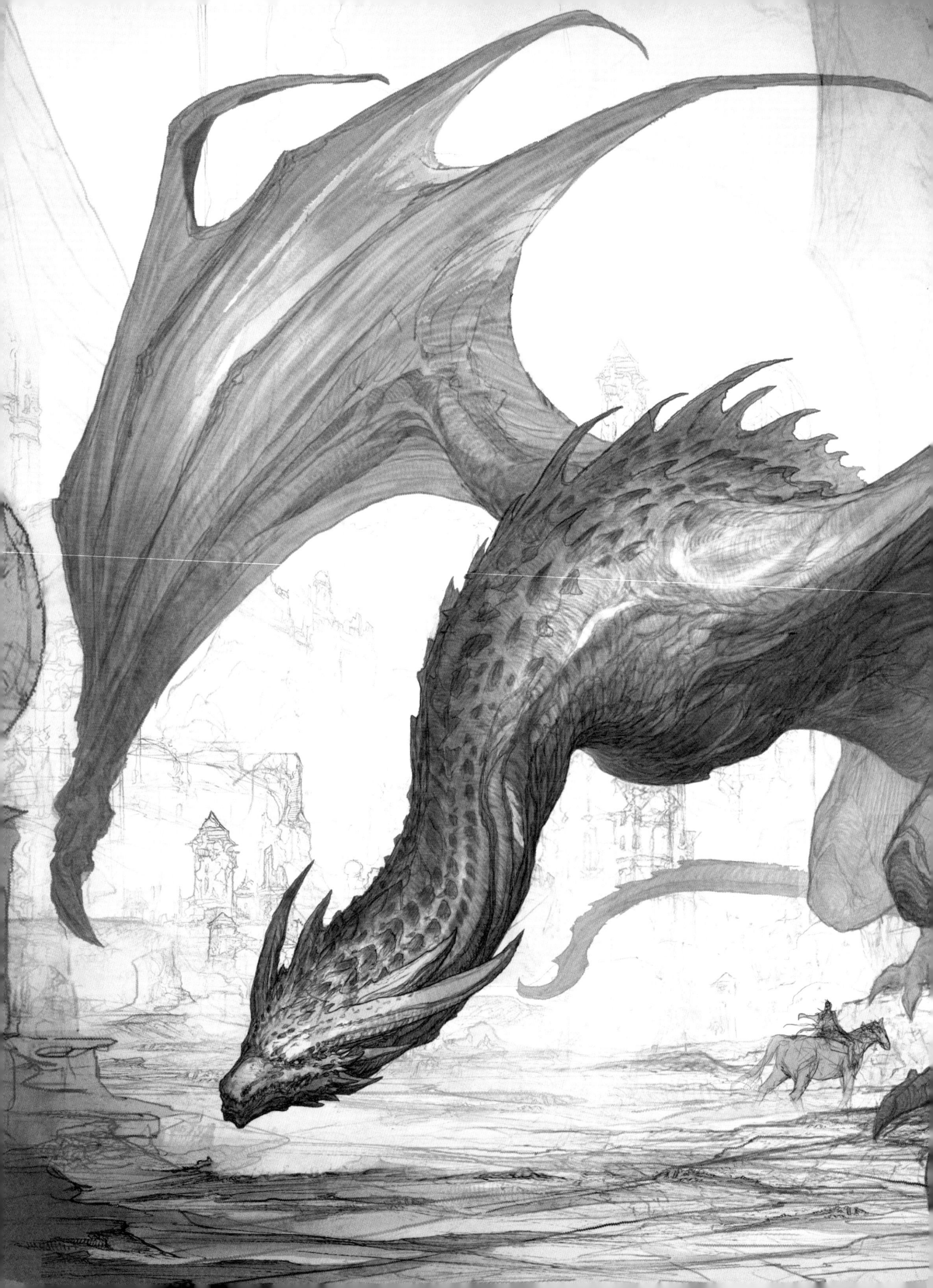

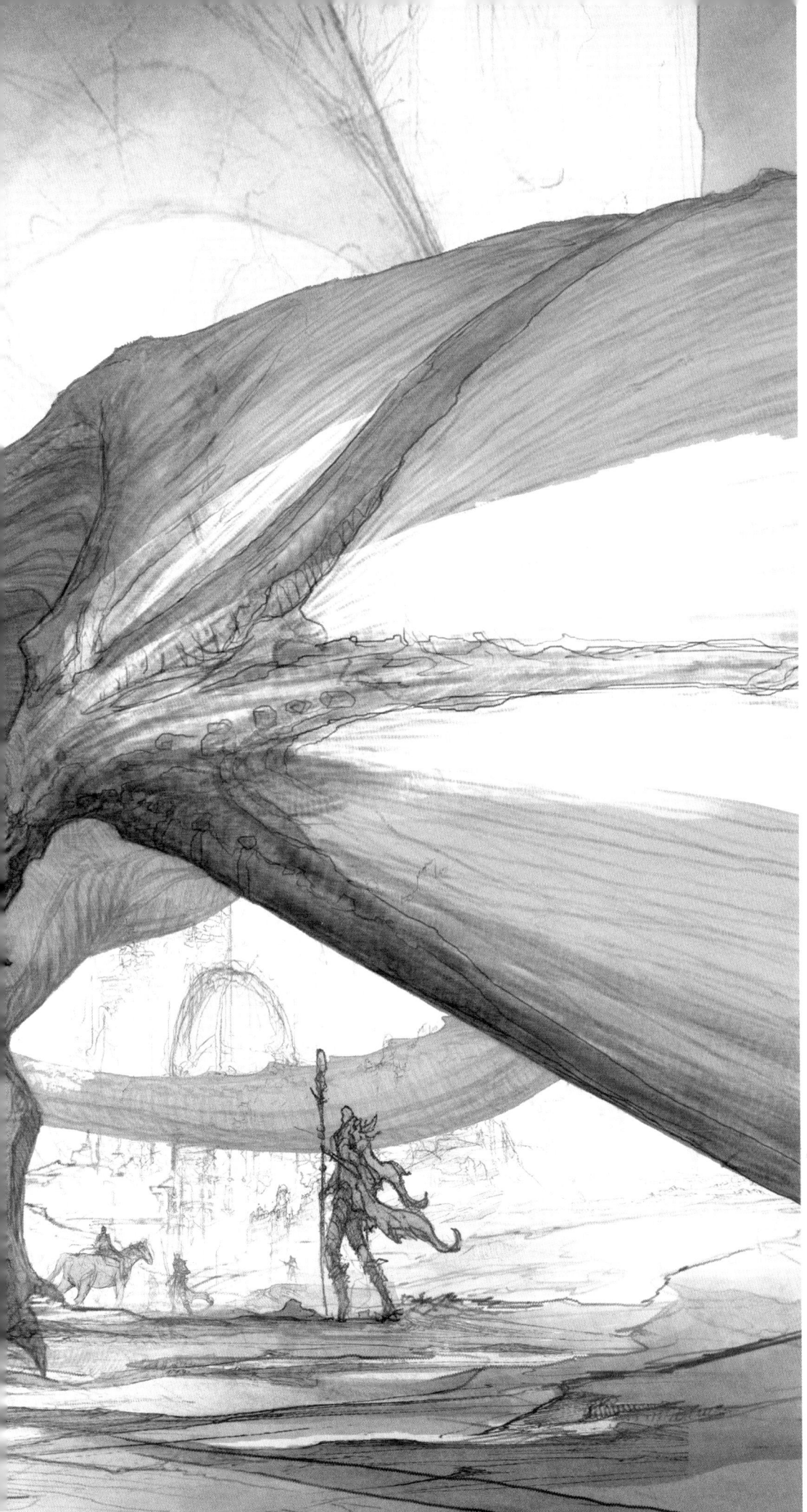

The scale

I always imagine my dragons on a huge scale. Placing them in a setting so the viewer can appreciate their size can make your designs exciting and awe-inspiring.

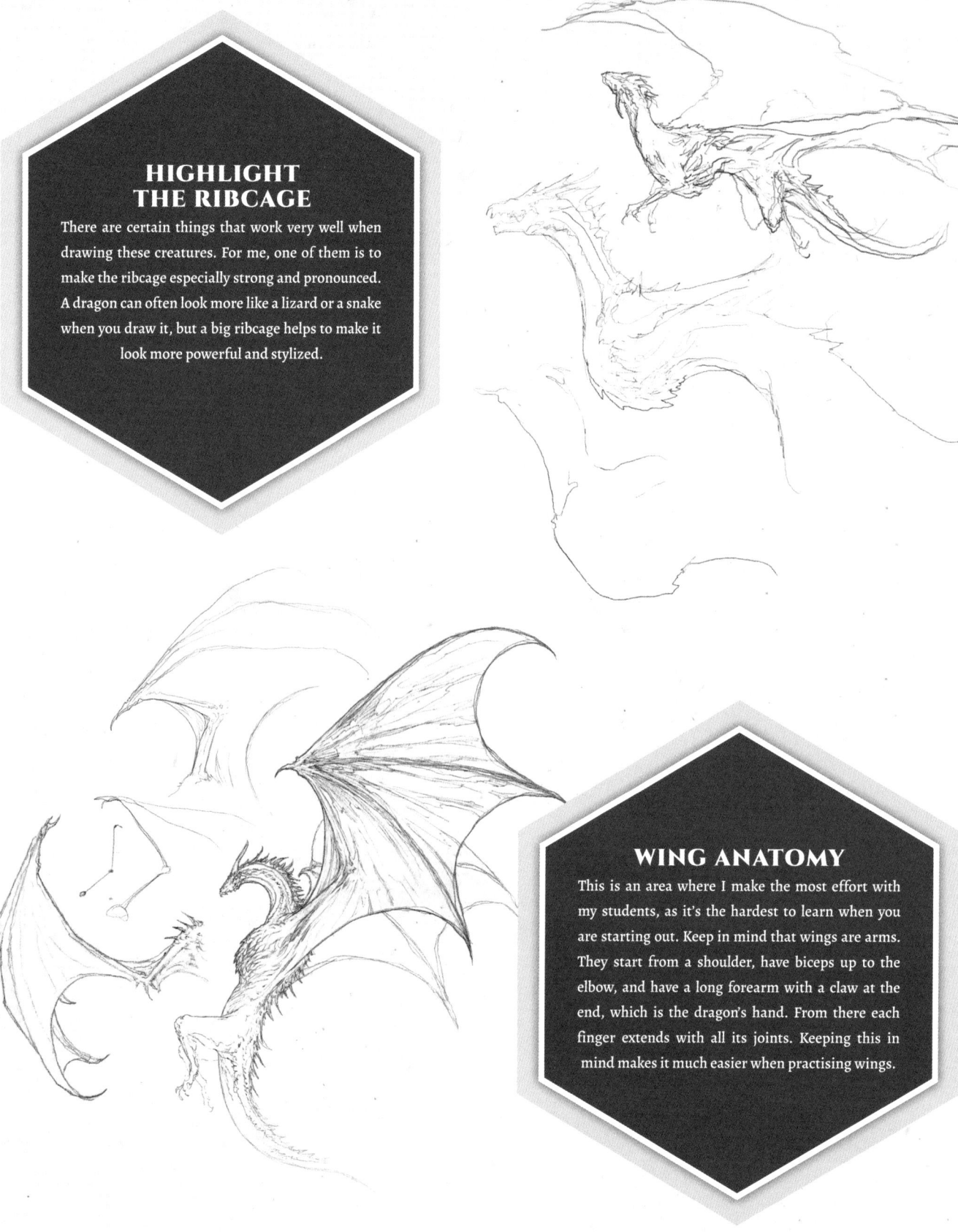

HIGHLIGHT THE RIBCAGE

There are certain things that work very well when drawing these creatures. For me, one of them is to make the ribcage especially strong and pronounced. A dragon can often look more like a lizard or a snake when you draw it, but a big ribcage helps to make it look more powerful and stylized.

WING ANATOMY

This is an area where I make the most effort with my students, as it's the hardest to learn when you are starting out. Keep in mind that wings are arms. They start from a shoulder, have biceps up to the elbow, and have a long forearm with a claw at the end, which is the dragon's hand. From there each finger extends with all its joints. Keeping this in mind makes it much easier when practising wings.

Elegance
Here the figure is stylized and the lines are varied –
soft in certain areas and hard in others to reinforce
certain parts. The texture of the pen is intact. It's an
unfinished process and that's what I like most.

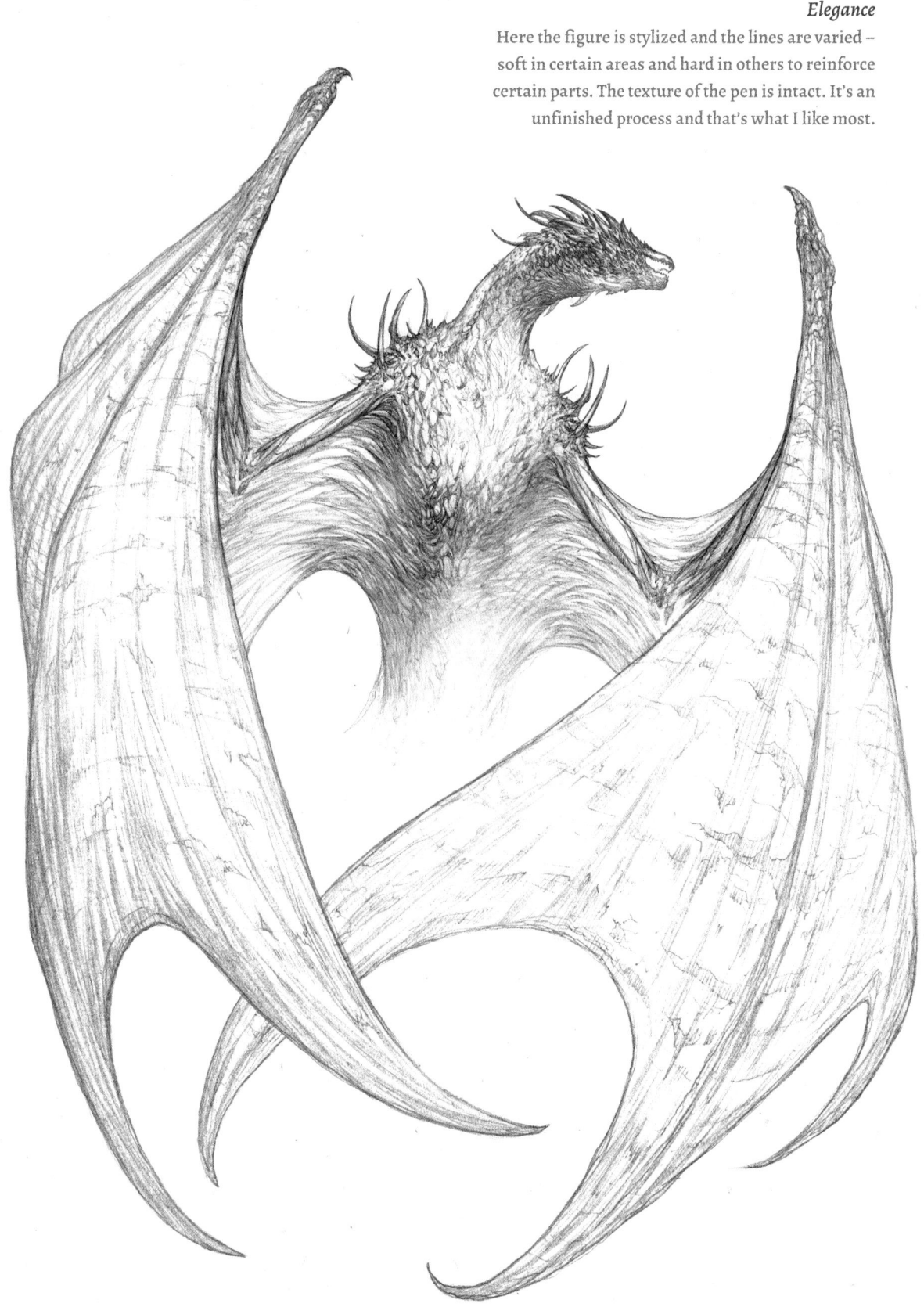

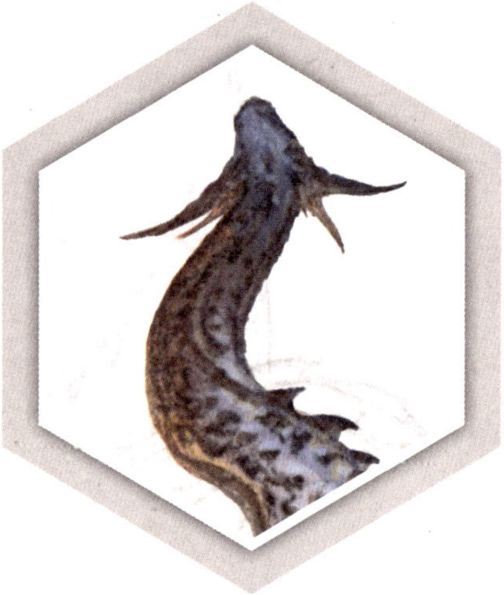

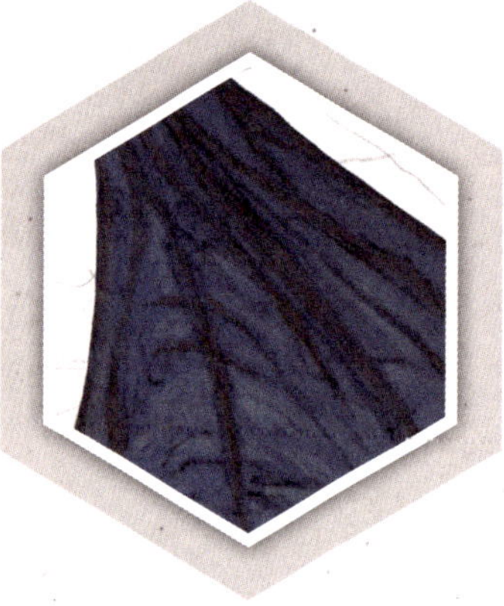

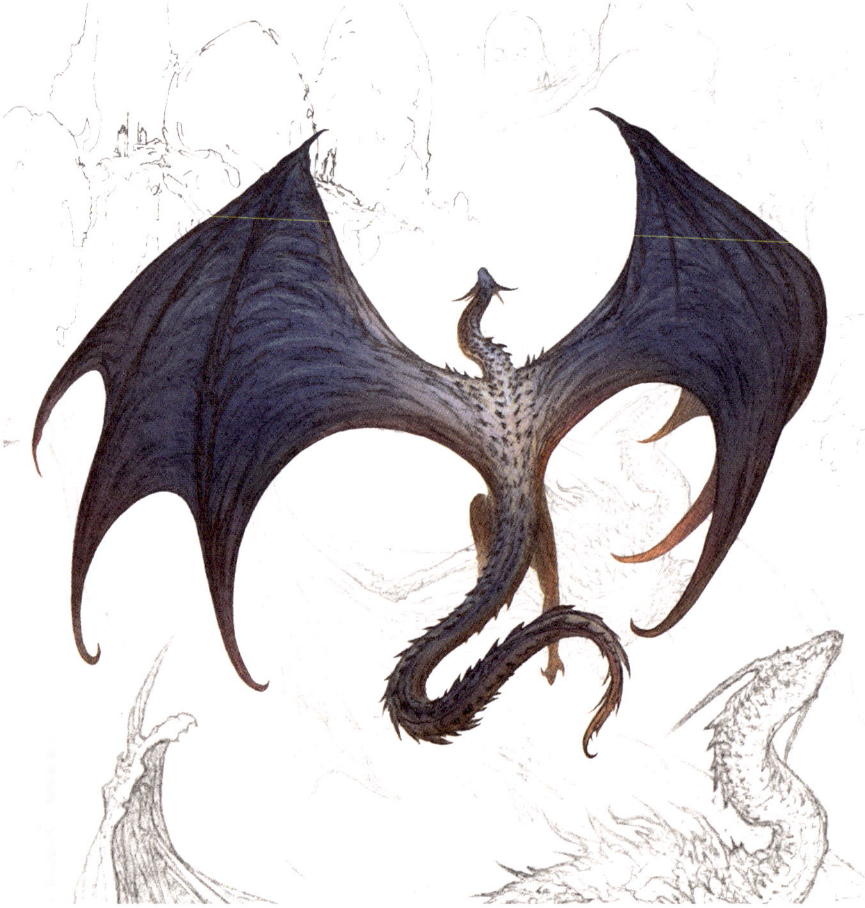

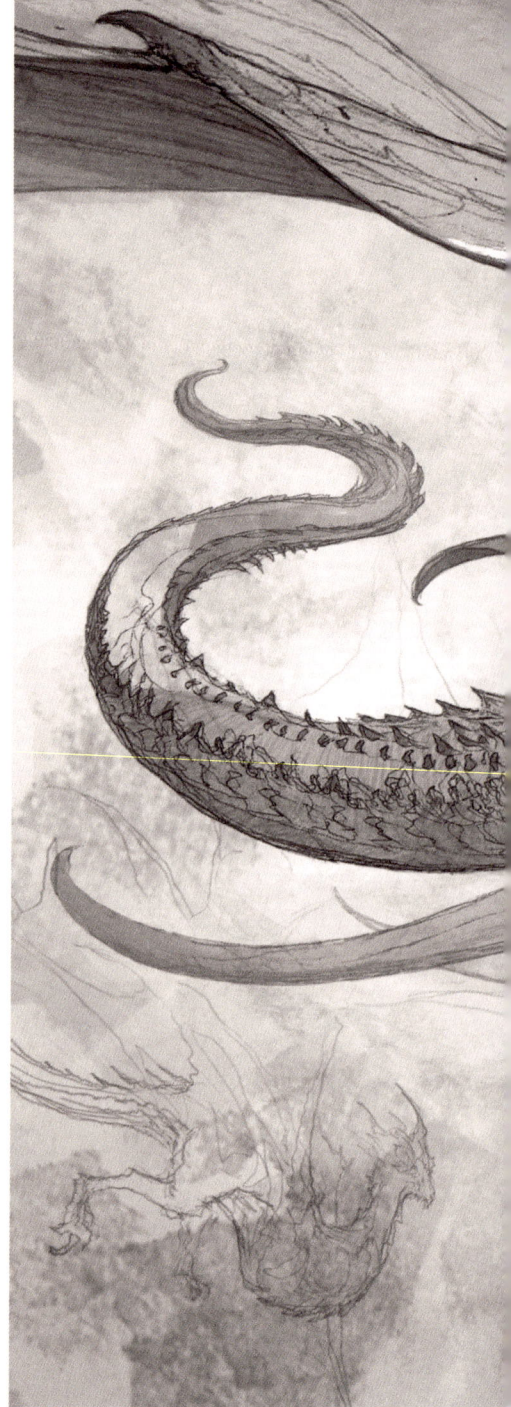

Small sketches

The sketchbook is the most important thing in my art. I do lots and lots of small sketches to improve on the dragon's anatomy, understand how his wings work, and keep refining the design.

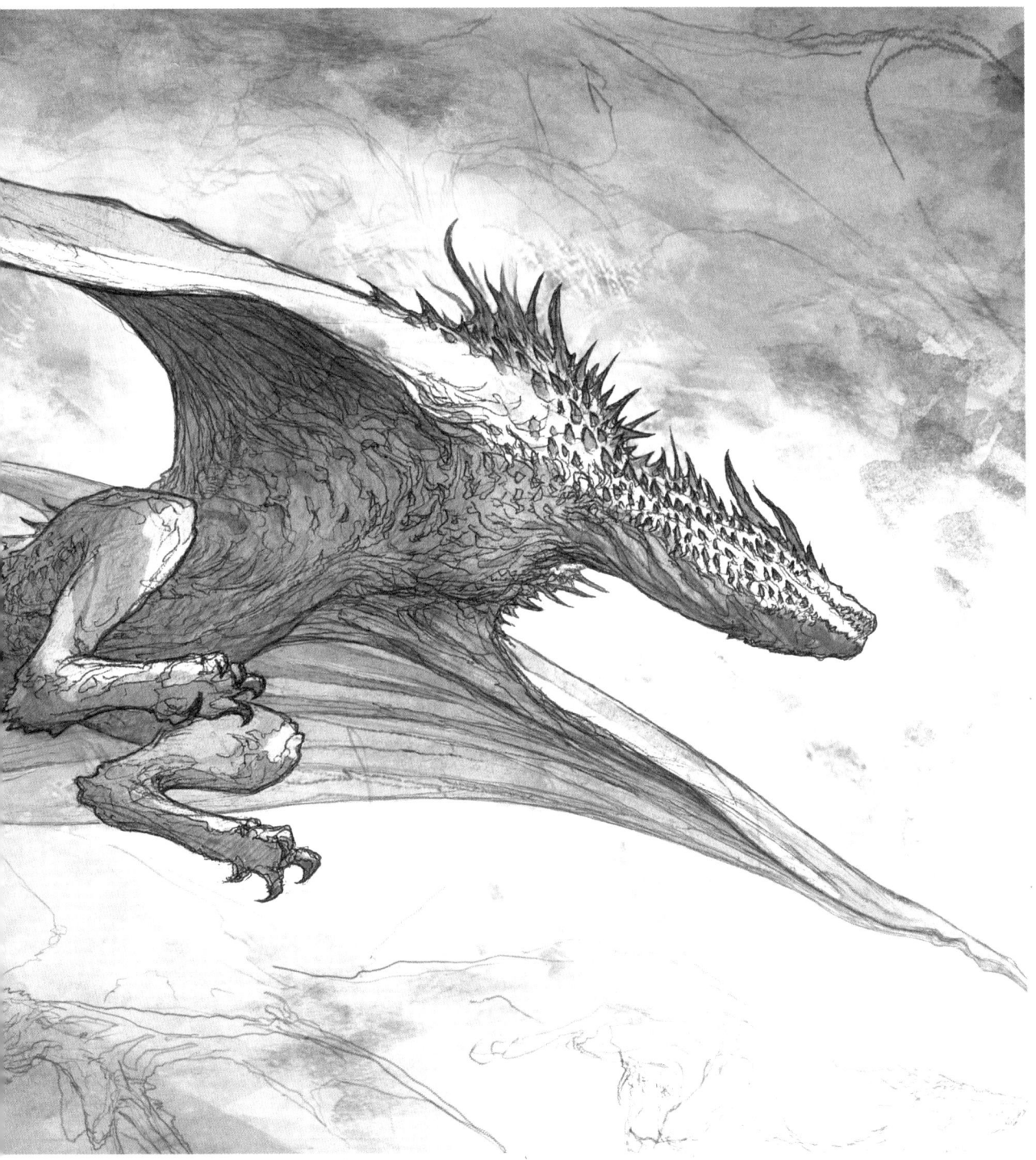

Evolution

A few years ago I would have been unable to draw something like this. I have learned a lot these last two years, which fills me with motivation. I want to keep learning and improving in what I like the most.

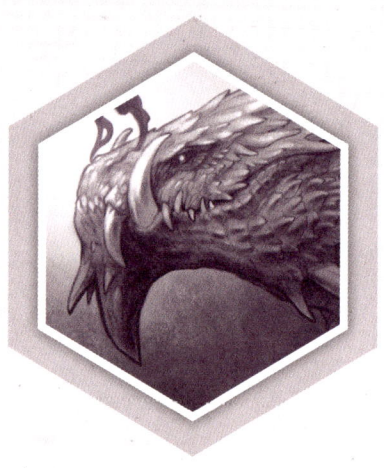

CHARLES HAMEL

This gallery includes a variety of dragon illustrations, from rough sketches to finished drawings, all done using Procreate. Previously I worked mostly with coloured pencils, and so one of my goals is preserving the feeling of traditional media in my digital work.

My passion for dragons comes from a childhood fascination; they captured my imagination through movies, books, and games. I found myself often doodling dragons in school, finding joy in coming up with different personalities and expressing their character in my design choices. As my own art progressed it has leaned towards a more naturalistic approach informed by dinosaur fossils and contemporary reptiles.

With an educational background in architecture, I grew to appreciate structure and how to communicate form through drafting. While it has been useful in designing dragons, there's a rigidity to this approach that conflicts with organic shapes. It's been an ongoing journey to loosen up and balance that design approach with drawing from life.

My favourite part of designing dragons is when they reach a point where I feel like they could really exist in their own world. There's something deeply magical about bringing a dragon to life through what already exists all around us.

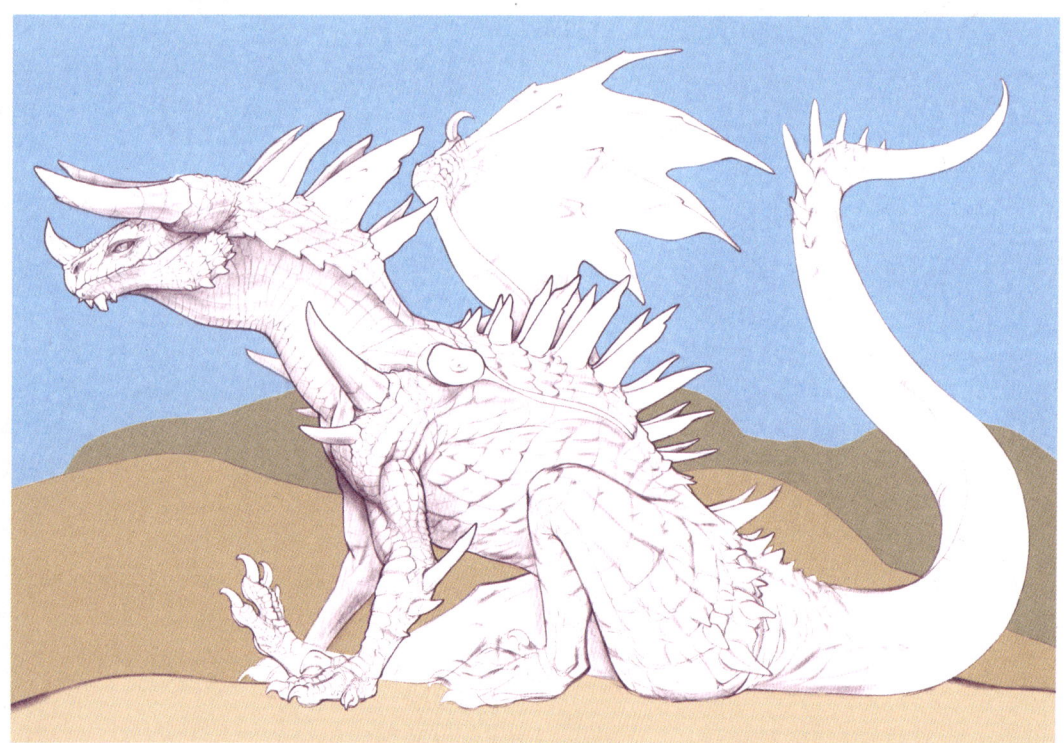

Horned Sand Drake
A combination of ideas I had about a swift desert predator. The vestigial wings can be used to help with manoeuvring and cooling off, while the spikes are for lacerating foes.

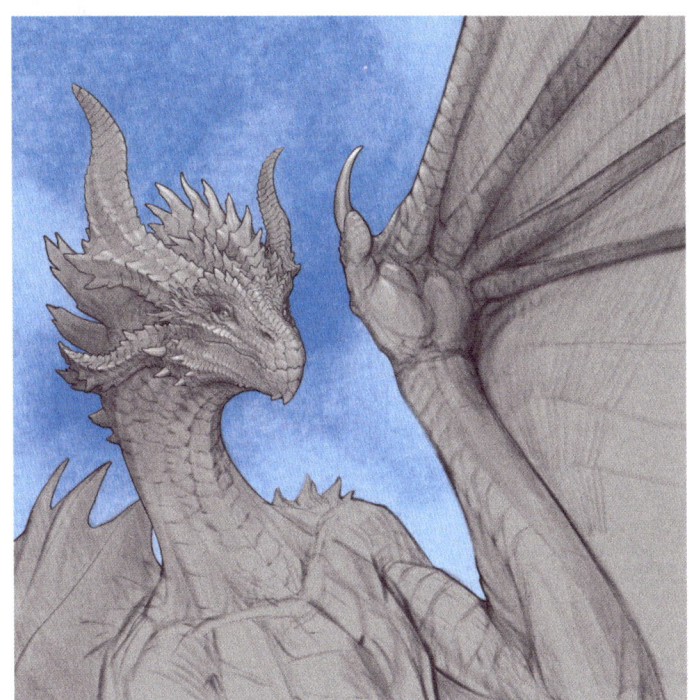

Learned Behaviours
If dragons are intelligent creatures, then perhaps they'd also mimic our behaviours. This light-hearted piece illustrates a wyvern returning a hand wave.

Return to the Sky
This elder dragon preparing for flight comes from an old pencil sketch I really enjoyed. Applying what I'd learned since then really helped to bring the piece to life.

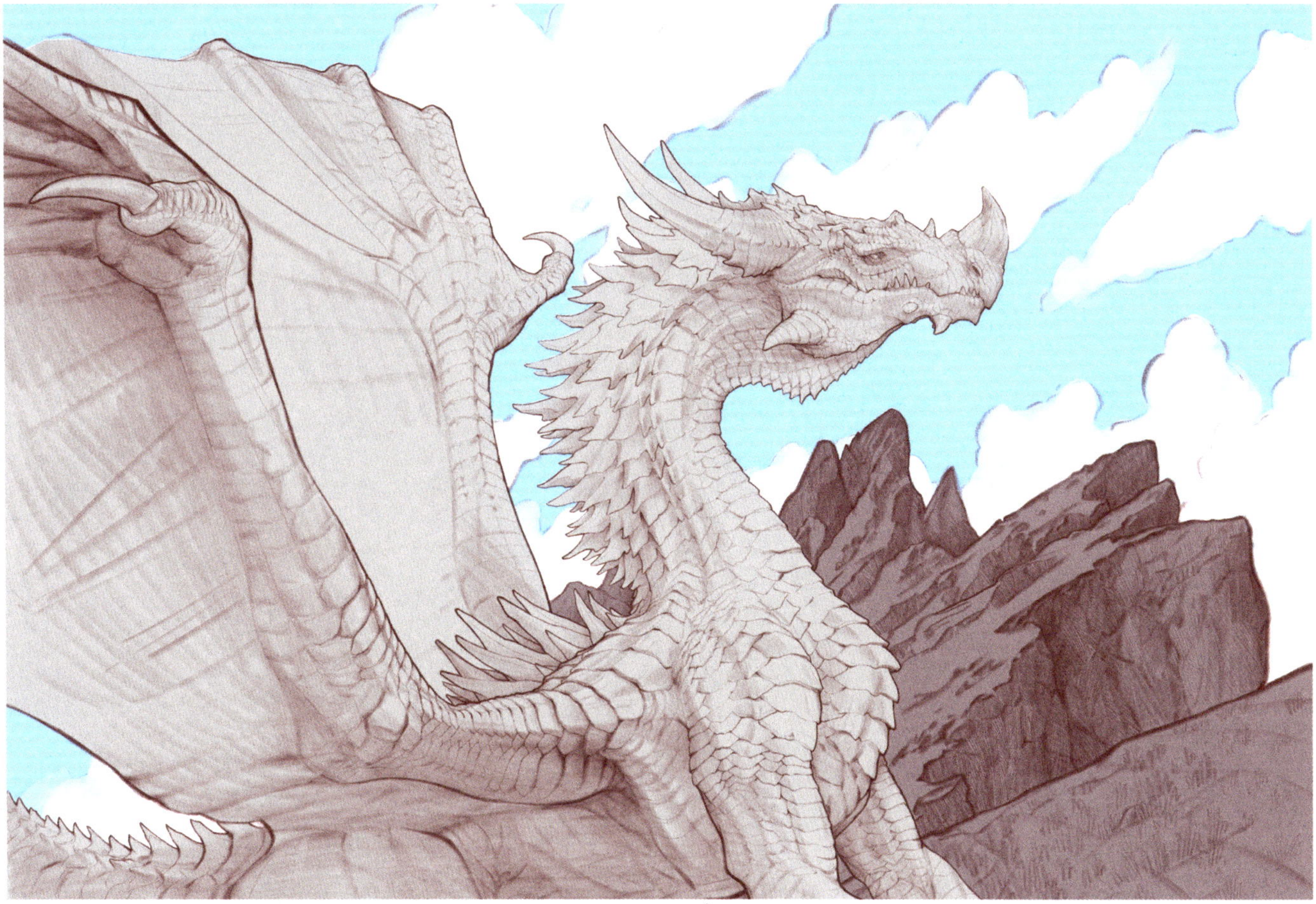

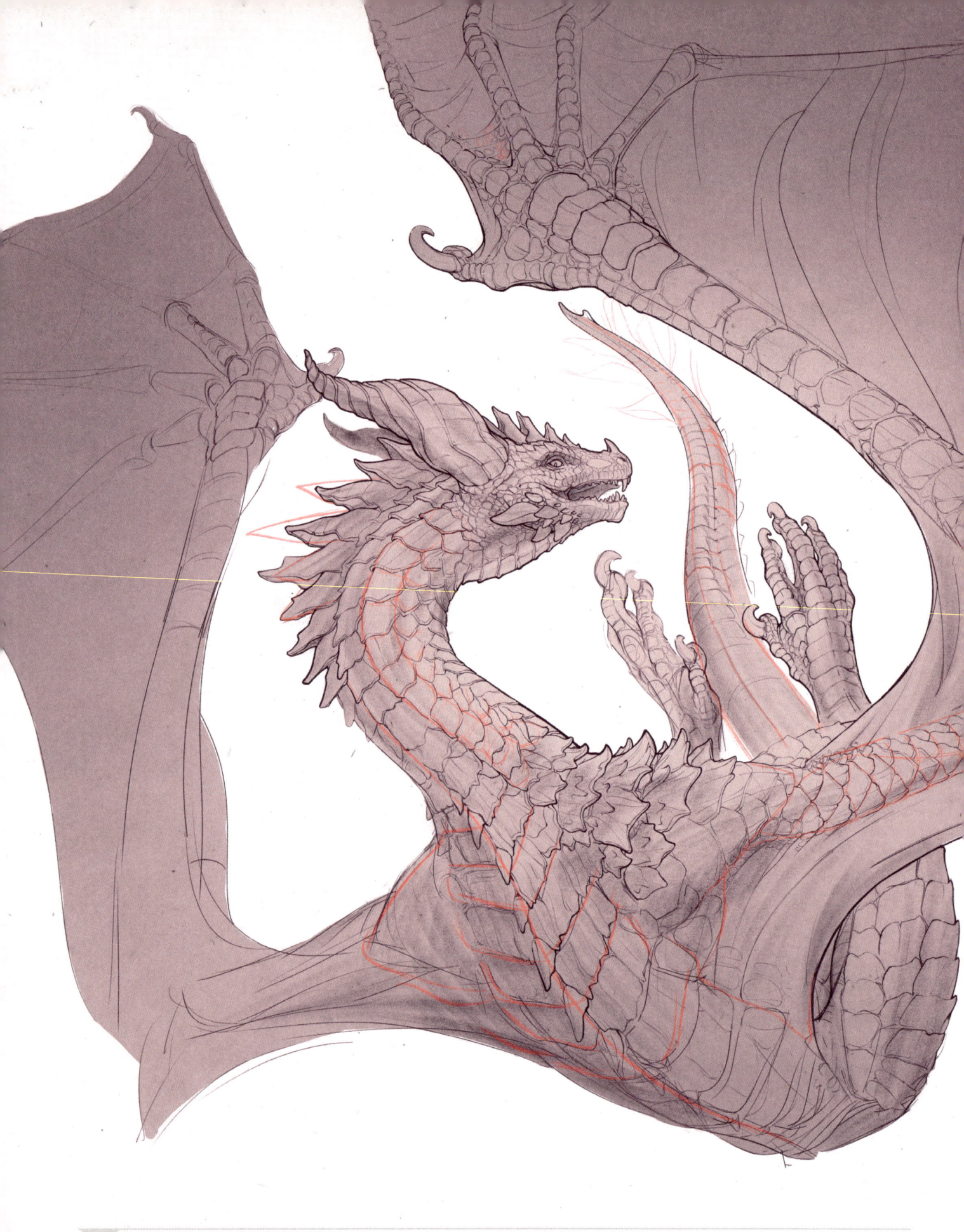

Tail Spin
A rougher work-in-progress exploring the playfulness of a dragon falling through the sky.

Crown of Feathers
Something caught this dragon's attention! I wanted to communicate a sense of tension through the twisting of the neck and how the scales would behave in this pose.

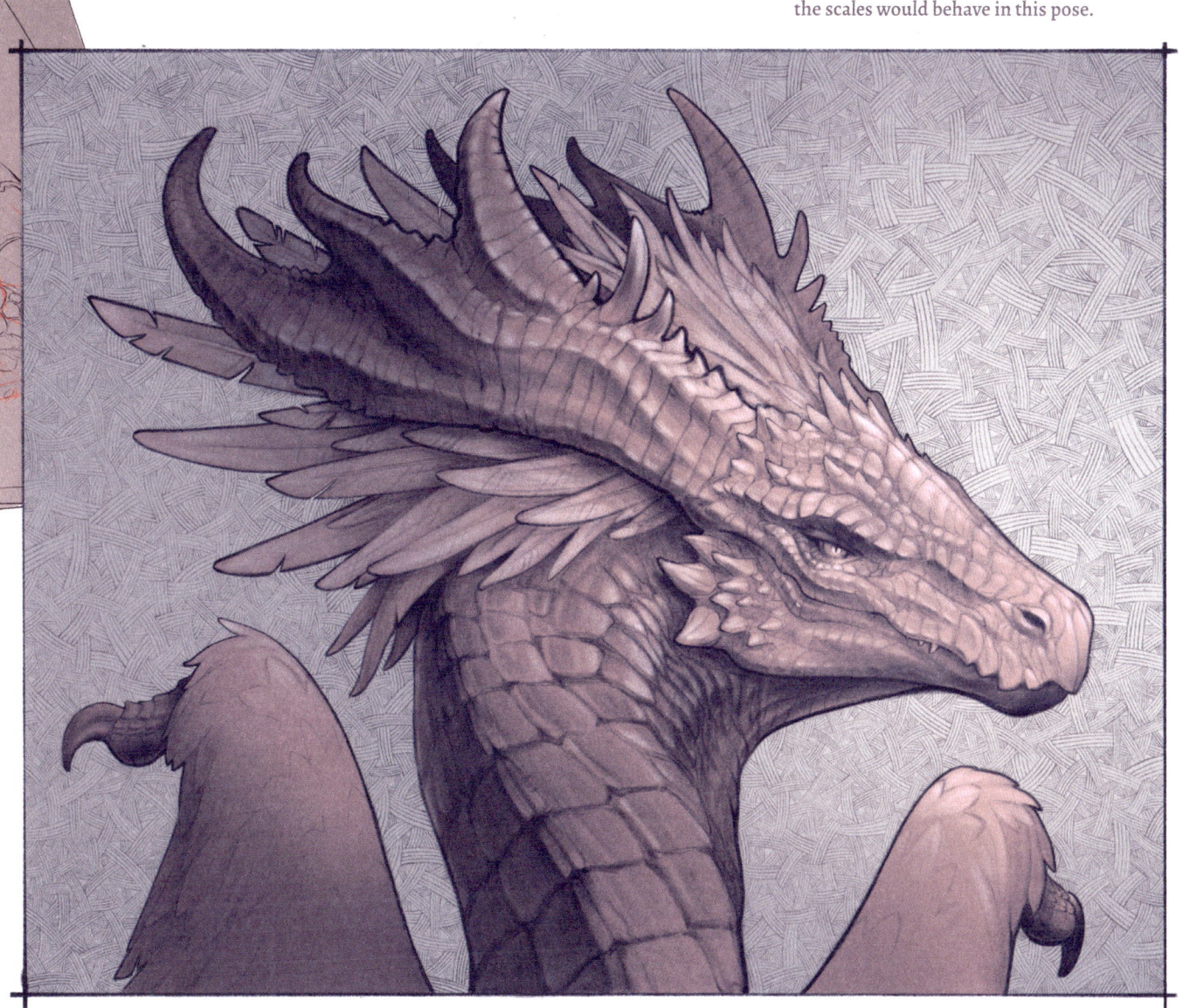

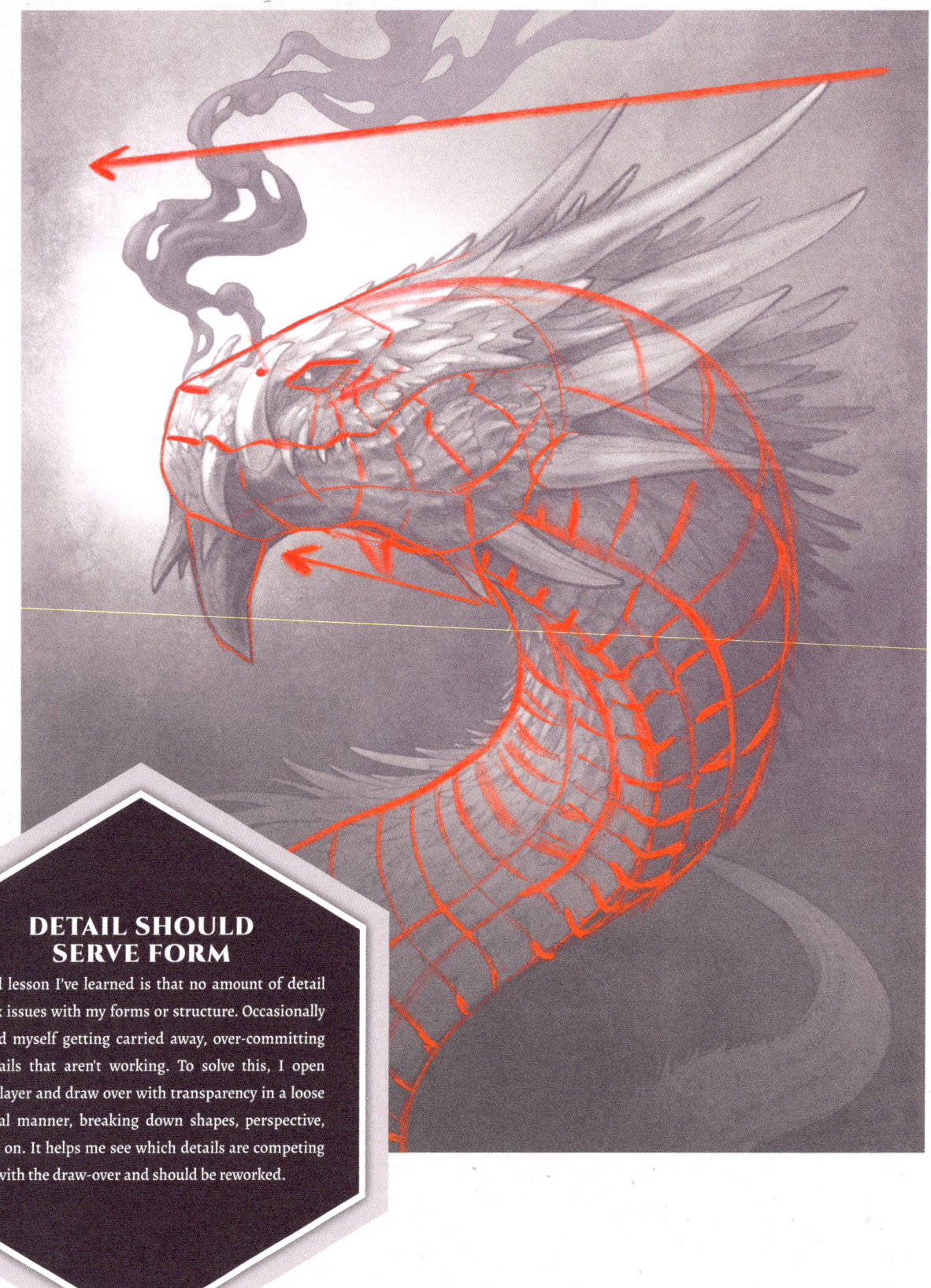

DETAIL SHOULD SERVE FORM

A hard lesson I've learned is that no amount of detail will fix issues with my forms or structure. Occasionally I'll find myself getting carried away, over-committing to details that aren't working. To solve this, I open a new layer and draw over with transparency in a loose gestural manner, breaking down shapes, perspective, and so on. It helps me see which details are competing with the draw-over and should be reworked.

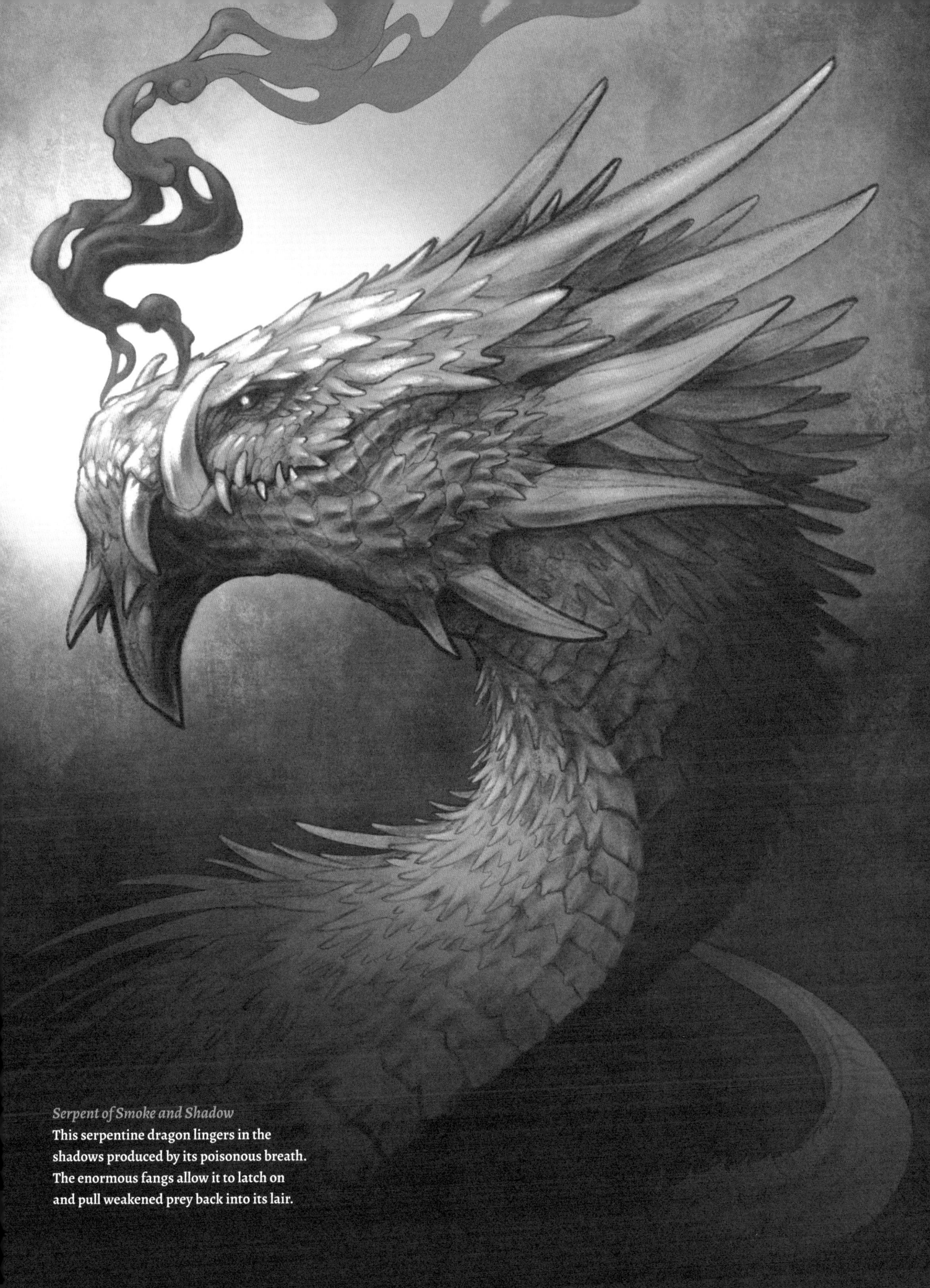

Serpent of Smoke and Shadow
This serpentine dragon lingers in the
shadows produced by its poisonous breath.
The enormous fangs allow it to latch on
and pull weakened prey back into its lair.

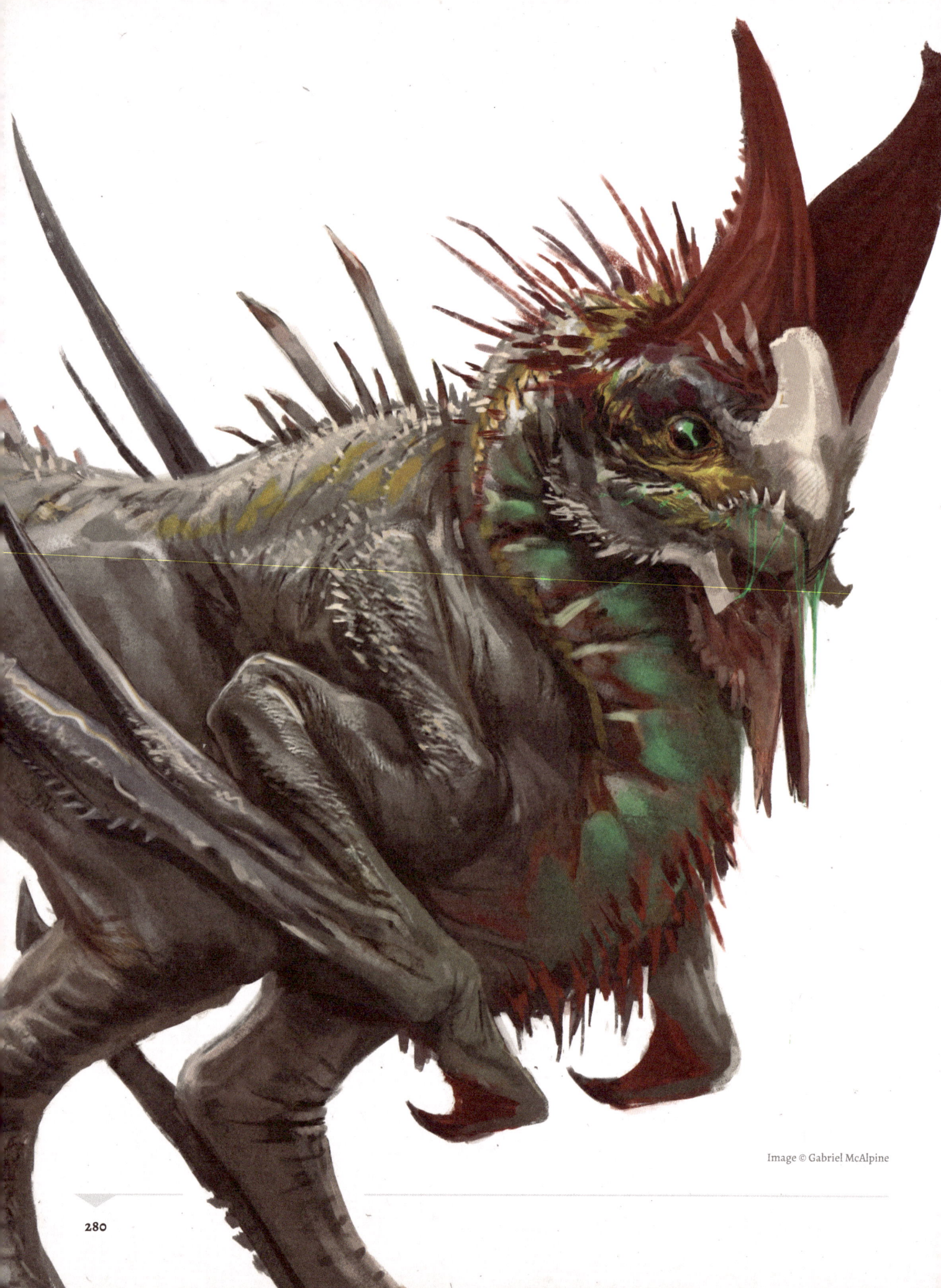

Image © Gabriel McAlpine

GLOSSARY

Anisodactyl
Having three toes at the front of the foot and one at the back, like a pigeon or chicken's foot.

Chimera
A mythical creature comprised from parts of different animals. In Greek mythology, a 'chimera' is specifically part lion, part goat, and part snake.

Chitin
The tough material that forms the exoskeletons and shells of many insects and crustaceans.

Drake
Another name for a dragon – often one with four legs and no wings.

Greyscale
An image or colour scheme composed of black, white, and grey values only.

Heraldry
The field concerning 'armorial bearings' – such as coats of arms and related elements – and their symbology and design.

Hue
The general 'family' that a colour belongs to, such as red or green, regardless of its lightness or darkness.

Local colour
The flat 'base' colours of something, without the influence of light or shadow.

Muscular hydrostat
A mobile body part that is mostly muscle with no skeletal structure, such as a tongue or tentacle.

Papillae
Small fleshy bumps such as those found on the human tongue or on the skin of some cephalopods.

Photobash
To compose a digital image from or with photographic elements – a technique commonly used by concept artists for rapid visualization.

Scute
A type of horned, bony plate or scale found on the skin or shell of some animals.

Sexual dimorphism
The condition of the sexes having very different appearances – for example, a peacock's plumage versus a peahen's.

Value
The lightness or darkness of a colour, with the brightest value being white and the darkest being black.

Wattle
A fleshy appendage found on the head or neck of several types of birds, most notably chickens.

Wyrm
Also worm or wurm. Another name for a dragon, especially a serpentine one without wings or legs.

Wyvern
Another name for a dragon, typically one with wings and two legs, as often seen in heraldry.

Zygodactyl
Having two toes at the front of the foot and two at the back, like an osprey or parrot's foot.

CONTRIBUTORS

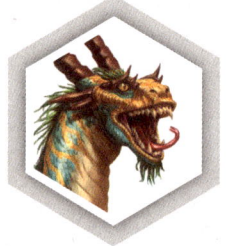 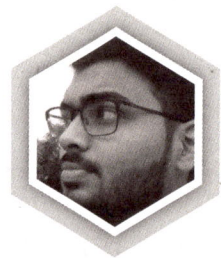

HAZEM AMEEN

artstation.com/caninebrush

Hazem Ameen is a freelance artist based in India. When he's not working for various clients abroad, he tends to make himself busy with his own projects.

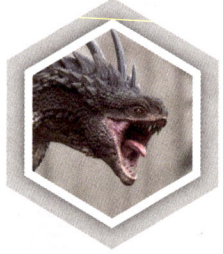 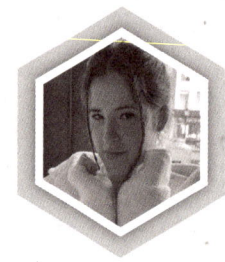

ROBIN BOONACKER

artstation.com/theredbirdart

Robin Boonacker, also known online as TheRedBirdArt, is a concept designer, illustrator, and 3D artist with a semi-realistic style focused on creature and character design.

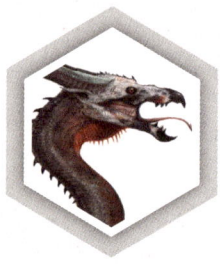 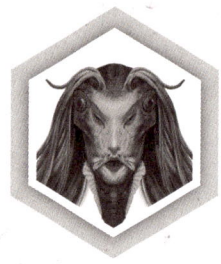

VINCENT COVIELLO

instagram.com/vincentcoviello

Vincent Coviello is a concept artist and illustrator whose work has been showcased in various projects and publications including *Magic: The Gathering* and *Fifth Journey*.

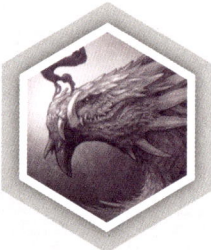 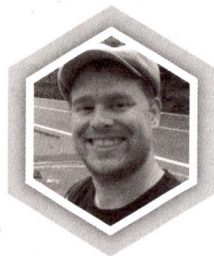

CHARLES HAMEL

instagram.com/Charles.Hamel

Charles Hamel is a freelance fantasy illustrator with a passion for bringing dragons to life through studying the natural world and a propensity for descriptive detail work.

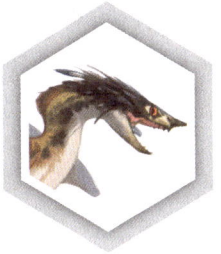 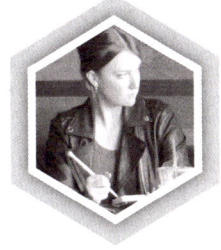

ALLIE IRWIN

allieirwinart.com

Allie Irwin is a concept artist who lives and works in Southern California, and whose past clients include Wizards of the Coast, Activision, and Darrington Press.

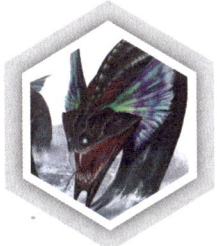 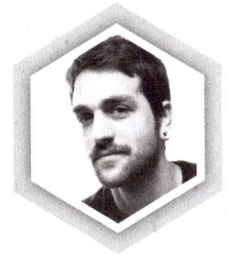

GIOVANNI LAZZARI

artstation.com/salus_art

Giovanni Lazzari has been drawing for as long as he can remember. When he's not drawing, he's fantasizing about what to draw next! He is a concept artist for video games, creating everything from creatures to props.

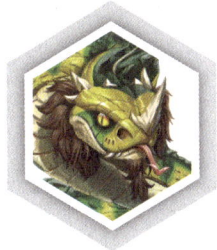 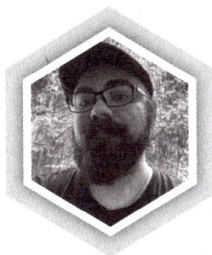

DAMIEN MAMMOLITI

boneandbrush.com

Damien Mammoliti is an illustrator for games and books, including tabletop RPGs and board games, specializing in lavish environments, maps, and creatures.

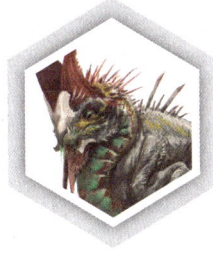 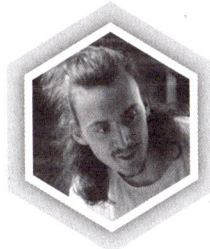

GABRIEL McALPINE

stray.design

Gabe McAlpine is currently Art Director at Stray Studios. Prior to this he worked as a concept artist specializing in character and creature design. Born in the UK, he has also lived in the USA and the Netherlands.

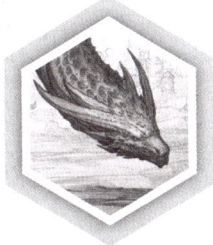 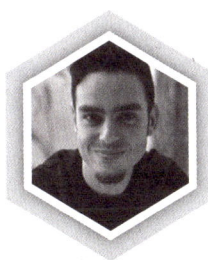

DIBUJANTE NOCTURNO

dibujantenocturno.com

Fran Garcés, aka Dibujante Nocturno, is a Spanish artist passionate about fantasy art. He has had a special love for dragons since he was a child – they are very present in all his sketchbooks.

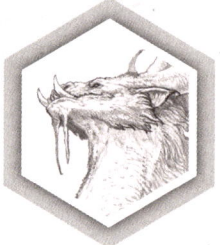 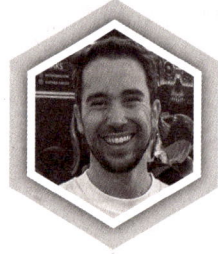

STEPHEN OAKLEY

artstation.com/artofoaks

Stephen Oakley is a concept artist for the entertainment industry. Raised in the woods of New Hampshire, he is now based in California, designing creatures for many titles including *God of War*, *Evolve*, and *Love, Death & Robots*.

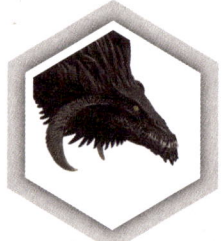 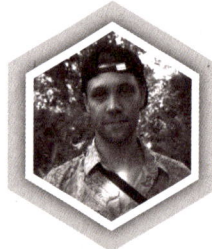

ALEXANDER OSTROWSKI

alexanderostrowski.com

Alexander Ostrowski is a concept artist and illustrator based in Germany, specializing in creature design for the entertainment industry. Clients include Karakter, West Studio, Ready at Dawn, Eidos-Montréal, and Wizards of the Coast.

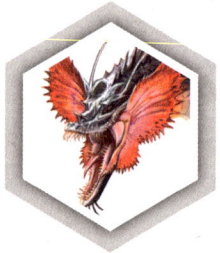 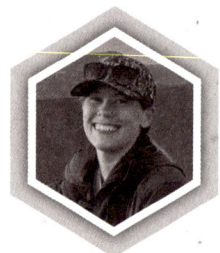

KATE PFEILSCHIEFTER

katepfeilschiefterart.com

Kate Pfeilschiefter is a multimedia creature specialist who loves working on the concept-design and illustrative side of creatures, as well as on full-production 3D models.

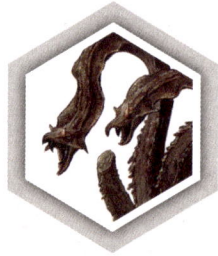 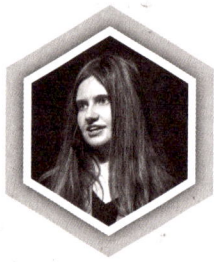

ANNA PODEDWORNA

artstation.com/akreon

Anna Podedworna is an illustrator and concept artist based in Warsaw. She has worked for studios such as CD PROJEKT RED, Riot Games, Jagex, Wizards of the Coast, Flying Wild Hog, Walt Disney Pictures, and Warner Bros. Pictures.

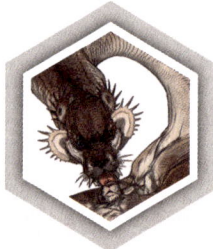 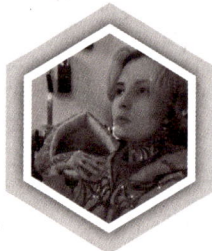

APRIL PRIME

instagram.com/april_prime

April Prime is a concept artist and illustrator based in Seattle. She grew up in rural Northern Australia, wrangling lizards and picking up bugs, which led to a lifelong obsession with creatures. Her work appears in many *Dungeons & Dragons* books and on several *Magic: The Gathering* cards.

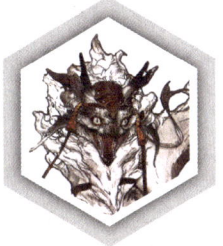
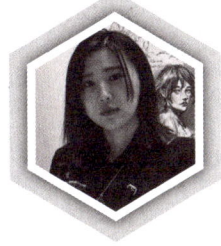

ENTEI RYU

instagram.com/badzrliuwt

Entei Ryu is a Tokyo-based artist and sculptor
for the film and games industry, and is currently
Lead Concept Artist at Kojima Productions.

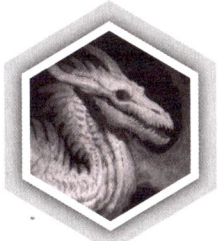
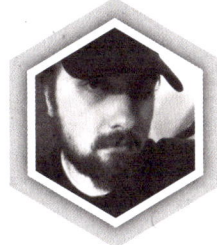

JOHN TEDRICK

artstation.com/tedrick94

John Tedrick is an illustrator and concept artist
living in Ohio, USA. His professional credits include
Magic: The Gathering and *Dungeons & Dragons*.

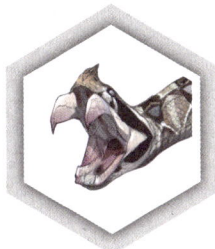
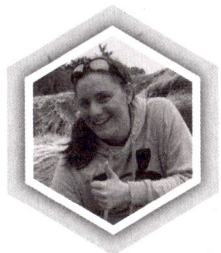

ALLISON THEUS

artstation.com/beastofoblivion

Allison Theus has been working as a concept artist
in the gaming space for over fifteen years and is
currently working on her own intellectual property.

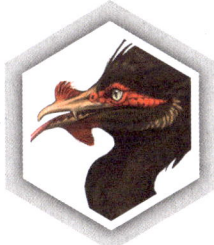
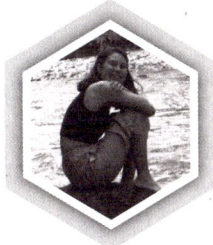

DOMINIQUE VASSIE

dominiquevassie.com

Dominique Vassie is a freelance artist and designer from
the United Kingdom, with a background in biology,
specializing in digital and natural-history illustration.

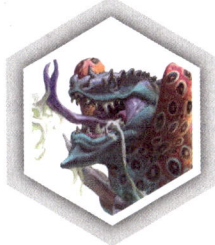
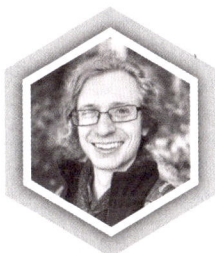

JORDAN K. WALKER

jordankwalkerart.com

Jordan K. Walker is an illustrator and fine artist with
a love for natural history. He has created illustrations
for clients such as Monte Cook Games, and numerous
creature-design tutorials for 3dtotal Publishing.

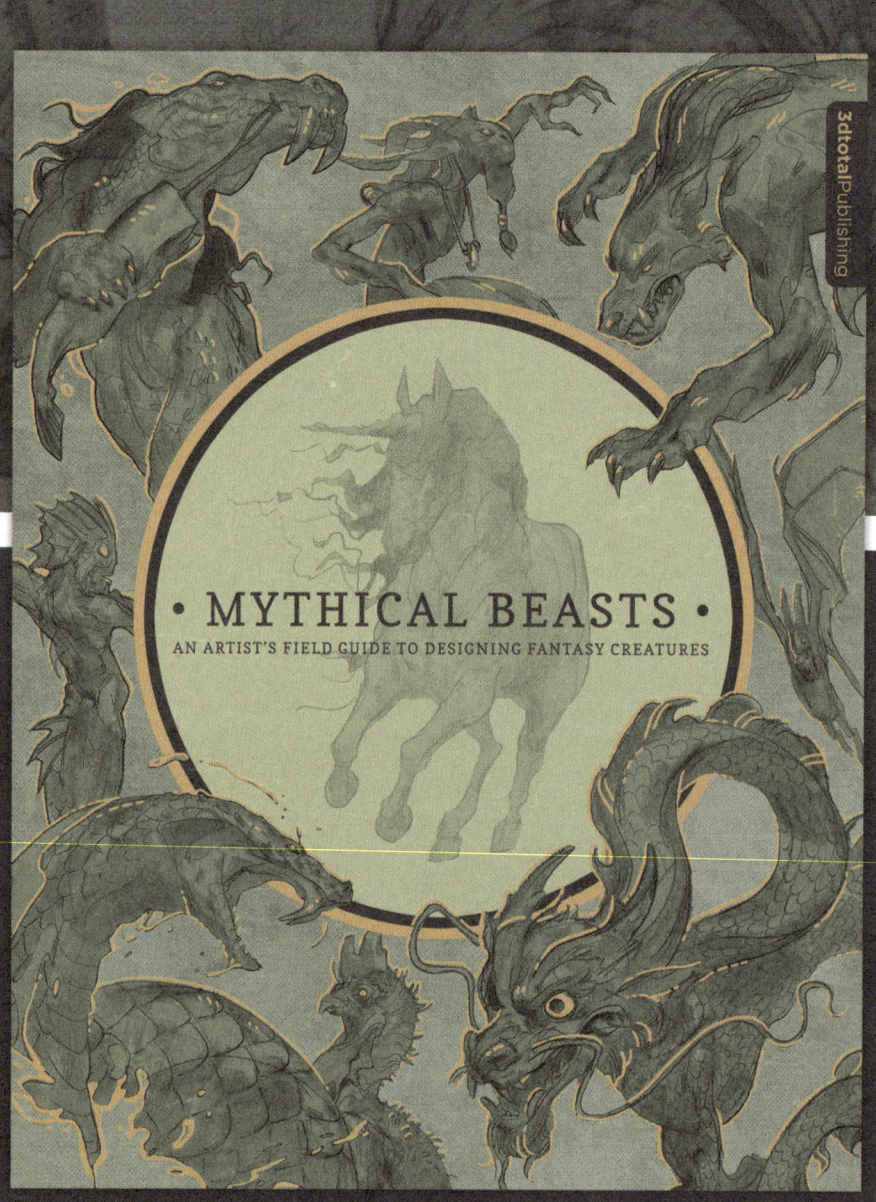

· MYTHICAL BEASTS ·

AN ARTIST'S FIELD GUIDE TO DESIGNING FANTASY CREATURES

3dtotalPublishing

Join thirty fearless artists as they explore and develop concepts for a treasure trove of fascinating mythical beasts. Journey around the globe and unearth the secrets of fantasy favourites and more provincial mysteries, including the legendary unicorn, the elusive yeti, the Slavic leshy, and the Japanese nue, to name just a few! Each creature has its own chapter that covers an overview of its history, how to detail main elements, such as fur and horns, and the thought process behind the artist's design. Let your imagination run wild and discover the captivating subspecies of each creature, such as the Arctic boggart and humpback kraken. *Mythical Beasts* is a spellbinding anthology for fantasy lovers, creature artists, or any intrepid adventurer looking to investigate the enchanting world of cryptozoology.

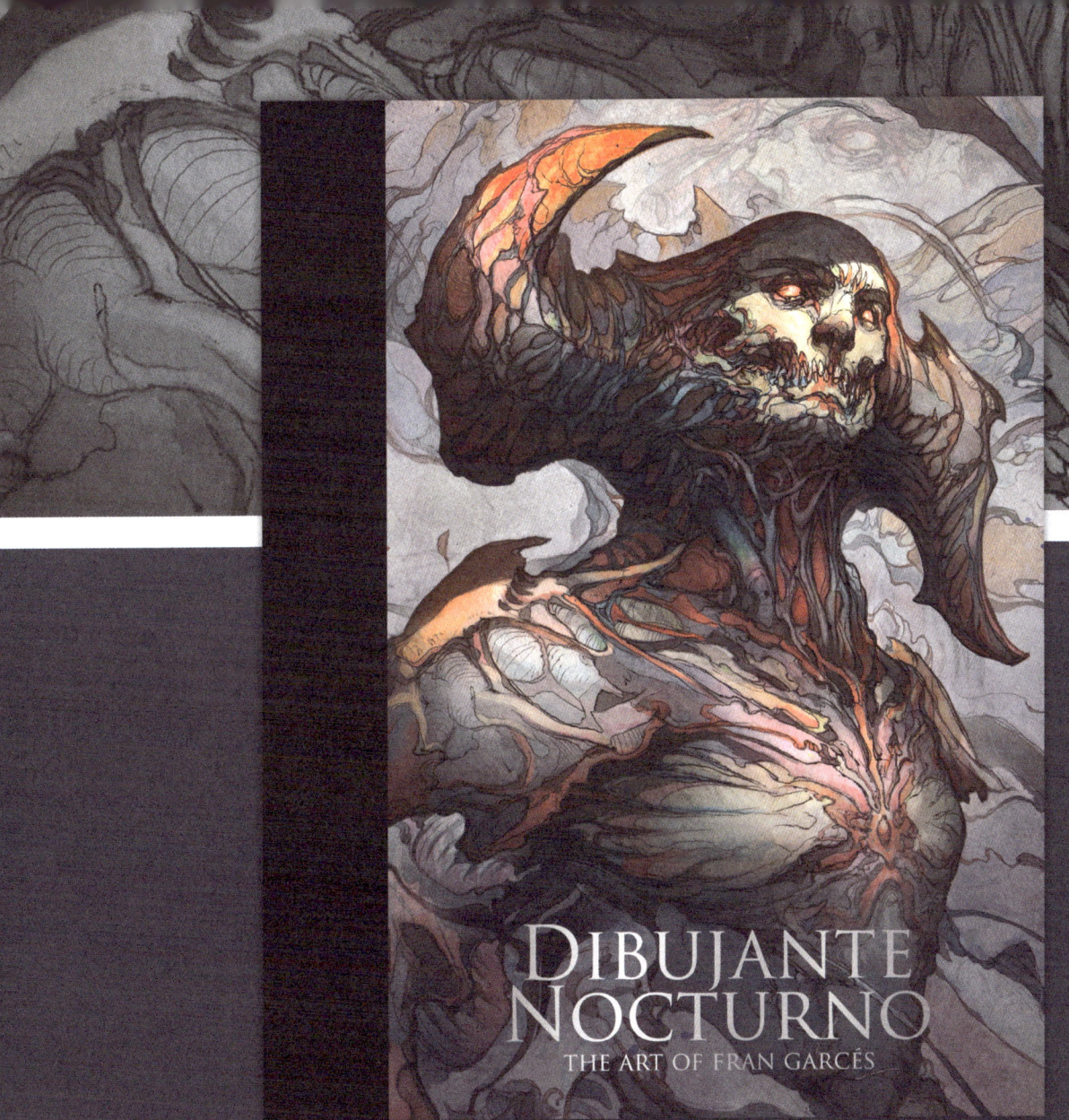

3dtotalPublishing

3dtotal Publishing is a trailblazing, creative publisher specializing in inspirational and educational resources for artists.

Our titles feature top industry professionals from around the globe who share their experience in skillfully written step-by-step tutorials and fascinating, detailed guides. Illustrated throughout with stunning artwork, these best-selling publications offer creative insight, expert advice, and essential motivation. Fans of digital art will enjoy our comprehensive volumes covering Adobe Photoshop, Procreate, and Blender, as well as our superb titles based around character design, including *Fundamentals of Character Design* and *Creating Characters for the Entertainment Industry*. The dedicated, high-quality blend of instruction and inspiration also extends to traditional art. Titles covering a range of techniques, genres, and abilities allow your creativity to flourish while building essential skills.

Well-established within the industry, we now offer over 100 titles and counting, many of which have been translated into multiple languages around the world. With something for every artist, we are proud to say that our books offer the 3dtotal package:

LEARN • CREATE • SHARE

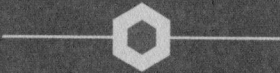

Visit us at store.3dtotal.com

3dtotal Publishing is part of 3dtotal.com, a leading website for CG artists founded by Tom Greenway in 1999.

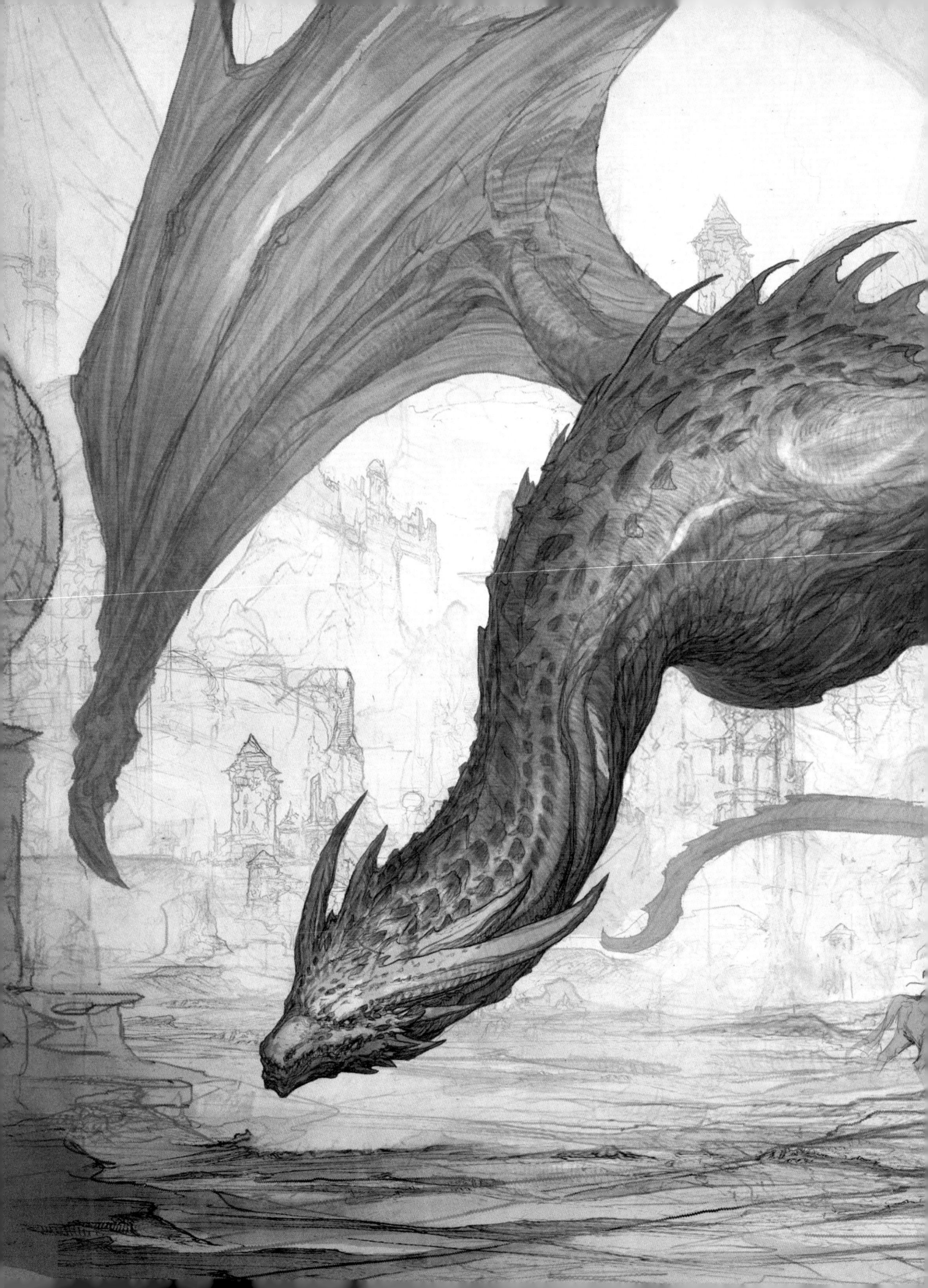